ASPA Classics

Conceived of and sponsored by the American Society for Public Administration (ASPA), the ASPA Classic Series publishes volumes on topics that have been, and continue to be, central to the contemporary development of the field. The ASPA Classics are intended for classroom use, library adoptions, and general reference. Drawing from the *Public Administration Review (PAR)* and other ASPA-related journals, each volume in the series is edited by a scholar who is charge with presenting a thorough and balanced perspective on an enduring issue.

Each volume is devoted to a topic of continuing and crosscutting concern to the administration of virtually all public sector programs. Public servants carry out their responsibilities in a complex, multidimensional environment, and each collection will address a necessary dimension of their performance. ASPA Classics volumes bring together the dialogue on a particular topic over several decades and in a range of journals.

The volume editors are to be commended for volunteering to take on such substantial projects and for bringing together unique collections of articles that might not otherwise be readily available to scholars and students.

ASPA Classics

Public Personnel Administration and Labor Relations
Norma Riccucci, ed.

Public Administration and Law
Julia Beckett and Heidi O. Koenig, eds.

Local Government Management:
Current Issues and Best Practices
Douglas J. Watson and Wendy L. Hassen, eds.

Public Personnel Administration and Labor Relations

An ASPA Classics Volume

Edited by

Norma M. Riccucci

M.E.Sharpe
Armonk, New York
London, England

Library of Congress Cataloging-in-Publication Data

Public personnel administration and labor relations / edited by Norma M. Riccucci.
    p. cm. — (ASPA classics)
  Includes bibliographical references and index.
  ISBN-13: 978-0-7656-1679-1 (cloth : alk. paper)
  ISBN-10: 0-7656-1679-3 (cloth : alk. paper)
   1. Public administration—United States—Personnel management. 2. Civil service—United States—Personnel
management. 3. Industrial relations—Government policy—United States. I. Riccucci, Norma. II. Series.

JF1351.P838 2006
352.60973—dc22   2006005850

Printed in the United States of America

The paper used in this publication meets the minimum requirements of
American National Standard for Information Sciences
Permanence of Paper for Printed Library Materials,
ANSI Z 39.48-1984.

BM (c)   10   9   8   7   6   5   4   3   2   1

CONTENTS

ACKNOWLEDGEMENTS

I would like to gratefully acknowledge the input and feedback from several colleagues, including Carolyn Ban, Marc Holzer, David H. Rosenbloom, and Frank J. Thompson. In addition, the support and assistance from executive editor Harry Briggs was invaluable. Also, many thanks to my graduate assistant Maria D'Agostino and especially to editorial assistant Madelene Perez, whose tireless efforts brought this classics anthology to fruition.

INTRODUCTION: PUBLIC PERSONNEL ADMINISTRATION AND LABOR RELATIONS

Norma M. Riccucci

Introduction

There is perhaps no area of public administration that has fundamentally shaped the realm of government as public personnel. Indeed, as the embodiment of civil service, it is the essence of government and public employment. Writing almost 70 years ago, in one of the first textbooks on public personnel administration,[1] William Mosher and J. Donald Kingsley (1936) argue that effective personnel management is the key to better government, and hence an enhanced quality of life for the American citizenry. They state that "the public business has become the foremost enterprise of the country" (Mosher and Kingsley 553). They go on to say:

> That it is bound to expand even farther no one who is alive to the far-reaching implications of the Rooseveltian "New Deal," will doubt. The long-cherished fiction that government is merely incidental to American life and engaged in supplying more or less routine services, must now be recognized as contrary to the facts, even by the most obtuse observer. If this great machine is to run smoothly, if the public whose welfare is so dependent on it is to be well served, it behooves the public in its own interest to elevate the status of governmental employment to the end that the more or most capable, the better or best trained, and the ambitious members of the citizenry will be attracted into it (1936: 41).

In their call for sound and effective public personnel administration and policy, Mosher and Kingsley (1936: 41) point to the importance of and need for highly qualified public servants; fair and equitable wages for all public employees; full rights of representation and a voice in determining the conditions of work; and elevating the prestige of public employment to the level of importance it deserves.

This template of concerns and issues characterizes the fields of public personnel and labor relations and is the topic of this book. The "classics" presented here trace the historical and evolutionary development of the fields of public personnel administration and labor relations in government from the point at which the first civil service law was passed—the Pendleton Act in 1883—through the twenty-first century. Critical issues surrounding the seminal concerns of civil service (e.g., keeping spoils out) to topics that the early reformers would never have envisioned (e.g., affirmative action and drug testing) are covered.

The classics appearing in this book represent some of the most critical, significant scholarship that has appeared in *Public Administration Review* (*PAR*) and other journals related to the American Society for Public Administration (ASPA), such as the *Review of Public Personnel Administration,* the *American Review of Public Administration,* and *Public Administration Quarterly.* These works continue to impact the writing and practice within the fields of public personnel and labor relations.

Organization of the Book

Something which is "classic" stands the test of time. It serves as a model or prototype, and has lasting significance. As such, it includes work which has contributed to the evolution and development of a field, as well as research which continues to impact the writing and practice within a field. Such classic articles are reproduced for this book. The anthology is comprised of two major sections. Section I presents articles on Public Personnel Administration and is organized into the following five parts: History and Politics; Institutions, Functions, and Process; Equal Employment Opportunity, Affirmative Action, and Representative Bureaucracy; Civil Service Reform; and Legal Developments.

Section II presents articles on Public Sector Labor Relations and is organized into four parts: History and Politics; Collective Bargaining, Impasse Resolution, and Strikes; Employee Participation and Labor Management Cooperation; and Critical Developments in Public Sector Labor Relations.

One of the most challenging aspects of working on this project has been space limitations. There were several classics that should have been included in this book, but restrictions of available space resulted in their exclusion. As such, the introductions to each topic area contain a listing of "additional classics" which are intended to provide further reading in respective areas.

Note

1. See White (1930; 1935); also see White (1926), a work which devoted considerable attention to personnel problems in government.

References

Mosher, William E. and J. Donald Kingsley. 1936. *Public Personnel Administration.* New York: Harper & Brothers Publishers.

White, Leonard D. 1926. *Introduction to the Study of Public Administration.* New York: Macmillan.

White, Leonard D. (ed.). 1930. *The Civil Service in the Modern State.* Chicago: University of Chicago Press.

White, Leonard D. 1935. *Government Career Service.* Chicago: University of Chicago Press.

SECTION I

PUBLIC PERSONNEL ADMINISTRATION

PART 1

HISTORY AND POLITICS

Public personnel administration, just like other spheres of government, is plagued with politics. Despite the early reformers' efforts to separate politics from administration, seeking to keep spoils or patronage out of government employment, politics is suffused in government personnel systems at every level. Notwithstanding, civil service systems have historically battled to limit the intrusion of politics and, at the same time, maintain merit-based public employment programs. However, as the articles in this first section all suggest, political considerations continue to prevail in public employment and, despite the merit system, the best and brightest are not always hired.

In the first article, Wallace Sayre observes from these personnel endeavors intended to minimize the incursion of politics that techniques have triumphed over purpose. Sayre's classic "The Triumph of Techniques over Purpose," is a review of a personnel textbook intended for use by business administration students. In his critique, Sayre argues that the rule of three, "split-digit" test rankings, and other quantitative techniques emanating from the scientific management school of thought to putatively eliminate political considerations have worked to dominate and dilute the very essence or goals of public personnel (e.g., hiring competent employees). He also observes that "[p]rivate personnel administration has not escaped similar pressures" (Sayre 1948: 135). Sayre urges, as others do in the articles presented in this section, that "both ends and means now urgently need fundamental reexamination" (Sayre 1948: 135), a theme which continues to have relevance for contemporary public personnel administration.

In the second article, David Levitan, writing during World War II, argues that "the search for political neutrality is a quest for the impossible" and that the government cannot expect "for a complete detachment of attitude toward the controversies of the public forum" (Levitan 1942: 323). Levitan, an administrator for the War Production Board,[1] states that "[t]here is a vital necessity . . . for a renewed devotion to political ideas and for the infusion of a spirit of dedication to ideals and concepts. The aim is . . . to avoid the decitizenation of hundreds of thousands of Americans" (Levitan 1942: 318). He goes on to say that "[n]or is this merely a wartime need. The war has simply made the need more apparent and more urgent" (Levitan 1942: 318).

In "Civil Service Versus Merit," Bernard Gladieux argues that the efforts to minimize spoils in the federal civil service system have resulted in major rigidity, ultimately confining the government's ability to make sound personnel choices. He states that more regulations do not lead to less patronage, and calls for the elimination of such formulas as the rule of three in order to provide the government with greater flexibility to hire quality employees. Gladieux argues that "[w]hile I deplore, as do all thoughtful observers, the introduction of political influence in employment matters, I think it too much to expect that in a dynamic democracy it will ever be possible to remove politics completely from public employment. We can only seek to minimize this factor" (Gladieux 1952: 174). He suggests that the efforts to curb spoils have produced mediocrity in public employment, and this is the greatest threat to democracy.

In "Public Personnel: Agenda for the Sixties," Felix Nigro writes about the "frustration gap" in public personnel administration. Nigro is referring to the disparity between reality and ideals in personnel work, and the struggle to narrow the gap. The constant effort to improve personnel programs is, as Nigro writes, an effort to improve the overall functioning of government. He writes about the vital role that personnel management plays in agency operations, stating that

> no longer . . . considered as just an adjunct to the agency program. On the contrary, it is now accepted to many as an indispensable part of the management equipment for carrying out the agency program successfully (Nigro 1961: 192).

Nigro outlines several issues that personnel managers and administrators should focus on to narrow the frustration gap, including among others increased attention to career service planning, performance evaluation, compensation, and labor relations.

Note

1. The War Production Board was the U.S. government agency established in January of 1942 by executive order to direct war production and the procurement of materials during World War II. It was abolished in November of 1945.

Additional Classics

Appleby, Paul A. "A Reappraisal of Federal Employment as a Career." 8 *Public Administration Review*, 85–90, 1948.

Belsley, G. Lyle. "Recruitment to the Public Service." 4 *Public Administration Review*, 2: 168–176, Spring 1944.

Cushman, Robert. "The Purge of Federal Employees Accused of Disloyalty." 3 *Public Administration Review*, 4: 297–316, Autumn 1943.

Epstein, Leon. "Political Sterilization of Civil Servants: The United States and Great Britain." 10 *Public Administration Review*, 4: 281–290, Autumn 1950.

Hays, Steven W. and Fred Carter. "The Myth of Hatch Act Reform." *Southern Review of Public Administration*, Winter, 1980.

Janowitz, Morris and Deil Wright. "The Prestige of Public Employment: 1929 and 1954." 16 *Public Administration Review*, 15–21, Winter 1956.

Klingner, Donald E. "Political Influences on the Design of State and Local Personnel Systems." 1 *Review of Public Personnel Administration*, 3: 1–9, Summer 1981.

Nalbandian, John. "From Compliance to Consultation: The Changing Role of the Public Personnel Administrator." 1 *Review of Public Personnel Administration*, 2: 37–52, Spring 1981.

Posey, Rollin. "The New Militancy of Public Employees." 28 *Public Administration Review*, 111–117, March/April 1968.

Smith, Russell L. "Representative Bureaucracy: A Research Note On Demographic Representation In State Bureaucracies." 1 *Review of Public Personnel Administration*, 1: 1–12, Fall 1980.

Van Riper, Paul P. "The Senior Civil Service and the Career System." 18 *Public Administration Review*, 3: 189–200, Summer, 1958.

Warner, W. Lloyd, Paul P. Van Riper, Norman H. Martin, and Orvis F. Collins. "A New Look at the Career Civil Executive." 22 *Public Administration Review*, 4: 188–194, December 1962.

White, Leonard D. "The Senior Civil Service." 15 *Public Administration Review*, 4: 237–243, Autumn 1955.

Zimmerman, Virgil B. and Dwight Waldo. "A Worm's Eye View of the Civil Service Commission." 2 *Public Administration Review*, 54–60, Winter 1942.

CHAPTER 1

THE TRIUMPH OF TECHNIQUES OVER PURPOSE

WALLACE S. SAYRE

I

The appearance of this book marks an important milestone in the development of personnel administration. It is the first successful effort to present, within the difficult requirements of a personnel textbook designed for general use, the significant findings and conclusions of the several groundbreaking monographs produced during the past fifteen years by the group known as the "human relations" school. The authors, who are professors of industrial relations at Massachusetts Institute of Technology, have themselves been important participants in this human relations movement. They have now undertaken the task of relating the concepts and methods of human relations to the theory and practice of personnel administration.

Pigors and Myers are primarily interested, as are most members of this group, with the administrative environment of private industry. This orientation reduces the initial appeal of their text for those readers who are absorbed in the tasks or in the study of public personnel administration. But the major barrier to the acceptance and influence which *Personnel Administration* deserves in the public field will arise from the wide gulf which divides its point of view and its method form many of the deep-seated stereotypes and cherished rituals of civil service administration. This resistance will be of minor concern to the authors, since they are assured of a gratifying influence in their chosen field of private industry; it is a more serious matter for the public administration fraternity, because they are now confronted with nothing less than the confirmation of Louis Brownlow's prediction, "a failure of the civil service institution to meet the needs of the peace."[1]

The concepts and the methodology of contemporary public personnel administration are, of course, the product of the dominant objectives set by, and for, the students and the practitioners of the craft. It is possible to identify these goals in separate terms, even though they overlap and have always exerted powerful reciprocal influences upon each other. For the purpose of demonstrating the values of the Pigors-Myers text, it is useful

---

From 8 *Public Administration Review*, 2: 134–137, 1948. Copyright © 1948 American Society for Public Administration. Reprinted with permission.

to restate the main streams in the evolution of the premises and techniques which now characterize personnel administration in public agencies.

The earliest of these, and still the source of the most distinctive public personnel practices, is the goal of eliminating party patronage from the management of the civil service. This definition of purpose has been the most enduring, the most widely understood and embraced, and consequently the most influential article of faith in the growth of the profession. From this premise the basic structure of civil service administration has been derived: central personnel control agencies, bipartisan commissions, quantitative techniques, the "rule of three," and the whole familiar arsenal of devices to neutralize and divert patronage pressures. On the whole, the means were once appropriate to the problem. But, as Gordon Clapp observed in this *Review* as early as 1941,[2] the merit system advocates having clearly won the day in most jurisdictions, the question now is what to do with the victory—which of these methods are today appropriate to the new priority objectives? And what are the new objectives?

A second, closely associated purpose was gradually made explicit in the development of the public personnel program. This goal is the guarantee of equal treatment to all applicants for public employment and among all public employees. This is clearly a positive ethic of great appeal in a democratic society, and it has won an increasing emphasis from public personnel specialists. The contribution of this goal to personnel methodology has been substantial. Its main effect has been to move personnel administration in the words of Gordon Clapp, "into the cold objective atmosphere of tests, scores, weighted indices, and split-digit ranking" so completely that "these technical trappings have become the symbols of the merit system" (p. 291).

Still another stream of influence has contributed to the fulfillment of this tendency. The logic of scientific management, the paramount ideology of articulate business management between the two wars, has also exerted a powerful attraction for the personnel administrators. The impersonal goals of management logic made the precise, quantitative techniques of the efficiency engineer plausible and attractive methods for the "scientific" personnel manager. Job classification, factor analysis, numerical efficiency ratings, formal promotion charts, and all their procedural relatives acquired a new and impressive endorsement—the personnel system could now lay claim to the combined virtues of merit, equality in competition, and scientific management.

Finally, public personnel policies and methods have been measurably affected by the goal of a public career service. Stated in its most positive terms, this objective represents an effort to provide the conditions of work which will attract and hold a public service of optimum talents. In its negative aspects, the goal has been translated into an elaborate system of protectionism. In the area of methodology the negative connotations have slowly but surely won the dominant position. The concept of status and the concept of rights earned by seniority, to use but two examples from a large network, have been molded from precedent to precedent into a personnel jurisprudence in which all but the most expert technicians lose their way.

In sum, the personnel administration produced by the confluence of these four streams of influence represents a triumph of techniques over purpose. This is not an unusual outcome in the field of administration. Nor does the conclusion mean that great historical accomplishments should not be recorded. What it does suggest is that both ends and means now urgently need fundamental reexamination.[3]

Private personnel administration has not escaped similar pressures. In particular, it has responded in its development to "scientific" management and to a modified version of careerism. The resulting complex of concepts and methods makes up a formidable system of quantitative techniques and format rules in private personnel administration. Here, too, one may conclude that the ends have been made captive by the means.

Personnel administration, then, has tended to become characterized more by procedure, rule, and technique than by purpose or results. In the public field especially, quantitative devices have overshadowed qualitative. Standardization and uniformity have been enshrined as major virtues. Universal (and therefore arbitrary) methods have been preferred to experiment and variety. From the perspective of the clientele (the public, the managers, and the employees), these traits increasingly connote rigidity, bureaucracy, institutionalism—and they are now beginning to evoke a reciprocal system of formal and informal techniques of evasion. Among personnel people there is an accompanying growth of frustration and a loss of satisfying participation in the real work of the organization.

Personnel administration, seen in this context, mirrors the dilemma of all orthodox administration. The traditional conceptual and methodological apparatus of administration has rested heavily upon the fallacy of an "administrative man" comparable to the synthetic, rational "economic man" of the classical economists. During the past fifteen years this fiction of the "administrative man" (which Elton Mayo so aptly called the "rabble hypothesis") has been steadily undermined not only by the painstaking inquiries of many students of human behavior but even more by the movement of great social forces. In the growth of personnel administration this rise of mature dissent may be traced, in large part at least, from its clearest beginnings in the reflections of John Dewey and Mary Follett upon the nature and structure of authority, in the efforts of Ordway Tead and Henry Metcalf to introduce more democratic precepts into the practice of personnel administration, and in the pioneering Hawthorne studies at Western Electric by Elton Mayo, F.J. Roethlisberger, and others. The efficiency engineer and the logician of management have slowly given way, at least at the level of administrative theory, to the psychologist, the sociologist, and other social scientists.

II

Dissent from the "rabble hypothesis" of traditional personnel administration is the central virtue of the volume by Pigors and Myers. With imagination and ingenuity they have woven into the familiar fabric of the personnel process the point of view and the basic concepts of human relations. It is difficult to condense into a few sentences the full measure of their accomplishment. Much of it, particularly for those concerned with public personnel, is implicit rather than explicit; that is, it must be translated into the specific terms and context of the public service. Perhaps something of the point of view and the method will be conveyed by the following brief excerpts from their introductory description of "basic variables" in personnel administration:

Experience in personnel administration indicates that the basic elements into which we need insight are (1) technical features, (2) the human element, (3) principles and policies, and (4) the time factor.

Technical Features. Modern management and engineering have brought the techniques of organization and productive enterprise to a high level of efficiency. In fact, progress in this direction has far outrun our capacity for dealing efficiently with people. More than that, the inclination to concentrate on mechanical systems and on the logic of efficiency has often led management to subordinate the individual to technical requirements. In what has been called the "machine age," human beings have too often been looked upon as mere functional entitles and adjuncts to machines. . . .

The Human Element. The individual in industry should be studied in two ways. First, the personnel administrator should think about the individual's needs and behavior as determined by his current situation. . . . What demand is the work situation making on him that he is unable to meet? Conversely, what demands is he making on his work situation that are not being satisfied? This approach may be called *person-centered thinking*.

Emphasis on the human element meant a step forward in the sense that management no longer defended the proposition that industrial progress can be achieved by a solution of purely technical problems. . . . A more comprehensive view attempts to balance and relate technical and human factors within an inclusive system.

Principles and Policies. The personnel administrator finds it useful to relate his observation of people and of the mechanical elements by means of his understanding of the general principles that apply to human situations. This approach may be called *policy-centered thinking*. Modern management thinks about such principles when formulating and administering policies for large-scale situations. These policies relate general principles to specific situations in such a way as to form a guide to action at all organizational levels. . . . Whatever the scale of relationships, clear and consistent policies enable us to act in a way that reconciles the different requirements made by the mechanical system and by the participating individuals. These policies form the basis for reasonable and consistent behavior.

. . . .

The Time Factor. In seeking understanding of human and technical elements, as well as of the principles that integrate both, the observer finds that he must also consider various aspects of the time element. How *far back* must we look in order to understand the meaning of what is happening now? What future events are we *moving toward?* What is the sequence of key facts? What *developmental* stage has been reached by this person or in this relationship? And how fast is the *pace?* . . .

. . . .

The practical answer to the question of where to begin is found in the situation and in its stage of development. For this reason, it is essential that a personnel worker be flexible and able to think on his feet (pp. 39–41).

The authors are not altogether successful in their attempt to transmute formal personnel procedures into useful human relations instruments.[4] This relative failure highlights one of the most difficult judgments which the human relations group must now make: to what extent can they accept and work within the present structure and methods of personnel administration? What are the hazards that any such acceptance will adulterate their concepts and inhibit further exploration and growth?

The answer, especially in public personnel administration, would seem to lie in a different perspective on the values and uses of quantitative techniques. It is not the techniques per se which have constructed the straightjacket that now imprisons so much of personnel administration. The basic techniques are, when properly used, of considerable value and of even greater potential promise. The real difficulty lies in the fact that (1) the techniques are usually inadequate for the full purpose they are relied upon to accomplish, yet accomplishment is gradually taken for granted; (2) the techniques are prematurely frozen into regulations and procedures for universal application in greatly varying administrative environments, thus stifling at birth the process of genuine research and technical development; and (3) the techniques gradually obscure the ends they were designed to serve. The contrast between this tendency of personnel specialists toward eager installation and canonization of rudimentary techniques and the stubborn experimentalism of the physical sciences is instructive. Even many of those who might be assumed to be the least susceptible to this tendency—the psychologists, with their strong experimental tradition—reveal their imprisonment within the system by devoting their energies to the refinement of the installed methods of testing skills and personality "traits" rather than to the working out of new techniques and applications in the fields of attitudes, motivation, and group dynamics.

The immediate trends as well as some of the most deeply imbedded concepts of public personnel administration are opposed to the human relations points of view. Although this is not the whole problem, it is a revealing index of the crisis in civil service administration. At a time when the urgency, difficulty, and complexity of governmental performance are daily increasing, at a time when industrial personnel administration is moving toward a recognition of the values of experimental and thorough inquiry into human behavior, tempered in application by informality and flexibility in the human relations of organized effort, the public service becomes steadily more dependent upon a cold, impersonal, rigid quantification of human ability and worth in public employment. Nor is even this the full measure of the inadequacy. The methods relied upon lack the objectivity which is their sole claim to usefulness; they provide merely the appearance, not the substance, of the relevant measurement of ability and merit. The variables of personnel administration are too many and too subtle to be contained within a purely statistical frame of reference. In contrast, a prime virtue of the human relations group is its relative lack of conceit and techniques.

Some readers may wonder whether this review overlooks the "new trends" in federal personnel administration. These trends need to be more carefully examined than opportunity here affords. However, some tentative observations are in order. During the war years, many useful explorations were made in the direction of personnel policies and methods which would be appropriate and adequate for the great tasks of federal administration. Some of these experiments still endure, but the surrounding climate is not encouraging. With perhaps the sole exception of TVA among the federal agencies, there has been uniformly a net loss of opportunity for the development of agency personnel programs responsive to the special needs of agency assignments and climate. The prewar pattern of uniform rules, designed to impose an artificial appearance of order and objectivity upon the federal establishments, has been restored and strengthened, not relaxed. "Decentralization" has been the main theme of "progress" in the postwar federal personnel program: It is relevant to inquire: what is the substance of the program being decentralized? The ultimate values of decentralization depend upon the quality of the program. The decentralization of work load under strict procedural instructions binding those who do the work is a dubious administrative economy; it certainly does not represent an important new trend in the development of an adequate philosophy and method of personnel administration.

Notes

This article was originally published as a book review: *Personnel Administration: A Point of View and a Method*, by Paul Pigors and Charles A. Myers. McGraw-Hill Book Co., 1947.

1. "Successes and Failures," in Leonard D. White, ed., *Civil Service in Wartime* (University of Chicago Press, 1945), p. 243.

2. "The Rule of Three, It Puzzles Me," 1 *Public Administration Review* 287–93 (Spring, 1941).

3. Those readers who find this judgment overdrawn are urged to examine anew *Better Government Personnel, Report of the Commission of Inquiry on Public Service Personnel* (McGraw-Hill Book Co., 1935), *the Report of the President's Committee on Administrative Management* (Government Printing Office, 1937), and the accompanying monograph by Floyd W. Reeves and Paul T. David, *Personnel Administration in the Federal Service* (Government Printing Office, 1937); *the Report of the President's Committee on Civil Service Improvement* (H. Doc. No. 118, 77th Cong. 1st Sess.); and J. Donald Kingsley's *Representative Bureaucracy; An Interpretation of the British Civil Service* (Antioch Press, 1944).

4. As a textbook, *Personnel Administration* acquires immeasurable additional value from the case materials included. These provide real-life illustrations for most chapters. The cases are presented with satisfying completeness (190 pages are devoted to 19 cases), and each one is accompanied by a series of searching and provocative questions for discussion.

CHAPTER 2

THE NEUTRALITY OF THE PUBLIC SERVICE

DAVID M. LEVITAN

This war has clarified many prevailing conceptions. A conflict of ideas and faiths neces-sarily brings into question much of what has been accepted. This is, therefore, an espe-cially appropriate time for a reexamination of some of the traditionally accepted notions concerning the proper role of the public servant under a party system of government. The author proposes to examine the prevailing conception of the proper political behavior of the public servant; to state some of the pitfalls which accompany the present notion; and finally, to suggest the beginnings of a code of political behavior for the public servant.

It is generally stated that the civil servant must adopt an attitude of impartially toward the conflicting philosophies of government espoused by the various political parties. This attitude has been termed the doctrine of the neutrality of the public service. Two propo-sitions are usually implied by this statement: first, that the public servant must abstain from any participation in the affairs of political parties while retaining the right of private discussion of political issues and of voting as he pleases; and second, that he is ethically and morally bound to administer the policy decisions of whichever party happens to be in power with equal zeal and determination. As to the former theory, it is recognized that, while the official under the American system is also a citizen and consequently entitled to the rights of a citizen, he may legitimately be deprived of the freedom to participate in the affairs of political parties. That limitation is simply a condition of employment. As to the second, it is open to question whether it can or should be applied in full vigor.

The development of the war program with the resulting expansion of the role of the federal government has dramatically illustrated the need for the establishment of a genuine career service in the federal government. The development of a career service necessitates a clear definition of the code of conduct of the career employee toward his political superior under our system of party government.

Foundations of Career Service

The elements which together constitute the foundation of a career service have been fully discussed elsewhere; some will be restated here. A career service must provide that

From 2 *Public Administration Review*, 317–23, 1942. Copyright © 1942 American Society for Public Administration. Reprinted with permission.

entrance into the service shall be based wholly upon merit, without any regard to political considerations. Also a career service must provide for permanence of tenure during good behavior and satisfactory performance and for an opportunity for promotion to the very top of the administrative hierarchy, exclusive of position involving policy determination. It is clear that if political parties are to comply faithfully with the spirit of these rules, the employee must refrain from participation in party affairs and, moreover, must adopt in attitude of neutrality regarding the policy decisions which he called upon to execute.

It requires little imagination to visualize the effect of employee participation in political affairs. Surely one could not expect a department head to place complete trust in an employee who in effect worked against his entrance into office or who worked for his removal from power. Aside from the personal antagonism which would arise, it would be natural for a department head to nourish at least a suspicion as to the employee's zeal in carrying out his orders and possibly a fear of sabotage by the employee. Nor is it enough that the employee be barred from actual political participation. Rather it is the supreme duty of the public servant in a democracy faithfully and zealously to administer the decisions of the administration in power so long as he remains in his position. That is simply the basic requirement of loyalty to a superior. The public servant in a democracy has, however, an additional obligation of loyalty. It is the duty of every citizen in a democracy to abide by the majority decision. Surely the public servant, the employee of the citizenry, has no special prerogatives giving him the privilege of disregarding the decisions of the majority.

Admirers of the British public service point with great pride to the record of complete impartially, devotion, and loyalty of the public service to the Labour party during its tenure in office in spite of the fact that most of the higher civil servants were, by temperament and orientation, devotees of the philosophy of the Conservative party.[1]

> . . . the British civil servant is famous, not in this country alone, for the zeal and ability with which he carries out the policy of the government in power, whatever it may be, and for the success which he represses his personal feelings and opinions inside and (were necessary) outside the conduct of official business. . . .[2]

The writer agrees thoroughly that members of the public service must abstain from political participation and are bound to execute with loyalty and devotion the policies of whatever party is in power—to effect the majority will. Civil service rules, the Hatch Act, and other statues and regulations have sought to incorporate the first of these conditions into law.

Because of the long history of political participation in the United States, especially by the higher administrative personnel, it was well for students of administration to stress the importance of the neutrality of public service. Today there is a distinct and urgent need for a change of emphasis. There is a vital necessity, especially among the groups in the lower level of the hierarchy, for a renewed devotion to political ideas and for an infusion of a spirit of dedication to ideals and concepts. The aim is not to make political debating clubs out of "stenographic pools" but to avoid the decitizenation of hundreds of thousands of Americans.

Nor is this merely a wartime need. The war has simply made the need more apparent and more urgent. In this connection it is necessary to distinguish between two groups of employees. One group, especially among the clerical and lower administrative series, may have strong ideological identification altogether. A second group, among the professional and higher administrative series, may have strong ideological identification but may become impressed with the need for repressing feelings and beliefs inside and outside of official business. The continuous emphasis on the neutrality of the public service has resulted in the development of an attitude of ideological indifference among a great portion of the public service. This in turn is conducive to the development of a bureaucratic mentality, to a complete absorption with "administrivia," and to a total divorcement from the basic philosophical, social, and political controversies behind the decisions which the public servant is called upon to execute.

Education in Citizenship

It is all too probable that the civil servant whose work does not bring him directly into touch with the broader questions of policy will develop just such an attitude of indifference. The typical person, it must be acknowledged, is not a political theorist; his limited thinking about ideological questions of a political nature arises only in the course of the discharge of his duties as a citizen, especially his participation in elections and his discussions of politics as they affect his immediate environment. The government employee in Washington is to a large extent deprived of the former outlet since few Washington employees of the federal government have an opportunity to vote. Some states do not permit absentee voting, and in those that do the procedure is cumbersome. Probably only a small percentage of government employees living in Washington exercise the right of suffrage.

The political discussions in which Washington employees participate, moreover, are not usually discussions of local community affairs as they affect people in their capacity as citizens but discussions among government employees of political affairs as they affect personal power and prestige or conditions and terms of employment. The unions of government employees tend to be more limited in their objectives than other unions, and preoccupation with these limited objectives tends to narrow the political and social consciousness of the government employees.

Consequently there is today an urgent need for a program of ideological education of government employees. It is true that the general program of "selling democracy," which is directed to the population as a whole, also reaches civil servants. That effort, however, is not sufficient, chiefly because the need is much more acute. A civil servant in a democracy cannot properly discharge his duties and responsibilities unless he has a firm appreciation of the meaning of democracy, of the dignity of the citizen, and of the concept of being a servant of the people. Some special effort is needed to convince employees in lower-grade positions detached from policy considerations and employees concerned largely with technical or professional considerations that their positions were established for the purpose of extending service to the people. It is hard for accountants or classification experts to appreciate sufficiently the part which their specialties play in the total complex machinery of public service. Such an appreciation must be our objective.

A great injustice is being committed against the public servant. The role of aircraft workers, tool- and diemakers, longshoremen, and other war laborers has been dramatized, and an effort has been made to develop in them a sense of identification with democracy, with the great ideals for which we are fighting. A failure by a stenographer in the priorities division of the War Production Board to get out in time a certain form or letter could paralyze an important segment of the war effort. Yet no real attempt has been made to make that employee fully conscious of the importance of his or her role and of the employee's responsibility in this struggle. The employee who appreciates the significance of the world struggle, and who is made proud of his role in it, will find new meaning in pounding the typewriter, operating office machines, or processing priority forms. It is remarkable in this connection that, with the spread of emphasis on training, nowhere does one find a general elementary course directed to an explanation of our system of government. Training courses are devoted to an explanation of the procedure of processing forms, to improving one's public speaking technique, or to developing an excellence in shorthand, typing, and operating office machines. This sort of training and job preparation, while very significant, totally overlooks the importance of the intangible and psychological factors which profoundly influence the employee's performance of his daily duties.

It is particularly necessary to adopt a program for the education of employees in the lower grades of the civil service regarding the policies and objectives of the agencies for which they work if we are to maintain in the American public service free opportunity for advancement from the lowest positions to the highest ones. Unless some special measures are taken, it is impossible to expect a person whose work is completely routine to acquire a broader point of view and the sense of responsibility that is necessary in the higher administrative positions. There need be no conflict between an educational program designed for this purpose and an attitude of impartiality between the political parties. Once Congress and the president have set up an agency to accomplish a certain purpose, we can properly expect its employees to be officially neutral as between political parties, but we should not expect them to look with equal favor on those who wish to accomplish the agency's purpose and those who wish to distort its purpose for party or group advantage.

The lower grades of the civil service, in short, are as urgently in need of "indoctrination" courses as are persons who are inducted into the armed forces and for the same reason, since by their effort they are contributing to the general victory program of the nation.

The higher grades of executive personnel, including administrative officials in the $4,600 per year range and up, are more closely concerned with matters of policy. Hence, it is even more necessary not to subject them to an indiscriminating interpretation of the doctrine of political neutrality. It is important to make a clear distinction between neutrality as applied to political parties and neutrality as applied to policies and principles.

Political Principles

All members of the public service must abstain from participation in party affairs. The same rule should not apply as to political principles. It is neither realistic nor advisable to expect the higher public servant to remain totally unconcerned with the political philosophy that he is called upon to administer. Is the public servant to be less militant, less honest about his political principles, than the normal citizen? Is the public servant expected to develop a split personality—to be one man in thought and belief and another in action as the administrative agent of political superiors? It is well recognized that people do their best only when they have genuine interest in and enthusiasm for their work. That enthusiasm can come only when they are engaged in work in which they genuinely believe.

The doctrine of neutrality was developed in England at a time when the chief basis for distinguishing different administrations was the name of the party in power, when the functions that were to be performed were generally accepted, and when all members of the civil service were assumed to have a right to life tenure. These conditions do not prevail in the United States, at least with respect to the work of some agencies, and during the past twenty years the difference in philosophy between the major parties in Great Britain has led even some British authorities to argue that neutrality is out of date. The complete doctrine of neutrality is an anachronism and a fiction which may well be discarded. It is based on misconceptions regarding the meaning of the professional attitude, regarding the nature of the science of public administration, and regarding the role and behavior of the higher civil servant. Even a career public servant, steeped in the tradition of neutrality, confessed that the public servant "cannot accomplish that remark able feat always and entirely [repressing his personal feeling], though he will always attempt it and never consciously fail in the attempt."[3]

As the functions of government spread into more controversial fields and as pressure groups and sometimes parties differ over specific programs, the *modus operandi* of the doctrine of political neutrality has been destroyed. Students of administration have emphasized the growth of the professional spirit among members of the public service and the influence of this development on the issue. They have pointed out that the professional spirit, the feeling that one is a member of a public service which transcends loyalty to any group, contributes to removing the public servant from the controversies of the market place. They have pointed out that it is part of the professional code of the career public servant thus to detach himself, that the civil servant must recognize that in a democracy policy decisions rest with the chosen representatives of the people, and that the role of the professional servant must be limited to the execution of these decisions.

In this connection it is interesting to note professor Carr's statement in his recent and highly challenging book, *Conditions of Peace*,[4] regarding the role of the civil servant in the modern state.

> The second and cognate cause of the decline in the reality of democratic rights has been the growth of bureaucracy. This is a symptom and consequence of the assumption of new functions by the state. To deplore or denounce it is futile; for the new economic functions of the twentieth-century state cannot be abandoned, and cannot be performed without a vast and complicated administrative machine. . . . As early as 1966 the German sociologist, Max Weber, wrote of this "new bondage," . . . The problem is twofold. In the first place, the House of Commons can no longer either discuss and criticize intelligently much of the highly technical legislation which it has to pass, or exercise even the most remote control over the processes of administration. Ministers are more dependent on their permanent civil servants than at any previous period, . . . By force of circumstances, the bureaucrat and the

specialist have very largely supplanted the minister and the member of Parliament as the managers of public affairs. Secondly—and as a corollary of this development—the ordinary voter is less able than ever before to feel that he is living under a system which makes him one of the governors as well as one of the governed. . . .

This analysis calls to our attention a serious trend, yet while the trend is inevitable the resulting situation is not. A public service highly conscious of its democratic responsibilities and in tune with the political philosophy of the administration in power will do much toward the reestablishment of a "ruler and ruled" identity in the public mind.

In some quarters there is a growing conception of administration as a science in the sense that the principles of administration are universally applicable. Therefore, it is alleged to the professional administrator it matters little what he administers. The philosophy, the ideology, the end, is immaterial. It is the function of the administrator to apply certain well-established and uniformly valid principles. That surely is too naïve an interpretation of the complexities of the administrative process.

Neutrality of the public official and continuance in office regardless of the administration in power are correct in theory and practice whenever party labels only are at stake and not fundamental policies or philosophies. Nor should an attitude of indifference, whether dignified by a label of professional spirit or not, be encouraged in the upper administrative corps even if it could be established. Men should not continue or be continued in positions where they will be called upon to advise and administer policies contrary to deeply rooted personal beliefs. The classic view is that though the career public servant is obligated to press forcefully his point of view to his political superior, yet if the superior insists on following another point of view, the civil servant must obey and is apparently expected to remain in his position and administer the decision.[5] Yes, obey he must as any other citizen simply because the decision is that of his government; but if it is a major decision and involves a major point of difference, then the civil servant should not remain responsible for the administration of that decision. He cannot fully execute that policy, and he should not be expected to. Naturally, this assumes that the civil servant has not been won over by his superior's logic and point of view—just overruled. There can be no continuance in his position if he accepts the philosophy he is to administer.

In an analysis of this problem it is important to bear in mind the role of the administrative personnel, other than the political heads of the agencies, in the administration of any program. Recent legislation provides for a great deal of administrative process. The administration of any large program gives rise to a great deal of what is commonly referred to as administrative interpretation even after the major policy decisions have been incorporated into the basic legislation and the political department heads have announced the over-all decisions. Through the use of such terms as "administrative interpretation" we tend to confuse and cloud the nature of the problem. The decisions and interpretations, though related to questions arising in the course of day-by-day administration, often have an important bearing on the program as a whole.

The attitudes and points of view of many officials often become apparent in the course of making what appear to be purely administrative decisions. To cite but one example, the case of procedure writers in the Railroad Retirement Board or in the Social Security Board, who are responsible for establishing the procedures for the registration or adjudication of unemployment claims. Here are a number of apparently simple administrative questions, yet the answer to these may well vary with the inarticulate premises of the employees. Should the procedure for registering a claim be made with emphasis on simplicity and accessibility to every potential claimant or should the emphasis be placed on what is termed "administrative feasibility"? The social attitude of the procedure writer will often determine the place of emphasis. Again, what constitutes "administrative feasibility" in turn depends on whether the official is more concerned with the plight of the unemployed citizen or with the smooth flow of papers.

The policy incorporated in the act or the policy of any board may be very liberal, yet a group of procedure writers may include so many rigid conditions for filing claims, hiding behind the fiction that it is the business of the person concerned to know all the requirements, that a great number of individuals may be deprived of payments although the act and the board intended that they should be compensated. We are not speaking of conscious violations of the spirit of the act but rather of unconscious deviations in the process of making simple decisions on details of administration. Legislation, in short, bequeaths discretion to administrators who, to a degree, are forced to participate in the refinement and restatement of policy. Can they be neutral in this portion of their task?

It cannot be too strongly emphasized that we do not propose a return to the spoils system or a limitation of the civil service system. We have attempted to distinguish between party partisanship and devotion to political principles. The significant matter is not what party is in power—it is the philosophy that is to be administered. Also, since some high administrative positions do not directly involve decisions related to political principles, the incumbents of these positions conceivably need not to be concerned at all with questions of policy. In any case, the decision whether to remain in a position should rest with the agency concerned. It is for the employee to search his conscience and to decide whether his political ideology is so strongly at odds with the program that he will be called on to administer as to make it impossible for him to give full, loyal, and zealous service. It is on this question that his professional ethics should be his guide. Can he remain on the job without detriment to the service? Can he continue to discharge the functions of the position effectively? Is he certain of his continued loyalty and devotion to his position? If he entertains any doubt as to the effectiveness with which he can continue to perform his duties then there remains but one course open to him—to step out of that position. It may very often be possible to transfer the employee to a position further removed from the forum of political controversy. Under any circumstances he must not remain in the former position. Should the disaffected employee choose to continue in his position under the new administration, his superior reserves the right to remove him in case of disloyalty or mal-administration, subject to the usual civil service removal procedures.

Conclusion

Throughout the civil service there is an acute need for a greater realization of the relationship between the administration of government and the broader social and political issues of the day. Some steps should be taken to educate the lower grades of the civil service not only in the general significance of the role of democratic government in world affairs today but in the relationship of their various agencies' programs to general government policy. Such an educational program would not only improve their attitude toward their current work but would make it more easily possible for them to fit themselves for the acceptance of broader responsibilities.

As for the higher administrative hierarchy, the search for absolute political neutrality is a quest for the impossible. There is still a need for political impartiality insofar as it concerns party participation. On the other hand, there is no need for a complete detachment of attitude toward the controversies of the public forum; such an attitude is not proof of the development of a professional outlook. It is time to stop pretending that it is a sign of a broad perspective and long-term vision to close one's eyes to controversies of the day simply because in the long evolution of mankind many of these have been automatically resolved by lapse of time and change of conditions. It is not a sign of vision or objectivity to detach oneself from the controversial problems of the day—such aloofness rather manifests a refusal to discharge one's obligation to his fellowmen, if not a lack of moral strength. Nor is it true that the scientific method requires concern only with questions removed from the arena of controversy—that it is impossible to investigate scientifically questions which are under public debate.

It should not be assumed that the public servant should concern himself with every issue that becomes the basis for public debate. There is need for a sense of evaluation and a capacity to distinguish the basic from the temporary. The public servant in an executive position must not permit himself to develop a sense of detachment from fundamental current controversies. As a citizen he is, of course, bound to obey the decisions of the government in power. He should not, however, continue as an instrument for the effectuation of those decisions if he finds himself completely at odds with the philosophy underlying them. He, like all citizens, must reserve the right to protest against policies which he considers detrimental to the public good even at the expense of resigning from public service.

Some line must be drawn between the two extremes of participation in party squabbles and cynical detachment from all personal interest in national policy. Perhaps the line may vary according to the nature of the various programs and the jobs themselves, but certainly the higher administrative official, even though he may be willing to adjust his general purposes to the judgment of his political superior, should not be required to adopt an attitude of indifference to the purposes themselves.

Notes

1. Hugh Dalton, *Practical Socialism for Britain* (George Routledge & Sons, 1935), pp. 11–14.

2. H.E. Dale, *The Higher Civil Service of Great Britain* (Oxford University Press, 1941), p. 46. See also Herman Finer and others, "The Administrative Class: Past and Future," 2 *Public Administration Review* 259–265 (1942).

3. Dale, *op. cit.*, p. 46.

4. Edward Hallet Carr, *Conditions of Peace* (Macmillian, 1942), pp. 28–29.

5. Finer, *op. cit.,* p. 261.

CHAPTER 3

CIVIL SERVICE VERSUS MERIT

BERNARD L. GLADIEUX

After many years of service in the federal government, I stepped out over a year ago into the fresh air of the free administrative world. My first pleasant awareness of the sharp contrast with the restrictive administrative system of the government came with the recruitment of staff for the operating office of The Ford Foundation in New York City. In this recruitment, no insistent demands from "the Hill" plagued me for the appointment of friends or constituents. There was no one from the White House or the Democratic National Committee informing me that he had just the right person for the job, or that someone else needed "to be taken care of." There was no one from the Civil Service Commission telling me that the person I had selected was not high enough on the register, or that the job classification was out of line, or that a displaced career person had been discovered who, by some abstruse process, was adjudged to possess the "minimum qualifications" for the position.

These limitations and outside influences simply did not exist for me any longer and I needed to concentrate only on the qualifications of the people I wished to employ.

In retrospect, I am now prone to wonder how the federal government is able to operate at all under the limitations of its personnel system. Badgered on the one hand by political demands and harried on the other by the ever growing network of personnel rules and restrictions, the responsible administrator must indeed be a paragon these days to maintain his administrative equilibrium and avoid the frustrations of public service.

Inflexibility Defeats Merit

Now, I would not claim that the federal government can dispense with a civil service system. Any public organization so huge and complex must have a central personnel control to help assure good executive management and the equitable treatment of employees.

Nevertheless, it is my basic thesis that the growing inflexibility of the civil service system of the federal government has not only served as a major impediment to the recruitment and retention of the best personnel for public service, but that these rigidities, so hopefully designed to eliminate political considerations, have failed in even this negative objective.

I realize there are many other conditions and situations which contribute to the present crisis—and I think "crisis" is the right word—in public employment. I refer to such matters as the statutory limitations under which the Civil Service Commission operates, the deteriorating political situation in the past few years which has hardly been conducive to a professional job of personnel management in the government, the absence of adequate financial inducement, and the abuse heaped on public officials.

Nevertheless, civil service inflexibility and unadaptability must, in my judgment, bear a considerable share of the blame for the general failure of our public personnel policies to meet the demands of our national interest in this crisis situation.

Moreover, I do not believe these limitations can be fully justified on grounds of "uniformity." Certainly the desirability of reasonable uniformity cannot be challenged in such matters as pay rates for comparable work, qualification standards, annual leave allowances, and other basic features of a personnel system. There are many limitations, however, which seem to the non-technician to exceed this objective of reasonable uniformity and to restrict the exercise of normal management judgment on the part of executives in personnel matters.

Politics and Civil Service

Historically, one of the principal motives for severely constricting the exercise of individual judgment by administrators in personnel actions has been the laudable objective of eliminating patronage. It is my contention that we have reached the point of diminishing returns in this matter and that there is no longer any assurance that more regulations will mean less patronage.

While I deplore, as do all thoughtful observers, the introduction of political influence in employment matters, I think it is too much to expect that in a dynamic democracy it will ever be possible to remove politics completely from public employment. We can only seek to minimize this factor.

Certainly the detailed and circumscribing regulations of the current civil service system have not succeeded in keeping political considerations out of personnel management. In spite of the increasing body of limitations, it is my observation that politics in employment is more prevalent now than when I first entered the government in the late 1930s. Most of us are aware, I'm sure, although those of you in the federal service are not in a position to say much about it, that there has been a considerable and deliberate increase in the pressures for, and in the volume of, political appointments in the last several years, despite civil service regulations and often within their framework.

This increase is particularly noticeable in the pressures generated within the executive branch, though political demands from the legislative side have hardly diminished. While these demands are usually not presented in the crude and bald forms of earlier years, they are nevertheless equally insistent. Agencies in the field of foreign affairs are somewhat exempt from the requests for "cooperation," but coping with these requests in most agencies is a major cross and one of the principal hazards of public life at the executive level.

No matter how tightly the federal personnel structure is drawn, political manipulators will always find loopholes. How many times a politically motivated supervisor or administrator has informed me with a grin of his success in appointing a favorite candidate "all strictly according to civil service!" There are other means of minimizing the political factor than burdening personnel management with cumbersome limitations.

Limitations of the Present System

Moreover, in this process of adding restrictions to keep pace with political inroads and justifying limitations improperly on grounds of uniformity, the civil service system has become so complex that only the few who concentrate on it full time are familiar with all the rulings and regulations which govern the system. Many administrators have long since given up any attempt to understand how civil service operates. It is simply left to "personnel experts" who become specialists in the vagaries of personnel procedures and regulations, but who are not permitted to join the top management team. By having to leave personnel matters so much to personnel technicians, the manager has become increasingly removed from one of the principal elements of management. To my mind, this is one of the most deplorable results of this administrative Gargantua into which the federal personnel system has grown.

The present rigidities place the administrator in a procedural and administrative jacket which is not conducive to public accountability. The poor administrator can always use the excuse that he has been handicapped by inability to obtain or retain the best people through the system. The able administrator cannot help but feel that some outside force is exercising more direct control and influence over the character of his organization than he himself. Acceptance of full accountability is understandably difficult under these circumstances.

The most significant inflexibility inherent in the present system is a conceptual one. Somewhere along the line many personnel officials have tended to lose sight of the original concept of "merit" in public service and to substitute the idea of "civil service" in which tenure and status are the primary considerations.

Under this concept, we have come to assume that merit and ability are synonymous with "status" and that if one has acquired civil service status, in no matter what obscure manner, then he belongs to the club of the anointed and is entitled to rise up the ladder under some special charm. Nothing short of disloyalty or malfeasance can dislodge him. All this makes for an "ingrown parochialism" among large segments of our public employees.

There has been a great deal of improvement in civil service recruiting techniques over the last several years, particularly of people in the lower administrative and professional levels. The present system, however, is generally not adapted to attracting or developing personnel for executive level positions. Recruitment at entrance levels is apt to be through examinations designed to reveal competence to handle junior level jobs only. Little effort is made in most instances to discover potentialities for executive level jobs which demand a more general operating capacity.

Most civil service selection is on the basis of written tests which measure intellectual and educational values but fail to evaluate personality characteristics and the ability to work within the dynamics of human relations. Yet our general administrators eventually must in large part be developed out of this group of individuals who originally came in through the specialized recruitment channels and who only by accident display administrative aptitude.

In my judgment, the Civil Service Commission has relied too exclusively on its own facilities and its own judgment for the recruitment of intermediate professional and executive talent. Although it has made efforts in the direction of using the facilities and learning the points of view of the departments through committees of expert examiners, this device needs to be greatly improved and expanded.

The latitude of the departments in the selection of personnel examined through the general civil service process needs to be broadened so that the responsibility of the operating agency for the selection of its personnel is more nearly equal to that of the central personnel agency. This would, in turn, place a heavier burden on the commission for coordination, standards, and the auditing of performance.

My greatest objection to the present civil service system is what might be called the rigidities of tenure. Persons who have been in high administrative posts know how really difficult it has become to dismiss a status employee short of charges of disloyalty or accusations of gross malfeasance. I think it is fundamentally wrong for the government to have to spend $50,000 or even $5,000 to dismiss an incompetent employee, and I can cite cases which have cost even more than the higher figure.

The effect of the present policy and practice of placing the burden of proof in dismissals so completely on the department or agency is to discourage the supervisor from initiating cases in all instances except of the highest extremity. The department serving the charges of incompetence or unsuitability is required to produce what is in effect evidence and testimony which would hold up under the standards of court litigation. If the defendant obtains a smart lawyer, he can prolong the case and harass the charging official to a point where he becomes discouraged and unwilling to face the persecution visited on him at the hands of opposing counsel. These hearings frequently degenerate into an attempt to discredit the supervisor by wild and unsubstantiated countercharges. As a result, the case is frequently dropped and the individual restored simply because the defendant and his attorneys wear out the government representatives.

I know of many administrators of high reputation and unquestioned integrity who practically refuse to serve a dismissal notice if it involves the filing of civil service charges on grounds of competence or suitability. They claim, with considerable justice, that it is they rather than the employee who must undergo trial and that life is too short and their time too valuable. This is a deplorable but widespread view.

Suggestions for Improvement

Not being a personnel technician, I need not pretend that I know all the answers. In general, I would suggest that the Civil Service Commission place much less reliance on absolute formulas in the selection and retention of federal employees and much greater reliance on the judgment of the commission and the employing agency. More specifically:

1. The "rule of three" should be abandoned as an archaic carry-over from the early days of the anti-spoils fight. Pro vision should be made for the certification of availability for appointment of all those ruled as qualified by the Civil Service Commission. A similar and alternative plan was recommended by the Hoover Commission three years ago. Under that plan applicants would not be given a numerical rating but would be grouped into categories such as "outstanding," "well qualified," "qualified," and "unqualified." These changes would clearly require the commission to establish higher standards of eligibility than now used.

   Such a plan would preserve the commission's authority for establishing standards and at the same time would give flexibility to appointing officials. Certainly it would force operating agencies to assume more responsibility for their appointment actions, and this in itself would be highly salutary.
2. The commission must also derive some better way of conferring civil service status on the non-civil-service employee who has proved his qualifications by performance. I am glad to know that plans are now being considered to save the best of the present group of temporary employees for continued government service. We must not repeat the mistakes made following 1945 in connection with war service employees. The public service will suffer for many years to come because of the uncompromising and destructive manner in which the war service employee, capable though he may have been, was indiscriminately rooted out of the government, frequently in favor of a much less qualified status employee.
3. The reduction-in-force regulations should be drastically revised. I know of no other practice so disruptive to good administration as the requirement that lay-offs be effected almost entirely on the basis of status and tenure. Frequently this practice has had the effect of forcing out a competent employee and replacing him with an incompetent or unqualified person. Only those who have had to administer the inflexible formula prescribed by the RIF regulations can understand the indescribable confusion and scrambling of jobs, men, and qualifications attendant on their application. The "chain bumping" which takes place through the uninhibited exercise of "retreat rights" in a reduction in force is better calculated to upset the stability of an organization than anything else yet devised in the field of civil service.
4. Promotions, even including within-grade promotions, should be based on a higher standard of merit as evidenced by performance and high efficiency ratings, with the factor of tenure de-emphasized. I do not suggest that this factor should be eliminated, but only that it should not be controlling.

The provision that only those receiving a rating of "good" or better are to be given automatic salary increases is practically meaningless in terms of merit. It is common knowledge that the efficiency rating "good" is frequently a cover for incompetence or worse.

5. Above all, the whole procedure and policy for dismissals needs a complete overhauling. Basically, this will involve a change in attitude on the part of the reviewing officers of the Civil Service Commission whose tendency is to favor the appellant and give him the benefit of every doubt. This is a matter which has evolved into a state of imbalance and needs to be rectified so that both the agency and the employee are treated equitably.

My suggestion is that all heads of agencies be given discretionary authority to dismiss anyone in their organizations on the basis of written charges and with an opportunity provided the employee to be heard by an appeals board appointed by the Secretary or other agency head. The Secretary's decision should not be reviewable, but the dismissed employee should have the right of a hearing before the Civil Service Commission to determine whether he may be declared eligible for appointment in some other agency of the government. The commission should not have the authority to direct restoration in the dismissing agency.

I appreciate the need for a career service which offers protection from arbitrary or capricious dismissal and which provides some hope that the competent and industrious employee can look forward to a rewarding and long-time career in the public service. Too many employees, however, have accepted all of the protections and privileges of federal service and have neglected their obligations as the holders of a public trust dependent on tax funds.

Current Evaluation of Civil Service

Under present trends, I fear we are drifting to the point in public employment where we consider the mediocre as adequate and the merely adequate as sufficient. In my judgment, the spreading paralysis of mediocrity constitutes more of a threat to our democracy than the recent disclosures of corruption in Washington, though these disclosures are far more spectacular. With the present-day emphasis on conformity and the restraints on imaginative positive action, our public employees are in danger of evolving into mere civil service eunuchs. It seems to me that the present civil service system fosters a leveling process in which the good and the bad are treated much alike, with diminishing incentives for the individual who has initiative and ability.

I wish to make it clear that I dissociate myself from those who make blanket accusations against the civil servants serving this nation. The view of some political demagogues that all government employees are incompetent bureaucrats, crooks, or disloyal persons is as fallacious as the view of some civil service apologists that there is nothing wrong with government that more civil service can't cure.

From my own experience, I know how many fine, capable, conscientious people are serving the government at all levels. The majority are carrying on in the best traditions of the public service and any blanket indictment of them is wholly unfair and not in conformance with the facts. They need to be rewarded and encouraged in larger measure than is now the case.

Yet there is a minority who are taking advantage of the protections and privileges of the civil service system in a way to discredit the career service. Unfortunately our civil service system does not give adequate protection against this type of employee.

Among top-level administrators there is a feeling that our current government personnel systems have generally failed to be responsive to administrative and operational needs. It is paradoxical that at a time when the concept of a career service based on merit is rather generally accepted by the public, the civil service system is encountering the most serious attack since the enactment of the Civil Service Act of 1883.

This attack is directed not at the merit concept as such. Although there are many politically motivated people who would favor some modern version of the spoils system, we can disregard this attack from political sources as not serious. What is serious is the attack on civil service by many able and intelligent public leaders sincerely interested in the improvement of government personnel.

Almost without exception, the high officials in Washington with whom I have been associated are privately critical of large segments of civil service practice. They feel that civil service frequently serves as a protective cloak to an entrenched bureaucracy. One of these days, this attack on the system may become open, and serious damage may be done when the intelligent critics of the system are joined by those politicians who will always favor a return to the more obtrusive forms of patronage.

I know that there are many able and sincere people in the Civil Service Commission who are making a real effort to improve government personnel practices. The commission, however, has created many of the inflexibilities that constitute a major barrier to its efforts to develop improved techniques of personnel administration.

I realize that personnel officials stand in an unenviable position between the advocates of more control and more restrictions on the one hand, and the advocates of laissez-faire on the other. I am confident there is a middle ground which will preserve high uniform standards across the government yet which will also give the responsible operator the latitude to acquire and keep the fully qualified people he must have to do the job and to screen out the incompetent and the mediocre.

To my mind, this is the most important management problem facing the professional administrative groups represented here. In a crisis age, it behooves us to find quickly the solutions which will make the career service synonymous with merit.

Note

This paper was presented at a session on "Flexibility in the Federal Civil Service" at the Annual Conference of the Society, March 8, 1952.

CHAPTER 4

PUBLIC PERSONNEL

Agenda for the Sixties

FELIX A. NIGRO

At the beginning, let me make clear that I do not plan to play the role of Messiah, leading my flock of personnel administrators to a happy decade of successes in the Sixties. My task is of another order. It is to report on the emerging goals in the public personnel field as I discern them from the many reports, articles, and other materials the trade kindly makes available to the textbook writer.

We can't talk about the Sixties without taking a long look into the past. I suggest we look back as far as the Thirties, for this will give us valuable perspective. Young or old, we are prone to forget or under-rate what has been accomplished in the past. We groan about present difficulties and despair of ever being able to solve some of them. Everyone could make a long list of important things, urgent things which still remain to be done in his jurisdiction and in the personnel field generally. A mountain of work looms ahead, but, if you think back on the past, you suddenly realize that this mountain is not as big as it used to be.

Before making this comparison, I want to refer to what Lawrence Appley refers to as "the frustration gap."[1] By this he means the contrast between ideals and reality and how discouraging this gap is as we struggle in the present to narrow it. Personnel practitioners usually don't think of themselves as idealists, but I know few of them who don't feel deeply that certain improvements should be made in personnel programs. There's no use denying that there is a "frustration gap" in personnel work; indeed, the difficulty of pointing to tangible measurements of what the personnel office has accomplished adds to this sense of despair. But note Appley's wise words: "what is significant in life is not how far human practice is from the ideal, but how much nearer it is to the ideal than it was at some previous time."

Personnel Administration in the Thirties

Important developments were taking shape by the late Thirties, particularly in the Federal government, but in general this is the picture of public personnel administration in the country as a whole at that time:

A preponderance of the daily working hours devoted to the routine aspects of appointments, records, and classification.

Centralization of most important personnel decisions in the Civil Service Commission and normal delays of several weeks in placing someone on the departmental payrolls.

Very little in-service training activity and, worse, the definite opinion of Congress, the General Accounting Office, and some personnel people themselves that the employee was responsible for his own training.

Only scattered evidence of interest in the improved personnel practices being developed in private industry, despite the obvious importance of some of these techniques and the possibility of using them in the government.

Very little career planning in the line departments, despite the rush of college graduates, attracted by the New Deal, to Washington.

Internships chiefly limited to those generously provided by the National Institute of Public Affairs (even though the NIPA paid the interns, even the legality of this program was questioned!).

Almost a complete neglect of the importance of good supervision and of the personnel responsibilities of line officials in general.

A fairly high percentage of supervisors whose basic conception of their role was "to get the work out of" their subordinates.

Very few personnel directors with any real voice in the management policies of their agencies.

Little attention to employee welfare and health, apart from some low-priced cafeterias, emergency rooms, bowling leagues, and softball.

Nagging restrictions (none of which could safely be questioned), such as no payment of moving of household effects, travel expenses of applicants called for interview, and, in general, a niggardly attitude towards payment of legitimate expenses of employees.

How Far Up the Hill?

Why is the picture so much better today? Most important of all, the whole concept of personnel administration has changed. Today there is far more recognition of the vital role that personnel management can play in accomplishing agency objectives. It no longer is considered as just an adjunct to the agency program. On the contrary, it is now accepted by many as an indispensable part of the management equipment for carrying out the agency program successfully.

To quote Appley again, management is personnel administration.[2] Many more people now accept this, and this is true in government, not just in industry. This description may seem to exaggerate the current rating of the personnel function. On the other hand, its present position, speaking generally for the nation as a whole, is one of relative strength and should not be under-rated.

What are some of the noteworthy improvements? The examination process is much faster; delays of several months in preparing eligible lists are no longer common. No self-respecting personnel administrator could get away with this nowadays. Even more important, the examinations themselves are substantially improved. In fact, there is good reason to believe that government does a better job of selection than most private companies. Recruitment efforts are both more intensive and more effective. In fact, we may have gone so far in this direction that some possible candidates, for example college students, are given an exaggerated sense of their importance. But certainly it is better to woo them as a group than to make no appeal at all to any of them.

Decentralization

Could the Civil Service Commission be persuaded to decentralize? This was a question many personnel people discussed anxiously before the outbreak of World War II. One personnel man present at a large meeting of Federal personnel workers during the War suggested that the Commission should allow the agencies to classify positions, subject to Commission standards and post-audit. Actually, to meet the War emergency the Commission had greatly speeded up approval of classification and appointment actions. Still the suggestion seemed Utopian at the time. It was thought that the Commission would never agree to this. Yet just a few years afterwards in 1949, such decentralization was provided for by law, with the Commission concurring. Perhaps there should be even more decentralization than there is today, but no one can deny that, whereas the Commission insisted on many prior approvals before the War, today its keynote is decentralization and reliance on agency initiative and responsibility.

Training

The contrast with the past is the greatest in the field of training. It is true that such astute observers as Gladys Kammerer have not found too much in the way of significant advance in training activities in many state governments.[3] Yet some state and local jurisdictions have progressed greatly in this area. The increasing tendency of local government units to pay tuition and related expenses for the further education of their employees in colleges, universities, and other outside facilities definitely is a development which reflects the spirit of the public personnel administration of the postwar days.[4] Even the less highly-rated state and local civil service agencies seem to find it necessary to do something, even if not very much, in the field of in-service training. They are at least conscious that this is a part of the personnel responsibility.

The biggest burst of training activity has taken place, of course, in the Federal government. What made this possible—the training legislation passed in 1958—was slow in coming, but, to illustrate the changed outlook, now the Commission is speaking of training as a continuing necessity for every employee. In other words, even the best workers never reach the point where they are in need of no improvement and therefore of no further training. When he was Chairman of the Commission, Roger Jones expressed that philosophy, and apparently it has growing acceptance whereas once few dared advocate it.[5]

We have even reached the point where orientation training of political, policy-making officials is a recognized responsibility of the personnel office. Few could have predicted this in the Thirties. Again, the personnel people now even have programs for briefing legislators and their staffs on the essential elements of the civil service system as it functions in the particular jurisdiction. Not too long ago many legislators would have been unreceptive to such briefing.

The Public View

Improvements are possible only when there is awareness of their need and desirability. So, understandably, at this point the emphasis shifts from an optimistic review of past gains to a sobering account of what still has to be done.

The key to further progress in public personnel administration, as in many other things, is the willingness of the public to invest more money in it. This obviously is not easy to achieve and it cannot, with justice, be said to be the total responsibility of the personnel administrator. Yet, more must be done in this vital area of public acceptance.

These are some of the questions which need to be asked:

> How effective is our liaison with the legislative body in general and with individual legislators in particular?
>
> What can be done to enlist and keep the support of the Chief Executive of the jurisdiction? How can he be persuaded to recommend more adequate funds for the personnel function?
>
> Can it honestly be said that personnel people lobby with the legislative body as strenuously as is the traditional practice of other administrative agencies? Can the same be said for our contacts with the Chief Executive and other influential political policy-making officials?
>
> Do personnel people try to build community support in the same thorough-going way, for example, as some public universities and colleges? (Agreed this comparison is unfair, but is it not at least suggestive?)
>
> Do personnel people use every opportunity available to join forces with public employee organizations in obtaining legislation and public support? Or do they stand aloof or refuse to compromise minor differences with such organizations?

These are the real problems of public relations. Recruiting campaigns, posters, brochures—all of these are very useful, but by themselves they cannot create real public understanding and support. True, luck plays an important role in shaping community attitudes. The two sputniks spurred Congress and some state legislatures to vote bigger appropriations for the support of public education and related activities, *such as training of public employees*. Charles E. Johnson, Counsel for the House Post Office and Civil Service Committee, has said that the Government Employees Training Act of 1958 might not have been passed "if it had not been for Sputnik."[6]

Well, luck or not, it is true that already in the Sixties there has been some about-face in traditional American ideas about what is practical and what isn't. Clearly, there is more willingness to spend money on, and devote time to, projects and activities which cannot be expected to produce results very quickly. It follows then, that a primary goal for the rest of this decade is to capitalize to the utmost on these stirrings of greater interest in improving the human resources of the country. Developing these human resources is the real business of personnel administration.

The Role of Personnel Research

Lawrence Appley, in a fine essay entitled "Time Invested v. Time Spent," developed a very simple theme: we can either use up our time with little or nothing to show for it, or we can sacrifice on present pleasures and invest it in hard efforts which bring future rewards.[7] Walter Lippmann and others have made the same point in referring to proposed additional public expenditures for schools, roads, and social security. Under one view, held by many taxpayers, this would be too expensive, but, as Lippmann points out, these are wise investments for the future. If a private company invests in future plant this is good American common sense. If the same is attempted in government, it is extravagance.

To the busy administrator, someone's talking of research may be as irritating as it is to some legislators. To many people, research means time lost in impractical theorizing. Besides, the personnel administrator is not supposed to give anyone the impression that he is interested in long-haired pursuits. He must show above all that he is interested in practical things and in people.

The fallacy here, of course, is that research can and does deal with practical things. It has also told us a good deal about people and their characteristics. Furthermore, no one expects any one personnel office to carry out more than a very small part of the total personnel research effort. Two recent publications bring out very well the tremendous dimensions of the unfinished business in this area: *Personnel Research Frontiers*, by Cecil E. Goode for the PPA, and *An Agenda for Research in Public Personnel Administration*, the latter prepared by Wallace S. Sayre and Frederick C. Mosher for the National Planning Association. A careful reading of both these reports shows very clearly that this large part of the unfinished business should be high on the list of goals for the Sixties and many decades ahead.

Goode defines personnel research as all research efforts aimed at improving worker productivity, satisfaction, and service. His findings were far from encouraging. Although he did discover that some $25 to $55 million a year was being spent on personnel or human relations research, he found that very little of it had a direct application to the public service. There is no need to repeat all of his detailed findings here, but one of them, distasteful as it may seem to some, is worth quoting. Goode puts it bluntly: "Practitioners do not have much understanding or knowledge of important new human research and insights."[8] By practitioners he means practicing personnel people.

Now the purpose in quoting the words of Goode is certainly not to indulge in the favorite sport of some teachers—castigating the practitioner. It would, among other things, be poor research to do so, because Goode also concludes that "many political scientists and public administration people are not interested in studying personnel problems." Everyone shares the blame for the scant attention given to personnel research. So, if everyone were to show more interest in it, it is more likely that legislatures and the public would do the same.

The Sayre-Mosher "Agenda" is downright frightening. Under many different headings, the authors list hundreds of specific problems and issues about which there is insufficient information. Of course, it is true that in many cases what they seek is more adequate information than is now available; it is not that there is no information or real knowledge in many important areas. Yet this "Agenda" projects enough research to absorb us and many others for quite a few years. It is clear that it could not all be accomplished in the Sixties!

Much of this research, of course, can and should be carried out by private foundations, universities, and similar organizations. Most of the items on the Sayre-Mosher "Agenda" are of this character, for they do not deal with the technical operating problems of immediate concern to the personnel practitioner.

At this point, the work of the recently-formed Municipal Manpower Commission should be noted. This Commission was established by the Ford Foundation to make a detailed analysis of the needs of urban governments for administrative, technical, and professional personnel. When it has finished its fact-finding, it will then recommend means for the education, recruitment, and utilization of such personnel.

Some practitioners already have completed questionnaires distributed by the staff of this Commission. I have seen at least one of these questionnaires and can now hardly wait to see the summaries and analysis of the answers. If all the queries are answered by the many jurisdictions involved, much more will certainly be known about present personnel practices in urban governments. As things now stand, there is no one place or person which has all this information for municipal government and the same is true for state governments.

Agenda for the Sixties

Apart from more effective public relations and vastly expanded personnel research in general, what are some of the specific problems or issues that personnel administrators should be, and are, placing on their "Agenda" for solution in the Sixties? That is, some of the vexing operating problems that daily confront the personnel administrator and technicians. High on the "Agenda" would be the following.

Public Service Careers: Increased attention to career service planning, particularly in state and local governments. The Federal government has certainly not reached the millennium in this regard, but it has definitely improved its drawing power, largely through its success with the Federal Service Entrance Examination.

Of course, the Federal service can offer better pay, but I have found that there is nothing most states offer which is in any way comparable to the FSEE. Today most college students, no matter what their major, can be shown that there is a possible career for them in the Federal service. It is much, more difficult to convince them of this in the case of state and local government.

Is it so very difficult to obtain the equivalent of the FSEE in state and local governments? There is no reason why this should be so, particularly in the larger and better-supported jurisdictions. Is enough attention being given to really intensive efforts to achieve the goal of career service? Some stock-taking here certainly is in order.

Merit versus Seniority: Improving the merit system by placing more emphasis on merit and less on seniority. Of course, civil service law and regulations usually tie the personnel office's hands as far as seniority is concerned. It may be required, for example, to give additional points in promotional examinations for length of service. It may have to lay off a first-rate employee and keep a much inferior one because the latter has more "seniority."

This may be true, but personnel people themselves have been sometimes lulled into too much acceptance of the seniority cult. Is it not perturbing that in merit systems the practice of basing promotions largely on seniority should not only exist but frequently be accepted as correct? How can this be reconciled with strict application of the merit principle in original recruitment? Why is selection of the best-qualified persons desirable in the one case and not in the other? And is it not true that one of the biggest obstacles to a true career system has been this undue emphasis on seniority? Surely the line should be held, at least, and any further inroads of the seniority principle opposed.

Compensation Plans: More willingness to depart from traditional practices in establishing and administering pay plans. Here again administrative discretion is limited, but strong recommendations can be made to the legislative body and the Chief Executive.

A high-priority objective in the Sixties should be to obtain acceptance of the principle of paying prevailing wages to white, as well as blue, collar employees. It has been perfectly obvious for some time that it is illogical for government to meet industry competition for skilled and unskilled workers in the trades and labor fields but not to do so in the case of executives, specialists in the different professions, and clerical workers.

The U.S. Civil Service Commission now not only accepts the prevailing wage principle but recommends its adoption immediately. It still remains, of course, for the Congress to act, but previously a serious obstacle had been lack of initiative within the Executive Branch in obtaining this kind of change. The legislature usually cannot be expected to take the initiative, and personnel people can help greatly in getting the ball rolling.

It also seems that many jurisdictions still devote much more time to the classification, than they do to the compensation, plan. Both are important, but more consideration should be given to such possible innovations as longevity increases and salary premiums for critical occupations. Some of these ideas, like salary premiums, may prove neither practical nor sound, but some local jurisdictions have already pioneered with good results.

Combining merit with automatic salary increases is one example. Using progressive instead of "level" increments is still another. Other examples could be cited, but the question here is how many jurisdictions are really weighing the advantages of and testing these new ideas in practice? It seems apparent that not enough jurisdictions are critically reexamining the traditional concepts of wage and salary administration.

Performance Evaluation: Development of much more reliable and acceptable systems of evaluating employee performance. It is no secret that little progress has been made in this area. The problem is difficult, but certainly better results should be possible than are now being obtained. Should it not at least be possible before the end of the Sixties to so improve service ratings that people won't snicker as they now do at the mere mention of such ratings? Can we afford this continuing embarrassment of ratings which nobody takes seriously?

The U.S. Civil Service Commission is supporting the proposals of the Second Hoover Commission to terminate summary adjective ratings and to discontinue the connection between the employee's last rating and decisions vitally affecting his future, such as whether or not he gets a raise. The system of "public rewards and penalties," as both Hoover Commissions pointed out so well, makes the service rating procedure distasteful and in the end produces no useful results, either to management or the employee. It is encouraging to see that, although the national Congress has as yet not acted to untie the knot between raises and the last rating, some state and local governments have done so.

The trend in private industry is clearly away from trait rating schemes, with their inherent vagueness, to plans based on an accurate identification of the main elements in the particular job and an evaluation of how effectively the employee carries them out. This principle is solidly accepted by many public personnel technicians, but the tendency still is to stick with the system already in use or not to make any thoroughgoing changes in it.

It is obvious that really good service rating systems won't be developed unless legislative bodies and the public come to recognize that much more money is going to have to be allocated to this part of the personnel job than at present. Like tests, evaluation of employee performance requires a good deal of study and experimentation, all of which costs money. If this had been recognized a long time ago, certainly much better results would have been achieved in this area.

Probation: Making the probationary period effective, instead of allowing it to remain the dead letter it is in most jurisdictions. The law and regulations usually make it easy to dismiss unsatisfactory employees during the working test period.

Of course, the fault is that of the supervisors; they simply won't be tough enough to recommend separating even a non-permanent employee. Is that any responsibility of the personnel office? Yes, because, while human nature is difficult to change, the supervisor can be prodded to discharge his personnel responsibilities properly. If he can be told he can't hire someone, why can't he be told that he has the responsibility to drop any probationer with whose performance he is not satisfied?

Too often, the supervisor justifies his failure to act by convincing himself that the personnel office would only supply him with an even less satisfactory employee. Meanwhile, the personnel office hears rumors about, or even has direct evidence of, the inefficiency of the probationary employee. It, however, washes its hands of the matter by deciding that it is up to the supervisor to act and that there is nothing that it can do. The personnel office ought to be able to get into the picture at the right time and to try, at least, to induce the supervisor to carry out this important part of his responsibility.

The Back Door: Dismissing permanent employees if they are clearly unsatisfactory. Here, of course, the employee's rights of appeal and a hearing provide the supervisor with a ready excuse: it is all so much trouble.

Yet, union agreements complicate the dismissal process in industry as well. It takes courage to discharge someone both in industry and government. In government, it may also take the patience of Job. It is also true that it should not be made possible for a supervisor to fire anyone just because he doesn't like him. And, just as in the case of the probationary employee, it is the responsibility of the supervisor to initiate the dismissal action. But supervisors need to be educated and encouraged and the personnel office should have a positive program for doing so.

There is a definite technique to preparing dismissal cases for hearing before the Civil Commission or other reviewing agency. Is as much time spent on this as the desired results deserve? It is all very annoying, but in the end worth it.

Employee-Management Relations: Developing machinery for systematic employee-management cooperations in improving personnel and carrying out the work of the in general. In most jurisdictions, numerous safeguards and protections exist for the individual employee. What very often is missing, however, is a recognized channel for registering and making effective the viewpoints of the employees as a group.

Management stands to gain when it regularly seeks the suggestions of the employee groups and sounds them out on proposed policies. Labor-management cooperation in industry has proved its value. Frequently, misunderstandings and friction arise simply because adequate channels for communication do not exist. Certainly, this is a problem area which cannot be neglected in the Sixties as pressures for union recognition and collective bargaining rights increase. The wisest policy is to anticipate these pressures and for personnel administrators and management in general to take the initiative in developing this machinery for mutual cooperation.

These problems need much more intensive treatment to do them justice than has been possible in this brief paper. However, one thing seems clear from placing the development, achievements, and goals of the personnel administration field in perspective. The personnel profession is in good shape to meet the challenges of the Sixties and significant progress in personnel administration is in prospect.

Notes

This article was originally delivered as a paper at the 1961 Central Regional Conference of the Public Personnel Association

1. Lawrence A. Appley, *Management in Action* (American Management Association, 1956), pp. 161–64.

2. Ibid., pp. 17–19.

3. Gladys M. Kammerer, "Opportunities Missed: The Little Hoover Commission' Reports," 21 *Public Personnel Review* 235–42 (October 1960).

4. Beatrice Dinerman and Eugene P. Dvorin, "Formal Education Programs for Local Government Employees," 20 *Public Personnel Review* 37 (January 1959).

5. Address by Chairman Roger W. Jones, U.S. Civil Service Commission, at the 1959 International Conference of the Public Personnel Association, October 5, 1959.

6. Charles E. Johnson, "The History of the Government Employees Training Act," in *Management of Employee Training*, 1959, proceedings of Training Officers Conference, Washington, D.C., p. 17.

7. Appley, op. cit., pp. 165–67.

8. Cecil E. Goode, *Personnel Research Frontiers* (Public Personnel Association, 1958), p. 91.

PART 2

INSTITUTIONS, FUNCTIONS, AND PROCESS

The heart and soul of public personnel administration can be characterized by its various functions and processes as well as the institutions it embodies and represents. Presented here are such classics which constitute the essence of public personnel. In the first article, "Understanding Attitudes Toward Public Employment," H. George Frederickson addresses the ageless issue of the quality of the public service and why individuals choose to enter it. Frederickson examines the attitudes of some 1,400 entry-level students of government at the University of Maryland toward the civil service. He found that such factors as the opportunity to get ahead and chances to be successful were significant in predicting students' attitudes toward and predisposition to enter public service at the federal, state, or local levels. He points to the importance of continuing this line of research or inquiry in order to build a high-quality public service.

In "Politics and Merit: Can They Meet in a Public Service Model?" Patricia Ingraham and Carolyn Ban address the important issue of political-career relationships at the federal level of government. Drawing an analogy to "politics and merit," they point out that the vitality of the public service "depends upon the value of *both* the career civil service and the political management system" (Ingraham and Ban 1988: 17, emphasis in original). They propose a new "Public Service Model" which supports not only a joint political-career commitment to serving public interests but also an ethos where both career civil servants and political appointees are equally recognized and valued.

Merit pay is a topic which continues to draw controversy in public personnel administration. As James Perry illustrates in "Merit Pay in the Public Sector: The Case for a Failure of Theory," merit pay systems tend to fail, not due to ineffective implementation or managerial incompetence, but because the theory on which they are based is flawed. Perry finds that three conditions—impractical performance contracts, breakdowns in information and communication, and poor coordination—contribute to failed pay-for-performance systems in government.

In a classic piece on participative management, Nicholas Lovrich writes about the inconsistencies between professed preference with and actual use of participative forms of management. Lovrich writes that administrators may extol the benefits of participative management but many have never relied on it or have abandoned it after experimenting with participatory forms of management. His study reveals that administrators' claims that employees may not be receptive toward participative management are not valid.

Critical personnel issues in the last few decades have centered around such managerial concerns as AIDS in the workplace as well as the drug testing of public employees. In "The Americans with Disabilities Act and the Workplace: Management's Responsibilities in AIDS-Related Situations," James Slack examines the responsibilities of managers in implementing Title I of the 1990 Americans with Disabilities Act (ADA). He argues that managers must create an environment where persons with HIV/AIDS are treated fairly and equitably. Public managers, he points out, have a major responsibility to ensure that the ADA is implemented effectively.

Donald Klingner and his colleagues, in "Drug Testing in Public Agencies: Public Policy Issues and Managerial Responses," address the policy issues surrounding the drug testing of government employees. They survey 300 personnel directors from federal, state, and local agencies across the country. Their research not only shows how prevalent drug testing has been in the public sector, but also the various circumstances under which public employers will administer drug tests (e.g., reasonable suspicion). They further report that while personnel directors view drug testing as a necessity, they also recognize that drug-testing programs may infringe upon the rights of public employees.

Additional Classics

Bowman, James S. "Whistle-Blowing in the Public Service: An Overview of the Issues." 1 *Review of Public Personnel Administration*, 1: 15–27, Fall 1980.
Elliott, Robert H. "Drug Testing and Public Personnel Administration." 9 *Review of Public Personnel Administration*, 3: 15–31, Summer 1989.
Finkle, Arthur L. "Can a Manger Discipline a Public Employee?" *Review of Public Personnel Administration*, Summer 1984.
Gabris, Gerald T. and William A. Giles. "Level of Management, Performance Appraisal, and Productivity Reform in Complex Public Organizations." 3 *Review of Public Personnel Administration*, 3: 45–61, Summer 1983.
Jos, Phillip H., Mark Tompkins, and Steven W Hays. "In Praise of Difficult People: A Portrait of the Committed Whistleblower." 49 *Public Administration Review*, 552–561, November/December, 1989.
Salzstein, Alan. "The Fate of Performance Appraisal: Another Death in the Bureaucracy?" 3 *Review of Public Personnel Administration*, 3: 129–132, Summer 1983.
Van Riper, Paul P. "Governmental Personnel Mobility: Basic Factors and Issues." 27 *Public Administration Review*, 4: 359–372, 1967.

CHAPTER 5

UNDERSTANDING ATTITUDES TOWARD PUBLIC EMPLOYMENT

H. GEORGE FREDERICKSON

Most students of public administration accept the notion that our civil services are less competitive in the manpower market than business and industry. There is also general agreement that the capacities of public organizations to achieve objectives are largely determined by the quantity and quality of the men who operate them. It follows, therefore, if the polity is less competitive for manpower than the private sector, government will be less effective.

The purpose of this writing is to give these claims an empirical warrant by considering in a detailed way some of the factors which appear to influence the competitive abilities of our governments in the manpower market. For heuristic purposes, a "predictive model" or "pattern of determinants" is presented which attempts to explain the sources of varying attitudes toward public employment at different levels in the government. First the variables which seem most likely to influence individual attitudes toward public service are examined. Second, key variables in the model are given detailed analysis by presenting the author's research on the determinants of such attitudes. These attitude variables are used as predictors of the likelihood that individuals will seek civil service employment. Public manpower policies and institutions are discussed as intervening variables in determining the ultimate quality of the public service.

Determinants of Attitudes Toward Public Employment

Figure 5.1 presents a heuristic model based on the hypothesis that the quality of our public service is *dependent* upon a complex series of independent and intervening variables.[1] The first order of variables has to do with the individual and the likelihood that he will seek public employment. It begins with a series of background characteristics, including the standard parental and personal measures such as occupation, sex, age, political affiliation and activity, education, religion, and the like. These independent variables are then linked with individual attitudes, perceptions, biases both of a general kind and those specifically associated with perceptions, and biases regarding government and questions

From 27 *Public Administration Review*, 5: 411–420, 1967. Copyright © 1967 American Society for Public Administration. Reprinted with permission.

Table 5.1

Group Differences in the Prestige Value of Public Employment (in percent)

Social Characteristics	Regard for Public Employment				
	High	Middle	Low	Unknown	Total
Income:					
Under $2,000	30%	42%	21%	7%	100%
Over $8,000	15	33	44	8	100
Social Class:					
Lower lower	37	38	21	4	100
Upper middle	14	34	43	9	100
Race:					
White	26	37	31	6	100
Negro	44	33	18	5	100
Education:					
Less than six grades	27	47	15	11	100
High school diploma	31	31	33	5	100
Beyond high school	14	34	47	5	100

Source: Adapted from Morris Janowitz, Deil Wright, and William Delaney, Public Administration and the Public (Ann Arbor: University of Michigan, Institute of Public Administration, 1958), Table XVIII.

of public policy. It is suggested that these attitude variables are the determinants of specific individual views of public employment and indicate or predict the probability that persons will consider employment in the public service.

These probabilities constitute the reservoir of individual skills, education, and motivation from which our public services must draw. Public personnel policies and institutions intervene, however, in this relationship. To give some precision to this argument and to be definitive about the relationships which have just been hypothesized, it is necessary to "flesh out" some of the model.

Factors Influencing Attitudes Toward Public Employment

What are the background characteristics which mold attitudes toward and perceptions of public employment?

Janowitz, Wright, and Delany found that in a metropolitan area variations in income, social class, race, and education are associated with variations in a "general regard for public employment."[2] As Table 5.1 indicates, persons of higher social class and education held a lower regard for public employment than did those with less schooling and lower social status, and whites a lower regard than did Negroes. The authors concluded that these differences "underline the real as well as the symbolic attractiveness of a government career and job for those who find themselves at the bottom of the economic and social pyramid."[3]

Figure 5.1 **A Heuristic Model of the Determinants of Attitudes Toward Public Employment and the Quality of the Public Service**

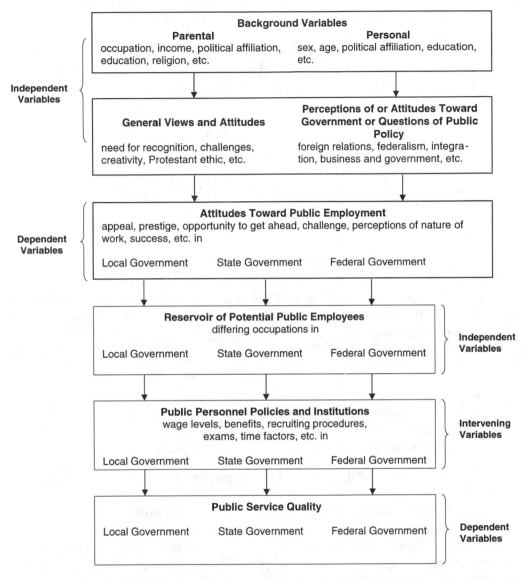

Kilpatrick, Cummings, and Jennings, in a more recent study with a wider data base, asked persons in the "general employed public" to rank their present occupation on a scale from 1 to 10. They were then asked to rank the same occupation but in the employ of the federal government. Women ranked public employment the same, while men rated it lower. Those who had not completed high school ranked the federal equivalent higher than their present private work; persons with a high school education or more rated public employment lower. Unskilled and semiskilled workers rated public employment higher; skilled, clerical professional, and managerial workers lower. Individuals making less than $4,000 annually rated federal work higher; those making more rated it lower.

Figure 5.2   **The Appeal of Public Employment at the Federal,
State, and Local Level (in percent, N = 1,424)**

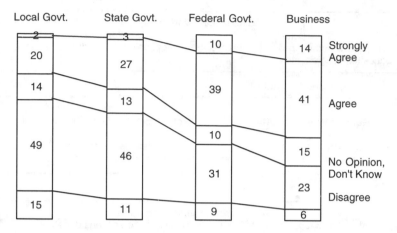

Negroes ranked federal service higher; whites rated it lower.[4] On the basis of their find-ings the authors concluded that "the [federal] government should find itself in a reason-ably competitive position when it seeks to hire janitors, maintenance workers, or postal workers. But to hire trained research scientists, potential executives, and engineers may sometimes be very difficult."[5]

The present author asked the following questions in a 1966 survey of 1,424 beginning government students at the University of Maryland:[6]

> All things considered, working for the federal government appeals to me.
> All things considered, working for a state government appeals to me.
> All things considered, working for a local government appeals to me.
> All things considered, working for a private firm appeals to me.[7]

As Figure 5.2 indicates, the appeal of public employment to early college students varied widely by level of government. Local government employment held the least appeal, while state governments were slightly more and the national government appre-ciably more appealing. None of the public employment categories was as appealing to beginning government students as private employment, although only a small difference existed between the appeal of federal and private work. Thus, though less competitive than the private sector for scientists, executives, and engineers, the federal government is more competitive generally than either state or local governments. These findings suggest that the reservoir of individuals inclined toward state and local government employment is rather limited compared to the pool of potential federal and private employees. And, if increases in education are generally associated with declines in positive attitudes toward public employment generally, as both the Kilpatrick and Janowitz studies have indicated, the pool of skilled potential state and local employees is even more shallow.

An attempt was made to determine if these varying views of public employment at different levels were associated with parents' income, occupation, and education. Little relationship was found. Similarly, neither parents' nor students' political and religious affiliations were associated with differing opinions of the appeal of public employment at any level. A student's sex and the level of his parents' political activity were, however, associated with differing opinions of civil service work. Generally, female students were mildly less inclined toward favorable views of public employment at any level than were male students. Students with politically active parents tended toward negative opinions of the appeal of public service at any level and positive opinions of the appeal of business employment.

On the basis of these findings it is hypothesized that:

1. Individual views of the appeal of public employment are associated more with present and personal socioeconomic conditions than with parental socioeconomic conditions.
2. High income, social or occupational status, and education are generally associated with low opinions of public employment.
3. Opinions of the appeal of public service vary by level of government, with local governments considered least desirable and the federal government most desirable, but all public employment less appealing than business work.

Attitudes Which Influence the Appeal of Public Employment

In the survey of the Maryland beginning government students, a series of questions were asked about attitudes toward public employment. There were five separate categories of four questions each. The first category of questions is presented in Figure 5.2. The remaining four follow. The only difference between the four questions in each category is the changing of the words "local," "state," or "federal" government or "private business corporation."

> A person who works for a local government (a state government, the federal government, a private firm) generally has a good chance to get ahead.
>
> Most jobs in local government (state government, the federal government, private business) are routine and monotonous.
>
> A young man of ability who starts work under local civil service (under state civil service, in the federal civil service, in a private business firm) has a good chance of ending up in one of the top-level jobs.
>
> For a young man of ability, his best chance for being *really* successful lies in working for local government (a state government, the federal government, a private business corporation).[8]

The responses to these questions are presented in Figure 5.3.

The students felt that local government employment would provide them with substantially less chance to get ahead than would jobs in business. Their opinions of getting

Figure 5.3 **Variations in Student Attitudes Toward Public Employment at Different Levels (in percent, N = 1,424)**

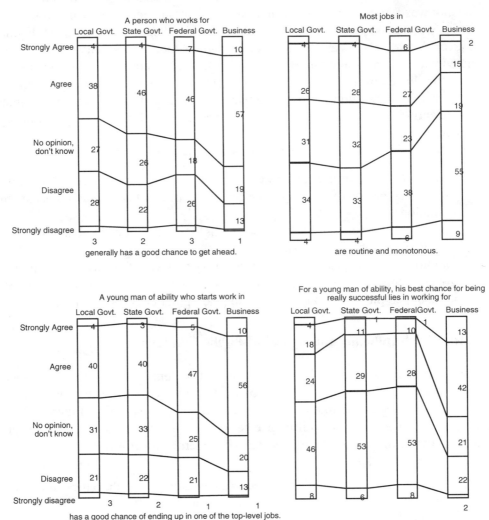

ahead in state and federal employment fell between these extremes. Notable in this array is the rather high percentage (26 and 27 percent) of students who felt they could not make judgments regarding state and local employment but appeared more confident in making such judgments about federal and business careers. This lack of opinion on state and local jobs probably indicates that these governments have not communicated their needs or opportunities as well as have their competitors.

A high percentage of these students held no opinion of the routine and monotony of state and local government work (32 and 31 percent respectively), but a lesser percent were unable to express opinions of the routine of federal employment (23 percent). This 10 percent difference is all reflected in the greater number who disagreed with the notion that federal work is monotonous. Students' opinions of the routine of business work were markedly less negative than their views on that of government work at any level. Government work may be no more routine than business jobs, yet it is perceptions rather than actualities which guide individuals in their career choices.

The pattern of responses to the "chance of ending up in one of the top-level jobs" question was very similar to that of the "generally has a good chance to get ahead" question. In general most students (about 75 percent) were pessimistic about public employment on both counts. The chances of getting to the top seemed less in state and local employment than in federal or business jobs. Also, many students (about one-third in each case) had no opinion on the chances of getting ahead in state and local government careers. Students' views of their chances of getting ahead were slightly less negative toward local work than toward state or federal jobs. This may suggest the possibility that working in smaller city or county jurisdictions is perceived as providing greater opportunity for the individual because of the fewer number of employees or the size of the community. The generally poor regard for the chances of being really successful in government work is underscored by the more than 50 percent who indicated that they felt the best chances for success were with business.

These findings clearly indicate that these students regarded state and local government employment as far less promising than federal or business work: In their opinion it provides less opportunity to get ahead or to be successful, less opportunity to end up in one of the top jobs, and it is more routine and monotonous. The findings show, in addition, that these students' attitudes toward state and local government careers were less well-formed than were their views of national government and business careers.

Some Determinants of the Appeal of Public Employment

What perceptions are most likely to influence the appeal of public employment at all three levels? Are feelings about routine and monotony the basic reason for having negative views of the appeals of state and local careers, or is it views of the chance to get ahead, or of ending up in one of the top jobs? How important are student opinions of the chances of being really successful in public employment in shaping their overall view of the appeal of careers in the civil service?

To answer these questions, four multiple linear regression equations were calculated, one for each level of government and one for business. (All statistical terms used in this paper are defined in the terminological note at the end of this article.) Students' views of the appeal of working for federal, state, or local government or a private firm, as presented earlier, were used as the dependent variables in these equations. Four independent variables were used in each of the four equations. They were student opinions of: (1) the chances to get ahead, (2) routine and monotony, (3) the chances of ending up in one of the top jobs, and (4) the chances of being really successful.[9] The results of these equations are shown in Table 5.2.

The local government findings indicate that those students who had positive attitudes toward the appeal of city and county employment were most strongly influenced by

Table 5.2

Some Indicators of the Appeal of Public and Private Employment (N = 1,424)

| Independent Variables | The Appeal of Employment in | | | | | |
| | Local Government | | | State Government | | |
	Reg. Coef.	Corr. Coef.	Beta	Reg. Coef.	Corr. Coef.	Beta
Chances to get ahead	.233	.293	.214	.234	.275	.191
Being really successful	.204	.240	.162	.231	.244	.174
Routine and monotonous jobs	.083	.202	.073	.205	.252	.177
Chance of a top-level job	.124	.187	.117	.072	.166	.059
	multiple R = .373, R^2 = .146			multiple R = .387, R^2 = .149		

| | Federal Government | | | Business | | |
	Reg. Coef.	Corr. Coef.	Beta	Reg. Coef.	Corr. Coef.	Beta
Chances to get ahead	.219	.329	.181	.129	.225	.096
Being really successful	.218	.297	.174	.291	.319	.259
Routine and monotonous jobs	.288	.331	.231	.191	.195	.152
Chance of a top-level job	.125	.251	.098	.080	.189	.061
	multiple R = .461, R^2 = .213			multiple R = .381, R^2 = .145		

their view that this work would provide them an opportunity to get ahead. At the same time, they did not feel that getting ahead in local public employment was an indication of "being really successful" or that they would necessarily have a chance for a "top-level job." Perceptions of the routine of local government work do not appear materially to influence student views of the appeal of that work.

The appeal of state government employment equation indicated that the "chance to get ahead" was again the most salient indicator. This, similarly, did not indicate opinions that they would have a good "chance for a top-level job," for this variable was a considerably less potent indicator of appeal. Both the "being really successful" and "routine jobs" variables were associated with the appeal of state employment, but to a lesser degree than was the "chances to get ahead" variable.

The most important indicator of the appeal of federal government employment to these students was their perception of routine and monotonous jobs in the national civil service. Those with positive views of the appeal of federal work tended to disagree or strongly disagree with the notion that this work was likely to be routine. Their views of the chances to get ahead and to be really successful were less influential in determining their perceptions of the appeal of federal jobs, and their opinions of the chances of a top-level job were even less influential.

The strongest determinant of the appeal of work for a private firm was students' perceptions of the chances of "being really successful." The other three independent variables were considerably less potent as indicators of the appeal of business employment.

What are the implications of these findings?

First, the "chances of being really successful" variable has a markedly different level of influence over the career preferences of these students. Those predisposed to business work were influenced significantly by this factor, while those with a favorable perception of the appeal of government work at any level were not so strongly influenced by the "success" variable. It is evident, then, that success is more attached to business or private employment than it is to civil service. Although this varies by the level of government under consideration, it is fair to generalize that the students most motivated toward their definition of success are least likely to be predisposed to government work. Clearly, the reservoir of individuals who indicate a favorable perception of the appeal of government work is made less rich by the absence of students who are strongly motivated toward success and who see little possibility of achieving it in government work. From these findings it appears that local government recruiting is most hampered and business recruiting is most advantaged by this set of attitudes, with state and federal civil service recruiting falling in between.

Second, it appears from these findings that those students indicating a favorable perception toward careers at the state and local level do so mostly because they feel it provides them a chance to get ahead, although they attach little "success" to such employment. It can be generalized, then, that the reservoir of those predisposed toward public work is likely to comprise more of those looking for chances to get ahead than of those seeking success.

Third, perceptions of the routine and monotony of work do not appear to influence markedly attitudes toward state, local, or business work, but they do influence views of federal employment. Persons predisposed to federal careers, covered in this survey, were more influenced by their impression that the work was not likely to be routine and monotonous than by their impressions about success, the chances to get ahead, or to achieve a top job. Among these students, the image of a national government career as being dull is not widely held, and those who are interested in the national civil service are interested because they feel it will not be dull. This is doubtless a great aid in federal civil service recruiting and explains in part why these students were more favorably impressed with the appeal of national as against state and local public employment.

Conclusions

At the beginning of this paper a heuristic model was presented. Implicit in this model was the assumption that the dependent variables, "attitudes toward public employment," were influenced by a variety of different types of independent variables. Personal background characteristics such as sex, income, and education were found to be associated with the variation in attitudes toward government work. Parental background variables were not found to be important determinants of opinions regarding public work. It was also found that attitudes toward "success," "chance to get ahead or get a top job," or "routine" influenced student opinions of the appeal of public employment. The mold under consideration should be modified accordingly.

The operations of all these variables, and doubtless many more, produce reservoirs of persons predisposed to seek public employment either at the local, state, or federal level. It was discovered that student views of the appeal of public employment varied widely on the basis of the level of government in question, and this variation in attitudes is determined by different independent variables on the basis of the level of government being analyzed. Consequently, differing levels of government draw their manpower from reservoirs which differ widely. The characteristics of the persons in these reservoirs are better understood because of demonstrated linkages between their backgrounds and opinions and their views of civil service jobs, and in this way the model has been made more precise.

To further develop the model we need to know how these attitudes vary from state to state. We also need to know the factors which seem to influence the step between having a positive opinion of public employment and actually applying for work. What types of persons are distilled out of the pools at this point, and why? We also need to know the influence of varying public service needs and how these needs are perceived by potential civil servants. In other words, how does the feedback process work in the model?

There are important intervening variables which must be measured, for they appear to influence the character of the manpower pool. How long does it take, in a given jurisdiction, between application for work and opportunity for examination; between notification of passage and an offer of employment; and between an offer of employment and taking a position? How many and what kinds of persons distill out during this process? What other civil service policies and institutions intervene to change the character of the reservoir? And what are the characteristics of those who finally take public employment as against the characteristics of those in the original pool?

For purposes of analysis, it is possible to conceptualize the reservoir of potential civil servants, broken down by level of government, as independent variables. These independent variables determine in part the quality of our public administration and thus the character of government. If we know the characteristics of the persons in the reservoir, we can make reasoned judgments of the quality of public service.

As has been demonstrated, local and state governments are at a pronounced disadvantage in the competition for manpower. Our national government is also at a manpower disadvantage compared to private employers. This disadvantage, coupled with the rapidly increasing demand for manpower, particularly by our local and state governments, creates a critical problem for the maintenance of a viable federal system. We need to know in much greater detail the nature of this disadvantage so as to make informed decisions in the hope of altering the state of affairs.

Notes

An earlier version of this paper was presented at the 1967 Conference of the American Society for Public Administration. Marver H. Bernstein, Milton C. Cummings, Jr., Samuel F. Thomas, and Paul P. Van Riper commented on the paper and provided valuable substantive suggestions.

1. This paper concentrates exclusively on pre-entry determinants of attitudes toward public employment and tends to emphasize the views and perceptions of college-level potential civil servants.

The actual characteristics of public employment are not considered. There have been two especially thorough studies of upper-level civil service in the federal government: Marver H. Bernstein, *The Job of the Federal Executive* (Washington, D.C.: The Brookings Institution, 1958) and W. Lloyd Warner, et al., *The American Federal Executive* (New Haven: Yale University Press, 1963).

2. Morris Janowitz, Deil Wright, and William Delaney, *Public Administration and the Public* (Ann Arbor, Michigan: University of Michigan, Institute of Public Administration, 1958), p. 68.

3. Ibid.

4. Kilpatrick, et al., *The Image of the Federal Service* (Washington, D.C.: The Brookings Institution, 1964), p. 94.

5. Ibid., p. 125

6. My former colleague Bob Zimring worked with me in the development and data-gathering phase of this research project, and his willingness to allow the presentation of these findings is sincerely appreciated. This questionnaire was administered in March 1966 to several sections of the Introduction to American Government course. In all, 1,742 students responded to the instrument, but only 1,424 responses were usable. The assistance and cooperation of Alan Cigler, R. D. B. Laime, and Alden Jay Stevens, graduate assistants at the University of Maryland, is gratefully acknowledged. The computer time used in the preliminary analysis of these data was donated by the Computer Science Center, University of Maryland, and the Computing Center, Syracuse University.

The students responding to this questionnaire were: 65 percent male, 35 percent female; 91 percent Maryland residents; 75 percent from the metropolitan Baltimore and metropolitan Washington, D.C. areas; 97 percent Caucasian; 46 percent Protestant. 25 percent Catholic, and 18 percent Jewish; 58 percent freshmen, 28 percent sophomores, 10 percent juniors, and 3 percent seniors.

For additional findings from this research project see H. George Frederickson, "Some Determinants of Attitudes Toward Public Employment," Mimeographed paper presented at the 1967 Conference of the American Society for Public Administration, Appendix II.

7. These questions were taken from Kilpatrick et al., op. cit.

8. These questions were taken from Kilpatrick et al., op. cit.

9. These Likert-type responses were assigned ordinal values as follows: The dependent variables and the independent variables, except the "routine and monotonous" question, "strongly agree" = 5, "agree" = 4, "no opinion" = 3, "disagree" = 2, "strongly disagree" = 1. The "routine and monotonous" question was assigned just the opposite values.

Terminological Note

The definitions presented here are not technically rigorous but are intended to convey, in simple language, the general meaning of the terms used.

Independent Variable: A variable used to explain or predict the values of the dependent variable.

Dependent Variable: The variable whose values are to be explained or predicted by the independent variable(s). The statistical "explanation" consists of determining how the dependent variable changes when there are changes in the independent variable(s).

Regression Equation: An algebraic equation which shows how, on the average, changes in a dependent variable are associated with or caused by changes in one or more independent variables.

Beta: The regression coefficient shows the average change in the dependent variable per unit of change in the associated independent variable. Because independent variables are not always stated in the same terms, beta is used to place all independent variables in the equation in one common term.

Regression Coefficient: A coefficient associated with an independent variable in the regression equation. It shows the average change in the dependent variable per unit of change in the associated independent variable (assuming the other independent variables are held constant).

Simple Correlation Coefficient: The regression coefficient, which is defined above, shows the direction and average amount of change in the dependent variable related to specified changes in the independent variable. In addition, it is desirable to know how close most of the observed values of the dependent variable will come to the values estimated by the equation. The simple correlation coefficient provides this information when only two variables are involved. It measures the degree of association between the dependent variable and the independent variable. The coefficient of simple correlation may range from -1 to +1. A negative coefficient means that one variable tends to decrease in value as the other increases. A positive coefficient means that one variable tends to increase in value as the other variable increases. If the coefficient is zero, there is no association between the variables.

Multiple Correlation Coefficient (R): A measure of the degree of association between a dependent variable and the combined effect of several independent variables. The multiple correlation coefficient may vary from 0 to +1.

Coefficient of Determination (R^2): The square of a simple or multiple correlation coefficient. The coefficient of determination shows the proportion of the total variation in the dependent variable associated with changes in the independent variable(s). For example, if the simple correlation coefficient equals .8, the coefficient of determination equals .64 (.8 squared). This means that approximately 64 percent of the total variation in the dependent variable is "explained" by changes in the independent variable and that 36 percent of the variation in the dependent variable remains unaccounted for.

CHAPTER 6

POLITICS AND MERIT

Can They Meet in a Public Service Model?

PATRICIA W. INGRAHAM AND CAROLYN BAN

Introduction

The passage of the Pendleton Act in 1883 was, in some ways, an affirmation of the *Federalist* arguments of Alexander Hamilton one hundred years earlier. A national government, Hamilton wrote, will be judged by the quality and strength of its administration. A strong national government, a strong executive, and a strong administration, he argued, will be inseparable components of a workable system (Hamilton et al. 1961:No. 70). One purpose of the Pendleton Act was to ensure the strength and merit of the career public service by separating some parts of its operation from the vagaries and abuse of the partisan political system. On the other hand, passage of the Pendleton Act reflected the conflicts inherent in the American view of the public service. The Act created only the nucleus of a career service, leaving the majority of public positions open to presidential appointment and removal, i.e., to politics.

In 1887, Woodrow Wilson acknowledged the profound tension that continued to exist between politics and merit. The purpose of administration, he wrote, was to "straighten the path of government" (Wilson 1978). In Wilson's view, and that of many theorists who followed him, the purpose of administration was to "balance" the purpose and impact of politics. Neutrality, stability, and expertise would offset undue political instability and frequent demand for change. The result would be a broader, longer term perspective on governmental policies and activities.

The practical and theoretical tensions are significant. First, a tension exists between democratic theory, which values openness and change, and administrative theory, which values predictability and stability. Second, there is an implicit tension in defining and serving the public interest. Is that interest defined and served by electoral politics and the policies which flow directly from them? Is the public interest better served by the long term perspective and commitment of public bureaucracies and their members? Or, as Wilson argued, is it better served by a combination of both? If so, how is that "jointness" achieved and maintained?

From 8 *Review of Public Personnel Administration*, 2: 7–19, Fall 1988. Copyright © 1988 Sage Publications. Reprinted with permission.

Past efforts to answer and resolve these questions have resulted in what Kaufman (1956:1060) terms a "cyclical and constant realignment" of public values. An early view that administration served a broader purpose through subservience to politics and elected officials was enhanced and strengthened by the work of the scientific management theorists and the report of the Brownlow Commission in 1937.

An argument for greater equality and for joint political participation—though in different kinds of politics—was advanced by the "Administration as Politics" writers of the 1940s (Appleby 1949; Dimock et al. 1958; Long 1978). Movement back toward the superiority of politics, interrupted briefly by the New Public Administration movement of the late 1960s, was jolted by Watergate and a renewed fear of political excess and wrongdoing. The Civil Service Reform Act of 1978 contained elements of both the politics and merit perspectives: "good management" initiatives to improve the performance and productivity of the career civil service and new provisions to allow greater political influence over the senior managers in that service. The Reagan administration moved strongly away from reliance on career expertise, arguing that careerists could not be trusted, but questionable activities by numerous high administration officials and the Iran affair have raised new concerns about where "trust" is appropriately placed.

We have not moved closer to solution. Moreover, increasingly complex and expansive governmental activities have recast the problem in even more difficult terms. As the issue has evolved, the activities and processes of both politics and administration have changed dramatically. The "politics" to which Paul Appleby and others so confidently turned for direction was perceived to be a majoritarian politics in which broader interests emerged from the interaction of specialized private interests (Bailey 1965). The "politics" at the bicentennial of the Constitution is more reflective of those narrow interests. Indeed, Newland (1987) argues that not only has politics itself changed, but that the "new politics" has deeply affected the politics-administration relationship because political patronage has again become so critical to political campaigns.

Administration too has changed, most obviously in size, but also in the problem-solving demands placed upon it. The issue of politics and administration *within* public organizations has become more complex. As ever greater numbers of public positions were included in the national civil service, presidential appointment power was dramatically curtailed. In the 1950s, the creation of Schedule C positions acknowledged that presidents were entitled to a somewhat broader authority. Use of that authority increased substantially under Presidents Nixon, Carter, and Reagan (Ingraham 1987). This increase was intended to strengthen presidential control of the public bureaucratic apparatus. One effect of larger numbers, however, has been to change the function of some political appointees and to place them in positions which are essentially administrative, rather than policy-oriented. Of broader significance, the increased tendency to rely on political appointees as agents of partisan political change within public bureaucracies has placed those appointees at the heart of the contemporary politics-administration debate.

The central question related to "correct" political-career relationships and broader purpose remains. Its solution is now closely related, however, to politics within the bureaucracy and to larger external issues. Most efforts at solution have suffered from two serious flaws. First, the responsibilities of political actors and administrative actors are most often identified and discussed in separate and isolated terms. Each is assigned specific responsibilities; joint responsibilities and duties are notably absent. Further, the emphasis is very clearly on *career* responsibilities, rather than those of political executives. Second, the public purpose of resolving the issue is often overlooked. In pursuing increased presidential control, improved organizational efficiency, or enhanced bureaucratic responsiveness, we often fail to ask: Why is it important (Ingraham and Ban 1986)? As in the overriding politics-administration debate, this failure trivializes the problem and sends us in pursuit of inappropriate solutions. This analysis examines some of those earlier solutions and, drawing from them, proposes one way of moving us toward resolution of the politics-administration problem. That proposal—the Public Service Model of political-career relationships—is based on the clearly normative assumption that both career administrators and political appointees have a legitimate role to play in the public policy process. A brief survey of existing models demonstrates, however, that normative assumptions are implicit in most of them. Specifying the underlying values of the various models assists in understanding both the parameters and the voids in the contemporary debate.

Where We Are: Models of the Political-Career Relationships

Management Models

An analysis of the literature related to working relationships between political and career executives suggests that three basic models have been advanced: the neutral competence model, the responsive competence model, and the managerial competence model (Ingraham and Ban 1986). The neutral competence model advocates the functional separation of politics and administration, with sole policy-making activity residing with elected officials and political appointees. The ascendant values in this model are economy and efficiency. Business principles play a key role in the achievement of both. Career expertise and longevity offset political instability and change.

The responsive competence model, as the name implies, places a high priority on complete career responsiveness to political direction. Career expertise and longevity are not intended to offset political influence, but are to be used as resources to achieve political goals. This model emphasizes change and complete career receptivity to frequent change.

The third model present in the literature emphasizes neither neutrality nor receptivity to change, but managerial competence and expertise. The managerial competence model is similar to the older neutral competence model. However, it relies on private-sector techniques and methods as the best way to achieve public sector efficiency and effectiveness.

The different emphases of all three models suggest different expectations of and by political executives and career managers. They also suggest very different general relationships and daily working interactions. They may suggest different policy outcomes for the public served by both career bureaucrats and political appointees. None of them address the issue of purpose, i.e., for what purpose do we wish to improve administrative functions? To examine a broader—or higher—public end, it is necessary to turn to ethical models.

Moral/Ethical Models

Ethical models of the public service are as important for what they exclude as for what they include among their component parts. The most notable inclusion is the consistent emphasis on the special quality of the public service. Hart (1984:112) observes:

> "Unlike a work of art, Administration is seldom a thing unto itself, sufficient in the doing. It is instrumental to, and justified by, a higher purpose. Thus, in a democratic system, "public" should refer to the citizens of the political community, with the rights and obligations of citizenship clearly understood by all. . . . Public Administration is that distinctive form of administration necessary (but not sufficient) for the realization of those values."

This special quality translates into duties and responsibilities for public administrators that are different from those of private-sector counterparts. It imbues administrative procedures and decisions with a broader purpose which must serve as a constant referent. Defining that "broader purpose," however, has been a continuing problem. Streib (1986) identifies three major categories of efforts to do so: the social equity model, the public interest model, and the regime value model.

The social equity model suggests that the narrow goals of the management models are inadequate for the public service. Efficiency, economy, and political responsiveness do not address larger democratic issues, such as social equity. This model is most closely associated with the "new public administration" of the early 1970s and with the theorists who emerged from that movement (Frederickson 1980; Marini 1971). Unlike the subservient expertise-oriented careerist envisioned by management models of the public service, the social equity model proposes an activist-administrator who, by virtue of the public responsibility inherent in her/his career choice, is driven by moral and ethical concerns for social justice.

John Rohr (1986) advances the second major ethical model, the "regime values model." This model argues that the values inherent in the U.S. Constitution are the appropriate anchor for discerning the public interest and for guiding administrative values and action. In Rohr's view, in taking the oath of public office, those in the public service inextricably bind themselves to constitutional principles and values. He writes: " . . . the oath of office legitimates a degree of professional autonomy for the administrator and . . . the object of the oath the Constitution, itself can keep this autonomy within acceptable bounds" (Rohr 1986:187).

The third major model present in the literature is the "public interest model." This approach identifies an emergent or perceived public interest as the overarching guideline for administrative action.[1] This model places an especially profound responsibility (or burden, depending upon one's perspective) on public administration. Though definition of the public interest is problematic, theorists in this group argue that definition is possible and provide alternative means of discerning it. Eggar (1965:312) offers the following: " . . . The public interest (is) compromise—the optimum reconciliation of competing claims of special and private interests." Wamsley and his Blacksburg co-authors (1987) simplify this definition to some extent by arguing that a clear "agency perspective" is necessary to clarify both policy and ethical constraints on compromise. The "agency perspective" is a particular view of the public interest (and the public service) derived from the programs, policies, and organizational culture of the agency in which the careerist is employed. Thus, it reflects commitment to a particular government function or service and to a particular segment of the citizenry. The combination of "agency perspectives" is a vital component of the larger public interest.

The ethical models, then, provide us with an exalted view of the public service: they describe a service which is, in Hart's (forthcoming) terms, "fameworthy." Individual morality and the public good are jointly served. Public service is a "calling," an opportunity to serve, an opportunity to be a part of a greater good.

As noted earlier, these models prescribe appropriate behavior and conduct for *career* civil servants, but do not include provisions which specifically address the particular responsibilities of political appointees. In addition, there is wide disparity in the career behavior deemed appropriate by the various technical models and that proposed by the more explicitly normative ethical models. The difference lies not only in the attributes and skills of career civil servants, but in the use of those skills to pursue goals and objectives which are not purely administrative. In the technical models, good administration is the end; in the ethical models, it is the means to a higher good.

It is strange, given the long-term awareness of the potential for political excess, that most of the models summarized above discuss career, rather than political or joints duties. Clearly, if careerists are to achieve either good administration or a higher public interest, they will do so only in cooperation with the political executives to whom they report. On the other hand, there is a continued need for the public service to counterbalance politics. A third set of models addresses this "balance" in terms of public policy processes and outcomes.

Policy Models

The third set of models present in the literature deals specifically with the relationship between political appointees and career managers and focuses on the appropriate public policy functions and responsibilities of each group. The rudiments of these models are contained in the work of Heclo (1977; 1984), Rourke (1984), Lynn (1984) and Pfiffner (1987). The key concern in these policy models is a policy system which often attempts to exclude career civil servants from important policy making functions and positions in the bureaucracy, but which does not foster the development of political managers whose skills and expertise are adequate to fill the void created. Heclo (1984) describes the American system as being "hollow at the center." Both Heclo (1984) and Rourke (1984) recognize the importance of policy networks and the critical need for effective political managers to create useful—and informed—working relationships, both within the bureaucracy and with important external actors. Lynn (1984) specifies the components of such a relationship, with specific emphasis on achieving policy change. He argues that managerial skills and experience, personality, opportunity to accomplish change, and expressed goals and intentions with respect to agency activities are components of a successful change model. He concludes: "Promoting change in government, far from requiring confrontation and conflict, is doubtless inhibited by adoption of a we-they attitude" (Lynn 1984:360). James Pfiffner (1987) concurs in this conclusion.

Nonetheless, models which explicitly advocate a "we-they" perspective do exist. The Administrative Presidency model advanced by Nathan (1983) and the recent variations advanced by Heritage Foundation theorists return to many of the basic assumptions of the politics-administration dichotomy. Arguing that, "as an independent political actor, the bureaucracy usurps power and function in violation of the framework of the Constitution and the principles of democratic accountability," Heritage theorists maintain that *full* control of policy processes and decisions must reside with political appointees (Rector and Sanera 1987:333). In this "presidential control" model, career managers offer expertise but do not advocate policy positions. Their primary function is to ensure full implementation of political directives.

The most fully developed policy model is based on empirical cross national survey research. Aberbach, Putnam, and Rockman (1981) describe four "images" of political career policy relationships. Images I and II essentially separate politics and administration, much as in the model advocated by Rector, Sanera, and others. Image III differs, in that both bureaucrats and politicians engage in policy-making but, " . . . in different settings—one relatively narrow and more concretely specified; the other broader and less easily defined" (Aberbach, Putnam, and Rockman 1981:85). Image IV portrays a relationship in which policy duties and responsibilities converge to produce a "pure hybrid" public executive. Noting that the first three images define tensions between politicians and bureaucrats, these authors argue that Image IV aims to make this tension "creative" rather than conquest oriented. They argue as well that both political and bureaucratic roles are crucial to successful policy outcomes.

This point is directly addressed by the public service model. In the public service model, the political-career tension is creative because both roles are valued and respected. Of equal significance, the tension is creative because neither political appointees nor career bureaucrats are limited by specific functions. Both roles are enhanced by a higher vision; both are informed and shaped by the public interest.

Where We Should Be: A Public Service Model

In initially arguing for a *public service model,* we wrote that the debate about how best to serve the public interest " . . . has always been at the heart of the public policy process; it is also an essential part of the public management process" (Ingraham and Ban 1986:159). Clearly, in taking such a position, we advocate a role for the public service that imposes a dual responsibility upon it. The responsibility to develop and maintain excellent management and program skills is still obvious. Less obvious, but of critical significance, is the constant responsibility to ask: Why are these skills important? For what purpose are they being utilized? Apparently even less obvious, given the dearth of its discussion in the literature, is that this dual responsibility resides with *all* the members of the public service. The responsibility to serve the public interest must be as keenly a part of the political public service as of the career service. Failure to recognize this duality seriously distorts administration and trivializes the political role in public management, no matter how many appointees there may be.

The ephemeral quality of the "public interest" is daunting. Yet for the larger political process, it has served a profound legitimating function. Cassinelli (1962:45) writes: "The public interest is a standard of goodness by which political acts can be judged; action in the public interest, therefore, deserves approval because it is good." Stephen Bailey (1962:97), while labeling the reality of the concept a myth, also notes the value of the ideal:

> "The phrase 'the public interest' is the decision maker's anchor rationalization for policy caused pain. . . . It is balm for the official conscience. It is one of society's most effective analgesics . . . ." He concludes that, " . . . 'the public interest' is the central concept of a civilized polity. Its genius lies *not in its clarity,* but in its perverse and persistent moral intrusion upon the *internal* and *external* discourse of rulers and ruled alike" (Bailey 1962:106, *our emphasis*).

It is this function, this "moral intrusion," that also causes the ideal of the public interest to be central to the politics-merit debate. The concept of the public interest does not mandate that there be perfect agreement between political appointees and careerists about either ends or means. It only ensures that the dialogue is carried out with the intent of achieving some larger, broader public good. Neither political control nor career expertise and objectivity are superior; both are simply component parts of necessary process. Each is, therefore, seasoned and tempered by the other.

The *jointness* of the tempering is critical. In the American system we have created public bureaucratic institutions with enormous power. There are serious precisions in the structure and leadership of those organizations, which neither the politicians nor the permanent bureaucracy have sole authority to resolve. *Joint* commitment and balanced actions are necessary.

What would be the characteristics of a model for the public service that achieved this jointness and balance? At a minimum, those characteristics must include the following:

1. *A consistent awareness of the public service as a democratic institution for political appointees and for career managers.* Such an awareness emphasizes the democratic role and function of the public service, and its various organizational functions. Further, it values the public service for these qualities and for the contribution an effective public service makes to the polity.
2. *A joint commitment to management competency which also recognizes the unique qualities and demands of public management.* This necessarily reduces emphasis on automatic transfer of private techniques to the public sector. It re-emphasizes the particular skills necessary for managing in a public/political environment.
3. *A mutual respect for the skills, perspectives, and values each set of managers brings to the organization.* Both are necessary and useful; both have value.

Utilized jointly, they will be constructive. Utilized separately, or in opposition to one another, they can be a serious detriment to a larger good. Underlying this component is a clear understanding of the different roles played by political appointees and career civil servants. Political executives care about partisan policy objectives, about immediate results, about responsiveness to short-term objectives. Career civil servants are, by definition, bureaucrats. Their perspective is longer term; their goals are often program related. Responsiveness is defined in terms of statutory and institutional constraints. Though each role is integral to the larger purpose of the public service, balancing them requires a special commitment.

4. *A consistent awareness of, and active concern for, the public interest, broadly defined.* The term is used in Bailey's "moral intrusion" sense. For political appointees, this will mean moving beyond election results. For career civil servants, it will mean moving beyond program survival and organizational stability. For both, it will mean working *with,* not around, the other set of managers.

The public service model differs from most of those presented earlier in several important respects. First, it explicitly includes political public servants and career public servants. It emphasizes that the roles and functions of each are important to the proper functioning of the larger democratic system. Second, it emphasizes the need for mutual, bilateral respect and collaboration between political executives and career managers. It emphatically underlines the need to utilize managerial efficiency and effectiveness for a higher, broader purpose, which crosses program, policy, and partisan lines. In that sense, it permits us to view the public service as a cohesive unit rather than as a loose assemblage of diverse parts. Finally, it consciously includes service to a larger public good in the definition of effective public service. That good is not achieved by simple subservience to technique, to efficiency, or to partisan politics. As in the larger democratic process, effective public service must be driven and constantly informed by broader societal concerns.

The public service model is an ideal, but one with strong implications for day-to-day government operations and for the long-term viability of our governmental system. Is it possible to move toward such an ideal? The next section addresses that potential.

How Do We Get There From Here? Is There a Yellow Brick Road?

The public service model depicts a situation in which both political and career executives view their task and function in terms of overarching societal purpose. The primary reason for continuing the search for an ideal, however, is the reality of the frequent failure of both political executives and careerists to do so. This is not because either group is necessarily evil. It is due, rather, to the nature of a system that forces two dramatically different perspectives into an organizational relationship that is, at best, tenuous.

The creation of the Senior Executive Service in 1978 was a notable attempt to address some aspects of the problem. Though the primary emphasis of the SES was again on career managers, there were serious efforts to create a structure to which both political appointees and senior career managers belonged. The emphasis, for example, on establishing an elite cadre of senior managers, much like the British higher civil service, was one effort to elevate the purpose of public management. The creation of "general" management positions which could be filled by either political or career executives was also part of the new system. There was an emphasis on joint policy functions and on the ability of senior careerists to move into high policy positions without jeopardizing career status or concerns. The specific attempt to create a common identity, or an *esprit de corps,* for this elite cadre was another concern. It must be noted that the provision to encourage appointment of career managers to significant policy positions was clear recognition of the need for jointness and for balance and tempering at the highest levels of public organizations.

At the same time, the Senior Executive Service reflected the continuing conundrum of the politics-merit debate. Language that proposed to create an elite cadre of generalist managers was accompanied by language which proposed to make them more directly responsive to political control. Any notion of a public service motivated by serving the public good was washed away in a sea of financial incentives designed to promote productivity by introducing competition to the ranks of public management (Ingraham and Ban 1984). Further, the implementation of the Senior Executive Service demonstrated the tenuous support for those provisions aimed at strengthening the institution of the public service and the strength of those aimed at increased political control. The presidential transition exacerbated that imbalance. Finally, the large budget and personnel cuts initiated by the Reagan Administration in non-defense agencies created a perception of siege, rather than institution building. Ten years later, there are numerous proposals for reform of the Senior Executive Service and for the larger system of political-career relationships. The simple existence of many reform proposals is testimony to serious problems in the SES. Indeed, early in its development, it was frequently termed a failure. Although more recent assessments have softened somewhat, the nature of the reform proposals indicates the serious obstacles encountered by even a small movement toward a higher public service encompassing both political and career managers.

Virtually all the proposed reforms begin with the assumption that the Senior Executive Service has *not* created a public service corps which values both political appointees and career civil servants. The elite, unified management cadre envisioned in 1978 has not emerged. Unfortunately, the SES may have succeeded in building more walls between politicians and bureaucrats than it has removed. Consequently, many reform proposals advocate new emphasis on the *institution* of the higher public service. Because of this emphasis, they contain many provisions that reflect the basic components of the Public Service Model. The newly appointed SES Advisory Board, for example, has recommended that renewed attention be directed toward 1) developing the SES as an *institution*, 2) enhancing executive excellence, and 3) ensuring that the incentives for joining and remaining in the public service are adequate to recruit and retain high-quality executives. Their report states: "Members of the Senior Executive Service have the challenge and responsibility of translating the Nation's laws and Administration policies into effective service to the public. This *demands* the ultimate in leadership, professional integrity and commitment to the highest ideals of public service" (U.S. Office of Personnel Management 1987:1, *our emphasis*).

Similarly, the Twentieth Century Fund analysis of the SES notes: "The government of the United States requires a competent, professional and spirited higher civil service to meet the challenges of the future. The demands on our political institutions have never been greater; the need for wisdom and experience in our administrative councils never more compelling" (Huddleston 1987:82). In this proposal for reform and in others, there is consistent focus on political executives and career civil servants. There is now in the House of Representatives legislation which goes one step further; that legislation mandates that political appointees possess appropriate management credentials and be trained in "how government and . . . how the civil service works" (Shroeder 1987:7).

There are other indications, too, of an increasing awareness that past efforts at bridging the politics-administration gap have led us down the wrong road. David Rosenbloom (1987:28) argues convincingly that there is an emerging administrative culture which is "compatible with the Constitution" and which "views public administration as government." He concludes: "An appropriate agenda for the third century of public administration is to recognize that the public-administration-as-government culture is already present in embryonic form, to embrace it and to define, develop, and refine it further" (Rosenbloom 1987:30). If Rosenbloom is correct—and many of the proposals for reforming the Senior Executive Service suggest that he may be—how do we move toward further development of the "public administration as government" culture and the public service model of political career relationships?

Conclusion

In the introduction to this paper, we noted that the tension between politics and merit has been a consistent element in the history of the American public service. In times of political excess and abuse we turn to the concept of a neutral career service for expertise and balance. In times of frustration with the slowness and isolation of the public bureaucracy, we turn to the dynamic political system for energy and balance. Were these shifts and realignments to occur smoothly, recognizing that the vitality of the system depends upon the value of both the career civil service and the political management system, all would be well and much of the above discussion would be moot. The history of the American public service for the last twenty years suggests that it is not. Embryonic administrative cultures and embryonic reforms have been buffeted by full-blown political forces. Redirecting and redefining those political forces will be a major task. It is a necessary task, however, and one that requires recognition and action in diverse quarters. For example:

(1) Politicians, both elected and appointed, must recognize that bureaucrat bashing has run its course, but has exacted a high toll. If the public service is to be valued, that value must necessarily develop in the larger political environment. Presidents cannot run "on the backs of the bureaucracy" and expect bureaucratic trust and cooperation on the day they assume office. Appointees cannot arrive at their appointed positions proclaiming that all bureaucrats are incompetent and

expect to be viewed as legitimate managers. Both elected and appointed officials must make a commitment to organizational policy change that is long term. The public service requires a full understanding of legitimate legal restraints on immediate actions, however well intended. This will undoubtedly require additional education for many political managers. It will be time well spent. In addition, those responsible for the political management system must make a serious commitment to management skills and expertise. Such a commitment does not currently exist. Finally, if political managers are to be viewed as organizational leaders and partners, they must commit to longer tenure in position. The public service is not a job market; properly viewed, it is a commitment to the public, not to individual advancement.

(2) Academics must commit, both in their research and in their teaching—but especially in their teaching—to an effort whose purpose is to ensure that future public administrators understand the role they will play in public policy and governance. We do no favors by glorifying technique to the exclusion of democratic and ethical concerns. The public service model mandates that career public servants recognize and consider the consequences of their actions. If we advocate a model of the public service that includes joint action for the public good, we are obliged to include training for such responsibilities in the education of future public administrators.

(3) Practitioners have a major and most difficult role to play. Despite the negativism currently surrounding much of the public service, it is necessary to maintain the objectivity and pride in service that has marked most of the history of the merit system. Members of the Senior Executive Service are especially important in this regard. They have suffered serious indignities at the hands of civil service reform and the political management system. There is evidence that their belief in the utility of a public service career has been shaken (Ingraham 1987). At the same time, however, many senior career managers continue to believe that, in performing their jobs, they are doing something important, not just for themselves or their agency, but for the public. This pride in purpose and in the ability of career civil servants to perform admirably in very difficult circumstances must be communicated. In many ways, the current "image of the public service" has not been informed by public servants themselves. It must be. Members of the Senior Executive Service—because of their visibility expertise, and the successes they have achieved in their careers—are in position to shape a more accurate image.

Just as the problems addressed by the Public Service Model are not new, neither are many of the proposals for moving toward its realization. This does not diminish the importance of continued efforts to achieve a higher purpose for the public service. If Rosenbloom and others are correct, a more basic awareness of the problem and a greater acceptance of solutions such as the Public Service Model may already be emerging in the larger system. If so, move toward the ideal may be enhanced; if not, the effort is even more important.

Notes

We are very grateful to Phillip Cooper, David Rosenbloom, Frank Thompson, and anonymous referees for helpful comments on earlier drafts.

1. There is not, however, agreement that the "public interest" can be discerned or can serve as a broad guideline for action. Schubert (1961) argues that it cannot. More recently, the authors associated with "The Blacksburg Manifesto" argue not only that it *can,* but that it *should* (Wamsley et al. 1987).

References

Aberbach, J., R. Putnam and B. Rockman (1981). *Bureaucrats and Politicians in Western Democracy.* Cambridge, MA: Harvard University Press.

Appleby, P.H. (1949). *Morality and Administration in Democratic Government.* Baton Rouge: Louisiana State University Press.

Bailey, S. (1962). "The Public Interest: Some Operational Dilemmas," pp. 96–106 in C.C. Friedrich (ed.) *Nomos V: The Public Interest.* New York: Atherton.

Ban, C. and P. Ingraham (1986). "Political Appointees and Career Bureaucrats: Adversaries Allies?" Paper prepared for presentation at the annual convention of the American Society for Public Administration, Anaheim, California.

Cassinelli, C.W. (1962). "The Public Interest in Political Ethics," pp. 44–53 in C.C. Friedrich (ed.) *Nomos V: The Public Interest.* New York: Atherton.

Dimock, M., G. Dimock and L. Koenig (1958). *Public Administration,* 2nd ed. New York: Rinehart.

Eggar, R. (1965). "Responsibility in Administration, an Exploratory Essay," pp. 299–302 in R.C. Martin (ed.) *Public Administration and Democracy.* Syracuse: Syracuse University Press.

Frederickson, G.H. (1980). *New Public Administration.* Scranton, PA: Chandler.

Hamilton, A., J. Madison and J. Jay (1961). *The Federalists Papers.* New York: New American Library.

Hart, D. K. (1984). "The Virtuous Citizen, The Honorable Bureaucrat, and 'Public' Administration." *Public Administration Review* 44: 111–119.

———— (Forthcoming). "Fame and Fameworthiness." *Administration and Society.*

Heclo, H. (1977). *A Government of Strangers.* Washington, D.C.: The Brookings Institute.

———— (1984). "America's Higher Civil Service," in E.N. Sulieman (ed.) *Bureaucrats and Policy Making.* New York: Holmes and Meier.

Herring, P.E. (1936). *Public Administration and the Public Interest.* New York: Russell and Russell.

Huddleston, M. (1987). "Background Paper," in *The Twentieth Century Fund: The Government Managers.* New York: Priority Press.

Ingraham, P. (1987). "The President, the Appointees and the Bureaucracy: Building Bridges or Burning Them?" *Public Administration Review* 47:425–435.

Ingraham, P. and C. Ban (1984). *Legislating Bureaucratic Change: The Civil Service Reform Act of 1978.* Albany, NY: State University of New York Press.

———— (1986). "Models of Public Management: Are They Useful to Federal Managers in the 1980s?" *Public Administration Review* 46:152–160.

Kaufman, H. (1956). "Emerging Conflicts in the Doctrines of Public Administration." *American Political Science Review* 50 (December) 1057–73.

Long, N. (1978). "Power and Administration," reprinted in J.M. Shafritz and A.C. Hyde (eds.) *Classics of Public Administration.* Oak Park, IL: Moore Publishing.

Lynn, L.E., Jr. (1984). "The Reagan Administration and the Renitent Bureaucracy," pp. 339–370 in L.M. Salamon and M.S. Lund (eds.) *The Reagan Presidency and the Governing of America.* Washington, D.C.: The Urban Institute

Marini, F. (1971). *Toward a New Public Administration.* Scranton, PA: Chandler.

Martin, R.E. (ed.) (1965). *Public Administration and Democracy.* Syracuse: Syracuse University Press.

McKenzie, C. (ed.) (1987). *The In and Outers.* Baltimore: Johns Hopkins Press.

Nathan, R. (1983). *The Administrative Presidency.* New York: Wiley.

Newland, C.A. (1987). "Public Executives: Imperium, Sacerdotum, Collegium? Bicentennial Leadership Challenges." *Public Administration Review* 47: 45–56.

Pfiffner, J.P. (1987). "Political Appointees and Career Executives: The Democracy-Bureaucracy Nexus in the Third Century." *Public Administration Review* 47: 57–65.

Rector, R. and M. Sanera (eds.) (1987). *Steering the Elephant.* New York: Universe Press.

Rohr, J.A. (1986). *To Run a Constitution: The Legitimacy of the Administrative State.* Lawrence, KS: University Press of Kansas.

Rosenbloom, D.H. (1987). "Liberty, Law and Bureaucracy: Freedom and Responsibility in the Administrative State." Paper prepared for delivery at the annual meeting of the American Society for Public Administration, Boston, Massachusetts.

Rourke, F.E. (1984). *Bureaucracy Politics and Public Policy.* Boston: Little Brown.

Schubert, G.A. (1961). *The Public Interest.* Glencoe, IL: The Free Press.

Shroeder, P. (1987). Speech before the Federal Executive Institute Alumni Association, March 18.

Streib, G. (1986). "Ethics and Expertise in the Public Service: Maintaining Democracy in an Era of Professionalism." Paper presented at the annual meeting of the American Political Science Association, Washington, D.C.

U.S. Office of Personnel Management (1981). "Final Report: The Federal Employee Attitude Survey, Phase I." Washington, D.C.: Government Printing Office.

U.S. Office of Personnel Management and the President's Council on Management (1986). "Report from Senior Executive Development Seminar." Hunt Valley, Maryland, September.

Wamsley, G.L., C.P. Goodsell, J.A. Rohr, C.M. Steivers, O.S. White, J.S. Wolf (1987). "The Public Administration and The Governance Process: Refocusing the American Dialogue," pp. 291–320 in R.C. Chandler (ed.) *A Centennial History of the American Administrative State.* New York: The Free Press.

Wilson, Woodrow (1978). "The Study of Administration," pp. 3–16 in J.M. Shafritz and A.C. Hyde (eds.) *Classics of Public Administration.* Oak Park, IL: Moore Publishing.

CHAPTER 7

MERIT PAY IN THE PUBLIC SECTOR

The Case for a Failure of Theory

JAMES L. PERRY

Introduction

Merit pay has had a long history in the U.S. civil service. Graduated pay systems were introduced in the federal civil service shortly after passage of the Pendleton Act (Van Riper 1958). Step-in-grade systems enjoyed widespread popularity among all levels of government until the 1970s when they came under increasing attack (see, e.g., Patton 1974; Savas and Ginsburg 1973). They were criticized for being automatic and for failing to differentiate employee rewards based upon performance. These shortcomings led to a search for alternatives that resulted in the merit pay provisions of the federal Civil Service Reform Act of 1978 (CSRA) (Hunter and Silverman 1980; Perry et al. 1982) and similar reforms in a variety of states and localities (Griener et al. 1981).

The CSRA pay reforms were short-lived. In 1984, Congress approved the Performance Management and Recognition Act (also known as the Merit Pay Improvement Act) to correct a litany of problems in the CSRA systems. Among the problems were inadequate funding, pay inequities and ratings manipulation. The 1984 law restored the step-in-grade feature of the old system and instituted a new bonus program to reward performance.

Despite the recent rocky experience with merit pay, there is no indication that it has become less popular with political leaders or the public. The Reagan administration recently has introduced legislation to extend pay-for-performance principles to Grades 1–12 of the General Schedule (*Public Administration Times* 1986:1). The reported failures of public sector systems and the undaunted response of politicians to merit-pay experience parallel reactions to the failure of such systems in the private sector. Failures of merit pay in private sector organizations have variously been attributed to a lack of commitment to pay for performance (Patton 1972, Redling 1981), problems encountered when implementing the theory (Hamner 1975), or poor judgments which resulted in applying contingent pay to inappropriate situations (Lawler 1981, Patton 1972, Ungson and Steers 1984).

From 7 *Review of Public Personnel Administration*, 1: 57–79, Fall 1986. Copyright © 1986 Sage Publications. Reprinted with permission.

The prospect that merit pay failures are a sign of problems fundamental to the underlying theory has been explored by only a few scholars. Deci (1975) has argued that money is an ineffective motivator because it relies upon extrinsic rewards and, therefore, stifles intrinsic motivation. The ultimate result of diminished intrinsic motivation is to remove the most powerful and enduring motivators. Meyer (1975) has contended that merit pay damages employee self esteem. He concluded that an incentive system that lowers an employee's self esteem is more destructive than constructive.

In addition to these potential threats to merit pay, which are grounded in alternative theories about its psychology, there is another theoretical basis for questioning the viability of merit pay. Pay-for-individual-performance is based on the assumption that organizational performance is the simple additive combination of individuals' separate performances. Yet theorists note that organizations are intricate social environments that cannot be understood as simple aggregations of employees. Therefore, a mismatch exists between the simplicity inherent in merit pay programs and the complexities of organizations (Pearce, in press). This mismatch is at the root of many of merit pay's failures.

This article develops a critique of merit pay theory as it has been applied to government. At the outset, it is important to identify the scope of our theoretical critique. The focus is individually-contingent pay for public managers, what will be called pay-for-individual-performance or, simply, merit pay. The critique is not intended to apply to group-contingent pay or to non-managerial employees. The article begins with a brief discussion of the psychological theory that is the rationale for merit pay. An alternative theoretical framework is then presented for understanding the dynamics of pay-for-individual-performance in an organizational context. The predictions of this theoretical framework are discussed in light of research on merit pay in the public sector.

The Theory Behind Pay-for-Individual-Performance

Lawler (1971, 1981) developed the first and probably most compelling theoretical argument for the motivating potential of individually-contingent compensation. His psychological model of pay is based on Vroom's (1964) cognitive theory of motivation. Lawler (1971) argued that pay acquires a valence or importance as a function of its perceived instrumentality for obtaining other desired outcomes. Pay is probably one of the most powerful rewards that organizations can offer: "Because it is important to most people, pay has the power to influence their membership behavior and their performance" (Lawler 1981:5).

Because pay can be an attractive reward, it is assumed to motivate members' actions more effectively if it is made contingent on those actions. Using the expectancy theory argument, Lawler (1971, 1981) noted that individually-contingent pay plans tie a presumably valuable reward (pay) directly to an individual's performance and, therefore, should result in a high subjective probability that performance will result in receipt of the valued outcome. Thus, a powerful motivational effect will result when pay is based on individual job performance.

Although research on the effects of pay-for-performance has usually lacked methodological rigor and has concentrated almost exclusively on routine, non-managerial jobs, it generally indicates that contingent pay results in higher performance than non-contingent pay. Reports of improvements in individuals' productivity range from 12.2 percent (Roethlisberger and Dickson 1939), to 30 percent (Locke et al. 1980), to 39 percent (Viteles 1953). Based on a comprehensive review of prior research, Lawler (1971) concluded that individual incentive plans can potentially increase individuals' productivity between 10 to 20 percent.

Not all scholars contend that pay-for-individual-performance results in improved productivity. Research by Deci (1975) and Meyer (1975) is among the most critical. Deci conducted a series of laboratory studies on the effects of external-mediated rewards, such as pay, on subjects' intrinsic motivation. He concluded that contingent pay is undesirable because it reduces intrinsic motivation and leads individuals to develop strategies to achieve rewards with minimum effort. Meyer (1975) argued that most employees have a highly favorable self image, but that the feedback implicit in merit pay awards undercuts this self image. The effect is to damage employee self esteem, a factor important in individual and organizational productivity.

Lawler also acknowledges that merit pay is subject to negative side effects, including the restriction of output and conflict among employees working on interdependent tasks. Bass, Hurder and Ellis (reported in Bass 1965) found that individual monetary incentives resulted in increased performance by those engaged in a simple task, but *decreased* performance on a more complex one. Bass (1965) suggested that these subjects were already motivated and the addition of financial incentives resulted in a motivational level that was so high that it interfered with performance on the complex task. Similar results are reported by Konovsky and Podsakoff (1984) who found that individual incentives had no impact on performance on an interdependent laboratory task, and that contingent pay actually decreased performance on a task in which subjects' performances were interdependent.

Only one field study has been conducted on the performance consequences of individually-contingent managerial pay. Pearce, Stevenson and Perry (1985) tested the performance effects of the introduction of merit pay for federal managers. The performance measure included four indicators of the productivity of the offices for which these managers were responsible. Productivity measures were available two years before the commencement of merit pay and for the first two years that managers' merit increases were based on these performance measures. They found that office productivity gradually improved over the four-year period, but that the merit pay intervention did not result in a significant change in this trend. Thus, merit pay did not result in improved performance.

The generally favorable reactions merit pay has elicited from senior executives and politicians have impeded its critical assessment. The evidence about the limitations of merit pay presented above hints that its failures represent more than faulty implementation and, in fact, may reflect shortcomings of theories of individual motivation in complex organizations. A theoretical framework which helps to explain the frequent failures of pay-for-individual-performance is developed below.

An Alternative Theoretical Perspective

A series of theoretical statements which explain merit pay failure in government organizations is presented in Figure 7.1. It is necessary to begin with some initial premises[1] or axioms about organizations, managerial behavior and managerial jobs to explain the reasoning behind this set of theoretical linkages. The first premise is that public organizations are systems of cooperative activity which are chartered to act for some common interests. As a system of cooperative activity (Barnard 1938), a range of participants (e.g., employees, managers, suppliers and clients) contract with the organization, both implicitly and explicitly, to exchange their contributions (e.g., expertise, time, loyalty) for inducements the organization offers (March and Simon 1958). The inducements an organization offers for members' contributions are likely to vary among categories of participants.

Another premise underlying the theoretical statements is that managerial jobs are characterized by complexity and uncertainty, resulting from the nature of the work performed (Doeringer and Piore 1971; Mintzberg 1973; Williamson 1975). Mintzberg (1973) found that managerial activities were characterized by brevity, variety and discontinuity, indicative of the uncertainty and complexity of managerial work. By their very nature, managerial positions are designed to absorb uncertainty. The scope of managerial work requires a wide range of specific skills that enhances the idiosyncratic nature of managerial jobs. Furthermore, the problems created by uncertainty/complexity cannot be completely mitigated because a manager's rationality is bound by knowledge, skill and time limitations (Simon 1957).

The premises above are implicit in the theoretical relationships identified in Figure 7.1. The figure indicates that any one of three conditions—invalid contracts, information failure or diminished capacity to coordinate interdependence—are sufficient to produce merit pay failure. These three conditions and how they come about are discussed below.

Impracticality of Fixed Contracts

Simon (1957) has argued that open-ended employment contracts allow organizations the flexibility to respond to future uncertainty. Open-ended contracts permit employers to call upon the undifferentiated time of employees. Given this flexibility, organizations are ideally situated to respond to uncertainty.

Merit pay involves a significant restriction of an organization's flexibility. The fixed-performance contracts characteristic of merit pay, such as those developed under the Civil Service Reform Act of 1978 (CSRA), are difficult to adapt to changing internal and external circumstances. Williamson (1975) contends that fixed contracts are rigid and completely unsuited for circumstances characterized by uncertainty, a condition that is typical for managerial work, particularly in the public sector. If managerial performance requirements are indeed uncertain, fixed contracts restrict the ability of managers to respond to changes. These contracts can, at best, cover only a portion of desired actions,

68

Figure 7.1 **A Model of the Sources of Merit Pay Failure in Government Organizations**

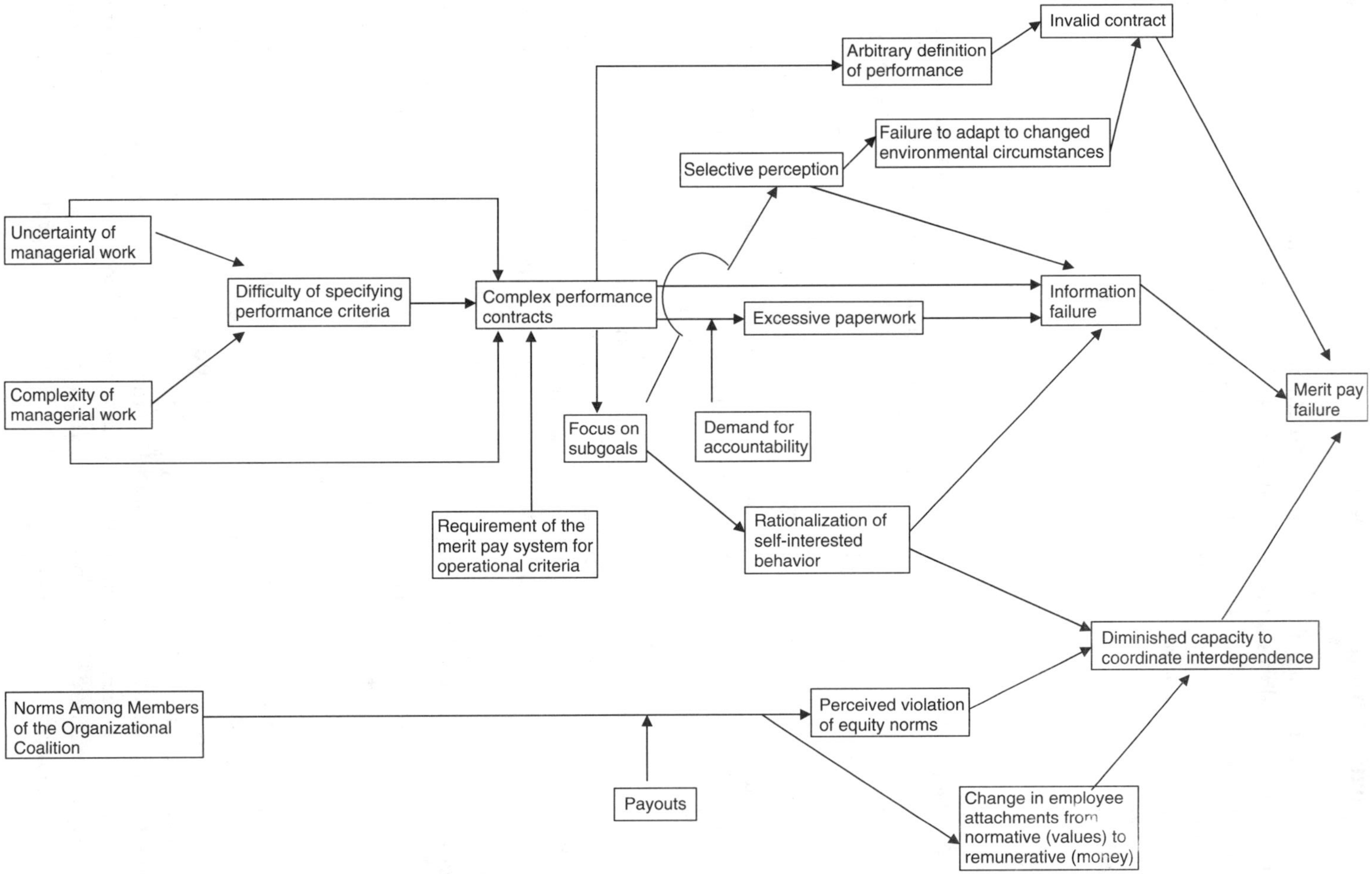

and, therefore, are artificial representations of the kind of performance that would be most effective for an organization. A related and equally serious liability of fixed contracts is that they discourage deviations from performance agreements even when such deviations may be necessary or appropriate (O'Toole and Churchill 1982).

Experience in the federal government illustrates the artificiality of fixed contracts. For example, Social Security Administration field offices experienced significant disruptions because of efforts to develop objective performance indicators such as processing time (Pearce and Perry 1983). Although this is a very specific illustration of the artificiality of fixed-performance contracts, it was not an isolated instance of the difficulty of writing performance contracts under CSRA. The General Accounting Office (United States General Accounting Office 1984b) found in a two-year study of three agencies that despite the legal requirement that performance appraisals rely on objective criteria, less than half the performance standards contained objective measures.

Despite the very real limitations of fixed contracts, many organizations behave as if these shortcomings can be overcome by establishing elaborate control systems which are used to write comprehensive contracts for their managers. Reports about the consequences of such contracts have largely been anecdotal, but they do not appear to remedy, and perhaps exacerbate, performance management problems. For example, one of the side effects of CSRA-mandated merit pay was an estimated billion dollars for operating costs in the first year (Harron 1981), partly attributable to supervisory effort in developing elaborate performance agreements. Federal agencies consistently reported excessive paperwork as a result of merit-pay performance appraisals (Perry and Porter 1980).

Although it may be impossible to predict future states of affairs given uncertainty/ complexity and, therefore, to write adequate fixed contracts, it is conceivable that such contracts could be re-written periodically to reflect new circumstances. This strategy also imposes significant costs on managers. The costs of re-writing the contract and re-formulating the pay-for-performance linkage are likely to be prohibitive, particularly if change is rapid. GAO reports (United States General Accounting Office 1984a) that in 1982 the responsibilities of 20 percent of federal senior executives changed during the rating period, but a majority (55 percent) did not have their plans revised. Thus, the contracts of more than 10 percent of senior executives, and probably a much larger proportion of subordinates reporting to them who were covered by merit pay, were invalid simply because they were not updated.

As an alternative to re-writing the contract, individually-contingent pay programs are frequently adapted to uncertainty by combining subjective and objective measures (Lawler 1981). This adaptation helps to preserve flexibility, but it has other consequences for pay-for-performance. For example, Carroll and Schneier (1982) note that the more subjective the rating criterion, the more rater judgment is required not only regarding the degree to which the rate meets the criterion, but also regarding what the measure actually means. The combination of objective and subjective measures is probably an unreliable solution to the performance measurement problem in government. Public sector performance environments are likely to impose severe strain on a manager's ability to make successful subjective determinations because of real or perceived concerns about politicization (Pagano 1985).

Information Failure

Fixed contracts are not only likely to be invalid when applied to managerial work, but the information that is the rationale for fixed contracts is likely to be a focus for manipulation. The manipulability of information could occur under several circumstances which are inherent in the situation. A supervisor's lack of expertise in a subordinate's job content or difficulty obtaining feedback about a subordinate's performance could permit a subordinate to withhold negative information or pass along positive information, thereby enhancing the subordinate's evaluation. For instance, a subordinate's attempt to beat the appraisal system by seeking an easy contract, reportedly a problem encountered in both federal (O'Toole and Churchill 1982) and local (Griener et al. 1981) merit pay systems, is possible when there is unequal information between superior and subordinate. Performance measurement and occupational characteristics of the public sector context (Perry and Porter 1982) tend to increase the probability of such information asymmetries occurring.

Merit pay exacerbates the tendency of individuals to adhere to subgoals which, in turn, reinforces the problems of information acquisition discussed above. Merit pay tacitly legitimizes self-interested behavior by defining performance in terms of organization subgoals. According to March and Simon (1958), individuals tend to adhere to these subgoals, even when the goals conflict with those of the larger organization, because of selective perception and rationalization. These processes could produce situations in which a subordinate shirks non-contractual obligations or challenges a superior's interpretation of the contract.

When a manager perceives that it is necessary to deviate from the contract and act in accordance with a broader conception of organizational good, he or she incurs the risk of going unrewarded even when the manager perceives that the spirit of the contract has been satisfied. This appears to be precisely how many public managers have responded. A widespread result of CSRA performance appraisals (Gaertner and Gaertner 1985, Pearce and Perry 1983, United States Merit Systems Protection Board 1981) were systems that employees simultaneously rated "accurate" and "fair," but not "helpful" or conducive to "improved agency effectiveness." Managers acquired a clearer understanding of the criteria on which they were judged, but were not convinced that the criteria were the best ones to promote improved performance or agency effectiveness. One can only infer that one reason the original CSRA merit pay system failed was the decision of many managers to maximize their personal development or agency effectiveness rather than their appraised performance.

Another result of information problems is that supervisors may not closely tie pay to individually-measured performance because they are unable to judge definitively the relative contributions of employees given the limitations of performance appraisals. The difficulty of making definitive judgments about performance is particularly true for managerial jobs. The small numbers of managerial positions (Williamson 1975) and the uniqueness of managerial jobs increase the power of managers to control the assessments levied by significant others (Thompson 1967). This phenomenon helps to explain why raters tend to minimize differentials in rated performance and to inflate ratings (see, e.g., Gaertner and Gaertner 1984), thus limiting the strength of pay-for-performance relationships. The propensity to minimize appraisal differentials is likely to be reinforced because supervisors bear a large part of the cost, in terms of information acquisition and interpersonal conflict, of justifying performance appraisal decisions to their subordinates.

Reduction of Coordination

Individual performance contracts will diminish coordination by altering patterns of inter-dependence among organizational members. Coordination problems originate with individual performance contracts and their attention to organizational subgoals. The subgoal focus is a necessary pre-condition for linking pay to performance because of the need to hold managers responsible for results within their control (March and Simon 1958). The focus on subgoals, however, tends to undermine the organization as a unit of cooperative activity by undermining interdependencies among organizational members.

Thompson (1967) identified three types of interdependence, pooled, sequential, and reciprocal, which, he asserted, represented ascending complexity and coordination requirements. Pooled interdependence is the dependence of each segment of the organization on the others for the well-being of the organization. Sequential interdependence involves situations in which a part of the organization depends upon another for supply of inputs, for disposal of outputs or both. Finally, reciprocal interdependence involves situations in which each unit poses a contingency for the other.

Field and laboratory research have documented the detrimental effects of merit pay upon sequential (Babchuk and Goode 1951, Whyte 1955) and reciprocal interdependence (Miller and Hamblin 1963), the two most complex forms. The detrimental effects of merit pay in the public sector involve pooled interdependence as well. Merit pay undermines pooled interdependence in public organizations in at least two ways: (1) by altering an individual's attachment to the organization and (2) by creating conflicts or inequities among segments of the organization coalition.

Merit pay systems undermine involvement because they treat the manager as a labor contractor and undermine the flexibility of traditional authority relations (Barnard 1938, Simon 1957). Such contracts communicate that the organization is only concerned with the employee's performance as it is reflected in the contract measures. In effect, organizations signal indifference to past contributions and to any extenuating circumstances that may have influenced the recent performance measures. Employees come to focus on the pay delivery and performance measurement system rather than the organization's tasks or mission.

This contention is supported by an assessment of merit pay for federal managers. CSRA required that managerial performance contracts be drawn up before the performance period, and that half of the money made available for raises be tied directly to rated individual managerial performance. Pearce and Porter (1986) reported the effects of this new pay and performance measurement system for federal managers and employees at two agencies. They divided their sample into those who received "outstanding" and "above average" ratings (55 percent) and those who received "fully successful" (45 percent) ratings. They found that whereas the organizational commitment of the relatively highly rated managers was stable over the 30-month period, the commitment of the "average" managers dropped significantly after their first merit rating and remained at this reduced level when retested a year later in both of these agencies. Their findings indicate that merit pay significantly reduced the psychological attachments of a large subgroup of satisfactory performers.

Additional evidence of the potential for merit pay to alter pooled dependence is provided by Perry and Pearce (1985) who traced how CSRA has led to a proliferation of new interest groups. The primary purpose of these new groups is the protection of members (e.g., merit pay managers, senior executives) whose employment status was modified by CSRA. The most prominent of these groups, the Senior Executive Association (SEA), sued for restoration of bonuses to original statutory levels after Congress reduced eligibility for bonuses in the summer of 1980 from a maximum of 50 percent of Senior Executive Service (SES) positions to a maximum of 20 percent. The development of SEA and the subsequent suit vividly illustrate how pay-for-performance can alter the focus of employee attachments from the organization's mission to the pay delivery system.

Merit pay also affects pooled interdependence through its influence upon organizational climate (James and Jones 1974) or atmosphere (Williamson 1975). Climate and atmosphere are concepts that explain linkages between a specific transaction and attitudes that have broader organizational consequences. The relevance of these concepts to the relationship between merit pay and pooled interdependence arises from the fact that inducements for some members of an organization are primarily remunerative and for others are primarily social or moral. Within government such variations are quite common. Nevertheless, expectations among participants about appropriate rewards for other participants are likely to have significant attitudinal implications. For example, taxpayers may have a great deal of difficulty accepting large contingent financial rewards for government managers because they perceive such rewards as "squandering their taxes."

Attitudes of other groups within the organizational coalition may operate in a preemptive fashion by influencing the design of merit pay systems. The result is often a design compromise that radically diminishes the probability for merit pay success. A dramatic illustration of this process occurred during the implementation of CSRA merit pay systems. Congress imposed a cap on merit pay funding because of the political sensitivity of federal pay levels. OPM [Office of Personnel Management] developed a merit-pay-funding formula which liberally interpreted congressional intent. Simulations of the system indicated that few employees would be worse off and most would be better off (Hunter and Silverman 1980). Agency and employee reaction to these simulations was favorable, primarily because of OPM's liberal assumptions about the payout formula. However, GAO forced OPM to rescind its formula in favor of one awarding less money shortly before the first payout because the OPM formula did not adhere to the "no-new-money" limitation in the statute. It is important to remember that, although this particular episode has been labeled an "implementation problem" by many (see, e.g.,

Pearce and Perry 1983, Silverman 1983), the OPM-GAO controversy originated because of statutory language which represented prevailing norms about appropriate reward levels for federal managers.

Conclusion

This article has presented a theoretical view of why merit pay has failed in many public organizations. It was argued that three conditions, i.e., invalid contracts, information failure, and diminished coordination, prevent contingent pay from contributing to improved organizational performance. The theoretical framework is useful for understanding implementation problems that accompany pay-for-performance. Such problems are, in fact, inherent in this form of motivational program in government programs.

An issue related to this analysis is whether pay-for-group-performance would fare better in light of the theory we have presented. It is quite obvious that some of the limitations of pay-for-performance are common to both individual and group programs, particularly the problem of specifying a performance contract. However, group incentives may affect individual behavior and allocate the costs of information acquisition differently than do individual incentives, thereby producing different outcomes. The relative effectiveness of individual versus group incentives clearly deserves further research.

The present analysis does not refute the instrumental value of pay as a motivator. Pay is undoubtedly a primary consideration in an individual's decision to join an organization and perform on its behalf (Nash and Carroll 1975, Ellig 1982, Wallace and Fay 1983). Although there is evidence that individuals entering public organizations are relatively less motivated by money than their private sector counterparts (Rawls et al. 1975), pay remains a significant factor in employee motivation. An organization's compensation system conveys a variety of signals to current and potential employees, including information about its fairness, the rewards for long-term loyalty and performance, and its labor market competitiveness. All of these factors are relevant to performance in organizations. The arguments in this paper suggest that also requiring a public organization's compensation system to harness pay for motivating short-term managerial performance is not realistic.

Notes

This paper grows out of my collaboration with Jone Pearce. My thanks to her for permitting me to borrow liberally from her ideas. See Pearce, in press.

1. The use of the term premises follows Hage (1972). Premises are very general assumptions that help to explain why a particular theoretical relationship occurs.

References

Babchuk, N. and W. J. Goode, (1951). "Work Incentives in a Self-Determined Group." *American Sociological Review* 16: 679–687.

Barnard, C. I. (1938). *The Functions of the Executive.* Cambridge, MA: Harvard University Press.

Bass, B. M. (1965). *Organizational Psychology.* Boston: Allyn and Bacon.

Carroll, S. J. and C. E. Schneier, Jr. (1982). *Performance Appraisal and Review Systems: The Identification, Measurement, and Development of Performance in Organizations.* Glenview, IL: Scott, Foresman.

Deci, E. L. (1975). *Intrinsic Motivation.* New York: Plenum.

Doeringer, P. and M. Piore (1971). *Internal Labor Markets and Manpower Analysis.* Boston: D. C. Heath.

Ellig, B. R. (1982). *Executive Compensation: A Total Pay Perspective.* New York: McGraw-Hill.

Gaertner, K. H. and G. H. Gaertner (1984). "Performance Evaluation and Merit Pay: Results in the Environmental Protection Agency and the Mine Safety and Health Administration," pp. 87–111 in P. I. Ingraham and C. Ban (ed.) *Legislating Bureaucratic Change: The Civil Service Reform Act of 1978.* Albany, NY: State University of New York Press.

——— (1985). "Performance-Contingent Pay for Federal Managers." *Administration and Society* 17 (May): 7–20.

Griener, J. M., H. P. Harry, M. P. Koss, A. P. Millar and J. P. Woodward (1981). *Productivity and Motivation.* Washington, D.C.: The Urban Institute Press.

Hage J. (1972). *Techniques and Problems in Theory and Construction in Sociology.* New York: John Wiley and Sons.

Hamner, W. C. (1975). "How to Ruin Motivation with Pay." *Compensation Review* 7 (3): 17–27.

Harron, M. (1981). "Another View of the Merit Pay System." *Management* 2 (Fall): 18–20.

Hunter, R. W. and B. R. Silverman (1980). "Merit Pay in the Federal Government." *Personnel Journal* 59 (December): 1003–1007.

James, L. R. and A. P. Jones (1974). "Organizational Climate: A Review of Theory and Research." *Psychological Bulletin* 81 (12): 1096–1112.

Konovsky, M. A. and P. M. Podsakoff (1984). *Effects of Individual and Group Incentive System and Task Interdependence on Group Productivity.* Academy of Management Meetings, Boston, MA.

Lawler, E. E., III. (1971). *Pay and Organizational Effectiveness: A Psychological Review.* New York: McGraw-Hill.

——— (1981). *Pay and Organization Development.* Reading, MA: Addison-Wesley.

Locke, E. A., D. B. Feren, V. M. McCaleb, K. N. Shaw and A. T. Denny (1980). "The Relative Effectiveness of Four Methods of Motivating Employee Performance." pp. 363–388 in K. D. Duncan, M. M. Grunsberg and D. Wallis (eds.) *Changes in Working Life.* New York: John Wiley and Sons.

March, J. G. and H. A. Simon (1958). *Organizations.* New York: John Wiley and Sons.

Meyer, H. H. (1975). "The Pay for Performance Dilemma." *Organizational Dynamics* 3 (3): 39–50.

Miller, L. K. and R. L. Hamblin (1963). "Interdependence, Differential Rewarding, and Productivity." *American Sociological Review,* 28: 768–778.

Mintzberg, H. (1973). *The Nature of Managerial Work.* New York: Harper & Row.

Nash, A. N. and S. J. Carroll Jr. (1975). *The Management of Compensation.* Belmont, CA.: Wadsworth.

O'Toole, D. E. and J. R. Churchill (1982). "Implementing Pay-for-Performance: Initial Experiences." *Review of Public Personnel Administration* 2 (Summer): 13–28.

Pagano, M. (1985). "An Exploratory Evaluation of the Civil Service Reform Act's Merit Pay System for the GS I3–15s: A Case Study of the U.S. Department of Health and Human Services," pp. 161–176 in D. H. Rosenbloom (ed.) *Public Personnel Policy: The Politics of Civil Service.* Port Washington, NY: Associated Faculty Press.

Patton, A. (1972). "Why Incentive Plans Fail." *Harvard Business Review* 50 (3): 58–66.

———. (1974). "Governments' Pay Disincentive." *Business Week* January 14.

Pearce, J. L. (in press). "Why Merit Pay Doesn't Work: Implications for Organization Theory," in Gomez-Mejia and D. B. Balkin (eds.) *Compensation: An Applied Perspective.* Reston, VA: Reston Publishers.

Pearce, J. L. and J. L. Perry (1983). "Federal Merit Pay: A Longitudinal Analysis." *Public Administration Review* 43: 315–325.

Pearce, J. L. and L. W. Porter (1986). "Employee Responses to Formal Performance Appraisal Feedback." *Journal of Applied Psychology* 71: 211–218.

Pearce, J. L., W. B. Stevenson and J. L. Perry (1985). "Managerial Compensation Based on Organizational Performance: A Time Series Analysis of the Impact of Merit Pay." *Academy of Management Journal* 28 (June): 261–278.

Perry, J. L., C. Hanzlik and J. L. Pearce (1982). "Effectiveness of Merit-Pay-Pool Management." *Review of Public Personnel Administration* 2: 5–12.

Perry, J. L. and J. L. Pearce (1983). "Initial Reactions to Federal Merit Pay." *Personnel Journal* 62: 230–237.

——— (1985). "Civil Service Reform and the Politics of Performance Appraisal," pp. 146–160 in D. H. Rosenbloom (ed.) *Public Personnel Policy: The Politics of Civil Service.* Port Washington, NY: Associated Faculty Press.

Perry, J. L. and L. W. Porter (1980). *Organizational Assessments of the Civil Service Reform Act.* Washington, D. C.: U. S. Office of Personnel Management.

——— (1982). "Factors Affecting the Context for Motivation in Public Organizations." *Academy of Management Review* 7 (January): 89–98.

Public Administration Times (1986). "Reagan Recommends Federal Pay Reform." 9 (May 15): 1.

Rawls, J. R., R. A. Ulrich and O. T. Nelson, Jr. (1975). "A Comparison of Managers Entering or Re-entering the Profit and Nonprofit Sectors." *Academy of Management Journal* 18 (December): 616–622.

Redling, E. T. (1981). "Myth vs. Reality: The Relationship Between Top Executive Pay and Corporate Performance." *Compensation Review* Fourth Quarter: 16–24.

Roethlisberger, F. J. and W. Dickson (1939). *Management and the Worker.* Cambridge, MA: Harvard University Press.

Savas, E. S. and S. G. Ginsburg (1973). "The Civil Service: A Meritless System?" *The Public Interest* 32: 70–85.

Silverman, B. R. (1983). "Why the Merit Pay System Failed in the Federal Government," *Personnel Journal* 62 (April): 294–302.

Simon, H. A. (1957). *Administrative Behavior.* Second Edition. New York: Free Press.

Thompson, J. D. (1967). *Organizations in Action.* New York: McGraw-Hill.

United States General Accounting Office (1980). *Postal Service Program Should Provide More Incentive for Improving Performance* (GGD-81-8). Washington, D. C.: U. S. Government Printing Office.

——— (1984a). *An Assessment of SES Performance Appraisal Systems* (GGD-84-16). Washington, D. C.: U. S. Government Printing Office.

——— (1984b). *A 2-Year Appraisal of Merit Pay in Three Agencies* (GGD-84-1). Washington, D. C.: U. S. Government Printing Office.

United States Merit Systems Protection Board (1981). *Status Report on Performance Appraisal and Merit Pay Among Mid-Level Employees.* Washington, D. C.: Office of Merit Systems Review and Studies.

Ungson, G. R. and R. M. Steers (1984). "Motivation and Politics in Executive Compensation." *Academy of Management Review* 9: 313–323.

Van Riper, P. P. (1958). *History of the United States Civil Service.* Evanston, IL: Row, Peterson.

Viteles, M. S. (1953). *Motivation and Morale in Industry.* New York: Norton.

Vroom, V. H. (1964). *Work and Motivation.* New York: Wiley.

Wallace, M. J., Jr. and C. H. Fay (1983). *Compensation Theory and Practice.* Boston: Kent.

Williamson, O. E. (1975). *Markets and Hierarchies: Analysis and Antitrust Implications.* New York: Free Press.

Whyte, W. G. (1955). *Money and Motivation.* New York: Harper and Brothers.

CHAPTER 8

THE DANGERS OF PARTICIPATIVE MANAGEMENT

A Test of Unexamined Assumptions Concerning Employee Involvement

NICHOLAS P. LOVRICH, JR.

Introduction

The once radical cry for increased participation by employees in the workplace has now become the conventional wisdom for public sector management in the 1980s. Whereas the teachings of McGregor (1960) and Likert (1959) were once considered progressive, they are now treated as "classics" in textbooks and readers on personnel administration. Notwithstanding the ubiquity of these ideas of democratic/egalitarian/participative forms of management, and despite the wide scope of agreement that this style of administration is generally more appropriate than traditional bureaucratic/authoritarian forms, many administrators nevertheless continue to use nonparticipatory management practices. When questioned about such practices, non-participative supervisors or managers are quite likely to express support for participative management in principle while offering some rather compelling circumstantial reasons why participative practices would be fatal in their own situations (Schein 1974).

The most common underlying theme heard from those numerous administrators who know about, have regard for, but do not *practice* participative management is that there is little employee interest in participation in the management function (Kilbridge 1960). Some would go so far as to say that their employees would dislike being imposed upon in this regard (Dubin et al. 1975)! In elaborating their view as to the lack of genuine interest in participation among employees, these administrators are likely to cite one or more of the following six common reasons also pointed to in the personnel literature: 1) employees have little faith in essential management processes being addressed through participative practices [e.g., performance appraisal, career

From 5 *Review of Public Personnel Administration*, 3: 9–25, Summer 1985. Copyright © 1985 Sage Publications. Reprinted with permission.

planning, determination of unit goals and objectives, etc.] (Simonds and Orife 1975); 2) employees who have been evaluated less well or promoted less often than they believe they deserve will have little interest in unit management problems (Wilcox 1969); 3) employees who think poorly of their supervisors will shun involvement (Kaplan 1976); 4) employees who have a low interest in their work will avoid engagement (Centers and Bugental 1966); 5) employees who see the organization as a whole as one providing a non-participative climate are not likely to respond to offers of involvement at the work unit level (Kaplan and Tausky 1977); and 6) employees lacking in the "Protestant work ethic" will not attach sufficient value to their work to make involvement personally salient (Friedlander 1965).

This listing of reasons for putting off—or avoiding altogether—the implementation of participative management practices will doubtless sound familiar to personnelists, training officers and academics and consultants who have dealt with the task of convincing supervisors and managers to adopt one or another aspect of participative management. All of these six reasons can be offered as evidence that participative management "won't work here," that the degree of employee involvement will be so lacking that the supposed benefits of participation will be miniscule—and at the cost of lost supervisory and managerial discretion! Common complaints include such expressions as: "they don't know enough to participate"; "they don't get along well enough with management to communicate effectively"; "they have too little attachment to the agency (or city, county, state) to care about participating"; or "they're so disinterested in their work they won't see much value in participating in its management."

Are these all valid, proven reasons for assuming that participative management practices ought to be avoided where such disadvantageous conditions obtain? Is it true that employees who lack faith in basic management processes, or who think poorly of their supervisors, or who have a low interest in their work, or who lack commitment to hard work will be less interested in participating in the management of their work if given the choice? If so, then there are many situations in which such participative practices should be avoided. If, on the other hand, it is true that there is little evidence of such effects, then it is likely that the range of applicability of participative management practices is quite wide—perhaps wider than many hesitant administrators might admit. Fortunately, data collected as part of a statewide, I.P.A.-funded effort to institute participative management practices in the area of performance appraisal in the state of Washington offer an opportunity to assess the empirical evidence on the question of the validity of these common, yet unexamined assumptions concerning barriers to participative management.[1]

Participatory Management Reform in Washington State

In keeping with the prevailing emphasis upon employee participation in performance appraisal processes, the state of Washington designed and implemented a new, "participatory" performance appraisal system made operational in 1979 (Lovrich et al. 1979). The key feature of the new system entails the use of both supervisory ratings and employee self-evaluations as the first stage of performance assessment. Both the employee and his/her supervisor are required to assess the employee's performance over the past year independently, and to use those separate assessments in the composition of a final performance appraisal report which records the employee's ratings (plus dissenting comments where desired) and a set of agreed upon goals and objectives for the coming year. At any point in the process either the employee or the superior has the right to request the next higher level of supervision to mediate differences on ratings, goals, work assignments, etc. In this new system neither employees nor their superiors are given much choice—i.e., both are required to participate jointly in the task of performance appraisal.

This system was implemented statewide after a thorough testing in three pilot and three control agencies (Lovrich et al. 1980). It is now used in over fifty state agencies, affecting approximately 30,000 state employees. Merit pay has not been attached to the performance appraisal process, although periodic attempts to do so have emerged in each legislative session since the advent of the participative system. After nearly a year of operation under the new participatory system, a random sample of state employees from all state agencies (except those "contaminated" by the pilot study interventions) were surveyed to assess their attitudes toward the new system. Of 1,200 employees surveyed, 781 responded for a 66 percent response rate. Since state government experiences a near constant turnover rate of approximately 13 percent, about 72 percent of the deliverable questionnaires were returned for analysis. The analysis below is based on responses recorded in this random sample survey of November/December 1979.

The survey questionnaire included two widely used and well-established diagnostic measures: 1) John Newman's (1977) measure of organizational climate—*Perceived Work Environment* (see also Lawler et al. 1974); and 2) *the Survey of Work Values*—Wollack, Wijting and Smith's (1971) survey for the assessment of work values relating to the Protestant work ethic. The survey also contained a number of specific questions designed to assess reactions to the participatory practices introduced in this specific project, as well as a series of demographic items commonly included in survey research. The measurement instruments will be discussed in somewhat more detail below.

The Proposed Virtues of Participatory Forms of Performance Appraisal

Why make this application of participatory management to the area of performance appraisal? The desirability of allowing subordinates to become involved in their own performance appraisal interviews has been advocated for a number of years by several respected voices (Likert 1959; McGregor 1957; Dossett et al. 1979; Hillery and Wexley 1974; Latham and Yukl 1976; Burke and Wilcox 1969). Studies which have experimentally manipulated the degree of participation in appraisal interviews (French, Kay and Meyer 1966; Wexley, Singh and Yukl 1973) have supported the notion of the beneficial effects of participation. French et al. (1966) found that higher levels of participation improved the supervisor-subordinate relationship. Wexley et al. (1973) found that greater participation by subordinates resulted in greater motivation and satisfaction following the appraisal. These findings are consistent with those on participative leadership (e.g., Vroom 1960) and with recommendations for the conduct of management appraisals (Meyer, Kay and French 1965).

Marion E. Haynes, in his 1973 article "Do Appraisal Reviews Improve Performance?" reaches the conclusion that a collaborative model, with its sharing of decision making power, is the most effective in evoking satisfaction with the decision and a sense of responsibility to carry it out on the part of the employee. Likewise, the respected researchers Meyer, Kay and French (1965), in an evaluation of the General Electric Company performance appraisal program, reached similar conclusions. They found that mutual goal setting—rather than criticism—generally improved performance, and that participation by the employee in goal setting procedures helped produce favorable results as compared to both more directive and totally undirected modes of performance assessment.

Victor Vroom, in *Work and Motivation* (1964:226), surveyed various investigations on the effects of participation in decision making and came to the following broad conclusion:

> "When the entire pattern of results is considered, we find substantial basis for the belief that participation in decision making increases productivity. There is experimental and correlational evidence indicating that higher levels of influence by the worker in decisions that they are to carry out results in higher productivity . . ."

Thus, the literature in this area points to greater worker satisfaction, increased motivation and increased productivity as among the benefits of participatory performance appraisal.[2]

Olsen and Bennett, in a 1975 *Management Review* article, listed the following benefits from participatory performance appraisal:

- Participatory performance appraisal reflects the influence of the increasing degree of participation occurring in our society and our more advanced knowledge of human behavior and motivation.
- Participatory performance evaluation acknowledges that satisfaction of the employee's needs for fulfillment and self-actualization through work is essential for the well-being of the organization.
- Employee participation in formulating work objectives uses development of commitments for the future as a way of enhancing motivation and providing a framework for productive behavior.
- Participatory performance appraisal enhances employee/employer communication.
- Participatory performance appraisal emphasizes such approaches as performance standards and goal setting; training and development activities also increase in importance to help employees to develop and prepare for future opportunities.

As judged from a thorough evaluation of the pre- and post-implementation attitudes of Washington State employees, many of these positive effects of participation in performance appraisal (with respect to organizational climate, work satisfaction, and work values) were realized in the Washington participatory performance appraisal system (Lovrich et al. 1981, 1983).

Table 8.1

Distribution of Responses on the Measure of Employee Receptivity to Direct Participation in Performance Appraisal

Preface: The opportunity for *direct participation* in the performance appraisal process is provided by means of the self-evaluation procedure.

Question: How do you feel about the *employee self-evaluation* portion of the new performance appraisal process?

Response Categories	Dislike		Undecided		Like
	1	2	3	4	5
Percent	13.7%	11.0%	23.6%	27.3%	24.4%
N	(99)	(79)	(170)	(197)	(176)

N = 721

Testing Unexamined Assumptions Regarding Affinity for Participation

Even though Washington State employees were quite receptive to the new, participative performance appraisal system, as witnessed by the results of evaluation surveys, there was clear evidence of variation in the extent to which the employee participation aspect of the new system was welcomed or regretted. The lack of unanimity in responses to a questionnaire item dealing with receptivity to the employee self-evaluation portion of the process—the key element of participation instituted by the new appraisal system—is most important. This variation in receptivity raises the prospect of covariates of receptivity; that is, the possibility arises that factors such as those mentioned above are associated with differing degrees of receptivity to participation. Evidence of such associations could then be taken as supporting the proposition that such factors as distrust of supervisors, lack of interest in work, and weak commitment to work values do constitute reasonable grounds for avoiding the use of participatory management procedures. Table 8.1 sets forth the distribution of responses on the key item of receptivity to direct employee participation. Since employee receptivity to participatory schemes has been proposed as both a prerequisite to effective implementation (Anthony 1978) and a requirement for the effective operation of appraisal systems (Yoder and Heneman 1974), this survey item takes on particular significance.

The Operationalization of Supposed Inhibitors to Employee Involvement

Attitude Toward Administrative Practices

The importance of an employee's general attitude toward management practices is frequently cited as a factor influencing attitudes toward participatory management schemes. It is reasonable to suppose, for example, that if an employee feels that performance appraisal *per se* is a questionable process, this fact will color his or her thinking toward *any* performance evaluation system. A measure of employee attitudes in this area can be developed from items used in the Washington State survey. An index can be constructed on the basis of the following five survey questions, all of which used the Likert, five-response format (dislike very much through like very much).

- How much do you like or dislike being evaluated?
- Some people believe that a good performance appraisal system *can* improve *individual performance*. How much do you agree or disagree with this opinion?
- Some people believe that a good performance appraisal system *can* improve *agency effectiveness*. How much do you agree or disagree with this opinion?
- Some people believe that a good performance appraisal system *can* improve *employee morale*. How much do you agree or disagree with this opinion?
- Some people believe that a good performance appraisal system *can* meet *employee needs for long-term development*. How much do you agree or disagree with this opinion?

The five items of the "general attitude toward performance appraisal" scale are highly intercorrelated, as evidenced by a very respectable .87 coefficient alpha computed for this scale.

Perceptions of Fair Treatment

A second major source of anticipated difficulty stems from the fear that employees who feel under-appreciated—as evidenced by earlier evaluations—will shy away from subsequent evaluative procedures. In illustration, J. B. Miner (1969) suggests that one major difficulty of performance review is that employees who do not anticipate a favorable rating are likely to oppose the whole evaluation process—which they may perceive as a direct personal threat or reminder of under-appreciation on the part of the superior and/or the organization. T. H. Stone (1973) asked employees whether or not they liked being evaluated (and why?) in two separate studies. In the first sample, 35 percent stated they disliked being evaluated, with 12 percent of those respondents having listed "receiving a negative evaluation" as a primary reason. In the second sample, 13 percent of the 17 percent who expressed a dislike for being evaluated listed receiving a negative evaluation as a reason. These studies provide some support for the investigation of this factor as a possible correlate of employee receptivity to self-evaluation in the new, participatory performance appraisal system. In order to investigate this factor as a possible influence upon receptivity to self-evaluation, answers to the following survey item can be used:

How would you describe the level of agreement on the final ratings recorded for your performance?

Low   1_____2_____3_____4_____5   High

Regard for Supervision

A third often-cited complicating circumstance in the implementation of participatory management practices is that of poor supervisory-employee relations, typically involving low respect for supervisors on the part of employees. The importance of this dimension of attitude has been suggested by Raymond Falcione (1973). He argues that a supervisor who allows subordinate participation and has a low degree of credibility in the eyes of his subordinates will be perceived either as "weak" or as being involved in a deceptive plot to exploit his subordinates. Falcione found that subordinates who viewed their supervisors as credible were likely, in contrast, to support their supervisor's goals and welcome further participation. Robert Cherry (1970) and M. M. Greller (1975) have also pointed to the centrality of supervisor-employee mutual perceptions in their separate analyses of conditions supportive of (and inimical to) participatory management.

Given this strong support for the notion that supervisor-employee mutual perceptions are an important element in participatory management, it is reasonable to assume that an employee's perception of his or her supervisor will strongly influence that employee's evaluation of a participatory performance appraisal system. To determine the significance of this claim we can use a number of questions pertaining to supervisory climate taken from the "Perceived Work Environment" inventory (Newman 1975; 1977). Each of the following eleven questions permits responses on a five-position scale, with position 1 labeled "never true" and position 5 labeled "always true."

- The supervisor is flexible when necessary.
- Employees know what their supervisor expects of them.
- Supervisors take a personal interest in the employees under them.
- Individuals can count on their supervisor to back them up.
- The supervisor gives recognition for work well done.
- Employees feel free to talk openly with their supervisor.
- Praise is given for doing a good job.
- The best way to get along with your supervisor is to not rock the boat.
- Individuals get helpful information about their job performance.
- The supervisor emphasizes good human relations among the employees.
- Employees are able to speak frankly with the supervisor.

Scoring of these questions depends, of course, on the positive or negative connotation of each term. The combination of these items into a single scale has produced a high degree of reliability in other studies, and this is again the case here with a very strong coefficient alpha of .92.

Task Characteristics

Yet another area of likely concern is that of low commitment to task on the part of employees. Frederick Herzberg (1959; 1966) has been both eloquent in advocacy of, and prodigious in providing empirical support for the view that it is the character of *the task itself* which determines one's dedication to work more than any other factor available to management. His studies have repeatedly documented the importance of employee perceptions of their own tasks vis-à-vis variety, challenge, inherent value to society, etc. for developing an attachment to, and interest in, the place of work and its successful operation. If Herzberg's studies offer a true indication of the significance of task-character perceptions, it should follow that employees who express a low degree of interest in their work would be unlikely to view participation in management practices as an important or welcomed development. On the other hand, it seems reasonable to assume that employees possessing a high degree of interest in their work would also welcome the opportunity to take part in administrative processes affecting that work (see Hackman et al. 1981).

Again, we can assess this potentially important factor by using the Perceived Work Environment inventory to measure the employee's perception of his own work task. Scoring of the following nine items was on the basis of a five-position scale, with position 1 labeled "never true" and position 5 "always true."

- There is the opportunity to do challenging work.
- The work requires a lot of technical training.
- There is the opportunity to do a number of different things.
- Employees have variety in their work tasks.
- There are opportunities to use skills and abilities.
- There is the opportunity to attain status.
- There is the opportunity to accomplish something worthwhile.
- There is the opportunity to develop power and use it.
- There is the opportunity for personal growth.

Again, scoring on this item depends on the positive or negative wording of the question. Once more, the combination of these items produces a measure with strong reliability, as evidenced by a coefficient alpha of .82.

Organizational Climate Regarding Participation

Some administrators who are fearful of utilizing participatory practices in their particular work unit point to the absence of participatory practices in the larger organizational setting. Such objections appear to have some basis in empirical research as well. For example, French, Kay, and Meyer (1966) found that the prevailing level of organizational participation was significantly associated with success in the implementation of participative forms of performance appraisal. Both mutual understanding and the acceptance of negotiated job goals were higher for those employees who were accustomed to a high level of participation in organizational decision making. French and his associates also found that individual employees who perceived their organizations to be generally open to employee participation were more likely to express favorable attitudes toward participative appraisal systems than those employees who viewed their organizations as offering little opportunity for employee involvement.

In a similar vein, Robert Cherry (1970) observes that attempts to implement participative performance appraisal processes under conditions where a non-participatory general management style predominates very often lead to counter-productive results. He argues that even with the adoption of "tricks" of the counseling trade (e.g., frequent eye contact, manifestation of a concerned attitude, employment of "good listener" techniques, etc.), the most likely effect of the adoption of limited scope participative processes is the further alienation of employees who suspect management of insincere, patronizing and manipulative purposes. In contrast, Gray and Starke (1984:282) have noted that the trial of participative methods in organizational settings where established patterns of autocratic governance have become institutionalized often results in the innovator being seen as "soft" and unduly subject to influence from all sides, hence appropriately to be disparaged.

In light of these observations then, it might well be concluded that the presence of an open decision making atmosphere (or lack thereof) may produce a strong influence upon a subordinate's attitude toward participatory performance appraisal. To assess the significance of this factor, the following four questions can be extracted from the Perceived Work Environment inventory:

- There is the opportunity to take part in deciding what the work methods, procedures and goals will be.
- Important decisions are made by employees closest to the situation.
- Most employees take part in making decisions that affect their unit.
- Managers and supervisors ask for the advice of their employees when making decisions that affect their employees.

As with the other items in the Newman inventory, these questions were also answered along a five-position scale running from "never true" to "always true." Once more the reliability of the index created by the combination of these items is respectable, in this case registering a coefficient alpha of .76.

Personality Factors—Character and Values

A final area of potential concern is that of employees' personalities, an area typically involving two related but separate aspects. On the one hand, it is argued that employee dedication to the "Protestant work ethic" may be a necessary condition for the successful operation of participatory management procedures (Greenberg 1977). Employees lacking this ethic will likely allow calls for involvement in work-related deliberations to fall on deaf ears.

A second aspect of this concern for work values also relates to personality make-up, but this time focusing upon the characterological prerequisites to effective employee/supervisor collaboration (Vroom 1960, Wexley et al. 1973). It is argued that persons who have low self-esteem, are introverted rather than extroverted, are rigid rather than flexible, are outer- rather than inner-directed, and who are security seeking rather than risk-oriented will be likely to shy away from rather than embrace opportunities for participation (Super 1962). Chris Argyris (1978) has gone so far as to suggest that the true tragedy of traditional, hierarchical bureaucratic forms of organization is that they reinforce "immaturity" and preclude the development of mature, healthy, self-directed personalities among employees.

The Washington State evaluation survey instrument contained sections pertaining to both of these aspects of personal character—commitment to the work ethic and personality inclinations supportive of participative interaction. On the first count, four of the six scales (pertaining to the need to keep busy, desire for upward mobility, pride in work and relative importance of one's job versus other life concerns) developed by Wollack, Goodale and Wijting (1971) were used to assess the significance of Protestant work ethic considerations. On the second count, the abbreviated personality inventory developed by Rosalind Forbes (1979) was used to assess the roles of self-esteem, extrovertism, flexibility, risk seeking and inner-directedness in determining receptivity toward participative practices.

Findings from a Bivariate Analysis

A preliminary analysis investigates the degree to which each of the factors thought to be important influences employee receptivity to participatory practices. To the degree that the operationalized indexes of these factors are correlated with variations in attitude toward the self-evaluation opportunity in the participative performance process, there is supporting evidence for the proposition that such factors are valid qualifiers to the applicability of participative management practices. Table 8.2 sets forth the findings on such a bivariate analysis.

The findings in Table 8.2 are striking for their *lack* of impressiveness; *none* of the hypothesized factors manifest a strong relationship to the central measure of receptivity to participation. The two factors showing the strongest association—general attitude toward performance appraisal and perception of fairness of the last evaluation—are both subject to implementation *training* in ways that the other supposed participation-inhibiting factors are not. These findings would appear to support those who contend that participatory management methods have a wide rather than narrow scope of applicability.

At this point it might well be objected that the practice of self-evaluation itself is more threatening than participation *per se,* and that this indicator of receptivity to participation is a poor criterion. While self-evaluation can be seen as a difficult task, it should be noted that all forms of *meaningful* participation involve the placement of self before the view of others (Goffman 1959; 1961). Whether it be a matter of saying one's piece in public, making a proposal for action before a group, venturing an opinion on a proposed course of action before colleagues—all of these involve exposing one's own ideas to the approval/ disapproval of others. It might even be argued that rather than being a poor indicator of receptivity to participation, this measure of receptivity is a particularly good criterion for the assessment of factors related to genuine, meaningful employee involvement.

Whatever the virtues or weaknesses of this particular measure of employee receptivity to participation, yet another objection might be raised to the analysis presented here. It might be argued that none of these supposed participation-inhibiting factors *taken alone* may relate directly to receptivity toward involvement, but that *in combination* they define dimensions of organizational climate which are determinative of employee receptivity to participatory management. In order to assess this possibility, then, it is necessary to use factor analysis in order to search out any underlying, undetected dimensions of organizational environment that might otherwise be hidden from notice. Coincidentally, by adding

Table 8.2

Bivariate Analysis of Relationships Between Receptivity to Participation and Hypothesized Determinants of Receptivity

	Correlation Coefficient (Pearson's R) with Attitude Hypothesized Determinants Toward Self-Evaluation*
General attitude toward performance appraisal	.34
Perception of fair evaluation in past assessment	.27
Perception of supervisory climate	.06
Perception of degree of enrichment of work task	.08
Perception of opportunity for participation [organization-wide]	.09
Personality factors	
Protestant work values	
• Desire to stay busy at work	.04
• Desire for upward mobility	.08
• Pride in work	.05
• Importance of job in one's life	.18
Character traits	
• Self-esteem	.05
• Introvert/extrovert	.04
• Flexibility/rigidity	.08
• Inner/outer directedness	.11
• Security/risk seeking	.06

*Calculations based upon 690 to 720 cases, with all cases where either of the two variables in question are missing being excluded from the determination of correlation coefficients.

the measure of participatory receptivity to the factor analysis it is possible to determine the degree of association between that criterion of receptivity and any hidden, underlying dimensions of the organizational setting which might obtain (Kim and Mueller 1978).

Findings from a Factor Analysis

The findings from such a factor analysis are reported in Table 8.3. This Table displays the results of the measure of employee receptivity to participation, along with all of the separate hypothesized influences upon receptivity within a single principal component, varimax rotated factor analysis (by means of *Statistical Package for the Social Sciences* software). The results of the factor analysis suggest the presence of three identifiable underlying factors, and the hint of a fourth, separate dimension.

Table 8.3

Factor Analysis Results: Factors Identified in a Principal Components, Varimax Rotated Factor Analysis Containing Receptivity to Employee Participation and Factors Hypothesized to Predict Such Receptivity

	Factor 1	Factor 2	Factor 3	Factor 4
	"Character traits"	"Work setting"	"Work values"	"Performance appraisal"
Variables				
Character trait—self-esteem	64	-.04	.01	-.05
Character trait—introvert/extrovert	.61	-.12	-.10	-.04
Character trait—flexible/rigid	.63	.01	.05	-.08
Character trait—inner/outer directed	51	-.19	-.08	-.11
Character trait—security/risk seeking	.78	.05	-.11	-.06
Perception of supervisory climate	-.13	.88	.06	.11
Perception of degree of enrichment of work	-.12	.52	.14	.10
Perception of opportunity of participation	-.14	.73	.08	.13
Variables				
Work values—desire to stay busy at work	-.04	.05	.69	-.01
Work values—desire for upward mobility	-.21	-.12	.31	08
Work values—pride in work	-.02	.09	.73	-.05
Work values—importance of one's job	-.21	.20	.45	.18
Attitude Toward Participation in Appraisal	-.12	-.01	-.06	.68
General attitude toward performance appraisal	-.03	.09	.13	.52
Perception of fairness in past assessments	-.13	.21	.01	.39
Eigenvalue	3.26	1.74	1.30	.86
% of variance	38.7	20.7	15.4	10.2

As might be expected, the several scales dealing with "character traits" fall on a single dimension, constituting the most important dimension (accounting for 38.7 percent of the total variance) identified in the factor analysis. The existence of a single factor uniting these separate aspects of personality lends support to Rosalind Forbes' (1979) contention that the element of stress-proneness underlies all of these separate aspects of character. However, with respect to receptivity to participation in performance appraisal, there is little evidence that such personality factors have anything to do with such receptivity. The item dealing with receptivity has only a –.12 loading on this first factor.

The second factor is quite interesting, for it contains three separate hypothesized inhibitors of receptivity to participation—namely, attitude toward supervision, perception of organizational openness to participation, and perception of degree of enrichment of one's work task. The presence of this factor suggests that these three characteristics tend to be interrelated, and that quite possibly this underlying "work setting" dimension might very well be a good predictor of employee receptivity to participation. Such is not the case, however, for the item on receptivity toward participation in performance appraisal shows a loading of only –.01 on this second factor! Once more the hypothesized influence of these job-setting conditions upon participatory receptivity does not surface to any noteworthy degree.

The third factor is again quite interpretable on *a priori* grounds; the four aspects of "work values" constitute a single factor as might be expected from their common use in combination as a measure of the "Protestant work ethic." While the third factor is easily interpretable in terms of a hypothesized factor of relevance to participatory phenomena, it is once more proven not to relate strongly to the measure of receptivity to participation. The item in question relates to this third factor with a loading of –.06, again indicating no noteworthy interrelationship.

The fourth and final factor turns out to be of the greatest interest in understanding the dynamics of receptivity to participation in this area. The central, key item serving as the criterion for receptivity to participation shows the highest loading on this fourth factor, with only two of the other measures showing covariation along the same underlying dimension. These two concerns—general attitude towards performance appraisal, and perception of fairness of previous appraisals—are both *immediate, remediable* attitudinal predispositions which constitute fit subjects for implementation training efforts. It would seem that a well-designed and adequately financed effort to sell the virtues of a participative, fair, and constructive appraisal system would likely influence these particular attitudes, while such efforts would scarcely affect work values, personality traits or basic supervisorial and organizational customs.

Conclusion

Both the bivariate and factor analytic approaches to the claims concerning the supposed inhibitory consequences for participatory management of particular organizational circumstances produce the same results. To wit, there is little evidence to support the most typical objections raised to the use of participatory management practices. At least with regard to the views of Washington State employees pertaining to their receptivity to participative performance appraisal, it does not appear that a poor assessment of supervisors, a weak commitment to the work ethic, a non-enriched job, or a low regard for organization-wide openness to employee involvement have much bearing upon employee receptivity to participatory management.

Since it appears that there is little evidence to support the claims of some public sector administrators who, though professing sympathy for participative management in the abstract, do not use such practices for reasons of "special, inauspicious circumstances," it follows that the probable area of application of such practices is quite a bit wider than often presumed (Hesper and Woll 1976). Perhaps the several reasons given as to why participative management practices are inappropriate in some particular, always "unique" setting should be viewed more often than not as reflecting an ill-founded fear of change. At least with regard to performance appraisal, and probably equally so in other less threatening areas of potential employee involvement, the would-be obstacles to effective implementation among non-receptive employees are largely a figment of ever-active imaginations. More research is certainly indicated in areas other than performance appraisal, and perhaps there are additional hypothesized participatory inhibitors to be investigated. This first study suggests, however, that a good deal of skepticism is in order when apparently plausible reasons are offered as to why the adoption of more participatory administrative practices cannot be undertaken.

Notes

1. A preliminary study of this question is presented by Carolyn Cron Ogden (1980) in an unpublished M.A. thesis, "An Analysis of Factors Affecting Employee Attitudes Toward a Participatory Performance Appraisal System."

2. Though there is a high degree of support for the adoption of participative management forms in the personnel literature, there exists among personnel scholars an articulate and insightful minority of critics; among them see particularly Pelz and Andrews (1966), Hunt and Hill (1969), Mott (1972), and Kaplan and Tausky (1977).

References

Anthony, W. (1978). *Participative Management.* Reading, Mass.: Addison-Wesley Publishing.

Argyris, C. (1978). "Organizational Behavior," pp. 182–186 in J. Shafritz and A. Hyde (eds.) *Classics of Public Administration.* Oak Park, Ill.: Moore Publishing.

Burke, R. J. and D. S. Wilcox (1969). "Characteristics of Effective Employee Performance Review and Development Interviews." *Personnel Psychology* 22 (Autumn): 291–305.

Centers, R. and D. Bugental (1966). "Intrinsic and Extrinsic Job Motivations Among Different Segments of the Working Population." *Journal of Applied Psychology* 50 (June): 193–197.

Cherry, R. (1970). "Performance Reviews: A Note on Failure." *Personnel Journal* 49 (May): 398–403.

Dossett, D. L., G. P. Latham and T. R. Mitchell (1979). "The Effects of Assigned vs. Participatively Set Goals, Knowledge of Results, and Individual Differences on Employee Behavior When Goal Difficulty is Held Constant." *Journal of Applied Psychology* 64 (June): 291–298.

Dubin, R., J. Champoux and L. W. Porter (1975). "Central Life Interests and Organizational Commitment of Blue-Collar and Clerical Workers." *Administrative Science Quarterly* 20 (September): 411–421.

Falcione, R. (1973). "The Relationship of Supervisor Credibility to Subordinate Satisfaction." *Personnel Journal* 52 (September): 800–803.

Forbes, R. (1979). "Job Stress and Personality." *Western's World* (September/October): 40–43, 64–67, 71.

French, J., E. Kay and H. Meyer (1966). "Participation and the Appraisal System." *Human Relations* 19 (February): 3–20.

Friedlander, F. (1965). "Comparative Work Value Systems." *Personnel Psychology* 18 (Spring): 1–20.

Goffman, E. (1959). The Presentation of Self in Everyday Life. New York: Doubleday.

——— (1961). *Encounters: Two Studies in the Sociology of Interaction.* Indianapolis: Bobbs-Merrill.

Gray, J. L. and F. Starke (1984). *Organizational Behavior: Concepts and Application,* 3rd Ed. Columbus, Ohio: Merrill.

Greenberg, J. (1977). "The Protestant Work Ethic and Reactions to the Appraisal Interview." *Journal of Applied Psychology* 62 (December): 682–890.

Greller, M. (1975). "Subordinate Participation and Reactions to the Appraisal Interview." *Journal of Applied Psychology* 60 (October): 544–549.

Hackman, J., G. Oldham, R. Janson and K. Purdy (1981) "A New Strategy for Job Enrichment," pp. 230–250 in Donald E. Klinger (ed.) *Public Personnel Management: Readings in Contexts and Strategies.* Palo Alto, Calif.: Mayfield Press.

Haynes, M. (1973). "Do Appraisal Reviews Improve Performance?" *Public Personnel Management* 2 (March/April): 128–132.

Hesper, G. and T. Woll (1976). "The Demand for Participation Among Employees." *Human Relations* 29 (May): 411–428.

Herzberg, F. (1959). *Motivation to Work.* New York: John Wiley.

——— (1966). *Work and the Nature of Man.* New York: Thomas Crowell.

Hillery, J. and K. Wexley (1974). "Participation Effects in Appraisal Interviews Conducted in a Training Situation." *Journal of Applied Psychology* 59 (April): 168–171.

Hunt, J. C. and J. W. Hill (1969). "The New Look in Motivation Theory and Organizational Research." *Human Organization* 38 (Summer): 100–109.

Kaplan, M. (1976). *Alienation and Identification.* New York: The Free Press.

Kaplan, R. H. and C. Tausky (1977). "Humanism in Organizations: A Critical Appraisal." *Public Administration Review* 37 (March/April): 171–180.

Kilbridge, M. D. (1960). "Do Workers Prefer Larger Jobs?" *Personnel* 37 (January/February): 45–48.

Kim, J. and C. Mueller (1978). *Introduction to Factor Analysis.* Beverly Hills, Calif.: Sage Publications.

Latham, G. and G. Yukl (1976). "Effects of Assigned and Participative Goal Setting on Performance and Job Satisfaction." *Journal of Applied Psychology* 61 (April): 166–171.

Lawler, E., D. Hall and G. Oldham (1974). "Organizational Climate: Relationship to Organizational Structure, Process and Performance." *Organizational Behavior and Human Performance* 11 (February): 139–155.

Likert, R. (1959). "Motivational Approach to Management Development." *Harvard Business Review* 37 (July/August): 75–182.

Lovrich, N., D. Bishop, R. Hopkins and P. Shaffer (1983). "Participative Performance Appraisal in a Municipal Setting: A Pre- and Post-Implementation Study." *State and Local Government Review* 15 (Winter): 24–31.

Lovrich, N., P. Shaffer, D. Yale and R. Hopkins (1979). "Participative Performance Appraisal in the State of Washington." *Intergovernmental Personnel Notes* (May/June): 13–16.

——— (1980). "Do Public Servants Welcome or Fear Merit Evaluation of Their Performance?" *Public Administration Review* 49 (May/June): 214–222.

——— (1981). "Quasi-Experimental Pilot Study of a Participative Performance Appraisal System in Six Washington State Agencies: Effects Upon Job Satisfaction, Agency Climate, and Work Values." *Review of Public Personnel Administration* 1 (Summer): 51–73.

McGregor, D. (1957). "An Uneasy Look at Performance Appraisal." *Harvard Business Review* 43 (January/February): 123–129.

Miner, J. B. (1969). *Personnel and Industrial Relations: A Managerial Approach.* New York: Macmillan Publishers.

Mott, Paul E. (1972). *The Characteristics of Effective Organization.* New York: Harper and Row.

Newman, J. (1975). "Understanding the Organizational Structure—Job Attitude Relationship Through Perceptions of the Work Environment." *Organizational Behavior and Human Performance* 14 (December): 371–397.

——— (1977). "Development of a Measure of Perceived Work Environment." *Academy of Management Journal* 20 (December): 520–534.

Ogden, C. (1980). "An Analysis of Factors Affecting Employee Attitudes Toward a Participatory Performance Appraisal System." Unpublished M. A. Thesis, Washington State University.

Olsen, L. and A. Bennett (1976). "Performance Appraisal: Management Technique or Social Process? Part II—Social Process." *Management Review* 65 (January): 22–28.

Pelz, A. and F. Andrews (1966). *Scientists in Organizations.* New York: John Wiley and Sons.

Schein, E. (1974). "The Hawthorne Group Studies Revisited: A Defense of Theory Y." M.I.T.
Sloan School of Management Working Paper No. 756–74. (December) [reprinted in Judith Gordon (ed.)
   A Diagnostic Approach to Organizational Behavior. Boston: Allyn and Bacon (1983)].
Simonds, R. and J. Orife (1975). "Worker Behavior Versus Enrichment Theory." *Administrative Science
   Quarterly* 20 (December): 606–612.
Stone, T. (1973). "An Examination of Six Prevalent Assumptions Concerning Performance Appraisal,"
   Public Personnel Management 2 (November/December): 408–414.
Super, D. (1962). "Structure of Work Values in Relation to Status, Achievement, Interests and Adjust-
   ment." *Journal of Applied Psychology* 46 (August): 231–239.
Vroom, V. (1960). "Some Personality Determinants of the Effects of Participation." *Journal of Abnormal
   and Social Psychology* 59 (November): 322–327.
———— (1964). *Work and Motivation.* New York: John Wiley and Sons.
Wexley, K., J. Singh and G. Yukl (1973). "Subordinate Personality as a Moderator of the Effects of
   Participation in Three Types of Appraisal interviews." *Journal of Applied Psychology* 58 (February): 54–59.
Wilcox, H. G. (1969). "Hierarchy, Human Nature, and the Participative Panacea." *Public Administration Review* 29 (January/February): 58–61.
Wollack, S., J. Goodale, J. Wijting and P. C. Smith (1971). "Development of the Survey of Work Val-
   ues." *Journal of Applied Psychology* 55 (August): 331–338.
Yoder, D. and H. Heneman (1974). *Staffing Policies and Strategies: Handbook of Personnel and Industrial Relations,* Vol. I. Washington, D. C.: Bureau of National Affairs.

CHAPTER 9

THE AMERICANS WITH DISABILITIES ACT AND THE WORKPLACE

Management's Responsibilities in AIDS-Related Situations

JAMES D. SLACK

Because it protects over 43 million people, the Americans with Disabilities Act (ADA) of 1990 has the potential of being the most significant piece of civil rights legislation enacted in the last three decades. ADA is comprehensive in its coverage, but Title I is of particular importance because it guarantees one of the fundamental rights demanded by every group and individual citizen in America: the right to have equal access to jobs and career opportunities. Organizations that are covered by ADA, private entities and public agencies that employ at least 15 full-time workers,[1] are prohibited from discriminating against otherwise qualified disabled Americans in selection, retention, retirement, and termination policies and practices. In addition, otherwise qualified disabled individuals cannot be denied access to various job-related opportunities, such as participation in training programs and workshops or career advancement and professional development activities.

The ADA protects everyone within the Human Immunodeficiency Virus (HIV) spectrum; from individuals just testing positive for the retrovirus to people who have contracted Acquired Immunodeficiency Syndrome (AIDS).[2] Nearly 500,000 Americans have contracted AIDS since the late 1970s; of these, approximately 97 percent are of working age, and 75 percent are in the prime working cohort of 25 to 44 years old (Centers for Disease Control and Prevention, 1995). Although estimates vary,[3] it is quite probable that more than one million Americans are unknowingly infected with HIV. Given the demographic trends of AIDS, it is reasonable to expect the same proportion of people who are HIV asymptomatic to be (or have the potential of being) in the work force and, therefore, contributors to the economy.

This makes the AIDS epidemic a central workplace issue in both the public and private sectors. Although the numbers of HIV-infected people certainly vary according

From 55 *Public Administration Review*, 4: 365–370, 1995. Copyright © 1995 Sage Publications. Reprinted with permission.

to location, this disease represents a national problem with severe consequences for every community. Considering the social stigma so often attached to having AIDS,[4] as well as the pattern of discrimination against job applicants and employees who are HIV challenged, the promise of protection under this piece of legislation is perhaps more treasured by members of the AIDS community than by any other group of disabled Americans.

To what degree, and in what manner, will the ADA be applied to workplace situations involving HIV-challenged job applicants and employees? As is the case with so many other pieces of legislation (Van Meter and Van Horn 1975; Pressman and Wildavsky 1979, Nakamura and Smallwood 1980), particularly those that deal with antidiscrimination laws (Saltzstein 1986, Bullock and Lamb 1984), ADA will only protect the rights of those in the HIV spectrum if it is understood and implemented effectively at the local level. This article examines management's responsibilities in ensuring the workplace rights of job applicants and employees who have HIV/AIDS.

The Bishop and Jones Study

Peter C. Bishop and Augustus J. Jones (1993) were first to analyze the potential effectiveness of the ADA. Using "prospective implementation analysis," they looked at several factors commonly found to be critical in the implementation process: participation of beneficiaries, clarity of policy goals, specificity of compliance standards, and ability of agencies to monitor and regulate implementation. According to Bishop and Jones, "Congress clearly stated its intent, regulatory agencies developed detailed compliance standards and enforcement mechanisms, and potential beneficiaries are engaged in the process" (1993:127). Hence, the analysis led them to predict successful implementation.

Because the study was conducted shortly after the passage of ADA, Bishop and Jones admittedly focused only on those variables which tend to affect the early stages of implementation—those at the federal end of the process (1993:122). Although they did not examine the impact of the local (in this study, workplace-level) implementors, Bishop and Jones suggested that one barrier to effective implementation would be litigation over such issues as reasonable accommodation and undue hardship (1993:127). The outcome of these issues is affected directly by efforts at the local end of the implementation process.

Furthermore, Bishop and Jones did not focus on the AIDS community as a target group. Major AIDS organizations joined in with other associations of disabled Americans to provide congressional testimony, but it remains unclear whether job applicants and workers in the HIV spectrum will actually use ADA protections. The nature of HIV and the history of AIDS-related discrimination suggest that enthusiastic target group support at the policy-making stage might not translate directly into the full exercise of newly acquired rights at the point of implementation. The fundamental question is, will HIV-challenged job applicants and employees feel sufficiently safe and secure in their respective workplaces to seek the benefits available under the ADA?

In order for the ADA to be implemented effectively in HIV/AIDS-related situations at the workplace, the disposition of the implementors—the knowledge-base and actions of top-level administrators as well as first-line supervisors—will be an extremely critical factor throughout the process. That is, a central responsibility of management will be to develop a thorough understanding of the legislations applicability to HIV-challenged job applicants and employees. As in the case of dealing with all disabled Americans in the work force, managers will need to know the intricacies of the law. But effective application in the age of AIDS will also be a function of management's ability to understand the nature of the retrovirus as well as the many workplace ramifications of its resultant multiple diseases.

ADA and AIDS

Although people with HIV/AIDS are protected by ADA, the disease is unlike many other disabilities. The complex nature of HIV and the multiplicity of AIDS-related illnesses require greater levels of understanding of both the general medical symptoms and the ways in which the legislation should be applied to situations involving specific individuals who are within the HIV spectrum. The need for such understanding becomes readily apparent when three critical components of the law are examined within the context of AIDS: (1) the definition of "disability," (2) the prerequisite of "notification and documentation," and (3) the need to develop specific, "reasonable accommodations."

First, ADA uses the same language as the Vocational Rehabilitation Act to define disability. According to Section 3 of ADA, a disabled person is someone with:

A. a physical or mental impairment that substantially limits one or more of the major life activities;
B. a record of such an impairment; or
C. being regarded as having such an impairment.

To understand how someone in the HIV spectrum can claim to be disabled under ADA, one needs familiarity with the progression of this retrovirus. Typically, HIV occurs in four stages. The first stage, known as acute HIV, occurs six days to six weeks after infection and is characterized by short-term mononucleosis-like symptoms. Generally people are unaware that they have acute HIV. Some people feel like they just have the flu, and others simply do not acquire any of the short-term symptoms.

The second, asymptomatic stage, is characterized by reasonably normal health. People can remain asymptomatic for varying amounts of time, typically anywhere from two to ten years. The length of time spent in the asymptomatic stage is dependent upon a variety of factors, including one's ability to cope with the tremendous levels of stress which normally accompany the knowledge of being infected, the initial strength and stability of one's immune system, the extent to which the immune system continues to be abused, the quality of health and social services available, and the type of medication prescribed and treatment followed.[5]

The third stage is known as persistent generalized lymphadenopathy (PGL). The clinical representation of this stage is the enlargement of various lymph nodes throughout the body.[6] This stage also can last for years, with the person experiencing prolonged swelling of glands. PGL typically marks the beginning of a decline in the number of CD4 T-cells, the cell that fight off diseases and viruses. It is the CD4 T-cells which explain why glands initially swell (a result of fighting the virus) and the reason why glands remain swollen (a result of the declining number of cells which become insufficient to kill the virus). Hence, the loss of CD4 T-cells culminates in the deterioration and ultimate destruction of the body's immune system. As in the previous stage, the rate of decline in CD4 T-cells results from many factors.

The fourth stage, full-blown AIDS, is defined by a CD4 T-cell count of 200 or less, whereas most healthy people who are not HIV challenged have a CD4 T-cell count of over 1,200. This final stage can also be clinically represented by a host of opportunistic infections, such as pneumocystis carinii pneumonia PCP, and cytomegalovirus (CMV), which cause infections in the lungs, eyes, and other parts of the body. It is also characterized by malignancies, like Kaposi's Sarcoma (KS), purplish plaques that can also occur throughout the body.[7] The final stage typically lasts between two to four years—again, depending on a variety of immunal and environmental conditions. Death is generally delayed until sometime after the development of full-blown AIDS.

Given the various stages of HIV, a job applicant or employee in the HIV spectrum may claim disability under each of the three definitions provided by Section 3 of the ADA.[8] Someone with either PGL or full-blown AIDS qualifies as a disabled worker under the first definition: having an actual physical or mental impairment. However, it is fairly typical for an individual with full-blown AIDS to beat temporarily one or a combination of the opportunistic diseases. The person, for instance, might have KS, but it may be in a state of remission. As such, she or he qualifies under the second definition: having a record of a physical or mental impairment.

An individual who is seropositive but asymptomatic also qualifies as a disabled worker under the third definition: being regarded as having a physical or mental impairment. This situation can include a wide variety of persons who are in the HIV spectrum, ranging from those who are in the asymptomatic stage to people with CD4 T-cell counts below 200 (full-blown AIDS) but do not have as yet any symptoms. People in these circumstances are still regarded as disabled under ADA because of the 100 percent fatality rate of HIV infection. Given that perhaps millions of people are unknowingly HIV positive and asymptomatic, this category of disability will become the one most commonly used in the future.

The second issue deals with the ADA requirement of notifying employers, and providing verifying documentation, about specific disabilities (56 Fed. Reg. 35,748, July 26, 1991). While some disabilities are readily apparent and need little further verification, others may not be so evident. This is often the case for people in the HIV spectrum.

Because the majority of HIV-challenged people are asymptomatic, only a nonanonymous blood test can prove the existence of the disability. Even in the case of individuals at more advanced stages, many symptoms and conditions are either psychological or physically unobtrusive.[9] For example, one might not necessarily detect the disfiguring lesions which result from KS except when they emerge on the hands or face. The effects of PCP or pulmonary CMV might also remain unnoticed with the use of prophylaxes. Moreover, the depression which frequently results from constant, swollen lymph nodes, or from learning about another decline in the CD4 T-cell count, may be noted but misinterpreted by management as simply employee moodiness. Hence, PGL or AIDS employees with hidden conditions will also have to provide documentation.

Management is not obligated to protect the rights of disabled individuals when it is unaware of the existence of specific impairments. When verification does not occur, it is possible that some managers will wrongfully discharge the employee; this could be based simply on stereotypes about the disability or fear of imminent health care costs. Hence, the notification and documentation requirement of ADA highlights one of the many ironies of the AIDS epidemic. While the price of protection rests largely on the act of self-disclosure, the social stigma attached to AIDS makes it extremely difficult for many individuals to "stand up" and empower themselves. This situation is exacerbated by the absence of readily apparent and uniquely shared characteristics which, if present, would afford the HIV challenged an opportunity enjoyed by individuals in most other protected groups in society: gaining additional strength and courage from knowing that one is not alone in a particular setting. Regrettably each person in the HIV spectrum must decide in a relative vacuum whether to become a "Rosa Parks" in his or her specific workplace or to simply remain silent and fundamentally unprotected.

The third component, underscoring the complexities and difficulties involved in applying the ADA to HIV/AIDS-related situations in the workplace, deals with the issue of "reasonable accommodation." ADA docs not define reasonable accommodation, but offers suggestions and guidelines on how to develop such accommodations. Section 101 (7) indicates that reasonable accommodations may include:

1. making existing facilities used by employees readily accessible to and usable by individuals with disabilities; and
2. job restructuring, part-time or modified work schedules, reassignment to a vacant position, acquisition or modification of equipment or devices, appropriate adjustment or modifications of examinations, training materials or policies, the provision of qualified readers or interpreters, and other similar accommodations for individuals with disabilities.

The law assumes that the responsibility for making the initial attempt at providing reasonable accommodation is in the hands of management. ADA requires employers to take into consideration the nature of the specific job setting as well as the many characteristics and symptoms of the specific disability. However, management is not obligated to provide reasonable accommodation if such modifications do not facilitate satisfactory performance of the essential functions of the job, or if the modifications result in undue hardship for the organization.

Here, too, the nature of HIV complicates the application of reasonable accommodation requirements. Because AIDS is a fatal disease with no cure in the foreseeable future, it is not unusual for the initial diagnosis of HIV to cast the person into a state of shock for a period lasting from several months to well over a year. The only recourse for someone testing positive for HIV is to remain as healthy as possible, minimize the level of stress, find a knowledgeable physician with whom a treatment strategy can be devised,[10] and hope that a cure or at least more effective treatments are developed before he or she dies. It is because of the fundamentally life-taking nature of the retrovirus that HIV-positive job applicants and employees require reasonable accommodations—even in the absence of clinical symptoms. Under ADA, they have a right to receive workplace-related assistance that will help them cope with having a fatal disease and keep them healthier, hence in the asymptomatic stage longer.

The many illnesses related to full-blown AIDS also complicate the rendering of reasonable accommodations. As the immune system deteriorates, opportunistic diseases begin to attack the body sequentially and in combination. Someone with fungal infections, such as candidiasis or histoplasmosis, might require different kinds of reasonable accommodations than someone with viral infections like CMV or shingles. As suggested above, learning that one's CD4 T-cell count has dropped dramatically might require additional, temporary accommodations similar to those needed immediately following the initial diagnosis of either HIV or AIDS. Each illness and situation—indeed, each individual—will have to be analyzed carefully in order to determine appropriate and effective reasonable accommodations.

Action Needed by Management

What should managers do to facilitate the effective implementation of the ADA in the case of employees with HIV/AIDS? They need to develop a workplace environment that supports and encourages the empowerment of employees in the HIV spectrum. Three specific activities can help establish and maintain this environment. First, management should establish a plan of action for dealing with HIV at the workplace. The plan should be tailored to the particulars of each workplace, but generally should include the following four components: (1) a statement supporting the workplace and civil rights of HIV-challenged employees and job applicants, (2) a set of procedures for helping these individuals, (3) general examples of reasonable accommodations which might assist HIV employees and their immediate supervisors in devising specific accommodations, and (4) a plan for providing education to employees and training for supervisors (Slack and Luna 1992:306). To further strengthen a supportive workplace environment, the specifics of the plan should be developed and approved by both management and labor. The plan should then be distributed to every employee as part of the personnel handbook.

Second, the education and training component of the plan must go well beyond "AIDS 101." Rather than underscoring only those topics which pertain to modes of transmission and strategies for prevention, focus must be on increasing the level of understanding about those aspects of the retrovirus that have a direct bearing on the productivity, morale, and health of the work force, as well as the processes and practices that are designed to address those aspects of AIDS in a more proactive, supportive, and effective manner. One example of a training workshop that focuses on workplace ramifications of AIDS is in the Appendix.

Finally, workplace managers must devise reasonable accommodations that are job-specific and meet the needs of each individual in each stage of the disease. This is a difficult task, but one which is absolutely essential to prolonging the health of the employee as well as maintaining high levels of morale and productivity. Here are a few suggestions.[11]

Beginning at the asymptomatic stage, reasonable accommodations should focus on minimizing the amount of stress at the workplace and, therefore, helping the employee to maintain a stronger immune system. Having a plan of action in place is the first step in relieving stress and anxiety in that it will help to reassure the HIV-challenged employee of a positive workplace environment. Additional stress reduction measures might include: facilitating the creation of HIV support groups at the workplace, permitting more flexibility in use of sick days for dealing with shock and depression, transferring workers out of jobs that bring them into contact with pollutants or infectious materials, and counseling employees about the negative health consequences of working overtime. Paradoxically, management should try to keep workplace conditions as normal as possible and thereby help to provide a psychological familiar routine.

Employees with PGL or full-blown AIDS will need an increasing amount of time away from the workplace. Hence, accommodations might entail working at home more often, downgrading to part-time employment while still maintaining benefits, or greater use of flexitime. Because sick-day use will increase, management might consider ways to pool unused sick days from other employees. Depending on symptoms, reasonable accommodations might also entail such simple acts as moving the HIV-challenged employee's work station closer to restrooms, allowing for additional work breaks to recapture his or her strength, or providing brief opportunities for privacy and reflection during the work day. At all stages of the disease, communication between management and the HIV-challenged employee is central to providing not simply reasonable, but effective, accommodations.

Conclusions

It is to be hoped that Bishop and Jones (1993) are correct in projecting success in the implementation of the ADA. After all, the law is supported by a wide variety of interest groups, including those within the AIDS community. Furthermore, both Congress and the Equal Employment Opportunity Commission have provided clear definitions and administrative guidelines. And unlike many other pieces of legislation, the ADA is accompanied with straight-forward oversight and compliance mechanisms.

As with past attempts to implement antidiscrimination legislation, however, local actors will certainly have to play a major role in the process. Especially given the stigma and fears attached to the AIDS epidemic, the responsibilities of the workplace manager in assuring effective implementation of the ADA will be even greater than is the case with other laws. Politics, after all, affects the quality of life for people with HIV/AIDS more than the morbid afflictions that come part-and-parcel with this retrovirus. If managers pursue the spirit of the law, then HIV-challenged individuals will grow increasingly comfortable in exercising their rights under the letter of law. This, it seems, is management's ultimate responsibility.

Notes

The author is grateful for suggestions and helpful comments made about earlier drafts of this article by several anonymous *PAR* referees, the editor of *PAR,* and Professor Gregory Butler of New Mexico State University.

1. The ADA does not cover federal employees, Native American tribes, and private membership clubs (except for labor organizations). Federal employees in the HIV spectrum, however, are protected from workplace discrimination and are due reasonable accommodations under the Vocational Rehabilitation Act. *(School Board of-Nassau County v. Airline, 1987; Alexander v. Choate, 1985; and Chalk v. United States District Court, Central District of California, 1988.)*

2. The legislative history makes this very clear ("House Committee on Education and Labor Report" at 52 and "Senate Committee on Labor and Human Resources Report" at 22, 136 *Congressional Record* S9697, July 13, 1990).

3. Estimates range from just a few hundred thousand persons (Fumento 1990) to perhaps over ten million persons (telephone interview with counselors at the Gay Men's Health Crisis and the San Francisco AIDS Hotline). The CDC estimates that, in the United States, 1 in every 100 men and 1 in every 150 women are probably within the HIV spectrum. All estimates are speculative because the only way to determine the number of HIV-challenged people is by testing everyone at least once every three months.

4. This is due primarily to cultural responses to the disease's initial connection with homosexual behavior and IV-drug use.

5. Several of these factors are supposition. That is, no study indicates conclusively the exact extent to which factors like stress reduction delay the progression of the disease. To one extent or another, however, there is consensus in the medical community that stress has an effect on the health of everyone's immune system Furthermore, most physicians treating people in the HIV spectrum prescribe activities (support groups, sleep, rest, etc.) designed to minimize the level of stress.

6. PGL is more of a sign than a symptom and, therefore, it is possible for some people to be within the PGL stage (decreasing CD4 T-cell count) and remain asymptomatic. For the vast majority of people with PGL, this stage is characterized by prolonged swelling (equal 10 or greater than 1 cm) of the lymph nodes with no other signs of AIDS (Stine 1993; and Cohen et al. 1990).

7. Full-blown AIDS also includes many other symptomatic manifestations, including wasting syndrome, fever, night sweats, and deterioration of the peripheral nervous system.

8. The exception is for individuals in the acute HIV stage. There are simply insufficient levels of antibodies to test positive of HIV at this stage.

9. Psychological issues change with the changes in the disease. The following list is from James Dilley (1984:62–76; in Dilley 1990:2–5.13.1):

New Diagnosis

- Affective numbing vs. affective discharge; "denial"
- Need for emotional, financial, social support; self-esteem
- Fear of contaminating family, friends

- Fear of rejection; family, friends
- Pressure to make complicated treatment decisions
- Feelings of guilt and self-blame; illness as retribution
- Is there sex after diagnosis? Life-style changes

Mid-stage

- Loss of hope; emotional exhaustion
- More derailed grief work: anticipating and mourning loss of important people and objects
- Extent of treatment; pain control
- Unfinished business: life review; putting one's affairs in order

Terminal Care

- Adequate pain control; personal contact
- Work with family, friends
- Death and dying: honoring the patient's wishes

10. Commonly such treatment strategies entail decisions about antiviral drugs (either azidothymidine, AZT—also referred to as zidovudine, ZDV, or the brand-name Retrovir—dideoxyinosine (ddI), and dideoxycytidine (ddC), PCP prophylaxis (Bactrim or Intron A), and other important secondary prevention strategies such as TB screening.

11. These suggestions are based on conversations with counselors and HIV-challenged people associated with The Living Room (Cleveland), the Gay Men's Health Crisis (New York), the San Francisco AIDS Hotline, the HIV Coordinating Council of New Mexico (Albuquerque), and the Southwest AIDS Committee (Las Cruces, NM, and El Paso, TX).

References

Alexander v. Choate, 1985. 469 U.S. 287.

Bishop, Peter C. and Augustus J. Jones, Jr., 1993. "Implementing the Americans with Disabilities Act of 1990: Assessing the Variables of Success." *Public Administration Review,* vol. 53 (March/April), 121–128.

Bullock, Charles S. and Charles U. Lamb, 1984. *Implementation of Civil Rights Policy.* Monterey, CA: Brooks/Cole Publishing.

Centers for Disease Control and Prevention, 1995. *HIV/AIDS Surveillance Report,* no. 2

Chalk v. United States District Court Central District of California, 1988., 840 F.2d 701, 9th Cir.

Cohen, P.T., et al., 1990. *The AIDS Knowledge Base: A Textbook on HIV Disease from The University of California, San Francisco, and the San Francisco General Hospital.* Waltham, MA: Medical Publishing Group.

DeSario, Jack P., Sue Faerman, and James D. Slack, 1994. *Local Government Information and Training Needs in the 21st Century.* Westport, CT: Quorum Books.

Dilley, James, 1984. "Treatment Issues and Approaches in the Psychological Care of AIDS Patients," In S. Nichols and D. Ostrow, eds., *Psychiatric Aspects of AIDS.* Washington, DC: American Psychiatric Press, pp. 62–76.

———, 1990. "Psychological Impact of AIDS: Overview." In P.T. Cohen, et al., eds., *The AIDS Knowledge Base: A Textbook on HIV Disease from The University of California, San Francisco, and the San Francisco General Hospital.* Waltham, MA: Medical Publishing Group.

Federal Register, 1991. "Equal Employment Opportunity for Individuals with Disabilities; Final Rule." Equal Employment Opportunity Commission, vol. 56, pp. 35725–35756.

Fumenro, Michael, 1990. *The Myth of Heterosexual AIDS.* New York: Basic Books, Inc.

Nakamura, Robert T. and Frank Smallwood, 1980. *The Politics of Policy Implementation.* New York: St. Martin's Press.

Pressman, Jeffrey L and Aaron B. Wildavsky, 1973. *Implementation.* Berkeley, CA: University of California Press.

Saltzstein, Grace H., 1986. "Female Mayors and Women in Municipal Jobs." *American Journal of Political Science,* vol. 30 (February), 140–164.

School Board of Nassau Country v. Airline, 1987. 480 U.S. 273.

Slack, James D. and Anelia Luna. 1992. "AIDS-Related Documents from 96 American Cities and Counties." *Public Administration Review,* vol. 52 (May/June), 305–308.

Stine, Gerald J., 1993. *Acquired Immune Deficiency Syndrome: Biological, Medical, Social, and Legal Issues.* Englewood Cliffs, NJ: Prentice-Hall.

Van Meter, Donald S. and Carl E. Van Horn, 1975. "The Policy Implementation Process: A Conceptual Framework." *Administration and Society,* vol. 6 (February), 445–488.

Appendix

Managing the Workplace Ramifications of AIDS

Purpose: To prepare management for dealing with workplace situations involving HIV and AIDS.

Goal: By end of training session, participants will have (1) epidemiological, legal, and interpersonal knowledge about HIV and AIDS and (2) understanding of how to apply knowledge of HIV/AIDS to their specific work settings.

Time: This is a one-day (8 hour) workshop.

Module 1. Understanding HIV and AIDS

The general purpose of module 1 is to familiarize workshop participants with (1) some of the fears and myths about AIDS which may impact workplace performance and (2) the realities of what HIV-infected employees experience, which impact workplace performance.

Specific topics include:

1. What is HIV and AIDS?
2. Modes of transmission
3. Progression from HIV to AIDS
4. AIDS-related diseases
5. Keeping workers healthy and productive

Module 2. Managing the Workplace

The general purpose of module 2 is to familiarize workshop participants on how to maintain a productive and healthy workplace. Topics center on the Americans with Disabilities Act (ADA) as it applies to AIDS.

Specific topics include:

1. ADA and the specific work setting
2. Nondiscrimination of HIV-infected employees
3. Reasonable accommodation issues and application to specific workplace and job descriptions.
4. Undue hardship issues and application to specific workplace and job descriptions.

Module 3. Dealing Effectively with both HIV-Challenged and Noninfected Employees

Module 3 shifts focus from the agency level to the supervisor-subordinate level. Using case law in the areas of labor relations, work force management, and AIDS, as well as workplace experiences of HIV-challenged individuals from the community, this module familiarizes workshop participants with one-to-one situations.

Topics include:

1. ADA's requirements of documentation of HIV
2. Sensitivity in dealing with HIV-challenged workers
3. ADA's modification of confidentiality
4. Knowledge about community-based assistance programs
5. Controlling rumors, fears, and behavior of employees who are not HIV challenged.

Module 4A. Developing an AIDS Plan for the Workplace

Workshop participants are divided into two groups. Managers participate in module 4A. Here the basic components of an AIDS plan for the workplace is discussed and applied to each work setting and at the job-specific level. It is emphasized that the purpose of the plan is to maintain a healthy and productive work force while avoiding AIDS-related litigation.

Module 4B. Training the Trainer about AIDS and the Workplace

Training Staff participate in module 4B, which focuses on strategies for educating the entire work force on the issue of AIDS. This module includes discussions on how to present AIDS in nonthreatening and nonoffensive ways, yet in ways that are direct and provide derailed information. It also focuses on how the training staff can tap local expertise and resources, as well as how to disseminate information in an effective manner.

Source: Adapted from DeSario, Faerman, and Slack (1994).

CHAPTER 10

DRUG TESTING IN PUBLIC AGENCIES

Public Policy Issues and Managerial Responses*

DONALD E. KLINGNER, NANCY G. O'NEILL, AND MOHAMMED GAMAL SABET

Drug and alcohol abuse is a tremendous problem in our society, from a legal, economic, social, medical, political, and managerial perspective (Harwood et al. 1984; Levin-Epstein and Sala 1986; Rowland 1985). Liability risks, economic costs, and public demands for effective performance have led many public agencies to initiate drug and alcohol testing, and to establish Employee Assistance Programs (EAPs) to treat employees (IPMA 1988, Masi 1987, Greenberg 1987, Hartsfield 1986, Curran 1987, Chiabotta 1985, Starr and Byram 1985).

While substance abuse is a societal problem with significant implications for public agencies and their employees, there is a lack of previously published baseline data on a range of research questions related to public agency drug testing. There is no uniform data base from which we may determine which public agencies test applicants or employees, and what they do with those who test positive.

This article presents the results of a survey of 300 public agency personnel directors. It describes the testing policies and procedures their agencies now use, and evaluates the implications of testing public agency employees for substance abuse in the workplace for three critical public policy concerns—public employees' right to protection against violations of their Constitutional rights to privacy and due process, elected officials' demands for enforcement of the public's right to an effective public service, management's need to mitigate the effects of employee substance abuse in order to reduce liability risks and increase program effectiveness.

Methodology

The Clearinghouse on Drug and AIDS Testing was created in 1986 by the American Society for Public Administration's Section on Personnel Administration and Labor Relations

From 10 *Review of Public Personnel Administration*, 1: 1–10, Fall 1989. Copyright © 1989 Sage Publications. Reprinted with permission.

(ASPA-SPALR). In November 1987, the Clearinghouse undertook a comprehensive survey of public agency drug testing policies and procedures, using a sample of 300 personnel directors from public agencies at all levels of government in the United States.[1]

The sample is not random. Rather, it is designed to include those jurisdictions which are most likely to be developing managerial responses to the critical public policy issues raised by drug testing. It comprises the 50 states, the 100 largest cities, all counties over 500,000 population, and all federal cabinet-level departments and independent agencies. It was compiled with the help of membership directories provided by the International Personnel Management Association (IPMA) and the National Association of Counties (NACO).

This study is designed to answer a range of questions about how public agencies have responded to demands that they create managerial policies and practices related to substance abuse. Specifically, its objective is to present baseline data which will acquaint public administrators with current policy and practice in this area, and guide them in further investigating the relationship of substance abuse testing in the workplace to the human resource management policies and personnel practices of public agencies.[2] The questionnaire employed in this study was designed and used by the IPMA to solicit their individual and organizational members' responses to drug testing.[3] It was utilized in this Clearinghouse study to enable eventual comparison of our results with those previously obtained by the IPMA and because both Clearinghouse staff and outside evaluators felt that the questionnaire was a valid instrument for measuring public agency responses to drug testing.[4]

The overall return rate was remarkably high (208 useable questionnaires returned out of a sample of 300, or 69.3 percent).[5] This was due to the salience of the issue, and to the persistence of Clearinghouse personnel in encouraging nonrespondents to contribute their information.

Data Analysis and Findings

Three types of statistical tests were applied to the data collected. First, descriptive analysis was conducted to determine overall frequencies and percentage distributions of responses. This type of analysis was most appropriate for determining the answers to research questions 1, 3, 5, 7, 8, 9, 10, and 12 (see footnote 2).

1. *Do public agencies' personnel directors consider substance abuse a significant problem?* Thirty-two percent of the respondents consider alcohol/drug abuse among their employees to be a serious problem, 26 percent do not, and 39 percent are not sure (N=208).
3. *Do public agencies have substance abuse policies in place? If not, are they considering adopting them?* Sixty-five percent have substance abuse policies in place, or are considering adopting them, 35 percent neither have them in place nor are considering them (N=208).
5. *Do public agencies test employees and/or applicants?* Sixty-six percent of the governments which have a substance abuse policy in place, or who are

developing one, test applicants, 34 percent do not (N=122). Forty-six percent of all respondents test employees under some circumstances (N=208).

7. *For which positions are public agencies most likely to test applicants?* Sixty-three percent of the 67 public agencies which test applicants test applicants for public safety positions (police and firefighters). Agencies are more likely to test applicants for these positions than for any others.

8. *When are public agencies most likely to test employees?* Sixty-eight percent of public agencies that test employees do so following performance incidents or upon the supervisor's reasonable suspicion (N=95).

10. *What provisions are taken to ensure the protection of employee rights?* Ninety-one percent of those public agencies that test employees verify positive results on the initial test with a second test before taking disciplinary action (N=85). Discipline, which includes termination, may vary for 35 percent of the respondents based on the employee's level of concentration (N=80), 51 percent based on job class (N=82), or 50 percent based on prior performance evaluations (N=81).

12. *To what extent are Employee Assistance Programs (EAPs) used in detection or treatment of substance abuse?* Eighty-five percent of respondent public agencies have a program to provide employees with counseling and medical help with substance abuse problems (N=205).

Second, inferential analysis techniques were used to measure the association between variables. Chi-square was selected as the appropriate statistic for measures of the significance of differences between observed and expected frequencies for two nominal variables; phi or Cramer's V was used to normalize values for different table dimensions (Blalock 1979). Kendall's tau beta was selected as the appropriate statistic for symmetric measures of association between variables measured along ordinal scales (Andrews et al. 1986). The level of significance was set at .05. These types of analysis were most appropriate for determining the responses to research questions 2, 4, 6, 9, 11, and 13:

2. *Which level of government is most likely to consider substance abuse a significant problem?* Cities and counties are more likely than other levels of government to view drug/alcohol abuse as a serious problem (Kendall's tau beta = .23473, significance = .0000, N=204).

4. *Which public agencies are most likely to have policies in place, or to be considering adopting them?* Cities and counties are more likely than other levels of government to have testing policies in place (Kendall's tau beta = .16228, significance = .0059, N=203). But this difference is disappearing as other levels of government develop testing policies—there is no significant association between level of government and whether a jurisdiction has a policy in place or is considering adopting one (Kendall's tau beta = −.01183, significance = .4265, N=207). Those governments which view the drug/alcohol problem as significant are more likely to have a policy in place, or to be developing one (Chi-square = 13.08944, df = 4, significance .0108, Cramer's V = .25393, N=203).

6. *Which public agencies are most likely to test applicants?* Cities and counties are more likely than other levels of government to test applicants (Kendall's tau beta = .05051, significance = .0000, N = 51). Governments which have a substance abuse policy in place, or which are adopting one, are more likely to test applicants than those without policies (Chi-square = 6.89051, df = 1, significance = .0087, Cramer's V = .23863, N=121).

9. *What do public agencies do with those employees or applicants who test positive?* Public agencies with a policy in place are more likely to refuse employment to applicants who refuse to be tested (Chi-square = 3.6996, df = 1, significance = .0544, phi = .22668, N=72). However, these agencies are not more likely to know what types of disciplinary action they will take against employees who test positive (Chi-square = 2.19571, df = 5, significance = .8215. Cramer's V = .16671, N=79).

11. *Are governments which have substance abuse policies in place, or are planning to adopt them, more likely than other governments to protect the rights of applicants and/or employees in the substance abuse testing process?* No. Governments with policies in place, or those planning to adopt them, are not more likely to inform applicants in advance that they will be tested (Kendall's tau beta = .05544, significance = .3157, N=71), nor are they more likely to require written consent of applicants (Chi-square = .1148, df = 1, significance = .9942, Cramer's V = .04022, N = 71).

13. *Is there a relationship between the development of a testing policy and the utilization of EAPs by public agencies?* Those governments that have or are contemplating the adoption of an alcohol/drug abuse testing policy are more likely to have an Employee Assistance Program (EAP) (Chi-square =16.78288, df = 1, significance = .0000, phi = .28683, N=204). And their EAPs are more likely to assist in evaluation and rehabilitation of referred employees (Kendall's tau beta = .17151, significance = .0124, N=147).

Third, discriminant analysis was used to determine which variables, taken together, are the best predictors of whether a public agency has a substance abuse policy in place, or is considering adopting one (research question #14).[6] Discriminant analysis techniques are appropriate to test for the significance of several predictor variables simultaneously.[7]

Three discriminant variables are statistically significant predictors of whether or not a government has a policy in place, or is considering adopting one. They are: whether the EAP itself conducts tests (v37), whether an EAP exists (v33), whether the EAP assists in evaluation and rehabilitation (v36), and whether the personnel director perceives the problem as significant (v4).[8]

Recommendations for Further Research

This descriptive and inferential analysis of baseline data makes it clear that public agencies are heavily involved in substance abuse testing of applicants and employees. Several critical questions which the authors believe merit further investigation also emerge from this study.

Given the pervasiveness of alcohol and drug abuse in our society, why do most respondents neither consider this a serious problem in their agency, nor have a testing policy? The most likely answer seems to be that respondents are often uncertain how to view substance abuse, and are therefore unable to develop clear policies toward it. If substance abuse is viewed as a moral issue, the key question is whether testing and threat of disciplinary action for those who test positive is a useful or appropriate method of behavioral change. The primary legal issue is whether society or employers should distinguish between legal drugs (alcohol and prescription drugs) and illegal ones. From a productivity perspective, personnel directors are justifiably doubtful that substance abuse is the primary factor that affects employee job performance. If productivity is really the issue, why not focus on personalities, family problems, debts, mental illness, or other probable causes of employee performance problems as well? And once personnel directors admit that agency employees have a substance abuse problem, the agency is legally and politically bound to do something about it (though the economic costs of treatment and the legal risks of liability may make an "ostrich" approach more attractive to management).

Since current employees are usually protected by collective bargaining agreements or due process provisions which make disciplinary action difficult, and since applicants have no such rights, it is not surprising that those agencies which admit that substance abuse problems exist respond to it by letting applicants. But then why do most respondents consider the testing of applicants to be merely a selection criterion (like a physical exam or reference check) rather than a broad area of personnel practice requiring underlying policy direction? The most obvious response is that personnel managers may prefer to use the blood and urine samples already collected in pre-employment physicals to detect substance abuse, without advising applicants that these samples may be used as the basis for selection decisions. But there are disturbing managerial, ethical, and legal implications of using substance abuse tests as a selection criterion without explicitly defining this as an agency policy to applicants, managers, and the public.

Most personnel directors report that they do not hire applicants who refuse to be tested. But they also state that under some circumstances they will consider applicants who test positive for future employment. Have agencies in fact hired applicants who previously tested positive, or will they do so in the future? The implicit alternative is that applicants who test positive will be "blacklisted" and not considered for future employment, even though personnel directors cannot admit publicly that this policy exists. The disturbing implications of a two-tier employment market, with the top tier closed to applicants who have ever tested positive for substance abuse, make this a significant question for future research.

Those respondents who test current employees do so primarily based upon incidents or reasonable suspicion, as defined by the supervisor. But because governments with policies are not more likely to know what to do with employees who test positive than governments without policies, it does not seem possible to conclude that the presence of a testing policy will provide greater structural definition of "critical incidents" or "reason-able suspicion" which would make it easier for supervisors to exercise discretion. For employees who test positive, the outcome is subject to considerable discretion, depending on level of concentration, job class, or employee performance. Therefore, it does not seem reasonable to expect that supervisors can identify or refer suspected substance abusing employees skillfully and equitably, particularly in the face of union opposition and due process protections. Instead, in the absence of clear guidelines and rewards, they are more likely to avoid these risks by declining to identify suspected substance abusers or to refer them for testing and treatment. How these expected supervisorial behavior patterns can be detected and changed is an issue which must be faced if substance abuse testing is to be successfully implemented in public agencies.

Most employers report that they have employee assistance programs (EAPs), and that these assist employees with drug/alcohol abuse problems. These are commendable responses. However, the propensity of public agencies to deal with emergent issues by creating special organizational units to deal with them, and then "solving" the issue simply by referring all related items to the special unit, has been well established in the past with respect to such issues as affirmative action, comparable worth, or sexual harassment. Thus, the effectiveness of EAPs is more likely to rest on the adequacy of their organization location, mission, and budget. In this regard, a majority of these EAPs are generic in focus rather than directed specifically toward substance abuse problems, and a plurality of EAPs are off-site and run by outside contractors. Given the uncertain adequacy of their location, mission, budget, and objectives, can EAPs provide the quality of testing and rehabilitative services needed to meet this crisis, at a price agencies and their employees can afford?

Finally, it must be acknowledged that while many public personnel directors view substance abuse testing of applicants and employees as a necessity, they legitimately see it as a risk because it confronts them with unavoidable conflicts among key human resource management values—responsiveness to elected officials, administrative efficiency, and protection of employee rights. But testing also presents them with an opportunity to play a critical role in the resolution of these emergent public policy issues. Discriminant analysis shows that the significance which the personnel director attaches to workplace substance abuse correlates highly with whether the agency has developed policies in this area, or is considering doing so. Given this correlation, how can public personnel directors be encouraged to maintain their pre-eminent role as shapers of managerial responses to the public policy issues raised by drug testing?

Notes

*Released by the Clearinghouse on Drug and AIDS Testing.

1. The Clearinghouse wishes to thank ASPA and its former President Robert Denhart for supporting the drug testing survey, and SPALR and its former Chair Dalmas Nelson for supporting the survey and providing initial financial support for questionnaire printing and distribution.

2. The research questions examined in this study are the following:

1. Do public agencies' personnel directors consider substance abuse a significant problem?
2. Which level of government (federal, state or local) is most likely to consider substance abuse a significant problem?
3. Do public agencies have substance abuse policies in place? If not, are they considering adopting them?
4. Which public agencies (federal, state, or local) are most likely to have policies in place, or to be considering adopting them?
5. Do public agencies test employees and/or applicants?
6. Which public agencies (federal, state, or local) are most likely to test employees and/or applicants?
7. For which positions are public agencies most likely to test applicants?
8. When are public agencies most likely to test employees?
9. What do public agencies do with those employees or applicants who test positive?
10. What provisions are taken to ensure the protection of employee rights?
11. Are governments which have substance abuse policies in place, or are planning to adopt them, more likely to protect applicants' or employees' rights in the substance abuse testing process?
12. To what extent are Employee Assistance Programs (EAPs) used in detection or treatment of substance abuse?
13. Is there a relationship between the development of a testing policy and the utilization of EAPs by public agencies?
14. Which factors, taken together, are the best predictors of whether a public agency has a drug/ alcohol policy in place, or is considering adopting one?

3. The six-page questionnaire contained four sections with closed-ended questions; answers were coded as cither ordinal or interval (Likert-type scale) data:

(I) *General:* Answered by all respondents (N=208). Six questions on level of government; number of agency employees; perceived significance of employee substance abuse; whether or not the agency has a policy in place; or whether or not the agency is considering adopting one; and whether the agency tests applicants.

(II) *Pre-employment Testing:* Answered only by those respondents who report that their agencies test applicants (N=122). Thirteen questions on the extent of applicant testing; which types of positions are covered; when the applicant is informed that testing will be conducted; whether written consent is required; whether refusal to submit to testing is grounds for ineligibility; whether the applicant is informed of positive test results; whether a second test is conducted to verify initial positive results; whether positive test results cause rejection of the application; whether the applicant is made aware of the fact that positive test results were the basis for refusing employment; whether positive test results are ever made available informally to other jurisdictions; whether the applicant who tested positive will ever be considered for future employment; whether conditional employment will be offered to applicants who test positive if they enroll in a treatment program; and whether this conditional employment offer is offered only to applicants for certain job classes.

(III) *Testing Current Employees:* Answered only by those respondents who report that their jurisdictions test current employees (N=95). Thirteen questions on the circumstances under which employees are tested; which employees are subject to testing; which job classes (if any) are subject to random testing; whether advance notice of random testing is given; whether refusal to take a test results in disciplinary action, and if so which type; whether a second test is conducted to verify a positive result in the first test before disciplinary actions are taken; whether disciplinary action varies if test results are positive (depending on level of concentration, job class, or performance evaluations); what types of disciplinary action are taken if employees test positive; where employees are tested; and what type of test is used.

(IV) *Employee Assistance Programs:* Answered only by those respondents who report that their agency has an employee assistance program (EAP) to provide employees with counseling and medical help with alcohol and drug abuse problems (N=171). Four questions on the location of the EAP; what range of services it provides; whether it assists with evaluation and rehabilitation of employees who are substance abusers; and whether the EAP itself conducts tests.

4. The Clearinghouse wishes to thank Sandra Biloon, former President of the IPMA, for generously allowing the adaptation of its questionnaire by the Clearinghouse. Sally Williams (past President of SPALR) and Rosslyn Kleeman (Senior Associate Director of the U.S. General Accounting Office) edited the questionnaire.

5. Sample and Return Rate

Level of Government	Sample	Return	Percent
Municipal	99	76	76.8%
Country	62	42	69.3%
State	49	45	91.8%
Federal	90	45	50.0%
Total	300	208	69.3%

6. The questionnaire included separate questions asking whether the agency had a substance abuse testing policy in place (v3), or was considering adopting one (v5). Because several respondents ambiguously answered both questions affirmatively, the researchers analyzed each variable separately and also created a dummy variable (v38) for which a positive response to either question (v3 or v5) was coded as a "yes," and a negative response to both questions was considered a "no."

7. The literature is ambiguous on the appropriateness of discriminant analysis for different levels of data. Dillon and Goldstein consider it appropriate only for ordinal data (Dillon and Goldstein 1984). Aldrich and Cnude (1975) consider discriminant analysis most appropriate for nominal data, probit for ordinal data, and regression analysis for interval data.

8. The proportion of variance in the discriminant function explained by the two groups is about 43 percent (a canonical correlation of 0.4366). The Wilks' Lambda degree of separation between the two groups was 0.2391. The unstandardized canonical discriminant function coefficient (used for predicting if an agency has a policy or not) is formed by multiplying the agency's scores on each of these six variables by its coefficient, adding these partial scores to get a discriminant score, and then comparing the discriminant score to the mean avenge for agencies in Group 1 (those having a policy) and Group 2 (those without a policy). The Group 1 mean is -0.35274 and the Group 2 mean is 0.66138, based on the following unstandardized and standardized canonical discriminant function coefficients for each variable:

Discriminant Analysis

Var.	Classification Function Coefficient		Canonical Discriminant Function Coefficient	
	Drug Policy	No. Policy	Standarized	Unstand.
1	1.308370	1.196931	-0.16629	-.1098866
2	3.136055	3.364998	0.30157	.2257551
4	2.769251	3.250845	0.46911	.4748871
33	15.38467	16.77325	0.48930	1.369249
36	0.8434998	.108360	0.38682	.2611717
37	2.111595	1.720396	-0.63132	-.3857509

Continued

Continued

Var.	Classification Function Coefficient		Canonical Discriminant Function Coefficient	
	Drug Policy	No. Policy	Standarized	Unstand.
constant:				
	-25.42523	-28.65859	-3.03401	

Therefore, knowing the responses of each agency to these six variables, it is possible to predict inclusion in Group 1 with 73.3 percent accuracy (99 out of 135 cases), and in Group 2 with 62.5 percent accuracy (45 out of 72 cases). Overall, 69.57 percent of the grouped cases can be correctly classified using discriminant analysis.

9. The Clearinghouse is currently conducting additional research on the relationship to substance abuse testing of other variables such as agency structure, functions of the personnel department, and the professionalism of public personnel directors.

References

Aldrich, J. and C.F. Cnude (1975). "Probing the Bounds of Conventional Wisdom: A Comparison of Regression, Probit, and Discriminant Analysis." *American Journal of Political Science* 19 (August): 571–608.

Andrews, F.M., L. Klem, T.N. Davidson, P.M. O'Malley and W.L. Rodgers (1981). *A Guide for Selecting Statistical Techniques for Analyzing Social Science Data.* Chicago, IL: Institute for Social Research, University of Michigan.

Blalock, H.M., Jr. (1979). Social Statistics. New York: McGraw-Hill.

Chiabotia, B. (1985). "Evaluating EAP Vendors." *Personnel Administrator* 30 (August): 39–43.

Curran, W. (1987). "Compulsory Drug Testing: The Legal Barriers." *The New England Journal of Medicine* 316 (February): 318–321.

Dillion, W.R. and M.G. Goldstein (1984). *Multivariate Analysis: Methods and Applications.* New York: John Wiley & Sons.

Greenberg, E. (1987). "To Test or Not to Test: Drugs and the Workplace." *Management Review* 76 (January): 18–20.

Hartsfield, W. (1986). "Medical Examination as a Method of Investigating Employee Wrong Doing." *Labor Law Journal* (October): 692–702.

Harwood, H.J., D.M. Napolitano and J.J. Collins (1984). *Economic Costs to Society of Alcohol and Drug Abuse and Mental Illness.* Research Triangle Park, NC: Research Triangle Institute.

International Personnel Management Association (1988). *Drug Testing in the Workplace.* Washington, D.C.: International Personnel Management Association.

Levin-Epstein, M. and S. Sala (1986). *Alcohol and Drugs in the Workplace: Costs, Controls and Controversies.* Washington. D.C.: U.S. Chamber of Commerce.

Masi, D. (1987). "Company Response to Drug Abuse from the AMA's National Survey." *Personnel* 63 (March): 40–46.

Norusis, M. (1986). *The SPSS Guide to Data Analysis.* Chicago, IL: SPSS, Inc.

Reynolds, H.T. (1984). *Analysis of Nominal Data.* Beverly Hills, CA: Sage Publications.

Rowland, A. (1985). "The Cost to the U.S. Economy of Drug Abuse." *Hearings Before the Subcommittee on Economic Goals and Intergovernmental Policy of the Joint Economic Committee.* U.S. Congress. Ninety-ninth, First Session (August 6–8) MC#5522.

Starr, A., and G. Bryam (1985). "Cost/benefit Analysis for Employee Assistance Programs." *Personnel Administrator* 30 (August): 55–60.

PART 3

EQUAL EMPLOYMENT OPPORTUNITY, AFFIRMATIVE ACTION, AND REPRESENTATIVE BUREAUCRACY

One of the most hotly debated issues in public personnel management has been the issue of affirmative action (AA). Since the U.S. Supreme Court issued its landmark ruling in 1978, *Regents of the University of California v. Bakke* (438 U.S. 265), practitioners and scholars of public personnel have grappled with the legality and constitutionality of employment programs to promote affirmative action, which has assumed a range of specious labels including "reverse discrimination" and "preferential treatment." And, despite the 2003 ruling by the Supreme Court in *Grutter v. Bollinger* (123 S. Ct. 2325), which upheld the constitutionality of AA, opponents continue to question the validity of its use. Critics maintain that equal employment opportunity (EEO) programs, which call for strict adherence to legal mandates such as the Civil Rights Act of 1964 as amended, are more than adequate to ensure equal access to the workplace. History and experience, however, indicate that EEO alone has never been sufficient.

Many scholars and practitioners of public personnel management have viewed AA as an essential way to promote social equity and representative bureaucracy. As seen in the following classics, representative bureaucracy has been defined, in the "passive" sense, as ensuring that the social composition of public workforces mirrors the social or demographic composition of the populations they serve and represent. "Active" representation, on the other hand, asks whether ascribed characteristics of an individual (e.g., race, gender, or ethnicity) relate to or predict policy preferences as well as actions in order to achieve certain policy *outcomes*. In this sense, the policy interests of a particular group (e.g., women) are actively represented by government.

Presented here are articles that address concerns surrounding ethnicity, race, and gender in the workplace. In the first piece, Lloyd Nigro writes in his introduction to a symposium on affirmative action that public managers have the responsibility to set standards and structure rules and procedures in order to give "affirmative action its behavioral and, therefore, socially consequential meaning." He further notes, however, that there is no consensus among personnel directors as to the precise meaning of affirmative action. In his concluding remarks he observes that

> the message that unifies all the statements on affirmative action in this symposium is that effective public administration in a democratic society relies heavily on the existence of genuinely representative bureaucracies. In other words, to be truly effective, our public

organizations must be representative in the most positive and meaningful sense of the word (Nigro, 1974: 245).

N. Joseph Cayer and Lee Sigelman in "Minorities and Women in State and Local Government" examine the status of women and people of color in state and local government jobs from 1973 to 1975. They find that women and people of color were underrepresented in high-level, policy-making positions, and were concentrated in jobs traditionally and historically held by them (e.g., housing, public welfare, and sanitation and sewage). The picture remains quite the same today.

In "A Symposium: Minorities in Public Administration," Adam Herbert makes several critical observations regarding people of color in government bureaucracies. One is that the "intellectual and operational contributions of minorities to the public service have not been accurately or adequately reflected in the theory, literature or teaching of public administration" (Herbert 1974: 519). In addition, as Herbert explains, racial and cultural biases continue to impede opportunities for people of color in government. Moreover, public agencies will become more responsive to the citizens they serve only when people of color are better represented in both administrative and elective posts in government.

Nesta Gallas, in her introductory remarks to "A Symposium: Women in Public Administration," suggests that there are a variety of interests and concerns that arise around women in public administration. Notwithstanding, however, Gallas points to the three common concerns which pervade the topic of women in public administration: discrimination against women, underrepresentation of women, and underutilization of women in public administration. She introduces articles which contribute to the advancement of women in public administration.

Writing almost twenty years after Gallas, Mary E. Guy contributes a classic, "Three Steps Forward, Two Steps Backward: The Status of Women's Integration into Public Management," which shows that women continue to be underrepresented and underutilized in government. Her research finds that women continue to be underrepresented in high-level decision-making positions in public administration, and that the integration of women into American governance is marked by ebbs and flows. Guy concludes that women still have a long way to go before they will reach parity with men in public administration.

One area where disparities continue to prevail between women and men is pay. Comparable worth took the concept of "equal pay for equal work" to the next logical level, one where women and men performing different jobs of comparable value or worth to an employer would be paid equal wages. Although now virtually defunct on substantive grounds as a result of a decision by the U.S. Court of Appeals for the Ninth Circuit, *AFSCME v. State of Washington* (770 F. 2d 1401, 9th Cir. 1985), a flurry of articles on comparable worth appeared in the 1980s. One such article is "Equal Pay for Comparable Work: Stimulus for Future Civil Service Reform," by Lois Friss. In this abridged version of her article, Friss identifies the key issues associated with the comparable worth debate, and addresses the key lawsuit from Washington State. Despite the appellate court ruling in Washington, a number of states and municipalities rely on comparable worth strategies to close the pay gap between women and men in government jobs.

Additional Classics

Carnevale, David G. "Recruitment Strategies in the Federal Government: Missing Links and Representative Bureaucracy. 11 *Review of Public Personnel Administration*, 1, 2: 112–120, Fall 1990/Spring 1991.

Corson, John J. "Comparable Pay for Comparable Work?" 21 *Public Administration Review*, 4: 198–205, 1961.

Daley, Dennis. "Political and Occupational Barriers to the Implementation of Affirmative Action: Administrative, Executive, and Legislative Attitudes Towards Representative Bureaucracy." *Review of Public Personnel Administration*, Summer 1984.

Doherty, Mary Helen and Ann Harriman. "Comparable Worth: The Equal Employment Issue of the 1980s." *Review of Public Personnel Administration*, Summer 1981.

Frederickson, H. George. "Public Administration and Social Equity." 50 *Public Administration Review*, 2: 228–237, 1990.

Harrison, Evelyn. "The Working Woman: Barriers in Employment." 24 *Public Administration Review*, 2: 78–85, 1964.

Johansen, Elaine. "Managing the Revolution: The Case for Comparable Worth." 4 *Review of Public Personnel Administration*, 2: 14–27, Spring 1984.

Kellough, James E. and Susan Kay. "Affirmative Action in the Federal Bureaucracy: An Impact Assessment." 6 *Review of Public Personnel Administration*, 2: 1–12, Spring 1986.

Lewis, William G. "Toward Representative Bureaucracy: Blacks in City Police Organizations: 1975–1985." 49 *Public Administration Review*, 3: 257–268, May/June 1989.

Naff, Katherine C. "ProgressToward Achieving a Representative Federal Bureaucracy." 27 *Public Personnel Management*, 2: 135–147, 1998.

Meier, Kenneth J. and Lloyd G. Nigro. "Representative Bureaucracy and Policy Preferences: A Study of Attitudes of Federal Executives." 36 *Public Administration Review*, 4: 458–469, 1976.

Nachmias, David and David H. Rosenbloom. "Measuring Bureaucratic Representation and Integration." 33 *Public Administration Review*, 6: 590–597, 1973.

Saltzstein, Grace Hall. 1979. "Representative Bureaucracy and Bureaucratic Responsibility." *Administration and Society*, 10: 465–475.

Selden, Sally Coleman, Jeffrey L. Brudney and J. Edward Kellough. "Bureaucracy as a Representative Institution. 42 *American Journal of Political Science*, 3: 719–744, 1998.

CHAPTER 11

A MINI-SYMPOSIUM

Affirmative Action in Public Employment

LLOYD G. NIGRO

Introduction

"Affirmative action" is a term deeply embedded in the language of today's public personnel administration. Nonetheless, its precise meaning for administrative thought and action is elusive. What is affirmative action? Does it mean doing something or not doing something? How does it relate to the functions of public agencies and to the role of government in our society?

Ambiguity can be useful. It allows room for maneuver and the flexibility needed to adapt and innovate in new or changing circumstances. However, it can also be counter-productive. Misunderstandings lead to unfulfilled expectations, mistrust, and conflict. The implementation of policies and programs can be blocked or sidetracked. Like the emotion-charged symbols of "pornography" and "national security," affirmative action has many meanings. It also shares their capacity to fragment and paralyze social systems.

Public administrators on all levels of government are at the centers of decision arenas wherein the *operational* definition of affirmative action is literally being created. They are participants in policy-making processes which set standards and structure rules and procedures. Perhaps most importantly, their day-to-day behavior is giving affirmative action its behavioral and, therefore, socially consequential meaning.

Yet, as a social group, public administrators are far from general agreement on what affirmative action is or should be. Witness these abstracts from an exchange between a U.S. Civil Service Commission regional director and a city director of personnel.

Director of Personnel: "The reason we apparently are not in compliance with U.S. Civil Service Commission standards is that we have been successful in hiring fully qualified minorities and women in various uniformed and civilian positions in our Fire Department, our Police Department, and several other departments through the use of our civil service rule permitting selective certification."

Excerpted from 34 *Public Administration Review*, 3: 234–237, 1974. Copyright © 1974 American Society for Public Administration. Reprinted with permission.

Regional Director: "For you to imply . . . that success in bringing about the employment of minorities and women in departments where they have been unrepresented or under-represented does not comply with our Standards is thus a major misrepresentation of fact. What we have stated . . . is that certification or non-certification of eligibles solely on the basis of race or sex is discriminatory per se, and hence contrary to the merit principles embodied in the law and in our prescribed Standards for a merit system."

Director of Personnel: "During the past three years, I have been forced to conclude that the traditional ranking and certification process has an adverse effect that cannot be defended as valid in many competitive situations where there are large numbers of candidates and no prior knowledge or experience necessary for the relatively few vacant positions available. With this conclusion, the only ethical course of action open to me was to recommend the adoption of the selective certification rule to the Civil Service Board."

Regional Director: "We fully appreciate the aims of the Civil Service Board . . . in approving the selective certification rule. There can be no question that we are all working toward a public service in which all groups in our society are fairly represented. . . . No matter how laudatory the purpose, however, we cannot give our approval to a method which we find to be illegal, as well as contrary to the principles of merit service."

This exchange between sincere and well-meaning administrators serves as an illustration of the kinds of difficulties encountered when the concept of affirmative action in public employment must be broken down into specific criteria for evaluating personnel policies, programs, and procedures. If anything approaching a working consensus is to be established, viewpoints, information, and experiences must be shared. The process of communication should reach and actively involve as many of those concerned as possible.

This mini-symposium on affirmative action is intended to contribute in a modest way to this objective. Contributions were solicited with an eye toward presenting a variety of opinions and information. As anticipated, the participants have approached their topic from different but complementary perspectives.

CHAPTER 12

A MINI-SYMPOSIUM

Affirmative Action in Public Employment

LLOYD G. NIGRO

Some Concluding Observations

One of the most frequently heard criticisms of affirmative action is that it displaces the primary goal of public personnel administration—the staffing of public agencies with people who are best able to run these organizations effectively. Yet the message that unifies all of the statements on affirmative action in this symposium is that effective public administration in a democratic society relies heavily on the existence of genuinely representative bureaucracies. In other words, to be truly effective, our public organizations must be representative in the most positive and meaningful sense of the word.

Roughly defined, " . . . the term representative bureaucracy is meant to suggest a body of officials which is broadly representative of the society in which it functions, and which in social ideals is as close to the grass roots of the nation" or community it serves.[1]

At least in theory, representative bureaucracy performs two important functions for a democratic society. First, public personnel practices which establish and maintain truly open employment opportunity systems reinforce egalitarian norms relating to the value of the individual, open paths to socioeconomic mobility, and free competition for meaningful jobs on the basis of culturally accepted definitions of merit. Second, the existence of representative public organizations is more likely to assure high levels of responsiveness and responsibility than are external controls on administrative action. Representativeness is counted on to act as a sort of internal "thermostat" on administrative behavior, keeping it within the boundaries set by societal values and attitudes.[2] It is this concept which moved the U.S. Commission on Civil Rights to state that,

> . . . the civil servant, in performing government's routine chores and housekeeping duties, makes many policy and administrative decisions which have a concrete and often immediate effect on the lives of the people living within the particular jurisdiction. If these decisions are to be responsive to the needs and desires of the people, then it is essential that those making them be truly representative of all segments of the population.[3]

Excerpted from 34 *Public Administration Review,* 3: 245–246, 1974. Copyright © 1974 American Society for Public Administration. Reprinted with permission.

Affirmative action in government, as a part of the total effort to develop a societywide structure of equal employment opportunity, is therefore a potentially valuable contributor to the social effectiveness of public administration on all levels of government. Through the concept of representative bureaucracy and its functions, there is a bridge between the policies and practices called "affirmative action" and the efforts to realize democratic values which have characterized the American experience.

A pervasive structure of equal opportunity employment is a prerequisite to a stable pattern of representative bureaucracy. Equal opportunity, as all of our symposium participants have emphasized, is a basic element of true merit systems. The "open door" is fundamental to the merit philosophy as it has evolved in the United States. That "door" must really be open to everybody, and the procedures and techniques used to select personnel have to be carefully evaluated and adapted to reflect new knowledge about their consequences for administrative effectiveness.

Experience tells us that simply opening the door is not enough to guarantee equal opportunity or representative public agencies. The public employer must move through the door into the environment, search out, attract, and *develop* a representative and competent manpower base for the public service. Representativeness and competence are not contradictory. They are mutually reinforcing and can be integrated if administrative resources, knowledge, and imagination are brought to bear on the task. In the final analysis, this challenge is the essence of affirmative action.

Notes

1. Paul P. Van Riper, *History of the U.S. Civil Service* (Evanston, Ill.: Row, Peterson and Co.), p. 552.

2. *Ibid.*, pp. 549–564.

3. Introduction, U.S. Commission on Civil Rights, *For All the People . . . By All the People.* Clearing House Publication No. 18, November 1969.

CHAPTER 13

MINORITIES AND WOMEN IN STATE AND LOCAL GOVERNMENT

1973–1975

N. JOSEPH CAYER AND LEE SIGELMAN

With the passage of the Equal Employment Opportunity (EEO) Act in 1972, federal prohibitions against discrimination in hiring, firing, promotion, compensation, and other conditions of employment were extended for the first time to state and local governments. Since then, precisely what is entailed by "equal employment opportunity" and the related (if even more controversial) policy of "affirmative action" has become the focus of heated debate. Nevertheless, the Equal Employment Opportunity Commission (EEOC), the federal agency that monitors and enforces the implementation of the 1972 act, has left little room for doubt about what it expects of state and local governments. Employers are advised that:

> The most important measure of an Affirmative Action Program is its RESULTS.
>
> Extensive efforts to develop procedures, analyses, data collection systems, report forms and file written policy statements are meaningless unless the end product will be *measureable, yearly improvements in hiring, training and promotion of minorities and females in all parts of your organization.*[1]

This explicit "results orientation" provides the immediate context for the present analysis of the employment of minorities and women in state and local governments across the country. Two basic questions guide our analysis. First, in the most recent year for which data are currently available, where did minorities and women stand with respect to state and local government employment? Because this question has both quantitative and qualitative dimensions, our analysis deals not only with the sheer number of minority and female employees, but also with the extent to which these groups have entered more responsible, prestigious, and remunerative government positions. Second, to what extent did the employment status of these groups change after the EEO Act went into effect?

Our ability to answer these questions stems from the EEO Act's requirement that state and local governments file annual reports on the status of minorities and women in their personnel systems. The only major category of employees excluded from the "EEO-4" reporting system is composed of employees of public elementary and secondary school systems and higher educational institutions; the annual EEOC surveys cover

From 40 *Public Administration Review,* 5: 443–450, 1980. Copyright © 1980 American Society for Public Administration. Reprinted with permission.

employees in every other functional area associated with state and local government in the United States.

Prior to the establishment of the EEO-4 work force reporting system, only scattered and often noncomparable data were available on minority and female employment in state and local jurisdictions.[2] Since the advent of the EEO-4 reporting requirements, EEOC has published three annual reports on the employment of minorities and women by states and localities. In the style typical of statistical compendia published by federal agencies, each annual report consists of several volumes of undigested computer printout—hundreds and hundreds of pages of extremely detailed descriptive information, with no attempt whatever at analysis. Two of these annual reports (the first one, published in 1974, and the most recent one, published in 1977) are the data sources for the present analysis.[3]

The 1974 report relates to the employment of minorities and women as of mid-1973, and the 1977 report provides parallel information for mid-1975. Thus, our analysis focuses on the three-year period immediately following enactment of the EEO Act. Three years is not a very long span of time—far too short for the composition of the work force to have changed in a truly fundamental fashion. As a result, ours is an early assessment of post-EEO Act trends. We do not believe that it is too early to undertake such an analysis, particularly because of EEOC's announced insistence on measurable yearly improvement. Indeed, Rose and Chia have recently published a most informative study of the EEO Act's impact on black employment in the federal service, based on data from only the 1973 and 1974 EEOC surveys.[4]

We recognize that the EEO Act is only one part of a whole series of separate yet inter-related forces which have worked to bring about changes in the employment prospects of minorities and women. The increased incidence of equal opportunity and affirmative action litigation, voluntary changes on the part of governmental jurisdictions, increased numbers of women seeking jobs, job training and retraining programs, unemployment in the private sector, and pressures from increasing numbers of elected minority officials are only a few of the other factors which affected affirmative action efforts. Nonetheless, the EEO Act provides the basic legal framework supporting most or all of these other forces and requiring action on the part of employers. Thus, we evaluate trends in equal employment opportunity since passage of the EEO Act, recognizing that it is only one of many factors but also believing that it is a major part of the environment shaping these equal employment trends.

The Question of Reliability

Before turning to the substance of the EEOC surveys, we must briefly consider their reliability. The EEOC data are subject to error for two reasons: (1) the agency does not survey each jurisdiction every year, but rather samples jurisdictions; and (2) response rates, though very high, are not perfect. EEOC stratifies jurisdictions according to the number of people they employ, and surveys all the largest jurisdictions and lesser proportions of the smaller ones. Of the approximately 5,500 jurisdictions that received EEO-4 forms in 1975, roughly 96 percent returned completed forms. Based on the size and response rate of each stratum, EEOC weights the data it receives in order to produce estimates for the population of state and local governments. It is these estimates which are published in the yearly reports and which form the basis of the present analysis.

Because of the sheer size of the yearly samples, the sampling errors associated with overall population estimates in the EEOC surveys are very small. For example, a 95 percent confidence interval for the 1973 and 1975 estimates of the total number of full-time employees indicates that these estimates were within one-tenth of one percent and three-tenths of one percent, respectively, of the true figures. Estimates based on subtotals (e.g., the number of black employees or the number of minority firefighters) are subject to greater error. For the 1975 survey, for example, one could be 95 percent confident that an estimate that there were 500,000 employees in some group was within 7,300 (1.5 percent) of the true figure. For smaller subpopulations, sampling error becomes more problematic: for example, in 1975, the standard error for an estimate that 5,000 employees were in some subgroup would have been 370, or 7.4 percent. The same principle holds for EEOC estimates of median salary levels. The 1975 median salary estimate of $9,827 for the almost four million state and local employees should, at the 95 percent level of confidence, have been off by no more than $42 one way or the other; but the median salary estimate of $9,361 for the 10,882 Indian employees was subject to much greater error, with the lower and upper bounds of the 95 percent confidence interval each being about $520 away from the estimated median.

Obviously, then, the fact that the EEOC reports are based on samples means that the figures they contain are approximations. As long as our attention is restricted to groups that comprise a sizeable proportion of the total number of state and local government employees, sampling error does not loom as a very large problem. Estimates for very small subgroups of the overall population are potentially more troublesome. For this reason, when our analysis focuses on employment within specific functional areas, we lump employees into much more inclusive categories (i.e., "minority" and "female" rather than "black male" or "Indian female"). Doing so sometimes lumps together employees from groups whose employment situations are quite dissimilar, but more refined breakdowns would be subject to sampling errors we consider unacceptably high.

In sum, none of the EEOC estimates should be taken at face value, but some estimates are a good deal more reliable than others. The presence of error makes comparative statements especially risky: for example if we know that both a 1973 estimate and its 1975 counterpart were subject to error, then we should recognize that our ability to estimate change between 1973 and 1975 is doubly subject to error. Accordingly, small differences should not be taken very seriously, particularly if the comparison groups were themselves small. This caveat must clearly be borne in mind as we address the questions posed above.

The Overall Picture

The Quantitative Dimension

The racial and sexual composition of the state and local government work force did change somewhat between 1973 and 1975, as Table 13.1 reveals. In both proportional

Table 13.1

Composition of State and Local Employment, 1973–1975

	1973		1975	
Group	No.	%	No.	%
White male	2,084,225	(54.7)	1,993,154	(51.1)
White female	1,031,060	(27.1)	1.109,119	(28.4)
Black male	287,230	(7.5)	317,374	(8.1)
Black female	236,112	(6.2)	284,369	(7.3)
Spanish-surnamed male	86,266	(2.3)	98,285	(2.5)
Spanish-surnamed female	38,331	(1.0)	49,159	(1.3)
Asian male	11,671	(0.3)	13,565	(0.3)
Asian female	10,096	(0.3)	12,661	(0.3)
Indian male	6,803	(0.2)	6,868	(0.2)
Indian female	3,347	(0.1)	4,014	(0.1)
Other male	10,221	(0.3)	6,262	(0.2)
Other female	3,146	(0.1)	4,450	(0.1)
Total	3,808,538	(100.1)*	3,899.280	(99.9)*

*Varies from 100.0 percent due to rounding. Data in this table and all ensuing tables are from EEOC, *Minorities and Women in State and Local Government 1973,* vol. I: *United States Summary* (Washington, D.C: Government Printing Office, 1974); and EEOC, *Minorities and Women in State and Local Government 1975,* vol. I: *United States Summary* (Washington, D.C: Government Printing Office. 1977).

and absolute terms, there were fewer white male employees in 1975 than there had been in 1973. In fact, the number of white males fell by more than 90,000, and the percentage of state and local employees who were white males dropped from 54.7 percent to 51.1 percent. With the single exception of the small "other male" category, every other group saw the number of positions its members held increase at least slightly, and some of the increases were fairly substantial.

The most noteworthy 1973–1975 gains were made by women. Both absolutely and proportionately, women's share of government jobs increased faster than that of males in each racial group except the Spanish-surnamed. White women were the greatest beneficiaries of this trend, increasing their numbers by approximately 78,000 and their work force percentage by 1.3 percent. Black women did almost as well, increasing the number of jobs they held by almost 50,000 and their work force percentage by 1.1 percent. Among males, the greatest gains were made by blacks, who held some 30,000 more positions in 1975 than they had in 1973.

So the first three years of affirmative action hiring do appear to have brought some changes. Nevertheless, by 1975 state and local jurisdictions were still a long way from reflecting the demographic makeup of the American population. The continuing

Table 13.2

Minority and Female Representation in State and Local Government Employment, 1973–1975

Group	Percent of General Population 1970	Percent of State and Local Bureaucracy 1973	1973 Representativeness Ratio	Percent in Bureaucracy 1975	1975 Representativeness Ratio
White male	40.0	54.7	1.37	51.1	1.28
White female	41.6	27.1	0.65	28.4	0.68
Black male	5.4	7.5	1.39	8.1	1.50
Black female	5.7	6.2	1.09	7.3	1.28
Spanish-surnamed male	2.9	2.3	0.79	2.5	0.86
Spanish-surnamed female	3.1	1.0	0.32	1.3	0.42
Asian male	0.2	0.3	1.50	0.3	1.50
Asian female	0.2	0.3	1.50	0.3	1.50
Indian male	0.5	0.2	0.40	0.2	0.40
Indian female	0.5	0.1	0.20	0.1	0.20

underrepresentation of women and certain minority groups becomes quite evident when the "representativeness ratios" contained in Table 13.2 are consulted. Representativeness ratios, which have been used in several previous studies of workforce composition,[5] were calculated by dividing each group's percentage of government jobs by the percentage each group comprises of the general population. Thus, a ratio of 1.0 means that a group occupied the same proportion of government jobs that it did of the general population; a lower ratio signifies numerical underrepresentation, and a higher ratio overrepresentation.[6]

Table 13.2 indicates that women and black and Spanish-surnamed men made some employment progress in state and local governments between 1973 and 1975. However, Spanish-surnamed, Indian, and white women and Spanish-surnamed and Indian men remained well below population parity in their levels of representation. By 1975, white women were represented at only 68 percent of their proportion of the population, while the counterpart figures for Spanish-surnamed and Indian women were 42 percent and 20 percent. By contrast, black and Asian women were numerically overrepresented in 1975, as they had been in 1973. Among men, the overrepresentation of whites, blacks, and Asians continued, although the white ratio did fall from 1973 to 1975. Indian males remained badly underrepresented, and so, to a lesser extent, did Spanish-surnamed males.

These figures, however, tell us only about overall levels of employment, and reveal nothing about the status of these groups within the state and local work force. Our analysis now turns to this qualitative dimension.

Table 13.3

Median Salary and Advantage Index, By Group, 1973 and 1975

	1973		1975	
White male	$9,873	(1.00)	$11,631	(1.00)
White female	$7,069	(.72)	$8,250	(.71)
Black male	$7,912	(.80)	$9,444	(.81)
Black female	$6,886	(.70)	$7,925	(.68)
Spanish-Surnamed male	$7,976	(.81)	$9,613	(.83)
Spanish-Surnamed female	$6,540	(.66)	$7,668	(.66)
Asian male	$12,663	(1.28)	$14,496	(1.25)
Asian female	$9,114	(.92)	$10,353	(.89)
Indian male	$8,778	(.89)	$10,482	(.90)
Indian female	$6,679	(.68)	$7,883	(.68)
Other male	$8,976	(.91)	NA	
Other female	$7,415	(.75)	NA	
Total	$8,568	(.87)	$9,827	(.84)

The Qualitative Dimension

While some progress was made in the number and proportion of female and minority employees in state and local government, the status of these groups within state and local government agencies is quite another matter. One very tangible indicator of group status in an organizational hierarchy is the monetary compensation group members receive. Table 13.3 summarizes the median salaries and presents a salary advantage index for each group. The advantage index was calculated by dividing the median salary for each group by the median salary for white males during the same year. Thus, the advantage index for white males is 1.00, and variations above or below the median white male salary are reflected by advantage ratios higher or lower than 1.00.

According to Table 13.3, women and minority group members made little headway in the first three years of equal employment opportunity and affirmative action programs toward offsetting the salary advantage enjoyed by white males. Within each racial category, men received higher median salaries than did women. This male-female salary differential was smallest for blacks, but even among blacks, men outearned women by some $1,500. The largest male-female differentials were found among Asians ($4,143) and whites ($3,381). With the exception of Asians, each group of males earned within 20 percent of the median white male salary. Asian males, on the other hand, earned almost 25 percent more than the median salary for white males.

Median salaries for all groups rose between 1973 and 1975 by an average of approximately $1,300. However, in all groups except Indians, women actually *lost* salary ground to white males. That is, women's salaries were higher in 1975 than they had been in 1973, but their salaries increased more slowly than those of white males—a striking finding in light of the larger salary base from which white males began. In a sense, then, both the rich and the poor got richer, but the rich did so faster than the poor. On the other hand, males in all minority groups except the Asians gained ground on white males. As for the exceptions, the gain among Indian women was miniscule, and Asian men remained far above the median white male income with their advantage score of 1.25.

Some of the advantage ratios, and particularly those found among women, are substantially below 1.00. Spanish-surnamed, black, and white women earned only 65.9 percent, 67.8 percent, and 70.9 percent, respectively, of the median white male salary in 1975. Relative salary changes were slight between 1973 and 1975. No male group earned less than 81.2 percent of the white male median, indicating once again the advantage males enjoyed in the employment arena. There was a difference of only .078 on the advantage scale between the *highest* advantage score for women and *lowest* for male minority members. On the other hand, the advantage scale difference between the lowest score for women and the highest for men was a huge .587, which represented a salary differential of more than $6,800.

The Functional Areas

A more refined perspective on the quantity and status of the jobs held by women and minorities in state and local government can be gained by classifying jobs according to function. Table 13.4 shows the racial and sexual distribution of state and local employees in each of 15 functional areas. What Table 13.4 reveals, in general terms, is that whites numerically dominated each functional area in both 1973 and 1975, and that males were predominant in the great majority of areas. However, let us couch our discussion of these figures in terms of representativeness ratios rather than figures on the sheer number of employees of various types in each functional area.

According to Table 13.5, minorities had representativeness ratios above 1.0 in 1973 and 1975 in only five of the 15 functional areas: public welfare, hospitals and sanitariums, housing, utilities and transportation, and sanitation and sewage. All of these are relatively labor-intensive fields which employ large numbers of unskilled laborers, and two of these areas (public welfare and housing) employ large numbers of clericals as well. Between 1973 and 1975, minorities actually increased their degree of overrepresentation in four of these five functional areas. The exception here was hospitals and sanitariums, where the largest number of professionals were employed.

In both 1973 and 1975, minorities were numerically underrepresented in five other functional areas: financial administration, streets and highways, natural resources, and, most notably, police protection and fire protection. Interestingly enough, these are areas in which professional training is important or in which unions or employee organizations have been relatively powerful. The effects of previous discrimination in denying women and minorities access to professional training almost certainly helps explain some of this underrepresentation. Additionally unions have traditionally been very resistant to equal employment opportunity programs, although their positions have been changing recently. Unions and employee organizations are especially strong in police and fire services, where

Table 13.4

Composition of State and Local Employment, By Function, 1973 and 1975

Function	1973		1975			
	% Minority	% female	% Minority		% female	
Financial administration	11.4	52.8	13.6	(+2.2)	51.5	(-1.3)
Streets and highways	11.8	7.1	12.5	(+0.7)	8.4	(+1.3)
Public welfare	23.6	71.8	26.2	(+2.6)	72.9	(+1.1)
Police protection	9.3	12.0	11.0	(+1.7)	14.0	(+2.0)
Fire protection	5.0	1.3	6.7	(+1.7)	1.6	(+0.3)
Natural resources	15.9	18.7	17.2	(+1.3)	19.8	(+1.1)
Hospitals and sanitariums	30.4	71.0	29.6	(-0.8)	70.2	(-0.8)
Health	17.8	60.6	21.8	(+4.0)	63.7	(+3.1)
Housing	34.6	27.3	42.7	(+8.1)	26.9	(-0.9)
Community development	15.1	32.3	18.8	(+3.7)	32.3	(0.0)
Corrections	18.7	26.9	20.7	(+2.0)	27.9	(+1.0)
Utilities and transportation	22.7	11.3	26.8	(+4.1)	12.1	(+0.8)
Sanitation and sewage	38.8	2.7	40.1	(+1.3)	3.4	(+0.7)
Employment security	18.7	54.8	18.6	(-0.1)	56.7	(+1.9)
Other	18.9	40.9	18.5	(-0.4)	45.9	(+5.0)
Total	18.2	34.7	20.4	(+2.2)	37.5	(+2.8)
N =	3,808,538		3,899,280			

minorities were most underrepresented in both 1973 and 1975. Representativeness ratios did, however, increase slightly for minorities in each of these functional areas between 1973 and 1975, indicating some improvement in the minority employment situation. In the remaining five areas (health, community development, corrections, employment security, and other), minority representativeness ratios hovered around 1.00 in 1973 and registered slight increases by 1975.

With respect to the employment of women, many of the same types of agencies that had the poorest employment records for minorities also employed the smallest percentage of females. As of 1975, women fared particularly poorly in six functional areas (streets and highways, police protection, fire protection, natural resources, utilities and transportation, and sanitation and sewage), all but the last two of which were also areas of minority under-representation. These functional areas involve work that is physically taxing, dangerous, or both, and have long been regarded as male preserves. However, between 1973 and 1975 women do appear to have made some employment inroads in each of these six areas.

Women were somewhat better represented in four other functional areas (housing, community development, corrections, and other), but 1973–1975 rates of improvement in these areas were much more mixed. In the remaining five areas (financial administration,

Table 13.5

Representativeness Ratios, By Function, 1973 and 1975

Function	1973		1975	
	Minority	female	Minority	female
Financial administration	0.62	1.04	0.74	1.01
Streets and highways	0.64	0.14	0.70	0.16
Public welfare	1.28	1.41	1.42	1.43
Police protection	0.51	0.24	0.60	0.27
Fire protection	0.27	0.03	0.36	0.03
Natural resources	0.86	0.37	0.93	0.39
Hospitals and sanitariums	1.65	1.37	1.61	1.38
Health	0.97	1.19	1.18	1.25
Housing	1.88	0.54	2.32	0.53
Community development	0.82	0.63	1.02	0.63
Corrections	1.02	0.53	1.13	0.55
Utilities and transportation	1.23	0.22	1.46	0.24
Sanitation and sewage	2.11	0.05	2.18	0.07
Employment security	1.02	10.7	1.01	1.11
Other	1.03	0.80	1.01	0.90
Total	0.99	0.68	1.11	0.74
N =	3,808,538		3,899,280	

public welfare, hospitals and sanitariums, health, and employment security), women were numerically overrepresented. These are areas dominated by jobs that are often stereotyped as "women's work"—nurses, social workers, secretaries, and clerical employees. In two of these areas (financial administration and hospitals and sanitariums), women experienced a falling-off between 1973 and 1975 in their proportion of the work force, but in none was their numerical overrepresentation jeopardized.

Turning to the qualitative dimension, Table 13.6 reveals some substantial differences within and between groups.[7] In each of the four groups, median salaries varied widely across the 15 functional areas. Among white males, median salaries were highest in police and fire protection, housing, community development, and utilities and transportation, and lowest in streets and highways, natural resources, hospitals and sanitariums, and sanitation and sewage. Among black males much the same situation applied: police and fire protection and utilities and transportation had the highest median salaries, and streets and highways, natural resources, hospitals and sanitariums, and sanitation and sewage had the lowest. For women the salary differences across functions were much less marked. There was, for example, only a $1,000 difference between the median salary for white females in the least

Table 13.6

Median Salary and Advantage Index,* for Selected Groups, By Function, 1975

Function	All Employees	White Male	White Female	Minority Male	Minority Female
Financial Administration	$9,391	$12,358 (106.3)	$7,962 (68.5)	$9,549 (82.1)	$7,883 (67.8)
Streets and Highways	$9,528	$9,896 (85.1)	$8,016 (68.9)	$8,342 (71.1)	$7,887 (67.8)
Public Welfare	$9,201	$11,415 (98.1)	$8,810 (75.7)	$9,638 (82.9)	$8,492 (73.0)
Police Protection	$12,448	$13,195 (113.4)	$7,907 (68.0)	$12,519 (107.6)	$8,070 (69.4)
Fire Protection	$12,800	$12,933 (111.2)	$8,192 (70.4)	$12,035 (103.5)	$8,175 (70.3)
Natural Resources	$9,588	$10,518 (90.4)	$8,059 (69.3)	$8,484 (72.9)	$7,453 (64.1)
Hospitals and Sanitariums	$8,281	$9,505 (81.7)	$7,999 (68.8)	$8,328 (71.6)	$7,789 (67.0)
Health	$8,894	$11,210 (96.4)	$8,482 (72.9)	$8,312 (71.5)	$7,364 (63.3)
Housing	$10,551	$12,892 (110.8)	$8,530 (73.3)	$10,040 (86.3)	$7,900 (67.9)
Community Development	$11,202	$13,109 (112.8)	$8,801 (75.7)	$10,082 (86.7)	$8,687 (74.7)
Corrections	$10,551	$11,421 (98.2)	$8,782 (75.5)	$10,929 (94.0)	$8,763 (75.3)
Utilities and Transportation	$12,399	$12,944 (111.3)	$8,963 (77.1)	$12,741 (109.5)	$10,012 (86.1)
Sanitation and Sewage	$9,461	$10,523 (90.5)	$8,181 (70.3)	$8,402 (72.2)	$7,720 (66.4)
Employment Security	$10,134	$12,375 (106.4)	$8,842 (76.0)	$10,450 (89.8)	$10,096 (86.8)
Other	$9,245	$11,099 (95.4)	$8,201 (70.5)	$8,853 (76.1)	$7,650 (65.8)
Total	$9,827	$11,631 (100.0)	$8,250 (70.9)	$9,623 (82.7)	$7,964 (68.5)

*Base salary for computing advantage index for each group is 1975 median for each group as reported in Table 13.3.

remunerative (police protection) and the most remunerative (utilities and transportation) functions. There was a greater difference between the lowest and highest median salaries for minority women, but the median salary figures for the best-paying areas (utilities and transportation and employment security) were based on a very small number of cases.

Without a single exception, in 1975 white males drew the highest median salaries in each functional area of state and local government. With only one exception (health), minority males ranked second in median salary levels, averaging approximately $2,000 less than the median salary for white males. Among females, whites outearned minority members in 12 of the 15 functional areas, although these differences tended to be small. Among both white and minority females, median salaries tended to be some $1,500 below those of black males and $3,500 below those of white males.

Conclusion

This barrage of figures adds up to several conclusions about the status of minorities and women in state and local government and the probable effects of equal employment opportunity and affirmative action programs. Generally, it can be said that the gains registered by minorities and women between 1973 and 1975 emanated from two distinct sources. First, the state and local government work force expanded by more than 90,000 positions. Second, at the same time that the work force was growing, the number of white males in the work force fell by more than 91,000. White and "other" males together accounted for approximately 95,000 positions open to women and minorities, or 106 percent of the number of new positions in state and local government during that period. This figure also represents 51 percent of the gains made by women and minorities between 1973 and 1975. As a result, more jobs for one minority group did not result in fewer jobs for another.[8] The burden of greater minority and female employment was borne by (1) taxpayers, who underwrote the 90,000 new positions, and (2) white males, who as a group lost 91,000 positions and "other" males who lost 4,000.

White males probably bore most of the burden because they no longer receive automatic preference. Instead, they have to compete with other qualified individuals, white or non-white, male or female. While we cannot be certain on the basis of the information provided here, it also seems likely that reverse discrimination—an orientation away from white males—has played some role. Whatever the cause, it is clear that on the quantitative dimension the employment situation for minorities and women has improved relative to white males. If these trends continue, minorities and women should increasingly share in higher level positions as they gain experience and seniority in the public service.

White females made the greatest gains by far, with over a 1.3 percent improvement in the number of positions. Blacks followed with .6 percent for males and 1.1 percent for females. Other smaller gains were registered by Spanish-surnamed males (.2 percent) and females (.3 percent). Thus, while women were still badly underrepresented in the state and local work force (holding only 74 percent of the jobs that would have been theirs on the basis of their share of the population), they did make some substantial gains between 1973 and 1975 in terms of the sheer number of positions held. During the first three years of federally mandated equal employment opportunity and affirmative action programs, the female portion of the work force increased from 34.8 percent to 37.5 percent, and particularly rapid progress was made by white and black women. Nonetheless, men still held more state and local jobs than women. This male-dominant pattern held up within racial groups, with males enjoying greater representation in each racial category. In some groups (especially whites, the Spanish-surnamed, and Indians), the differential was on the order of two-to-one.

Comparison of levels of employment of men and women also suggests a continuing pattern of gender stereotyping of jobs. In areas such as police and fire protection, women were still very scarce in 1975. On the other hand, women remained highly represented in such traditional female employment areas as health and social work.

Perhaps more significantly, by 1975 women's salaries continued to be lower than those of men and, except for Indian females, actually fell further below the median salary for white males from 1973 to 1975. Within every racial group the same trend was apparent, suggesting a long, difficult struggle before women achieve financial equality with men. These disparities have no doubt resulted from the longer job tenure of males, the fact that new female employees come in at low, entry-level salaries, and the continued clustering of women in more menial positions, as well as outright salary discrimination against women. If salaries are compared within functional areas the same pattern prevails.

These figures tend to follow the pattern of female employment of federal agencies. Recent studies indicate that women are disproportionately employed in lower grades of the federal civil service and occupy very few positions at the higher GS grades.[9] State and local patterns are consistent with practices at the national level, and the reasons that were cited above probably rule in both national and state and local levels.

Minority employees have experienced similar difficulties in gaining equity and in some respects have fared even worse than women. Between 1973 and 1975 minority groups registered some gains, but for minority males, in particular, the gains were less dramatic than for women. Among minorities overall, employment increased from 17.9 percent to 20.1 percent. Minority males went from 10.3 percent to 11.1 percent of state and local employees, while minority females increased their proportion of the workforce from 7.6 percent to 9.0 percent. Asian and black Americans continued to be highly overrepresented, while the Spanish-surnamed and particularly American Indians continued to be badly underrepresented. Just as with females, minorities tended to be better represented in certain functional areas of employment. In particular, they were highly overrepresented in sanitation and sewage and housing, and least represented in police and fire protection. In most functional areas, however, they did make gains between 1973 and 1975. With the exception of highly-paid Asians, minority males gained some salary ground on white males between 1973 and 1975, although these gains were not very large.

It is worthy of re-emphasis that ours is an early assessment of the progress of equal opportunity and affirmative action in state and local governments, and that truly fundamental changes could not realistically have been anticipated in such a brief period of time. However, certain changes in the composition of the state and local government workforce did take place between 1973 and 1975, changes that primarily concerned the sheer number of minority and female employees. Should such changes continue into the 1980s, the overall composition of the work force would come much closer to reflecting the racial and sexual make-up of the American population. In order to achieve the results expected by EEOC, however, state and local jurisdictions must not only continue to hire more and more minority and female employees. They must also see to it that progress is made toward integrating these groups into all organizational levels and functional areas. In that regard the 1973–1975 record provides much less room for optimism.

Notes

1. Equal Employment Opportunity Commission, *Affirmative Action and Equal Employment: A Guidebook for Employers*, Vol. 1 (Washington, D.C.: EEOC, January 1974), p. 3.

2. See, e.g., Grace Hall and Alan Saltzstein, "Equal Employment in Urban Governments: The Potential Problem of Inter-minority Competition," *Public Personnel Management*, 4 (November-December 1975), 386–393; Grace Hall and Alan Saltzstein, "Equal Employment Opportunity for Minorities in Municipal Government," *Social Science Quarterly*, 57 (March 1977), 864–872; Commission on Civil Rights, *For ALL the People . . . By ALL the People* (Washington, D.C.: Government Printing Office, 1969); Commission on Civil Rights, *To Eliminate Employment Discrimination*, Vol. 5: *The Federal Civil Rights Enforcement Effort—1974* (Washington, D.C.: Government Printing Office, July 1975); Lee Sigelman, "The Curious Case of Women in State and Local Government," *Social Science Quarterly*, 57 (March 1976), 591–604; and Lee Sigelman and Albert K. Karnig, "Black Education and Bureaucratic Employment," *Social Science Quarterly*, 58 (March 1977), 858–863.

3. EEOC, *Minorities and Women in State and Local Government 1973*, Vol. I: *United States Summary* (Washington, D.C.: Government Printing Office, 1974); EEOC, *Minorities and Women in State and Local Government 1975*, Vol. I: *United States Summary* (Washington, D.C.: Government Printing Office, 1977).

4. Winfield H. Rose and Tiang Ping Chia, "The Impact of the Equal Employment Opportunity Act of 1972 on Black Employment in the Federal Service: A Preliminary Analysis," *Public Administration Review*, 38 (May/June 1978), 245–251. Data from early EEO-4 surveys are also cited in Harry Kranz, *The Participatory Bureaucracy* (Lexington, Mass.: D.C. Heath and Co., 1976), and Nijole V. Benokraitis and Joe R. Feagin, *Affirmative Action and Equal Opportunity: Action, Inaction, Reaction* (Boulder, Colo.: Westview Press, 1978). An extremely brief presentation of 1973 and 1975 EEO-4 data appeared recently in Lenneal J. Henderson, "The Impact of the Equal Employment Opportunity Act of 1972 on Employment Opportunities for Women and Minorities in Municipal Government," *Policy Studies Journal*, 1 (Winter 1978), 234–239. A state-by-state analysis of the same data appears in Kenneth Meier, "Constraints on Affirmative Action," *Policy Studies Journal*, 1 (Winter 1978), 208–213.

5. See, e.g., Sigelman, *op. cit.*; Sigelman and Karnig, *op. cit.*

6. Population figures were derived from the 1970 census, and may thus not perfectly reflect the composition of the population as of 1973 and 1975.

7. Table 13.6 pertains only to 1975, because comparable figures are not available for 1973.

8. For detailed early examinations of this question, see Hall and Saltzstein, "Equal Employment in Urban Government" and David H. Rosenbloom, "A Note on Interminority Group Competition for Federal Positions," *Public Personnel Management*, 1 (January–February 1973), 43–48.

9. See Debra Stewart, "Women in Top Jobs: An Opportunity for Federal Leadership," *Public Administration Review* 36 (July/August 1976), 357–364, and the other articles in the "Symposium on Women in Public Administration" edited by Nesta M. Gallas on pp. 347–389 of the same volume.

CHAPTER 14

A SYMPOSIUM

Minorities in Public Administration

ADAM W. HERBERT

Introduction

Historically, few issues in America have generated such controversy as governmental requirements for "integration," "equal rights," "equal employment opportunity," and "affirmative action." While efforts to circumvent these obligations persist in a number of governmental jurisdictions and agencies, the list of minority public administrators and elected officials at all levels of government is growing at an impressive rate. With this growth have come a number of significant challenges for both minority administrators and public bureaucracies. This symposium represents an effort to document some of these challenges, particularly as they affect/have affected minority groups.

It is critical that the reader recognize that the views and perceptions of minority group peoples vary considerably relative to the good will of public administrators and the efforts of governmental agencies to address the broad social and economic needs of the American people. Any symposium of this type which fails to reflect cynicism and discontent on the one hand, and the pragmatic guarded optimism felt by others would be less than intellectually honest, or factually accurate. The articles in this symposium do reflect this range of views. They all are written, however, in the context of how the public affairs profession and educational institutions can be made more responsive to a set of established societal objectives and needs which have not been adequately understood or addressed. In this context, four themes seem to emerge from the essays included herein:

1. The intellectual and operational contributions of minorities to the public service have not been accurately or adequately reflected in the theory, literature, or teaching of public administration.
2. Before public agencies will become more responsive to their needs, minority group people must become more active and visible in both administrative and elective governmental positions.

From 34 *Public Administration Review*, 6: 519–563, 1974. Copyright © 1974 American Society for Public Administration. Reprinted with permission.

3. Racial and cultural biases continue to be major factors delimiting the opportunities of minority group people in many governmental agencies to be hired or to advance to professional or high-level administrative positions.

4. Universities, and particularly those with substantial minority group constituencies, have a major role to play in training more minority administrators who possess the skills necessary to research problems, analyze, advocate, and implement public policies which address the needs of low-income people.

In the first article, Deryl Hunt argues that public administration is experiencing an "identity crisis" which must be addressed by the profession. In this context, he suggests that particular attention should be given to the attitudes of administrators towards clients of their agencies. Central to this attitudinal change is a public policy and administrative emphasis on "collective" needs as opposed to "individual" aspirations or demands.

In the second article, on black elected administrators, William Nelson and Winston Van Horne identify some of the most significant problems these officials have encountered, including a review of the strategies they have utilized to overcome the problems. Their analysis suggests that those problems confronting black elected administrators are not encountered by their white counterparts. The authors offer suggested improvements which might address the conditions about which they voice concern.

The third article, prepared by Maria Diaz deKrofcheck and Carlos Jackson, describes the forms of discrimination experienced by Chicanos—Spanish-surnamed Americans—in public personnel systems at all governmental levels. Their article suggests that "nativism" is frequently more subtle than racism, and calls for greater recognition of the causes and effects of this form of discrimination.

Cheryl Dobbins and Dollie Walker examine the role black colleges and universities can play in training students and addressing problems facing low-income peoples. They point out the need for institutional cooperation, and suggest roles for NASPAA (National Association of Schools of Public Affairs and Administration), ASPA (American Society for Public Administration), foundations, and predominately white academic institutions in the quest for policies which are more responsive to the needs of "all" people.

Rose Robinson describes the conditions and perceptions which led to the creation of the Conference of Minority Public Administrators (COMPA). She refutes the arguments that COMPA is separatist in nature, and illustrates how it seeks make to strengthen the public affairs profession.

The final essay, by the symposium editor, focuses on the roles and responsibilities of minority administrators. It identifies several of the pressures brought to bear on the minority administrator, and suggests the need for a new bureaucratic perspective with regard to role expectations of the minority professional. It presents the argument that minority administrators have a unique role in the formulation and implementation of public policies which they must assume in a more vigorous effective manner, and which public bureaucracies should encourage.

The challenge of identifying a representative set of issues and perspectives related to minorities and public administration has been a major one. Added to this conceptual problem has been the length restrictions placed on *Public Administration Review* symposia.

I do not believe that we have covered herein "all" of the significant issues or problems to be considered in this important subject area, and certainly not in the depth desired. This symposium, however, does constitute an important step in the effort to identify and place into a clearer perspective the contributions minority group people have made, and must continue to make to the public service.

CHAPTER 15

A SYMPOSIUM

Women in Public Administration: Introductory Comments

NESTA M. GALLAS

When asked to serve as editor of this symposium, I accepted with alacrity. My enthusiasm for the project was shared by members of ASPA's Committee on Women in Public Administration, with whom plans for the Zsymposium were discussed. My condition soon turned to alarm as I read my mail following a *P.A. News and Views* announcement of symposium plans. I had not anticipated the volume of suggestions (and prescriptions) both in number and intensity—nor the sharp differences of opinion as to appropriate coverage.

Women in public administration became an elusive subject compounded by the uniqueness and individuality of the women in public administration who contacted me—practitioners, academics, students, and combinations of each.

An attempt to synthesize suggestions (and prescriptions) was abandoned in favor of finding a focus that permeated divergencies. Three were found: There has been and is discrimination against, underrepresentation of, and underutilization of women in public administration. Despite the foci identified, pandemonium prevailed as I sorted and resorted the materials submitted for consideration. Analyses of why conditions of discrimination, underrepresentation, and underutilization exist and remedies for their removal covered the spectrum of beliefs and concerns.

The manuscripts selected for inclusion only sample the complexities of the subject, the diversities, and the heterogeneity of those having an interest in and a commitment to advancing the cause of women in public administration. All, however, project a positive stance rather than negative rhetoric.

The restrictions of available space resulted in the exclusion of several articles that hopefully may be published at a later date. Criteria for selection became one of balance in presentation and the extent to which each complemented the substance or significance of the others. If both conflict and consensus—hidden or exposed—are seen by *PAR* readers, it will be par for the course this symposium has traveled.

From 36 *Public Administration Review*, 4: 347–389, 1976. Copyright © 1976 American Society for Public Administration. Reprinted with permission.

The articles included are placed against two backdrops. The first is an article on the women's movement in ASPA by Joan Bishop, a pioneer activist in this effort. The second is a selected profile of women in public administration by Andrea Stoloff, my research assistant, who has worked with me on affirmative actions.

These are followed by four articles that explore discrimination, underrepresentation, and underutilization and their removal from varied vantage points—both general and specific.

Debra Stewart focuses on the dilemma of why so few women have been able to move into top jobs. Three theses are advanced for analyzing the blockages to female entry into high level decisional posts: The political, biological, and sociological. Some directions for federal leadership in removing existing barriers are suggested.

Mary Lepper presents a timely overview on the status of women in the United States and their search for justice and equity. Affirmative action processes are weighed against other means of ending the unequal position of women in employment.

Peggy Newgarden describes and critiques the federally recommended process for determining affirmative action goals and suggests a more workable set of criteria for reaching measurable goals. The application of these criteria to a local government setting is provided, based on work done in Sacramento, California.

Nancy R. Hooyman and Judith Kaplan concentrate on a specific occupational area in which women predominate but have little visibility and exert little influence as administrators in the human services profession. The focus here is on how women can enhance their influence by removing internal, interpersonal, and structural obstacles. A training model for modifying barriers to career advancement and effective performance is presented.

The next two articles turn to women and women's groups as the vehicle for exploring behavior in complex organizations. The first of these, by Robert B. Denhardt and Jan Perkins, relates concepts of administrative man to alternative theories of organization emerging from the women's movement—both women's rights groups and radical feminists. This "women's way" analysis may seem to some to be blatantly sexist. That women have been able to form effective work groups, however, is evidenced by the strength and number of the divers pieces that are labeled the women's movement.

The final article by Jennifer Dorn Oldfield presents a case study of women as the makers of policy and designers of programs dealing with women's rights. Connecticut's Permanent Commission on the Status of Women is the focus of the study. An issue raised is whether the "status of women" provides a unified goal for organizing a government program. A second issue is whether an advocacy role can be performed by a government agency.

Lurking throughout each of these articles is the specter of sexism in traditional strongholds, i.e., everywhere, at high levels and in the processes designed to combat it. In these times of transition in public administration generally and for women in public administration specifically, a variety of options are open to women for surfacing and confronting sexism—whether overt or covert. Through litigation, negotiation, socialization, enthusiasm, commitment, and competence in their public service roles, the imbalances and plateaus are being challenged.

This symposium sets forth some selected stances for scrutinizing women in public administration. If you wish to read more, Joan Bishop (and I) suggest the following references.

References

Amundsen, Kirsten, *The Silenced Majority: Women and American Democracy* (Englewood Cliffs, N.J.: Prentice-Hall, 1971).

Andreas, Carol, *Sex and Caste in America* (Englewood Cliffs, N.J.: Prentice-Hall, 1971).

Babox, Deborah, and Madeline Belkin (eds.). *Liberation Now: Writings from the Women's Liberation Movement* (New York: Laurel, 1971).

Bernard, Jessie, *Women and the Public Interest: An Essay on Policy and Protest* (Chicago & New York: Aldine-Atherton, 1971).

Bird, Caroline, and Sara Welles Briller, *Born Female: The High Cost of Keeping Women Down,* Rev. Ed. (New York: David McKay Co., Inc., 1974).

Bullough, Vern L., and Bonnie Bullough, *The Subordinate Sex: A History of Attitudes Toward Women* (Urbana: University of Illinois Press, 1973).

Cafe, William Henry, *The American Woman: Her Changing Social, Economic and Political Roles, 1920–1970* (New York: Oxford University, 1972).

Carden, Maren Lockwood, *The New Feminist Movement* (New York: Russell Sage Foundation, 1974).

Catt, Carrie Chapman, and Nettie Rogers Shuler, *Woman Suffrage and Politics, the Inner Story of the Suffrage Movement* (Seattle: University of Washington, 1970).

Chesler, Phyllis, *Women and Madness* (New York: Doubleday, 1972).

————, and Emily Jane Goodman, *Women, Money and Power* (New York: William Morrow & Co., Inc., 1976).

Cudlipp, Edythe, *Understanding Women's Liberation* (New York: Paperback Library, 1971).

Epstein, Cynthia Fuchs, *Woman's Place: Options and Limits in Professional Careers* (Berkeley: University of California, 1971).

Ferns, Abbott L., *Indicators of Trends in the Status of American Women* (New York: Russell Sage, 1971).

Firestone, Shulamith, *The Dialectic of Sex: The Case for Feminist Revolution* (New York: Bantam Books, 1970).

Flexner, Eleanor, *Century of Struggle: The Women's Rights Movement in the United States* (New York: Atheneum, 1970).

Freeman, Jo, *New Thoughts on Women* (Berkeley: National, 1974).

————, *The Politics of Women's Liberation: A Case Study of an Emerging Social Movement and Its Relation to the Policy Process* (New York: David McKay Co., Inc., 1974).

Friedan, Betty, *The Feminine Mystique* (New York: Dell, 1963).

Githers, Marianne, and Jewel L. Prestage (eds.), *A Portrait of Marginality: The Political Behavior of the American Woman* (New York: David McKay Co., Inc., 1974).

Gornick, Vivian, and Barbara K. Morgan (eds.), *Women in Sexist Society: Studies in Power and Powerlessness* (New York: Basic Books, Inc., 1971).

Holt, Judith, and E. Levine, *The Rebirth of Feminism* (New York: Quadrangle, 1971).

Huber, Joan (ed.), *Changing Women in a Changing Society* (Chicago: University of Chicago, 1973).

Jacquette, Jane E. (ed.), *Women in Politics* (New York: Wiley, 1974).

Kanowitz, Leo, *Women and the Law, The Unfinished Revolution* (Albuquerque: University of New Mexico, 1969)

Klein, Viola, *The Feminine Character: History of an Ideology* (Urbana: University of Illinois, 1971).

Kraditor, Aileen S., *The Ideas of the Woman Suffrage Movement, 1890–1920* (Garden City, N.Y.: Doubleday, 1971).

———— (ed.), *Up From the Pedestal: Selected Writings in the History of Feminism* (Chicago: Quadrangle, 1970).

Kreps, Juanita, *Sex in the Market Place: American Women at Work* (Baltimore and London: Johns Hopkins Press, 1971).

Lifton, Robert Jay (ed.), *The Women in America* (Boston: Beacon, 1967).

Mead, Margaret, *Male and Female: A Study of the Sexes in a Changing World* (New York: Dell, 1949).

Millett, Kate, *Sexual Politics* (Garden City, N.Y.: Doubleday and Company, Inc., 1970).

Mitchell, Juliet, *Woman's Estate* (New York: Pantheon Books, 1971).

Morgan, David, *Suffragists and Democrats: The Politics of Woman Suffrage in America* (East Lansing, Mich.: Michigan State, 1972).

Morgan, Robin (ed.), *Sisterhood is Powerful* (New York: Vintage, 1970).

Murphy, Irene L., *Public Policy on the Status of Women: Agenda and Strategy for the 70s* (Lexington, Mass.: Lexington Books, 1973).

Myrdal, Alva, and Viola Klein, *Women's Two Roles: At Home and Work* (New York: Humanities, 1968).

Oltman, Ruth M., *Campus 1970: Where Do Women Stand* (Washington, D.C.: American Association of University Women, December 1970).

O'Neil, William L., *Everyone Was Brave: A History of Feminism in America* (Chicago: Quadrangle, 1969).

———— (ed.), *The Woman's Movement: Feminism in the United States and England* (Chicago: Quadrangle, 1971).

Perrucci, Carolyn C., and Dena B. Targ (eds.), *Marriage and the Family: A Critical Analysis and Proposals for Change* (New York: David McKay Co., Inc., 1974).

Rapoport, Rhona, and Robert Rapoport, *Dual-Career Families* (New York: Penguin, 1972).

Reeves, Nancy, *Womankind: Beyond the Stereotypes* (Chicago: Aldine-Atherton, 1971).

Riegel, Robert E., *American Women: A Story of Social Change* (Cranbury, N.J.: Fairleigh Dickinson University, 1970).

Roberts, Joan I. (ed.), *Beyond Intellectual Sexism: A New Woman, A New Reality* (New York: David McKay Co., 1976).

Rossi, Alice S., and Ann Calderwood (eds.), *Academic Women on the Move* (New York: Russell Sage, 1973).

Samuels, Catherine, *The Forgotten Five Million: Women in Public Employment* (New York: Women's Action Alliance Inc., 1975).

Sargent, Alice G. (ed.), *Beyond Sex Roles* (St. Paul, Minn.: West Publishing Co., 1975).

Schneir, Miriam (ed.), *Feminism: The Essential Historical Writings* (New York: Vintage, 1972).

Scott, Ann Firor (ed.), *The American Woman: Who Was She?* (Englewood Cliffs, N.J.: Prentice Hall, 1971).

Scott, Ann Firor, and Andrew M. Scott, *One Half the People: The Fight for Woman Suffrage* (Philadelphia: J.B. Lippincott Co., 1975).

Sochen, June (ed.), *The New Feminism in Twentieth-Century America* (Lexington, Mass.: D.C. Heath, 1971).

Sullerot, Evelyn, *Women, Society and Change* (New York: McGraw-Hill, 1971).

Tanner, Leslie B. (ed.), *Voices from Women's Liberation* (New York: New American Library, 1970).

Theodore, Athena, "The Professional Woman: Trends and Prospects," in *The Professional Woman*, Athena Theodore (ed.), (Cambridge, Mass.: Schenkman, 1971), pp. 1–35.

CHAPTER 16

THREE STEPS FORWARD, TWO STEPS BACKWARD

The Status of Women's Integration into Public Management

MARY E. GUY

Today, as in the past, women must convince men that their demands for governmental action are legitimate before their desires are transformed into policies, programs, and services. This is because men hold the vast majority of decision-making positions in government. In legislative chambers and top-level career posts, women's voices are still mostly heard indirectly through the mouths of their husbands, fathers, brothers, and sons. When Abigail Adams reminded her husband to "remember the ladies" as a new nation was being founded, he responded in jest to her. The thought of treating women as full-fledged citizens was considered frivolous. Two hundred years later, women's political status has improved, but women remain largely dependent on the goodwill of the men around them. This is true in policy implementation and program management as well as in the political arena.

In this article, I outline the pattern of women's integration into public management. I characterize the pattern as being not unlike that of women's integration into society at large—"three steps forward, two steps backward." Each series of advances toward equality for women is followed by a backlash of restraint and a yearning for a social order that lurks in archetypes from an era long gone.

Challenges to Contemporary Public Administration

To borrow from Paul Appleby's (1949) argument, public administration is the enterprise of making a mesh of things. In today's world, "to make a mesh of things" means integrating the strengths that diverse interests and forces bring to governing. If the differentness of women and men makes a difference in the workplace, then those strengths that are attributed to women, such as mediating, facilitating, and consensus building are too

---

From 4 *Public Administration Review*, 53: 285–292, July/August 1993. Copyright © 1993 American Society for Public Administration. Reprinted with permission.

valuable to ignore. The fact that women pay attention to the human dimension is exactly the reason they should have a place on center stage as this nation grapples with a changing work force, the transition from an industrial economy to a service economy, a troubled educational system, an inadequate health care system, an unsettled Eastern Europe, a changing international economy, and a world in which environmental hazards threaten not just the nation but the planet. If ever there were a need for building bridges, it is now. If ever there were a need to build on the skills that women have always been characterized as bringing to management, it is now.

Why, then, are women still on the outside looking in when it comes to managing government's interests? Government, in combination with economic forces, is the train that engineers social change. In the case of women entering managerial levels in the public service, the train forces change, and accommodation to it, by treating jobs as resources and redistributing them. This, in turn, creates changes in behavior and changes in attitudes coincident with the behavioral changes. No organizations, least of all public agencies, operate in a vacuum devoid of the pushes and pulls that societal values exert.

As much as diversity is the wave of the future, a backlash of reaction against it occurs periodically (Faludi 1991). Images of the past creep into the national consciousness and promote a yearning for lifestyles of the past. As recently as the 1992 Republican Convention, platform speeches were still encouraging the outmoded Norman Rockwell image of the traditional family, including a husband who is the breadwinner for the family, a wife who is a contented mother and happy housewife, and healthy children who are well dressed and well adjusted. The fact is that too much has changed in American society to turn the clock back. By 1986, the so-called "typical" American family of husband earner, wife homemaker, and two children accounted for 3.7 percent of all the nation's families (U.S. Dept of Labor 1987, Kosterlitz 1988).

Women's Entry into the Work Force

A thumbnail sketch can describe women's entry into the world of work and into public administration: By the mid-1800s, it had become acceptable for women to fill clerical positions in the public service (Van Riper 1976). Women stenographers were described as especially capable because of their ability to radiate sympathetic interest, agreeableness, and courtesy in the office (Kanter 1977). The growth of administration brought women into numerical dominance in the office, placing them in clerical but not managerial positions. Prior to World War II, women left the work force when they became pregnant, not to return. The period between the end of World War II and the mid-1960s were watershed years, however, for they heralded what has come to be the norm. Women entered the work force upon completion of their formal education and stayed in the work force, with only brief absences associated with childcare responsibilities. Economic and social pressures had combined in such a way that women started to climb the career ladder and knock on doors for higher level jobs.

By the mid-1960s, the nation started paying attention to this phenomenon. In 1963, an article in the *Wall Street Journal* argued that it was advantageous to have women in management positions because they were "good listeners" and "sympathetic in nature" and thereby brought a "humanizing" influence to managerial ranks. Just as with secretarial positions, women were credited with humanizing organizations. But convincing employers that women were capable of effective performance in more powerful positions has been, and continues to be, a difficult process. Legislation has helped. The Civil Rights Act of 1964 provided a milestone for women's employment in the federal government by prohibiting job discrimination on the basis of sex. The Equal Employment Opportunity Act of 1972 amended the Civil Rights Act of 1964 by bringing state and local governments, governmental agencies, political subdivisions, and any governmental industry, business, or activity within its coverage (Grossman 1973). Rapid spurts soon increased the proportion of women in the public service, especially in the higher grades.

In 1972, another *Wall Street Journal* article declared that employers were coming to grips with demands for women's equality on the job. The article closed with a quote that "You might as well face it—women aren't going to go away" (Morgenthaler 1972: 17). That was in 1972. Over 20 years have passed and it will still be many years before the number of women in management is proportionate to the number of women in the workplace. The workplace is marked by vertical sex segregation. Women are able to make much greater inroads into lower paid positions than into higher paid male-dominated ranks. In fact, if progress toward integrating women into top management continues at the pace set by the first six years following passage of the Equal Employment Opportunity Act of 1972, *it will take until the year 2040* for women to gain perfect representation among career agency leaders (Dometrius 1984).

Moreover, sex segregation has been a remarkably stable feature of the American workplace during the 20th century both in the private sector and in the public sector (Lewis and Emmert 1986, Powell 1988). In 1900, 67 percent of the total work face would have had to change jobs for sex segregation to be eliminated. By now, about 60 percent of the work force, both public and private, would have to switch jobs for sex segregation to be eliminated (Lewis and Emmert 1986, Powell 1988). Although the proportion of women ad men employed in professional and technical jobs is roughly the same for both sexes, women are more likely to be employed in traditional female jobs such as health, human services, and education (Diamond 1987). For instance, as of 1986 women were two-thirds of the employees in the U.S. Department of Health and Human Services (Kaplan 1987).

Regardless of whether or not the work force of an agency is majority female, the top ranks are invariably filled with men. When tracing women's integration into public management, we see a pattern of rapid progress in the middle and late 1970s, followed by a period of quiescence in the mid-1980s. The late 1980s and early 1990s, however, are showing enhanced progress once again. Thus, women's integration into the public service is marked by spurts of progress followed by periods of redefinition, a sequence that is best described by the expression "three steps forward and two steps backward."

Three Steps Forward

Projections show that women will continue their climb into decision-making posts. For example, between 1976 and 1986 the number of women in federal General Schedule (GS) jobs at grades 13 through 15 doubled from 5 percent to 12 percent of the total workers in those grades (Barnes 1988). And between 1976 and 1986, the female share of new entrants to the federal work force who were under the age of 35 tripled to 27 percent. In 1970, women made up only 1.4 percent of all federal employees in the top grades (GS 16–18). By 1985, women composed 6.1 percent (Fox 1987). Table 16.1 shows the impact of equal opportunity initiatives which, when combined with underlying social forces (or vice versa), significantly affected the composition of the federal work force. In 1960, for example, only 1 percent of the women in the federal work force were in grades 9 or above. By 1987, this proportion had increased to 28 percent.

Table 16.1

Percentage of Women in the Federal Work Force and in Federal GS Grades, Selected Years, 1910–1987

Federal Work Force

Year	Percent	Year	Percent
1910	10	1960	25
1939	19	1968	34
1945	37	1978	37
1947	24	1987	48

Federal GS Grades

Year	GS 8 or below	GS 9 or above
1960	99	1
1987	72	28

Source: Guy 1992a.

Windows of opportunity open in ironic ways. Between 1976 and 1986 the increase in General Schedule jobs held by women increased by 6.5 percent while the white male share of these jobs decreased from 50.2 percent to 41.8 percent (Lewis 1988). These were the years in which candidates for President campaigned for office by railing about the inadequacies of the federal bureaucracy. They were years of low morale and declines in real pay. Thus, it appears that societal biases against government provided an opportunity for women to make greater than usual inroads into the public service.

The gradual integration of women into federal managerial levels is mirrored at the state and local levels. The information in Tables 16.2, 16.3, and 16.4, which is drawn from data provided by the U.S. Equal Employment Opportunity Commission (1982, 1985, 1990), provides a look at new hires and salaries across all levels by gender. Table 16.2 shows that women are now entering the public work force in greater numbers than men.

Table 16.2

New Hires in State and Local Government, 1980, 1985, and 1989 (in Percent)

Year	Women	Men	Difference
1980	50.5	49.5	+1.0
1985	49.0	51.0	-2.0
1989	51.4	48.6	+2.8

Source: U.S. EEOC 1982, 1985, 1990.

Table 16.3

Percentage of New Hires in Six State Governments, 1980, 1985, 1989

	Women	Men	Difference
Alabama			
1980	49.1	50.9	-1.8
1985	44.5	55.5	-11.0
1989	54.6	45.4	9.2
Arizona			
1980	48.2	51.8	-3.6
1985	47.8	52.2	-4.4
1989	52.3	47.7	4.6
California			
1980	52.5	47.5	5.0
1985	54.1	45.9	8.2
1989	54.5	45.5	9.0
Texas			
1980	47.8	52.2	-4.4
1985	47.1	52.9	-5.8
1989	53.1	46.9	6.2
Utah			
1980	48.4	51.6	-3.2
1985	46.3	53.7	-7.4
1989	47.6	52.4	-4.8
Wisconsin			
1980	48.9	51.1	-2.2
1985	49.1	50.9	-1.8
1989	56.7	43.3	13.4

Source: U.S. Equal Employment Opportunity Commission 1982, 1985, 1990.

Table 16.4

Full-Time Median Salary for Officials/Administrators in State and Local Government, 1980, 1985, 1989

Year	Women	Men	Difference	Wage Gap (Percent)
1980	$17,493	$23,150	-$5,657	75
1985	$26,440	$33,370	-$6,930	79
1989	$32,686	$40,469	-$7,783	81

Source: U.S. Equal Employment Opportunity Commission 1982, 1985, 1990.

In a spot check of states, these same trends are represented in different regions of the United States. Table 16.3 shows new hires in states in the southeast, southwest, west, and upper midwest.

Data in Tables 16.2 and 16.3 show that women have made the greatest strides in gaining employment in state and local government toward the end of the 1980s. In all the states shown except Utah, more women than men were hired in 1989. The increase is anything but steady throughout the decade, however. In 1980, the only state shown in which there were more women than men hired was California. In 1985, the gap continued in most states, and grew wider in many. By 1989, though, the numbers show a turnaround. More women than men were hired in Alabama, Arizona, California, Texas, and Wisconsin. If the past informs the future, then it is obvious that the rate by which women will move into key posts will be anything but steady.

Two Steps Backward

By the beginning of the 1960s, it had become socially acceptable to question the wage disparities between women's and men's earnings. It was in 1963 that Congress passed the Equal Pay Act requiring that women receive equal pay for equal work. Despite legislation, sexual inequality in earnings has remained a telltale sign of the status of women in the workplace (Cooney, Clague, and Salvo 1980, National Committee on Pay Equity 1989, Smith and Ward 1984). Fully employed women high school graduates with no college had less income in 1979, on the average, than fully employed men who had not completed elementary school. And in that same year, women with four years of college had less income than men with only an eighth grade education. By the latter 1980s, the inequity had not changed substantially and the wage gap persisted, with women earning $.65 for every $1.00 that men earned.

In fact, since 1955 the female-male average annual earnings gap of full-time, year-round workers in the United States has hovered around 60 percent. It has been as low as 57 percent in 1973 and 1974 and as high as 65 percent in 1987 (National Committee on Pay Equity 1989). Administrative positions in state and local government have done a little better than this (Table 16.4). According to data gathered by the U.S. Equal Opportunity Commission (1982, 1985, 1990), in 1980 the median salary for men who held administrative positions in state and local government was $23,150; for women it was

$17,493, leaving women's average earnings at just 75 percent of men' average earnings. Ten years later, the median salary for men in the same type of positions was $40,469; for women it was $32,686, a gap of $7,783. This represents a narrowing of the wage gap to 81 percent. If salary is a windsock for indicating progress, then only a slight breeze is blowing. Salary figures reflect not only the lack of pay equity between the sexes but also the fact that women are often relegated to working in lesser valued missions that pay lower wages. In fact, Lewis and Emmert (1986) report that one-third of the male-female earnings gap is attributable to occupational sex segregation.

The fact that societal pushes and pulls results in women's gaining entrance to administrative positions while the wage gap continues reveals the relationship between gender and salary (Ahn and Saint-Germain 1988, Welch, Karnig, and Eribes 1983). One scenario goes like this: As government employment is maligned by elected officials and public opinion, those nearing retirement (men) remain at higher wages, while those newly hired (women) are paid less for they have fewer years' experience. Although this is plausible, it risks oversimplifying the facts of the matter. The systemic causes of this phenomenon are better explained by the differential effect of opportunity, power, and numbers.

Opportunity, Power, and Numbers

Opportunity, power, and numbers are three significant features that differentiate men from women in the workplace. The consequences of high or low opportunity, high or low power, and high or low numerical representation affect public administration and program implementation. Rosabeth Moss Kanter (1977) generated a rich set of hypotheses related to these structural determinants of behavior in organizations. These factors also help to reveal and explain women's status in public administration. For example, Kanter hypothesized that people low in career opportunity behave differently than people high in career opportunity. Opportunity relates to expectations and future prospects for mobility and growth. Those with high opportunity have high aspirations, are more attracted to high-power people, are competitive, and are more committed to the organization and to their careers. They value their competence, and become impatient or disaffected if they do not keep moving. On the other hand, those in low opportunity positions limit their aspirations, seek satisfaction in activities outside of work, and have a horizontal orientation rather than a vertical orientation. They find ways to create a sense of efficacy and worth through personal relationships, they resign themselves to staying put, and they are concerned with basic survival and extrinsic rewards.

Kanter also developed notions about power, which she defined as the capacity to mobilize resources. People low in organizational power tend to foster lower group morale, behave in more authoritarian ways, and use coercive rather than persuasive power. They are more controlling and more critical. People high in organizational power foster higher group morale, behave in less rigid ways, and delegate more control. They allow subordinates more latitude and discretion and are more often seen as helping rather than hindering.

Kanter called a third characteristic "proportions." This concept relates to the composition of people in approximately the same situation. It is a numerical matter of how many people of a kind are present, so that differentness is, or is not, noticeable. People whose type is represented in very small proportion tend to be more visible, that is, they are "on display." They feel more pressure to conform and to make fewer mistakes, they find it harder to gain credibility, they are more isolated and peripheral, and they are more likely to be excluded from informal peer networks. Thus, they are limited in their source of power-through-alliance. Furthermore, they are stereotyped and placed in role traps that limit effectiveness. People whose type is represented in very high proportion tend to "fit in" and find it easier to gain credibility in positions beset by high uncertainty. They are more likely to be accepted into the informal network, to form peer alliances, and to learn the ropes from peers. They are also more likely to be sponsored by higher status organization members and to acquire mentors easily.

These three possessions, opportunity, power, and numbers, combine to produce self-perpetuating cycles. Thus, those with high opportunity behave in ways that generate more opportunity, which in turn produces further inducement for the behavior. High opportunity is accompanied by more power. Both opportunity and power coincide with being a member of a group that constitutes a large enough proportion of the work force so that any one member of the group is not immediately noticeable as "different." The confluence of opportunity, power, and proportion, then, produces upward cycles of advantage or downward cycles of disadvantage. The cycle of high opportunity, power, and numbers makes it very difficult for newcomers (such as women) to break into the managerial work force. The cycle of low opportunity, powerlessness, and tokenism is also difficult to break because of its self-perpetuating nature.

The glass ceiling that prevents women from reaching top positions is partially explained by the combined effects of tokenism and sex-role expectations. When Frances Perkins, the first woman to be appointed to a cabinet post, was named Secretary of Labor in 1933, she was wary of being identified as a special champion of women. She felt everyone was watching her to see if she appointed too many women. Consequently, she went to great lengths to quell such fears by not catering to concerns of women in the department's Women's Bureau (Sealander 1983). Such is the dilemma of tokens. If they respond too directly to the expectations of the group that they represent, they lose credibility in the eyes of the dominant group. If they ignore the expectations of their own group, they are accused of being mere tokens. If women are too assertive, they are castigated as being too aggressive and "unfeminine," making them unworthy representatives of their gender. If they are too cooperative and conciliatory, they are seen as being too weak to be an effective representative of their gender.

The Gendered Workplace

Gender infuses organizational processes and shapes our interpretations of behaviors and events (Kelly 1991). Although we take it for granted, it is important to understand that policy implementation is conducted by gendered instruments, women and men. The reason women are so few in top levels of state administrative positions flows from the innumerable small influences that shape the way we organize, along with who decides how we do it. To aid our understanding of this, career managers in state agencies have been surveyed in seven states: Alabama, Arizona, California, Texas, Utah, and Wisconsin (Guy 1992b; Kelly, Guy et al. 1991) and Florida (Newman 1992). These surveys provide a systematic comparison across organizational and political units. The results show that gender is more predominant than geographic boundaries or political traditions when it comes to affecting one's status in public management.

Although the cultural foundation upon which women's and men's experiences are based is generally the same, it is the differences that are most visible. Thus, even though differences show up as only one point, or a fraction of a point on a Likert scale, the direction of the differences persists across the states. The patterns are inescapable and haunting. They appear in regard to career advancement, personal background, family obligations, access to mentors, exposure to sexual harassment, fitting into the organizational culture, management style, and policy preferences. The differences between the sexes are the visible part of women and men in public management. The invisible part is the commonality that arises from being socialized in the same culture, living in the same communities, working in similar surroundings, and sharing the same overriding views about American government and democracy in general. Thus what women and men have in common is much greater than what they do not have in common. This is why the differences that occur are so remarkable.

Even with all the homogenizing influences of television, public education, and cultural and workplace socialization, a consistent pattern of differences shows up in all the states surveyed over most of the issues included in the questionnaire. Job titles provide an example. For instance, the survey results show that people hold jobs in their agencies in sexually coded positions and locations. Power titles, such as "administrator," "chief," and "director" are dominated by men, even in agencies that address traditional women's issues, such as health and human services. This holds true even when states differ politically, culturally, and economically (Guy and Duerst-Lahti 1992). Patterns such as these prevail in all the states studied. A brief review of findings related to career advancement, workplace policies, personal background, family obligations, and mentoring uncovers the components that influence gender roles in the managerial workplace.

Career Development

The career paths of women and men are different. The pattern in the state is that women tend to move into management at a younger age than their male counterparts. The women who make it are promoted from one position to another in less time than men are (Kelly, Guy et al. 1991; Bullard and Wright 1991). Thus, for the very small portion of women in the public work force who break into the high opportunity cycle, they break into it early. Women managers, however, receive lower pay than men in each state surveyed, are under-represented in traditionally "male" occupations, and are over-represented in public welfare, health care, and employment security agencies.

Workplace Policies

Policies affecting workplace reform, such as affirmative action programs, prohibitions against discrimination and harassment, and moves toward pay equity and childcare, affect women and men differently. Changes in these policies alter the workplace and level the playing field for women and men in public administration. As one might expect, workplace policies that treat all workers as if they were men get the most support from men. Policies that favor advancing women's interests received the most support from women. Women express a greater preference for workplace reforms related to proportionate representation of women and for issues related to childcare and pay equity.

Women and men disagree over whether or not there is equal opportunity for both sexes. While men believe that discrimination against women is diminishing, women believe that it is increasing. In fact, Simon and Landis (1989) report a study that asked about employment discrimination in general. They conclude from their findings that the percentage of women perceiving discrimination against them has increased from 46 percent to 56 percent between 1975 and 1987; but the percentage of men perceiving discrimination against women decreased from 50 percent to 46 percent.

Personal Background

The positions that public managers achieve are influenced by their background. Women and men who have attained equally high positions in state government differ in their educational achievement and socioeconomic status. The similarity between the effects of genders across the states cannot be overstated. Regardless of political traditions, economic differences, systemic differences, and geographic differences, the same patterns prevail. Women who make it to the top managerial ranks in state agencies tend to come from more advantaged backgrounds than do the men who make it into those ranks. In the states surveyed, as many as 58 percent of the male managers held an advanced degree beyond the bachelor's degree, while as many as 76 percent of the women held such degrees. As many as 28 percent of the women managers had mothers who held professional or managerial jobs, whereas only as many as 13 percent of male managers' mothers had such a work history. As many as 44 percent of female managers' fathers held professional or managerial jobs, while only as many as 32 percent of the male managers' fathers held such jobs. While as many as 29 percent of the female managers reported that they had grown up in an upper-middle or upper class setting, only as many as 11 percent of the men reported such a background. Finally, as many as 32 percent of female managers said they had grown up in a lower-middle or lower class background, whereas as many as 59 percent of male managers reported such a background.

What does this information tell us? It says that while the average man is able to climb the bureaucratic ladder, the average woman is shut out. She needs to be above average in order to make it. The networks provided by one's socioeconomic status, family connections, and education, apparently help women to crack the barriers that they meet and gain a toehold where things without such networks are more likely to fail.

Family Obligations

Public work and private lives intersect in the careers of top-level public servants. The personal is political because conventional career patterns assume a particular relationship to family/private life obligations that pose problems for women who pursue careers. The fact is that men in top-level positions tend to live traditional family lives, while women disproportionately live nontraditional lives. Women who lead traditional lives carry an extra burden of family obligations and are less likely to be promoted into management ranks. Women who do not lead traditional lives carry an extra burden of being "different" from most women. As many as 71 percent of female managers reported they had no dependents while only as many as 48 percent of male managers reported this. About 50 percent of the women managers were married, while over 80 percent of the men were married. Women are caught in a Catch-22: a woman's power is diminished by being "different" once she arrives in a management post. On the other hand, if she is not different, then she will have family obligations that are likely to prevent her from being promoted to management.

Mentoring

Because there are so few women in top posts, women who aspire to such posts find few mentors to turn to for advice. Although as many as 57 percent of men in management positions in state agencies reported having a male mentor at the agency director level, only as many as 35 percent of the women reported having a woman mentor at that level. There are so few women who hold management positions that senior women mentors are hard to find. Although women benefit from having male mentors, they also need mentors who have successfully forded the barriers that confront women but which men may not even be aware exist.

Conclusion

Regardless of whether one evaluates the status of women in public administration from a political, psychological, or sociological paradigm, the realities are clear (Stewart 1990). We know that women are making advances into management posts. But there is a long way to go before women will hold management positions proportional to their representation in the work force, let alone their representation in the population. We know that women in management in state and local government earn only 80 percent to 90 percent of what men earn. We know that women who live traditional lives are not nearly as likely to progress up the career ladder as are nontraditional women. We know that both women and men rely on mentors to assist their advancement, but that women have few senior women to look to for mentoring. We know that the higher a woman goes in the organization, the more likely it is that she has not only heard about sexual harassment happening to those around her but that she has actually experienced it. In terms of management style, we know that sex role stereotypes seem to sculpt what are thought to be appropriate styles for women and men. When we closely examine styles, however, we see that what is thought to be real often fades into fantasy. We know that women in management ranks are concentrated in only a few agencies. In sum, the structure of the workplace militates against women having opportunities equal to those of men. But these structures are not immutable and it is within our reach to adjust these structures to accommodate the needs of the changing work force and to breathe life into the ideal of a representative bureaucracy.

It is time to think "out of the box" about new leadership styles and new structures for classifying positions. We need to rest our career structures on assumptions that go beyond simple gender dualisms. What levers would have to be pulled to correct the differences between the sexes that disadvantage women? Three come readily to mind. They pertain to loosening rigid position classifications to accommodate women's career paths, encouraging agencies to be representative bureaucracies vertically as a well as horizontally, and to promote affirmative action in deed as well as in word.

Systems that use broad-band classifications to signify skill levels without the lock step progression that inheres in more rigid systems provide at least some degree of flexibility toward this end (National Academy of Public Administration 1991, *PA Times* 1991). The incorporation of flexitime and job sharing opportunities also expand opportunities for women to continue working and accruing experience when their family obligations cannot accommodate a standard 40-hours per week work schedule. A theory of career development, Larwood and Gutek (1987) remind us, needs to be "roomy" enough to allow for breaks in service for women to accommodate childcare responsibilities. By facilitating childcare and parental leave, employers remove a major obstacle for employees whose family obligations interfere with their promotion potential.

Vertical representation is currently missing. Women occupy the lower rungs on the agency ladders and men occupy the upper rungs. Although giving the appearance of being representative in terms of sheer numbers, most agencies are anything but representative in their decision-making processes. While the number of state agencies with a significant number of women in the upper grade levels is increasing, many agencies and departments still have no women in these top grades. The promise, as yet unrealized, of the notion of representative bureaucracy is that policy implementation should be directed by women and men, not just men.

Practicing affirmative action means much more than merely adhering the letter of the law in terms of considering applicants for promotion. It means *affirmatively* reinforcing equal opportunity in the workplace by actions as well as words. It means promoting qualified women into positions even though there may never have been a woman who held that position before. It means making reasonable accommodations to the workplace so that women who are qualified for promotion are not penalized for being female. Only when such measures are taken can an unfair system be altered so that women are treated as equals when they compete for management positions. It means setting the stage for women to enter the high opportunity cycle, rather than the low opportunity cycle.

The legitimacy of governmental action depends upon broadening the scope of vision in order to understand the confluence of opportunity, power, and numbers. Integrating women into public administration requires reweaving the fabric of societal expectations about the rightful place of women. The 200-year record of the women's movement for equal rights and opportunities in the United States tells us that initiatives that seem eminently reasonable to women have only been secured by persistent, patient pushing. History tells us that the path of change is marked by three steps forward and two steps backward.

Note

Portions of this article are excerpted from the author's following works: Guy 1992a and 1992b. An earlier version of this article won a Lilly Award for Outstanding Research at the 1992 Annual Meeting of the American Society for Public Administration.

References

Ahn, Kenneth K. and Michelle A. Saint-Germain, 1988. "Public Administration Education and the Status of Women." *American Review of Public Administration,* vol. 18(3), pp. 297–307.

Appleby, Paul H., 1949. *Policy and Administration.* Tuscaloosa, AL: University of Alabama Press.

Barnes, Lesley, 1988. "The Work Force of the Future." *Government Executive,* November, pp. 56–57.

Bullard, A. and D. Wright, 1991. "Circumventing the Glass Ceiling? Women Executives in American State Government(s)." Paper presented at the Southeastern Conference on Public Administration, Charlotte, NC.

Cooney, Rosemary S., Alice S. Clague, and Joseph J. Salvo, 1980. "Multiple Dimensions of Sexual Inequality in the Labor Force: 1970–1977." *Review of Public Data Use,* vol. 8, (October), pp. 279–293.

Diamond, E.E., 1987. "Theories of Career Development." In B.A. Gutek and L. Larwood, eds., *Women's Career Development.* Newbury Park, CA: Sage, pp. 15–27.

Dometrius, N.C., 1984. "Minorities and Women Among State Agency Leaders." *Social Science Quarterly,* vol. 65, pp. 127–137.

Faludi, Susan, 1991. *Backlash: The Undeclared War Against American Women.* New York: Crown Publishers.

Fox, S. F., 1987. "Rights and Obligations: Critical Feminist Theory, the Public Bureaucracy, and Policies for Mother-Only Families." *Public Administration Review,* vol. 47(5), pp. 436–440.

Grossman, Harry, 1973. "The Equal Employment Opportunity Act of 1972, Its Implications for the State and Local Government Manager." *Public Personnel Management,* vol. 2(5), pp. 370–379.

Guy, Mary E. 1992a. "The Feminization of Public Administration: Today's Reality and Tomorrow's Promise." In Mary T. Bailey and R. Mayer, eds., *Public Administration in an Interconnected World: Essays in the Minnowbrook Tradition.* Westport, CT: Greenwood Press, pp. 91–115.

Guy, Mary E. 1992b. *Women and Men of the States: Public Administrators at the State Level,* Armonk, NY: M.E. Sharpe.

Guy, Mary E. and Georgia Duerst-Lahti, 1992. "Agency Culture and Its Effect on Managers." In Mary E. Guy, ed., 1992b, *Women and Men of the States: Public Administration at the State Level.* Armonk, NY: M.E. Sharpe, pp. 157–188.

Kanter, Rosabeth Moss, 1977. *Men and Women of the Corporation.* New York: Basic Books.

Kaplan, Paul A., 1987. "Affirmative Employment Statistics for Executive Branch (Non-Postal) Agencies as of September 30, 1986." *Employment and Trends as of . . . ,* May, pp. 69–75, available from U.S. Office of Personnel Management.

Kelly, Rita M., 1991. *The Gendered Economy.* Newbury Park, CA: Sage Publications.

Kelly, Rita M. and Mary E. Guy with J. Bayes, G. Duerst-Lahti, L. Duke, L. Duke, M. Hale, C. Johnson, A. Kawar, and J. Stanley, 1991. "Public Managers in the States: A Comparison of Career Advancement by Sex." *Public Administration Review,* vol. 51(5), pp. 402–412.

Kosterlitz, Julie, 1988. "Family Cries." *National Journal,* vol. 20(16), pp. 994–999.

Larwood, L. and B.A. Gutek, 1987. "Toward a Theory of Women's Career Development." In B.A. Gutek and L. Larwood, eds., *Women's Career Development.* Newbury Park, CA: Sage, pp. 170–183.

Lewis, Gregory B., 1988. "Progress Toward Racial and Sexual Equality in the Federal Civil Service?" *Public Administration Review,* vol. 48(3), pp. 700–707.

Lewis, Gregory B. and Mark A. Emmert, 1986. "The Sexual Division of Labor in Federal Employment." *Social Science Quarterly,* vol. 67(1), pp. 143–155.

Morgenthaler, Eric, 1972. "Under Pressure, Firms Try Upgrade Status of Women Employees." *Wall Street Journal,* March 20, pp. 1, 17.

National Academy of Public Administration, 1991. *Modernizing Federal Classification: An Opportunity for Excellence.* Available from NAPA, 1120 G St., NW, Washington, DC 20005.

National Committee on Pay Equity, 1989. Briefing Paper no. 1: *The Wage Gap.* 1201 Sixteenth St., NW, Suite 420, Washinton, DC 20036.

Newman, Meredith, 1992. "Career Advancement: Does Gender Make a Difference?" Paper Presented at the Annual Meeting of the American Political Science Association, Chicago, IL.

PA Times, 1991. "Report Calls for New Federal Classification." September 1, p. 15.

Powell, G.N., 1988. *Women and Men in Management.* Newbury Park, CA: Sage.

Sealander, Judith, 1983. *As Minority Becomes Majority.* Westport, CT: Greenwood Press.

Simon, R.J. and J.M. Landis, 1989. "Women's and Men's Attitudes About a Woman's Place and Role." *Public Opinion Quarterly,* vol. 53(2), pp. 265–276.

Smith, James P., and Michael P. Ward, 1984. *Women's Wages and Work in the Twentieth Century.* Santa Monica, CA: The Rand Corp., R-3110-NICHD.

Stewart, Debra W., 1990. "Women in Public Administration." In Naomi B. Lynn and Aaron Wildavsky, eds., *Public Administration: The State of the Discipline.* Chatham, NJ: Chatham House Publishers, pp. 203–227.

U.S. Department of Labor, 1987. "Over Half of Mothers with Children One Year Old or Under in Labor Force in March 1987." Press Release, August 12, USDL 87–345.

U.S. Equal Employment Opportunity Commission, 1982. *Job Patterns for Minorities and Women in State and Local Government,* 1980. Washinton, DC: Government Printing Office.

———, 1985. *Job Patterns for Minorities and Women in State and Local Government, 1985.* Washington, DC: Government Printing Office.

———, 1990. *Job Patterns for Minorities and Women in State and Local Government, 1989.* Washington, DC: Government Printing Office.

Van Riper, Paul P., 1976. *History of the United States Civil Service.* Westport, CT: Greenwood Press.

Wall Street Journal, 1963. "More Women Conquer Business World's Bias, Fill Management Jobs." February 25, pp. 1, 16.

Welch, Susan, Albert K. Karnig, and Richard A. Eribes, 1983. "Correlates of Women's Employment in Local Governments." *Urban Affairs Quarterly,* vol. 18(4), pp. 551–564.

CHAPTER 17

EQUAL PAY FOR COMPARABLE WORK

Stimulus for Future Civil Service Reform

LOIS FRISS

Introduction

The magnitude and the persistence of the earnings gap between men and women has stimulated international, federal, state, and local interest. England, Canada, and Australia have confronted the problem; over 80 member nations of the International Labor Organization have ratified Convention 100, a statement of principle for equal pay for work of comparable value. In this country, the Equal Employment Opportunity Commission (EEOC) requested that the National Research Council examine the issues involved in the comparable worth concept of job compensation. The recently released report of the Council's Committee on Occupational Classification and Analysis assessed whether (and to what extent) current practices of assessing the worth of jobs and assigning relative pay rates incorporates discriminatory elements.

The *Manual on Pay Equity* developed by the Conference on Alternative State and Local Policies (Grune 1980) described studies of sex discrimination in wage and job structures in five states: Connecticut, Washington, Michigan, Minnesota, and Nebraska. General studies of the compensation and classification systems in Idaho, New Jersey, Wisconsin, Iowa, and Georgia have been conducted. The consistent findings are that (1) women are segregated into low-level jobs, and (2) there is a substantial differential between predominantly female occupations and comparable male occupations (Doherty and Harriman 1981: 29).

The most publicized local jurisdictional action was the three-week strike by city workers represented by the American Federation of State, County, and Municipal Employees (AFSCME) in San Jose, California. Alleging male-female inequity, AFSCME filed suit. The city settled for a $1.5 million phased-insettlement. AFSCME now has similar suits filed with the EEOC on behalf of locals representing clerical workers and librarians in Los Angeles and clerical employees in Connecticut. The charges include discrimination on the basis of sex through assignment, compensation, and promotional opportunities.

Excerpted from 2 *Review of Public Personnel Administration*, 3: 37–48, Summer 1982. Copyright © 1982 Sage Publications. Reprinted with permission.

Table 17.1

Female Federal Employment by Grade 1978

		Total	No. Women	% Women
GS	1–4	280,887	218,185	78
GS	5–8	438,319	272,512	62
GS	9–11	346,331	102,967	30
GS	12–13	271,510	27,270	10
GS	14–15	92,790	4,780	5
GS	16–18	6,598	260	4

Source: Federally Employed Women (1980).

However else the participants in the debate may disagree, the evidence suggests that employers and employees at all levels of government agree that equal pay for work of comparable worth is a public policy issue with high visibility. . . .

Issues

Three basic issues exist. First, is there discriminatory pay inequity related to being female? That is, how much of the wage difference between men and women cannot be explained by defensible human capital and productivity difference such as education, experience or longevity? Second, if employer actions do perpetuate pay inequity, what approaches should be considered, i.e., should comparable worth strategies be pursued? The third question centers around the extent to which a managerial commitment exists to deal with the problem.

Question 1: Is There Discriminatory Pay Inequity?

The report *Women, Work, and Wages: Equal Pay for Jobs of Equal Value* prepared by the Committee on Occupational Classification and Analysis of the National Research Council, National Academy of Sciences (Treiman and Hartmann 1981: 41–42) provides the most timely answer. Briefly, it concludes:

> The existence of wage differentials is not in dispute; the causes are. Apparently, human capital and productivity differences explain only 25–50 percent of the wage gap. Job segregation which is pronounced appears to explain only part of the earnings gap.

Table 17.1 documents that job segregation occurs in the U.S. civil service system which mirrors the larger society (a finding discovered in several state studies). The largest proportion of women are employed in the lowest grades; as the GS grade increases, the proportion of women declines precipitously (*Federally Employed Women* 1980). The existence of job segregation, which is in part the result of complex cultural and economic forces, does not by itself prove discriminatory hiring and promotion practices, but it does suggest a need for scrutiny. . . .

Question 2: What Are the Available Strategies?

A National Academy of Sciences report states (Treiman and Hartmann 1981: 65–67, 89–90):

A. Concerning the institutional features of labor markets, the committee concludes that market wages include discrimination effects as well as many institutional factors. Therefore, (a) market wages cannot be used as the sole standard for judging relative worth, (b) policy intervention to alter market outcomes may be required, and (c) actions intended to have one result may turn out to have other perverse consequences. Further, since equal access to employment opportunities may be expected to be more effective for new entrants than for established workers and more effective for those who have invested less in skills, the strategy of comparable worth merits consideration as an alternative policy of intervention in the pay setting process.

B. There are two approaches to detecting and correcting discrimination in pay rates: improve the design and implementation of job evaluation plans in use and statistically adjust pay rates to estimate and remove the effects of sex, race, and ethnic composition of job categories. These approaches depend on two assumptions: that the base on which jobs are paid at different rates can be made explicit and measurable, and that whatever cannot be measured does not favor any sex, race, ethnic group. . . .

Question 3: Does a Management Commitment Exist?

The four critical components of an equitable pay system are: determining job worth, collecting job content information, writing a job description, and designing a pay structure (Henderson and Clarke 1981). But, having an administrative policy commitment to fair pay precedes all of these. Recent court decisions should stimulate managerial sensitivity about their policies. . . .

In *Gunther v. County of Washington* (1981) four women employees were employed as matrons in the Washington County (Oregon) jail. Their duties were to guard female prisoners. Males were employed as guards to guard the male prisoners and were paid a substantially higher rate. The women lost their suit in district court, but the Ninth Circuit Court sent it back to the lower court to be heard on its merits. The Appeals Court found that Title VII did not limit sex-based pay claims to the equal work standard of the Equal Pay Act, but merely permitted the employer in a Title VII case to defend an unequal pay policy on any of the exceptions set forth in the Act.

The Court held that "although decisions interpreting the Equal Pay Act are authoritative where plaintiffs suing under Title VII raise a claim on equal pay, plaintiffs are not precluded from suing under Title VII to protest other discriminatory compensation practices unless the practices are authorized under one of the four affirmative defenses contained in the Equal Pay Act and incorporated into Title VII by Section 703(h)." The Court remanded the case to district court for further proceedings to afford plaintiffs the opportunity to establish a claim for sexual discrimination apart from an equal pay claim.

On June 8, 1981 the U.S. Supreme Court affirmed the judgment of the Court of Appeals by a 5 to 4 vote in *County of Washington et al. v. Gunther* (1981). What this means is that the courts will not turn their back on wage disparities between men and women where the employer has studied the value or market for the respective jobs and found jobs to be equal. Suits can be brought under Title VII even if they do not strictly meet the provisions of the Equal Pay Act. . . .

Conclusion

At a time when the personnel function is asked to be more accountable, more responsible, more goal oriented, more identified with achieving public objectives, the fundamental issue is whether incrementalism or inaction followed by major upheaval will occur. Incrementalism is difficult; the more active agencies may experience the most immediate public dismay, both from activists and traditionalists. But the dimensions are clear and not new: job analysis, job classification, wage setting, and entry/promotion based on fair criteria.

The primary problem is not the lack of feasible alternatives, but the belief system which argues that none of the proposals is feasible. The underlying trend which needs recognition is that the emphasis has shifted from concern with process to concern with outcomes. As a baseline, for any policy to be effective, it will need to:

1. stem from a commitment to achieve pay equity;
2. identify areas where change is most likely to succeed;
3. recognize that special groups (aged, minorities, and women) have differing perceptions;
4. specify strategies needed to overcome inequities in job evaluation (including classification) and wage setting by occupational level; and
5. be sensitive to negative short-term dislocations.

Notes

1. The seminal articles which argue for and against equal pay for equal work are by Blumrosen (1979, 1980) and Nelson, Opton, and Wilson (1980, 1981). It is beyond scope of this paper to provide full exploration of economic theory about occupational crowding, relating legislative history, and intent. Similarly, those interested in the review of job analysis should refer to Treiman (1979), National Academy of Sciences (1980) and Miller et al. (1980).

2. Court-ordered affirmative action, however, must take precedence over seniority during layoffs (*Public Administration Times* 1981: 11; Bent 1978: 318–326).

References

Bent, A. and T.Z. Reeves (1978). *Collective Bargaining in the Public Sector.* Menlo Park, California: Cummings Publishing.

Blumrosen, R.G. (1979). "Wage Discrimination, Job Segregation, and Title VII of the Civil Rights Act of 1964." *Journal of Law Reform* 12 (Spring): 399–502.

Blumrosen, R.G. (1980). "Wage Discrimination, Job Segregation and Women Workers." *Employee Relations Law Journal* 6 (Summer): 77–136.

Borjas, G.J. (1980). *Wage Policy In The Federal Bureaucracy.* Washington, D.C.: American Enterprise Institute for Public Policy Research.

County of Washington et al. v. Gunther et al. (1981). Supreme Court No. 80–429.

Doherty M. H. and A. Harriman (1981). "Comparable Worth The Equal Employment Issue of the 80's." *Review of Public Personnel Administration* 1 (Summer): 26–29.

Federally Employed Women (1980). Statement of Federally Employed Women for Equal Employment Opportunity Commission Hearings on Wage Discrimination. Washington, D.C.: (April 29).

Fogel, W. and D. Lewis (1974). "Wage Determination in the Public Sector." *Industrial and Labor Relations Review* 21 (April): 410–432.

Friss, L. (1981). "Work Force Policy Perspectives: Registered Nurses." *Journal of Health Politics, Policy and Law* 5 (Winter): 696–719.

Raskin, A.H. (1976). "Conclusion: The Current Political Contest." in A.L. Chickering. *Public Employee Unions.* Lexington, MA: D.C. Heath: 203–232.

Thomsen, D.J. (1978). "Eliminating Pay Discrimination caused by Job Evaluation." *Personnel* 55 (September/October): 11–22.

Treiman, D.J. (1979). *Job Evaluation: An Analytic Review.* Washington, D.C.: National Academy of Sciences.

Treiman, D.J. and H.I. Hartmann (eds.) (1981). *Women, Work and Wages: Equal Pay for Jobs of Equal Value.* Washington, D.C.: National Academy Press.

U.S. Department of Labor (1972). *Manpower Report of the President.* Washington, D.C.: U.S. Government Printing Office.

PART 4

CIVIL SERVICE REFORM

Efforts to improve and reform civil service systems are a perennial part of the history of public personnel administration. Sometimes political, sometimes administrative in nature, reforming civil service systems at the federal, state, and local levels is a common theme, because of a belief that there is always room for change and improvement.[1] Indeed, beginning with President William Howard Taft's Keep Commission in 1905, presidents have continually sought to reform the system of government employment in order to minimize bureaucratic power over public policy formulation and implementation. One of the more ambitious efforts was that of President Jimmy Carter with the Civil Service Reform Act of 1978. This act simplified methods for firing federal workers, increased managerial flexibility and mobility, and created the Senior Executive Service (SES), comprising the highest levels of career administrators in the federal service. This latter change sought to strengthen executive leadership in a number of ways in order to make federal bureaucrats more responsive to the President and to political appointees.

In "A Symposium on Civil Service Reform," James Bowman outlines the various changes brought about by the Civil Service Reform Act of 1978. As he notes, "The changes seek to strike a balance between providing administrators with flexibility to improve organizational productivity and protecting employees from unfair personnel practices" (Bowman 1982: 1).

Felix Nigro, in "The Politics of Civil Service Reform," points out that the contours of the civil service system, as delineated by the Pendleton Act of 1883, have been altered a good deal with passage of the Civil Service Reform Act of 1978. Nigro provides a comprehensive review of the reform law signed by President Carter, as well as its implications for public personnel administration.

In 1987, the first National Commission on the Public Service, also referred to as the Volcker Commission for its Chair, Paul A. Volcker, was established to rebuild America's trust in the public service.[2] The Commission emphasized the importance of strengthening leadership for governance, recruiting the best and brightest for government service, and strengthening the government's commitment to performance through, for example, adequate pay, accessible training, and decent working conditions.

Following the efforts of the Volcker Commission at the federal level, the National Commission on the State and Local Public Service, better known as the Winter Commission after its Chair, William Winter, was created in 1991 to improve and revitalize the public service at the state and local levels of government. In the report of "The Winter Commission Report: Deregulation and Public Personnel Administration," Frank Thompson outlines the various recommendations of the Winter Commission. Ten major recommendations were offered under the broad themes of removing the barriers (1) to executive leadership, (2) to lean and responsive government, (3) to a high-performance workforce, and (4) to meaningful citizen involvement. One of the major institutions targeted by the Winter Commission for change was civil service.

In the last piece, "Reinventing the Federal Civil Service: Drivers of Change" Carolyn Ban begins with an examination of the recommendations of the formal "reinvention" efforts under the National Performance Review (NPR), the intensive study of the operations of the federal government in 1993 spearheaded by Vice President Al Gore. As Ban points out, however, reinvention can also be seen as a broader process to reform the culture of human resources in the federal government. By looking at reinvention efforts from this broader perspective, Ban shows that the civil service system has undergone many more changes than those instituted as a result of the NPR's formal reform efforts.

Notes

1. In the last several years, Georgia, Texas, and Florida have made significant changes to their civil service systems, essentially abolishing merit protections for state employees.

2. A second National Commission on the Public Service, also chaired by Paul Volcker, was created in 2001 to continue the work of revitalizing the public service at the federal level of government. The Commission's report, *Urgent Business for America: Revitalizing the Federal Government for the 21st Century*, was issued in January 2003 by the Brookings Institution, Washington, D.C.

Additional Classics

Ban, Carolyn, Edie Goldenberg, and Toni Marzotto. "Firing the Unproductive Employee: Will Civil Service Reform Make a Difference?" *Review of Public Personnel Administration*, 2: 87–100, Spring 1982.

Bellone, Carl. J. "Structural vs. Behavioral Change: The Civil Service Reform Act of 1978." *Review of Public Personnel Administration*, 2: 59–67, Spring 1982.

Carroll, James D. "The Rhetoric of Reform and Political Reality in the National Performance Review. 55 *Public Administration Review*, 3: 302–312, May 1995.

Colby, Peter W. and Patricia W. Ingraham. "Civil Service Reform: The Views of the Senior Executive Service." 1 *Review of Public Personnel Administration*, 3: 75–89, Summer 1981.

Dresang, Dennis L. "Diffusion of Civil Service Reform: The Federal and State Governments." 2 *Review of Public Personnel Administration*, 2: 35–47, Spring 1982.

Facer, Rex L. II. Reinventing Public Administration: Reform in the Georgia Civil Service." 22 *Public Administrations Quarterly*, 1: 58–73, Spring 1998.

Rosen, Bernard. "Revitalizing the Federal Service." 49 *Public Administration Review*, 5: 501–506, September/October 1989.

Thompson, James R. "Reinvention as Reform: Assessing the National Performance Review." 60 *Public Administration Review*, 6: 508–521, November/December 2000.

CHAPTER 18

A SYMPOSIUM ON CIVIL SERVICE REFORM

JAMES S. BOWMAN

Introduction

The Civil Service Reform of 1978 and accompanying Reorganization Plan No. 2 constitute the most comprehensive effort to revise the federal merit system since its beginning
nearly one hundred years ago. If the objective of the initial reform era, symbolized by
the Pendleton Act of 1883, was a single-minded effort to replace the spoils system, the
new era contains an extensive array of reforms. The changes seek to strike a balance
between providing administrators with flexibility to improve organizational productivity
and protecting employees from unfair personnel practices.

Among these changes are:

- the creation of the Office of Personnel Management and the Merit Systems Protection board to replace the Civil Service Commission;
- the delegation of personnel management authorities to agencies, notably in the area
  of performance appraisal;
- a streamlining of the process used to discharge employees as well as a strengthening
  of procedures to protect those who uncover fraud, waste and abuse;
- establishment of a Senior Executive Service for top-level decision-makers;
- passage of a comprehensive, statutory framework for the conduct of labor-management relations;
- expansion of training programs; and
- authority to establish a merit pay system for middle-level supervisors based on
  performance rather than longevity.

Now that this set of policies has been adopted, the challenge and opportunity for the
personnel profession focuses on the political will and organizational capacity necessary
to administer these reforms. This, then, forms the core of the symposium; each of the
areas noted above (and more) is addressed by the contributors.

From 2 *Review of Public Personnel Administration*, 2: 1–4, Spring 1982. Copyright © 1982 Sage
Publications. Reprinted with permission.

As a result of a national call for papers and subsequent refereeing process, this project brings together recognized and new authors, academicians and practitioners into one area for an examination of how government manages itself. The product of this collective effort is the identification of strategies to make personnel management more effective. Together, the studies furnish a contemporary record of the most compelling issue in the public service today, civil service reform. They are, therefore, a timely contribution to the literature as well as a research tool for future use.

Two lessons from the American bureaucratic experience might be recalled as we embark on this exploration of implementation of civil service reforms. First, our history is riddled with the unintended, frequently ironic, consequences of reform. Second, delay in implementation of programs is a common, sometimes fatal, problem in administrative innovation. The Civil Service Reform Act marked a new beginning for personnel management in the federal government. While its passage left many ambiguities, the authors in these pages shed light on the impact of the law. What emerges is the sense that if the problems identified herein are not dealt with, the 1978 reforms will be no more successful than previous attempts to improve the public bureaucracy.

Due to space limitations, the symposium is divided into two issues of the *Review of Public Personnel Administration*. The present issue consists of two forums, one on structural context, the other on specific areas of reform. The next issue of the *Review* will be devoted to a forum on compensation followed by a reference section consisting of an assessment of evaluation techniques and an annotated bibliography.

The symposium begins with Kenneth W. Kramer's excellent analysis of the development of the Federal Act. On the premise that the future of the reforms should be based on an understanding of their conception, he identifies their seeds of success and failure in the origins of the legislation. By exposing commonly-held assumptions about reorganizations and reform—promises, promises—Vera Vogelsang-Coombs and Marvin Cummins contend that change is a myth, that reorganization alters bureaucratic structure but not necessarily political reality. They argue, in a well-documented analysis, that reformers are simply incorrect in presuming that the bureaucracy problem can be solved.

Dennis L. Dresang, in the third article, considers the environment of reform by cataloguing activities in state governments before and after enactment of the 1978 federal law. "Foreign Systems, Familiar Refrains," by Mark W. Huddleston, isolates common themes in public service reform and discusses how they have shaped change in personnel systems here and abroad. Finally, Carl J. Bellone provides an appropriate transitional essay from this section to the next by investigating the important differences between structural and behavioral change. He weighs the assumptions that lead to the reform legislation, the structural changes contained therein, and the apparent lack of any behaviorally-oriented change strategy to accompany organizational reform.

These broad-ranging analyses from academe set the stage for more specific and functional studies in the second forum in Part One of this symposium. Office of Personnel Management executive, Robert W. Brown, presents a theory-directed assessment of administrative reform. By identifying conditions necessary for effective policy implementation, Brown's study of performance appraisal has implications for other functional areas in personnel management as well. Managers and professors combine efforts in the next article by Carolyn Ban, Edie Goldenburg, and Toni Marzotto. Reviewing current policies vis-à-vis unproductive employees, they concur with Bellone in suggesting that simply creating new procedures is insufficient to deal with the problem.

"Individual Motivations and Institutional Changes Under the Senior Executive Service" by Professors Peter W. Colby and Patricia W. Ingraham argues that members of the service do not perceive improvements in areas that the reform was designed to solve. Finally, Loretta R. Flanders, a government official, and Rudi Klauss, a professional association analyst, examine executive development activities since the enactment of the 1978 law. After tracing the recent institutionalization of training programs, they express concern that executive development may not receive adequate support in the years ahead.

Due to the substantial interest in and importance of compensation issues in public management, the first section of Part Two of this symposium is devoted to a four-article forum on pay. In a technical piece, James L. Perry and his colleagues scrutinize management strategies for implementing merit pay plans presented by Daniel E. O'Toole and John R. Churchill. Foreshadowing the next article in the forum, they conclude that "it would be both ironic and tragic if a tool intended to foster efficiency actually achieved the opposite effect." In a provocative analysis, Office of Personnel Management administrator Buddy Silverman contends that merit pay is inordinately expensive, complicated, and inequitable. The last article in the forum introduces a compensation issue that transcends many other problems in this field. Noting that the 1978 Act uses the comparable worth concept, Dr. Lois Friss discusses equal pay for work of comparable value and establishes benchmarks to be used to gauge progress in this increasingly controversial dimension of personnel management. (e.g., Bellone, Colby and Ingraham, and Flanders and Klauss).

A reference section appropriate for the entire symposium is presented in the second section of this issue. Health and Human Services official Mark A. Abramson and his academic colleagues offer an evaluation design used in assessing the impact of the Reform Act and the Senior Executive Service. An annotated bibliography compiled by Charolette Hurley of the General Accounting Office closes this inquiry into civil service reform.

As editor of this project, I wish to thank the authors for their contribution to our knowledge of bureaucratic reform. The anonymous referees of their manuscripts must not go unrecognized for their careful decisions to recommend revisions for or rejection of the manuscripts sent to them. I am grateful, therefore, to:

Ronald L. Usher, County of Sacramento
Joseph Stewart, Jr., Rice University
Glenn Rainey, Eastern Kentucky University
Priscilla Levinson, Office of Personnel Management
Brian E. Donnelly, Southern Illinois University at Edwardsville
Lea P. Stewart, Rutgers University
William Thompson, University of Nevada-Las Vegas
N. Joseph Cayer, Arizona State University
William B. Eddy, University of Missouri-Kansas City
James W. Evans, University of San Diego
Robert B. Denhardt, University of Missouri-Columbia
W. Bartley Hildreth, Kent State University

Paula Gordon, Silver Spring, Maryland
Steven W. Hays, University of South Carolina
Toni Marzotto, Towson State University
John Dempsey, College of Charleston
H. Brenton Milward, University of Kentucky
John S. Robey, East Texas State University
Charles T. Goodsell, Virginia Polytechnic Institute
Peter W. Colby, SUNY-Binghamton
Naomi Lynn, Kansas State University
Charles F. Wicker, General Accounting Office
Fran Burke, Suffolk University
Rosslyn Kleeman, General Accounting Office

Appreciation is also expressed to the people who responded to the call for papers, but whose interests could not be accommodated within the confines of the symposium. Finally, I am glad to acknowledge *The Public Administration Times,* and *P.S.* for listing the announcement for this volume.

CHAPTER 19

THE POLITICS OF CIVIL SERVICE REFORM

FELIX A. NIGRO

Between passage of the Civil Service Act of 1883 and almost a century later of the Civil Service Reform Act of 1978, the conception of civil service reform has changed greatly.[1] Reform in 1883 meant starting the process of eliminating the spoils system and of implementing a merit system based on the use of competitive examinations in filling federal jobs. In 1978, there was full awareness that the danger of political subversion of the personnel operation still existed, for memories of such systematic subversion during the Nixon administration were still fresh. However, the predominant objective of reform had become to make merit a reality rather than a meaningless label for a personnel system which was widely viewed as so enmeshed in red tape, so inflexible, and so inefficient that it was largely responsible for the failure of government to "work."

The Civil Service Act of 1883 was the culmination of a moral crusade by reformers anxious to remove from American society the evil of spoils and its attendant corruption. The Civil Service Reform Act of 1978 represented the initiative of a President with a strong moralistic bent but also an overwhelming managerial interest in improving government organization and efficiency. When Governor of Georgia (1970–1974), Jimmy Carter had made reorganization of government his first priority. Upon assuming the presidency in 1976, he had many priorities, but in 1978 he made civil service reform the centerpiece of his plans to reorganize the government.

Carter's Proposals

The Civil Service Reform Act of 1978 correctly has been referred to as a complicated piece of legislation. For those with a special interest in personnel administration, it is essential reading in all its detail, because it covers components of the personnel process such as recruitment, compensation, performance evaluation, discipline, career management, and employee organizations. In this article, the focus is on the political aspects of Carter's proposals and on the strategy followed to deal with the opposition and to obtain passage of the legislation. Obviously, the political decision-making process started with the determination within the administration as to what the legislation should include.

Excerpted from 3 *Southern Review of Public Administration,* 2: 196–239, September 1979. Copyright © 1979 Southern Public Administration Education Foundation, Inc. Reprinted with permission.

These determinations were of a bold character, as seen in the following principal elements in the bill presented to Congress in early March, 1978[2]:

1. Replacement of the United States Civil Service Commission by an Office of Personnel Management directly under the President and by an independent Merit Systems Protection Board. The Civil Service Commission, established in 1883 as part of the Civil Service Act, was a venerable federal institution which had been a model for many state and local governments.

The reason for the change was that the Commission lacked credibility in its combined roles of adviser to the President and to agency managements, on the one hand, and the protector of employee rights and interests, on the other. Many employees and the unions had come to regard the Commission as an arm of management that too often favored management over the employee. At the same time, the President lacked the direct line of control a Chief Executive must have in the initiation and implementation of basic personnel policies. The solution was to create both an Office of Personnel Management (OPM) directly under the President, and an independent Merit Systems Protection Board (MSPB) to enforce merit principles, hear employee appeals, and generally protect employees from unfair treatment.

The President would appoint the OPM Director, subject to Senate confirmation, and the Director would serve at the President's pleasure. The President was to name the three members of the MSPB, with Senate confirmation, and the members could be removed by the President only for misconduct, inefficiency, neglect of duty, or malfeasance in office.

2. Clear statements of both merit principles and prohibited personnel practices and provision of enforcement machinery to prevent such practices. Existing provisions of law did not adequately define merit principles to be observed and violations to be prohibited.

A Special Counsel in the MSPB would assist in enforcing merit principles. Named by the President with Senate confirmation, the Special Counsel would investigate charges of prohibited personnel practices and recommend corrective action to the agency and OPM. The Special Counsel could order a stay of any proposed personnel action not otherwise appealable to MSPB that would have a substantial and adverse economic impact on the employee and, if reprisal action had been taken against whistleblowers, the Special Counsel could order the agency head to cancel such action.

3. Substantial curtailment of veteran preference. Under existing law, nondisabled veterans who passed the examination received five preference points. Disabled veterans got ten preference points and, except for scientific and professional positions at grade GS-9 and above, their names were placed at the top of the employment register. In reductions-in-force, in a given tenure category (e.g., permanent career, career-conditional, or temporary), no veterans in a given grade or type of work could be laid off before all nonveterans in that same grade or type of work had been terminated.

The bill provided that, after October 1, 1980, preference in hiring for nondisabled veterans would be limited to a period of ten years following separation from military service. Absolute retention for them in reductions-in-force was to be given only during the three years following their initial appointment. Disabled veterans were to continue to receive ten points preference in examinations and to rise to the top of lists except for professional and scientific positions at GS-9 and above. They would also continue to have the same absolute retention rights in reductions-in-force.

The first veteran preference legislation in the federal service was passed in 1865 and, as policy, has antecedents as far back as colonial times. By World War I, veterans preference was solidly established at all levels of government.

4. More latitude for agency managements in personnel matters. The OPM Director was authorized to delegate to agency heads *any* of the functions vested in the Director, including preparation and administration of competitive examinations. Appointing authorities were authorized to select for appointment from the highest seven eligibles on the employment register available for appointment; further, the OPM could authorize selection from broad categories such as "outstanding," "very good," and "good."

Existing law required selection to be made from the top three names on the register. The administration believed the rule of seven would not only provide more choice for appointing authorities but also result in the appointment of more women and minority group members.

5. Modification of adverse action procedure. In employee appeals of dismissals, demotions, and other disciplinary actions, the MSPB would uphold the agency unless the employee could show either that 1) the agency's procedures contained errors that substantially impaired his or her rights or 2) the action was taken for reasons of racial or other discrimination, or 3) it was arbitrary or capricious. Under existing procedures, agencies had to prove to Civil Service Commission appeals officers, by a preponderance of evidence, that the action was justified. The burden of proof would now be placed on the employee.

6. New performance appraisal systems. Pursuant to regulations issued by the OPM, each agency was to develop one or more appraisal systems, and employees were to be rated in accordance with performance standards clearly communicated to them at the beginning of each appraisal period. Agencies could at any time demote or remove employees whose performance they found unacceptable.

The employee was to be given 30 days' advance written notice of the proposed action, such notice to identify the expected standard of performance and the aspects in which his or her performance was considered unacceptable. The employee was entitled to reply to the notice orally and in writing. A decision to retain, remove, or demote the employee was to be made within 30 days after the expiration of the notice period. The employee could appeal to the MSPB which, in considering the appeal, would be governed by the standards stated in point 5 above.

7. Merit pay for supervisors and managers in grades GS-13 through GS-15. Existing law provided for employees in General Schedule grades (1–18) to receive periodic within-grade increases dependent upon receiving satisfactory performance ratings. Since about ninety-five (95) percent got satisfactory ratings, in effect these increases were granted for length of service. Merit pay was to be introduced into the government by providing it first for supervisory and managerial positions in grades GS-13 through 15, estimated as numbering about 72,000. These positions were considered particularly important for the effective administration of federal programs. Annually, federal employees receive comparability increases in base pay, based on comparison with private sector compensation. Within-in grade or step increases are in addition to the comparability adjustment. Step increases were to be eliminated for supervisors and managers in grades GS-13 through 15, and instead they were eligible for merit increases ranging from the minimum to the maximum rate of the particular grade. Within-grade increases in the GS Schedule are much smaller, starting at approximately three (3) percent and increasing at the higher grades.

Annually, OPM, in consultation with the Office of Management and Budget (OMB), would determine what proportion of the amount of the comparability pay adjustment for all white-collar employees would automatically be allocated to employees under the merit pay system. The remaining amount was to be combined with money that otherwise would have been used for step increases, and the total would constitute the "merit pay pool."

8. Creation of a Senior Executive Service (SES). The SES would include all managers above GS-15 and below level III of the Executive Schedule (the latter Schedule includes the highest policy-making officials in the executive branch). Initially, about 9,000 managers would be in the SES, and it was to include both career and noncareer officials. For the government as a whole, not more than ten (10) percent of the SES was to consist of noncareer officials.

SES members were to be deployed between and within agencies, wherever needed at a particular time. GS grades 16–18 would be eliminated, and SES executives were to be compensated within a broad salary band, ranging from step 6 of GS-15 to the salary for Executive Level IV. Since rank was to be in the person, not the position, the possibility of being downgraded in order to accept a reassignment, ever present in GS Schedule position classification system, would not exist, thus eliminating this obstacle to mobility. The President would establish at least five executive salary rates for SES executives, and agency heads would set the salaries to be paid to individual SES members. There would be no length-of-service increases, instead pay rewards based on performance, including cash bonuses of as much as twenty (20) percent of base pay and also merit stipends in substantial amounts for those judged to be "meritorious" or "distinguished" executives.

Present executives could choose whether or not to become SES members; if they decided to do so, no review of their qualifications was necessary. Future executives' positions would all be in SES, and those aspiring to them would have to undergo qualifications review in accordance with OPM regulations. SES members would not have tenure. Their performance would be appraised annually and, on the basis of these evaluations, consistently mediocre members would be weeded out. Someone dropped from the SES for reasons other than misconduct, neglect of duty, or malfeasance would be guaranteed placement in a continuing career position equivalent to at least GS-15.

Under existing law, employees could appeal any reassignment that involved a reduction in grade, salary, or rank. This had proved a serious deterent to transfer of executives in accordance with agency needs, because the executive could argue that the position to which he or she was to be assigned was not as responsible as the one currently occupied. Under the SES, executives could freely be transferred to positions within the equivalent of five grades (GS-16–18 plus Executive Levels IV and V). Although they lacked tenure, SES members could advance rapidly in salary and would receive pay commensurate with their accomplishments. The criticism had long been made that outstanding and mediocre executives were paid the same and advanced at the same rate.

9. Placing the federal labor relations program on a statutory basis. In January of 1962, President Kennedy issued an executive order providing for collective bargaining between agency management and employee organizations. This program, which excluded negotiation of salaries and fringe benefits, had continued on an executive order basis although the employee unions had sought legislation making collective bargaining a matter of law, not presidential discretion. The employee leaders wanted a broader scope of negotiations and other provisions advantageous to the unions, such as the agency shop. Under the union shop, employees in the bargaining unit who are not members of the majority union must become members within a specified time period or else lose their jobs. The agency shop does not require them to join the union but, to retain their jobs, they must pay the equivalent of the union dues.

When Carter presented his civil service reform proposals to Congress, he did not include a title on labor relations. Instead, he directed his administration to work with the appropriate congressional committees and with federal employee representatives in preparing a legislative proposal on labor relations. On May 10, 1978, Carter recommended to Congress a labor-management title (Title VII) to be added to the bill. Title VII codified into law provisions of the executive order (Executive Order # 11491, as amended). It also provided for binding resolution by independent arbitrators of removals and other adverse actions excluded from arbitration under the executive order. Title VII also provided for establishment of an independent Federal Labor Relations Authority, similar to the National Labor Relations Board. Under the executive order, the policy-making body was a Federal Labor Relations Council, consisting of the chairman of the Civil Service Commission, the OMB Director, and the Secretary of Labor—administration officials the unions considered biased in favor of management.

Political Context of the Proposals

Viewed in their entirety, Carter's proposals were bold ones from the political standpoint. Viewed individually, they were also bold, although, of course, the opposition to some of them, for example, curtailment of veterans preference, could be expected to be greater than to others.

Carter proposed abolishing a 95 year-old agency, one identified with the principles of merit instead of spoils, and making drastic changes in long-established personnel policies, such as tenure in the job for executives and very strong protections for employees in dismissal cases. The administration had decided that no personnel system could be so constructed as to eliminate all possibilities of political abuse, that the objective should be to strengthen the protections against such possibilities, at the same time making the system more flexible, responsive, and efficient.

Many employees and union leaders believed that the lessons of the Nixon and previous administrations were very clear: agency managements should have less, rather than more, discretion. In fact, Carter's recommendations were surprising to many persons in view of the climate of strong suspicion of the White House and of the agency managements. Plans similar to the SES had been recommended by both Presidents Eisenhower and Nixon, and proposals to redistribute personnel functions and split the Civil Service Commission into two agencies had also failed. The belief was widespread that employees and the unions clearly had sufficient strength to prevent enactment by Congress of such sweeping changes. When it was known that the reform package would include recommendations for substantial curtailment of veterans preference, predictions were freely made that this would sink the entire bill.

On the other hand, dissatisfaction with government and antipathy for the "bureaucracy" had intensified throughout the country. The climate on Capitol Hill had changed, and support for the federal employee and the employee unions was in a down spiral. The administration made clear that it considered most federal employees to be dedicated and productive. The political challenge was to capitalize on the prevailing public anti-bureaucratic mood, but not in the process to create irreparable alienation on the part of the employees toward the administration.

While there was much sentiment in Congress that, as expressed by Senator John C. Stennis,[3] the time for civil service reform had come, some members were apprehensive that the administration would accept amendments making too many concessions to the unions. Particular concern was expressed that the administration might agree to the agency shop and to relaxation of the prohibitions on political activities of federal employees contained in the Hatch Act. The Defense Department was strongly opposed to granting union demands for a larger role. It had to deal with the unions at its many installations and it was determined to maintain its right to manage these installations without, as it considered, cumbersome union restrictions.

The biggest anticipated obstacle to moving the bill in Congress was the House Committee on Post Office and Civil Service. (The Senate Committee on Post Office and Civil Service had been abolished and its functions absorbed by the Senate Committee on Governmental Affairs.) Historically, the political complexion of the House Committee and its former counterpart in the Senate had evolved as one of friendliness to the federal employees and of serving as their protector against possible mistreatment by administrative branch officials. Several of its members were from districts in Virginia and Maryland heavily populated with federal employees. Representatives Gladys N. Spellman (Md.) and Herbert E. Harris (Va.) being two examples.

The Committee also had a liberal, pro-labor Democratic wing, represented prominantly by William D. Ford (Mich.), William Clay (Mo.), and Stephen J. Solarz (N.Y.). They had sponsored bills for a statutory labor relations program with a broad scope of bargaining and an employee right to strike, and they obviously would not be satisfied with a bill that simply codified the executive order into law and only slightly strengthened the position of the unions. Furthermore, the Committee much reflected the attitude in Congress as a whole: civil service reform was not as important as many other issues before the lawmakers, and it lacked strong voter appeal. In the language commonly used, it was not a "sexy issue," which the administration itself granted and knew was a minus factor.

A further difficulty was that Committee Chairman Robert C. Nix (Pa.) faced a difficult campaign in the primaries and could not be expected to have the time to do an effective job of managing the bills within committee and on the House floor. Committee Vice-Chairman Morris K. Udall (Ariz.) had opposed Carter in the presidential primaries, and relationships between the two were presumed not to be very close.

Carter had not had dramatic successes with his legislative proposals. He wanted to make good on his campaign promise to reinvigorate the bureaucracy and, in late 1977, it appeared to him and his political advisers that "civil service reform was a possible winner" (Sugarman 1979: 10).

The Administration Strategy

The administration's political strategy was to develop support within the executive branch, in the country as a whole, and in Congress. Thorough planning and careful attention to detail characterized this effort in which Civil Service Commission Chairman Alan K. Campbell played a prominent role.

The process of building support within the executive branch had started long before submission of the legislation to Congress. After naming Campbell as Chairman and Jule M. Sugarman as Vice-Chairman of the Commission, Carter had told them to work with OMB on plans for civil service reform, and that he wanted the "bulk of the people in this effort" to be career employees. Experienced federal employees knew the personnel problems the best and recommendations they produced "would more likely be credible with the rest of the public service" (Sugarman 1979: 4).

Accordingly, a Personnel Reorganization Project was established under the joint leadership of Campbell and of Wayne Granquist, OMB Associate Director for Management. Most of the more than 100 persons assigned to the project were career employees, including managers and personnel generalists, and the project was headed by a highly-respected retired federal executive, Dwight Ink. In Sugarman's opinion, one of the most significant decisions made in carrying out this project was to hold hearings, 17 in all, at field locations throughout the country. (About 87 percent of all federal employees are stationed in the field.) At these hearings, agency field personnel testified and gave their opinions as to what the problems were and the changes needed in the personnel system. These views were forwarded to project task forces in Washington which had been studying different personnel areas and consulting with many organizations and individuals. The task forces put together all this information and prepared seven option papers that were sent for comment to about 1,500 individuals and groups, within and outside the government. Thus, when the task forces made their recommendations to Campbell and Granquist, the point of view of the federal employee and of numerous interested persons had been ascertained (Sugarman 1979: 5–8).

In Washington, a Working Group was established, consisting of the Assistant Secretaries for Administration in each department and major agencies. According to Sugarman (Sugarman 1979: 8, 9):

> . . . that group became in effect a steering committee for the full effort. We decided that we should not propose anything that did not have full support of the members of that committee. . . The reason for our decision was that civil service legislation had typically gotten nowhere in the Congress because among other reasons it had been torn apart by the agencies, and it really didn't have their support. So we started very early with the belief that we needed to have a government-wide position, not simply a position of the Commission and OMB.
>
> There were major changes that occurred because the Assistant Secretaries said, "no that's not workable, that's not practicable in terms of the way we think our departments have to operate. . ." At two points in the process we met with the Under-secretaries and at three points. . . the President actually devoted part of the cabinet meeting to discussion of these recommendations.

Also in Washington, a legislative task group was established to coordinate contacts with members of Congress and plan strategies for reaching the media and other support sources. It included Richard A. Pettigrew, Assistant to the President for Reorganization; representatives of the White House Congressional Liaison Office, the White House Press Office, and the White House Domestic Policy Staff; and designees of OMPB and the Civil Service Commission. This voluntary arrangement was particularly needed because many members of Congress were not familiar with the details of federal personnel management.

The legislative task group held briefing sessions with members of the House and Senate Committees considering the legislation and with their professional staffs. Committee staff were provided with extensive background information on the proposed legislation. Members of the legislative task group also arranged for and attended meetings between President Carter and these congressional committee members.

President Carter directly involved himself in the efforts to develop support for the bill. For example, he asked Cabinet members to make known their interest in the bill to their congressional contacts. Campbell relates (Campbell 1979: 3):

> There was a great deal of surprise and interest by members of the Armed Forces and the Foreign Affairs Committees when they got calls from Secretaries Brown and Vance saying they very much wanted the civil service reform passed because it was terribly important to them in the running of their departments. And that was done, by the way, with the leadership of the President, who said to the Cabinet, quite correctly, that this was a matter which is not the responsibility of a particular department or agency. This was something that related to all of us; therefore, all of us had to work for it.

THE POLITICS OF CIVIL SERVICE REFORM 173

Successful efforts were made to obtain the support of a diversity of business, labor, public interest, professional, civic, civil rights, and other organizations. Two organizations usually at opposite poles, the Business Roundtable, an association of business executives, and Common Cause, a very active public interest organization, both supported the bill. The strange spectacle was seen of representatives of the Roundtable and of Common Cause visiting members of Congress to lobby for the bill. Sugarman comments, "to my knowledge they have never agreed on anything else in history" (Sugarman 1979: 22).

Campbell and the administration realized that, although support for civil service reform was broad-based, it was not intense. Quoting Campbell again (Campbell 1979: 1),

> Yet these were not groups that would give a lot of time and effort to this because it wasn't in their direct line of interest . . . So the mobilizing and orchestrating of that support had to come from us, and we started out very early to do that. I met with editorial boards of literally dozens of major newspapers across the country. Out of that came overwhelming editorial support from newspapers like the *New York Times, Chicago Tribune, Chicago Sun-Times, Washington Post,* and *Los Angeles Times.* More than 200 editorials were written in favor of civil service reform. There's no question that helped us . . . because we had some difficulty arousing substantial interest on the Hill in the legislation.

The *St. Louis Globe-Democrat* wrote: "Congress should recognize that the great majority of Americans will support President Carter on the civil service reform plan" (*St. Louis Globe-Democrat* 1978: March 3). Only a handful of newspapers opposed the bill as a whole. The *Federal Times,* a Washington, D.C. weekly that is read by many federal employees and reflects their concerns, published numerous editorials attacking the proposals. Its theme, which mirrored widespread employee fears, was that the administration wanted to politicize the civil service system and desired "yes" people in the top executive posts. The SES scheme could only intimidate executives, because OPM would screen in executives and force out others for political and other non-merit related reasons. Lower level employees would be dismissed on the same basis. As consideration of the bill reached successive critical stages, there were new bursts of favorable editorials. Employee unions and other opponents of the legislation referred to the "slick public relations job" but granted its effectiveness.

Strategy with the Unions

The administration carefully formulated its plan for dealing with the employee unions. The four unions representing the largest number of federal workers are the American Federation of Government Employees (AFGE), an AFL-CIO affiliate; the National Federation of Federal Employees (NFFE); the National Association of Government Employees (NAGE); and the National Treasury Employees Union (NTEU) which recently has been organizing employees in other federal agencies as well. AFGE represents about 700,000 employees, NFFE close to 139,000, NAGE some 78,500, and NTEU about 99,000.

NFFE, NAGE, and NTEU early took strong positions against the bill. Vincent L. Connery, NTEU President, said the bill presented the "potential for unchecked political manipulation of the civil service by the White House." He claimed the OPM Director would become the "personnel czar of the entire Federal government" (House Committee on Post Office and Civil Service 1978: 160). NFFE President James Peirce thought Carter was honorable and decent but that "laws should be written not only to provide for the good and the honorable, but also to guard against the abuses of a Watergate" (House Committee on Post Office and Civil Service 1978: 279). Alan K. Whitney, NAGE Executive Vice-President, stated that "civil service reform as embodied in these proposals equals the ruination of the merit system in Federal employment" (House Committee on Post Office and Civil Service 1978: 657).

The administration plan was to concentrate on getting at least the qualified support of AFGE and of the AFL-CIO Executive Council and then to negotiate with them on their objections to parts of the legislation. Passage of the bill would be easier if accommodation with the unions could be reached, and Carter, who had been elected with AFL-CIO backing, preferred that the legislation pass with labor support.

Kenneth Blaylock, AFGE President, wanted a much stronger Title VII than the administration had proposed, a view shared by the AFL-CIO, but AFGE and the parent union also wanted very much a statutory basis for the labor relations program. They knew that Congress had become more conservative, reflecting the public mood, and that there was no reasonable prospect of passage of separate legislation providing this statutory basis. Only if made a part of the reform bill could this long-delayed goal of the unions be achieved. AFGE's rival unions had so many objections to the reform bill that they did not think the price was worth it. Blaylock paid dearly within AFGE for his willingness to work with the administration on the bill, rather than to oppose it outright. At the summer 1978 annual convention of AFGE, the delegates passed a resolution instructing its officials not to negotiate any further on the bill, and Blaylock was almost defeated for re-election as AFGE's President. However, the AFGE Executive Council later authorized him to continue his negotiations to obtain a stronger Title VII. . . .

Final Enactment

On September 13, 1978, the House passed the bill by a vote of 385 to 10. Five of the negative votes were registered by members from the Washington, D.C. area and from Maryland.

Among the differences to be resolved by Senate-House conferees were: (1) the House standard for sustaining adverse actions was preponderance of evidence, the Senate's was reasonable evidence; (2) the Senate bill called for government-wide implementation of the SES, without any time limitation, but the House bill would launch the SES as a two-year experiment in only three agencies; (3) the Senate bill would allocate to a merit increase pool part of the annual comparability increases for GS-13 through 15 supervisors, whereas the House measure would automatically grant the comparability increases; (4) the House bill would require agencies to pay employee attorney fees in cases of successful appeals to the MSPB, provided such payment was warranted. The Senate bill would require agencies to pay such fees if the MSPB rules that the agency had taken the adverse action in bad faith; and (5) the Senate wanted the OPM Director to be appointed for a four-year term, coterminous with that of the President, and to be removable only for cause, while the House bill contained no such provision.

The conferees agreed that the standard of proof in misconduct cases would be "preponderance of evidence." Because of the "difficulty of proving that an employee's performance is unacceptable," they provided for a "lower standard" in performance cases, namely, the agency would be upheld "if the action is supported by substantial evidence in the record before the MSPB" (*Civil Service Reform Act of 1978, Conference Report* 1978: 139).

The experimental approach for introducing the SES was rejected, and the SES was to go into effect nine months after the bill's enactment. Five years from the SES's effective date, Congress could, by concurrent resolution, disapprove its continuation (*Civil Service Reform Act of 1978, Conference Report* 1978: 149).

The conferees provided that employees under the merit pay system would automatically receive half of the amount of annual comparability adjustments and that OPM could in its discretion "pass along additional portions of the full adjustment increases" (*Civil Service Reform Act of 1978, Conference Report* 1978: 151). As to payment of attorney's fees, it was authorized "in cases where employee prevails on merits and the deciding official determines that attorneys' fees are warranted in the interest of justice, including a case involving a prohibited personnel practice or where the agency's action was clearly without merit" (*Civil Service Reform Act of 1978, Conference Report* 1978: 142). Finally, the President could remove the OPM Director for reasons other than cause, but the Director would have a four-year term, not necessarily coterminous with that of the President (*Civil Service Reform Act of 1978, Conference Report* 1978: 132).

A newspaper report is revealing: "Conferees will meet Tuesday to wrap up some loose ends, but they urged dissenting lobbyists not to bother changing any minds over the weekend. They stressed that yesterday's agreements are final" (Sawyer 1978).

Summary of the Provisions of the Legislation

As signed into law by President Carter, the Civil Service Reform Act of 1978 included:

1. Establishment of an Office of Personnel Management, an independent establishment in the Executive Branch. The OPM Director is appointed by the President, subject to Senate confirmation, and he or she serves for a four-year term. The OPM Director is authorized to delegate any of his or her functions to executive agency heads, except the authority for competitive examinations for position with requirements "common to agencies in the Federal Government." In exceptional cases, justified by considerations of economy and efficiency, "in which such delegation will not weaken the application of the merit system principles," authority for such examinations may be delegated.[4]

2. Creation of a three-member bipartisan Merit Systems Protection Board, the members to have seven-year nonrenewable terms, to be appointed by the President with Senate confirmation, and to be removable only for inefficiency, neglect of duty, or malfeasance in office.

3. Clear statements of both merit principles and prohibited practices and provision of enforcement machinery to prevent such practices. The position of MSPB Special Counsel is created, the Counsel to be named by the President, with the Senate's approval, for a five-year term, and to be removable by the President only for inefficiency, neglect of duty, or malfeasance in office.

The MSPB is empowered to review OPM rules and regulations and to veto rules it believes constitute prohibited personnel practices. The Special Counsel is authorized to receive and investigate allegations of prohibited personnel practices and to recommend corrective action to the MSPB if he or she determines that there are reasonable grounds to believe a prohibited practice has occurred. The MSPB is authorized to order appropriate corrective action by the agency or individual involved, as well as disciplinary action (removal, reduction in grade, disbarment from federal employment for not more than five years, suspension, reprimand, or a civil fine of not more than $1,000).

Prohibited personnel practice includes reprisal against an employee for disclosure of information that he or she "reasonably believes evidences" a "violation of any law, rule, or regulation, or. . . mismanagement, a gross waste of funds, an abuse of authority, or a substantial and specific danger to public health or safety."[5] Any MSPB member may stay personnel actions temporarily, and the MSPB indefinitely, if it agrees with the Special Counsel after hearing oral or written presentations by the Special Counsel and the agency concerned.

4. Elimination of veterans preference for nondisabled military retirees at or above the rank of Major or Lieutenant Commander. Veterans with disability of thirty (30) percent or more may receive noncompetitive appointments to positions that may lead to career employment. This latter provision has been recommended by the administration.

5. Continuation of the rule of 3 in certifying names from eligible lists. The administration's proposal for a rule of 7 and other flexibility was rejected.

6. Modification of adverse action procedures. The employee may appeal to the MSPB, and the burden of proof rests with the agency. In cases of alleged misconduct by the employee, the agency must be supported by a preponderance of the evidence. If the charge against the employee is alleged incompetence, the agency must show substantial evidence for its action.

Agencies must give an employee at least 30 days advance notice in writing of proposed dismissal or demotion because of unacceptable performance. The agency must make its final decision, in writing, within 30 days after expiration of the notice period.

7. New performance appraisal systems. Each agency is required to develop one or more performance appraisal systems, to encourage employee participation in establishing performance standards, and to use the results of the appraisals as a basis for training, rewarding, and removing employees.

Pursuant to OPM regulations, each performance appraisal system shall provide for performance standards to serve as the basis for evaluating employee performance, such standards to be communicated to the employee at the beginning of each appraisal period. Notice of reduction in grade or removal for unacceptable performance shall conform to the notice requirements stated in (6) above. The employee must be advised of the specific instances of unacceptable performance upon which the proposed action is based and given reasonable time to answer orally or in writing. If, because of improved performance, the employee is not reduced in grade or removed during the 30 day notice period, and if the employee's performance continues to be acceptable for one year from the date of the notice period, any notation of the proposed action shall be removed from the agency record relating to the employee.

8. A merit pay system for managers and supervisors in GS-13 through 15, to be phased in gradually and go into effect in all agencies by October 1, 1981. At least half of each annual comparability increase must be granted, and OPM is authorized to grant more than half if it so desires. Superiors of GS 13–15 managers and supervisors will review their performance annually and decide what size merit increase to grant them. Funds for these increases will come from a merit pay pool built from the remaining comparability pay, plus funds that otherwise would have been spent on step increases, which are eliminated.

9. Creation of a Senior Executive Service. The SES, consisting of approximately 8,000 persons formerly in grades GS 16–18 and in levels IV and V of the Executive Schedule, is government-wide, although a few agencies like the FBI are exempted. Five years after the SES's effective date, Congress can, by concurrent resolution, discontinue the SES.

The SES includes two types of positions: (1) career reserved—-may be filled only by career employees; and (2) general—-may be held by career or noncareer employees. The number of career-reserved positions may not be less than the number of SES positions which, at the time of the passage of the legislation, were in GS 16–18 and were filled by competitive examination. Not more than ten (10) percent of SES positions in the government, nor more than twenty-five (25) percent of such positions in any one agency, may be noncareer (except in a few agencies that had a higher percentage of noncareer employees on the date of enactment).

The individual agencies designate the positions to be included in SES. Employees in these designated positions were given 90 days to decide whether or not to join SES or remain in their present positions. SES candidates must have five years of current continuous service, but, to bring in new talent, up to thirty (30) percent of SES appointees can be exempted from this requirement. . . .

10. Placing the federal labor relations program on a statutory basis. Title VII enacts into law the provisions of the executive order labor relations program, adding provisions contained in the Udall amendment. The program is administered by a Federal Labor Relations Authority, the three members of which are appointed by the President, with Senate confirmation, for 5-year terms and who may be removed only for cause. The President also appoints an FLRA general Counsel, with the approval of the Senate for a 5-year term. The General Counsel, whom the President may remove at any time, is responsible for investigating and prosecuting charges of unfair labor practices by unions or agency managements.

Summary Remarks

In a television interview with correspondent Bill Moyers, President Carter, in recounting the accomplishments of the administration, mentioned bringing the bureaucracy under control. Chief executives, particularly new ones, often reason that one of the first obstacles to their leadership to be removed must be holdover agency top career officials. The chief executive's thinking is that many of these officials can be expected to be unresponsive to the policy changes sought by new administrations and some of them may even sabotage the new directions. While this feeling is particularly strong if there has been a change in political party control of the government, it also exists when a new president of the same party is elected.

Chief executives do not view their attempts to "control the bureaucracy" as politicization, but the line of distinction between responsiveness and politicization is a blurred one. During the Senate debate, Stevens of Alaska cited John F. Kennedy as one example: "He found himself surrounded by an administration which he felt was unsympathetic to his views. In order to get the best results out of his New Frontier program, he wanted to find ideological sympathizers to fill policymaking positions. Kennedy appointed the Special Assistant for Congressional Relations to 'clear out the executive branch' of all persons whom he felt could not be trusted politically."[6] Stevens cited other examples, and certainly there are many such examples in American history.

Many career employees and, except for AFGE and the AFL-CIO, the unions strongly opposed the reform bill because they were convinced that it meant politicization in Carter's or future administrations. Their view of "management flexibility" was very different from that of the administration. To them, such flexibility sooner or later led to political abuses. Of course, employees and unions were concerned about job security, but many of the employees opposed to the bill were known as competent and dedicated. The conflict was basically one of differing perspectives of the reality. Union leaders indicated that any federal executive who wanted to dismiss or transfer an employee could do so without undue difficulty under existing regulations; the will was lacking not the means.

Although Carter prevailed, the question remained: was his conception of the difficulties by an "unresponsive" bureaucracy accurate? While the relationship between noncareer and career officials is often one of mutual distrust, is the resistance of career officials a major explanation of why "government doesn't work?" Perhaps this is largely a fiction carried in the minds of chief executives; perhaps the real explanation of the failure of government programs is the basic complexity of the societal problems with which government attempts to deal. This is not an argument against the changes made by the new legislation, for an improved bureaucracy is desirable in every way. Rather, it is a question of accurate diagnosis of the most important reasons why "government doesn't work."

With approval of the reform bill, the Carter administration destroyed several political myths. One was that comprehensive personnel system changes could not succeed politically, nor could any legislation opposed by most of the unions, nor could any attempt to curtail veterans preference come even close to succeeding. . . .

The planning of the administration's strategy for gaining approval of the legislation was a model of thoroughness. Execution of that strategy with the press and the various business, civic, professional, and other organizations was very good. Some criticisms of ineptness were made of the lobbying with Congress, but in the main it was carried out effectively by Campbell, Pettigrew, and other members of the administration. Udall's management of the bill was superb. Of course, it was good fortune for the administration that he was available and willing. . . .

Notes

1. Prepared for delivery at the 1979 Annual Meeting of The American Political Science Association, The Washington Hilton Hotel, August 31–September 3, 1979. Copyright 1979 by Felix A. Nigro, Athens, Georgia.

2. S. 2640, 95th Congress, 2nd Session.

3. Conversation between John C. Stennis and Felix A. Nigro, March 10, 1979.

4. Public Law 95–454, 95th Congress, October 13, 1978, 92 Stat. 1120.

5. Public Law 35–454, 95th Congress, October 13, 1978, 92 Stat. 1125.

6. Congressional Record-Senate, S 14273, August 24, 1978.

References

"Campbell Reflects on Reform Process," (1979). *Public Administration Times* 2 (January 16):3.

"Documentation," (1971). *Public Administration Review* 31 (March/April).

Heclo, Hugh (1977). *A Government of Strangers: Executive Politics in Washington*. Washington, D.C.: Brookings.

House Committee on Post Office and Civil Service (1978). *Civil Service Reform*, 95th Congress, 2nd Session. Washington, D.C.: Government Printing Office.

Mace, Don (1978). "Carter's Reform Bill Floundering on Hill." *Federal Times*, August 18.

Nigro, Felix A. and Lloyd G. Nigro (1976). *The New Public Personnel Administration*, Itasca, Ill.: Peacock.

Sawyer, Kathy (1978). "Panel Clears Civil Service Revision Bill." *Washington Post*, September 29.

Senate Committee on Governmental Affairs (1978). *Civil Service Reform Act of 1978 and Reorganization Plan No. 2 of 1978*, 95th Congress, 2nd Session. Washington, D.C.: Government Printing Office.

——— (1978). *Appendix*. Washington, D.C.: Government Printing Office.

St. Louis Globe-Democrat (1978). March 3.

Stanley, David T. (1964). *The Higher Civil Service: An Evaluation of Federal Personnel Practices*. Washington, D.C.: Brookings.

Sugarman, Jule M. (1979). "Remarks." Congressional Operations Seminar for Managers, April 5.

Van Riper, Paul P. (1958). *History of the United States Civil Service*. New York: Harper and Row.

Vaughn, Robert (1972). *The Spoiled System: A Call for Civil Service Reform*. Washington, D.C.: Public Interest Group.

CHAPTER 20

THE WINTER COMMISSION

Deregulation and Public Personnel Administration

FRANK J. THOMPSON

On June 24, 1993, the National Commission on the State and Local Public Service presented its first report, *Hard Truths/Tough Choices: An Agenda for State and Local Reform,* to President Bill Clinton at the White House. The commission (customarily referred to as the Winter Commission after its chair, William Winter) offered ten major recommendations under the basic themes of removing the barriers to executive leadership, to lean and responsive government, to a high-performance workforce, and to meaningful citizen involvement. It also called for reducing fiscal uncertainty for states and localities through health care reform.

While the Winter Commission's proposals targeted a range of institutions, none was more central than the civil service systems that do so much to shape human resource management. In this regard, the report's fifth recommendation called for an "end to civil service paralysis" by deregulating governments' personnel systems. It noted that "sadly, many state and local governments have created such rule-bound and complicated systems that merit is often the last value served." Designed "to protect against failure" these "hidebound" systems had quashed "the spirit of innovation" (pp. 24–25). The report went on to recommend several changes, most of which sought to usher greater flexibility into the personnel system. These included:

- Greater decentralization of the merit system;
- Less reliance on written tests;
- Rejection of the rule of three and other requirements that stringently restrict managerial discretion in picking from an eligible list;
- Less deference to seniority and veterans preference;
- Reduction in the number of job classifications;
- More streamlined procedures for removing employees from positions;
- More portable pension systems to facilitate mobility across governments;
- Greater freedom to award extra pay for outstanding performance by work teams.

From 14 *Review of Public Personnel Administration*, 2: 5–10, Spring 1994. Copyright © 1994 Sage Publications. Reprinted with permission.

The Winter Commission is not, of course, alone in calling for less rule-bound public personnel management. Its predecessor, the Volcker Commission, had also endorsed greater managerial flexibility in this area (National Commission on the Public Service 1989). Moreover, shortly after the release of *Hard Truths/Tough Choices,* President Clinton's National Performance Review (1993) (with Vice President Gore in the lead) released its diagnosis and prescription. Among other things, the report pointed to the reams of rules that tied the hands of federal personnel managers. Aside from commissions, others joined the deregulation chorus in the early 1990s. For instance, Garvey and DiIulio (1994: 26–27) in a Brookings Institution volume stressed the need to reduce or eliminate "personnel rules and work regulations that sap public employees' productivity and make careers in public service unattractive to talented, energetic potential candidates" (see also Osborne and Gaebler 1992). In sum, the notion that administrators ought to have more opportunity to choose among meaningful possible courses of action or inaction in managing personnel has become a central tenet of the "reinvention" movement.

Springboard to Inquiry

The Winter Commission was not a turnkey commission, releasing its report and then disbanding. Instead, it has pursued a vigorous dissemination strategy, including challenge grants focused on specific jurisdictions, to galvanize action on the recommendations of *Hard Truths/Tough Choices*. But the Winter Commission report should be seen as more than a prescriptive, action-oriented document. It can also help shape the research agenda for specialists in public personnel administration and lead to the development of more satisfying theory. The intellectual strands embedded in the Winter Commission report and the "reinvention" literature more generally comprise a rich set of working hypotheses which need additional testing. This spirit of inquiry animates this symposium. It takes the Winter Commission hypothesis on deregulation seriously and then proceeds to examine its implications in several different jurisdictions. State and local governments provide a wonderful laboratory for exploring hypotheses related to deregulation because they vary so much along this dimension. To some degree quantitative studies can help us understand the implications of this variation (e.g., Elling 1992, Hays and Kearney 1991). But greater insight also depends on systematic qualitative comparison jurisdictions with an eye toward what difference, if any, the degree of rule intensiveness makes.

This symposium can lay no claim to having captured the full range of internal regulation present in state and local personnel systems. It does not draw on a random sample of jurisdictions. But the five governments analyzed do vary considerably across the spectrum of deregulation. At the regulated end of the continuum, Steven Cohen and William Eimicke describe the rule-dense, highly constraining personnel system of New York City. Carolyn Ban and Norma Riccucci continue on this theme with their analysis of rule intensive system in New York State government. At the other end of the continuum, the city of Indianapolis described by James Perry, Lois Wise and Margo Martin, has always been a non-regulated system—one substantially free of the encumbrances that so concern the Winter Commission. St. Louis city government, described by Lana Stein, has personnel processes subject to substantial regulation but with nowhere near the rule density of the two New York systems. Finally, Bart Wechsler captures the dynamics of reform in Florida's substantially decentralized personnel system, where officials boldly set out to reinvent merit practices.

A Sampler of Lessons

What conclusions flow from this symposium concerning the dynamics, potential and limits of deregulation? Among the propositions and lessons embedded in these studies, five deserve particular emphasis.

First, highly regulated personnel processes generate much improvisation to "beat the system" in part because managers want more flexibility and in part because of the substantial costs involved in sustaining the internal regulatory apparatus. Ban and Riccucci note, for instance, how the managerial quest for greater control over promotions led to the proliferation of small, special classifications in New York State. That way, these officials could reach the person they wanted on the eligible list. For their part, Cohen and Eimicke show how the great numbers of provisional appointments in New York City (those exempt from merit system requirements) substantially derive from sheer overload on the personnel staff agencies. To require elaborate testing for virtually all positions is expensive; financially hard-pressed policymakers are unlikely to invest the monies needed to surmount the backlog. Personnel agencies cannot, therefore, keep up with the demand for testing and other required activities. This leads to an alternative system based on provisional appointments which managers often prefer, but which union leaders resent.

Patterns like these may prompt the view that informal means almost invariably arise to make highly regulated personnel systems livable. But this view ignores the costs of gaming the system. Maneuvering to get around the rigidities of the personnel procedures eats up time and effort that might be more productively devoted to the core tasks of the agency. It can also encourage an agency culture excessively disrespectful of existing rules and procedures. Emphasizing that officials can only succeed by skirting the rules can undermine respect for authority more generally. The informal adjustments may also divert energy from more serious efforts to reform the personnel systems.

Second, non-regulated or deregulated personnel systems become more vulnerable to patronage pressures by elected politicians, but in many settings these politicians have little incentive to pursue this end. Stein's analysis of the fairly regulated system in St. Louis—a "city of friendships" and a "city of favors" with a heritage of machine politics, southern style—suggests that massive deregulation might well whet the appetites of politicians to penetrate personnel practices in undesirable ways. It remains open to question, however, whether incremental steps toward deregulation would unleash destructive politicization in St. Louis. Stein acknowledges, for instance, that certain reforms of the classification system might well be productive. The assessment of non-regulated Indianapolis by Perry, Wise, and Martin depicts a system with a strong tradition of partisan politicization of personnel processes moving steadily toward greater professionalism and merit. In fact, the mayor wants to be on the cutting edge of the reinvention movement. Their analysis suggests that less regulated personnel systems probably have greater upside and downside potential in the quest to promote efficient and responsive governance. The inclinations of the chief executive and other top executives may well be the most critical factor influencing whether these systems move to the high or low road in terms of patronage.

Several factors reduce (but do not eliminate) the risk of downside problems in non-regulated systems. Supreme Court decisions over the last 20 years have made it more difficult to incorporate overt partisan preferences into hiring and firing decisions (e.g., *Rutan v. Republican Party of Illinois* 1990). Moreover, elected officials in many settings realize that the best politics is "good management"—respecting competence and striving for efficient and effective service delivery. Finally, politicians bent on rewarding their friends and supporters often have more alluring plums to provide than government jobs—namely, the allocation of lucrative contracts to private firms.

Third, reinvention politics may impose deregulation solutions on settings where rule-intensiveness is not the critical problem. One of the boldest personnel reform initiatives of the post-Reagan period occurred in the State of Florida, which sunsetted its merit system in the early 1990s. Yet, as Wechsler describes, the State of Florida has a decentralized personnel system with much less of a regulatory superstructure than New York State or New York City. This mismatch between solution and problem limited the accomplishments of the Florida reform initiative. This is not to suggest that issues of deregulation are irrelevant in Florida. Wechsler's analysis reminds us that in decentralized personnel systems, the line agencies may still generate rules and an organizational culture that leaves managers feeling highly constrained.

Fourth, major reform directed toward deregulation will not come easily in personnel systems, but quiet, constructive change can occur in even the most difficult settings. The articles on New York City and New York State hammer home how difficult it can be to forge change. Adversarial labor relations rooted in a culture of mistrust makes it almost impossible to secure even modest steps toward deregulation (e.g., slight expansion of the rule of three). Players in this arena adhere to a kind of domino theory of labor relations where any concession is interpreted as sign of weakness and vulnerability. Yet even in such gridlocked settings as those in New York, Ban and Riccucci show how administrative and technological change has occurred.

Finally, the deregulation of civil service systems should not be seen as the grand elixir for better human resource management in the public sector. As Wechsler's analysis of Florida reminds us, low pay and inadequate investment in training and education can quickly scuttle the benefits of deregulation. The entire repertoire of "reinvention" tools will do little to help in jurisdictions that pay so poorly that they cannot attract and retain skilled personnel. Moreover, competitive pay scales can help mitigate problems with the most regulated systems. For instance, New York State agencies manage to get by and occasionally achieve high levels of innovation and effectiveness partly because they attract many quality personnel with salaries and benefits that rank among the highest offered by state governments (Gold and Ritchie 1993). Consistent underinvestment in training and education can also undermine deregulation. Union leaders repeatedly and appropriately complain that granting more discretion to managers will have negative effects if these administrators do not grasp the rudiments of human resource management. In emphasizing the importance of creating "a learning government," the Winter Commission called for a training and education budget amounting to at least three percent of total personnel costs. Taking this recommendation seriously and working to ensure a high-quality learning experience would create a more favorable milieu for the benefits of deregulation to be realized.

These five propositions comprise only a sampler of those embedded in this symposium. Subsequent research on deregulating public personnel administration can derive some benefit from focusing on comparisons between the public and private sector. But I believe that even greater knowledge dividends will result from targeting the great variation present within our federal system. For all the talk about states and localities being the laboratories of democracy, systematic comparative inquiry into civil service systems to develop and test better theory tends to be the path not taken. This symposium takes a few steps down this path in the hope that others will follow and travel a farther distance.

References

Elling, R.C. (1992). *Public Management in the States*. Westport, Conn.: Praeger.

Garvey, G.J. and J.J. Dilulio, Jr. (1994). "Sources of Public Service Overregulation," pp. 12–36 in J.J. Dilulio, Jr. (ed.) *Deregulating the Public Service*. Washington, D.C: Brookings.

Gold, S.D. and S. Ritchie (1993). "Compensation of State and Local Employees: Sorting Out the Issues." pp. 163–196 in F.J. Thompson (ed.) *Revitalizing State and Local Public Service*. San Francisco: Jossey-Bass.

Hays, S.W. and R.C.Kearney (1991). "Public Personnel Values in State Civil Service Systems: A Preliminary Examination and Ranking." Paper delivered at the Annual Meeting of the American Political Science Association. Washington, D.C.

National Commission on the Public Service (1989). *Leadership for America: Rebuilding the Public Service*. Washington, D.C.: National Commission on the Public Service.

National Commission on the State and Local Public Service (1993). *Hard Truths/Tough Choices: An Agenda for State and Local Reform*. Albany, N.Y.: Rockefeller Institute of Government.

National Performance Review (1993). *From Red Tape to Results: Creating a Government That Works Better and Costs Less*. Washington, D.C.: Government Printing Office.

Osborne, D. and T. Gaebler (1992). *Reinventing Government*. Reading, Mass.: Addison-Wesley.

Rutan v. Republican Party of Illinois (1990). 110 S. Ct. 2729.

CHAPTER 21

REINVENTING THE FEDERAL CIVIL SERVICE

Drivers of Change

CAROLYN BAN

Introduction

As others have noted, the formal NPR [National Performance Review] process had two
major streams. It encompassed both an attempt to improve the management of government and a focus of cutting the size of government, frequently an uneasy juxtaposition.
Increasingly, the NPR effort has shown what Kettl (1994) termed as a preoccupation
with savings over improvement of performance. While the good government strand of
the NPR included explicit attempts to revamp the civil service system, the NPR effort to
cut government focusing heavily upon the staff functions, including personnel, may have
had an even greater effect than the efforts directed specifically at civil service reform. The
response to drastic cuts was mediated by two other factors: the availability of sophisticated
new technology and ongoing efforts to change the culture of human resources. Finally,
the Government Performance and Results Act (GPRA), currently being implemented,
will have an increasing effect on the civil service system. Let us look at each of these
drivers of reform in turn and then examine their cumulative effects.

The NPR Recommendations

The NPR overall report, *Creating a Government that Works Better and Costs Less,* and
the specific report on *Reinventing Human Resources Management* provide an extensive
laundry-list of recommended reforms in the civil service system. But, taken as a whole,
they focus on three key themes: deregulation, decentralization, and delegation. First,
the NPR calls for elimination of the *Federal Personnel Manual* (FPM), the 10,000-page
guideline to personnelists on how to implement Title 5 (the law governing the civil Service
system) and the *Code of Federal Regulations* (CFR) (the official regulations implementing that law). Describing the current system as "complex and rule-bound" (NPR 1993a:

From 22 *Public Administration Quarterly*, 1: 21–34, Spring 1998. Copyright © 1998 Southern
Public Administration Education Foundation, Inc. Reprinted with permission.

22), the NPR called not only for eliminating the FPM but also for scrapping all agency implementing directives.

A second focus of the NPR recommendations was decentralization. In particular, the NPR recommended that OPM abandon its traditional role of gatekeeper of the civil service system. OPM would no longer conduct exams centrally and maintain central registers. Instead, it would delegate authority to agencies to do all their own examining, expanding a movement begun as a result of the Civil Service Reform Act (CSRA) of 1978 (Ban and Marzotto 1984). In addition, job candidates would no longer be required to complete the Standard Form (SF) 178; they could simply submit a resume.

Third, the NPR called for delegating more responsibility for managing the human resources function to line managers themselves. Giving managers more authority in hiring, classifying, and assessing the performance of their employees was seen as an integral part of breaking through the traditional culture of control that characterized the civil service system. The NPR's call for reform of the classification system (1993b: 19–27) was consonant with this goal; adopting broadbanding, which has been tested by the Navy and National Institute of Standards and Technology (NIST) through demonstration projects, would both simplify one of the more convoluted aspects of the civil service system and provide managers more authority to set pay to assist in recruiting and rewarding top performance.

The NPR: Status of Implementation

The NPR as a whole addressed many areas of government management. While some NPR recommendations have led to dramatic reform, formal reform efforts in the civil service area have been constrained by the political environment, particularly since the Republicans took control of Congress in 1994. To be sure, some reforms could be made administratively and some of these have had real impact. OPM has really gotten out of the business of maintaining standing registers and only conducts hiring tests under contract to agencies. Thus, the hiring system has become almost totally decentralized.

But other reforms may be more apparent than real. The administration abolished the *Federal Personnel Manual* with considerable fanfare and press coverage showing stacks of regulations being piled over a front-loader for disposal. Has it really made a difference? Reports are decidedly mixed. Based on this author's interviews with a range of informants in Washington, there is widespread recognition that the FPM is still out there and being consulted by personnelists. As a senior Hill staff told this author:

> The FPM was tossed out the window, but people still live by it, so it was more symbolic than anything else. Title 5 and the CFR are still here, so without changing the fundamental rules, you've not helped them by eliminating the FPM. But if you want to make a symbolic gesture, I accept that.

An analyst in an oversight agency pointed out that the FPM may be dying because it is not being updated. Others observe that abolishing the FPM without providing any replacement did not make life easier for personnelists who are still charged with upholding the law.

Reports on efforts to delegate more personnel authority to managers are also mixed. Oversight agencies have surveys out in the field now. Final results are not in but it is clear that agency experiences here differ sharply. Some agencies are delegating aggressively while, in others, managers report that little has changed. And, in some agencies, managers are rejecting the additional authority (and responsibility) being offered.

At the same time that NPR proposed giving managers broader personnel authority, it called for "delayering," reducing the number of line managers. These proposals have been criticized as putting an undue burden on managers: at the same time that managers were asked to take on more responsibility, they were also expected to handle a broader span of control (Ban 1997b). In fact, compliance has been uneven. While hard figures are still not in, there is substantial evidence that, in some agencies, first-line supervisors have simply been relabeled "team leaders," officially defining them as non-managers but not actually changing their responsibilities.

But while some changes are, indeed, being made administratively, others require legislation. Initially, Congress was supportive of at least some aspects of NPR. It passed the Federal Workforce Restructuring Act (sometimes referred to as the "Buyout Bill") to facilitate downsizing government (Ingraham 1996, Foreman 1995) as well as the Federal Acquisition Streamlining Act which deregulated the federal procurement system. But legislation on civil service reform was not introduced until after the 1994 congressional election gave Republicans control of Congress; it fell victim to divided government and, according to some informants, failure on the part of the administration to push the legislation effectively. That means that more fundamental system reform, such as adopting broadbanding government wide, is not likely to take place soon.

Cutback Management: The Up Side of Downsizing

While NPR's specific proposals to reinvent civil service have had limited effect, the sharp cuts in the size of human resource staffs appear to have had a much more far reaching effect. The shrinkage in human resource staffs has, indeed, been dramatic. From 1992 to 1996, the number of people employed in personnel occupations declined by 18 percent. In comparison, procurement staff declined by 12 percent and budgeting staff by six percent (MSPB 1997). The cuts varied somewhat in individual agencies with some reducing personnel staff by over one-quarter. Some critics have expressed the concern that such sharp cuts, without the deregulation and resulting administrative efficiencies that were their justification, could seriously weaken government capacity, increasing the 'hollowing" of government (Pfiffner 1997).

Given the severity of the cuts, it was obvious to HR directors that business as usual would not permit them to offer the service levels needed with the remaining staff. Their responses have taken two directions.

First, although early indications were that several agencies intended to decentralize the personnel function, even breaking up existing centralized offices, the most common strategy for coping with severe cuts has been to create centralized personnel processing offices. The Department of Veterans Affairs, the Departments of Agriculture, and Transportation have moved to a more centralized model. The Department of Defense recently announced that it was centralizing in six sites as major processing centers (see NAPA 1996, for discussions of change at Veterans Affairs and the Department of Defense).

When this author asked her informants whether this tendency was not in conflict with the stated values of NPR, especially decentralization and delegation to managers, she got very consistent responses. As one of them told her, "I don't think there's a necessary contradiction between centralizing personnel offices and decentralizing decision-making. Operations is just that—getting papers done, boiler-room stuff. It can be done anywhere."

The second response to severe cuts has been increased contracting out to the private sector or "franchising," i.e., internal contracting to other government agencies to perform routine personnel functions such as processing appointment forms or managing payroll. This trend shows up, for example, in the continued growth of the National Finance Center administered by the Department of Agriculture and located outside of New Orleans. It now processes paychecks for about 70 agencies and bureaus (NAPA 1996).

In sum, severe cuts are, as this author argued elsewhere (Ban 1997b: 278), a two-edged sword. While they are very traumatic for the individuals and organizations involved and can have a negative effect on morale and productivity, they "may force organizations to restructure or to try new approaches."

Two additional drivers have reinforced the changes triggered by reinvention in the HR (human resources) workforce. First is the availability of new technology. Agencies are moving rapidly to adopt complex new software that will permit much more sophisticated management of personnel. Thus, while routine processing is being centralized, new technologies, according to one informant, "actually makes it easier to decentralize the personnel function, and the technology allows you to push it right down to the manager's desk, using expert systems and access to data bases."

As she reported:

> There is more going on in this area than anyone expected this soon. Agencies are learning from each other. At least 80 percent of government has committed to new systems, either PeopleSoft or Oracle. The roll outs are from 1997 to 2000. The implications are tremendous. Traditional service delivery required personnel officers where the records were. Now records can be anywhere. It's better for quality control and accessibility to centralized records.

An additional driver of reform has been a changing approach to human resources management with far greater focus on customer service and on strategic human resources management. Personnelists have long been caught in the dilemma of trying to provide good customer service while still upholding the rules (Ban 1995). A number of agencies had already adopted the credo of customer service. While the NPR supported and reinforced this movement, it did not initiate it and many agencies had already moved quite far in this direction (Ban 1995, 1997a).

Some had implemented Total Quality Management (TQM) while others had stressed improved training and professionalism of personnel staff (Ban 1995). That movement has only intensified since the NPR recommendations appeared. Agency personnel staff, even under conditions of extreme scarcity, are using the combination of centralized routine processing and decentralized decision-making supported by new technology to provide what they hope will actually be better service to customers.

In addition, personnelists are looking for a place at the table, that is, the ability to participate in major agency decisions that have broader HR implications. As Perry and Mesch (1997: 26) explain, this is one of the key elements of what is being termed "strategic human resources management":

> One means for making the human resource function more supportive of mission accomplishment is to integrate human resources considerations into the strategic planning process. In order to accomplish this, human resources managers must become strategic partners with management and play an integral part on the strategic team in the initial stages of planning. . . . This means senior management must recognize the importance of the human resources contribution to the organization's strategic goals and must allow the human resources senior manager the same status and power as other top team players.

Results are mixed regarding the willingness of top agency management to accept the concept of strategic HR management. Anecdotal evidence, based on the author's interviews, is that, in some agencies, human resources directors perceive that they are only brought into the discussion when top officials want something (such as higher classifications for a group of employees).

GPRA and NPR: Cooperation or Collision?

A final driver of change is the Government Performance and Results Act (GPRA). GPRA's focus is on developing clear measures of government performance and holding managers accountable. GPRA mandated that, by September 30, 1997, all agencies would develop five-year strategic plans linked to annual performance plans with objective, quantifiable outcome measures. Agencies are currently embroiled in the difficult process of developing standards by which to measure what they do (Kravchuk and Schack 1996).

GPRA intersects the personnel function in two ways. First, agencies must find ways to measure the efficiency and effectiveness of their line functions. There appears to be little if any centralized effort to develop standards that could be applied across agencies. As one outside observer told this author, "There has been no substantial research on evaluation programs or measurement processes, as opposed to compliance [with civil service rules]. OPM hasn't been able to develop a new model of measurement, [although] 'HR Accountability,' OPM's recent publication . . . makes big strides." Only when agencies release their standards will we be able to examine the extent to which they have developed standards in this area.

Second and more importantly, agencies are busy developing standards to measure organizational performance but they are not linking them to individual performance standards, making it hard to hold specific individuals (especially managers) accountable for agency success or failure in meeting its standards. In fact, one of the NPR recommendations for decentralization and deregulation advocated allowing agencies to design their own performance management programs. According to the NPR (1993b: 33), HR report, "At least two levels of performance must be identified: meets and does not meet expectations." This recommendation has been implemented and several agencies are moving from their former Performance Appraisal systems (many developed as a result of CSRA) to pass-fail systems.

Senior staff on the Hill have raised serious questions about how a pass-fail system would work in a Reduction in Force (RIF) since the current rules require that performance be taken into consideration. But more important is the overall problem of linking individual and organizational performance. Several observers raised this as a problem that is looming and several attributed the problem to "ownership" of different systems by different central management agencies. As one explained:

> You need to decide whether to link employee performance management and organizational management in the GPRA context. Parallel systems are becoming more dramatic because GPRA is supposed to be fully in place this year. The two systems don't link. If they do, it's happenstance. Employee performance—the key is contribution to performance *of* mission. Usually the CFO [Chief Financial Officer] is in control *of* GPRA. HR is not designing standards linked to this. The OMB people are against linkage because they don't like the employee performance system. GPRA is owned by OMB and performance management by OPM.

A senior official at an oversight agency raised similar concerns: "GPRA has sort of bumped up against NPR. And they are sort of two branches of government competing efforts toward results-oriented management and better approaches of managing the government, and the intersection may become a full-blown collision in the next year or so."

Multiple Drivers of Change: Their Combined Effects

As we have seen, recent changes in the federal civil service system and in the management of human resources stem from several different sources. Separating out their effects is nearly impossible because agencies are reacting simultaneously to multiple pressures for change. While formal system change has been somewhat disappointing, nevertheless NPR has made a difference both directly through deregulation and delegation and indirectly through sharp cuts in the HR workforce. As a result, OPM looks very different and so do agency personnel offices.

OPM has been cut in half; it has simply stopped doing such things as maintaining centralized registers. And other OPM functions have been hived off. The training function was taken over by the Department of Agriculture Graduate School. Investigation of new federal employees was handed over to an ESOP (an employee-owned private firm). Jim King, Clinton's appointee to head OPM, initially tried to focus on the more positive role of consultant and coach to agencies, downplaying OPM's traditional oversight role (Lane and Marshall 1995). Only under congressional pressure has OPM focused effort on oversight of agency personnel practices and here it is relying heavily of self-assessment by the agencies themselves. OPM has been criticized for being a "non-player in the reform effort" (Ingraham 1996). While that may be overstrong, even in the area of human resources OPM is clearly the dominant force, particularly in the implementation of the Government Performance and Results Act (GPRA). But, overall, the NPR implementation effort has been highly decentralized making it both uneven and difficult to track (Ingraham 1996).

Agency personnel offices are still very much in the middle of the change process. Still adjusting to massive cuts while taking on new functions, they are restructuring (often by centralizing), moving rapidly to adopt new technologies, and changing their internal cultures at the same time.

Demos, PBOs, and FAA: The Break-Up of Title 5?

Most of our models of civil service reform are still based on the assumption that the system is unitary and that change means changing the system as a whole. But agency responses to the changes described above have been anything but standard with agencies moving in different directions and at different speeds. For at least 10 years, some reformers have taken a more radical stance, arguing that the time for a centrally managed, unitary set of rules governing human resources management in all federal agencies has passed and that agencies need the authority to develop their own systems to reflect their specific needs.

One could imagine two different ways of moving from a unitary model to a more flexible personnel system or set of systems. The first is the path of comprehensive reform with Congress passing legislation permitting agencies to tailor personnel systems to fit their unique circumstances perhaps by implementing new approaches tested via demonstration projects such as the Navy demonstration. This author wrote some time ago about the puzzling failure to attempt to pass legislation to permit agencies to adopt broadbanding, even though the demonstration project had apparently been a success (Ban 1991). Current congressional opposition to such legislation is focused particularly on the cost implications of such a move. As a senior Hill staff member told this author, "Government-wise, broadbanding is dead because it's too expensive. . . . The reason why people want to get away from the current system is because they want to pay more, not less."

Facing a political environment inimical to sweeping legislative reform, a number of agencies have gone a second route pushing for piece-meal reforms that would help them solve their own problems. The net effect of a series of such reforms may be the gradual whittling away of the traditional civil service system (known as Title 5 by the section of federal law that governs civil service). Agencies are requesting, and in some cases getting, either exemption from some provisions of Title 5 or full movement out of coverage by Title 5. In the former category are agencies that have successfully requested authority to move permanently to new systems tested through demonstration projects. That includes both the Navy labs covered by their demonstration projects and NIST.

The NPR HR report recommended expansion of the demonstration project provision of the law. Increasingly, demonstration projects are being seen not as a chance to test out reforms that could be implemented government-wide but rather as an opportunity for agencies to fix their own problems by getting dispensation from the constraints of the law which might eventually be made permanent if the agency so wishes.

Even more dramatically, some agencies are successfully opting out of coverage by Title 5 moving, in technical terms, from the competitive service to the excepted service.

Over the years a number of agencies have won congressional approval for developing their own personnel systems. The largest of these is the Postal Service (which is now a government corporation) but many other agencies, ranging from the TVA to the Department of Veterans Affairs, have developed their own personnel systems. These systems typically have many of the standard features of the competitive service and operate as merit systems but with variants fitting agency specifications. Excepted-service agencies are not subject to oversight by OPM (Office of Personnel Management).

The most recent agency to join this list is the Federal Aviation Administration (FAA) which won the right to develop its own personnel system as part of the legislation separating it from the Department of Transportation in 1995. It is far too soon to pass judgment on the effects of this change but some observers have remarked that the FAA appears to be recreating the system that it left.

The newest approach to changing civil service systems piece-meal is the creation of Performance-Based Organizations (PBOs). PBOs reflect, in many ways, the philosophy underlying both GPRA and NPR. They are agencies that can function as independent cost centers run on a quasi-business model. The key elements of the PBO model are substantial deregulation and incentives to improve performance. Chief Operating Officers are hired under contract and rewarded based on performance. They vary somewhat from government corporations in that they are not required to be financially self-sustaining (NPR 1997b).

While FAA is not technically a PBO, much of the language justifying removing it from Title 5 reflects a similar philosophy. Legislation to convert the St. Lawrence Seaway Corporation (part of the Department of Transportation) to a PBO called the St. Lawrence Seaway Development Corporation was submitted to Congress in May 1997. Other organizations being considered as candidates for PBO status include three separate parts of the Department of Commerce (the National Technical Information Service, Patent and Trademark Office, and National Ocean Service), two parts of HUD (Housing and Urban Development) (the Government National Mortgage Association and Federal Housing Administration), the Defense Commissary Agency within the Department of Defense, the processing of federal retirement benefits within the Office of Personnel Management, and the U.S. Mint (NPR 1997a).

The draft legislation being used as a model for PBOs includes substantial flexibility in personnel management, detailing some areas where agencies could implement changes without OPM approval, including moving to a broadbanded classification system and eliminating the ten steps in the General Schedule, establishing category ratings (i.e., zone scoring) rather than numerical ratings for job applicants, establishing longer probation periods for certain positions (up to three years), and shortening the notice period preceding a dismissal for poor performance or for violation of rules.

Other changes could be made only with OPM approval. These might include establishing one or more alternative job evaluation systems, providing for variations from grade and pay retention for employees who are bumped down in a Reduction in Force, and providing for variations from the law governing recruitment and relocation bonuses and retention allowances (NPR 1997b).

Many of the most important flexibilities would be available, in short, to PBOs without any need for OPM prior approval. These organizations would be able to implement many of the new approaches tested out by demonstration projects out close to 20 years, none of which have been incorporated in Title 5. If PBOs take off and if they are deemed successful over time, the pressure to grant these flexibilities to other agencies could become overwhelming.

Conclusions

This brief examination of the current state of efforts to reinvent the federal civil service leads this author to some general conclusions both about the state of the civil service and more broadly about the reform process.

Previous attempts to reform the civil service, most notably the Civil Service Reform Act of 1978, have assumed a rational-planning model. Some of the CSRA reforms, such as the creation of the Senior Executive Service, were top-down while reforms in performance appraisal and merit pay were predicated on the assumption that agencies should be able to design their own systems with considerable input from managers.

This author should note that the latter reforms, in particular, were not successful; neither the performance appraisal systems nor the CSRA approach to merit pay have lasted. In particular, the original model of the demonstration projects assumed that reforms could be tested, evaluated scientifically, and then accepted as government-wide policy. The assumptions underlying this rational model were naive. In the complex political environment of federal personnel management, no demonstration project has led to system-wide reform (Ban 1991).

The NPR reform process is messier, more bottom-up in many ways, and more driven by the exigencies of the political process and by the related need to cut the size of the federal workforce. Because it is so decentralized, it threatens established values such as equity and uniformity across the system (Kellough 1998). Indeed, it is likely to speed the breakup of the traditional standard civil service system (i.e., Title 5). There are strong arguments in support of moving to a more decentralized, flexible system that allows agencies to design personnel systems that meet the needs of the agencies. But we need to be explicit about the values embedded in such a change and the tradeoffs involved.

It is also clear that, like the CSRA, the NPR rhetoric is based on adapting to the public sector private-sector models which are presumed to lead to more efficiency in organizations. But the assumptions underlying such a technology transfer have been criticized for years. Without reopening the debate over the differences between the public and private sectors, here too we need to examine the underlying values embedded in reforms. The proposals for PBOs, for example, raise serious questions about the relative weight of efficiency versus democratic control and due process. It remains to be seen whether both the Congress and the American public will accept such a radical change in the accountability structure of government.

In sum, while the formal changes in the personnel system as a result of the National Performance Review have not been as sweeping as in other administrative areas, particularly procurement, the reinvention movement taken as a whole is changing the face of the federal civil service in some very profound ways. It is clear that the personnel management system of the future will be leaner and technologically more sophisticated. It is likely that at least some organizations will be managing within more flexible personnel systems. It is too early to say whether the result will be a high quality civil service protected from political abuse and dedicated to the values of public service.

References

Ban, Carolyn (1991). "The Navy Demonstration Project: An 'Experiment in Experimentation'," in Carolyn Ban and Norma M. Riccucci (eds.). *Public Personnel Management: Current Concerns, Future Challenges*, 1st ed. White Plains, NY: Longman.

———— (1995). *How Do Public Managers Manage? Bureaucratic Constraints. Organizational Culture, and the Potential for Reform*. San Francisco: Jossey-Bass.

———— (1997a). "Hiring in the Public Sector: 'Expediency Management' or Structural Reform?," in Carolyn Ban and Norma M. Riccucci (eds.). *Public Personnel Management: Current Concerns, Future Challenges*, 2nd ed. New York: Longman.

———— (1997b). "The Challenges of Cutback Management," in Carolyn Ban and Norma M. Riccucci (eds.). *Public Personnel Management: Current Concerns, Future Challenges*, 2nd ed. New York: Longman.

Ban, Carolyn and Toni Marzotto (1984). "Delegations of Examining: Objectives and Implementation," in Patricia Ingraham and Carolyn Dan (eds.). *Legislating Bureaucratic Change: The Civil Service Reform Act of 1978*. Albany: State University of New York Press.

Foreman, Christopher H. Jr. (1995). "Reinventing Capital Hill." *The Brookings Review* (Winter): 34–38.

Gore, Vice President Al (1996). *The Best Kept Secrets in Government: A Report to President Bill Clinton*. Washington, D.C. Government Printing Office.

Ingraham, Patricia W. (1996). "Reinventing the American Federal Government: Reform Redux or Real Change?" *Public Administration* 7 (Autumn): 453–457.

Kellough, J. Edward (1998). "The Reinventing Government Movement: A Review and Critique." 22 *Public Administration Quarterly*, 1: 6–20.

Kettl, Donald F. (1994). *Reinventing Government? Appraising the National Performance Review*. Washington, D.C.: Brookings Institution.

Kravchuk, Robert S. and Ronald W. Schack (1996). "Designing Effective Performance Measurement Systems under the Government Performance and Results Act of 1993." *Public Administration Review* 56(4) (July/August): 348–358.

Lane, Larry and Gary Marshall (1995). "Reinventing OPM: Adventures, Issues, and Implications." Paper presented at the ASPA National Conference, San Antonio, Texas.

National Academy of Public Administration (NAPA) (1996). *Improving the Efficiency and Effectiveness of the Human Resources Management*. Washington, D.C.: Author.

National Performance Review (1993a). *From Red Tape to Results: Creating a Government that Works Better and Costs Less*. Washington, D.C.: Government Printing Office.

———— (1993b). *Reinventing Human Resource Management*. Washington. D.C.: Government Printing office.

———— (1997a). Current PBO Candidates, as of July 1997. Listed on NPR's web site (www.npr.gov).

———— (1997b). *Performance-Based Organizations: A Conversation Guide*. Washington, D.C.: Government Printing Office.

Perry, James and Debra Mesch (1997). "Strategic Human Resource Management," in Carolyn Ban and Norma M. Riccucci (eds.). *Public Personnel Management Current Concerns, Future Challenges*, 2nd ed. New York: Longman.

Pfiffner, James P. (1997). "The National Performance Review in Perspective." *International Journal of Public Administration* 20(1): 41–70.

U.S. Merit Systems Protection Board (MSPB) (1977). Calculations of OPM's Central Personnel Data File.

PART 5

LEGAL DEVELOPMENTS

Certainly, legal issues undergird every aspect of public personnel administration. From the point at which Justice Oliver Wendell Holmes uttered his celebrated dictum, that a police officer has the right to talk politics but "has no constitutional right to be a policeman," the legal as well as political landscapes of public personnel were forever transformed. The statutory and constitutional frameworks for public personnel administration have thus been analyzed and written about extensively. Beginning when public employment was seen as a privilege to the point where legal and constitutional provisions were advanced to protect the rights of public employees, students of public personnel administration have recognized the paramountcy of law to the field.

In the first piece, David Rosenbloom provides a comprehensive analysis of U.S. Supreme Court decisions involving the public employment relationship. As he shows, the Court has been divided over issues pertaining to public employees' constitutional rights. He also points out that the role of adjudication as a means for assessing constitutional requirements for public employment has grown considerably. As Rosenbloom observes, these trends are related to the general tensions between our administrative and constitutional states. Who sets the contours for the public employment relationship? The courts or professionally trained public personnel administrators? These are the questions addressed by Rosenbloom.

In "Due Process and Public Personnel Management," Deborah Goldman examines the U.S. Supreme Court's treatment of public employees' constitutional rights to due process when adverse employment actions are taken. As she shows, the Court has focused primarily on procedural issues, and further, the Court has defined these interests in a very narrow fashion. As such, public personnel managers have had significant flexibility in dismissing public employees. Goldman finds that the primary procedural due process barrier to termination is retaliatory actions by employers for an employee's exercise of a protected substantive constitutional right.

One of the early concerns in public personnel after passage of the Pendleton Act of 1883 was the degree to which patronage or partisan politics would seep through the walls of the merit system. Would government officials continue to reward political supporters with public jobs? Yes, they would, but the U.S. Supreme Court has served as a watchdog over such practices. With such decisions as *Elrod v. Burns* (427 U.S. 347, 1976), *Branti v. Finkel* (445 U.S. 506, 1980), and *Rutan v. Republican Party of Illinois* (497 U.S. 62, 1990), the Supreme Court has curbed the use of patronage appointments. In "Curbing Patronage Without Paperasserie," Christopher Daniel addresses the issue of political patronage in public employment. Daniel suggests ways in which public employers can curb patronage without the imposition of unwieldy paperwork or "red tape." In so doing, as he concludes, "reformers may finally be able to avoid letting technique triumph over purpose, as creative antipatronage efforts help revive the personnel function and invigorate the public service" (Daniel 1993: 389).

Statutory and constitutional developments in public personnel ranging from such issues as racial and gender discrimination to drug testing have defined the contours of the public employment relationship. Some of these issues (e.g., HIV/AIDS, race and gender discrimination) were addressed elsewhere in this reader (see articles presented in Section I, Part 2, "Institutions, Functions, and Process" and Section I, Part 3, "Equal Employment Opportunity, Affirmative Action, and Representative Bureaucracy"). Two additional legal and constitutional concerns of great interest to public employees and employers are drug testing and sexual harassment.

In her article, Norma Riccucci provides a legal analysis of drug testing in the public sector. She examines the laws and constitutional provisions governing drug testing, provides a comprehensive review of the two major drug-testing decisions issued by the U.S. Supreme Court in 1989 (*Skinner v. Railway Labor Executives' Association* and *National Treasury Employees Union v. Von Raab*), and assesses the state of drug testing in government workforces.

In "The Legal Evolution of Sexual Harassment," Robert Lee and Paul Greenlaw examine the legal status of sexual harassment policy in the United States. They provide an analysis of existing caselaw and discuss the various legal issues upon which sexual harassment cases revolve. In particular, Lee and Greenlaw examine the form of sexual harassment known as "hostile environment." This refers to unwanted, unwelcome sexual conduct of a verbal, nonverbal, or physical nature which unreasonably interferes with a person's work performance or creates a hostile, offensive, or intimidating work environment even though the harassment may not result in tangible or economic job consequences. They conclude from their study that "Cases involving public employment can be considerably more complex than private sector cases, because public workers may enlist rights beyond those guaranteed by Title VII" (Lee and Greenlaw 1995: 363).

Additional Classics

Dotson, Arch. "A General Theory of Public Employment." 16 *Public Administration Review*, 3: 197–211, Summer 1956.

Hildreth, W. Bartley, Gerald J. Miller and Jack Rabin. "The Liability of Public Executives: Implication for Practice in Personnel Administration." 1 *Review of Public Personnel Administration*, 1: 45–56, Fall 1980.

Ingraham, Patricia W. and David H. Rosenbloom. "The New Public Personnel and the New Public Service. 49 *Public Administration Review*, 2: 116–125, March/April 1989.

———. "The Political Foundations of the American Federal Service: Rebuilding a Crumbling Base." 50 *Public Administration Review*, 2: 210–219, March/April 1990.

Jones, Walter J. and James A. Johnson. "AIDS in the Workplace: Legal and Policy Considerations for Personnel Managers." 9 *Review of Public Personnel Administration*, 3: 3–14, Summer 1989.

Leidlein, James E. "In Search of Merit." 53 *Public Administration Review*, 4: 391–392, July/August 1993.

Levine, Charles H. "The Public Personnel System: Can Juridical and Administrative Manpower Co-Exist?" 35 *Public Administration Review*, 1: 98–107, 1975.

Newland, Chester A. "Public Personnel Administration: Legalistic Reforms vs. Effectiveness, Efficiency, and Economy." 36 *Public Administration Review*, 5: 529–537, 1976.

Rosenbloom, David H. "Public Personnel Administration and the Constitution: An Emergent Approach." 35 *Public Administration Review*, 1: 52–59, January/February, 1975.

———. "The Sources of Continuing Conflict Between the Constitution and Public Personnel Management." 2 *Review of Public Personnel Administration*, 1: 3–18, Fall 1981.

Rosenbloom, David H. and Carole C. Obuchowski. "Public Personnel Examinations and the Constitution: Emergent Trends." 37 *Public Administration Review*, 1: 9–18, January/February, 1977.

CHAPTER 22

THE PUBLIC EMPLOYMENT RELATIONSHIP AND THE SUPREME COURT IN THE 1980s

DAVID H. ROSENBLOOM

During the 1980s, Supreme Court decisions regarding the public employment relationship continued to be an important feature of public personnel administration in the United States. The relationship is distinctive to the public sector because it seeks "...to accommodate the dual role of the public employer as provider of public services and as a government entity operating under the constraints . . . " of the Constitution (*Rankin v. McPherson* 1987: 5021; Rosenbloom 1971). Although there has been a " . . . common-sense realization that government offices could not function if every employment decision became a constitutional matter" (*Connick v. Myers* 1983: 143), there is also a broad recognition that public employees have significant constitutional protections against the actions of their governmental employers. Moreover, by the 1980s, judicial decisions became increasingly cognizant of " . . . the impact of the public employment relationship on the public at large" (*Harvard Law Review* 1984: 1748). Yet, adjudicating the competing claims of governmental employers for effective control of their work forces and those of public employees for the retention of basic constitutional rights within the context of their employment, while also assessing the public interest in the functioning of the public service, has perplexed the judiciary.

Understandably, public administrators cannot always be certain as to the requirements of the public employment relationship. This essay analyzes the Supreme Court's recent decisions concerning the relationship in four areas of centrality to contemporary public administration: (1) public employees' substantive constitutional rights, (2) their rights to procedural due process, (3) equal protection in public employment, and (4) public administrators' personal liability for breaches of individuals' constitutional and/or federally protected statutory rights. It concludes that the Court has continued to "constitutionalize" the relationship by holding that public employees have rights that cannot be abridged, constitutionally, by their governmental employers. However, instead of developing broad constitutional doctrines that comprehensively define the scope of these rights, the Court,

From 8 *Review of Public Personnel Administration*, 2: 49–65, Spring 1988. Copyright © 1988 Sage Publications. Reprinted with permission.

beset by deep divisions and competing views,[1] has opted for approaches that often require case-by-case adjudication and complicate public personnel administration.

Historical Background

Historically, the public employment relationship has been related to the contest between politics and merit as bases for organizing public personnel administration (Rosenbloom 1971). During the period from 1829 to 1865, when patronage was at its peak in the federal government, the political community generally accepted the proposition that public employees had few, if any, constitutional rights within the context of their jobs. Patronage dismissals were institutionalized. Public employees were often coerced to electioneer and vote for the political party in power as well as to support it financially through political assessments. At times, employees were inhibited from expressing " . . . any opinion, however privately, which might offend those in power, lest stories be carried, and dismissals follow" (U.S. Civil Service Commission 1941: 21). Ironically, abuse of public employees' rights was so egregious under the spoils system that the restrictions later imposed by merit reforms upon civil servants' participation in partisan political activities were frequently considered to be protective measures. This was true of an anti-assessment statute of 1876 and of the Hatch Acts of 1939 and 1940. Once an activity was declared illegal for public employees, superordinates and party bosses had more difficulty forcing them to engage in it.

But if the merit system did not guarantee public employees the same First Amendment rights that other citizens have, it did provide a logical basis for extending procedural due process and equal protection rights to them. Once the civil service was viewed as a *public* institution, rather than an adjunct of political parties, the development of a constitutional interest in public personnel administration was virtually inevitable. By 1976, the Supreme Court even held that patronage dismissals can be unconstitutional infringements on public employees' First and Fourteenth Amendment rights (*Elrod v. Burns* 1976). The merit system's insistence on political neutrality was at least partially constitutionalized.

Although the public employment relationship evolved in conjunction with these shifting concepts of public employment, its specific modern development was deeply affected by the federal loyalty-security program of the late 1940s and early 1950s. The program sought dismissal of federal employees whose thoughts and/or actions were disloyal to the United States or subversive of it. In practice, the program proscribed many beliefs challenging the status quo. Favoring peace, civil liberties, and racial equality; reading the *New York Times*; and being nonreligious were sometimes considered relevant to loyalty-security investigations that might result in dismissal from the federal service. In response, by the mid-1950s, the Supreme Court was well on its way to rejecting the corpus of case law, called the "doctrine of privilege," that failed to protect public employees from such actions on the basis that public employment was a voluntarily accepted privilege rather than a right. The Court squarely held that even though there is no constitutional right to be a public employee, public employees do have some constitutional protections within the context of their employment.

Despite much adjudication during the 1960s and 1970s, however, the Supreme Court did not define the rights of public employees comprehensively (Rosenbloom 1975, 1977). Consequently, as the 1980s approached, the scope of public employees' rights and the extent to which the Constitution constrained public personnel administration lacked clarity. In an increasingly litigious society and a government in which verbal attacks on public employees and elaborate strategies for dominating them have become routine, there was little doubt that the public employment relationship would remain an important area of constitutional adjudication.

Substantive Constitutional Rights

During the 1980s, the Supreme Court handed down decisions of importance to public employees' substantive constitutional rights in the areas of freedom of speech, association, and privacy. *Connick v. Myers* (1983) addressed speech. In a 5 to 4 holding, the Court restated a familiar framework of constitutional analysis, but, at the same time, seemed to place greater weight on the governmental employer's interests in efficient and effective operations.

> For at least 15 years, it has been settled that a State cannot condition public employment on a basis that infringes the employee's constitutionally protected interest in freedom of expression . . . Our task, as we defined it in *Pickering* [*v. Board of Education* (1968)] is to seek "a balance between the interests of the [employee] [sic], as a citizen, in commenting upon matters of public concern and the interest of the State, as an employer, in promoting the efficiency of the public services it performs . . . " (*Connick v. Myers* 1983: 142). The Court emphasized that the threshold requirement is that the employee's speech be on a matter of public concern: " . . . when a public employee speaks not as a citizen upon matters of public concern, but instead as an employee upon matters only of personal interest, absent the most unusual circumstances, a federal court is not the appropriate forum in which to review the wisdom of a personnel decision taken by a public agency allegedly in reaction to the employee's behavior" (*Connick v. Myers* 1983: 147). Nor did the Court consider everything that pertains to the operation of a government office to be a matter of public concern.

Assuming that the employee's expression meets the threshold test it becomes necessary to strike the appropriate balance in determining whether the speech is constitutionally protected. *Connick* laid down some broad guidelines. First, "when close working relationships are essential to fulfilling public responsibilities, a wide degree of deference to the employer's judgment is appropriate" (*Connick v. Myers* 1983: 151–152). It is not necessary for the employer to wait until an office is disrupted or working relationships are destroyed before taking action. Second, "when employee speech concerning office policy arises from an employment dispute concerning the very application of [a] policy to the speaker, additional weight must be given to the supervisor's view that the employee has threatened the authority of the employer to run the office" (*Connick v. Myers* 1983: 153). Finally, the majority suggested that the degree of deference accorded to the employer might be inversely related to the extent to which the employee's speech involves matters of public concern. In other words, had the employee's speech dealt more comprehensively with such matters, the Court might have afforded less deference to the employer's claims.

The majority in *Connick* claimed that its holding was " . . . no defeat for the First Amendment" since the Court was merely rebuffing " . . . the attempt to constitutionalize the employee grievance . . . " (*Connick v. Myers* 1983: 154). However, the dissenting opinion, which emphasized that the speech in question involved matters of public concern, predicted that "The Court's decision . . . inevitably will deter public employees from making critical statements about the manner in which government agencies are operated for fear that doing so will provoke their dismissal" (*Connick v. Myers* 1983: 170).

If *Connick* seemed to presage a narrower range of free speech for public employees, *Rankin v. McPherson* (1987), another 5 to 4 holding, may carve " . . . out a new and very large class of employees—i.e., those in 'nonpolicymaking' positions—who . . . can never be disciplined for statements that fall within the Court's . . . definition" of public concern (5024). Rankin, a probationary employee in a constable's office had no policymaking responsibilities and only very limited opportunity for contact with the public. Upon hearing of an assassination attempt on President Ronald Regan, she said, " . . . if they go for him again, I hope they get him" (*Rankin v. McPherson* 1987: 5020).

Her statement was made privately to a fellow employee, who was her boyfriend, and in the context of a discussion about Reagan's policies. Another employee overheard the comment, became upset, and reported the incident to Constable Rankin. After questioning McPherson about the remark, Rankin dismissed her. In ruling that McPherson's remark was constitutionally protected, the Court's majority reasoned that 1) it was on a matter of public concern, and 2):

> . . . in weighing the State's interest in discharging an employee based on any claim that the content of a statement made by the employee somehow undermines the mission of the public employer, some attention must be paid to the responsibilities of the employee within the agency. The burden of caution employees bear with respect to the words they speak will vary with the extent of authority and public accountability the employee's role entails. Where, as here, an employee serves no confidential, policymaking, or public contact role, the danger to the agency's successful function from that employee's private speech is minimal (*Rankin v. McPherson* 1987: 5023).

The dissent, by contrast, argued that " . . . the statement at issue here did not address a matter of public concern, and . . . even if it did, a law enforcement agency has adequate reason not to permit such expression . . . " (*Rankin v. McPherson* 1987: 5026).

It is obvious that the Supreme Court has given public administrators much think about regarding the scope of public employees' constitutionally proved speech. At the very least, the following must be considered: whether the marks in question involve a matter of public concern; the context in which they are uttered; the nature of the employee's position with reference to confidentiality, policymaking, and public contact; and the remarks' disruptive quality. To these concerns must be added others from earlier case law, including whether the speech involves prohibited political partisanship, is so without foundation that the employee's basic competence is properly at issue, or evinces disloyalty to the United States (*Civil Service Commission v. National Association of Letter Carriers* 1973; *Pickering v. Board of Education* 1968). Under such circumstances, it is not really surprising that the *Rankin* case was " . . . considered five separate times by three different federal courts" (*Rankin v. McPherson* 1987: 5024), or that the Supreme Court itself has admitted that "competent decisionmakers may reasonably disagree about the merits of [a public employee's] First Amendment claim" (*Bush v. Lucas* 1983: note 7). On the other hand, in *Rankin* five members of the Court could agree on the principle, of limited applicability, that " . . . a purely private statement on a matter of public concern will rarely, if ever, justify discharge of a public employee" (*Rankin v. McPherson* 1987: 5022, note 13). In practice, though, the Court's decisions in this area of the public employment relationship are apt to encourage public personnel administration by adjudication (see *Bush v. Lucas* 1983, for an example).

Public personnelists face a less complicated task in assessing the scope of public employees' constitutionally protected freedom of association. Two of the Supreme Court's decisions during the 1980s are especially important. *Branti v. Finkel* (1980) concerned the constitutionality of patronage dismissals of public servants employed as public defenders. It extended and clarified an earlier decision, *Elrod v. Burns* (1976), which lacked a majority opinion, in holding that such dismissals violate the First Amendment's guarantee of freedom of belief unless the " . . . hiring authority can demonstrate that party affiliation is an appropriate requirement for the effective performance of the public office involved" (*Branti v. Finkel* 1980: 518). A 6 to 3 majority of the Court was insistent that simply labeling those dismissed for their partisan beliefs or affiliations as "policymakers" or as employees in "confidential" positions would be constitutionally insufficient. The Court's decision applies well beyond the specific job title involved and pertains to employees regardless of whether they are in a merit-based personnel system.

A second case, *Chicago Teachers Union v. Hudson* (1986), concerned the constitutionality of coercing public employees to support specific labor unions. Previously, in *Abood v. Detroit Board of Education* (1977), the Supreme Court " . . . rejected the claim that it was unconstitutional for a public employer to designate a union as the exclusive collective-bargaining representative of its employees, and to require nonunion employees, as a condition of employment, to pay a fair share of the union's cost of negotiating and administering a collective bargaining agreement" (*Chicago Teachers Union v. Hudson* 1986: 243–244). But the Court also held that " . . . nonunion employees do have a constitutional right to 'prevent the Union's spending a part of their required service fees to contribute to political candidates and to express political views unrelated to its duties as exclusive bargaining representative'" (*Chicago Teachers Union v. Hudson* 1986: 244). In the *Hudson* case, a unanimous Court (with a concurring opinion) strengthened the latter right considerably. It held that unions must follow certain procedures to enable nonmembers to challenge the amount of the assessed fees: "We hold . . . that the constitutional requirements for the Union's collection of agency fees include an adequate explanation of the basis for the fee, a reasonably prompt opportunity to challenge the amount of the fee before an impartial decisionmaker, and an escrow for the amounts reasonably in dispute while such challenges are pending" (*Chicago Teachers Union v. Hudson* 1986: 249).

From an historical perspective, it is striking that the public employment relationship now includes constitutional protection against patronage dismissals and the improper assessment of agency shop fees. Both *Branti* and *Hudson* represent considerable extensions of public employees' constitutional rights. *Hudson's* requirement that an impartial decisionmaker be available to rule on the propriety of fees also introduces, on a constitutional basis, an additional adjudicatory function into public personnel administration.

During the 1980s, the Supreme Court also brought the Fourth Amendment to bear squarely upon the public employment relationship. Although the Court was unable to formulate a majority opinion, in *O'Connor v. Ortega* (1987) all its members appeared to agree with the general proposition that public employees retain Fourth Amendment protections within the context of their employment. The case originated when O'Connor, the Executive Director of a state hospital became aware of alleged improprieties in Dr. Ortega's management of the hospital's resident training program. While Ortega was placed on leave, hospital staff searched his office and " . . . seized several items from Dr. Ortega's desk and file cabinets, including a Valentine's card, a photograph, and a book of poetry all sent to Dr. Ortega by a former resident physician" (*O'Connor v. Ortega* 1987: 4407). The purpose of the search and seizure was unclear and the investigators found it impossible to separate all of Ortega's personal property from state property. Instead, everything was boxed-up together. No formal inventory of the property was ever made. Subsequently, Ortega was dismissed, though the search appears to have had no significant bearing on the charges against him.

Justice O'Connor announced the Court's judgment to remand the case for trial at the district court level. O'Connor's plurality opinion was joined by Chief Justice Rehnquist, Justice White, and Justice Powell. She reasoned that "individuals do not lose Fourth Amendment rights merely because they work for the government instead of a private employer" (*O'Connor v. Ortega* 1987: 4408). But the scope of those rights depended upon two considerations. First, whether the employee had a reasonable expectation of privacy in the work place. In O'Connor's view, this matter required an idiographic, if not adjudicatory determination: "Given the great variety of work environments in the public sector, the question of whether an employee has a reasonable expectation of privacy must be addressed on a case-by-case basis" (*O'Connor v. Ortega* 1987: 4408). Second, even if the employee did have such an expectation, his/her rights would not be violated if the government could show that " . . . both the inception and the scope of the intrusion . . . [were] reasonable" (*O'Connor v. Ortega* 1987: 4410). The latter standard was more appropriate than requiring warrants or probable cause, she argued, because " . . . public employees are entrusted with tremendous responsibility, and the consequences of their misconduct or incompetence to both the agency and the public interest can be severe" (*O'Connor v. Ortega* 1987: 4409).

Justice Scalia concurred separately in the Court's judgment. He argued that " . . . the offices of government employees, and *a fortiori* the drawers and files within those offices, are covered by Fourth Amendment protections as a general matter" (*O'Connor v. Ortega* 1987: 4411–4412). But in his view, as a general rule, " . . . searches to retrieve work-related materials or to investigate violations of workplace rules—searches of the sort that are regarded as reasonable and normal in the private-employer context—do not violate the Fourth Amendment" (*O'Connor v. Ortega* 1987: 4412). Having formulated a general principle, Scalia berated the plurality for its " . . . formulation of a standard so devoid of content that it produces rather than eliminates uncertainty in the field" (*O'Connor v. Ortega* 1987: 4411).

Justice Blackmun's dissent, joined by Justices Brennan, Marshall, and Stevens, agreed that "[i]ndividuals do not lose Fourth Amendment rights merely because they work for the Government instead of a private employer" (*O'Connor v. Ortega* 1987: 4413). He also agreed that "given . . . the number and types of workplace searches by public employers that can be imagined—ranging all the way from the employer's routine entry for retrieval of a file to a planned investigatory search into an employee's suspected criminal misdeeds—development of a jurisprudence in this area might well require a case-by-case approach" (*O'Connor v. Ortega* 1987: 4412, note 2). However, he argued that the plurality was too quick to substitute a reasonableness standard for the more traditional Fourth Amendment requirements involving warrants or probable cause. Indeed, he thought a warrant would have been "perfectly suited" for the search in the case at hand (*O'Connor v. Ortega* 1987: 4415).

The Fourth Amendment rights of public employees are virtually certain to be clarified as the judiciary faces the progeny of *O'Connor v. Ortega* and cases involving drug testing. In the meantime, however, many public administrators lack adequate guidance concerning searches of their own and their coworkers' offices. When is an expectation of privacy reasonable? When is a search reasonable in its inception and scope? These are the questions with which administrators contemplating searches in the workplace should now be preoccupied.

Procedural Due Process

The Supreme Court's actions in cases dealing with the substantive constitutional rights of public employees are bound to leave public personnel administrators with considerable uncertainty. By contrast, the Court clarified the constitutional right to procedural due process within the public employment relationship. Here, too, the Court displayed a preference for adjudicatory process in public personnel administration. *Cleveland Board of Education v. Loudermill* (1985), concerned the dismissal of a security guard by the Cleveland Board of Education on the grounds that he lied on his job application in stating that he was never convicted of a felony. Under Ohio law, Loudermill was a "classified civil servant," who could be fired only for cause and was entitled to an administrative review of any such discharge. The issue before the court was whether Loudermill's constitutional right to procedural due process was violated by the school board's failure to afford him an opportunity to respond to the charge against him *prior* to his dismissal.

The Supreme Court, per Justice White, held that Loudermill's due process rights depended upon whether the Ohio civil service statute gave him a property interest in his job. Upon finding that the law did so, White argued that deprivation of the interest was controlled by the Constitution, rather than by the *statute's* provisions for dismissals:

> The point is straightforward: the Due Process Clause provides that certain substantive rights—life, liberty, and property—cannot be deprived except pursuant to constitutionally adequate procedures. The categories of substance and procedure are distinct . . . . "Property" cannot be defined by the procedures provided for its deprivation any more than can life or liberty. The right to due process "is conferred, not by legislative grace, but by constitutional guarantee. While the legislature may elect not to confer a property interest in [public] [sic] employment, it may not constitutionally authorize the deprivation of such an interest, once conferred, without appropriate procedural safeguards" (*Cleveland Board of Education v. Loudermill* 1985: 541).

Having established that Loudermill's due process rights were governed by the Constitution, the Court next applied a traditional analysis in finding that he was constitutionally entitled to a pre-termination hearing (*Matthews v. Eldridge* 1976). Though such a procedure was necessary, it " . . . need not definitively resolve the propriety of the discharge. It should be an initial check against mistaken decisions—essentially a determination of whether there are reasonable grounds to believe that the charges against the employee are true and support the proposed action" (*Cleveland Board of Education v. Loudermill* 1985: 545–546). Justice White noted, however, that the extent of due process required prior to dismissal in this case was related to the opportunity for a more elaborate post-termination hearing under Ohio's law.

The *Loudermill* decision is part of the Court's general tendency, during the 1980s, to constitutionalize public personnel administration and to promote adjudicatory processes within it. Both aspects of this tendency were addressed in separate opinions in *Loudermill*. Justice Rehnquist's dissent voiced opposition to constitutionalization, whereas separate opinions by Justices Marshall and Brennan expressed preferences for a more elaborate pre-termination procedure.

Equal Protection

The guarantee that no person shall be denied equal protection of the laws is clearly a fundamental part of the contemporary public employment relationship. In several cases during the 1980s, the Supreme Court sought to negotiate the tensions between equal protection and affirmative action. Specifically, the Court addressed the constitutionality of affirmative action that is imposed as a remedy for admitted or proven past illegal and/or unconstitutional discrimination. It also suggested, but did not actually rule upon, the conditions under which affirmative action that is voluntarily adopted by a public employer to redress social imbalances in its workforce might be constitutional. For the sake of legal and constitutional analysis, it is important to distinguish between "voluntary" and "remedial" affirmative action. Voluntary affirmative action may seek to overcome the effects of past discrimination, but it is not a "remedy" in the legal sense since it is not based on a legal finding or admission of past unconstitutional and/or illegal practices.

United States v. Paradise (1987) is the Supreme Court's most recent wide-ranging effort to deal with the constitutionality of remedial affirmative action. It grew out of a federal district court decision in 1972, holding that Alabama had unconstitutionally excluded blacks from its force of state troopers for almost four decades. The district court issued an order requiring the Department of Public Safety to refrain from discriminating and it imposed a quota hiring system as a remedy for past discrimination. Although blacks had been hired pursuant to the order, by 1979 there were still no blacks in the department's upper ranks. In that year, the department entered into a consent decree requiring it to promote blacks. By 1981, however, no black troopers had been promoted. A second consent decree was then approved by the district court. It specified that a promotion exam would be administered to applicants and that the results would be reviewed to determine whether there was an adverse impact on blacks. The test had such an impact and, in 1983, the district court ordered the department to submit a plan to promote at least 15 qualified candidates in a manner that would not adversely affect black troopers seeking promotions. The department proposed that 4 blacks be among 15 troopers promoted. The district court rejected this plan and ordered that, "for a period of time," at least 50 percent of those promoted to the rank of corporal be black, if qualified black candidates were available. It also imposed a 50 percent promotional requirement in the other upper ranks, but only on the conditions that (1) there were qualified black candidates, (2) in the ranks covered less than 25 percent of the workforce was black, and (3) the department failed to establish a promotion plan for the rank involved that did not have an adverse impact on blacks (*U.S. v. Paradise* 1987: 4211). The district court also ordered the department to submit a realistic schedule for developing promotional procedures for all its ranks. The department proceeded to promote 8 blacks and 8 whites under the district court's order. The United States, that is, the Solicitor General, appealed the district court's order on the grounds that it violated the Equal Protection Clause. The Court of Appeals affirmed and subsequently the Supreme Court took the case on writ of certiorari.

The high court upheld the order, but it failed to formulate a majority opinion. Justice Brennan announced its judgment in plurality opinion joined by Justices Marshall, Blackmun, and Powell. Brennan had little difficulty in finding the remedial affirmative action ordered by the district court to be constitutional. In his view, "It is now well established that government bodies, including courts, may constitutionally employ racial classifications essential to remedy unlawful treatment of racial or ethnic groups subject to discrimination" (*U.S. v. Paradise* 1987: 4215). But two issues remained. First, was the plan sufficiently "narrowly tailored." Brennan responded affirmatively because it was "temporary and flexible" and applied " . . . only if qualified blacks are available, only if the Department has an objective need to make promotions, and only if the Department fails to implement a promotion procedure that does not have an adverse impact on blacks" (*U.S. v. Paradise* 1987: 4220).

Second, was the district court's order realistically related to the percentage of blacks in the relevant workforce? Brennan noted that the 50 percent promotional quota was intended to fulfill a goal the district court had established earlier of having 25 percent black representation in the department's entire personnel complement. Thus, " . . . the 50 figure is not itself the goal; rather it represents the speed at which the goal of 25 will be achieved" (*U.S. v. Paradise* 1987: 4219). Since the 25 percent figure was realistic, the district court's order was deemed satisfactory.

Justice Stevens concurred in the Court's judgment, but he objected to Brennan's concern with narrow tailoring: " . . . the record discloses an egregious violation of the Equal Protection Clause. It follows, therefore, that the District Court had broad and flexible authority to remedy the wrongs resulting from this violation—exactly the opposite of the Solicitor General's unprecedented suggestion that the judge's discretion is constricted by a 'narrowly tailored to achieve a compelling governmental interest' standard" (*U.S. v. Paradise* 1987: 4222).

Justice O'Connor dissented in an opinion joined by Chief Justice Rehnquist and Justice Scalia. She argued that the plurality had inappropriately adopted " . . . a standardless view of 'narrowly tailored' far less stringent than that required . . . " (*U.S. v. Paradise* 1987: 4223). Her view seemed diametrically opposed to that of Stevens:

> There is simply no justification for the use of racial preferences if the purpose of the order could be achieved without their use . . . . Thus, to survive strict scrutiny, the District Court order must fit with greater precision than any alternative remedy . . . . The District Court had available several alternatives that would have achieved full compliance with the consent decrees without trammeling on the rights of nonminority troopers (*U.S. v. Paradise* 1987: 4224).

For instance, the district court could have appointed a trustee to develop a proper promotion procedure, or it could have held the department in contempt and imposed stiff fines or other penalties on it.

The Supreme Court revealed further fragmentation. Justice White dissented separately on the basis that the district court had exceeded its equitable powers. Justice Powell, joined in the plurality's opinion, but also concurred separately. He emphasized that the district court's order was narrowly drawn and properly scrutinized by the plurality.

In *Paradise*, the burden imposed on (or the advantage taken away from) nonminority troopers involved the opportunity for promotion. In other cases the burdens may be heavier or the advantages more costly to forfeit. This may affect the legality of affirmative action plans. For instance, in *Wygant v. Jackson* (1986), which involved voluntary affirmative action, the Supreme Court reached the judgment that a collective bargaining agreement providing for layoffs based on a racial classification that favored minorities was in violation of the Equal Protection Clause. In *Firefighters Local v. Stotts* (1984), the Court overturned a district court's injunction against laying off black employees as a means of preserving the intent of a consent decree formulated to remedy past discrimination in hiring and promotional practices.

Paradise did not address the constitutional issues posed by voluntary affirmative action. *Johnson v. Transportation Agency* (1987) established that such affirmative action, intended to redress sexual imbalances in a public employer's workforce, can be legal. Presumably, this conclusion holds for imbalances involving racial, ethnic, and religious minorities as well. Johnson also strongly suggests but does not hold, that voluntary affirmative action can be constitutional. Due to the way the case was argued, "no constitutional issue was either raised or addressed . . . " (*Johnson v. Transportation Agency* 1987: 4380).

Johnson involved an affirmative action plan adopted by Santa Clara County (California) intended to " . . . remedy the effects, of past practices and to permit attainment of an equitable representation of minorities, women and handicapped persons" (*Johnson v. Transportation Agency* 1987: 4380). Apparently, the past practices to which the plan referred did not include actual discrimination for as Justice Scalia pointed out in dissent, the District Court concluded that the Agency " . . . has not discriminated in the past, and does not discriminate in the present against women in regard to employment opportunities in general and promotions in particular" (*Johnson v. Transportation Agency* 1987: 4391). Rather, the plan was a forward-looking, voluntary effort to overcome sex segregation in " . . . job classifications in which women have been significantly underrepresented" (*Johnson v. Transportation Agency* 1987: 4380). The plan was flexible and utilized short-range goals. When Diane Joyce was promoted Paul Johnson, who had scored slightly higher than she in a promotion procedure, filed a sex discrimination complaint with the Federal Equal Employment Opportunity Commission. Eventually, his case reached the Supreme Court.

A majority of the Court upheld the plan's legality, primarily on the grounds it was flexible, did not set aside a specific number of positions for women or establish quotas, and did not trammel on the rights of male employees or absolutely prevent their promotion. Justice Brennan's majority opinion relied on statutory construction and private sector interpretation and precedent, notably *Steelworkers v. Weber* (1979). Yet, the Court's decision has implications for the constitutionality of voluntary affirmative action. Justice O'Connor's concurrence asserted that " . . . the proper initial inquiry in evaluating the legality of an affirmative action plan by a public employer under Title VII [of the Civil Rights Act of 1964, as amended] is no different from that required by the Equal Protection Clause" (*Johnson v. Transportation Agency* 1987: 4388). Similarly, Justice Scalia's dissent, joined by Chief Justice Rehnquist and partially by Justice White, noted that " . . . it is most unlikely that Title VII was intended to place a lesser restraint on discrimination by public actors than is established by the Constitution" (*Johnson v. Transportation Agency* 1987: 4393). Nonetheless, since the now retired Justice Powell joined the majority opinion while Justice O'Connor concurred separately and three justices dissented, it would be imprudent to assume that the constitutional question has been all but resolved. Until the Court does hand down a definitive decision regarding the constitutionality or public sector voluntary action, public administrators will remain somewhat uncertain as to the requirements of equal protection with respect to a whole range of personnel functions, including recruitment, testing, selection, classification, pay, training, promotion, and layoffs.

Public Employees' Personal Liability

The personal liability of public employees for violation of the constitutional or statutory rights of individuals upon whom their official actions bear is a final feature of the public employment relationship that merits attention. Historically, by virtue of their working for the sovereign, public employees were given a cloak of nearly absolute immunity from civil suits for damages arising from their official performance. Such immunity was based on a combination of common law and constitutional interpretation. During the 1970s, the Supreme Court modified the presumption of absolute immunity regarding most public officials to one of qualified immunity only.[2] In so doing, the Court reduced an important protection that the public employment relationship had once afforded public administrators generally. In the 1980s, the Court further refined the standards for immunity and liability.

In *Wood v. Strickland* (1975), the Supreme Court established a two prong analysis of public employees' immunity. An employee would not be immune from civil suits for damages " . . . if he knew or reasonably should have known that the action he took within his sphere of official responsibility would violate the constitutional rights . . . " of the individuals acted upon. Nor would the employee be immune "if he took the action with the malicious intention to cause a deprivation of constitutional rights or other injury . . . " (*Wood v. Strickland* 1975: 322). The second prong enabled insubstantial claims to go to trial, including by juries, because it is relatively easy to charge public officials of acting with impermissible intentions. The other prong, by contrast, involved an objective standard (that is, appropriate knowledge of others' rights) that facilitated summary judgment. In *Harlow v. Fitzgerald* (1982), the Court opted to eliminate the issue of intentions and to restate the objective standard: "We . . . hold that government officials performing discretionary functions generally are shielded from liability for civil damages insofar as their conduct does not violate clearly established statutory or constitutional rights of which a reasonable person would have known" (*Harlow v. Fitzgerald* 1982: 818).

The *Harlow* standard for immunity was subsequently augmented in *Davis v. Scherer* (1984). There the Supreme Court emphasized that "A plaintiff who seeks damages for violation of constitutional or statutory rights may overcome the defendant official's qualified immunity only by showing that those rights were clearly established at the time of the conduct at issue" (*Davis v. Scherer* 1984: 197). In theory, this standard relieves public administrators of the need to anticipate or predict future judicial holdings defining individuals' rights. However, in at least one case, *Pembaur v. Cincinnati* (1986), liability was attached to a municipality even though the rights it violated had never previously been declared.

Harlow and *Davis* establish the basis upon which public administrators may be considered immune from civil suites for damages. If such immunity is no available to them, that is, if their conduct did violate clearly established statute rights of which a reasonable person would have known, a plaintiff may be able to recover actual (compensatory) and punitive damages. Actual damages are intended to compensate the individual for the harm he/she suffered, such as loss of pay, as a result of the official's action. In general, actual damages will not include an assessment of the value or importance of the substantive constitutional rights abridged (*Memphis Community School District v. Stachura* 1986). Assessing punitive damages, which are intended to punish the culpable official and to deter others from acting in a similar fashion, presents a more complicated problem.

The Supreme Court confronted the matter of punitive damages in *Smith v. Wade* (1983). A majority held that juries could assess such damages " . . . when the defendant's conduct is shown to be motivated by evil motive or intent, or when it involves reckless or callous indifference to the federally protected rights of others" (*Smith v. Wade* 1983: 56). Consequently, should the plaintiff overcome the defendant official's qualified immunity, the issue of the official's intent may take on great importance. The potential impact of the Court's ruling was emphasized by Justice Rehnquist in dissent: "Because punitive damages generally are not subject to any relation to actual harm suffered, and because the recklessness standard is so imprecise, the remedy poses an even greater threat to the ability of officials to take decisive, efficient action" (*Smith v. Wade* 1983: 88).

A number of additional rulings helped to sort out the issues pertaining to immunity and liability. In *Nixon v. Fitzgerald* (1982), a fragmented Supreme Court held that the President of the United States is entitled to absolute immunity from civil liability for damages predicated on his acts. But, such immunity does not extend to the president's aides (*Harlow v. Fitzgerald* 1982). For the most part, federal managers and personnelists are not liable for breaches of federal employees' constitutional rights, at least if there is an alternative statutory scheme through which the aggrieved employee can seek a remedy (*Bush v. Lucas* 1983). However, state officials remain potentially liable for violations of state employees' federally protected statutory and constitutional rights. In *Clevinger v. Saxner* (1985), members of a prison disciplinary committee were brought under the qualified immunity standard.

Conclusion

This analysis of Supreme Court decisions involving the public employment relationship during the 1980s prompts several observations. First, it is obvious that the Court has been seriously divided, indeed sometimes fragmented, on several issues pertaining to public employees' constitutional rights. In *Ortega* and *Paradise*, the Court was unable to formulate a majority opinion. Other cases were decided by narrow margins and with vigorous dissents and separate concurrences. Yet, a general pattern does emerge. The Court has continued the trend, beginning in the 1950s, of affording public employees constitutional protections within the context of their employment. *Connick* rejected the notion that employee grievances should be constitutionalized, but *Branti, Hudson, Loudermill,* and *Ortega* extend constitutional protections to public employees. Arguably (in the dissenters' view), Rankin does the same. *Paradise* and *Wygant* indicate that public personnel practices can be very much regulated by the Constitution. The immunity and liability decisions go even further in bringing the Constitution to public administration by providing public employees with a strong personal incentive to know and avoid violating others' constitutional rights.

Second, the growth of constitutional rights in the public sector workplace has been accompanied by a greater reliance on adjudication as a means of assessing precisely what the Constitution requires. In *Ortega*, the Court was candid about its preference for a case-by-case jurisprudence. *Hudson* and *Loudermill* directly incorporate adjudicatory procedures, minimal though they may be. *Connick* and *Rankin* are very likely to promote adjudication in civil service appeals systems, where they are available. Who but the courts can decide what knowledge an official reasonably should have under *Harlow* and *Davis*? The cases involving affirmative action require an evaluation of "narrow tailoring" and an assessment of the costs imposed on nonminority employees.

These tendencies are part of a much larger set of developments that are related to the tensions between our constitutional and administrative states. During the past three decades or so, public administration has been partly characterized by major changes in doctrine and practice that bring constitutional values and processes into its core (Rosenbloom 1987b). There has been a vast expansion of the constitutional rights of individuals vis-à-vis public administrative activity. The growth in public employees' constitutional protections against their governmental employers has been part of this development. Concern with the representativeness of the public service has also intensified dramatically. Statutes such as the federal Civil Service Reform Act of 1978 call for a socially representative workforce. In *Paradise* and *Johnson*, the Supreme Court speaks of minority and female representation and underrepresentation. But social representation is only part of the larger concern, which includes citizen participation and public representation in in administrative processes (Gormley 1986). The demise of the presumption of absolute immunity makes many public employees personally responsible for their actions abridging individuals' federally protected rights. This, too, is part of a large process that moves public administration away from mere hierarchical accountability (*respondeat superior*) to individualized personal responsibility. It is related the legitimization of whistleblowing and may eventuate in a solid right of principled administrative disobedience (Vaughn 1977). With administrative discretion comes not only political power, but demands for representation and personal accountability and responsibility. Thus far, during the 1980s, the development of the public employment relationship by the Supreme Court has largely coincided with these broader administrative changes.

Impending changes in the composition of the Supreme Court may have marked impact on the public employment relationship, especially as so much doctrine is unsettled or imprecisely defined. However, in view of the Supreme Court's evident difficulty in defining the constitutional rights of public employees comprehensively during the recent past, there is some prospect that public personnelists will be able to exert considerable influence on the judiciary's approach to the public employment relationship in the future. Judicial deference to administrative expertise is common in many areas, including public personnel. In *Johnson v. Transportation Agency*, the Supreme Court accepted the American Society for Personnel Administration's position, filed in a friend of the court brief, that " . . . [i]t is a standard tenet of personnel administration that there is rarely a single 'best qualified' person for a job" (*Johnson v. Transportation Agency* 1987: 4386, note 17).

At least two conditions would seem to enhance public personnelists' influence on the judiciary. First, their positions should be consistent and formulated with a coherence that encompasses public personnel concerns as a whole. Second, these positions should be expressed in the terms that the courts have already applied to the public employment relationship. Both conditions require some rethinking of traditional personnel procedure. Personnel concepts, such as the competitive service, probationary or temporary status, position classification, and insubordination, have not generally been those of the constitutional law pertaining to public employees' rights. The judiciary thinks in terms of individuals' rights, motives, intentions, and knowledge of constitutional law. It looks toward the burdens imposed upon persons adversely affected by public personnel procedures.

The courts often look far beyond matters of organizational efficiency and administrative convenience in assessing the public interest. Public personnelists' professional associations can be excellent vehicles for promoting these conditions. In sum, perhaps the main thrust of the Supreme Court's decisions regarding the public employment relationship during the 1980s should be taken as assuring that concern with public employees' constitutional rights will be viewed as a central aspect of contemporary personnel administration.

Notes

1. See David Lauter (1986: S2–S4), whose analysis indicates that during the 1985–1986 term there were 143 dissents and 105 separate concurrences in the 147 cases in which opinions were written. According to Marcia Coyle (1987: S2–S3), during the 1986–1987 term, there were 116 dissents and 99 separate concurrences in the 145 cases in which opinions were written.

2. For a full discussion see *Harvard Law Review* (1977). State and local public administrators' liability under federal law flows generally from 42 U.S. Code section 1983. Federal employees are liable directly under constitutional interpretation. There is currently no significant distinction in the terms of qualified immunity for federal and nonfederal public employees. Some public administrators, including those charged with adjudicatory functions, may still retain absolute immunity. Political subdivisions also face liability, but their situation is outside the scope of this essay as they are not "employees." For a more general interpretation of liability/immunity, see Rosenbloom (1987a).

References

Abood v. Detroit Board of Education (1977). 431 U.S. 209.
Branti v. Finkel (1980). 445 U.S. 507.
Bush v. Lucas (1983). 462 U.S. 367.
Chicago Teachers Union v. Hudson (1986). 89 L. Ed.2d 232.
Civil Service Commission v. National Association of Letter Carriers (1973). 413 U.S. 548.
Cleveland Board of Education v. Loudermill (1985). 470 U.S. 532.
Clevinger v. Saxner (1985). 54 LW 4048.
Connick v. Myers (1983). 461 U.S. 138.
Coyle, M. (1987). "Major Liberal Victories Dominate Rehnquist Term." *National Law Journal* (August 17): S2–S3.
Davis v. Scherer (1984). 468 U.S. 183.
Elrod v. Burns (1976). 427 U.S. 347.
Firefighters Local v. Stotts (1984). 104 S.Ct. 2576.
Gormley, W. (1986). "The Representation Revolution." *Administration and Society* 18 (August): 179–196.
Harlow v. Fitzgerald (1982). 457 U.S. 800.
Harvard Law Review (1977). "Developments in the Law—Section 1983 and Federalism." Volume 90: 1133–1361.
——— (1984). "Developments in the Law—Public Employment." Volume 97: 1611–1800.
Johnson v. Transportation Agency (1987). 55 LW 4379.
Lauter, D. (1986). "A New Polarization for the High Court." *National Law Journal* (August 11): S2–S4.
Matthews v. Eldridge (1976). 424 U.S. 319.
Memphis Community School District v. Stachura (1986). 54 LW 4771.
Nixon v. Fitzgerald (1982). 457 U.S. 731.
O'Connor v. Ortega (1987). 55 LW 4405.

Pembaur v. Cincinnati (1986). 89 L.Ed.2d 452.

Pickering v. Board of Education (1968). 391 U.S. 563.

Rankin v. McPherson (1987). 55 LW 5019.

Rosenbloom, D. H. (1971). *Federal Service and the Constitution: The Development of the Public Employment Relationship*. Ithaca, NY: Cornell University Press.

———(1975). "Public Personnel Administration and the Constitution: An Emergent Approach." *Public Administration Review* 35 (January/February): 52–59.

——— (1977). "The Public Employee in Court: Implications for Urban Government," pp. 57–82 in Charles Levine, (ed.). *Managing Human Resources*. Beverly Hills: Sage.

——— (1987a). "Public Administration and the Judiciary: T he 'New Partnership.'" *Public Administration Review* 47 (January/February): 75–83.

——— (1987b). "Liberty, Law, and Bureaucracy." Presented at the American Society For Public Administration Conference, Boston, Massachusetts, March 29–April 1. Forthcoming in P. Van Riper and F. Burke (ed.), *Three Centuries of Public Administration*.

Smith v. Wade (1983). 461 U.S. 30.

Steelworkers v. Weber (1979). 443 U.S. 193.

U.S. Civil Service Commission (1941). *History of the Federal Service*. Washington, D.C.: Government Printing Office.

United States v. Paradise (1987). 55 LW 4211.

Vaughn, R. (1977). "Public Employees and the Right to Disobey." *Hastings Law Journal* 29 (November): 261–295.

Wood v. Strickland (1975). 420 U.S. 308.

Wygant v. Jackson (1986). 90 L. Ed. 2d 260.

CHAPTER 23

DUE PROCESS AND PUBLIC PERSONNEL MANAGEMENT

DEBORAH D. GOLDMAN

Introduction

The federal judiciary has given a great deal of attention to the issues posed by the application of procedural due process to adverse actions against public employees. On the surface, it has frequently appeared that federal judges were trying to control both the substance and process through which public employees were disciplined. Indeed, public managers and politicians occasionally complain that it is becoming increasingly difficult to manage the public sector as a result of judicial intervention of this nature.

However, a more thoroughgoing analysis of the content of Supreme Court decisions concerning the due process rights of public employees indicates that the Court has not generally attempted to substitute its judgment for that of executive branch officials on the merits of whether an individual civil servant should be dismissed. Rather, for the most part, the Court has sought to establish guidelines for the constitutional treatment of public employees in adverse action cases. Thus, most of the Court's attention has been paid to matters of procedure. Although it is sometimes argued that the process required by the judiciary in adverse action cases has become so elaborate that public managers are deterred from undertaking it except in extreme instances, there is reason to believe that this view is considerably overstated (Merrill 1973). In reality, judicial involvement in this area of public personnel management has been far more limited than is sometimes perceived. Moreover, at the present time the Supreme Court appears to be reducing the relevance of procedural due process to public employment even further.

Procedural Due Process

One of the difficulties generally confronting public personnel managers in trying to apply procedural due process in adverse actions is determining precisely what the constitution and court require. Indeed, the judiciary has not developed a rigid definition of procedural

From 2 *Review of Public Personnel Administration,* 1: 19–27, Fall 1981. Copyright © 1981 Sage Publications. Reprinted with permission.

due process. For instance, in *Hannah v. Larche* (1960: 442) the Supreme Court specifically addressed the amorphous character of procedural due process: "'Due process' is an elusive concept. . . Whether the Constitution requires that a particular right obtain in a specific proceeding depends upon a complexity of factors. The nature of the alleged right involved, the nature of the proceeding, and the possible burden on that proceeding, are all considerations which must be taken into account." Generally, however, procedural due process involves at least the right to notice of the proposed government action, the reasons for it, and an opportunity to respond. It often goes further by affording the injured individual a hearing before an impartial official. The hearing may include the right to counsel, confrontation, cross examination, and the subpoena witnesses. It may also have to be open to the public.

Historically, the Supreme Court has been extremely reluctant to make procedural due process applicable to adverse actions against public employees. The reasons for this appear to be primarily twofold. Firstly, from the 1830s through the 1950s, the Court's reluctance could be attributed to its adherence to the then prevailing doctrine of privilege, as noted by Rosenbloom in his essay ["The Sources of Continuing Conflict Between The Constitution and Public Personnel Management." 2 *Review of Public Personnel Administration*, 1 (Fall 1981): 3–18]. For example, in *Bailey v. Richardson* (1951) the Court sustained the opinion of a lower court that allowed a federal employee to be dismissed for disloyalty after a procedure in which she was denied the right to confront and cross examine the informants against her, who were also unknown to the Loyalty Board hearing her case. Secondly, and more recently, the Court has sought to reduce its role in defining the procedural rights of public employees in an effort to avoid over-burdening public personnel management with excessive judicial intervention and also in order to reduce the pressures on the federal courts' crowded dockets. In fact, the Court has explicitly announced that the federal judiciary is not the appropriate forum for the resolution of mistakes by public personnel managers. During the 1960s and early 1970s, however, the Supreme Court expressed a markedly different view.

The doctrine of privilege was never confined to public employment. It defined the constitutional relationship between the individual and the government in most situations where some form of governmental largess was being distributed (Reich 1964; Van Alystyne 1968). Its demise by the 1960s coincided with a period of remarkable judicial activism in which the rights of individuals generally underwent a widespread expansion. In the area of the procedural due process rights of public employees, the doctrine's influence eroded primarily as a result of two factors. Firstly, the abuses of the loyalty-security program in the 1950s led the Supreme Court to reconsider the rights of an individual whose dismissal from government impugned her or his reputation. For instance, in *Cafeteria Workers v. McElroy* (1961: 898) the Court had occasion "to acknowledge that there exist constitutional restraints upon state and federal governments in dealing with their employees," although it declined to apply these to the facts before it. Nevertheless, the Court's discussion was a major step away from the confines of the doctrine of privilege.

Secondly, the Court's decision in cases involving other kinds of government largess led to a different view of the procedural due process rights of public employees. In *Goldberg v. Kelly* (1970: 262–263), for example, the court articulated a general standard for the application of due process to instances of deprivation of governmental benefits: "The extent to which procedural due process must be afforded the recipient is influenced by the extent to which he may be 'condemned to suffer grievous loss' . . . and depends upon whether the recipient's interest in avoiding that loss outweighs the governmental interest in summary adjudication." But, based on this concept, under what circumstances will a public employee's loss in an adverse action be considered sufficiently "grievous" so as to trigger a right to procedural due process?

The Supreme Court's initial answer came two years after its decision in *Goldberg v. Kelly*. In *Board of Regents v. Roth* (1972), it delineated the grounds upon which a public employee whose employment was terminated could assert a right to procedural due process. These were:

1. Where the employees had a "property interest" in the job.
2. Where the termination infringed upon an employee's liberty interests by harming her or his reputation and/or adversely affecting her or his future employablility.
3. Where the termination was in retaliation for the exercise of protected substantive constitutional rights, such as freedom of speech or assembly.

Almost immediately upon defining these conditions, however, the Court was confronted with complexities of applying them to specific circumstances. Indeed, in the process of using them as guidelines, it has drastically limited the applicability of procedural due process to public personnel management.

The first signs of difficulty in applying the *Roth* ruling appeared in *Arnett v. Kennedy* (1974). The case presented at least five complex questions involved in the termination of a federal employee and the Court found itself unable to develop a majority opinion on how these should be answered. Mr. Kennedy was a non-probationary federal employee with the Chicago regional office of the Office of Economic Opportunity. Employee Kennedy was dismissed because he publicly accused Supervisor Arnett of attempting to use federal money to bribe a third party to make false accusations against him. Pursuant to statutory and Civil Service Commission regulations Kennedy was notified of the action and afforded an opportunity to respond in writing. However, he refused to abide by this process, asserting instead that he had a right to a trial type hearing before and impartial hearing officer prior to the dismissal. The Supreme Court divided 5 to 4 on the matter of whether Kennedy should be reinstated, holding against him. But Kennedy's circumstances perplexed the justices greatly.

One complex issue was the applicability of due process. Three justices, Rehnquist, Burger, and Stewart, the authors of the *Roth* decision, thought that Kennedy had no constitutional right to procedural due process. They argued that he had no property right in his position because the prevailing statute, the Lloyd-LaFollete Act of 1912, allowed dismissals for such cause as would promote the "efficiency" of the service. This opinion argued that the dismissal procedure established by Congress in that statute was controlling, since to the extent that federal employees had a property interest in their jobs it was created by that act. As Rehnquist expressed it, "Where the grant of a substantive right is inextricably intertwined with the limitations on the procedures which are to be employed in determining that right, a litigant in the position of appellee must take the bitter with the sweet" (*Arnett v. Kennedy* 1974: 153–155).

The remaining members of the Court disagreed with this approach. Presumably, they agreed with the gist of Justice Powell's opinion, which was joined by Justice Blackmun. Powell reasoned that: "While the legislature may elect not to confer a property interest in federal employment, it may not constitutionally authorize the deprivation of such an interest, once conferred, without appropriate procedural safeguards" (*Arnett v. Kennedy* 1974: 167). In this view, then, once a legislature confers a property interest upon public employees by statutorily limiting the grounds for their removal, the procedure by which dismissals can take place is controlled by the Constitution, not the statute. However, Powell did not believe that the Constitution required the kind of hearing Kennedy sought prior to his actual dismissal.

The division of the justices on the matter of whether the Constitution or the statute should control the termination of a property interest was of great importance. It indicated that despite the *Roth* decision, at least three members of the court were dissatisfied with the notion that constitutional due process should be afforded to civil servants whose tenure was protected by statute.

Justice White concurred in part and dissented in part. In terms of procedural due process he argued that Kennedy had the constitutional right to be dismissed by an impartial official, and not by the very individual he publicly accused of committing a crime.

Justices Marshall, Douglas, and Brennan dissented on several grounds. They believed that a balancing of the government's interests against those of the employee required that Kennedy be afforded a full evidentiary hearing before an impartial official prior to termination. They also argued that the Lloyd-LaFollette Act was unconstitutionally vague and overbroad because it deterred federal employees from exercising their first amendment rights, for fear that their public speech would be construed as detracting from the efficiency of the federal service.

For the most part, the Court's action in the *Arnett* case suggested that its construction of the principles developed in *Roth* would be very narrow. Only three justices thought that Kennedy's dismissal violated both procedural and substantive constitutional rights. On the other hand, three justices considered the constitutional due process to be almost wholly irrelevant to the facts at hand. The remainder of the members of the Court found the Constitution to be applicable, but of these only Justice White thought it required a fairer process than Kennedy received. Future cases have limited the requirements of procedural due process even further.

"Property Interests"

Bishop v. Wood (1976) seems to have marked a clear turning point in the Supreme Court's approach to the procedural due process rights of public employees. The case involved the dismissal of police officer Bishop in Marion, North Carolina. Bishop was classified as a "permanent employee" under a city ordinance that afforded such employees a right to notification of the deficiencies in their work in dismissals for unsatisfactory performance. Bishop was not afforded a hearing to determine the sufficiency of the cause for his discharge prior to his dismissal. In addressing the issue of whether Bishop had a property interest in his job by virtue of being classified as a "permanent employee," the Court, per Justice Stevens, held that "a property interest in employment can, of course, be created by ordinance, or by an implied contract. In either case, however, the sufficiency of the claim of entitlement must be decided by reference to state law" (*Bishop v. Wood* 1976: 344). The Court appears to have reached this conclusion in an effort not to overburden state personnel management with restraints imposed by the federal judiciary and the Constitution. In Stevens' words, "The ultimate control of state personnel relationships is, and will remain, with the States; they may grant or withhold tenure at their unfettered discretion" (*Bishop v. Wood* 1976: 344).

Under this construction, therefore, the Court's task was to determine whether the ordinance under which Bishop was classified as a permanent employee could be interpreted to convey a property interest. In addressing this question, the court took a narrow view of the concept of property interest. Following the District Court and an equally divided Court of Appeals, both of which had decided the case earlier, it held that despite the ordinance, the employee held his position at the will and pleasure of the city. It reasoned that even though the ordinance specifically allowed dismissals of permanent employees for negligence, inefficiency, or unfitness, it did not prevent them for other legitimate causes. Needless to add, perhaps, that it is highly unusual for the Supreme Court to look for authority in an equally divided lower court.

In sum, *Bishop v. Wood* considerably reduced the likelihood that a public employee would be able to assert a "property interest" which would trigger a constitutional right to procedural due process in dismissals. The case had ramifications for "liberty interests" as well.

"Liberty Interests"

Part of the issue in *Bishop v. Wood* was whether Bishop's dismissal harmed his reputation and future employability to such an extent that it violated his "liberty interests" in the absence of a pre-termination evidentiary hearing. In this context, too, the Court was unsympathetic to the public employee. Bishop was dismissed for failure to follow orders, poor attendance at training sessions, and unbecoming conduct. However, given the way the case was framed, the Supreme Court concluded that "we must . . . assume that his discharge was a mistake and based on incorrect information" (*Bishop v. Wood* 1976: 348). Nevertheless, it held that Bishop's constitutional right to procedural due process was not violated because "it would stretch the concept [of procedural due process] too far to suggest that a person is deprived of "liberty" when he simply is not rehired in one job but remains as free as before to seek another. This same conclusion applies to the discharge of a public employee whose position is terminable at the will of the employer when there is no public disclosure of the reasons for the discharge" (*Bishop v. Wood* 1976: 348). Consequently, since the city did not publicly release the reasons for Bishop's dismissal, it did not infringe upon his liberty interests. Justices Brennan and Marshall dissented on this point, arguing that the Court was allowing the government to tell the employee one set of reasons for his dismissal, while effectively remaining free to tell prospective employers another.

What accounts for the Supreme Court's unsympathetic stance toward public employees' procedural due process rights in the *Bishop* case? Perhaps the answer is best conveyed in the Court's own words:

> The federal court is not the appropriate forum in which to review the multitude of personnel decisions that are made daily by public agencies. We must accept the harsh fact that numerous individual mistakes are inevitable in the day-to-day administration of our affairs. The United States Constitution cannot feasibly be construed to require federal judicial review for every such error. In the absence of any claim that the public employer was motivated by a desire to curtail or to penalize the exercise of an employee's constitutionally protected rights, we must presume that official action was regular and, if erroneous, can best be corrected in other ways. The Due Process Clause of the Fourteenth Amendment is not a guarantee against incorrect or ill-advised personnel decisions (*Bishop v. Wood*, 1976: 349–350).

In short, the Court was calling a halt to the expansion of judicial involvement in the procedural aspects of public personnel management.

The essence of this approach was reiterated in *Codd v. Velger* (1977), which reduced the scope of an employee's liberty interests even further. Velger was a probationary patrolman who was dismissed from his position for having placed a revolver to his head in an apparent suicide attempt while a trainee. He was not afforded a hearing, but asserted that he had a right to one due to the stigmatizing effect of certain material placed by the city in his personnel file. This information subsequently brought about his dismissal from a position with a private police agency and severely injured his employability.

In addressing the issue of whether the principles developed in *Roth* required that Velger be afforded a hearing, the Court reasoned that "the hearing required where a nontenured employee has been stigmatized in the course of a decision to terminate his employment is solely 'to provide the person an opportunity to clear his name.' If he does not challenge the substantial truth of the material in question, no hearing would afford a promise of achieving that result for him . . . Only if the employer creates and disseminates a false and defamatory impression about the employee in connection with his termination is such a hearing required" (*Codd v. Velger* 1977: 627)

Violation of Substantive Constitutional Rights

The *Bishop* and *Codd* decisions considerably narrowed the scope of the *Roth* ruling with regard to matters of property and liberty interests. On the other hand, however, the Supreme Court has not substantially reduced the scope of procedural due process where an employee's dismissal violates substantive constitutional rights, such as those protected by the first amendment. If anything, the Court has expanded public employees' substantive rights and has not shown signs of allowing their erosion at the hands of public personnel managers through inadequate procedural protections (*Elrod v. Burns* 1976; *Mt. Healthy City School District Board of Education v. Doyle* 1977; *Givhan v. Western Line Consolidated School District* 1979; *Branti v. Finkel* 1980; Rosenbloom and Gille 1975). The clearest example of the Court's desire to protect substantive rights through procedural due process was presented in *Mt. Healthy City School District Board of Education v. Doyle.*

Doyle was an untenured school teacher who also headed the Teachers' Association. He was involved in several incidents which apparently led to his dismissal for "a notable lack of tact in handling professional matters . . . [and] much doubt as to . . . sincerity in establishing good school relationships" (*Mt. Healthy City School District Board of Education v. Doyle* 1977: 283). Among Doyle's alleged misdeeds was informing a radio station of the issuance of an official memorandum pertaining to teacher dress and appearance. He was also argumentative with his colleagues and students, sometimes provoking physical violence and obscenity.

Upon dismissal, Doyle claimed that the School Board had violated his First and Fourteenth Amendment rights. The Supreme Court addressed the issue in the following fashion: "Doyle's claims under the First and Fourteenth Amendments are not defeated by the fact that he did not have tenure. Even though he could have been discharged for no reason whatever, and had no constitutional right to a hearing prior to the decision not to rehire him . . . he may nonetheless establish a claim to reinstatement if the decision not to rehire him was made by reason of his exercise of constitutionally protected First Amendment freedoms" (*Mt. Healthy City School District Board of Education v. Doyle* 1977: 283–284). The question, then, was whether Doyle was fired in retaliation for the exercise of constitutionally guaranteed rights or whether his dismissal was based on conduct not protected by that document. Since Doyle very well could have been discharged for the latter alone, it was incumbent upon the Court to develop a standard for dealing with such instances.

In so doing, the Court developed an approach which implies a substantial amount of procedural due process protection for public employees in such circumstances. It held that:

> Initially, in this case, the burden was properly placed upon respondent [Doyle] to show that his conduct was constitutionally protected, and that, this conduct was a "substantial factor"—or, to put it in other words, that it was a "motivating factor" in the Board's decision not to rehire him. Respondent having carried that burden, however, the District Court should have gone on to determine whether the Board had shown by a preponderance of the evidence that it would have reached the same decision as to respondent's reemployment even in the absence of the protected conduct (*Mt. Healthy City School District Board of Education v. Doyle* 1977: 287).

But where is the employee to show that constitutionally protected conduct was a substantial factor in his dismissal? The answer appears to be either in federal district court or in some kind of administrative hearing before an impartial hearing officer. And, if the employee carries this initial burden, the employer will be compelled to respond in the same forum. In either event, it is evident that extensive procedural due process will be afforded the employee. Thus, where substantive constitutional rights, such as making public or private statements about an employer, are implicated in a nonretention or dismissal, in practice the public employee may be afforded elaborate procedural due process.

Conclusion

The public employee's constitutional right to procedural due process in terminations currently appears to be rather limited. Although this right can be triggered by breaches of the employee's property or liberty interest, the Supreme Court has construed these in a narrow fashion. Its decisions in *Bishop v. Wood* and *Codd v. Velger* establish substantial barriers to the public employee who would claim such interests have been infringed. This is a reality that may be somewhat misunderstood by public personnel managers. Despite much publicity to the contrary, they currently enjoy considerable constitutional flexibility in terminating public employees. At the moment, the major barrier in terms of procedural due process arises where a termination involves the possibility of retaliation for the exercise of a protected substantive constitutional right. In such instances, under the logic the *Mt. Healthy* ruling, the employee must be afforded a forum in which to show that her or his dismissal infringed upon such a right.

Despite the limited applicability of procedural due process, however, public personnel managers may afford such protections as a matter of policy. And, as Rosenbloom argues in his essay, in the long-run such an approach might be desirable as a means of reducing some of the incompatibilities between public administrative theory and constitutional values.

References

Arnett v. Kennedy (1974). 416 *U. S.* 134.
Bailey v. Richardson (1951). 341 *U.S.* 918.
Bishop v. Wood (1976). 426 *U. S.* 341.
Board of Regents v. Roth (1972). 408 *U.S.* 564.
Branti v. Finkel (1980). No. 78-1654 (March 31).
Cafeteria Workers v. McElroy (1961). 367 *U.S.* 886.
Codd v. Velger (1977). 429 *U. S.* 624.
Elrod v. Burns (1976). 427 *U. S.* 347.
Givhan v. Western Line Consolidated School District (1979). 99 *S.C.* 693.
Goldberg v. Kelly (1970) 397 *U. S.* 254.
Hannah v. Larche (1960). 363 *U. S.* 420.
Merrill, R. (1973). "Procedure for Adverse Actions Against Federal Employees." *Virginia Law Review* 59 (February): 196–287.
Mt. Healthy City School District Board of Education v. Doyle (1977). 429 *U.S.* 274.
Reich, C. (1964). "The New Property." *Yale Law Journal* 73: 733–787.
Rosenbloom, D.H. and J.A. Gille (1975). "The Current Constitutional Approach to Public Employment." *Kansas Law Review* 23 (Winter): 249–275.
Van Alstyne, W. (1968). "The Demise of the Right-Privilege Distinction in Constitutional Law." *Harvard Law Review* 81: 1439–1464.

CHAPTER 24

CURBING PATRONAGE WITHOUT PAPERASSERIE

CHRISTOPHER DANIEL

Antipatronage reform is a perennial issue that refuses to go away. Systemic patronage continues in many counties, some cities, and at least a few states. Stahl (1990: 309) discerns renascent patronage amid "a profound weakening of the federal career service." Of course, some political hiring and firing is legitimate. This commentary uses the term "patronage" to refer only to politically motivated appointments made at the entry and middle organizational levels. Patronage appointments of upper level policy makers and their confidential assistants is easily justified, but extension of the principle to others reduces organizational effectiveness and violates First Amendment rights protected by *Rutan v. Republican Party of Illinois* (1990).

Patronage continues to adversely affect the efficiency of the public service. It has become anachronistic as public jobs have become more complex, professionalism has grown, and new approaches to organizing for productivity have emerged. Many organizations pursue quality and productivity by developing mission-oriented cultures and fostering decision making by production-level workers and their supervisors. Unfortunately, patronage practices stifle such efforts. Decisions to select or promote individuals send strong signals about real priorities, be they mission fulfillment, cronyism, or supporting campaigns.

Patronage reinforces bureaucratic centralism; instead of eliciting production-level participation, it sends supervisors and employees the message that their views do not matter much. The National Academy of Public Administration (1983), Ingraham and Rosenbloom (1990), and Carnevale (1991) have advocated increasing the personnel authority of line managers, but such efforts are not likely to succeed unless patronage pressures are restrained.

Despite their architects' virtuous intentions, civil service reforms sometimes create new problems, enmeshing public personnel in a control mentality emphasizing "the triumph of technique over purpose" (Sayre 1948). Such systems produce excessive paperwork, which the French aptly call *paperasserie* (Sharp 1952). In some jurisdictions, restrictive practices have outlived the abuses they were designed to curtail; improvement may be accomplished there by loosening the controls. A dilemma occurs,

---

From 53 *Public Administration Review,* 4: 387–390, July/August 1993. Copyright © 1993 American Society for Public Administration. Reprinted with permission.

however, in jurisdictions where patronage endures despite the presence of restrictions. Which threat is greatest to such organizations' effectiveness, the dysfunctions of patronage or those associated with traditional remedies? There are traditional patronage jurisdictions, such as some rural counties, have never experimented with reform. How should their innovations proceed? Perhaps fresh reform approaches can address these dilemmas.

To curb patronage while minimizing *paperasserie,* jurisdictions should be pragmatic, not moralistic, emphasizing monitoring of employee perceptions, decentralization of hiring, and increased use of assessment technology. Sired by reform movements and invigorated recently by the courts, antipatronage efforts have often been ambitious and moralistic, seeking to completely eliminate problematical practices. Litigants and unions often describe patronage and merit issues in terms of individual rights, justifying draconian remedies. If patronage supports a political "evil" or violates citizen or employee "rights," then logically, great effort should be made to eliminate it. When, however, the primary goal is to enhance organizational effectiveness, then merely curbing the practice, reducing its incidence, may be satisfactory.

Controls designed to prevent officials from basing decisions on patronage frequently produce inefficiencies of their own, so officials must accept tradeoffs. To comply with the *Shakman II* court decree, the city of Chicago battled patronage during the mid-1980s through a Detailed Hiring Plan (Freedman 1988, Hoskins 1989). While lauding the plan's effectiveness against patronage, Freedman also described dysfunctions one would expect to encounter whenever controls are imposed bureaucratically. Chicago officials implemented the hiring plan by documenting more personnel decision making (i.e., producing more red tape) and requiring approval by the personnel department for many routine decisions. Consequently, the time required to fill a position in Chicago increased from two to ten weeks. Perhaps such measures were justifiable, especially if they were temporary and no other means could successfully combat well-entrenched patronage institutions. At some point, centralized control costs become excessive, however, and line managers must be *trusted* to act appropriately without being constantly scrutinized. Officials must strike a balance, achieving an optimal combination of controls, trust, and acceptance of an intractable residue of patronage activity.

Chicago's hiring plan was reviewed using a process modeled after systems of financial accountability, requiring documentation of rationale for personnel transactions, followed by record audits. Financial systems can trace cash and goods, but it is very difficult for reviewers to second guess hiring and promotional decisions. At best, the written record can only provide clues about whether particular decisions were based upon patronage, amicism, predicted job performance, or the simple desire to fill vacancies quickly. Rather than emphasizing accountability through documentation it may sometimes be preferable to promote accountability for perceptions, *surveying* informed observers about the norms guiding selection and promotion. As Freedman noted, Chicago conducted a survey as an additional method of monitoring compliance with *Shakman,* obtaining responses from newly hired employees, newly promoted employees, and rejected applicants. Such individuals' interpretations of decision making are useful, especially when comparisons can made among departments and over time. Individuals sometimes perceive events erroneously, but overall survey findings illuminate organizational climate. Disseminating such data may have a positive influence on elected administrations, since those accountable to the electorate prefer to avoid negative publicity. The Merit System Protection Board has actively pursued accountability for perceptions by surveying federal managers and personnel officers repeatedly during the 1980s, asking whether they have observed prohibited patronage practices, sex discrimination, and racial discrimination (Ban and Redd 1990).

Ideally, antipatronage reform efforts should reduce, or at least not increase, bureaucratic centralism. Ironically, both patronage mechanisms and some reform counter measures (clearances from civil service boards, personnel department policing) increase central control.

To ensure that positions and promotions are given only to the politically faithful, patronage systems implement high level clearance systems. Consider, for example, the extreme centralization that led to the *Rutan* case in Illinois (Katz 1991). Originally justified on fiscal control grounds, a hiring freeze was extended for ten years, requiring *all* employment decisions to be approved by the governor's office. Obviously, if cost cutting had been the freeze's only objective, it could have been accomplished by having cabinet-level officials establish ceilings, or approve the existence of position *openings,* without personally evaluating production-level individuals. What rationale other than patronage could have justified directly involving gubernatorial aides in selection and promotion of a geographically dispersed work force of 60,000?

Ironically, Harold Washington's administration was accused of exercising patronage while it simultaneously executed major reforms through Chicago's Detailed Hiring Plan (Freedman 1988). Accusations centered on the activities of a mayoral liaison who personally approved all sewer department hires. Whatever the reality may have been in that instance, such arrangements look suspicious because they violate sound management principles. Selection and promotion should be based upon appraisals of applicants' future performance, requiring decision makers to know as much as possible about both candidates and jobs. Unless an organization is very small, lower level supervisors are much more likely to possess such knowledge than are those at the top.

As with other forms of human endeavor, patronage requires its own administrative infrastructure to succeed on a systemic scale. Several state managers in Kentucky have described structures to this writer closely resembling those discerned by Katz (1991) in Illinois:

> The governor's patronage director relied on a network of people in each agency to provide information about job openings and the partisan inclinations of applicants. The designated informer within an agency was known as the "key person." He or she was usually an administrative assistant to the agency director. The key person operated separately from the agency's regular personnel office.

Obviously, the effectiveness of patronage operatives is enhanced when hiring and promotion decisions are highly centralized within an agency, with all hires and promotions, no matter how humble, requiring top approval. So, decentralization of these functions within line agencies may dent the covert infrastructure, reducing the incidence of patronage, while empowering supervisors and middle managers. In other words, it may sometimes be possible to curb patronage without resorting to stifling bureaucratic controls.

Reform should not simply reduce the incidence of patronage, but should make selection as demonstrably job related as possible, emphasizing supervisory-level use of assessment technology. Professionally developed tests remain important, but they should be supplemented with structured interviews and performance simulation activities developed by line officials. This may require personnel staff to alter their roles, shifting from policing modes to a consulting and service orientation. Assessment devices developed by lower level officials are sometimes imperfect, but are better than the status quo alternative—informal interviewing. Traditional, informal interviews have little or no validity (Arvey and Campion 1982), but structured interviews have corrected validity up to .62 (Wiesner and Cronshaw 1988: 284), accounting for up to 38 percent of applicants' later variations in job performance. Structured interviews can be conducted in a variety of ways, but the more time-consuming approaches, emphasizing job analysis and creation of scoring guides, seem to produce the most validity.

Adding structure to interviews can also reduce legal vulnerability (Gatewood and Feild 1990). Technically, all interviews are tests, so plaintiffs sometimes challenge their outcomes in civil rights (Title VII), age (AREA), and disability (ADA) discrimination suits. Informally conducted interviews are vulnerable to legal challenges because interviewers discuss topics not related to the job at hand, sometimes inadvertently making statements interpretable as discriminatory. A recent study by the Assessment Council of the International Personnel Management Association (Feuquay 1990) identified structured interviewing, work sample tests, and biodata instruments as promising techniques producing relatively high validity without imposing adverse impact on racial minorities.

Contemporary reformers possess resources their Progressive-era forbearers did not enjoy. Technical tools of surveying, assessment, and decentralized management can now be deployed against patronage, and computer and communications technologies assist dissemination of information about position openings. Tests, long effective tools, have benefited from research by several generations of industrial psychologists. Informed by past experiences with red tape, reformers may finally be able to avoid letting technique triumph over purpose, as creative antipatronage efforts help revive the personnel function and invigorate the public service.

References

Arvey, Richard D. and James E. Campion, 1982. "The Employment Interview: A Summary and Survey of Recent Research." *Personnel Psychology,* vol. 35, pp. 281–321.
Ban, Carolyn and Harry C. Redd III, 1990. "The State of the Merit System: Perceptions of Abuse in the Federal Civil Service." *Review of Public Personnel Administration,* vol. 10, no. 3 (Summer), pp. 55–72.
Carnevale, David G., 1991. "The Learning Support Model: Personnel Doctrine the Mass Production Paradigm." Paper presented at the National Conference of the American Society for Public Administration. Washington, DC.

Daniel, Christopher and Bruce J. Rose, 1991. "Blending Professionalism and Political Acuity; Empirical Support for an Emerging Ideal." *Public Administration Review,* vol. 51, no. 5 (September/October), pp. 438–441.

Feuquay, Jeffrey P., ed., 1990. *Recent Innovations in Public Sector Assessment.* Personnel Assessment Monographs. Alexandria, VA: International Personnel Management Association-Assessment Council.

Freedman, Anne, 1988. "Doing Battle with the Patronage Army: Politics, Courts, and Personnel Administration in Chicago." *Public Administration Review,* vol. 48 (September/October), pp. 847–859.

Gatewood, Robert D. and Hubert S. Feild, 1990. *Human Resource Selection.* Chicago: Dryden Press.

Hoskins, Jesse E., 1989. "Chicago Personnel Administration: A Management Process." *Public Administration Review,* vol. 49, no. 1 (January/February), pp. 93–94.

Ingraham, P. W. and D. H. Rosenbloom, 1990. *The State of the Merit System in the Federal Government.* Occasional paper presented to the National Commission on the Public Service. Washington, DC.

Katz, Jeffrey L., 1991. "The Slow Death of Patronage." *Governing* (April), pp. 59–62.

National Academy of Public Administration, 1983. "Revitalizing Federal Management Managers and their Overburdened Systems." Washington, DC.

Newland, Chester A., 1979. "Public Personnel Administration: Legalistic Reforms vs. Effectiveness, Efficiency and Economy." In Alan Saltzstein, ed., *Public Employees and Policy Making.* Pacific Palisades, CA: Palisades Publishers, pp. 236–247.

Rutan v. Republican Party of Illinois, 1990. 110 S. Ct. 2729.

Savas, E. S. and Sigmund G. Ginsburg 1979. "The Civil Service: A Meritless System." In Alan Saltzstein, *ed., Public Employees and w Making.* Pacific Palisades, CA: Palisades Publishers, pp. 223–236.

Sayre, Wallace S., 1948. "The Triumph of Techniques Over Purpose." *Public Administration Review,* vol. 8 (Spring). pp. 134–137.

Sharp, Walter Rice, 1952. "Procedural Vices: la Paperasserie." In Robert K. Merton, Ailsa P. Gray, Barbara Hockey, and Hanan C. Selvin, eds., *Reader in Bureaucracy.* Glencoe, IL Free Press, pp. 407–410.

Stahl, Glenn, 1990. "A Retrospective and Prospective; the Moral Dimension." In Steven W. Hays and Richard C. Kearney, eds., *Public Personnel Administration; Problems and Prospects.* Englewood Cliffs, NJ: Prentice-Hall, pp. 308–321.

Wiesner, Willi H. and Steven F. Cronshaw, 1988. "A Meta-Analytic Investigation of the Impact of Validity Format and Degree of Structure on the Validity of the Employment Interview." *Journal of Occupational Psychology,* vol. 61, pp. 275–290.

CHAPTER 25

DRUG TESTING IN THE PUBLIC SECTOR

A Legal Analysis

NORMA M. RICCUCCI

A priority in American domestic policy over the past few years has been to win the battle against drug use in our society. Efforts to combat drugs seemed to have reached full throttle in 1986 when the President's Commission on Organized Crime recommended drug testing in the work place as one method for stopping the use of illegal drugs (Dale 1987; Elliot 1989). Since then, a number of controversial political and legal actions have been taken to operationalize the commission's recommendations.

Is the government, either as an employer or regulator of private sector employment, within legal and constitutional bounds when it requires employees to undergo drug testing? This question has been addressed extensively by lower courts and, more recently, by the U.S. Supreme Court in two cases. In this essay, the substantive questions of law that are raised by testing public sector employees for drug use primarily are examined. Private sector employees also receive some attention insofar as the government develops laws and regulations for certain industries (e.g., railroad) for the purpose of protecting and promoting the safety and health of the general public. In recent years, a component of such regulations is a requirement that the employees of that regulated industry be tested for drug use. The article closes with forecasted legal trends in drug testing and the implications for public as well as private sector employers.

Legal Theories of Drug Testing

Questions about the legitimacy of drug testing have been raised under several legal theories. For example, some employees have challenged the legality of drug-testing programs under Title VII of the Civil Rights Act of 1964 as amended (Martin 1988; Moore 1987). In one such case, *The Shield Club v. City of Cleveland* (1986), black police cadets alleged that the use of urine tests to detect drugs has a disparate impact against blacks. Their argument was based on the theory that melanin, the hormone responsible for skin tone, creates fragments within urine that closely resemble cannabinoids (*Shield*

From 20 *The American Review of Public Administration*, 2: 95–106, June 1990. Copyright © 1990 Sage Publications, Inc. Reprinted with permission.

Club 1986: 277), and the darker the skin tone, the greater amount of melanin fragments will appear in urine samples. To the extent that this theory is correct, drug testing would have a disproportionately harsh impact on racial minorities, thereby calling into question its legality under Title VII.

Drug testing also may fall within the scope of the Rehabilitation Act of 1973. Specifically, Section 504 of this Act proscribes discrimination against persons who are "otherwise qualified" but have or are perceived to have a disability within the meaning of "physical or mental impairment." Thus it may be unlawful for an employer to make employment decisions based on a positive drug test if the employer cannot demonstrate that the drugs are the actual cause of impaired job performance (Zimmerman 1989; but see, for example, *American Federation of Government Employees v. Dole* 1987 and *American Federation of Government Employees v. Skinner* 1989).

Aside from these statutes, drug testing also poses a threat to public employees' due-process rights under the Fifth and Fourteenth Amendments to the U.S. Constitution. For example, a requirement that job applicants list all of the drugs they are currently using or have used raises due-process concerns (Moore 1987; Weeks 1988). It is important to note, however, that relatively few cases have been decided based on these premises (due-process concerns around the accuracy of tests and employment decisions made when employees test positive for drug use will be discussed in a later section). In addition, the case law under Title VII and the Rehabilitation Act has yet to unfold. Yet it is very timely to examine the constitutionality of drug testing under the Fourth Amendment since the preponderance of legal challenges to drug testing thus far have been brought under this body of law.

The Constitutionality of Drug Testing Under the Fourth Amendment

There appears to be general agreement in state and federal courts that drug testing falls within the purview of the Fourth Amendment to the Constitution, which provides protection "against unreasonable searches and seizures." That is, because drug testing involves "seizing" individuals in order to obtain and analyze their blood and/or urine, the testing procedures constitute a "search" and "seizure" as prescribed by the Fourth Amendment (Dale 1987; Sculnick 1989).

The basic thrust of the Fourth Amendment is to protect the privacy rights of individuals. In this Amendment, however, is the explicit recognition that the government, under certain circumstances, may need to intrude upon individuals' expectations of privacy for the benefit, protection, or safety of the general public. Thus, although the Fourth Amendment proscribes "unreasonable" searches, it implicitly permits reasonable ones that seek to promote governmental interests. It is the definition of unreasonable and reasonable that has created questions and confusion around the constitutionality of drug testing.

In general terms, as Cooper (1988: 316) has pointed out, "unreasonable is defined as lacking a valid search warrant"—that is, one that has not and cannot be justified by "probable cause" (Rosenbloom 1983).[1] The flip side of this, of course, is that the government can reasonably and legally intrude upon individuals' privacy if the searches and seizures are conducted with a warrant or showing of probable cause. Once such requirements are fulfilled, the courts generally will rule that the government's interest in protecting the public outweighs the privacy rights of the individual.

Over the years, however, courts have permitted searches and seizures to be conducted without a warrant or probable cause, especially in administrative contexts, if the circumstances would make such requirements impractical.[2] Drug testing has been an area in which most courts have been willing to waive the warrant or probable-cause requirements in balancing governmental interests against individual privacy rights.

These courts instead have created three categories to judge the "reasonableness" and, hence, constitutionality of drug testing under the Fourth Amendment. The categories are (1) reasonable suspicion—or the stricter standard of individualized suspicion, (2) administrative search warrant exception, and (3) security and safety hazards. Key to each strategy is a balancing test whereby the courts will weigh the government's interest in protecting the public against the privacy rights of the individual.

The reasonable-suspicion standard, perhaps the strictest of the three, essentially requires the employer to have some reasonable grounds for suspecting that the employees are on drugs. This might require, for example, direct observation by a coworker or an undercover narcotics agent that the targeted employees have taken drugs. Most lower courts have not upheld drug-testing programs unless the employer has demonstrated reasonable suspicion of drug use (Dale 1987). According to these courts, then, for the government's interest in protecting the health and safety of the public to outweigh the intrusiveness of drug testing on individual privacy rights, there must be a showing of reasonable suspicion.

Some courts have constructed an even higher threshold for determining the constitutionality of drug testing by requiring the employer to produce evidence of *individualized* suspicion (Zimmerman 1989). This requires reasonable suspicion that an *individual,* rather than a group of employees, is impaired by drug use (Sculnick 1989; Tschirn 1988).

The administrative search exception is another category in which the courts have said that the Fourth Amendment's warrant and probable-cause requirements are unnecessary or impractical. Under this approach, lower courts as well as the U.S. Supreme Court, as will be discussed, have allowed warrantless searches in highly regulated industries such as horse racing (*Shoemaker v. Handel* 1986), coal mining (*Donavan v Dewey* 1975), and the armed forces (*Committee for G.I. Rights* 1975; also see Cooper 1988). These courts have reasoned that, by virtue of employment in a highly regulated industry, employees have a diminished expectation to privacy. Therefore, the government's interest in promoting the integrity of a work force or ensuring the safety of the general public outweighs the already-reduced privacy rights of employees. Ultimately, drug-testing programs in highly regulated industries are uniformly found constitutional under the Fourth Amendment.

The final category in which the courts have upheld the constitutionality of drug testing in the absence of a warrant or showing of probable cause is when security or safety risks are involved. For example, the Appeals Court for the Eighth Circuit in *McDonell v. Hunter* (1987) upheld a drug-testing program for correctional officers who had daily contact with inmates. The court reasoned that safety and security risks are posed if the employees responsible for prison security are themselves drug users. In this sense, courts have ruled that the government's interest in safeguarding the public from safety and security hazards outweighs the privacy rights of certain employees.

These categories provide a context for the U.S. Supreme Court's 1989 decisions on the constitutionality of drug testing under the Fourth Amendment. In the following section I will briefly examine these two cases.

The U.S. Supreme Court's 1989 Decisions on Drug Testing

In March 1989, the Supreme Court upheld the constitutionality of drug testing under the Fourth Amendment in two cases. The first case, *Skinner v. Railway Labor Executives' Association* (1989), involved a mandatory drug-testing program, instituted by the Federal Railroad Administration (FRA), for employees involved in certain types of train accidents. The FRA also adopted regulations that authorized the railroad industry to test employees violating certain rules (e.g., speed limits) for drug use.

The Court majority in *Skinner* began by providing a rationale for waiving the warrant and probable-cause requirements. It stated that the "government's interest in regulating the conduct of railroad employees to ensure safety . . . presents 'special needs' beyond normal law enforcement that may justify departures from the usual warrant and probable-cause requirements" (*Skinner* 1989: 4328–4329). Moreover, the Court said that "the burden of obtaining a warrant is likely to frustrate the governmental purpose behind the search" in that "the delay necessary to procure a warrant . . . may result in the destruction of valuable evidence" (*Skinner* 1989: 4329).

Once the court deemed the warrant and probable-cause requirements unnecessary and impracticable, it then conducted a balancing test, weighing the government's interests against the privacy rights of the railroad employees. As noted earlier, three categories often have been employed for determining the reasonableness and, hence, constitutionality of drug-testing programs in the absence of a warrant or probable cause requirement. The Court did not choose to rely on the reasonable suspicion or individualized suspicion standards, despite the fact that the Appeals Court found such a requirement essential. The Supreme Court (*Skinner* 1989) issued the following opinion:

> In limited circumstances, where the privacy interests implicated by the search are minimal, and where an important governmental interest furthered by the intrusion would be placed in jeopardy by the requirement of individualized suspicion, a search may be reasonable despite the absence of such suspicion. We believe this is true of the intrusions in question here. (p. 4330)

Rather, the Court opted to apply the other standards of reasonableness discussed above—warrantless search exception in regulated industries and safety and security hazards. The Court said, for example, that "the expectations of privacy of covered employees are diminished by reason of their participation in an industry that is regulated pervasively to ensure safety" (*Skinner* 1989: 4330). In addition, it suggested that drug abuse among railway employees poses serious safety hazards for the general public. The Court said that the government has an important goal "of ensuring safety in rail transportation" and thus "may take all necessary and reasonable regulatory steps to prevent or deter [the] hazardous conduct" presented by drug use (*Skinner* 1989: 4332).

The *Skinner* Court concluded that the government's interest in regulating the railway industry in order to promote the safety of the general public outweighs the already-diminished privacy rights of railroad employees. The drug-testing program was thus found reasonable or constitutional under the Fourth Amendment.

The conclusions of law were very similar in the U.S. Supreme Court's *National Treasury Employees Union v. Von Raab* (1987) decision. This case involved mandatory drug testing of Customs Service employees who handle classified material, who are required to carry firearms, or who seek transfers or promotions to jobs directly involved in the interdiction of drugs.

The *Von Raab* Court said that the standard of individualized suspicion is not a necessary component for measuring the reasonableness of a drug-testing program. Instead, the Court stated that the government has "compelling interests in safety and in the integrity of our borders" (*National Treasury* 1989: 4342). It went on to rule that

> in light of the extraordinary safety and national security hazards that would attend the promotion of drug users to positions that require the carrying of firearms or the interdiction of controlled substances, the [Customs] Service's policy of deterring drug users from seeking such promotions cannot be deemed unreasonable. (p. 4343)

The *Von Raab* Court concluded that the drug-testing program was constitutionally firm because governmental interests in minimizing safety and security hazards for the general public outweigh the privacy rights of at least those Customs Service employees that carry firearms or seek promotions to positions involving the interdiction of drugs. Based on the evidence presented, however, the Court did not find the testing of employees who handle classified material reasonable.

Drug Testing After Skinner and Von Raab

The standards employed by the U.S. Supreme Court in *Skinner* and *Von Raab* for determining the reasonableness of drug-testing programs have been applied by lower courts to several cases. For example, the U.S. Court of Appeals for the D.C. Circuit has applied them to three cases, as of this writing. It is interesting to note at the outset that the measures of reasonableness were deemed applicable despite the fact that these cases involved *random* drug testing.

In *Harmon v. Thornburgh* (1989), for example, the D.C. Circuit was called upon to judge the constitutionality of a random drug-testing program devised by the U.S. Department of Justice (DOJ) for three categories of employees: (1) prosecutors in criminal cases, (2) employees that have access to grand jury proceedings, and (3) employees with top secret national security clearances (*Harmon* 1989).

Relying upon the Supreme Court's rulings in *Skinner* and *Von Raab,* the appeals court upheld the constitutionality of the DOJ's random drug-testing program at least for the employees holding national security clearances.[3] The court reasoned that the government's interest in minimizing the security hazards that are posed by drug use among personnel in top secret posts outweighs the privacy interests of these employees.

Note that the court did not find the random nature of the program controlling. It stated that although "the random nature of the . . . testing plan is a relevant consideration [it does not require] us to undertake a fundamentally different analysis from that pursued by the Supreme Court in *Von Raab*" (*Harmon* 1989: 10). Although seemingly extreme, this aspect of the ruling actually comports with decisions issued by other appellate courts that generally have upheld random drug testing in occupations (e.g., corrections) in which there are heightened safety or security risks (see, for example, *McDonell v. Hunter* 1987).

In another case, *National Federation of Federal Employees v. Cheney* (1989), the Court of Appeals for the D.C. Circuit ruled on the constitutionality of a random drug-testing program developed by the Army for certain classes of workers (e.g., air traffic controllers, pilots, aircraft engine mechanics, police, and guards). Again, the court ruled that the random quality of the program was not controlling. The court upheld the legality of the program for those workers in aviation and police/guard positions on the grounds that the government's interest in ensuring the safety of the public outweighs the privacy interests of these particular employees.

In its most recent decision, the D.C. Circuit Court in *American Federation of Government Employees v. Skinner* (1989) upheld the constitutionality of a random drug-testing program for employees in the Department of Transportation who are involved in air, highway, water, and rail transportation on the grounds that their positions "bear a 'direct and immediate impact on the public health and safety, the promotion of life and property, law enforcement, or national security'" (p. 4).

There have been cases other than those ruled on by the D.C. Circuit that also are noteworthy. In particular, the federal district court judge in *American Postal Workers Union v. Frank* (1989) ruled that mandatory drug testing of applicants to the Boston branch of the U.S. Postal Service was unconstitutional under the Fourth Amendment. The court first ruled that the American Postal Workers Union (APWU) had a standing to file suit on behalf of job applicants, notwithstanding the fact that job applicants are not yet union members nor are they members of the bargaining unit.

The court's ruling here was based on APWU's ability to meet the following three criteria set forth by the court:

> 1) [APWU's] members . . . have standing to sue in their own right; 2) the interests the union seeks to protect are germane to the organization's purposes; and 3) neither the claim asserted nor the relief requested require the participation of individual members in the lawsuit. (*American Postal Workers Union* 1989: 89)

The court then addressed the substantive issue raised by the case—that is, the constitutionality of the drug-testing program. The court found this particular program unconstitutional because the Postal Service could not demonstrate individualized suspicion of drug use. The court, relying on the U.S. Supreme Court's decisions in *Skinner* and *Von Raab*, reasoned that the Postal Service is not a highly-regulated industry nor are the jobs in question safety or security sensitive. As such, without a showing of individualized suspicion, the drug-testing program was "an unreasonable intrusion into the privacy of applicants and thus, a violation of the Fourth Amendment" (*American Postal Workers Union* 1989: 90).

This is an important ruling because it suggests that employers who cannot justify their drug-testing programs on the grounds that the industry is highly regulated or that the jobs are sensitive to safety and security risks must show reasonable or individualized suspicion of drug use by employees or job applicants. As noted earlier, this appears to be the strictest standard created by the courts and, compared to the other standards, is difficult to demonstrate. It should be further noted, however, that the case is on appeal, so the ultimate outcome remains to be seen.

One of the most recent developments at this writing involves the U.S. Supreme Court's refusal to grant certiorari to three appellate court rulings, including *Guiney v. Roache* (1989), and two cases discussed earlier, *National Federation of Federal Employees v. Cheney* (1989) and *Harmon v. Thornburgh* (1989, sub nom *Bell v. Thornburgh*).

In *Guiney v. Roache,* the First Circuit Court of Appeals, relying on *Von Raab,* upheld a random drug-testing program for police officers who carry firearms and are responsible for drug enforcement. The court reasoned that police officers who carry firearms and participate in drug interdiction are no different than customs officers (the employees involved in *Von Raab*) who have the same responsibilities. Because the Supreme Court refused to review this case, as well as the others mentioned above, the appellate court rulings will stand.

It should be noted that the Boston Police Department's drug-testing policy applies to "all sworn and civilian personnel of the Boston police department" (*Guiney* 1989: 1558). The appeals court, however, did not rule on the constitutionality of drug testing as it applies to employees who do not carry firearms and are not involved in drug interdiction. The court instead remanded the case to the district court on this point. It will be interesting to see if the district court, similar to the *American Postal Workers Union* court, will rule that a showing of individualized suspicion is necessary to justify legally the drug-testing program for these other employees in Boston's police department.

Implications for Public and Private Sector Employers

Based on the case law to date, it now appears well established that mandatory as well as random drug-testing programs in the public and private sectors will be found constitutional if the employees are involved in heavily regulated industries such as transportation or if they hold jobs that are sensitive to public safety and security risks. But, as Mazo (1987) has pointed out, the legal concerns raised by drug testing do not end once the courts have ruled that employers can constitutionally and legally test employees for drug use. There are other concerns as well.

Perhaps the three issues that will be of most concern to the courts and hence, public and private sector employers in the coming years are (1) the procedures employed for drug testing, (2) the employment decisions made when employees test positive for drug use, and (3) the categories of employees tested.

Aside from the government's interest in drug testing, which was made clear by the U.S. Supreme Court in *Von Raab* and *Skinner,* the courts will also scrutinize the *procedures* used for testing. At the extreme end are employers who test without authorization by formal policy or regulation. In *Capua v. City of Plainfield* (1986), for example, there was no written departmental policy on the procedures for collecting and testing the urine samples of firefighters or on how the results of the test would be used. The district court in *Capua* found this ad hoc type of drug testing to be unreasonable and. hence, unconstitutional under the Fourth Amendment

Lower court rulings issued after *Von Raab and Skinner* also suggest that procedural issues surrounding drug testing will not be overlooked by the courts. The Seventh Circuit Court of Appeals in *Taylor v. O'Grady* (1989) for example, has stated that "while urinalysis may be within the government's prerogative in a given circumstance, the manner in which the program is carried out may be so unnecessarily intrusive as to render it constitutionally intolerable" (p. 1195).

In particular, the courts will pay close attention to such procedural issues as the act of urination, which does, indeed, implicate privacy interests. The appeals court in *Von Raab* (1987), for example, has said that

> there are few activities in our society more personal or private than the passing of urine. Most people describe it by euphemisms if they talk about it at all. It is a function traditionally performed without public observation; indeed, its performance in public is generally prohibited by law as well as social custom. (p. 175)

Notwithstanding, some courts have further said that there is a diminished expectation to privacy in the act of urination in highly regulated industries and occupations that involve a risk to public safety (Moore 1987). Indeed, the U.S. Supreme Court in *Skinner* seemed to support this position. Although the drug-testing program at issue in the case did not require that urine samples be furnished under direct observation of a monitor, the Court recognized that "the process of collecting the sample to be tested . . . may in some cases involve visual or aural monitoring of the act of urination . . ." (*Skinner* 1989: 4328).

For those employees who do not work in highly regulated industries or safety-sensitive jobs, employers, in an effort to minimize intrusions on workers' privacy rights, may seek alternatives to urinalysis for drug testing. One such alternative is hair analysis. With this type of test, strands of hair, taken from the head, face, or elsewhere on the body, can reveal traces of drug residue, which is carried to hair roots by the circulation of blood (Gesensway 1989).

At this writing, the courts have not yet been called upon to assess the legality or constitutionality of such tests. However, although the procedures involved with hair analysis may not be as humiliating or degrading as those involved with urinalysis, an argument certainly could be made that collecting hair samples represents some degree of intrusion upon an individual's reasonable expectations to privacy.

Another concern revolves around the actions employers take when employees test positive for drug use (Klingner, O'Neill and Sabet 1989). If employers punish or discipline such employees by, for example, terminating them, due-process concerns are raised

(Mazo 1987; Weeks 1988). As Moore (1987) has pointed out, "due process protections are . . . required where an employee may only be dismissed for cause and thereby has a property right in his [or her] employment and . . . reputation and good name" (p. 766).

This concern is heightened because drug-testing procedures are often inaccurate or unreliable (Mazo 1987; Thompson, Riccucci and Ban, in press). That is to say, there tends to be a high risk of "false positives," which occur when employees' tests erroneously are positive for drug use. As such, dismissing an employee who tests positive in error further implicates due-process rights. Although some courts have recognized this and continue to be concerned with it, the case law to date suggests that it may not be pivotal in every case. In an early decision, *Greenholtz v. Nebraska Penal & Correctional Complex* (1979), the U.S. Supreme Court said that "there is simply no constitutional guarantee that all executive decisionmaking must comply with standards that assure error-free determinations" (*Greenholtz* 1979: 2104). More recently, the Supreme Court in *Skinner* (1989) said that "it is impossible to guarantee that no mistakes will ever be made in isolated cases . . . We deal therefore with whether the [drug] tests contemplated by the regulations can ever be conducted" (p. 4332, note 10).

Nonetheless, a more progressive approach to addressing drug use or abuse in the work place is gaining support from the personnel community—for example, rehabilitation or counseling, such as that provided through Employee Assistance Programs (EAPs) (Elliott 1989; Klingner et al. 1989). This is not only a more humane approach for dealing with employees with drug-dependency problems, but it also guards against potential due-process violations. This approach also may be seen as more acceptable to employee unions, another force that has a very strong interest in drug-testing programs and the decisions that emanate from positive test results (Casey 1988; Cochran 1989).

In sum, the courts may require formal, written policies to authorize drug-testing programs as a condition of their constitutionality. Other procedural issues that courts are likely to monitor on a *case-by-case* basis include the actual process of collecting urine samples for testing and the employment decisions made when employees test positive for drug use.

Another issue that will be of concern to the courts and employers in the coming years is the categories of employees to be tested. As the case law to date suggests, the courts are willing to waive the individualized suspicion standard for employees in highly regulated industries and safety- or security-sensitive jobs. It seems clear, however, at least from the appellate court rulings issued after *Skinner* and *Von Raab,* that if employers cannot justify their drug-testing programs under these standards, the courts will hold employers to the individualized suspicion standard. For example, in the *American Postal Workers Union* case, as discussed earlier, the court ruled that drug testing for any postal applicant or employee would be permitted if there is a showing of reasonable or individualized suspicion. The district court in *Guiney* may issue a similar ruling.

Alternatively, courts may create new or additional standards for judging the reasonableness of drug testing for certain employees. The appeals court in *Harmon v. Thornburgh,* for example, was willing to permit drug testing for certain U.S. Department of Justice employees in order to ensure the integrity of the department's work force. The court

(*Harmon* 1989) reasoned that in light of the government's integrity interests, "it seems quite possible that the Department might constitutionally fashion a random drug-testing program for all DOJ employees having substantial responsibility for the prosecution of federal drug offenders" (p. 13).

Thus it seems clear that the courts are willing to uphold the drug testing of a broad range of employees in public and private sectors if certain conditions are met. It may be that the courts' motivations here are tied directly to the politics surrounding the government's efforts to combat drug use in our society. In any event, this issue no doubt will be of concern to the courts and employers in the coming years.

The case law on employee drug testing is just now beginning to unfold. In the coming years, the courts will continue to refine the contours of the law and public policy surrounding employee drug testing on a case-by-case basis. This holds true particularly for the testing of employees who do not work in highly regulated industries or safety/security-sensitive positions. Much more research is needed in this volatile, contested area of public law and employee relations. In particular, research is needed on the politics of court involvement in drug testing, as noted earlier. It would appear that the rote of the judiciary in these matters, as in other areas of public employment and management, is expanding, thereby contributing to, as Rosenbloom (1983) might argue, the constantly evolving nature of legal and constitutional doctrines affecting public employment.

Notes

1. Probable cause exists when there is "good reason" to believe that a particular unlawful act has occurred.

2. It is important to note that, as Cooper (1988) has pointed out, the standard of probable cause is and always has been much stricter in criminal cases as compared to administrative ones.

3. The court, however, did not uphold the DOJ's drug-testing program as it pertained to the other categories of employees. It rules that the privacy interests of these particular employees outweighed the government's interest in promoting the safety and integrity of its work force. A discussion of the categories of employees that can be tested will follow in a later section.

References

American Federation of Government Employees v. Dole, 670 F. Supp. 445 (1987).
American Federation of Government Employees v. Skinner, 885 F. 2d 884 (D.C. Cir. 1989).
American Postal Workers Union v. Frank, 725 F. Supp. 87 (1989).
Capua v. City of Plainfield, 643 F. Supp. 1507 (D.N.J. 1986).
Casey. D. L. (1988). Drug testing in a unionized environment. *Employee Relations Law Journal*, 73(4), 599–613.
Cochran, K. M. (1989). Union challenges to testing. In Decresce, R. P., Lifshitz, M. S., Ambre, J., Mazura, A. C., Tilon, J. E. & Cochran, K. M. (Eds.) *Drug testing in the workplace* (pp. 165–222). Washington, DC: Bureau of National Affairs.

Committee for G.I. Rights v. Callaway, 518 F. 2d 466 (D.C. Cir. 1975).

Cooper P. J. (1988). *Public law and public administration* (2nd ed.) Englewood Cliffs, NJ: Prentice Hall.

Dale, C. V. (1987). *Constitutional analysis of proposals to establish a mandatory federal employee drug testing program.* Washington, DC: Congressional Research Service, The Library of Congress.

Donovan v. Dewey, 452 U.S. 594 (1981).

Elliott, R. H. (1989). Drug testing and public personnel administration. *Review of Public Personnel Administration,* 9(3), 15–31.

Gesensway, D. (1989, November 12) Hair a new way to test for drugs. *Albany Times Union,* A1, 4.

Greenholtz v. Nebraska Penal & Correctional Complex, 99 S. Ct. 2100 (1979).

Guiney v. Roache, 873 F. 2d 1557 (1st Cir. 1989). *cert. denied,* 110 S. Ct 404 (1989).

Harmon v. Thornburgh, 878 F. 2d 484 (D.C. Cir. 1989). *cert. denied,* sub nom *Bell v. Thornburgh* 110 S. Ct. 865 (1990).

Klingner, D. E., O'Neill, N. G., & Sabet, M. (1989). Drug testing in public agencies: Public policy issues and managerial responses. *Review of Public Personnel Administration,* 70(1), 1–10.

Martin. A. A. (1988). Title VII discrimination in biochemical testing for AIDS and marijuana. *Duke Law Journal,* 729, 129–153.

Mazo, D. P. (1987). Yellow rows of test tubes: Due process constraints on discharges of public employees based on drug urinalysis testing. *University of Pennsylvania Law Review,* 735, 1623–1656.

McDonell v. Hunter, 809 F. 2d 1302 (8th Cir. 1987).

Moore. T. (1987). Constitutional law: The Fourth Amendment and drug testing in the workplace. *Harvard Journal of Law & Public Policy,* 10(3), 762–769.

National Federation of Federal Employees v. Cheney, 884 F. 2d 603 (D.C. Cir. 1989).

National Treasury Employees Union v. Von Raab, 816 F. 2d 170 (5th Cir. 1987).

National Treasury Employees Union v. Von Raab (1989, March 12). *Law Week* 57, 4338–4347.

Rosenbloom, D. H. (1983). *Public administration and law.* New York: Marcel Dekker.

Sculnick, M. W. (1989). Key court cases. *Employment Relations Today,* 5, 141–146.

The Shield Club v. City of Cleveland, 647 F. Supp. 274 (N.D. Ohio 1986).

Shoemaker v. Handel, 795 F. 2d 1136 (3d Cir. 1986). *cert. denied,* 107 S. Ct. 577(1986).

Skinner v. Railway Labor Executives' Association (1989, March 21). *LawWeek* 57, 4324–4338.

Taylor v. O'Grady, 888 F. 2d 1189 (7th Cir. 1989).

Thompson, F. J., Riccucci, N. J., and Ban, C. (in press). Biological testing and personnel policy: Drugs and the federal workplace. In C. Ban & N. J. Riccucci (Eds.), *Public personnel management: Current concerns, future challenges.* White Plains, NY: Longman.

Tschirn, L A. (1988). *National Treasury Employees Union v. Von Raab:* Specimen surveillance. *Loyola Law Review,* 33, 1148–1162.

Weeks, J. D. (1988). Public employee drug testing under the Fourth and Fifth Amendments. *The Urban Lawyer,* 20(2), 445–474.

Zimmerman, C. (1989). Urine testing, testing-based employment decisions and the Rehabilitation Act of 1973. *Columbia Journal of Law and Social Problems,* 22, 219–267.

CHAPTER 26

THE LEGAL EVOLUTION
OF SEXUAL HARASSMENT

ROBERT D. LEE, JR. AND PAUL S. GREENLAW

In this article, we examine the legal evolution of sexual harassment in the workplace. The U.S. Supreme Court's 1993 unanimous decision in *Harris v. Forklift Systems, Inc.*, clarified some aspects of law. Here, a lower court ruling was overturned that would have restricted the chances of persons successfully bringing sexual harassment suits. Just prior to the handing down of this decision, the Equal Employment Opportunity Commission (EEOC) issued proposed guidelines intended to clarify what constitutes harassment and what obligations employers have in preventing and eliminating harassment. The guidelines apply broadly to "harassment based on race, color, religion, *gender,* national origin, age, or disability" (emphasis added). The Supreme Court regarded the proposed regulations sufficiently authoritative to discuss them in the *Harris* decision. As will be seen, the judicial and executive branches of the government have begun developing a coordinated approach to combating sexual harassment in the workplace.

The discussion here, as the tide of this article suggests, is primarily legal in nature. A thorough review of the literature is forgone for an examination and analysis *of primary* legal sources. These sources include decisions made by the federal courts and guidelines issued by the Equal Employment Opportunity Commission. Major emphasis is given to what is known as hostile-environment harassment, since the subject has been the main focus of attention in sexual harassment court cases.

Sex Discrimination, Sexual Harassment, and the *Harris* Case

The existence of sex discrimination in employment is well documented. Women's salaries are typically lower than those of men (Lee 1989; Willoughby 1991), and discrimination often presents a glass ceiling that thwarts women in advancing their careers (Bullard and Wright 1993; Guy 1993; Kelly et al, 1991; Merit Systems Protection Board 1992). Those who are sexually harassed can experience severe harm in terms of their careers, personal

From 55 *Public Administration Review*, 4: 357–364, July/August 1995. Copyright © 1995 American Society for Public Administration. Reprinted with permission.

finances, and mental health (Kreps 1993; McCann and McGinn 1992; Wagner 1992). Discrimination can lead to lower overall productivity of an organization's work force.

A wide assortment of laws has addressed sex discrimination. The Equal Pay Act of 1963 required equal pay for equal work between the sexes (*Aldrich v. Randolph Central School District* 1992; Greenlaw and Lee 1993). Title VII of the Civil Rights Act of 1964 prohibited sex discrimination with respect to terms, conditions, and privileges of employment (such as in hiring, promoting, and firing employees). An amendment to Title VII, the Pregnancy Discrimination Act of 1978 prohibited discrimination based on pregnancy, childbirth, or related medical conditions (*Gedulig v. Aiello* 1974; *General Electric v. Gilbert* 1976). The U.S. Supreme Court in two Title VII-based cases banned sex discrimination with respect to retirement plan contributions and benefits (*City of Los Angeles, Department of Water and Power v. Manhart* 1978; *Arizona Governing Committee for Tax Deferred Annuity and Deferred Compensation Plans v. Norris* 1983). Special protections against various forms of sex discrimination are available to government workers through the due process clause of the Fifth and Fourteenth Amendments, and the equal protection clause of the Fourteenth Amendment. In addition, state and local cases may be filed using the Civil Rights Act of 1871. The cases are known as Section 1983 suits, since the 1871 legislation is codified at 42 U.S.C. 1983.

The topic of sexual harassment is of increasing importance as women—the usual subjects of harassment—have come to constitute a greater proportion of the work force. In a study of federal workers, 42 percent of the women reported being sexually harassed within a two-year period (Merit Systems Protection Board 1988: 2). Half or more of working women can expect to be sexually harassed during their careers (National Council for Research on Women 1991: 9). In 1989–1990, sexual harassment cases accounted for 5.4 percent of all cases filed before the EEOC and state human rights commissions; that number increased to 8.0 percent in 1992–1993. In this time period, the number of cases rose from 6,127 cases to 11,908, nearly a doubling of complaints (unpublished data from EEOC). All too often the investigation of complaints seems excessively slow, and those filing the complaints report they become the subjects of reprisals (General Accounting Office 1993).

The nation's attention has been fixed on harassment charges in several recent high-profile situations. Highly publicized cases include the 1991 Clarence Thomas nomination hearings for the Supreme Court, the Navy's 1991 Tailhook convention in Las Vegas, the 1994 investigation of Senator Bob Packwood (R, OR), and the 1994 suit filed against President Clinton for allegedly engaging in sexual harassment while governor of Arkansas. Clearly, sexual harassment is one of the most prominent employment issues of the 1990s.

Sexual harassment, particularly the hostile-environment type, which will be fully explained later, has had a stormy legal history. In 1980, the EEOC issued guidelines declaring sexual harassment to be a form of sex discrimination and in violation of Title VII of the Civil Rights Act. Not until 1986—22 years after passage of the Civil Rights Act and 6 years after the issuance of EEOC's guidelines—did the Supreme Court rule that sexual harassment violated the prohibition against sex discrimination. However, the Court's 1986 decision in *Meritor Savings Bank v. Vinson* did not resolve such issues as what form of behavior constituted harassment and what degree of proof must be provided in order to prevail in court. By 1993, the circuit courts were in disarray concerning the degree of severity which had to underlie hostile environment claims for the plaintiff to prevail. The *Harris* case involved a woman who worked for an equipment rental company and alleged repeated abuses by the company's president. The specific question in the *Harris* case was whether the hostile environment had to be so intense that it caused grave psychological harm. As will be seen, the Supreme Court took a middle ground between the positions of the circuits. The outcome of the case applies to all employers, including the federal, state, and local governments.

Types of Sexual Harassment

Sex was of comparatively minor concern in drafting the Civil Rights Act of 1964, and legislative intent regarding sex discrimination was unspecified in the law, and left largely unspecified in hearings and the like. Over time, the Title VII ban against sex discrimination has been interpreted to include sexual harassment, of which there are two basic types—quid pro quo and the hostile (or abusive) work environment.

Quid Pro Quo

Quid-pro-quo harassment involves tangible aspects of an employee's job. "Here the plaintiff attempts to prove that the harasser has denied job benefits, such as a promotion, [or] salary increase . . . because sexual favors were not granted; or the harasser has taken away job benefits (e.g., discharge or demotion) because sexual favors on the part of the employee were not forthcoming" (Greenlaw and Kohl 1992: 164–165). Quid-pro-quo sexual harassment is also sometimes referred to as sexual extortion.

Not until ten years after the passage of the Civil Rights Act did a quid-pro-quo sexual harassment case reach the federal courts. Then a federal employee claimed to have been discharged for refusing to have an affair with her supervisor (*Barnes v. Train* 1974). The court, however, ruled that this was "not the type of discrimination purposed by the Act and found no basis for the suit" (Woerner and Oswald 1990: 786). In 1976, a turning point was reached when a district court ruled quid-pro-quo harassment was actionable under Title VII; the case involved employees in the Department of Justice (*Williams v. Saxbe* 1976). Quid-pro-quo cases continue to the present. Current and former employees of the District of Columbia Department of Corrections filed suit in 1994 alleging "supervisors demanded sex from their female subordinates, made threats against employees who refused their advances, and retaliated against employees who complained" (*Neal v. Ridley* 1994; also see *Karibian v. Columbia University* 1994).

Quid-pro-quo actions, unlike those involving a hostile environment, have never been heard by the Supreme Court. This is probably because the issues involved are fairly straightforward as opposed to the difficulty of defining "hostile environment."

In 1980, the EEOC adopted *Guidelines on Discrimination Because of Sex,* which covered both types of sexual harassment. The guidelines define sexual harassment as follows:

Unwelcome sexual advances, requests for sexual favors, and other verbal or physical conduct of a sexual nature constitute harassment when (1) submission to such conduct is made either explicitly or implicitly a term or condition of an individual's employment, (2) submission to or rejection of such conduct by an individual is used as the basis for employment decisions affecting such individual, or (3) such conduct has the purpose or effect of unreasonably interfering with an individual's work performance *or creating an intimidating, hostile, or offensive working environment* (emphasis added) (Equal Employment Opportunity Commission 1980).

The first two items listed are of the quid-pro-quo form of harassment and the third is of the hostile-environment type, which is discussed shortly.

Sexual harassment was deemed to be a form of sex discrimination in the landmark Supreme Court decision of *Meritor Savings Bank, FSB v. Vinson* (1986). The Court's opinion strongly endorsed the EEOC 1980 guidelines, pointing out that although they were not controlling on the courts, the guidelines did represent a body of experience and judgment which the courts could use. The Court relied upon a circuit court decision involving discrimination against an Hispanic person (*Rogers v. Equal Employment Opportunity Commission* 1971), noting this was "the first case to recognize a cause of action based upon a discriminatory work environment." The Court stated that subsequent to Rogers, courts had applied the law to harassment involving race, religion, and national origin and concluded that it was appropriate to extend the law to sexual harassment.

Hostile-Environment Harassment

In order to prevail in a claim of hostile-environment sexual harassment, one must show five conditions; "(1) she belongs to a protected group, (2) she was subject to unwelcome sexual harassment, (3) the harassment was based on sex, (4) the harassment affected a term, condition or privilege of employment, and (5) [the employer] knew or should have known of the harassment and failed to take proper remedial action" (*Burns v. McGregor Electronic Industries, Inc.* 1993a: 564; also see *Stafford v. Missouri* 1993, involving the Missouri Department of Corrections).

The EEOC's proposed 1993 guidelines classify harassing behavior into two categories. The first refers to "epithets, slurs, negative stereotyping, or threatening, intimidating, or hostile acts" (EEOC 1993). In the *Meritor Savings* case, a female employee alleged she was fondled by her supervisor, followed into the women's lavatory, and was forcibly raped. In the 1993 Supreme Court case of *Harris v. Forklift Systems, Inc.*, a woman employee was expected to obtain coins from her supervisor's front pants pockets and was told that the two of them should go to a local motel to negotiate her pay raise. Sexual harassment can occur in a variety of circumstances, including after the dissolution of a mutually consenting relationship; a male supervisor might decide to harass a female subordinate after their sexual partnership ends, as apparently happened in *Babcock v. Frank* (1992) involving two Postal Service workers.

According to the proposed EEOC guidelines, employees are protected even when the harassing behavior "is not targeted specifically at them." For instance, a woman could file a sexual harassment charge if she repeatedly witnesses a male supervisor openly harassing another female employee. However, the courts have ruled that such third parties are not necessarily protected when mutually consenting relationships exist and sexual conduct occurs off the job. For example, a woman working for a county government failed in a hostile environment suit when she alleged a co-worker had romantic liaisons with various supervisors during nonbusiness hours; she contended these liaisons created a sexually charged work environment (*Candelore v. Clark County Sanitation District* 1992).

The second category under the EEOC guidelines consists of "written or graphic material that denigrates or shows hostility or aversion toward an individual or group . . . and that is placed on walls, bulletin boards, or elsewhere on the employer's premises or circulated in the workplace" (EEOC 1993). Instances can include posters showing people explicitly engaged in sexual acts, E-mail messages of a sexual nature broadcast to employees, and employee clothing, such as tee shirts, with sexual drawings or slogans.

Special Facets of Hostile-Environment Harassment

Several specific issues have emerged regarding hostile-environment harassment. Topics include gender-based discrimination, the severity and pervasiveness of discrimination, the reasonableness of a harassment complaint, and harassment's effects on employment.

Gender and Sex

Hostile-environment sexual harassment can be nonsexual. In other words, the environment can be negatively focused against a gender without reference to sexual behavior. In the eyes of the courts, Title VII bars "any harassment or other unequal treatment of an employee . . . that would not occur but for the sex of the employee" (*McKinney v. Dole* 1985: 1138). In a case of women flag personnel at road construction sites, the use of vulgar names and less overtly sexual behavior (such as a man urinating in a woman's water bottle and men using surveying equipment to watch women urinating in ditches) was considered gender-based harassment (*Hall v. Gus Construction Co., Inc.* 1988). Slapping a woman on the buttocks and making references to women as being intellectually inferior to men is prohibited behavior (*Campbell v. Board of Regents of the State of Kansas* 1991; *Campbell v. Kansas State University* 1991).

The 1993 *Harris* case included important gender-harassment behavior as well as behavior of a sexual nature. On several occasions, the woman employee, in the presence of other employees, was told by her supervisor "You're a woman, what do you know." She was told "We need a man as the rental manager" and was called "a dumb ass woman." Comments such as these are sex based but not sexual in content.

In its 1993 proposed harassment guidelines, the EEOC specifically notes that "sex harassment is not limited to harassment that is sexual in nature, but also includes harassment due to gender-based animus" (Equal Employment Opportunity Commission 1993: 51267). The commission went on to note that these proposed broad guidelines dealing with race, age, and other forms of harassment as well as sexual harassment would not replace the existing guidelines on sexual harassment, since the latter "raises issues about human interaction that are to some extent unique in comparison to other harassment" (Equal Employment Opportunity Commission 1993: 51267). Both the EEOC and the Supreme Court are adopting virtually identical stances regarding gender harassment.

At least two key questions are raised in this regard. First, is there really a single continuum of harassment ranging from highly explicit sexual behavior to somewhat overtly sexual to gender-motivated behavior or are there two different continua, with one for sex and one for gender? Second, will problems arise with sexual harassment being treated in two separate, albeit closely related regulations, and would one set of guidelines on sexual harassment be preferable to two? For the moment, the two sets of regulations appear well meshed, but whether gaps between the two will emerge in litigation is, of course, to be determined.

Severity and Pervasiveness

In order to establish the existence of a hostile environment, the plaintiff must show that the environment was "sufficiently severe or pervasive" (*Meritor Savings* 1986). One must show that severe sexually harassing behavior existed and/or that sexually harassing behavior existed over time and pervaded the work setting. A few harassing events over a short period fail to constitute a hostile environment (*Babcock v. Frank* 1992), such as a supervisor simply uttering an epithet (*Fazzi v. City of Northlake* 1994). In the case mentioned above about a woman being slapped on the buttocks, that action by itself might not have established a hostile environment but the supervisor's repeated threats to slap her did. Once the supervisor carried out this threat, the employee appropriately was continually concerned that the behavior would be repeated. In another case, a male supervisor and female subordinate met socially after work, he "rubbed his hand along her upper thigh" and kissed her, a few weeks later, they walked together during the lunch period, and he "lurched" at her from behind some bushes. This behavior, while inappropriate and warranting employer intervention, was not found to be "so pervasive or debilitating as to be considered hostile" (*Saxton v. American Telephone and Telegraph* 1993).

Given the vast array of human behavior that is possible, setting an explicit standard for when a hostile environment exists may be impossible, and therefore, the EEOC has a policy of treating situations on a case-by-case basis. According to the guidelines adopted in 1980, "The Commission will look at the record as a whole and at the totality of the circumstances, such as the nature of the sexual advances and the context in which the alleged incidents occurred" (EEOC 1980). This same position is taken in the proposed 1993 guidelines.

Similarly, the Supreme Court in *Meritor Savings* held that "the record as a whole" must be examined to consider the "totality of circumstances." The Court further enunciated this standard in its 1993 *Harris* decision: "Whether an environment is 'hostile' or 'abusive' can be determined only by looking at all the circumstances. These may include the frequency of the discriminatory conduct; its severity; whether it is physically threatening or humiliating, or a mere offensive utterance; and whether it unreasonably interferes with an employee's work performance" (371).

Reasonableness and the Reasonable Woman

The proposed harassment guidelines of the EEOC provide that conduct will be judged using a "reasonable person" standard, namely what is regarded as socially acceptable behavior. The use of the term "reasonable person" goes back at least to 1988 in sexual harassment cases (*Bennett v. Corron & Black Corp.* 1988). One immediate problem in applying such a standard is that behavior considered to be acceptable in some work sites, and therefore might be regarded as "reasonable," might well be considered unreasonable to others. For example, the construction industry has been notoriously sexist, often condoning behavior that would be intolerable elsewhere.

Further complicating the situation is that which may seem reasonable to men is not necessarily reasonable to women (Thacker and Gohmann 1993). *Ellison v. Brady* (1991), a circuit court of appeals case involving a complaint by a U.S. Treasury Department employee, formally recognized the standard of the "reasonable woman." The alleged harassment entailed a male co-worker giving a woman handwritten notes. This correspondence was largely nonlascivious but more expressive of strong affection: "I know that you are worth knowing with or without sex. . . . Leaving aside the hassles and disasters of recent weeks [sic]. I have enjoyed you so much over these past few months. Watching you. Experiencing you from O so far away. Admiring your style and elan . . ." (874). While the man might have thought the correspondence was innocent, the woman thought he was "crazy," and the court ruled that a reasonable woman would be frightened by such behavior.

Recognition of the "reasonable woman" doctrine in *Ellison* was not without controversy. Circuit Judge Stephens, in his dissent in the case, strongly criticized the "reasonable woman" concept and supported the "reasonable man" term "as it is used in the law of torts" referring to the "average adult person" (884). Judge Stephens added, "Title VII presupposes the use of a legal term that can apply to all persons" (884).

Since the *Ellison* decision and despite the Stephens dissent, the standard of the reasonable woman has gained major acceptance. In a nonemployment case, the reasonable woman standard was used in considering the practice of male prison guards searching fully dressed female prisoners (*Jordan v. Gardner* 1993). The proposed EEOC harassment guidelines state, "The 'reasonable person' standard includes consideration of the perspective of persons of the alleged victim's race, color, religion, gender, national origin, age, or disability" (EEOC 1993).

Of particular significance, the reasonable woman standard was integral to the Supreme Court's 1993 *Harris* decision. The Court quoted at length from the district court opinion which noted that the behavior involved was harmful to women whereas it probably would have been only offensive to men but not so severe as to affect work performance. While not specifically supporting the reasonable woman standard, the Court gave the impression of supporting it; certainly, the case could have been used as an occasion for striking down the standard, had it so wished. One can anticipate the reasonable woman standard cutting in two directions in future cases. Hostile environments will be recognized where men saw no harm but women did. Also, some women may lose cases in which it is ruled that they were too easily offended and that a reasonable woman would not have been.

In concurring with the *Harris* decision, Justice Scalia expressed concern that reasonableness may provide little real guidance in determining what is a hostile work environment. He also expressed concern that the Court had used the term "abusive" apparently as a synonym for "hostile" in the context of a work environment. The lack of definition of these terms, in his opinion, allows "virtually unguided juries [to] decide whether sex-related conduct engaged in (or permitted by) an employer is egregious enough to warrant an award of damages" (372). However, the justice admitted to having no alternative substitute that would clarify the situation.

Harassment's Effects on Employment

In order to prevail in a hostile-environment case, a plaintiff often attempts to show the severity of the harassment by indicating its effects on employment. Issues have arisen whether harassment has resulted in reduced work performance, economic or other tangible loss, psychological harm, and loss of employment due to dismissal, forced resignation, or what is known as constructive discharge.

While quid-pro-quo discrimination typically affects economic aspects of a job, such as being denied a promotion or threatened with firing if not complying with sexual advances, hostile environment harassment has no such requirement. The Supreme Court ruled in the 1986 *Meritor Savings* case that economic or tangible discrimination need not be shown and that non-economic injury could violate Title VII. In the road construction case, the women employees were convincing in identifying an extensive series of events that forced them to resign (*Hall v. Gus Construction Co., Inc.* 1988). Circuit courts will overturn district courts, finding that a set of circumstances was insufficient to result in constructive discharge (*Burns v. McGregor Electronic Industries, Inc.* 1993), but also will vacate jury awards of damages when the jury is found not to have been "reasonable" and to have concluded that an employee was forced to resign because of harassment (*Stafford v. Missouri* 1993). In a 1994 district court case involving "full body hugs" and "sexual innuendos, sexual advances, sexual talk, and admitted unwelcome touching," the court found that any reasonable person, male or female, would have had little choice but to resign (*Currie v. Kowalewski* 1994).

One line of argument that plaintiffs have used is that the environment was so intensely hostile that it caused grave psychological harm. The circuit courts were in disagreement on this matter, sometimes ruling that the offensive conduct had to be "sufficiently severe and persistent to affect seriously the psychological well-being of an employee," as in the case of alleged harassment in the Federal Aviation Administration (*Downers v. FAA* 1985: 292). Another court ruled that the environment would have to "seriously [affect] the psychological well-being of a reasonable employee" to be deemed hostile (*Rabidue v. Osceola Refining Co.* 1986: 620; also see *Vance v. Southern Bell Telephone and Telegraph Co.* 1989). In contrast, the important case of *Ellison v. Brady,* discussed above regarding the reasonable woman standard, concluded, "Surely, employees need not endure sexual harassment until their psychological well-being is seriously affected to the extent that they suffer anxiety and debilitation" (878).

The Supreme Court's 1993 *Harris* decision is important in this regard. The Court said it was taking a "middle path between making actionable any conduct that is merely offensive and requiring the conduct to cause a tangible psychological injury." In other words, a person might allege such injury to document the severity of the harassment but is not obligated to show psychological injury. In the words of the Court, Title VII comes into play before the harassing conduct leads to a nervous breakdown. A discriminatorily abusive work environment, even one that does not seriously affect employees' psychological well-being, can and often will detract from employee's job performance, discourage employees from remaining on the job, or keep them from advancing in their careers (370–371).

In a case subsequent to the *Harris* decision, a district court found that a female FBI employee who had suffered a mental breakdown had not linked that condition with her employment, despite a lengthy list of events on the job that supposedly had caused her illness. In referring to *Harris,* the district court held that "abnormal sensitivity" could not be the basis for a charge of sexual harassment (*Sudtelgte v. Reno* 1994). Similarly, another district court found against a plaintiff, who alleged a hostile environment had resulted in "suffering from depression, inability to concentrate, sleeplessness, high blood pressure, and chest pains" but failed to offer "any evidence of sexual advances, sexual or gender-based comments, or any demeaning references to women" (*Laird v. Cragin Federal Bank* 1994: 7–9, 12).

Employer Responsibilities

The 1980 EEOC guidelines indicate that an employer is responsible for the acts of its "agents and supervisory employees." In addition, the employer can be responsible for sexual harassment between fellow employees and by nonemployees.

Supervisors, Co-Workers, and Nonemployees

The Supreme Court in its 1986 *Meritor Savings* opinion left ambiguous the extent of employer responsibility.

> Congress' decision to define "employer" to include any "agent" of an employer . . . surely evinces an intent to place some limits on the acts of employees for which employers under Title VII are to be held responsible. For this reason, . . . employers are [not] always automatically liable for sexual harassment by their supervisors. . . . For the same reason, absence of notice to an employer does not necessarily insulate that employer from liability (*Meritor Savings* 1986; 72).

The courts have attempted to resolve the seeming incongruence between the guidelines, which hold employers responsible for harassment, and *Meritor Savings,* which provides an escape hatch for employers. The prevailing trend of case law "seems to hold that employers are liable for failing to remedy or prevent a hostile or offensive work environment of which management level employees knew, or in the exercise of reasonable care should have known" (*Equal Employment Opportunity Commission v. Hacienda Hotel* 1989: 1515–1516). "Knew" can be read here as having received notice, while "should have known" refers to harassment which is so pervasive that management "could not have helped knowing about it" (Greenlaw and Kohl 1992: 169).

The guidelines proposed by the EEOC provide greater detail regarding employer responsibility. An employer is responsible for the acts of its supervisors if (1) the employer "knew or should have known of the conduct and failed to take immediate and appropriate corrective action" or (2) independent of the previous condition, the supervisors were "acting in an 'agency capacity.'" This condition is met when supervisors act with "apparent authority" and (a) the employer does not have "an explicit policy against harassment" or (b) the employer does not have "a reasonably accessible procedure by which victims of harassment can make their complaints known to appropriate officials" who can take corrective action.

Meritor Savings held that simply having an antidiscrimination policy and a grievance procedure was not necessarily sufficient for protecting an employer from liability. The proposed guidelines emphasize the point that both harassment policy and grievance procedure must be in place and that they must be treated seriously by the employer. As the EEOC explains in its draft regulations, without these two conditions "employees could reasonably believe that a harassing supervisor's actions will be ignored, tolerated or even condoned by the employer."

With regard to co-workers and harassment, employers are liable when supervisors "knew or should have known of the conduct" and did not correct the situation. An employer in a 1994 district court case was found not liable for acts of co-workers because the behavior was not reported to supervisors; a woman was allegedly hugged and kissed by a co-worker and was raped by an unknown attacker (*Doe and Doe v. Donnelley Sons* 1994).

Employers may be responsible for the acts of nonemployees when supervisors "knew or should have known of the conduct" and had some control over the nonemployees. The latter situation might involve harassment by welfare recipients, unemployment insurance clients, and others.

Types of Employers

While Title VII and the ban on hostile environment sex harassment apply to all forms of employers, other legal provisions complicate the situation. As a result, the law pertaining to hostile environment harassment varies among private employers, state and local governments, and the federal government.

With regard to private employers, not only may the company be liable but so may other parties. For example, the individual supervisor or foreman may be named in the suit (*Hall v. Gus Construction Co., Inc.* 1988), and the owner of a professional corporation being the "alter ego" of the firm can be named as an individual (*Janopoulos v. Harvey L. Walner & Associates, Ltd* 1993).

State and local governments not only must comply with Title VII but they also can be liable under the equal protection clause of the Fourteenth Amendment. Moreover, state officials may be sued as individuals under Section 1983, and local governments and local officials also may be sued under Section 1983. In these cases, the plaintiff's claim their civil rights as guaranteed under 42 U.S.C. §1983 were denied them "under color of law" (*Campbell v. Board of Regents of State of Kansas* 1991). The courts have held that when both Section 1983 and Title VII claims are treated together, the Title VII verdict must be consistent with the jury's decision in the Section 1983 portion of the case (*Ways v. City of Lincoln* 1989; *Stafford v. Missouri* 1993). (The due process clause of the Fourteenth Amendment is also a possible avenue, in which a plaintiff would claim a property right—his or her job—was denied without due process of law.)

Federal cases can become extremely complicated due to several laws possibly applying to a given situation. Besides Title VII applying, other laws include the Federal Tort Claims Act of 1946, the Federal Employees Liability Reform and Tort Compensation Act of 1988 (the Westfall Act; see *Westfall v. Erwin* 1988), and appropriate state tort laws (*Mitchell v. Carlson* 1990; *Bartlett v. United States* 1993; *Jamison v. Wiley* 1994).

Corrective and Preventive Actions by Employers

Employers must not only have a procedure by which employees can complain of harassment but that procedure must lead to corrective action. When an employee complains about being harassed by her supervisor, that complaint should not be followed by even more numerous and "intense" sexual advances (*Davis v. Tri-State Mack Distributors, Inc.* 1992). In a Postal Service case, the agency was found to have taken corrective action each time a woman employee complained of sexual harassment (*Babcock v. Frank* 1992). Additionally, the employer is obligated to take sufficiently strong measures to prevent the recurrence of harassment. An example of insufficient action involved a woman employee of the Veterans Administration having been harassed by a co-worker. The agency responded by having the co-worker undergo counseling, and subsequent harassment only resulted in further counseling, which failed to halt the worker's harassing behavior (*Intlekofer v. Turnage* 1992; also see Butler 1994).

Preventing sexual harassment, of course, is preferable to taking remedial action once harassment has occurred. This is the position of both the EEOC 1980 guidelines and the proposed harassment guidelines. The 1980 guidelines call for "affirmatively raising the subject, expressing strong disapproval, developing appropriate sanctions, informing employees of their rights to raise and how to raise the issue of harassment under Title VII, and developing methods to sensitize all concerned" (EEOC 1980). The proposed guidelines recommend "an explicit policy against harassment that is clearly and regularly communicated to employees, explaining sanctions for harassment, developing methods to sensitize all supervisory and nonsupervisory employees on issues of harassment, and informing employees of their right to raise, and the procedures for raising, the issue of harassment under Title VII" (EEOC 1993). The Supreme Court's 1993 *Harris* decision, which rejected the notion that an employee would need to show psychological harm resulting from a hostile environment, is seen as underscoring the need for employers to prevent abuse, because plaintiffs are more likely to be successful in the post-*Harris* era.

Ignorance of the law is unavailable as a defense for employers. Employers are expected to comply with statutes, EEOC guidelines, and court decisions. Information is available from EEOC to help employers learn what is expected of them, including policy guidance that interprets pertinent court decisions (Equal Employment Opportunity Commission 1990).

As an example of what can be done, Minneapolis recently replaced its existing sexual harassment policy with a more definitive one, with supervisors being held to a higher standard than other workers. To dramatize the seriousness with which the city views sexual harassment, the new policy requires that within one day of the filing of a complaint, an investigation must be begun. A supervisor who fails to enforce the policy will receive a final warning (i.e., not an initial warning) or will be discharged on the first offense of failing to enforce the policy ("New Minneapolis Sexual Harassment Policy" 1994).

Conclusion

Harris v. Forklift Systems, Inc. (1993) marks the second time that the Supreme Court has dealt with the hostile environment form of sexual harassment (the other case being *Meritor Savings* 1986). The subject perhaps has demanded the attention of the Court because of the greater ambiguity associated with this form of harassment than the quid-pro-quo form. The *Harris* case reiterated earlier findings that the entire circumstances of a situation need to be reviewed in determining whether a hostile environment exists. The Court clarified the matter somewhat by offering examples of what factors to consider such as the frequency of events and whether conditions were humiliating. Importantly, the Court resolved a conflict among the circuits by ruling that plaintiffs need not show psychological injury stemming from harassment, a factor that may lead to more suits against employers and more victories. The Court for the first time acknowledged the standard of the reasonable woman but did not explicitly endorse it.

The proposed guidelines of the Equal Employment Opportunity Commission cover "gender harassment" as distinguished from the possibly more narrowly defined "sexual harassment," although the courts have found that sexual harassment only needs to be sex based and not of a sexual nature. The proposed guidelines mesh well with the Harris decision on such important matters as considering what behavior is reasonable, including from the perspective of the victim of harassment, and as not requiring psychological injury be shown. The guidelines place strong emphasis upon the responsibilities of employers to prevent harassment and to correct it. Federal agencies and state and local governments can be held responsible for their supervisory personnel, workers, and even nonemployees. Preventing harassment is the first line of defense, while the second is taking sufficiently strong action when harassment occurs to insure it will not recur.

Numerous ambiguities remain. As Justice Scalia noted, what the word "hostile" means is still unresolved, and the concept of "reasonableness" may provide little guidance to a jury. While the Supreme Court has recognized the existence of the reasonable woman standard, the Court has avoided explicitly endorsing it. Public employers can anticipate suits involving situations that may seem nonoffensive or reasonable to most of their men workers but not to their women workers. Cases involving public employment can be considerably more complex than private sector cases, because public workers may enlist rights beyond those guaranteed by Title VII.

Finally, legislative action may be forthcoming. Senator Patty Murray (D, Wash.) and Representative George Miller (D, Calif.) have introduced bills in Congress that would provide a definition of sexual harassment and would require employers to notify employees about their rights and how to file complaints with the Equal Employment Opportunity Commission.

References

Aldrich v. Randolph Central School District, 963 F.2d 520 (2nd Cir. 1992); cert. denied 113 S. Ct. 440 (1992).

Arizona Governing Committee for Tax Deferred Annuity and Defined Compensation Plans v. Norris, 463 U.S. 1073 (1983).

Babcock v. Frank, 783 F. Supp. 800 (S.D.N.Y. 1992).

Barnes v. Train, 13 FEP 123 (D.C.D.C. 1974).

Bartlett v. United States, 835 F. Supp. 1246 (E.D.Wash. 1993).

Bennett v. Corron & Black Corp., 845 F.2d 105 (5th Cir. 1988).

Bullard, Angela M. and Deil S. Wright, 1993. "Circumventing the Glass Ceiling: Women Executives in American State Governments." *Public Administration Review,* vol. 53 (May/June), 189–202.

Burns v. McGregor Electronic Industries, Inc., 955 F. 2d 559 (8th Cir. 1993a); 989 F. 2d 959 (8th Cir. 1993).

Butler, Suzanne R., 1994. "Sexual Harassment: Winning the War, but Losing the Peace." *Journal of Individual Employment Rights* vol. 2 (4), 339–362.

Campbell v. Board of Regents of State of Kansas, 770 F. Supp. 1479 (D.Kan. 1991).

Campbell v. Kansas State University, 780 F. Supp 755 (D.Kan. 1991).

Candelore v. Clark County Sanitation District, 975 F. 2d 588 (9th Cir. 1992).

City of Los Angeles, Department of Water and Power v. Manhart, 435 U.S. 702 (1978).

Civil Rights Act, ch.22, 17 Stat. 13, 42 U.S.C. 1983 (1871).

Civil Rights Act, P.L. 88–352, 78 Stat. 241, Title VII, 42 U.S.C. 2000e 2(a) (1964).

Currie v. Kowalewski, U.S. Dist. Lexis 909 (N.D.N.Y. I994).

Davis v. Tri-State Mack Distributors, Inc., 981 F. 2d 340 (8th Cir. 1992).

Doe and Doe v. Donnelley and Sons, U.S. Dist. Lexis 1561 (S.D.Ind. 1994).

Downes v. Federal Aviation Administration, 775 F.2d 288 (Fed. Cir. 1985).

Ellison v. Brady, 924 F.2d 872 (9th Cir. 1991).

Equal Employment Opportunity Commission (EEOC). 1980. *Guidelines on Discrimination because of Sex* 29 C.F.R. 1604.11.

———, 1990. *Policy Guidance on Current Issues of Sexual Harassment,* N-915–050.

———, 1993. *Guidelines on Harassment Based on Race, Color, Religion, Gender, National Origin, Age or Disability.* 58 Fed. Reg. 51,266; Proposed to be codified at 29 C.F.R. 1609.

Equal Employment Opportunity Commission v. Hacienda Hotel, 881 F.2d 1504 (9th Cir. 1989).

Fazzi v. City of Northlake, U.S. Dist. Lexis 610 (N.D.Ill. 1994).

Federal Employees Liability Reform and Tort Compensation Act (Westfall Act), PL 100–694, 102 Stat. 4563 (1988).

Federal Tort Claims Act, ch. 753, Title IV, 60 Stat. 842 (1946).

Gedulig v. Aiello, 417 U.S. 484 (1974).

General Accounting Office, 1993. *Federal Employment: Sexual Harassment at the Department of Veterans Affairs.* Washington: U.S. Government Printing Office.

General Electric v. Gilbert, 429 U.S. 125 (1976).

Greenlaw, Paul S. and John P. Kohl, 1992. "Proving Title VII Sexual Harassment." *Labor Law Journal,* vol. 43 (March), 164–171.

Greenlaw, Paul S. and Robert D. Lee, Jr., 1993. "Three Decades of Experience with the Equal Pay Act." *Review of Public Personnel Administration,* vol. 13 (Fall), 43–57.

Guy, Mary E., 1993. "Three Steps Forward, Two Steps Backward: The Status of Women's Integration in Public Management." *Public Administration Review,* vol. 53 (July/August), 285–292.

Hall v. Gus Construction Co., 842 F.2d 1010 (8th Cir. 1988).

Harris v. Forklift Systems, Inc., 114 S. Ct. 367 (1993).

Intlekofer v. Turnage, 973 F. 2d 773 (9th Cir. 1992).

Jamison v. Wiley, U.S. App. Lexis 558 (4th Cir. 1994).

Janopoulos v. Harvey L. Walner & Associates, Ltd, 835 F. Supp. 459 (N.D.Ill. 1993).

Jordan v. Gardner, 986 F. 2d 1521 (9th Cir. 1993).

Karibian v. Columbia University, 14 F.3d 773 (2nd Cir. 1994).

Kelly, Rim Mae et al., 1991. "Public Managers in the States: A Comparison of Career Advancement by Sex." *Public Administration Review,* vol. 51 (September/October), 402–412.

Kreps, Gary L., ed., 1993. *Sexual Harassment: Communication Implications.* Cresskill, NJ: Hampton Press.

Laird v. Cragin Federal Bank, U.S. Dist. Lexis 339 (N.D.Ill. 1994).

Lee, Yong S., 1989. "Shaping Judicial Response to Gender Discrimination in Employment Compensation." *Public Administration Review,* vol. 49 (September/October), 420–430.

McCann, Nancy Dodd and Thomas A. McGinn, 1992. *Harassed: 100 Women Define Inappropriate Behavior in the Workplace.* Homewood, IL: Business One Irwin.

McKinney v. Dole, 765 F.2d 1129 (D.C. Cir. 1985).

Meritor Savings Bank, FSB v. Vinson. 477 U.S. 57 (1986).

Merit Systems Protection Board, 1988. *Sexual Harassment in the Federal Government: An Update.* Washington: U.S. Government Printing Office.

————, 1992. *A Question of Equity: Women and the Glass Ceiling in the Federal Government.* Washington: U.S. Government Printing Office.

Mitchell v. Carlson, 896 F. 2d 128 (5th Cir. 1990).

National Council for Research on Women. 1991. *Sexual Harassment: Research and Resources.* New York: National Council for Research on Women.

Neal v. Ridley, No. 93–2420, filed 1/5/94, 32 GERR 76 (D.C.D.C. 1994).

"New Minneapolis Sexual Harassment Policy Specifies Conduct, Penalties" (1994). 32 GERR 13–14.

Pregnancy Discrimination Act, P.L. 95–955, 92 Stat. 2076 (1978).

Rabidue v. Osceola Refining Co., 805 F.2d 611 (6th Cir. 1986).

Rogers v. Equal Employment Opportunity Commission, 454 F. 2d 234 (5th Cir. 1971); cert. denied 406 U.S. 957 (1972).

Saxton v. American Telephone and Telegraph Company, 10 F. 3d 526 (7th Cir. 1993).

Stafford v. Missouri, 835 F. Supp. 1136 (W.D.Mo. 1993).

Sudtelgte v. Reno, U.S. Dist. Lexis 82 (W.D.Mo. 1994).

Thacker, Rebecca A. and Stephen F. Gohmann, 1993. "Male/Female Differences in Perceptions and Effects of Hostile Environment Sexual Harassment: 'Reasonable' Assumptions?" *Public Personnel Management,* vol. 22 (Fall), 461–472.

Vance v. Southern Bell Telephone and Telegraph Co., 863 F.2d 1503 (11th Cir. 1989).

Wagner, Ellen J., 1992. *Sexual Harassment in the Workplace.* New York: AMACOM.

Ways v. City of Lincoln, 871 F. 2d 750 (8th Cir. 1989).

Westfall v. Erwin, 484 U.S. 292 (1988).

Williams v. Saxbe, 413 F. Supp. 654 (D.C.D.C. 1976).

Willoughby, Katherine, 1991. "Gender-Based Wage Gap: The Case of the State Budget Analyst." *Review of Public Personnel Administration,* vol. 12 (September/December), 33–46.

Woerner, W. and S. Oswald, 1990. "Sexual Harassment in the Workplace: A View Through the Eyes of the Courts." *Labor Law Journal,* vol. 40 (November), 786–793.

SECTION II

PUBLIC SECTOR LABOR RELATIONS

PART 6

HISTORY AND POLITICS

The field of public sector labor relations is relatively new, despite the fact that unions representing certain categories of public sector employees (e.g., in federal naval shipyards) have existed almost since the birth of this nation. While there has been considerable resistance to labor unions in general in the United States, a long, convoluted history of labor uprisings eventually gave way to a comprehensive system of labor relations for private sector employees. Public employee unions, on the other hand, continue to this day to battle over the right to represent government employees in some jurisdictions. Moreover, even though many state and local workers ultimately won some legal standing to engage in collective bargaining over such fundamental issues as wages and working conditions, federal workers are still barred from negotiating over wages and terms and conditions of employment. In the realm of labor-management relations, public employees have lagged well behind their private sector counterparts.

Justifications to limit the labor rights of public employees abound, but perennial concerns turn on the sovereignty of governments, the existence of merit systems to protect employee rights, and also on what has been considered by many as to be the inappropriateness of various labor actions (e.g., striking) by public employees. These are some of the issues that will be addressed here. In one of the first labor relations' articles appearing in the public administration literature, Sterling Spero contrasts the practice of Whitleyism in Great Britain to the system of collective bargaining in the United States. Whitleyism refers to the system of collective negotiations in Great Britain, particularly in the public sector. In drawing his comparisons, Spero points to the increasing tendency in both federal and local government employment in the United States for labor negotiations, despite the lack of formal mechanisms to regulate or mandate such activity for public employees. He writes that "The parties bargain and reach agreements which they regard as morally binding on matters which fall within the area of administrative discretion and control" (Spero 1944: 166).

Felix Nigro addresses several important issues in "Collective Negotiations in the Public Service: The Implications for Public Administration." One issue is the doctrine of sovereignty, which has been historically invoked to deny public employees the right to engage in collective bargaining. Nigro (1968: 137–138) writes that the doctrine "is still invoked by many public officials, some of whom are really not sure exactly what it means but understand vaguely that it is something about government which makes collective negotiations both impossible and inappropriate." Nigro not only provides a comprehensive analysis of the legal basis for the sovereignty doctrine (or lack thereof), but he also examines labor relations in the broader context of public personnel administration.

In "Bilateralism and the Merit Principle," Paul Camp and W. Richard Lomax address a recurrent theme in public sector labor relations: Is collective bargaining consistent with merit principles? They point out that while government employers may see an inconsistency, union leaders view merit systems as offering limited protections to public employees because such systems are too paternalistic in nature to serve the full interests of workers. Camp and Lomax conclude that while there may be some degree of conflict between merit and collective bargaining, the accommodation of both systems is necessary for the full and effective operation of government workforces.

"Labor Unions and Collective Bargaining in Government Agencies," is a panel discussion on the question of the role of labor unions in government that took place in March of 1945 before the Chicago chapter of the American Society of Public Administration. Both government and labor union representatives participated. The panel addressed such questions as: Should public employees be allowed to join labor unions? Should supervisors or managers in government employment be allowed to join unions? What are the legal contours of the relationship between government and labor unions? The discussion is lively and illuminating and the viewpoints of both union officials and management have relevancy for contemporary labor relations.

In the final classic presented here, George Sulzner in "Public Sector Labor Relations: Agent of Change in American Industrial Relations?" addresses the broad changes occurring during the 1980s in labor-management relations in government. He argues that major improvements to the system of labor relations can serve as a paradigm for innovation and change in government and should thus elevate the status and importance of both the practice and scholarship of public sector labor relations.

Additional Classics

Leiserson, Avery. "Certification of Collective Bargaining Representatives." 2 *Public Administration Review*, 4: 292–301, Autumn 1942.

Posey, Rollin B. "The New Militancy of Public Employees." 28 *Public Administration Review*, 2: 111–117, March/April, 1968.

Seroka, Jim. "The Determinants of Public Sector Union Growth." 5 *Review of Public Personnel Administration*, 2: 5–20, Spring 1985.

Vietheer, George C. "The Government Seizure Stratagem in Labor Disputes." 6 *Public Administration Review*, 149–156, Spring 1946.

CHAPTER 27

WHITLEYISM AND COLLECTIVE BARGAINING

STERLING D. SPERO

This study of the methods and machinery of employer-employee relationships in the British civil service follows the general pattern of Professor Leonard D. White's path-breaking book *Whitley Councils in the British Civil Service*, published in 1933. Dr. Gladden discusses the functioning of the Whitley Councils, the operation of the Civil Service and activities of the staff associations. His book contains more intimate detail than Dr. White's work, but it lacks the latter's broad perspective.

The Whitley Councils constitute a highly formalized system of employer-employee consultation and negotiation which, since its inception in 1919, has effected an almost revolutionary change of attitude on the part of the administration toward the rank and file. Beatrice and Sidney Webb tell that, prior to World War I:

> When the Post and Telegraph Clerks Association attempted to study the methods by which the Post Office could increase the efficiency of its service to the public, and began to publish studies upon the postal cheque system, which is successfully in operation over a greater part of Europe, the Postmaster-General made it known that any such investigation, which might be held to imply criticism of the backwardness or apathy of the British Postal Administration, was regarded as a breach of official discipline; and steps were taken to prevent the study being proceeded with.

Contrast this incident with the declared objects of the Whitley system, and the revolution in the administration's attitude which made possible even the inception of Whitleyism becomes apparent. The constitution of the National Whitley Council states:

> The objects of the National Council shall be to secure the greatest measure of cooperation between the State in its capacity as employer and the general body of civil servants in matters affecting the Civil Service, with a view to increased efficiency in the public service combined with the well-being of those employed: to provide machinery for dealing with grievances, and generally to bring together the experience of different points of view of representatives of the administration, clerical and manipulative Civil Service.

As in the case of all reforms requiring drastic changes in established relationships and alterations in the accepted attitudes and habits of thought of those in control, Whitleyism

From 4 *Public Administration Review*, 3: 164–168, Summer 1944. Copyright © 1944 American Society for Public Administration. Reprinted with permission.

did not come as a gift from those in power to their subordinates. Two years of intensive pressure and agitation by the civil service unions were required to bring about its adoption. Originally, the Whitley system was not conceived as a civil service reform but as a device for improving labor relations in industry. Mr. J. H. Whitley, later Speaker of the House of Commons, presided over a Committee on Relations between Employers and Employed which issued a report in March, 1917, proposing the establishment of a system of joint industrial councils. Each industry was to set up by agreement between the employers' association and the trade-unions national, district, and works councils. These councils were to hold regular meetings to settle questions of wages and working conditions, to effect a better utilization of the practical knowledge of the employees, and to consider technical, educational, and legislative problems affecting the industry.

After studying the report Beatrice Webb expressed doubt as to whether the proposals would have much effect on labor relations in industry. But, she predicted, the government would sooner or later have to adopt the Whitley idea in its own services. Mrs. Webb was right. The influence of Whitleyism on British industry has been slight. On the other hand, the civil service employee organizations, even before they had heard of Mrs. Webb's prediction, sensed the importance of Whitleyism for the public services.

After more than a year of activity by the staff organizations, the government in July, 1918, at a meeting assembled to hear its decision, offered a scheme of advisory bodies whose conclusions would always be subject to veto by ministers. The staff representatives rejected the plan and continued to press for a scheme of plenary councils operating in effect as a system of collective bargaining. The persuasiveness and the political influence of the union spokesmen are indicated by the fact that the government, instead of assuming a "take it or leave it" attitude, consented to negotiate. After nearly a year of negotiation the representatives of the two sides reached an agreement in May 1919, which laid the basis of present Whitley system. These negotiations and the resulting agreement were in themselves a significant demonstration of the possibilities of Whitleyism. They were, in fact, one of Whitleyism's greatest accomplishments.

The heart of the new plan was contained in the following clause in the constitution of the National Whitley Council:

> The decisions of the Council shall be arrived at by agreement between the two sides, shall be signed by the chairman and vice chairman, shall be reported to the Cabinet, and thereupon shall become operative.

The councils thus became more than mere advisory or consultative agencies. Their agreements, subject to the overriding authority of Parliament, the powers of the Treasury, and the responsibility of the minister, were supposed to be carried out and not merely to serve as suggestions for the government to accept or reject.

Civil service Whitleyism has now been in operation for a quarter-century. It has weathered the major crisis of the General Strike of 1926 and the consequent enactment of Clause V of the Trade Disputes and Trade Unions Act of 1927 forbidding civil service unions to affiliate with the general labor movement. It is likely that without Whitleyism these events would have greatly weakened civil service unionism.

Despite the serious setback of 1927 the Whitley system has greatly strengthened unionism in the civil service because it is founded upon the principle of representation by employee organizations. The only way in which employees can obtain representation on a council at any level is through membership in an organization. As a result there has been since the establishment of Whitleyism a phenomenal growth in both the number and membership of civil service associations. Before the outbreak of the present war the number of service organizations has passed 330, while their membership today approximates 475,000.

These organizations, in groups, select representatives to the Staff Side of the National Whitley Council. The larger bodies, like the Union of Post Office Workers (156,000) and the Civil Service Alliance (173,000), have six seats each. The Executive Group of organizations has three, the Technical Group one. The Staff Side has twenty-three votes.

The Official Side consists of government representatives, usually top civil servants and permanent department heads. These officials act in the name and by the authority of the ministers. It is the ministers who decide what they will agree to or refuse to agree to. The Official Side registers their will. This is true in practice despite the fact that the Whitley constitution, according to some, implies acceptance by the ministers of agreements reached on their behalf. Frequently, therefore, there has been some feeling and expression of frustration on the part of the Staff Side when the Official Side have "nothing to add" to what they have said according to their instructions.

This indicates that there are in the British civil service, as in all governmental services, limitations on collective bargaining inherent in the governmental structure or practice. But these limitations in Great Britain are far more superficial than the limitations on collective bargaining in our federal service. President Roosevelt has spoken of the "insurmountable limitations" on collective bargaining "when applied to public personnel management." He declared:

> The very nature and purposes of government make it impossible for administrative officials to represent fully or to bind the employer in mutual discussions with government employee organizations. The employer is the whole people who speak by means of laws enacted by their representatives in Congress. Accordingly, administrative officials and employees alike are governed and guided, and in many instances restricted, by laws which establish policies, procedures or rules in personnel matters.

From a strict legal point of view, collective bargaining between administrators and employee organizations is subject to the overriding authority of the legislature in both national services. The great difference, however, is that in the United States, operating under a system of separation of powers, the limitation is always real. In Great Britain the limitations on the Official Side inhere in the practices which have grown up under the Whitley system rather than in the nature of the British government. The Official Side could receive larger grants of power and discretion; the ministers could come to more definite conclusions. The problem could be solved if the government wanted to solve it. In Britain an agreement reached in the National Whitley Council can become binding; for the government, barring extraordinary circumstances, has parliamentary authority behind it before beginning negotiations with the staff. In the United States an agreement reached between staff and administrators may readily be overridden in Congress by refusal to provide funds or by specific legislation.

Yet there has been developing in this country in recent years in both federal and local governmental employment an increasing tendency for administrators to deal with their employees through negotiation or collective bargaining. The parties bargain and reach agreements which they regard as morally binding on matters which fall within the area of administrative discretion and control. Of course, legislation may supersede these agreements. Some agencies have a freer area of bargaining than others, depending on the extent to which personnel matters are affected by legislation.

It is well to remember in this connection that employers and employees in private industry must also bargain collectively within the framework of the law. Collective agreements cannot alter or affect the Social Security Act, the Fair Labor Standards Act, the Labor Relations Act, and state factory laws and sanitary codes, to mention but a few overriding limitations on collective bargaining.

When the Whitley system was first adopted in Great Britain, trade unionists and administrators in America generally misunderstood it. Will H. Hays, who was Postmaster-General after Harding's election, set up a system of service relations councils, national and local, which superficially looked something like the Whitley Councils. Representation in the National Service Relations Council, like that in the Whitley Council, was based on employee organizations. Each national organization of postal employees had two representatives. There was no weighting for size and no distinction between regular trade unions affiliated with the organized labor movement and organizations which were anti-union in attitude and policy. Furthermore, organizations of officials had seats along with organizations of rank and file.

The big unions were afraid of the plan. Created as it was in a period of rising company unionism, these unions regarded the Hays organization as a disguised company union plan intended to undermine them. Nor did Mr. Hays' remarks to the convention of an unaffiliated (with AFL) association with a long record of anti-unionism help matters. Mr. Hays said that he hoped his plan would make affiliation of postal workers with the labor movement unnecessary. The big unions, therefore, set out to emasculate the service relations plan by confining its activities to narrower and narrower fields of mutual benefit and welfare work. They refused to permit the councils to deal with issues of wages or working conditions. Finally, they succeeded in circumscribing the system to such an extent that it passed out of the picture almost unnoticed.

It should not be overlooked that Whitleyism has not absorbed all the energy and activity of the British civil service labor movement. The associations bargain collectively through the Whitley machinery, but they also lobby and engage in publicity campaigns and bring organized pressure upon the government in much the same manner as bargaining agents in private employment use their power outside the conference room to bring reluctant employers into line. While such activity takes place outside of Whitley processes, the Whitley system has influenced it profoundly through the part played by the National Staff Side. This body is no mere grouping of association delegates on an official negotiating committee, but rather a true federation of the staff organizations. It has acted as their joint spokesman in almost every crisis or major effort affecting the service as a whole from the General Strike of 1926 to the recent war bonus campaign.

Of course, Dr. Gladden's book covers other aspects of the problem of staff relations in the British service. He discussed the work and accomplishments of Whitleyism in detail in the areas of both personnel and general administration. He analyzes the work of another important staff relations agency, the Arbitration Tribunal. He discusses the role of the staff in the administrative process. And he points out, as did Dr. White in his book, that professional trade-union leadership has limitations from the point of view of the student of public administration interested in harnessing staff energy for administrative reform. But, as Dr. White pointed out, "It is foolish to expect interest in administrative technique when the very necessaries of life are lacking, and the associations and unions would have failed in their obvious duty had they not bent their energy to secure improvements in the economic standing of the service."

The success of Whitleyism lies in the fact that it is an effective system for collective bargaining and negotiation on all matters affecting the staff and the service. The health of the system and of British civil service staff relations in general rests in the fact that they are based on a free civil service labor movement.

Note

This article was originally published as a book review: *Civil Staff Relationships*, by E.N. Gladden. Administrative Research Series, William Hodge & Co. Ltd., 1943.

CHAPTER 28

COLLECTIVE NEGOTIATIONS IN THE PUBLIC SERVICE

The Implications for Public Administration

FELIX A. NIGRO

The authors of [the] articles in this symposium have ably described and explained the recent developments in management-employee relations in the public service.[1] They have analyzed collective bargaining in the private sector, discussed some of the problems in adapting it to the government, examined the growing strike activity by public employees, and evaluated the impact of collective negotiations on the merit system. This final essay will deal with the implications of the heightened collective negotiations activity for public administration in general. Both doctrine and practice in public administration are undergoing significant change as the result of this development.

Under collective negotiations, management agrees to deal with organizations of employees, rather than with each employee individually, and to negotiate the terms of employment with representatives of these employee organizations. Personnel and other policies are not determined unilaterally by management; the process is one of joint decision making. There is no real difference between collective negotiations and collective bargaining; the first term is preferred in this symposium because as yet the strike weapon, although increasingly used, is not legalized as it is in the private sector.

Unless they have worked in private enterprise, managers in government generally have not thought much about the way decisions on personnel policies and procedures are reached in the private sector. In fact, some of them, convinced that industry is a "jungle" where the bosses treat the workers badly whenever they can "get away with it," see no reason to look to the private sector for new approaches to employee relations. What they overlook is that joint decision making, required by the Wagner Act of 1935 and since enlarged by Supreme Court decisions to cover many areas besides wages, hours, and fringe benefits, has limited greatly what the private entrepreneurs and managers can do to the worker without penalty. Moreover, they would be greatly surprised to learn that there are many voices in private management circles which state that collective bargaining has actually strengthened rather than weakened management.

From 28 *Public Administration Review*, 2: 137–147, March/April 1968. Copyright © 1968 American Society for Public Administration. Reprinted with permission.

Redefinition of Sovereignty

The doctrine of "sovereignty" was long the legal basis requiring and justifying unilateralism in the public service.[2] It still is invoked by many public officials, some of whom are really not sure exactly what it means but understand vaguely that it is something about government which makes collective negotiations both impossible and inappropriate. Most public personnel specialists, for example, are not at home in discussions of abstract concepts: they are inclined to accept without questioning the dogma which is handed down by the legal counsel and other interpreters of "what you can do in government."

Basically, the concept has been that, as the "sovereign employer," the government cannot be compelled to enter into a commitment, or even to respect one it has made if it later changes its mind. This stems from the English common law principles that the king could do no wrong and that no individual could sue the state without its consent. These ideas were carried over into the legal system of the American colonies, but only those who have carefully studied their later evolution and actual government practices know what "sovereignty" really means today. The government can do wrong and it knows it: for years now, based on legislation passed by the Congress and the state legislatures, private citizens have been able to sue the government for redress of alleged injuries.

The Doctrine Applied to Collective Negotiations

To sign a collective agreement with an employee organization is, of course, to limit the public employer's discretion. For years the prevailing opinion of the courts and the legal experts was that the government would in effect be giving away its sovereignty if it entered into such pacts. The argument went along these lines: terms of employment are at bottom a matter of legislative policy, so it is an illegal delegation of legislative power for representatives of administrative agencies to sign collective agreements with employees.[3] The courts also sometimes warned that accepting collective negotiations meant ultimately also accepting the employees' right to strike; the strike, of course, was a direct attack on the government and, therefore, its sovereignty. Logically, some of the judges argued, collective negotiations would also lead to binding arbitration of grievances, as in the private sector, and no sovereign government could agree to bind itself to accept the decisions of private parties (the arbitrators).

To illustrate the finality with which these rulings were made, a New York court said in 1943:

> To tolerate or recognize any combination of Civil Service employees of the Government as a labor organization or union is not only incompatible with the spirit of democracy, but inconsistent with every principle upon which our Government is founded. Nothing is more dangerous to public welfare than to admit that hired servants of the state can dictate to the Government the hours, the wages, and conditions under which they will carry on essential services vital to the welfare, safety, and security of the citizen. To admit as true that Government employees have power to halt or check the functions of Government, unless their demands are satisfied, is to transfer to them all legislative, executive, and judicial power. Nothing would be more ridiculous.

... Much as we all recognize the value and the necessity of collective bargaining in industrial and social life, nonetheless, such bargaining is impossible between the Government and its employees, by reason of the very nature of Government itself. ...

Collective bargaining has no place in Government service. The employer is the whole people. It is impossible for administrative officials to bind the Government of the United States or the State of New York by any agreement made between them and representatives of any union.[4]

Questions Are Raised About the Dogma

"Nothing would be more ridiculous." One wonders how many times courts and other bastions of the status quo have said this about ideas which not too much later came into general acceptance. Some people could not see why all of this was "obvious" (another word used by the above-mentioned court in pronouncing the "illegality" of collective bargaining in the public service). These people queried, What if the government decides it is a good idea to give the employees bargaining rights and to limit its discretion in specified areas, as detailed in the contract? If it decided years ago to allow itself to be sued, and yet its sovereignty survived, why could it not accept restrictions on its dealings with its own employees? If it were to sign a collective agreement, would it not be true that rather than having delegated its discretionary powers it would simply have agreed to limit them in certain respects and for a certain time, in pursuit of its own interest: better relationships with the employees? Furthermore, if it were absolutely necessary could it not abrogate the agreement without effective legal challenge by the employees? Are there not ample precedents for collective agreements in the numerous contracts government has signed with private contractors, some of which contain binding arbitration clauses for settling disputes over contract performance?[5]

Along another line of reasoning—political philosophy—others reminded that in a democracy sovereignty resides in the people. If the citizens' elected representatives were to pass laws authorizing collective negotiations, how could it be said that the government would lose its sovereignty in the process? Wilson R. Hart in the United States and Saul Frankel in Canada have brilliantly exposed the mistaken interpretations of "sovereignty." Pointing out that public agencies sign many contracts with private parties which in theory they could renege on but in practice never do, Hart calls "sovereignty" a "meaningless legislative circumlocution," because "a right which will never be exercised is the equivalent of no right at all."[6] Frankel grants that "the idea of sovereignty is a useful legal fiction" because "it provides for an ultimate authority within the state that may be invoked under certain conditions," but he reminds that the "notion of a monolithic, all-powerful sovereign is a thing of the past."[7] He reveals how it has been possible in Great Britain to "provide for the reality of arbitration while preserving the fiction of sovereignty." In that country since 1925 there has been an agreed-upon system of compulsory arbitration for settling disagreements between the government and civil service workers over pay and other conditions of work. This was accomplished simply by inserting the language in the formal arbitration agreement, "Subject to the overriding authority of Parliament the government will give effect to the Awards of the [arbitration] Court."[8] Parliament has never rejected any award, but it retains its power to do so, thus eating its cake and keeping it too!

The "Law" in 1958

In a paper delivered at a professional meeting in May 1958, Herbert W. Cornell reported that collective negotiations and written contracts were "outlawed in most states for the employees of states, counties, and cities." There were a few exceptions, "here and there," attributable to "peculiar circumstances."[9] Although the New York State Supreme Court had in 1956 upheld the right of the New York City Transit Authority to bargain collectively with its employees even in the absence of state enabling legislation, Cornell stated, "it does not seem likely that there will be a general acceptance of collective bargaining without legislative authorization or in some cases constitutional amendment."[10]

The Changed View of the "Law" in 1968

In 1958, no state had passed such legislation, but, as Rollin B. Posey has stated in his article above, 11 states, including New York, have since done so. This is not very many, but the significant development is that the legal doctrine is now emerging that public agencies can bargain collectively so long as there is no state law preventing it. In most states the law is silent, so this has opened up a big opportunity for public officials to embark upon collective bargaining, on the assumption that it is within their administrative discretion to do so. There are now more than a few states where the attorney generals and the courts have supported the view that an affirmative law is not necessary, although there are still some where the old views prevail. The great likelihood, however, is that the legal barriers to collective negotiations have suffered irreparable damage. How and why has this happened? The story needs to be told in detail, because it shows in striking fashion how the "law" changes in response to quick, but deeply felt, forces in the social environment.

The explanation in a real sense is that the employee organizations and public officials sympathetic to the principle of bilateralism have taken the bull by the horns. They have gone ahead with collective negotiations despite the absence of a statute specifically telling them that they could do so, because they considered it important to act to prevent a complete breakdown in management-employee relations. Mayor Wagner's 1958 Executive Order providing for full-fledged collective dealings in New York City is properly considered history-making. The provision in the state constitution on collective bargaining had been interpreted to apply to private workers only, and bills introduced in the legislature to extend this right to public employees had failed of passage.[11] In theory, Wagner's action was illegal, but nonetheless it was the reality and New York City did not need the statewide authorization for collective negotiations given in the Public Employees' Fair Employment Act of 1967 (Taylor Law).[12]

Quick Change, as Illustrated in Illinois

How rapidly the legal obstacles can be removed is revealed in the following newspaper report dated April 12, 1966:

> "Our hands are tied. We'd like to help you teachers but legally, election of a collective bargaining agent is out of the question."
>
> The board of Illinois' Thornton Fractional School District put it just about this plainly to local officials of the American Federation of Teachers (AFL-CIO) one day last March.

> Exactly one 2-day strike, one marathon 10 ½ hour night session, and one legal clarification later, the school board changed its tune. In addition to a pay raise for teachers, it announced that a collective bargaining election would take place in June.
>
> Illinois has no state law allowing or prohibiting collective bargaining for teachers, but a recent ruling by a circuit court judge here [Chicago] holds that election of a bargaining agent for teachers is legal.[13]

The Chicago Board of Education had also at first refused to bargain collectively, on the same grounds of legal inability, but it changed its mind and in September of 1965 issued a resolution authorizing a teacher referendum election to "select a sole collective bargaining agent concerning wages, working conditions, fringe benefits, and other professional problems."[14] The Chicago Division of the Illinois Education Association, an affiliate of the National Education Association, joined by an intervenor-plaintiff, James D. Broman, a citizen and taxpayer of Chicago, requested the circuit court to restrain the Board from holding the election, but the court upheld the Board, whereupon the case was appealed. The briefs submitted and the Appellate Court's decision rejecting the appeal tell a great deal about the new reasoning on collective negotiations.[15]

In the appeal, Broman disputed the contention of the Board and the intervenor-defendant, the Chicago Teachers Union (affiliated with the American Federation of Teachers, AFL-CIO), that "general legislation empowering the Board to contract and to do all things 'necessary or proper' for the operation of the schools" constituted all the authority it needed for engaging in collective negotiations. He argued that "'the courts of this state—like those in a majority of other jurisdictions—should leave to the legislature the many policy questions presented by the question of whether, and under what restrictions and conditions, the institution of collective bargaining should be imported into the public sector.'"[16] Broman maintained that since 1958 the courts in nine states had "reiterated" the basic principle that affirmative action by the legislature was necessary, and he noted that on ten occasions it had refused to enact "*general* authorization for public collective bargaining."[17]

On the basis of its review of state and federal legislation, the Board insisted that legislation was needed only to prevent the collective bargaining, not to permit it. As to illegal delegation of legislative powers and of its administrative discretion, it called attention to the part of the circuit court's decree which prohibited it from "'entering into any collective bargaining agreement under which it would abdicate or bargain away its continuing legislative discretion,'" or delegate "'its statutory duties or powers.'"[18] John Ligtenberg, AFT general counsel, had argued that "the fact that the board cannot delegate its functions or its authority does not necessarily lead to a conclusion that it cannot bargain collectively on subjects where the law does not foreclose its discretion. In the event an agreement is negotiated it is within the scope of its discretion to adopt such rules and regulations as are necessary to carry out the agreement and it does not thereby delegate anything. It does so no more than a private corporation under the same circumstances."[19] The Appellate Court stated simply that it agreed with the Board and the AFT, and today the Chicago Teachers Union is the exclusive bargaining agent for the Chicago schools, and other school boards throughout Illinois are signing collective contracts.

The Michigan Decision on Binding Arbitration

Since arbitrators are "outside" parties, frequently not even employed by the public juris-diction, in the past even those sympathetic to the principle of collective negotiations in government have had doubts about the legality of agreements with binding arbitration clauses. A recent decision in Michigan, however, suggests that this, too, can be justified, and that the long-standing belief that it represents an illegal delegation of governmental power may be in the first stages of disappearing.[20] The Benton Harbor School District had signed an agreement with Municipal Employees Local 953 containing such a clause as the final step in the grievance procedure, but, when the union requested arbitration of certain grievances concerning overtime pay and job posting, the school board backed out, saying it had no legal authority to agree to arbitration. The case was taken to the Berrien County Circuit Court which ruled in the union's favor.

The court's decision is an excellent illustration of the adaptation of the judicial process to social reality. Its first point was that the contract had been entered into voluntarily and that, while the arbitrator's decision would be final and binding, his powers were restricted to interpreting the meaning of the contract provisions and he could not modify or alter the provisions themselves. It then stated that the public interest was best served "'in educa-tion, as well as other activities,'" when a means was found of resolving disagreements over the meaning of the different contract clauses. Further, while Michigan did not have a statute expressly permitting or preventing school districts and other public employers from agreeing to binding arbitration, there was the implied power to do so in the Michigan Public Employment Relations Act of 1965.

The court's interpretation of the language in this act is most significant: "Had the leg-islature intended that binding arbitration within the terms of the labor agreement be not embraced in its use of the words 'collective bargaining,' it could have easily and briefly so stated. It did not do so, and this court must find that the right to collective bargaining includes the right to provide for binding arbitration. Had the legislature intended only to permit limited negotiations between the public employer and employee, it could have used specific terms and rights rather than the general term 'collective bargaining.'" Finally, the court dismissed the illegal delegation of authority argument as follows: "This is not a situation of passing to an individual [the arbitrator] the rights and duties of the state legislature or of the board of education of the defendant school district. *It is an amicable and more efficient means than resignation, walkout or strike by the employees to resolve any difficulties within a contract previously acceptable to and executed by the parties.*" (Italics ours) The implications of this decision are sweeping, because, as we shall see later, school board agreements sometimes make subject to binding arbitration not only provi-sions relating to economic benefits but also to educational policy, such as class size.

The Death of Weak Doctrine Under Strong Pressure

Without doubt the original hard-nosed doctrine of sovereignty had no real logic behind it. It survived only because there were few people inclined to expose it and, more impor-tantly, no social pressures strong enough to topple it. The judges in Illinois clearly must have been convinced that the way to prevent, or at least diminish, teacher strikes and boiling discontent was to give them bargaining rights. Moreover, to have marched the board of education, after it was ready to negotiate, back down the road of intransigence must hardly have seemed wise judicial policy making. The courts may be slow to move, but not when a real social revolution is under way. The public employee will no longer tolerate the old paternalism, and he will not be boxed out of his share in the affluent society.

The Redefinition

"Sovereignty" is not being discarded; rather, it is rapidly being redefined in such a way as to make it compatible with the supreme power of the State to show the supreme wisdom of doing the right thing! And, as to the government's always being able to terminate the agreements, New York City's Mayor Lindsay learned that this was like cherishing a handsome weapon which could never be used. Shortly after assuming office, Lindsay, appalled by the costs of the collective contracts his administration had inherited, indicated that the financially hard-pressed City might have to cancel some of them. When even the public employee strike-sensitive *New York Times* called him to task for not respecting the American tradition of "sanctity of contract," he retreated and decided to make that last effort to find the money.[21]

Administration and Policy—The Third Stage

The collective negotiations movement strongly suggests that government is moving into a third stage of the administration-policy relationship. In the first stage separation of administration from policy, although never the reality, was considered proper. In the second the essential and increasing policy-formulating role of the administrator in modern society was stressed; "administrative science" became greatly concerned with the value systems of administrators and with ways of improving the decision-making process. The third phase, not yet fully developed, but definitely emerging, is one of codetermination of policy by management and organized employees. It has its roots in the long-standing labor-management partnership policies of a few agencies like the Tennessee Valley Authority, but it now is being adopted and championed much more.

Ethos of the Movement

Strangely, up to now it appears also to be a development largely unappreciated by the public administration theorists. This is unfortunate, for it has a distinct ethos: a mixture of *democracy* (right of the workers to participate in determination of management policies), *justice* (an end to the paternalism which has made management the judge of the fairness of its treatment of the employees), *pragmatism* (the policies and the work results will be much better under the partnership arrangement), and *idealism* (levels of service to the public will be greatly improved because of the employees' constant pressure on management in that direction).

The Dynamics—More and More to Negotiate

In collective negotiations the scope of the codetermination is as wide as that of the bargaining. In this respect the experience in the private sector is very revealing. The Taft-Hartley Act, like the preceding Wagner Act, speaks only of bargaining over "wages, hours, and other terms and conditions of employment,"[22] but, as the result of Supreme Court decisions, the negotiations now cover many other areas besides economic benefits (e.g., automation and subcontracting). One labor expert has said that although "no court or the Board [National Labor Relations Board] has said it would go this far," "*all* decisions in an enterprise are potentially open to bargaining [since all affect the worker]."[23]

Under most present labor relations programs in government the bargaining scope is not that extensive, but the same potential exists to expand it greatly and invade hitherto relatively unchallenged areas of "management prerogatives." The reaction of some public officials to such employee pressures is sometimes plain amusing: "How can they ask to share in *our* jobs?" Basically, this is naiveté, for what they fail to understand is that, as demonstrated in the private sphere, this is the dynamics of collective negotiations. It is part of the ethos, as shown in the appeal of a Canadian labor leader for "recognition that in modern society the trade union has a greater role to play than just that of an economic bargaining agent for the employees."[24]

The Ultimate Limits of Bargaining: Need for Creativity

Immediately we are reminded again that "government is different," as it indubitably is. There are civil service and other laws which must be respected, as well as management responsibilities, like deciding on the budget, which cannot be waived to satisfy the employees' healthy appetite for codetermination. Many management rights have been preserved in industry; public management will simply have to hold the line at certain vital boundary points beyond which it is convinced that bilateralism would not be in the public interest.

Remembering Chester A. Newland's emphasis on creativity in collective negotiations, these boundary markers should not, however, be laid down at the same points in all kinds of public programs. The scope of the bargaining, and the consequent erosion of management rights, has undoubtedly been greatest in public education, yet it should bring solid improvements in the quality of the schools. Following are a few examples of provisions in recent teacher contracts, negotiated either by NEA or AFT affiliates: class size limits; duty-free lunch periods; a guaranteed number of preparation periods; teacher participation in textbook selection and curriculum planning; prohibition of classroom interruptions; and soundproofing of the band, chorus, and shop rooms.[25]

New Frontiers in Joint Decision Making

For the teachers to be able to make contract demands including class size certainly gives them a direct role in educational policy making. If they can do this, who really is running the schools? The answer is that in quite a few school districts now the teacher organizations are really sharing responsibility with the management for formulating and carrying out the educational program. The NEA is as adamant on this as the AFT.

As early as 1962 the Denver Classroom Teachers' Association (NEA) signed an agreement with the Denver school board providing for negotiations on any matter affecting the "'professional or economic'" improvement of teachers, the "'advancement of public education,'" or "'attainment of the objectives of the educational program.'"[26] Commenting on this and similar agreements, an American Bar Association Committee said that in education the "concepts of what is bargainable and non-bargainable, drawn from the decisions of the National Labor Relations Board, are irrelevant." In its view, "the central question" was "whether this concept of the scope of bilateralism in the relationship between school teachers and boards of education or an 'industrial relations' concept delineating between 'working conditions' and 'management prerogatives' will prevail."[27] In 1968, it is obvious that the teachers' view has prevailed.

Legislative Policy and the Content of Collective Agreements

Since bargaining is pressure, the very pertinent question arises, "When do the results of bilateralism violate or exceed the legislative mandates under which such programs as the schools function?" Because these mandates are often very broad, couched in terms like "the public interest," one man's opinion is usually as good as another's.

In May 1966, the Inkster (Michigan) Federation of Teachers and the local school board signed an agreement in which they mutually recognized that "the most significant social movement occurring in America today is the civil rights revolution." The board agreed to: purchase of "'integrated elementary text books to be used as the basic reading text'"; supply pupils in American history classes with teaching materials describing in detail the contribution of Negroes and other minority groups to the nation's development; prompt, full integration of the teaching faculties; elimination of the "class orientation" in achievement and intelligence tests; and establishment of a community action committee of union, board, civil rights, and church leaders to eliminate de facto school segregation.[28] Does a school board's responsibility extend into social movements? Strong opinions will naturally be expressed pro and con, but it is not the particular example which is important. *The significance for public administration is that the definition of administrative policy is likely to be very different when agreement must first be hammered out with the representatives of the employee organizations.* This is where the innovating force of bilateralism can breathe new life into sagging programs. In this third stage of the administration-policy relationship we may see quite a few examples of daring policy making: the decisions will not always be the soundest, but they will break new ground.

Program Improvements, the Contract, and Management Rights

Strong convictions about the inadequacy of existing programs may also lead employee organizations to seek to nail down improvements by having them written into the collective agreements. In January 1967 the Social Service Employees Union in New York City included in its contract demands the following: a 25 percent increase in welfare budgets; revision of the budgets of families on welfare in accordance with the Consumers' Price Index; automatic clothing grants to clients twice yearly; and creation of a "workload committee" of four union and four city representatives, to meet weekly "to discuss, review, and study all questions relating to any aspect of the work load affecting staff," with the welfare commissioner *required* to implement the committee's decisions.[29] They also wanted a contract provision pledging the welfare department to join it in requesting the state and federal governments to adopt more simplified grant-in-aid procedures. The welfare commissioner sympathized with some of these requests, but refused to negotiate on them, arguing that he was legally responsible for the welfare program, not the union or any joint union-management committee.[30]

In this kind of situation the department head knows that the mayor and/or the city council may see no possibility of finding the funds to make the desired program improvements, or they may not agree with the particular proposals. The commissioner also wants to run his own department and contrive his own tactics for dealing the most diplomatically with the grant-disbursing state and federal officials. And yet when unions make demands like these, they spur administrators to press harder for program improvements. The "nervy" request to put it in the contract may cause the administrator to get the "nerve" to take action he might never have attempted.

Union Pressures for the Wrong Policies

Unfortunately employee organizations sometimes seek (and obtain) contract provisions which, far from reflecting idealism, are purely selfish and tend toward lowering the quality of service to the public. In the summer of 1966 the Uniformed Firemen's Association in New York City requested that a fixed number of men always be available in a given area and not be moved around (one of several contract demands relating to work assignments).[31] Fire Commissioner Robert O. Lowery had started a new policy of shifting companies from lower Manhattan to nighttime duty in heavily populated areas like Brownsville, East New York, and the Bedford-Stuyvesant section of Brooklyn. His reasoning was that after business hours some of the fire equipment could be spared and used to make fire protection more effective in other parts of the city. *The New York Times* commented, "at the root of their reluctance to have companies shifted is moon-lighting, the off-duty employment permitted to firemen below a certain salary level. Commissioner Lowery has taken an initial step toward ending this highly questionable practice, which makes men unwilling to leave the neighborhood in which they have established part-time jobs."[32]

Illustrating that there is still a role for the management, when this issue was put to an arbitrator, he ruled that the city did not have to negotiate on such matters: "'the city, exclusively, determines what programs and services shall be furnished; what equipment shall be utilized; what employees shall perform the services; and when, where, and under what conditions they shall be performed.'"[33]

The administrator still retains his basic responsibilities; furthermore, even in areas where he is required to negotiate, he does not have to agree to all the employee requests. Nonetheless, one simply would not be reporting objectively if he left the impression that bilateralism will, except in stray cases, produce better administrative policies. Much depends, of course, on the employee organization and the quality of its leadership, as well as on the fibre of the management officials; but, bluntly, some of the demands frequently made by the employees do not augur well for the cause of an improved public service.

Public Personnel Administration: What Will It Be Like?

This is revealed in the impact on the merit system, as Paul M. Camp and W. Richard Lomax bring out so well in their analysis in this symposium. The "merit principle" is so widely identified with virtue that sophisticated employee leaders are quick to state their support for it. Unfortunately, "merit," like "democracy," has many meanings.

What Is Merit?

Many employee spokesmen argue that ability to do the particular job is the soundest evidence of merit. So far so good; but then they go on to say that the relative worth of the different workers can be measured validly by comparing their years of service.

The whole "science" of modern personnel administration is based on the conviction, supported by research evidence, that really good workers perform far better than those who simply meet minimum standards.[34] No matter how unimaginative in the past, the public personnel administrator usually has not equated "merit" with years of service. Although they contradict the principle of equal opportunity for public employment, the union and agency shops can be justified as benefiting the merit system in the long run provided the employee organizations gaining strength from the increased membership use their influence in the right way. The definition of seniority as "merit" is what makes it difficult to believe the employee leaders' protestations that they are for "merit." Instead of arguing for better tests and more rigorous ranking of candidates for appointment and promotion, some of them imply that "civil service" has been a flat failure and that nothing would be lost and a great deal gained if it were replaced by personnel systems based on collective contracts. They greatly exaggerate the past weaknesses of civil service at the same time that they brush aside the evidences of damage to good personnel policies in some of their points of view.

In New Castle, Delaware, the County Executive recently decided to enforce a merit system rule providing for mandatory retirement at the age of 70. Although this rule had been ratified by ordinance, for years political and other pressures had been so effective that quite a few employees over 70 were allowed to continue, to the point where 29 were on the payroll when the County Executive acted in late 1967. The county's contract with Locals 459 and 1607 of the American Federation of State, County, and Municipal Employees states that "the provisions of this Agreement shall be applied equally to all employees in the bargaining units without discrimination as to age, sex, marital status, race, color, creed, national origin, or political affiliation."[35] The locals announced that the county, in enforcing mandatory retirement, was discriminating on the basis of age, in violation of the contract! They forthwith initiated a grievance which they threatened to take to binding arbitration, and even published a funeral-type advertisement in the local newspaper mourning the impending departure of the 29. In a few days saner counsels prevailed: the AFSCME District Council president withdrew the grievance, explaining that his legal counsel had advised that the County Executive had the right under the contract to make this kind of management determination.

Need to Re-Consider Positions on Civil Service

It is not the ill-considered actions of local union leaders which cause the most concern. When AFSCME President Jerry Wurf in some of his statements more or less rejects "merit systems" for symbolizing a "unilateralism" which must be ended, then there is real cause for worry. If "civil service" and "bilateralism" are to coexist in a relationship which will benefit the workers, management, and the general public, the employee organizations should be willing to accept the principle of true competition in making appointments, promotions, and other changes in employee status. The advantages of "bilateralism," already evidenced in many places by improved salaries and fringe benefits, as well as a greater willingness by management to listen to employee grievances and do something about them, are so great that a frontal assault on "civil service" would be pure folly.

Personnel Men Should "Retool"

If public management can "contain" the employee organizations on this front, the public personnel administration of the future should be greatly improved, with the new element of collective negotiations infusing a dynamic quality long needed. Personnel men who do not want to deal with the "unions," and hope that the current "militancy" will die out, will have to change their outlooks if they are to represent progress rather than obsolescence in their profession. "The unions are here to stay"; the smart personnel worker realizes that he is being affected by a change in social technology: specifically, the fairly rapid substitution within the government of collective for individual dealings with employees. As a good "professional," he should "keep up," which means in this case that he must develop labor relations insights and skills. This retooling will take time, as it will for line officials who have to deal with the employee organizations. Obviously, schools of public administration and all those concerned with training for the public service should take note.

A Final Word

The point made about improved salaries and fringe benefits should be elaborated. The compensation of many public employees, particularly in state and local governments, has for long been much too low. For some groups, like teachers, nurses, and law enforcement officers, it has often been wretched. Under traditional practices for setting rates for jobs peculiar to the public service, information is collected on the salaries, fringe benefits, and working conditions of the same kinds of employees in other public jurisdictions. Generally, no one public employer has wanted to pay much more than the others: the salary-setting has been imitative, not innovative. For positions which do exist in the private sector, the wage data is based on questionnaires sent to selected firms with which the jurisdiction competes for workers. The trouble here is that in many places, including the federal service, it has been considered impractical to put into effect the comparability principle (paying as well as private employers for comparable jobs). The contention has been that the money is not available, but now the employee organizations are in effect saying, "look harder and you will find it." Finding all of it is, in truth, an impossibility in many cases, but the employee organizations have succeeded in getting some public employers to make faster strides towards "comparability." The evidence is convincing that collective negotiations and militancy do meet the pragmatic test of achieving results previously not obtainable. The economic gains have not been phenomenal, but they suggest that in the not too distant future the pay of many public employees may be considerably improved.

The other clear gain is in far better upward communication. There is nothing like an employee organization for making possible a frank presentation of employee views to the management. Paternalism basically means that the management is both blind and deaf: it sees and hears only what it wants to see and hear. The "union" talks loudly enough to be heard, and it is glad to take management by the hand and show it what the employees think is wrong. As we have seen, the new bilateralism presents certain perils, but it is proving effective in chasing paternalism out of public management.

Notes

1. For the literature on these developments consult the extensive annotated bibliography in Kenneth O. Warner and Mary L. Hennessy's *Public Management at the Bargaining Table* (Chicago: Public Personnel Association, 1967), pp. 435–474.

2. See Wilson R. Hart, *Collective Bargaining in the Federal Service* (New York: Harper and Row, 1961), pp. 38–54.

3. Herbert W. Cornell, "Legal Aspects of Collective Bargaining by Public Employee Groups," a paper presented at the Central Regional Conference of the Public Personnel Association, St. Louis, May 12, 1958.

4. Ibid., pp. 3–4. The case quoted is *Railway Mail Association vs. Murphy,* 44 N.Y. Supp. (2) 601.

5. See John Ligtenberg, "Legal Opinion on Collective Bargaining," reprinted by the American Federation of Teachers from *Chicago Union Teacher,* September 1963.

6. Hart, op. cit., p. 43.

7. Saul Frankel, "Employer-Employee Relations in the Public Service," *Public Personnel Review,* XXV (1964), 221.

8. Ibid., p. 222.

9. Cornell, op. cit., p. 1.

10. Ibid., pp. 4–5.

11. Ibid., p. 4.

12. Chapter 392 of the Laws of 1967 of the State of New York.

13. Lucia Mouat, "Teachers continue campaign for bargaining," *Christian Science Monitor,* April 12, 1966.

14. John Ligtenberg and Robert G. Andree, *Collective Bargaining in the Public Schools, a Hand-book of Information and Source Materials on Teacher Rights and Teacher Obligations* (Chicago: American Federation of Teachers Educational Foundation, Inc., 1966), p. 189.

15. Ibid., pp. 188–198 for text of Appellate Court's decision.

16. Ibid., p. 191.

17. Ibid., p.192.

18. Ibid., pp. 192–193.

19. Ligtenberg, "Legal Opinion on Collective Bargaining," *op. cit.*

20. "Michigan Court Rules in Favor of Grievance Arbitration for Public Employees," *The Public Employee,* November 1967, p. 5.

21. *New York Times,* editorial, January 22, 1966.

22. *Labor Management Relations Act, 1947, as Amended by Public Law 86–257, 1959.* Public Law 101, 80th Congress. Washington, D.C.: U.S. Government Printing Office.

23. Donald E. Cullen, *Negotiating Labor-Management Contract* (Ithaca: New York State School of Industrial and Labor Relations, Cornell University, 1956).

24. S. A. Little, "Union or Association Objectives: A Labor Viewpoint," in Kenneth O. Warner (ed.), *Collective Bargaining in the Public Service: Theory and Practice* (Chicago: Public Personnel Association, 1967), p. 60.

25. Pete Schnaufer, "Collective Bargaining Contracts, From the Houses of AFT & NEAT" *American Teacher,* March 1967. Special section.

26. American Bar Association, Section of Labor Relations Law, 1963 *Proceedings, Part II* (Chicago: American Bar Center, 1964), p. 150.

27. Ibid., p. 151.

28. *American Teacher,* June 1966, p. 9.

29. Thomas R. Brooks, "The Caseworker and the Client," *New York Times Sunday Magazine,* January 29, 1967, p. 72.

30. Ibid., p. *73.*

31. *New York Times,* August 13, 1966.

32. *New York Times,* editorial, September 9, 1966.

33. *New York Times,* October 11, 1966.

34. Albert H. Aronson, "A Look at Selection Methods," in The Federal Career Service (Washington, D.C.: Society for Personnel Administration, 1954), p. 35.

35. *Agreement between New Castle County and The American Federation of State, County, and Municipal Employees A.F.L.-C.I.O., Locals 459 and 1607,* p. 8.

CHAPTER 29

BILATERALISM AND THE MERIT PRINCIPLE

PAUL M. CAMP AND W. RICHARD LOMAX

IN THE PUBLIC SERVICE, we have seen the *unilateral* development of merit systems to guard against improper influence in the filling of career positions. The word "unilateral" is italicized because this is the key feature of merit systems to which the labor-affiliated and other public employee organizations now strenuously object. They grant that the record of merit systems shows substantial successes, as well as failures, but, even if "civil service" had been much more successful, they still would view it askance.

Civil service commissions and boards, the personnel administrators in the line agencies, are considered the representatives of a paternalistic public employer who refuses to share the decision-making process with them. The employee leaders recognize that the traditional merit systems offer protection to the employees, but only within this paternalistic framework. The system of protection which they prefer is the one which has proved itself in the private sector: collective bargaining, which means joint decision making, since both parties must agree before the contract can be signed. This is the best protection, because the terms of employment are not imposed on the workers; it is bilateralism, so infinitely superior to unilateralism. Merit system administrators, confronted with this now openly expressed attitude of employee organizations, are grappling with the difficult task of proving that it is possible both to junk the old paternalism and retain the essential elements of a merit system. The future of public personnel administration depends upon how successful they are in this effort.

Merit Systems and Union Contracts

Is collective negotiation theoretically consistent with merit principles? What do we mean by "merit"? Does it mean the traditional union concept of "seniority"? Since there are so many different employee organizations, it is doubtful that a generally accepted union definition could be found. Most of the unions on the federal scene have generally endorsed the merit principle, but in the specific application of this principle they have expressed views which some federal personnel administrators believe constitute a threat to "civil service."

From 28 *Public Administration Review*, 2: 133–137, March/April 1968. Copyright © 1968 American Society for Public Administration. Reprinted with permission.

To public personnel administrators and the general public, a "merit system" is "a personnel system in which comparative merit or achievement governs each individual's selection and progress in the service and in which the conditions and rewards of performance contribute to the competency and continuity of the Service."[1] Perhaps a more precise definition is: "The organization and administration of a method whereby jobs in a government service are filled by the orderly recruitment and examination of applicants; a plan having as one of its principles the promotion of employees on the basis of ability."[2]

The essential components of "merit" are set forth in the proposed Intergovernmental Manpower Act of 1967 which authorizes the President, "in programs that are financed in whole or in part from Federal funds and as a condition for the grant of such funds, to require State and local governments to provide for their employees systems of merit personnel administration." Specifically, it is provided that:

the President may establish appropriate standards consistent with such merit principles as:

- recruiting, selecting, and advancing employees on the basis of their relative ability, knowledge, and skills, including open consideration of qualified applicants for initial appointment;
- providing equitable and adequate compensation;
- training employees, as needed, to assure high-quality performance;
- retaining employees on the basis of the adequacy of their performance, correcting inadequate performance, and separating employees whose inadequate performance cannot be corrected;
- assuring fair treatment of applicants and employees in all aspects of personnel administration without regard to political affiliation, race, color, national origin, sex, or religious creed; and
- assuring that employees are protected against coercion for partisan political purposes and are prohibited from using their official authority for the purpose of interfering with or affecting the results of an election or a nomination for office.[3]

Union Testimony

At the hearings on the Proposed Manpower Act, some union officials expressed concern over the proposed merit standards on the ground that existing contract clauses covering grievances, appeals, and promotion plans might be nullified and these areas preempted from future bargaining. The views they expressed throw light on the specific stands they will take on the relationship between merit systems and collective contracts. Representatives of the Government Employees Council, AFL-CIO and of the American Federation of State, County, and Municipal Employees, AFL-CIO made clear that they were not opposed to merit personnel administration as such. What they feared was that the mandatory extension of merit systems would interfere with the opportunity of the public employee organizations to negotiate conditions of employment with state and local governments. Specifically, they wanted assurances that adoption by a state or local government of a merit system as a result of a federal requirement would not invalidate collective bargaining agreements already reached between any such government and its employees.

The Senate report on the bill contains the following significant statement: "new language was added providing that the bill shall not be construed to prevent participation by employees or employee organizations in the formulation of policies and procedures affecting the conditions of their employment, subject to the laws and ordinances of the State or local government concerned. The question of the effect of Federal requirements of merit systems on collective bargaining procedures or on existing agreements does not arise, since no such requirements are authorized in the bill."[4]

One must conclude that a degree of conflict exists between the principles of merit systems and those underlying collective negotiations as now practiced, or at least that some of the union leaders suspect that such a conflict exists. In our opinion, this does not preclude the accommodation of the systems to each other (as has been demonstrated in practice) since there are many features of public personnel systems which have been devised to create a desirable and effective career service which are not critical merit factors. In practice the nonmerit elements in public personnel systems vary widely in content and value, and it cannot be assumed that they are immune to bargaining.

Bilateralism and Promotion Policy

A principal area of concern in the federal service has been the impact of collective dealings on promotion policy. The Civil Service Commission's guidelines leave considerable latitude for innovation in the establishment of merit staffing plans through negotiations under Executive Order 10988. However, its basic guidelines prescribe fundamental elements of merit which must be adhered to in such staffing plans in order to ensure that positions are filled by the best-qualified persons available within or outside the federal service. Successes in the federal service under Executive Order 10988 have been based upon a parallel development of two systems, civil service and collective negotiations, originally designed for different purposes, and upon the mutual accommodation of these systems. It has been largely a matter of adjustment; in practice, however, this adjustment has been primarily made at the expense of inroads into existing concepts of merit and fitness for public office. Some of the unions have in effect pushed for seniority as the major consideration in promotions, and this cannot be reconciled with merit. Future successes will depend on several factors:

- The ability of these two systems to continue to accommodate each other: to adjust and to compromise.
- The demands made by the unions for further concessions, including the "right to strike," or a mechanism to substitute for this "right."
- Employee reaction to the direct values received by them in return for union membership and financial support.
- Public reactions to the changes in government organization and merit principles which will have to occur as further union activity develops.

Proposals of AFL-CIO

A preview of what is expected by organized labor may be obtained by reading the statements by George Meany, president of the AFL-CIO, in his testimony before the Presidential Review Committee on Labor-Management Relations in the Federal Service.[5] He expressed his belief that the basic policy represented by Executive Order 10988 has "been good for federal employees and for the labor organizations representing these workers," and that "this policy has been good for the federal government and for the public interest." At the same time, he repeated the comment he made in 1961 to President Kennedy's Task Force on Employee-Management Relations in the Federal Service: "We take the view that public employment is not so inherently different from employment in private industry as to require denial to employees of the Federal Government of rights of organization and collective bargaining which have long been guaranteed by law to employees in private industry." The authors of this article believe there are significant differences between public and private employment, and that the adoption of certain of Meany's specific proposals, such as the union shop, definitely would damage the merit system. Specifically, Meany proposed:

1. Abolition of informal union recognition. [Informal recognition is granted under Executive Order 10988 to qualified employee organizations, no matter how small their membership in the bargaining unit. It gives them the right to present their views to management on matters of concern to the members, but in practice has not meant much and has resulted in the agency managements having to deal with too many employee groups.]
2. Establishment of a system of effective "National Consultation." No organization except the one holding exclusive recognition at the national level would be entitled to National Consultation: it would have the right to *negotiate,* not merely to be consulted, "on all matters in agency regulations that deal with personnel policies."
3. Making "all matters subject to the collective bargaining under Section 6(b) of the Executive Order . . . negotiable items, as long as they are not inconsistent with present and future laws."
4. The assurance that when agreements are negotiated at the local level, the negotiators for the local activity or installation would have the necessary authority to sign the agreement.
5. The "sections of the E.O. referring to management rights—Section 7 and the last sentence of 6(b)—be amended to guarantee the rights of unions to protect the workers they represent."
6. The "negotiated grievance procedure . . . automatically preclude[s] the use of the agency procedure contained in the personnel manual." [As the situation now stands, when the agencies negotiate grievance procedures the agency procedure, established in conformance with Civil Service Commission standards, remains in effect for nonunion members or union members opting to use it.]
7. "All grievances and appeals . . . be subject to the negotiated grievance procedure except when a law requires a special procedure."

8. "Grievance arbitration . . . be final and binding."
9. "A Federal Service Disputes Panel be established for the purpose of resolving negotiation impasses."
10. "A Federal Service Labor-Management Relations Board be established for the purpose of administering the Executive Order."
11. "The Executive Order be amended to state explicitly that the federal government accepts the principle that unions and management in federal service . . . have the right to negotiate union-security agreements." The AFL-CIO believes there is no "legal or constitutional prohibition against the negotiation of labor-management security agreements which bring all workers in an appropriate unit into membership of the appropriately recognized labor organizations."
12. "Employees of the District of Columbia and employees of nonappropriated fund activities of the federal government . . . have all rights guaranteed by the Executive Order."
13. "The term 'employee organization' in the Executive Order . . . be replaced by the term 'labor organization.'"
14. "The revocation period for dues check-off be changed so as to occur once a year."
15. "The 60 per cent rule be abolished." [This requires that 60 per cent of the employees in the bargaining unit must vote for a representation election to be valid.]
16. "The Department of Labor provides services and collects and publishes data for well-informed and intelligent collective bargaining."

Some of these proposals, like the one for strengthening the authority of local installation heads, would improve both collective negotiations and ultimately the merit system. The problem is one of distinguishing between those union positions which can be squared with the merit system and those which cannot. A resolution introduced at the Seventh Constitutional Convention of the AFL-CIO states that "the Federal Government has lagged far behind private industry in the areas of wages and working conditions and . . . the resulting gap can be filled only by progressive and constructive legislative actions." It then goes on to make recommendations in almost every major area of personnel administration, including pay, overtime, wage board employment, union-management relations, retirement, political activities, automation, compensation for injury, promotions, health benefits, life insurance, leave, safety, use of military personnel, restoration of postal service, fire and safety standards, fire research, civil service procedures, uniform allowances, and payment for travel time. Clearly, the AFL-CIO has positive ideas as to what are the areas of legitimate concern to the unions, and some of these recommendations cannot but improve any merit system.

A Look at the Future

The authors believe that progress has been made in personnel administration because of the activities of unions. More progress will be made if, in the attempt to reconcile merit systems and collective negotiations, the following basic questions are asked:

- Why, when, where, and how did the merit system concept develop?

  - Is it doing its job?
  - Can it be modified further so as to do its job better?
  - Should a new concept be developed?
  - Is militant unionism this "new" concept?

- Why did unionism develop?

  - In the private sector?
  - How did it cross over into the public service?
  - Is it necessary in the public service if the merit system is doing its job?

Answers to the above questions will likely result in the raising of others, for example: Does either system, or both in concert, provide what the public service really needs?

There are different solutions to this dilemma:

- Continue the present practices with their attendant tensions. From the point of view of some of the union leadership, this might be desirable; one of the essential reasons for growth is tension, having something to fuss about, and being able to show some tangible benefits for the effort.

In our opinion, such a decision would result in further reductions in the traditional management and merit system prerogatives. It would create an extremely complicated, widespread proliferation of systems of personnel administration even within a given organization. This would be difficult to administer, especially on the federal level where ultimately the kind, scope, and dollar amounts available for employee benefits and programs are controlled by Congress. The same problems of fiscal and administrative coordination, on a lesser scale, face the state legislatures and local government councils.

- Recognize that a plateau has been reached, that most of the accommodations possible of achievement under the two systems have been made, and radically revise: (a) the merit system as it has developed and as we know it; or (b) the application of the techniques of collectivism and negotiations as now practiced by organized labor.

Unless further inroads are made by unions, specifically in those areas still considered management prerogatives, and unless a substitute for the "right" of public employees to strike is developed, there will be more and more labor stoppages. Last year's experience in the strike area was an eye opener for many heretofore passive public servants, and success stimulates success.

The International Executive Board of the American Federation of State, County, and Municipal Employees has approved a policy statement endorsing the "right of public employees—except for police and other law enforcement officers—to strike," with this weapon to be "exercised only under the most extreme provocation or as a final resort if an employer acts in an irresponsible manner."[6] There is no evidence to indicate at present that the leadership of the AFL-CIO, including the National Association of Letter Carriers, the United Federation of Postal Clerks, and the American Federation of Government Employees, intend to assert the right of federal employees to strike. It is, at present, generally recognized that to assert the right of federal employees to strike would be contrary to the intent of Congress as expressed in law, and that to claim such a right would jeopardize employee benefit legislation in Congress.

One cannot be at all sure, however, that the no-strike pledge of federal employees will not be tested in modem times as it once was in the early days of Navy Yard industrial relations, nor can one predict the effects of massive "civil service disobedience" on the federal personnel system. The present trend in public service indicates an erosion of the civil service commission's prerogatives on all levels, and a dwindling capacity of management at all levels to control its program destinies by the deployment and manipulation of its manpower.

A fresh approach must be found. Perhaps the development of a new unionism with techniques applicable to government is emerging. The traditional merit system is becoming more and more a refined selection process for initial employment. It may one day soon be confined to the selection of employees at the beginning level. The significance of Meany's proposals, listed previously, is that the unions are now pressing for the adoption of principles and techniques such as the union shop and binding arbitration which were rejected by the Kennedy Task Force as labor relations methods inappropriate to the federal service and any public employer. Much intensive analysis is now going into what is and what is not "appropriate." Certainly the decisions will have a great impact on public administration.

Notes

1. O. Glenn Stahl, *Public Personnel Administration* (New York: Harper and Row, 1962), p. 28.
2. W. Richard Lomax, *Public Personnel Glossary* (Bloomington, Ind.: Indiana University, 1950), p. 20.
3. *Intergovernmental Personnel Act of 1967, Intergovernmental Manpower Act of 1967.* Hearings before the Subcommittee on Intergovernmental Relations of the Committee on Government Operations, United States Senate, 90th Congress, First Session on S. 699 and S. 1485 (Washington, D.C.: U.S. Government Printing Office, 1967), p. 21.
4. 90th Congress, 1st Session, Calendar #684, Report 701 on S. 699, *Intergovernmental Personnel Act of 1967* (Washington, D.C.: U.S. Government Printing Office, 1967), pp. 11–12.
5. The *Federal Times* of November 8, 1967, summarizes Mr. Meany's testimony.
6. *Government Employee Relations Report*, Number 154, August 22, 1966, Bureau of National Affairs, Washington, D.C.

CHAPTER 30

LABOR UNIONS AND COLLECTIVE BARGAINING IN GOVERNMENT AGENCIES

A Panel Discussion

There is no unanimously accepted answer to the question of what the role of labor unions in government agencies should be. Nevertheless, it is of considerable interest to have stated the views of persons who are concerned in their everyday work with this aspect of public administration. The following discussion sets forth the views of three men who are responsible officials of unions of governmental employees and two men who stand in the role of "employer" in important governmental agencies. The viewpoints expressed are solely those of the participants and are in no way expressions of official attitudes or policies of the organizations with which they are connected.

The discussion took place on March 27, 1945, before the Chicago Chapter of the American Society for Public Administration. The members of the panel were: James W. Errant, executive secretary, Municipal Employees Society of Chicago, chairman; Samuel C. Bernstein, commissioner of placement and unemployment compensation, State of Illinois; George Cervenka, president, National Federation of Post Office Clerks, AF of L; Jack M. Elkin, president, Chicago Local No. 13, United Federal Workers of America, CIO; and Edgar L. Warren, chairman, Sixth Regional War Labor Board.

The transcript of the full discussion has been edited by Dean John Day Larkin of the Illinois Institute of Technology.

CHAIRMAN ERRANT: We in the public service are interested in the efficient operation of the administrative machine; any movement tending in that direction should be given serious consideration. The objectives of the civil service unions are handling grievances, improving wages and working conditions, protecting and promoting merit systems and pension systems, engaging in welfare activity for the benefit of union members, sponsoring in-service training programs, and, finally, professionalizing the civil service for the improvement of administration.

In order to limit our discussion, let us agree that public employees have the right to join unions and to be represented collectively through leaders of their own choosing. If

From 5 *Public Administration Review*, 4: 373–379, Autumn 1945. Copyright © 1945 American Society for Public Administration. Reprinted with permission.

we so agree, we should confine our discussion to those matters involving civil service unionism which may be open to question.

First of all, *is the neutrality of government employees, particularly in agencies which deal with employer-employee relations [such as the NLRG or the NWLB] endangered by membership of these employees in labor unions?*

MR. WARREN: The way that question is put, my answer would be definitely "No." I should amplify that some to say that, in those agencies which deal with labor disputes and jurisdictional questions, in my opinion the public feeling would be that if the employees are members of unions, such unions should not be affiliated with any of the major labor organizations—especially one having problems before that agency.

MR. ELKIN: It is proper to put this in its real perspective and note that the problem is a minor one, considering the government service as a whole. There are few government departments involved in adjudicating cases between rival unions. Even in that small realm we feel that the item of neutrality is exaggerated. Our organization claims that no case has ever been brought forward in which government employees holding membership in a union were affected by that membership in making a decision on policy. There is a dangerous precedent to be established in insisting on neutrality. While a man may not be a member of the union, one of his family may, and then the charge may be made that he is sympathetic to a particular union because of his family connection. If he is not a union man, then the charge can be made that he is, therefore, antiunion. So, we feel that these cases should be considered on their merits. If a man is a government employee, he accepts his job in good faith; if he violates his trust, there are ample remedies. You don't have to restrict his joining a union.

MR. BERNSTEIN: Until we get a greater public acceptance of the attitude expressed by Mr. Elkin, I would be reluctant to state that governmental agencies of the type of Mr. Warren's should have full organizational representation which would involve clashes between the two large labor union organizations. There is not any difficulty with respect to a union which is not affiliated with either side. It need not be a "company union"— meaning one dominated by the powers that be within the organization—but one with the usual attributes of a bona fide labor organization. This would be a lot more sensible in an agency such as the NLRB or the NWLB than one affiliated with one of the two national organizations.

MR. CERVENKA: I take the position that employees of a policy-making body should be neutral. If you have them belonging to one particular faction, you may have prejudiced orders and directives. Recently, charges have been made by the AF of L that some of the federal agencies have been controlled by the CIO. We take the position that such organizations should not be controlled by either AF of L or CIO; they should be absolutely neutral.

MR. WARREN: I would like to emphasize again that the question is a much larger one than our discussion thus far would indicate. The question is: "Is the neutrality of government employees endangered by membership of these employees in labor unions?" I still think the answer is definitely "No," if we except the small segment of government employees who deal with labor relations problems.

MR. ELKIN: You cannot guarantee neutrality by preventing a man from joining a union of his choice. A man joins a union because he has the general problem of wages, hours, working conditions, pay raises, promotions, and such. These problems are common to government employees in all agencies. The employee joins a union to find a solution to these problems. He would object to the charge that he ought not to join a union just because he happens to be in a particular job that requires adjudication between rival organizations. He might say, "Well, my sympathies are already established, and keeping me from joining a union is not going to guarantee my neutrality. Other remedies to insure neutrality already exist without instituting a system of thought-policing."

CHAIRMAN: Let us take up the next part of the question. *How far upward in the ranks of professional and administrative employees should union membership be permitted to go?*

MR. BERNSTEIN: According to a recent NLRB decision, foremen should be recognized for purposes of collective bargaining. With respect to the organization of government employees, there is no reason to limit the organization to so-called clerical employees, excluding those at the policy-making level. I am stating that in a general sense and getting away from those agencies, previously discussed, where the problem of neutrality is important. My experience has been there is no necessity of any clash between the responsible head in an agency and the individual who might be acting for him in a policy-making capacity by reason of the latter's affiliation with any particular union. I have been able to get the benefit of some of the things that my policy-making officials have gathered from union sources, things which helped in determining the proper steps to be taken—and I don't mean getting secrets or spying on the union. Officials who are union members pick up an employee attitude that should be imparted to the head of an agency. They have played fair with me, and I don't see any reason why any limitation should be placed upon organizational activities with respect to policy-making employees in an agency.

CHAIRMAN: Do I understand that you, as the head of an agency, could be included in a labor union?

MR. BERNSTEIN: I don't think the union would want me. Let's put it this way: we have said foremen might very well be included in industrial unions. We did not say that we were going to take the boss of the plant and put him in an industrial union. The head of a government agency would be acting in the same capacity as an employer in a plant. Below that level, individuals who are policy-making—who work on the decisions which the agency is called upon to make in its daily operations—should not be excluded from union membership.

MR. WARREN: Anyone should be eligible for membership who the union feels would not jeopardize their rights and privileges as union members. It is a matter for union determination.

MR. ELKIN: It is hard to draw a line in government service. Almost everybody supervises somebody. Our union will accept into membership anyone except an administrative official who has major responsibility for hiring and firing. This general rule would exclude the head of a department, the director of personnel, and, in large agencies, the bureau heads. This does not mean that these men do not have similar interests. It merely means that the grievance procedure may come to grief if these people are in the union. But the community of interest between employees and supervisors is greater in government service than in industry. For instance, the federal employees' pay-raise bill now pending before Congress, which our union is backing, affects all employees—the bureau chief as well as the rank and file of his staff. The same thing would not be true in industry.

MR. CERVENKA: The union organization in the post office is unique. In the post office everybody starts as a clerk, and the only men who are eligible for membership in our organization are clerks. After promotion to a supervisory position a man must resign from the organization or take out what is known as an honorary membership which makes it possible to keep up the sick benefit, the death benefit, and all that.

CHAIRMAN: *What limits does the law place on the power of government administrators to deal with unions?*

MR. WARREN: As far as I know, none at all.

MR. BERNSTEIN: In a meeting this afternoon with a regional organizer for one of the AF of L unions I asked him that specific question. He pointed out some instances in Illinois where local counsel, city attorneys, and several county attorneys have ruled that it is illegal for any of the local government agencies to enter into collective bargaining agreements with unions but cited also opposing examples, such as an agreement signed by the head of the city council and the mayor of a particular city in the east. I asked him whether he believed that gave the union any legal rights which were enforceable in court. He said, "No." He did not think it did, but he felt that the good faith of the two responsible officials was such as to be relied upon. He further stated that that agreement had been in effect for the last eight years and that the union had been operating under it successfully. If you are going to bargain with a municipality or some other government agency, the important thing is, not whether the agreement is in writing, but whether the ones making the agreement are in a position to enforce what they have agreed to and whether they are the type that can be relied upon.

CHAIRMAN: Our next question is: *Can and should government agencies sign formal contracts with unions with respect to collective bargaining rights and conditions of employment?*

MR. WARREN: I see no reason why government agencies should not sign formal contracts when the parties feel that they can operate better under a written agreement than without one. In some instances it may not be felt necessary to formalize an agreement in writing, but I see no reason why it should not be formalized if there is a desire for such written agreement.

CHAIRMAN: And, in line with what Bernstein has just said, even though it might not be a legally enforceable document it is a gentlemen's agreement.

MR. ELKIN: Government agencies not only can and should sign formal collective bargaining agreements with employee organizations, but they actually do. One of the most widespread collective bargaining agreements in the federal service exists in the TVA, a government corporation. The managers started right out with the idea of placing confidence in their employees and with the idea that the employees, through their organization, can contribute to the efficiency of operation of the Authority. President Roosevelt had occasion to praise that as a model of collective bargaining agreements in government service.

The Securities Exchange Commission signed an agreement with its employees some time ago. I single out that agreement because it was signed by Dean Landis and Mr. Douglas, now Justice Douglas.

MR. BERNSTEIN: Do they consider that an agreement or a declaration of policy?

MR. ELKIN: They consider it an agreement. They signed an agreement whereby they promised to discuss with the organization such matters as promotional opportunities, employee training, dismissals, posting of vacancies, and ventilation of the building.

In some cases the agency discusses new policies with the employee representatives before they are announced. These policies are not set out in written agreements but represent areas of negotiation between the administration and the union.

MR. CERVENKA: Our union has never signed a formal contract with the government agencies, but our national executive board does meet with the officials of the Post Office Department, and we submit memorials on all our grievances. Then we usually thrash out such grievances and have rulings made on them. They more or less become law after that, but we have no formal contracts. Our practice is a matter of policy, accepted for years, and is just as good as a signed contract.

CHAIRMAN: Now we come to the primary point: *Can and should government agencies enter into closed-shop agreements with labor unions?*

MR. WARREN: I suppose a closed-shop agreement would be contrary to civil service regulations. If you have a closed-shop agreement, that would mean that you could not employ anyone who is not a member of the union. That might be considered discrimination under civil service regulations.

MR. BERNSTEIN: Frankly, I think the question is largely academic for that reason. In government agencies you have methods of recruitment that are pretty well spelled out. You have to be guided by certain conditions which, by inference, preclude en-trance into a closed-shop agreement.

MR. CERVENKA: I am absolutely in favor of closed-shop agreements. The government insists on other people's having something of that type. We should have it. It is becoming chaotic in some of the departments of government where you have four, five, maybe a dozen different organizations claiming that they represent the employees. We should have the employees elect whom they should have represent them and have a closed shop. As far as civil service rules are concerned, you could have everybody take a qualifying examination and after he comes into the agency he should join the union.

MR. ELKIN: I could give some reasons why a closed shop would be a good thing, but the question is rather academic. None of the unions have raised it as a part of their programs. There is one instance of a ruling that was made with regard to a closed shop which occurred in the TVA. When the management decided to embark on its collective bargaining program, the question of the closed shop came up. Many of the unions with which they would have to deal had closed-shop agreements in industry. They submitted to the general counsel of the TVA the question as to whether a closed-shop agreement in a government agency would be illegal. His ruling was that it could be legal in those instances in which it could be shown on prima facie evidence that nonmembership in the union was tantamount to failure to establish competence in that particular field. I suppose it is a theoretical question, but conceivably you may have a union in a particular locality which embraces all of the workers in a particular craft or skill. Where the union has maintained a high standard of proficiency and experience and has embraced all of those possessing that degree of skill necessary to fill the positions, it might mean that all qualified persons employed would be of that union. Under these hypothetical circumstances, the general counsel said, such a closed shop would be legal.

CHAIRMAN: It is understood then, that public employees have the right to organize and bargain collectively but cannot enter into closed-shop agreements. Now we come to the question of affiliation. *Should unions of government employees affiliate with national labor organizations?*

MR. BERNSTEIN: With the exception of the incidents we discussed at the beginning of this meeting—with respect to agencies where neutrality must be maintained—I am definitely for affiliation of our employees with national labor organizations. Most programs now—even those of a state character—have national implications, and the program, even though administered by the states and by local governments, finds its duplication in practically every other state in the union. The problems of the employees are similar.

CHAIRMAN: What about the second part of that question? *Should government employees organize nationally in separate unions apart from specific craft or other unions found in private industry?*

MR. ELKIN: I want to go back to the previous question. Unions that are not affiliated with national organizations very easily become company unions. They do not have available the advice, guidance, and experience of national organizations in the field. They consider themselves a group apart. Experience has shown that such unions frequently become company unions in the particular establishment. Unaffiliated unions become too much involved with the petty irritations which confront the employees in daily operations. They begin to exaggerate the importance of petty grievances and fail to see the major problems which can be solved only on a national level.

MR. CERVENKA: I agree with Mr. Elkin. I think the best affiliation is with the national union of government employees. After all, government unions can't make individual contracts. They have to go to Congress for any wage increase—or they have to go to the head of the department in Washington for the improvement of conditions within the department.

MR. ELKIN: I don't disagree. You are talking about a national organization of government employees affiliated with the AF of L or the CIO.

MR. CERVENKA: We found a straight national union better for us than affiliating nationally with electricians, boilermakers, and so forth.

MR. BERNSTEIN: Do you feel, with respect to craft unions, that government employees in those trades ought to remain in such unions?

MR. ELKIN: We feel that government workers ought to be in a national government union which is affiliated with the AF of L or the CIO rather than in the respective craft unions which at present maintain departments in government service—as in the Navy

Yards or the TVA, for example. There are many government employees who are currently members of electrical workers', machinists', or boilermakers' unions. We believe the government employees should be in a government union which affiliates through its national organization with the AF of L or the CIO.

MR. BERNSTEIN: Has there been any question of jurisdictional disputes on that basis?

MR ELKIN: They don't become public but there is some difficulty at times. We feel that the government union is best qualified to handle matters involving civil service rules rather than the rules which machinists or boilermakers would normally find in industry.

MR. BERNSTEIN: As a practical matter in the state of Illinois, I know that the craft unions are in a better bargaining position than any so-called government union. The collective bargaining power of the craft unions is a lot more potent.

CHAIRMAN: *Should the right of government employees to strike be admitted and should the same policy apply to all government employees?*

MR WARREN: Certainly on a theoretical basis, I see no reason why government employees, simply because they are government employees, should not be entitled to the right to strike. I can see why people might argue that particular types of government employees should not be entitled to the right to strike; but on the basis of the same argument I see no more reason why the employees of a privately-owned power plant should be permitted to strike. The employees of the Bureau of Useless Documents, for example, could strike with much less injury to the public safety and welfare. Of course, under the present policy of the government, government employees cannot strike, and it is therefore somewhat of an academic question. Personally, I am not in agreement with the general policy.

CHAIRMAN: Could you designate the classes of employees that you think should have the right to strike?

MR. WARREN: I suppose it might be done, but I wouldn't want the job of saying who should have the right to strike and who should not.

MR. CERVENKA: I maintain that as long as employees in private industry have the right to strike, government employees should also have the right to strike—unless they are in a strictly "governmental" function such as running the Army, Navy, or comparable functions. I could never understand the arbitrary discrimination against government employees in the matter of strikes. I feel that there are many private industries which affect the public welfare as seriously as some government employments, and I see no good reason for the discrimination.

CHAIRMAN: *What is the proper role of labor unions in dealing with local, state, and federal legislative bodies? What types of lobbying and other legislative action are desirable and what types undesirable?*

MR. BERNSTEIN: Frankly, it seems to me that that is the real source of bargaining for governmental labor unions. In many situations where they bargain collectively with heads of governmental agencies, the scope of their bargaining is rather restricted because the legislative bodies have already taken care of the questions of hours, wages, and, in some measure, the working conditions. It is only within such prescribed limits that the head of an agency can operate. Therefore, if unions did not have the right to go to legislative bodies to present their grievances, they would really be foreclosed from the real source of relief in a situation where relief might be necessary. We know that we have taxpayers' associations which do not hesitate to bring pressure upon the legislatures to keep down public expenditures. If there were not pressure from the other side, you would have an artificial level placed upon such things as salaries of public employees.

MR. ELKIN: I don't think that there is much to be added to that statement. The right to lobby was established as far back as 1912 by the Lloyd-LaFollette Act, which was in the nature of an injunction against the Post Office Department, which had imposed a gag rule upon its employees, preventing them from petitioning Congress regarding certain wrongs and grievances under which the postal employees were suffering. That has become a landmark establishing the rights of government employees to lobby.

The effectiveness of the lobbying of government workers has been recognized. When the Ramspeck Automatic Pay Increase Bill was passed in Congress, Representative Ramspeck publicly announced from the House floor that if it had not been for the lobbying activities of the United Federal Workers—their buttonholing of congressmen and their postal card campaign—the bill probably would not have passed.

CHAIRMAN: How do the members of the panel feel about this final question? *Should civil service unions be permitted to engage in political activity?*

MR. WARREN: I see no reason why civil service unions should not be permitted to engage in political activity as long as it does not interfere with the official business of the employees.

CHAIRMAN: Would you call lobbying political activity?

MR. WARREN: It is possible to distinguish between lobbying and other types of political activity—as the Hatch Act does. However, if there were no Hatch Act, I see no reason why government employees should not be permitted to engage in political activity on behalf of a particular individual in a campaign.

CHAIRMAN: In short, you think it is proper for a civil service union to take after a congressman, a state legislator, or an alderman and unseat him if possible?

MR. WARREN: I think it would be proper if legal.

MR. ELKIN: We agree with Mr. Warren. We agree to the extent that we are taking a case to the Supreme Court of the United States to get rescinded that provision of the Hatch Act which prevents government employees from engaging in political activity. We feel that government employees are sufficiently branded with the mark of second-class citizenship without burning the brand deeper.

(Some time later in the discussion Mr. Cervenka returned to this topic.)

MR. CERVENKA: We public employees must remember that we cannot have our cake and eat it too. If we want civil service protection and certain rights under civil service, we have no right to become involved in politics. The average man engages in political activity to get something in return: either he wants a better job or something else. I don't favor political activity to gain favors. The man most active in getting somebody elected is the one who expects to be personally rewarded and is rewarded. So, I am somewhat against political activity for government employees. I would rather have our civil service protection, our seniority rights, and other protections accorded us under the law than be subject to the vicissitudes of politics. Let's keep out of political activity as far as campaigning goes.

CHAPTER 31

PUBLIC SECTOR LABOR RELATIONS

Agent of Change in American Industrial Relations?

GEORGE T. SULZNER

Introduction

Everywhere one turns, it seems, commentary about the changing nature of work, workers, and the workplace is prevalent in the daily media. Not surprisingly, employee relations as practiced in private and public organizations has had its share of attention. Current changes and their implications for the development of thinking about personnel management was the subject of a provocative essay recently in *Public Personnel Management* (Newland, 1984). A corresponding assessment of developments in industrial relations appeared at nearly the same time as a symposium in *Industrial Relations* (1984). Interest is not limited to the United States. In the western democracies (Barkin 1983) similar trends are changing the contours of industrial relations systems.

A common theme is that employee relations practitioners are facing challenges of an unprecedented nature, and that in America, at least, the legitimacy of collective bargaining is being confronted by management directly in ways that necessitate innovative responses by bargaining organization representatives. The predominant orientation of public employee relations specialists who engage in collective bargaining has been to replicate private sector practices wherever applicable. Generally, the source of innovation has been industrial relations as practiced in manufacturing concerns, and new concepts and techniques which have emerged there have been examined for adaptability to the public setting.

The burden of this essay is to suggest that it might be worth considering whether the contemporary condition will reverse this pattern of thinking. Is it possible that the public arena will be the environment that spawns the creativity needed for a viable evolution of the United States industrial relations system in the last decade of the twentieth century? In the rest of this paper I will set forth the reasons why I think this could be the case.

From 5 *Review of Public Personnel Administration*, 2: 70–77, Spring 1985. Copyright © 1985 Sage Publications. Reprinted with permission.

Macro Considerations

Union Growth

Certainly the public setting is going to be looked at even more closely by scholars and other specialists simply because it is an area where bargaining organization continues to grow (Garbarino 1984) in contrast to a 15 percent decline in union density since 1950 among nonagricultural employees in the private sector (Strauss 1984). Basic arithmetic indicates public employee unions are going to have more influence in the councils of the AFL-CIO as they experience slow growth while, at least for the immediate future, the private sector unions' membership is projected to decline further. Union research activity and experiments with new organizing techniques are likely, therefore, to be focused more in the public than in the private sector.

A main factor in the significant decline in private sector union density has been a big drop in the rate of union membership gains through NLRB elections, much of which is linked to growing management opposition to unions (Freeman 1983). This anti-union orientation, which has characterized the Reagan appointees to key labor relations positions and particularly at the National Labor Relations Board as well, is constricted in its impact on public sector dealings by the federal nature of governmental policy in the area. Further, the shift initiative to management in the private sector after 40 years, "during which most of the innovations in industrial relations came from unions," (Strauss 1984: 2) will not be a comparable shock to public union representatives. They have always functioned within a framework of statutory management rights prerogatives which limit the scope of bargaining and require competence in handling civil service and legislative procedures if employee interests are to be promoted. Thus, both in terms of attitudinal and resource flexibility, the public sector seems a more likely location, than in the past, for launching new directions in labor relations.

Political Action

As noted above, public sector labor relations has an explicit political dimension. "Government is not just another industry," Summers has written, " . . . in private employment collective bargaining is a process of private decisionmaking shaped primarily by market forces . . . in public employment it is a process of governmental decisionmaking shaped ultimately by political forces" (Summers 1974: 1156). The development of an increasingly constraining climate for collective bargaining in industry means that reliance upon it for gains in employee welfare has diminishing returns for private sector unions. Inevitably, it would seem, they will have to seek more of their remedies through political action. The AFL-CIO's decision to endorse Walter Mondale prior to the Democratic Party's presidential primaries is the most visible sign of this turning. Aaron has observed others. "Whether the emphasis of the AFL-CIO and its affiliates will turn from voluntarism and business unionism to political action designed to bring about favorable government action remains to be seen, but there are plenty of signs in the wind: demands for extended unemployment benefits, restrictions on imports, support for corporate bailouts, legislative regulations of plant closing and removals, etc." (Aaron 1984: 53). The movement of unions toward seeking legislative, administrative and judicial treatment of subjects historically covered by collective bargaining is bound to make the political action experience of government employee unions on these matters more relevant to strategic planning within the AFL-CIO hierarchy. As industrial action declines in utility for employee bargaining organizations in the private sector and political action gains, representatives of both parties are likely to look to the experiences of government employers and unions for guidance in manipulating public levers of power.

Demography and Technology

Increasingly, the workforce in the United States is composed of individuals who have not experienced industrials relations. Growing numbers of women and minorities are participants in the labor market, especially in service occupations, which have been subject to little union organizing activity. These employees often identify with goals that are not related to historical union objectives—job sharing, day care facilities, affirmative action, comparable worth—or have legitimately regarded labor organizations as obstacles to, rather than facilitators of, upward mobility (Strauss 1984). Moreover, with the introduction of sophisticated technologies into the plant and office, work itself is changing. The mental requirements associated with the professions is becoming a commonplace feature of more and more nonprofessional positions. Furthermore, the discretion associated with professional occupations—control over much of the timing and contents of jobs—is spreading to many employment situations. For example, it is estimated that by 1990 as many as 15 million people will be working half-days at home and half-days at their offices (Aaron 1984).

Public sector unions operate in settings that are more like future work environs than those of private sector unions. Public bargaining organizations represent professionals, supervisors, and in the education and public safety fields, even the top echelons of management. At universities and research institutes, unions develop competency in handling esoteric issues such as patent policy and related entrepreneurial rights, and deal with judgments concerning the relative merits of book length publications compared to serial publication in scholarly journals. Bargaining organizations representing social workers, public school teachers, public safety officers, nurses and other hospital professionals have consistently had to grapple with matters relating to the quality versus the quantity of service provision. Through the various grievance processes, they have articulated concerns about the degree and level of employee participation in public enterprise decisions. In organizing drives they have had to learn how to appeal to the interests of white collar service employees in potential bargaining units with large representation of women and minorities. Successful campaigns have led to bargaining organizations with significant numbers of women and minorities in leadership positions often interacting with similar management counterparts in public institutions. Whereas it was thought by many that real collective bargaining only took place in the private sector, this proposition may be reversed in the future. It seems obvious, at the least, that public sector practices should have considerable value to industrial relations specialists who are interested in discerning the likely evolution of the private sector system.

Micro Concerns

Decentralization

Recent developments seem to suggest that strategic planning by corporate management favors decentralized collective bargaining. Pattern wage bargaining is disappearing, especially in the transportation industry, and more attention is concentrated on the individual plant or facility as the proper location for industrial relations dealings (Kochan et al. 1984). This level of interaction has been the normal circumstance for many public sector relationships. Working conditions often differ according to individual facility and sometimes even by bargaining unit. Centralized economic bargaining is still the exception in most states, though it increasingly occurs within municipalities. Public unions are well aware that in this type of labor relations setting, personalities, perhaps even more than contract provisions, can have a primary influence on the quality of contacts between the parties and over time have adjusted to the fluidity in relationships that entail. Flexibility in handling diverse dealings is an increasingly esteemed skill for practitioners in both sectors.

Human Resource Policies and Legal Regulations

Human resources policies which are intended to increase employee motivation and job commitment are becoming more regular features of the corporate landscape. On the whole, they center on job enrichment, career ladders, incentives for increased productivity, and due process protections against arbitrary management action. Strauss comments, "These new policies have been most widely introduced in nonunion plants and especially in high technology industries. They have been talked about more than they have actually been adopted. Nevertheless, they seem to represent the wave of the future" (Strauss 1984: 4–5).

This development, coupled with the passage of new employment regulations (EEO, ERISA, OSHA) and the erosion of the employment-at-will doctrine in the private sector, has led some observers to conclude that an equally comprehensive employee welfare system is available to workers outside of collective bargaining. It undoubtedly has made union organizing more difficult throughout the United States (Strauss 1984). Unions, if they are to compete in the private sector, are undoubtedly going to have to put more emphasis on their watchdog role in contract administration and how it has equipped them to be expert overseers of the implementation process. " . . . The role of unions will shift," Aaron predicts, "from that of innovators to that of consolidators and enforcers. . . . The role of enforcer of employment guarantees will become increasingly important; but, as in Western Europe, most of those guarantees will be created by statute, administrative regulation, executive orders, and judicial decisions . . ." (Aaron 1984: 56).

Once more, it seems apparent that public sector operatives will find this future context somewhat familiar. They function in a world where understanding of civil service regulations and personnel procedures is mandatory for the effective conduct of employee relations. Nowhere is this more visible than at the national level where, deprived of the authority to bargain about wages and hours of work, federal unions have become expert in using all the available employment guarantees to represent employee interests through the grievance, administrative, and judicial processes (Sulzner 1979). Public unions have been quite successful in competing with alternative employee welfare systems by stressing their ability to use a multiple of networks and avenues in providing independent representation of bargaining unit members (Garbarino 1984). The necessity which forced them to move beyond the written agreement in their representation endeavors has served them well and may be of benefit to union organizing efforts in the private sector. Recent research indicates a majority of nonunion workers have an interest in supporting unions; that union members place a high priority on effective grievance representation; and that "complaint procedures" are used infrequently in nonunion firms, perhaps because of a lack of experienced, independent representation of employees, and independent review of decisions (Farber 1983, Kochan 1979, Foulkes 1980, Berenbeim 1980, Garbarino 1984).

Participation

Much is being written currently about the development of participatory plans structured to enhance worker identification with corporate well-being. These vehicles vary from the establishment of growing numbers of worker cooperatives, to increasing the availability of employee stock option plans, to large scale concern with the quality of work life and the formation of joint committees to study ways of improving products and productivity. Does all this activity foretell the beginning of an era of cooperation and good will between management and labor and a movement away form the adversarial relations of the past? Certainly some of the convergence in interests flows from the recent recession and the competitive rigors of an international market which affect more American businesses. Survival was at stake for many concerns and the parties were motivated by a "Dunkirk spirit" which, while deeply felt, can be quite transitory once the worst is overcome. For cooperation to last, the payoff must be clear; mechanisms for consultation must be in place, and trust must be present (Sulzner 1982; Strauss 1984). Some experienced practitioners think relationships and attitudes must change in American industrial relations. Unfortunately, most labor-management relations, as Stephen Schlossberg, former director of government affairs of the United Auto Workers, notes, "are still about yesterday" (Easterbrook 1983: 32). Too much of the dealings, he thinks, have been geared to an adversative history and built on assumptions of unimpeded growth. Certainly, at a minimum, more sharing of thinking about problems by the parties is necessary (Easterbrook 1983). The outcome of the ongoing negotiations in the automobile industry should be a good indicator whether industrial relations in the United States is heading in a new direction. My guess is that there will be more opportunities in the future for union representatives to share decision responsibility with their management counterparts and public sector unions have track records in this regard which the private sector should study.

One of the major distinctions of collective bargaining in the public sector is the number of professional employees who are organized by unions. These unions have operated for years in a grey area of enterprise decisionmaking. Some decisions, based on expertise, are in their members' domain. Others, based on location within the management hierarchy, are outside. Nowhere is this line blurred more than in higher education, though it exists in nearly all public fields of endeavor. Faculties traditionally exercise primary responsibility in academic matters through Senates or Councils. In unionized situations, this practice coexists with and, typically, mutually supports efforts to increase faculty input on matters relating to pay and working conditions. Many opportunities exist for "biting the apple" and, more importantly, the peaches, pears, and plums which show up at the table. Public unions and their members, in these situations, necessarily get involved with enterprise decisions in a manner—for example, coordinated joint lobbying—that has been quite foreign to the mainstream practice of industrial relations elsewhere.

The prospects for union growth in most areas of private employment may require a departure from the traditional "informed critic" role of American unions. It appears they are beginning to follow the lead of western European industrial unions and starting to deploy some of their collective resources to guarantee a voice in matters concerning company investments, production design and location, and managerial appointments. In the United States, the public sector labor relations experience may be the bridge for private sector unions to get from here to there.

Conclusion

Observers of the public labor-management scene might be disposed to argue that mature collective bargaining has arrived in numerous jurisdictions just at the time it is becoming passé in the private sector, and once more, public practices are destined to be behind-the-times. This analysis rests on a reading of the public sector experience which is too superficial. The organizing of government employees came late to the United States but, in a sense, has been a mixed blessing to public employee unions. They have been forced to face up to new issues and new attitudes at the work place in order to gain and hold the support of employee constituencies. The postures, positions, and techniques derived from this circumstance should stand them in good stead in a future in which all work environs are likely to become more rather than less similar to the ones in which they customarily function.

From this perspective, public sector dealings between the parties are establishing precedents which could govern future thinking about industrial relations in America. Regardless of whether public labor-management relations takes on the status of being the lead agent for change, labor-management relations' viability as a key element of the governance structure of work will ultimately depend on the orientation on the participants. Justice Brandeis' dictum in 1905 has added currency today. "Don't assume," he wrote, "that the interest of employer and employee are necessarily hostile—that what is good for one is necessarily bad for the other. The opposite is more apt to be the case. While they have different interests, they are likely to prosper or suffer together" (Easterbrook 1983: 31–32). Public sector practitioners have held this as an article-of-faith since the beginning.

References

Aaron, B. (1984). "Future Trends in Industrial Relations Law." *Industrial Relations* 23 (Winter, 1984): 52–57.

Barkin, S., ed. (1983). *Worker Militancy And Its Consequences,* 2nd ed. New York: Praeger.

Berenbeim, R. (1980). *Nonunion Complaint Systems: A Corporate Appraisal.* Report No. 770. New York: The Conference Board

Easterbrook, G. (1983). "Voting For Unemployment." *The Atlantic Monthly* (May): 31–44.

Farber, H. (1983). "The Extent of Unionization in the United States: Historical Trends and Prospects for the Future." Paper prepared for the M.I.T. Conference on Industrial Relations in Transition.

Foulkes, F.K. (1980). *Personnel Policies in Large Nonunion Companies.* Englewood Cliffs, NJ: Prentice Hall.

Freeman, R. (1983). "Why are Unions Fairing Poorly in NLRB Representation Elections?" Paper prepared for the M.I.T. Conference on Industrial Relations in Transition.

Garbarino, J.W. (1984). "Unionism Without Unions: The New Industrial Relations." *Industrial Relations* 23 (Winter, 1984): 40–51.

Kochan, T.A. (1979). "How American Workers View Labor Unions." *Monthly Labor Review* C11 (April): 23–31.

Kochan, T.A., R.B. McKersie and P. Cappelli (1984). "Strategic Choice and Industrial Relations Theory," *Industrial Relations* 23 (Winter, 1984): 16–39.

Newland, C.A. (1984). "Crucial Issues for Public Personnel Professionals." *Public Personnel Management* 13 (Spring, 1984): 15–46.

Strauss, G. (1984). "Industrial Relations: Time of Change." *Industrial Relations* 23 (Winter, 1984): 1–15.

Sulzner, G.T. (1979). *The Impact of Labor-Management Relations Upon Selected Federal Personnel Policies and Practices.* Washington D.C.: United States Office of Personnel Management.

——— (1982). "The Impact of Labor-Management Committee on Personnel Policies and Practices at Twenty Federal Bargaining Units." *Journal of Collective Negotiations in the Public Sector* 11, 1: 37–45.

Summers, C.W. (1974). "Public Employee Bargaining: A Political Perspective." *Yale Law Journal* 83: 1156–1200.

PART 7

COLLECTIVE BARGAINING, IMPASSE RESOLUTION, AND STRIKES

At the federal level of government, public employees gained the statutory right to collectively bargain with passage of the Civil Service Reform Act of 1978. Prior to this time, labor relations for nonpostal, federal employees was governed by a hodgepodge of executive orders (e.g., EO 10988 issued in 1962), court rulings, and "pattern and practice." At the state and local levels, Wisconsin was the first state in 1959 to grant public employees the legal right to engage in collective negotiations. Today most states allow their public employees some right to bargain collectively, but wide variation exists across governments around such issues as scope of bargaining (i.e., what can be bargained over), methods for resolving disputes, and the rights of supervisors to engage in collective negotiations. One of the long-standing controversial issues in public sector labor relations is the right of public employees to engage in strikes as a form of labor protest. The issue continues to be hotly debated, but over the years, a dozen states have provided some modified right for public employees to strike.

In "Collective Bargaining in Public Employment: Form and Scope," Sterling Spero addresses the growth of collective negotiations in government, with particular attention to the importance of law. He points out that while administrative practice and policy have relevance to labor relations, "the law continues to be a primary factor affecting the solution of practical problems" (Spero 1962: 2). In addition, Spero addresses some of the major distinctions between collective bargaining in the public and private sectors.

In the next selection, Arnold Zander, president of the American Federation of State, County and Municipal Employees (AFSCME), one of the largest public employee unions in the country, presents the union perspective on collective bargaining in government. He notes that

> The union wants collective bargaining because it is concerned with the general welfare of the public employee, raising wage levels in public employment, improving working conditions, and providing job security, and because it is equally concerned with improving the public service. The one is dependent on the other (Zander 1962: 5).

Zander addresses such key collective bargaining issues as union recognition, dues checkoff, arbitration and striking.

Gordon Nesvig, in his article "The New Dimensions of the Strike Question," examines the propensity of public sector unions to strike. He also addresses such issues as types of unions that are likely to engage in strikes, alternatives to striking (e.g., "blue flu"), and the debate over whether public sector unions should be afforded the legal right to strike.

In "Public Sector Collective Bargaining: Is the Glass Half Full, Half Empty, or Broken?" Donald Klingner examines the vitality of public employee unions at the bargaining table. He shows, on the one hand, that union membership in the public sector is on the rise. On the other hand, as Klingner shows, other indicators suggest an erosion to unions' power bases. For example, with the constant threat of layoffs and the inability to strike, unions' bargaining power has been severely hampered and depleted. Klingner suggests strategies (e.g., mobilizing public support) that unions could pursue in order to remain viable on a long-term basis.

The Southeast is one of the areas in the nation which has substantially restricted the rights of public employees to engage in collective bargaining and other labor activities. Richard Kearney, in "Public Employee Unionization and Collective Bargaining in the Southeast," examines the status of that region's collective negotiations. His study shows that the Southeast lags behind the rest of the country in terms of workers' propensity to join unions and the incidence of collective bargaining. Kearney also points to several factors which could lead to greater public employee unionization in the Southeast: heightened two-party competition, large nonwhite workforces, and increased per capita incomes.

Additional Classics

Delaney, John Thomas and Peter Feuille. "Collective Bargaining, Interest Arbitration, and the Delivery of Police Service." 5 *Review of Public Personnel Administration*, 2: 21–36, Spring 1985.

Elling, Richard C. "Civil Service, Collective Bargaining and Personnel Related Impediments to Effective State Management: A Comparative Assessment." 6 *Review of Public Personnel Administration*, 3: 73–93, Summer 1986.

Gellhorn, Walter. "Selecting Supervisory Mediators Through Trial by Combat." 8 *Public Administration Review*, 4: 259–266, Autumn 1948.

Johnson, Richard B. "Administrative Problems of Government Seizure in Labor Disputes." 11 *Public Administration Review*, 3: 189–198, Summer 1951.

Kearney, Richard C. and David R. Morgan. "Unions and State Employee Compensation," *State and Local Government Review*, 1980.

Newland, Chester A. "Collective Bargaining Concepts: Applications in Governments." 28 *Public Administration Review*, 2: 117–126, March/April, 1968.

Nigro, Felix A. "Managers in Government and Labor Relations." 38 *Public Administration Review*, 2: 180–184, March/April 1978.

Perry, James L. "Collective Bargaining: The Search for Solutions." 39 *Public Administration Review*, 3: 290–294, 1979.

Perry, James L. and David T. Methe. "The Impacts of Collective Bargaining on Local Government Services: A Review of Research." 40 *Public Administration Review*, 4: 359–371, 1980.

Sharpe, Carleton F. and Elisha C. Freedman. "Collective Bargaining in a Nonpartisan, Council-Manager City." 22 *Public Administration Review*, 1: 13–18, Winter 1962.

Terry, Newell B. "Collective Bargaining in the U.S. Department of the Interior." 22 *Public Administration Review*, 1: 19–23, Winter 1962.

CHAPTER 32

COLLECTIVE BARGAINING IN PUBLIC EMPLOYMENT

Form and Scope

STERLING D. SPERO

Labor management relations in the public service are moving toward the patterns prevailing in private employment. The traditional methods of determining working conditions by legislation or unilateral decision by the employing authority are slowly giving way to systems of collective bargaining analogous to those outside the government services. This development has been most marked in municipal employment. Philadelphia has signed union contracts covering all of its employees outside the uniformed forces. New York City adopted collective bargaining a few years ago. Its Board of Education is now in the process of installing formal bargaining arrangements for its 44,000 employees. More than 400 local and state government agencies as well as scores of school and special districts now have collective agreements with their employees. The federal government is implementing the report of a Task Force recommending the formal recognition of employee organizations for collective bargaining on all personnel matters within the competence of the employing agency.

Collective Bargaining or Collective Negotiation?

Yet opposition to determining the working conditions of government employees by negotiation and agreement between the employing authority and its organized workers is still strong in many quarters. The roots of this opposition lie in the theory of the sovereign state under which government as the custodian of ultimate authority in the community must exercise the right of final decision in all matters affecting its relations with its servants. The opponents of collective bargaining regard it as a process presupposing equality between the parties to the employment relationship which conflicts with the claims of the sovereign employer and runs counter to the "nature of the state."

This position was implied in President Franklin D. Roosevelt's statement in 1937:

From 22 *Public Administration Review*, 1: 1–5, Winter 1962. Copyright © 1962 American Society for Public Administration. Reprinted with permission.

> . . . . the process of collective bargaining as usually understood, cannot be transplanted into the public service. . . . The very nature and purposes of government make it impossible for administrative officers to represent fully or bind the employer in mutual discussions with government employee organizations. . . .

Many employing authorities have sought to justify their unwillingness to bargain collectively with employee organizations by seizing upon this statement as proof that it was "impossible" for them to do so. This attitude has persisted despite the fact that the President in dedicating the Chicamauga Dam of the Tennessee Valley Authority three years after he made this statement praised "the splendid new agreement between organized labor and the T.V.A." which had just been consummated, declaring, "collective bargaining and efficiency have proceeded hand in hand."

It should be noted that President Roosevelt specifically used the term "collective bargaining." Public administrators and employee organizations which engage in collective negotiation and are fully aware of the differences between public and private employment believe that the term accurately describes the labor relations process in which they engage. Others, however, prefer such terms as "collective negotiation," "collective dealing," "joint consultation and agreement," on the ground that "collective bargaining" has legal connotations applicable only in private enterprise.

The primary distinction between public and private labor-management agreements is the fact that the former are made subject to the overriding power of the government. The T.V.A. agreements to which President Roosevelt referred declare:

> The parties recognize that T.V.A is an agency of and is accountable to the government of the United States of America. Therefore T.V.A. must operate within the limits of its legally delegated authority and responsibility.

Similarly the Constitution of the Whitley Councils in Great Britain, which are highly formalized instruments for employee-management negotiation, provide that the agreements reached between the organized "staff side" and the government's representatives known as the "official side" shall become effective "subject to the overriding authority of Parliament and the responsibility of the minister."

While the legal differences between collective agreements in public and private employment are important, the tendency to regard collective bargaining in the public service as a question of law rather than as a matter of public policy has been a source of confusion. A central aspect of sovereign power is authority to make public policy decisions. A policy decision by governments to establish collective bargaining procedures in its service is itself a sovereign act.

Form and Scope of Collective Bargaining

Although the growth of public service collective bargaining moves consideration of the process from the realm of political and legal theory to the field of administrative policy and practice, the law continues to be a primary factor affecting the solution of practical problems.

Two such practical problems rooted in the law are the form and the scope of the public collective agreement. Both problems involve administrative discretion. In many instances courts or law officers have questioned the power of public authorities to enter into formal contracts either because they found no legal grant of power to do so or because they believed that a formal contract improperly delegated the authority of the employing agency and bound its freedom to administer. Although government in its dealings with business constantly enters into contracts which bind administrative discretion, courts and law officers have been reluctant to admit such contractual authority in personnel matters. In such circumstances when collective bargaining was desired by employing agencies the essence of the bargaining process has been sustained and the letter of the law preserved by publishing agreements in the form of unilateral statements of policy, executive directives, or memoranda of agreement. In some cities the results of collective bargaining agreements were published as resolutions or acts of the local legislative body.

The scope of collective bargaining likewise involves the issue of administrative discretion. Where an agency has a high degree of autonomy and fiscal independence, the scope of collective bargaining is virtually as wide as in private employment. Where, on the other hand, basic conditions of work are fixed by classification acts, time and leave laws, and statutory hiring and promotion procedures, the scope of collective bargaining is obviously far more limited. But even here the area of administrative discretion in the application of the laws is substantial. The manner in which the classification system is carried out, in which vacation dates are determined, in which assignments and promotions are made are all matters of deep employee concern. Employee-management agreements covering such matters in the postal service and government industrial works as well as in white collar agencies and public institutions on all governmental levels have been in effect for many yearn. As government services become larger and more complex, it becomes increasingly desirable to devolve discretion over personnel matters to administrators. Public employees want a voice in the exercise of this discretion for the same reasons as do employees in private industry.

Need for an Exclusive Bargaining Unit

No collective bargaining, whether of broad or more limited scope, can take place until there is a responsible employee bargaining agent with which to deal. Where the bargaining process concerns conditions of work, the recognition of a sole bargaining agent to represent all employees of a given category is clearly indicated. There can be only one system of working conditions in a jurisdiction. Objections have been raised to the recognition of exclusive bargaining agents on the ground that such recognition compels employees in an open employment system recruited on the basis of merit to be represented by an organization to which they may not wish to belong.

Negotiation between management and a multi-organization panel or committee has been suggested as an alternative. Such plans, however, have not proved satisfactory. They give rise to pulling and hauling among the competing groups within the negotiating panel. In the end, they tend to break down or to evolve into a system of sole representation.

The experiences of the New York Transit System, where a plural representation plan established in the 1940s was eventually abandoned in favor of an exclusive bargaining unit, is a striking example. The Tennessee Valley Authority had a somewhat similar experience with its white-collar employees. The Report of the President's Task Force on Employee-Management Relations in the Federal Service endorses exclusive representation for purposes of negotiation and agreement on working conditions where a union has the support of a majority in an agency, but reserves "informal recognition" and access to management for the presentation of views to minority groups.

After all, the problem of bargaining representation is a practical one. Majority rule in politics may give rise to many individual dissatisfactions, but it is a practical device. An exclusive bargaining agent freely chosen representing a majority of the employees concerned is a manifestation of majority rule and representative industrial government. Supervision of the choice of a bargaining agent can either be made the duty of the central personnel agency or another independent body.

The check-off of dues is usually regarded as a feature of exclusive bargaining. There are many unions in private employment in this country and abroad which prefer to have their agents circulate among their members and hear their gripes and learn their attitudes in the dues collecting process. However, the check-off has become a recognized practice in public employment. Sometimes the cost of the process is shared by the parties, sometimes it is borne by one or the other of them. The President's Task Force has recommended that Congress authorize a voluntary check-off in the Federal service.

Some employee organizations insist that the union shop under which all employees in the bargaining unit are required to join the union is the logical consequence of the recognition of an exclusive bargaining agent. The union shop, they hold, prevents "free riding" by individuals who receive the benefits of the union without paying dues or bearing the responsibilities of membership. The union shop is a device invented by the labor movement in private industry to prevent employers from weakening the union and undermining standards through the introduction of cheap non-union labor. Such tactics are possible in jurisdictions without merit systems, but highly unlikely, if not impossible, where recruitment is on a merit basis and standards are uniform and publicly declared. In such situations unions have generally been able to convince non-members to join by demonstrating the significance of their services. Although the union shop seems to be winning increasing acceptance in local governments and exists for practical purposes, without formal recognition, in some federal agencies, it is not an essential complement of collective bargaining in the public service.

It is essential, however, that procedures be available for the resolution of grievances and other disputes arising under the collective agreement. In industry labor-management contracts almost invariably provide for the settlement of disputes arising under them through final and binding arbitration by impartial third parties. Legal objections have at times been raised to such procedures in the public service on the ground that they permit outsiders to bind the administrative discretion of public officials. But ways have been found to overcome this obstacle by designating public officers or official bodies as arbitrators. Thus the Secretary of Labor serves as binding arbitrator on wages in the

T.V.A. and the Joint Committee on Printing performs the same function in the Government Printing Office. The State Legislature has clothed an outside arbitrator with official status in the New York Transit System. Many other examples might be cited. Final and binding awards under such circumstances derogate administrative authority no more than rulings on appeal to central personnel agencies or boards of review on ratings, discipline, or dismissals.

In practice final and binding awards under agreements have not proved necessary. Awards in the form of advice to the agency head are all that are normally required. The publicity attached to them has given the parties ample protection while the legal authority of the agency has remained intact.

Anti-Strike Policy: A Fact in the Public Service

The more difficult problem is that of resolving disputes regarding working conditions where the bargaining process results in an impasse. In private employment under such circumstances workers have recourse to the strike. In the public service strikes are outlawed either by legislation as in the case of the federal government and eleven states or by other sanctions such as the attitude of the public authorities, the courts, and the press. Many countries actually guarantee the right of their government employees to strike. The right has often been exercised and the governments concerned still stand. Yet, in the United States, the slogan "one cannot strike against the government" has become an article of faith to be accepted without question. This, despite the fact that strikes by many classes of workers in private industry could do far more damage to the community than strikes of certain classes of public employees. It is hardly logical for the government to guarantee the right to strike to transportation, communication and utility workers, and the handlers of perishable foods, who are private employees, and forbid it by law or practice to park attendants, charwomen in government buildings, or record office clerks, who are government employees. If it is not the convenience and welfare of the community but the continuous functioning of the public services which justifies anti-strike policy for public employees, then it should be noted that strikes by private utility or transport workers could interfere with the operations of government as directly as strikes by government employees.

However illogical anti-strike policy confined to public workers may be, it is nevertheless a fact. Equally important is the fact that, although strikes have occurred even in the face of drastic legislation, the strike is not a significant weapon in the American public service. All of the techniques for the settlement of disputes in private employment have been used in the course of public service negotiation. These have included mediation and conciliation, fact finding with and without recommendations, and advisory or final and binding voluntary arbitration.

Compulsory arbitration has been widely recommended as a socially desirable substitute for the strike. Private industry has generally rejected it. Many of the reasons given for such rejection are also applicable in the public service, particularly the objection that the compulsory process tends to discourage full and effective bargaining. Its very availability encourages the parties to dump their problems into the arbitrator's lap, relieving the principals from making difficult decisions and unpleasant concessions to be justified to their constituents. Compulsory arbitration has long been a feature of Australian and Canadian labor relations. It has been tried in the Canadian municipal services with so little success in some cases that the local governments concerned have recommended the recognition of the right to strike. This recommendation was based on the ground that the compulsory process not only discouraged effective bargaining pushing hard questions into arbitration, but also led employee organizations to make excessive demands in the belief that they could always be sure of getting a good part of what they asked from the arbitrators.

The Lever of Political Power

The most effective substitute for the strike in government service is the political power of the employees. The political environment in which public employee-management relations are carried on is quite different from the milieu of private labor relations. Pressure on the public official which ultimately might affect his job gives the public employee organization a leverage which is at least a partial substitute for the strike. Publicity by employee organizations through demonstrations, advertisements in the newspapers, broadcasts, and loud general screaming frequently provide the setting in which the process of bargaining takes place. The atmosphere thus created is intended not only to soften the administration but also to ease the way for deals with legislative and party leaders. Arrangements prior to formal bargaining between unions and elected officials in which political support is exchanged for promises of concessions to the employees are hardly unknown even under the most meticulously correct merit systems. This sort of thing is more common in local and state jurisdictions than in the Federal government, but it has its counterparts, though somewhat less bizarre, even there.

Traditionally, government employee unions on all governmental levels have used their political power to check or overrule the administration and to obtain legislation spelling out working conditions in detail. This greatly circumscribed the administrative discretion of operating officials, but it was exactly what the unions wished to do. They regarded the legislature as a buffer between themselves and their bosses, who with rare exceptions refused to recognize and deal with them, thus making recourse to the legislature their only alternative to accepting unchecked executive control over their working lives.

If civil service reform in this country had not begun at the wrong end, at the bottom with the clerks instead of at the top with the administrators (perhaps this was inevitable at the time) the country might long ago have developed a corps of government executives in whom the great body of employees had confidence. This now has begun to happen and the change is one of the reasons why employee negotiation with officials with broad administrative discretion can take the place of the traditional system of detailed legislative regulation.

Collective bargaining has had its best results in government employment in the agencies with a high degree of autonomy and broad discretionary authority. The test will henceforth be in the agencies which operate under tight personnel legislation. At the beginning the scope of possible negotiation will necessarily be limited. Success in this limited area can be expected to lead to the relaxation of legislative strictures and thus to widening the field open for employee-management agreement. This should give the employees greater influence over their working lives than they have under the legislative system and the administrator the freer hand in the operation of his agency that the complexity of modern public administration requires.

CHAPTER 33

A UNION VIEW OF COLLECTIVE BARGAINING IN THE PUBLIC SERVICE

ARNOLD S. ZANDER

Why does the union in the public service want collective bargaining? The union wants collective bargaining because it is concerned with the general welfare of the public employee, raising wage levels in public employment, improving working conditions, and providing job security, and because it is equally concerned with improving the public service. The one is dependent on the other. The union wants to represent and bargain for all employees in the unit involved in order to secure a continuous relationship and joint consideration of problems arising out of the bargaining contract. It wants more than meetings prior to the adoption of the annual budget; it wants consideration of day-to-day problems. The union wants collective bargaining to help do away with the spoils system, to correct the lag between the economic position of the public employee and that of the industrial worker.

Collective bargaining is the mutual participation by management and labor in the determination of the terms of employment and of the obligations and responsibilities of both management and the union. It is accomplished through negotiations in conferences between representatives of the employer and representatives of the employees, and it terminates in a collective bargaining agreement between the parties. It is a continuing process of bilateral accommodation on the part of labor and management. Collective bargaining is concerned not only with the economic status of the employee but also with the protection and extension of his rights and freedom. Constructive collective bargaining is based on peaceful negotiations, mutual understanding, and agreement. Constructive collective bargaining tends to reconcile the respective interests of management and the union. Without this relationship, there may result tension, quarrels, and bitter conflict between the parties, with their ultimate effect on the public.

Traditionally, public employee unions in the United States have not attempted the same collective bargaining procedures and techniques as have developed and continue to be developed in the non-governmental areas. They reacted to bad conditions with public appeals and if pressed hard they walked out in disorganized strikes, for which they were

From 22 *Public Administration Review*, 1: 5–13, Winter 1962. Copyright © 1962 American Society for Public Administration. Reprinted with permission.

later sorry; they wrote letters to newspapers; they met privately with those presuming political influence. They worked for the enactment of legislation regulating their conditions of employment. They exercised in a very elementary way the right of assembly and petition. They were ineffective and they did not prosper.

The American Federation of State, County and Municipal Employees started out in the tradition of other public employee unions. Today, it is the dominant union in the state and local government field with 220,000 members in forty-eight of the fifty states, the Commonwealth of Puerto Rico, and the Canal Zone. Its success is clearly the result of not having accepted the traditional forms of relationships between the sovereign government and its employees. It decided to discard the traditional techniques and through organization, the development of political effectiveness, and the development of new tools to bring collective bargaining to the public service. It found early that statutory regulation of conditions of employment was inadequate in the complex operation of government. AFSCME advocates the merit system at all levels of government, and the promotion of civil service legislation and career service in government is one of the objectives stated in its constitution. But civil service laws and rules were found to be too broad to care for the day-to-day problems of employees. Even a good civil service system must be policed through the collective bargaining process.

Collective bargaining and the civil service merit system are complementary. A growing number of civil service jurisdictions have found it expedient to enter into collective bargaining agreements covering their employees because they have discovered that the medium of the agreement is increasingly valuable in dealing with questions within the general framework of civil service law and rules. Many points of conflict and misunderstanding arise in the day-to-day relations of employees with their supervisors. These problems are much more satisfactorily handled at the departmental level through a procedure involving the employee union than through formal civil service appeal. Public officials are well aware that a more or less detached central personnel agency is much less apt to secure a satisfactory settlement of an employee's grievance than is a system which gets to the problem at its very inception and gives the employee assurance of representation from the outset. Even in those instances where the grievance comes to the civil service board, the employee needs the assurance of union representation.

Collective bargaining holds other advantages for the public employer. The union serves as a channel of communication. When conditions of work have been determined through collective bargaining, the union feels a responsibility for enforcement of the regulations which have been agreed upon. Employee morale is higher and efficiency greater if employees have had a voice in formulating policy. Improved standards and higher productivity brought about by employee participation result in economic gains not only for the employee but for the employer. Collective bargaining is a time-saving device for employers because it eliminates the process of never-ending individual bargaining. It insures a stable relationship between the employer and employees and it helps promote an orderly administration of government affairs. Collective bargaining when practiced in good faith has tended to reduce conflict and strife and has brought harmony in place of disorder. Collective bargaining is a vital and essential part of a healthy and democratic employer-employee relationship. The process of collective bargaining in the public service gives to the public employee social status and a sense of dignity essential for sound human relations. Moreover, employers by bargaining in good faith with the leadership and membership of democratic unions strengthen the mature and responsible leadership of the union and encourage the better employees to seek leadership positions, thus helping to insure the continued success of a responsible collective bargaining relationship.

The Instruments of Collective Bargaining

Most of the union devices used successfully in private employment can and are being projected into the public service. Despite the fact that the National Labor Relations Act exempts from its provisions federal, state, and local government employees, and despite the fact that no state or municipal government has yet adopted for public employees a thorough comprehensive code of labor relations, there has been increased legislative activity in the last few years in this area and a growing favorable climate is found in opinions of attorneys general and municipal attorneys throughout the country.

Union Recognition

The right of public employees to organize is a generally accepted principle in the public service. Formal union recognition, which is guaranteed employees in industry by the National Labor Relations Act, is gaining increasingly greater acceptance in the public employment field by law, by contract, by administrative or executive order, and by court decision. While AFSCME takes the stand that public employees have the right to organize and bargain collectively through unions of their choice in all areas, this position is, of course, strengthened by favorable legislation. Its goal is a well-drawn comprehensive code of labor relations governing public employees in each of the fifty states.

Dues Check-Off

Another union device which is used in industry has now become fairly widespread in state and local government, namely the check-off of union dues. Presently, there are thirty-eight states and the Commonwealth of Puerto Rico where the check-off for state or local government employees has been authorized either by legislation or administrative arrangement. More than 80 percent of AFSCME membership pays dues by the check-off method.

Exclusive Representation

In industry, exclusive representation by the union of all employees in a bargaining unit in negotiations on wages, hours, and working conditions is almost universal. While most public officials appreciate the practical advantage of exclusive representation by a majority union in achieving orderly relationships with their employees, many are hesitant to grant this full recognition to the union. However, exclusive representation elections are part of the New York City labor relations program covering city employees and are authorized by statute in Minnesota for the state and local governments; exclusive bargaining rights are granted AFSCME unions by collective bargaining agreement in 214 state, county, and city jurisdictions.

Grievance Procedure

The formal grievance procedure which is given great emphasis by unions in industrial employment is also found in an increasing number of public jurisdictions. The employer-employee relationship, whether in public or private employment, inevitably gives rise to disagreements which produce grievances. Civil service regulations, although they are important in such matters as appointment, classification, promotion, and discharge, are not so comprehensive that they dispel all causes for employee complaints. Grievance procedure in the public service is frequently inadequate because it is often part of the civil service mechanism which does not lend itself to quick, practical settlement of day-by-day irritations and complaints. Public employees need representation by their union at every stage of the grievance procedure and if it becomes necessary, final settlement of their grievances by outside neutrals. When part of the collective bargaining process, the grievance procedure is jointly determined by the union and the public employer and then issued as an administrative regulation by the employer or it may be part of a formal signed working agreement between the employer and the union. A multi-step grievance procedure, setting forth various steps for the orderly settlement of grievances of the employee, is found in 351 agreements negotiated by AFSCME locals.

Mediation

Mediation, or third party intervention in disputes in an effort to secure voluntary agreement of the parties, while common in industry is found to a lesser extent in the state and local government field. Several of the states have by legislation made available to public employers and public employees the facilities and services of their state labor mediation and conciliation departments. In Wisconsin, New York, Connecticut, and Massachusetts, there has been some use, on a voluntary basis, of state labor relations facilities despite the lack of specific statutory authorization for such use.

Arbitration

Arbitration, the terminal step in the grievance procedure, by which an unresolved dispute or grievance is submitted to a third disinterested party for final settlement, is used commonly in industry. Despite the general feeling in government that arbitration is an improper compromise of the government's sovereign position, arbitration of grievances has achieved some acceptance. AFSCME unions have collective bargaining agreements with 150 jurisdictions which provide for binding arbitration as the final step in the grievance procedure. Arbitration awards have been made under these agreements in a number of instances.

Union Shop

The union shop, whereby the employer agrees to keep only union employees on the payroll but may hire non-union persons provided they join the union within a designated period of time, usually thirty days, is fairly widespread in industry, except of course in the states with so-called "right-to-work" laws. The union shop is making some headway in public service with eighty-eight contracts negotiated by AFSCME locals containing this strongest form of union security provision.

Negotiation

Negotiation between the union and management on wages, working conditions, and grievances is practiced to varying degrees in public employment. The ultimate objective, collective bargaining, has been negotiated by AFSCME unions in well over 400 state, county, and municipal jurisdictions.

Strike

The strike, the basic union weapon in union negotiations in private employment, is the most questioned and the most controversial device in labor relations in public employment. We oppose strikes; they should not be necessary. To outlaw strikes will not eliminate them; bona fide negotiations will. Government is expanding and government functions are mushrooming; the line of demarcation between government and private enterprise is becoming more shadowy. Many services are performed interchangeably by public employees and by employees in private industry, and there is no logic in depriving such an employee of his right to strike simply because he is employed by a governmental unit. We recognize that in certain services restrictions may be necessary; for example, AFSCME charters to police locals contain a no-strike provision. However, the outright prohibition of the right to strike by public employees is a denial of a fundamental and inherent right. Behind almost every strike in public employment will be found refusal by a shortsighted, irresponsible public official to meet and discuss with organized public employees and their chosen representatives grievances and other matters of concern to both the public employee and the public. Certainly, it is unfair for government to require its employees to surrender the economic weapons of others unless impartial machinery is provided for settlement of employee grievances and for improving labor standards.

Meaning of Collective Bargaining Misunderstood

The greatest obstacle to organization and collective bargaining in public employment is the lack of clarification of the legality of officials dealing with unions and the failure of the government employer to spell out the right of employees to organize. Except for a few state and big city governments which are more attuned to present-day realities and show a more progressive approach to the problem, the area in large part is a no-man's land. Legislation is needed which will permit collective negotiations and contracts. Even in a collective bargaining situation, there is often a lack of clarification as to which city officials are responsible for conducting negotiations, for example, the legislative and executive branches.

This failure to spell out the rights of the worker in public employment is due to the timeworn and outmoded parochialism of many public administrators who cling to the theory that government is a sovereign employer. These administrators fear that the collective bargaining principle constitutes a delegation of power incompatible with their concept of sovereign government. At the roots of the attitudes expressed by these public officials is the complete misunderstanding of the meaning and essence of collective bargaining. Collective bargaining does not involve the surrender of sovereignty or the delegation of authority from the governmental body to the labor union. The government cannot in good conscience dodge its responsibility to face its problems simply on the grounds that it is the sovereign and that the assertion of any right by public employees is the delegation of its sovereignty. If it does so, public employees are then faced with extensive lobbying to secure piecemeal relief, litigation before the courts, and living under conditions autocratically and arbitrarily imposed until they become demoralized and either leave the service, lose all incentive for efficiency, or strike.

Actually, sovereignty resides in the people who have delegated its exercise partly to the government. The question is not one of surrendering sovereignty: the problem does not involve giving up something which the government has but rather is to create something which we have not had but which we imperatively need in employer-employee relations in government. When the government employer fails to keep abreast of conditions, some method of handling the situation must be devised. If the people who are the real source of sovereign power conclude that a new method should be devised, they are not surrendering anything; rather they are requiring law and order in a field where such law has never existed and an institution which will guarantee the rights of employees in public employment.

Obstacles to Collective Bargaining

Here then are two great obstacles to collective bargaining. One, the refusal of public officials to bargain because to do so would oblige them to surrender some of their "sovereign" authority and two, the refusal to bargain because they claim they do not possess the authority.

A third obstacle is no-strike legislation which has been enacted in eleven states. We have already discussed the failure of no strike laws to solve the problem of strikes and the use of substitute measures. A fourth obstacle is restriction of political activities on the part of public employees. Another limitation on occasion is that the union must be affiliated with the labor union movement. In some instances workers have been denied by law the right to organize; in other instances the right to organize has been forbidden to certain occupational groups, e.g., policemen.

Another obstacle is refusal of the public employer to recognize the union as exclusive bargaining representative for employees even where a majority belong to the union. Many public officials refuse to submit unresolved grievances to arbitration or to call in outside neutrals even for the purpose of fact finding or making recommendations. Another difficulty in the way of orderly development of public employee unionism is the existence in almost half our states of the spoils system which spreads fear among the workers and results in high turnover with higher cost and poorer service to the citizens.

A further obstacle to organization and collective bargaining is the presence of company unions sponsored and aided by management. They usually take the form of state, county, and city employee associations. We find in practice that these associations are dominated by supervisors who invariably align themselves with the employer in any showdown over employee demands and grievances.

Still another problem is the psychology of public employees. Fear is still amazingly widespread. Without any guaranteed protection of his right to join a labor union, the employee fears discrimination by the employer. Other obstacles are refusal by the employer to grant the union shop, refusal to grant check-off of union dues, insistence on the right of individual bargaining, all of which undermine the union and deny the union stability and security as a permanent institution with the result that the union is not free to devote enough time to constructive work which will benefit both the employee and the employer. Without these securities, namely, union recognition and a formal contract with security provisions for the union and the employees, the union tends to disintegrate as a benefit is won.

The Mechanics of Collective Bargaining

How do public service unions bargain? The collective bargaining relationship in public service may range all the way from participation in annual budget meetings to full scale collective bargaining on all matters relating to wages, hours, working conditions, and fringe benefits, culminating in a written agreement. Let us look at two areas where labor management relations have been well developed and where public officials have taken an open positive attitude to collective bargaining and have attempted to establish their relations in a pattern approaching that practiced in private industry.

Philadelphia Experience

Philadelphia is probably the outstanding example of such an area. There, a collective bargaining relationship has developed over the years to the point where in 1958 a contract was signed giving AFSCME Council 33, with which are affiliated ten separate locals, exclusive bargaining rights over all non-uniformed city employees. This year approval was given to a modified union shop agreement. This latest agreement establishes three categories of city employees—12,000 who must join the union as a condition of employment (10,500 of these were already members of the union at the time the agreement became effective), 4,800 for whom membership is voluntary, and 1,200 for whom union membership is prohibited.

Now what does all of this mean in Philadelphia? It means that Philadelphia instead of dealing with a multiplicity of unions, as is common in other cities, deals with only one union, AFSCME Council 33. The personnel director is directly in charge of labor relations and has been authorized by the civil service commission to engage in negotiations and to enter into agreements with District Council 33. Each department or other sub-unit of government of Philadelphia is considered a separate bargaining unit. However, these individual units do not bargain directly on major items such as wages, fringes, and general working conditions. In these areas, centralized negotiations are conducted between the city and our union.

The major participants on the city's side of the negotiation table are the personnel director and the labor relations consultant, the finance director, the managing director, who is the city manager, and the mayor's assistant. Prior to negotiations, preliminary meetings are held between the labor relations consultant and the union to clarify issues, to present data relating to the matters to be negotiated, or to explore matters of a detailed nature.

You may ask how the city council and the civil service commission fit into this picture. Neither of the two is directly involved in the bargaining and yet both must give their approval to various items, for example, the budget, and certain provisions in the form of civil service regulations. There is then a liaison activity between the participating city officials on the one hand and the members of the city council and civil service commission on the other.

Negotiations are on a continuing basis and are not limited to annual demands. Some negotiation takes place at the department or local unit level with regard to work rules and practices which are solely in the jurisdiction of the particular department or unit. The labor consultant is an important part of the collective bargaining relationship. His function is to provide advice on labor relations problems and handle grievances and special problems. He is responsible to the personnel director of the civil service commission.

Looking beyond the union security provisions of the agreement—exclusive representation and the modified union shop—we find the very important area of employee security and fringe benefits. There are generous provisions for holiday, vacation, and sick leave as well as a grievance procedure and job security provisions, but the most significant employee benefit provided by the contract is the health and welfare fund. This provision, improved constantly since its initial adoption, sets up a health and welfare program financed by the city with a $120 a year contribution by the city for each employee. The contribution covers the cost of ambulatory service provided by the AFL medical service plan in Philadelphia as well as health, surgical, and maternity care with some limits. Hospital benefits are paid for members and dependents at the rate of $11 per day up to a total of seventy days. Full costs for maternity benefits are paid for members and their wives at the medical center, with pre- and post-natal care included. If a member prefers another hospital, maternity benefits are paid up to $135. Surgical and medical benefits and medical services are paid for members, their wives, and their children up to the age of 19. Retired members receive the entire hospital, surgical, and medical coverage at a cost of $10.75 per month.

City officials in Philadelphia are happy in their relationship with the union. They have found that collective bargaining does work in the public service and they have repeatedly declared the value of Council 33 as an organization of "strong and responsible leadership, an excellent medium of communication and interpretation from management to employee as well as vice versa, and a continual source of strong support and sympathy for our program of ever-better government."[1] The pioneering of Philadelphia and our union in the exclusive bargaining relationship and the modified union shop was accomplished "in an atmosphere in which the paramount interest of the public and the need for efficient, good government has at all times been recognized and respected on both sides."[2]

Cincinnati Experience

The collective bargaining relationship which developed over a period of twenty-two years in Cincinnati emerged from a policy of tacit recognition of unions to culminate in a union-management agreement in April 1960. When AFSCME unions were first organized in Cincinnati, recognition by the city was provided only in the sense that if a business agent appeared he was allowed to talk. The city council first formally recognized unions in 1951, when the city council passed a resolution which declared a city wage policy and defined a system of collective bargaining between the city manager and employee representatives on all matters pertaining to wages and working conditions. The 1951 resolution came as a substitute form of recognition granted after labor unions had requested a formal collective bargaining agreement. The resolution declared it to be the policy of the city council, through the city manager, to "bargain collectively with city employees, their unions or other authorized representatives on all matters pertaining to wages and working conditions before determination is made by the city council." The resolution further defined collective bargaining as "the process whereby city employees, their unions or other authorized representatives and the city manager and his designated assistants shall make every effort to reach an agreement on all matters through negotiations . . ."

In 1957 the city manager announced a policy approved by the city council with regard to unions, which went a step further by providing exclusive recognition of a majority union and written record of results of agreements, subject to approval by city officials or bodies where necessary. The new contract signed in April 1960, after a series of meetings between AFSCME and city personnel officials, is evidence of mature, responsible labor relations in the city of Cincinnati. The significance of the exclusive bargaining rights clause is that management has agreed that it will make no change in the present working conditions or recommend any changes to the city council which would affect the bargaining unit without negotiating with AFSCME Council 51.

Immediately after the agreement was signed by the union and the city, the city manager issued a written statement of his policy with regard to the union, and meetings were set up with supervisors at every level in each operating agency affected by the agreement for the purpose of explaining the agreement and the city manager's policy statement which declared that recognition of the union is city policy requiring supervision's support. The city manager also emphasized that the concept of management prerogatives included in the agreement should not be stretched into a basis for refusing to discuss anything with unions. The city manager, in his statement, delegated to department heads the responsibility of dealing with unions on matters affecting their own agencies and named the personnel officer of the city responsible for review and approval of agency policy with regard to unions. The meetings with supervisors served to communicate the city's policy. About 500 supervisors were reached in thirty meetings. Prior to the meetings, supervisors were furnished a copy of the agreement, policy resolution, and the city manager's policy.

Political Pressure and Publicity Are Important Methods

What is the role of publicity and political pressure in the public employee movement? The labor movement does not lack for publicity, but unfortunately the press seldom finds space to talk about the public services of labor unions. Its treatment of labor affairs often creates conflict in the minds of the readers and a vague fear that labor unions are a threat, to be viewed with alarm. Somehow we must get across to the public that we are not isolated from the community, but that instead we are part of it. We must convince America that we are not a narrow pressure group, but instead a source for the social good and that we are performing a job for the people by community leadership, service, and by helping solve the economic problems of the community. Only by greater public service and by responsible actions made known to the public can unions build a better public image of themselves.

One of the most important channels used by public employee unions to support their programs is political pressure. AFSCME may have a ten-point legislative program in a particular state. A committee of our union meets with the controlling interests in the legislature, in some cases the political party leaders, in other cases, where one party is not dominant, a combination of people. Then we meet with the executive branch, the governor or his representatives, and we develop a program of what is possible, what the political powers will accept, and in some cases what we can do to support legislative bills in which they have an interest. In almost all instances, we have a legislative representative who follows the course of these bills, can speak for us in accepting adjustments and, where hearings are held, make the proper presentations. Often our legislative process starts at the political convention. We attempt to get the party to incorporate in the platform our program as pre-election commitments.

Seldom do public employee unions engage in direct political campaigning. Rather we are concerned with political education consisting mainly of presenting to the membership and to the public the voting record of legislators. Sometimes the union seeks out the views of legislators or candidates for political office toward pending legislation affecting public employees and gives publicity to the answers received.

Generally, we have found that political designations mean little in judging the fairness of public employers toward their employees. Some of our first and some of our best negotiated with conservative New England Republicans. Philadelphia's excellent reform administration is Democratic, but so are some of the large city administrations where the spoils system still operates. Enlightened public officials of both parties have recognized and bargained with AFSCME as the union chosen by the employees.

The labor union provides employees with a democratic vehicle for representation and articulation of their interests, and the union contract between the labor organization and the employer, covering the employee's legal rights in his job, his wages, and working conditions, gives him his bill of rights. It is true that collective bargaining is motivated to some extent by failure of many cities, counties, and states to provide proper pay, classification, and personnel procedures for their employees and by failure by many administrators to take into consideration the needs and desires of their employees. But a much stronger motivation is the need of the employee to have a voice in determining the economic conditions under which he works and to have job security.

The union movement in public employment has grown through the past twenty-five years to a position of strength, influence, and responsibility. In its building public employees are contributing much to the development of citizenship, to the preservation of democracy, and to social and economic justice for all of the people of the United States. Unions are a fundamental part of society and they are a fundamental part of government service bringing order and system to what otherwise might well be chaos in the increasingly complex area of labor relations in government.

Notes

1. Foster B. Roser, Personnel Director, City of Philadelphia.
2. Richardson Dilworth, Mayor of Philadelphia.

CHAPTER 34

THE NEW DIMENSIONS OF
THE STRIKE QUESTION

GORDON T. NESVIG

Mere numbers tell much of the story: 28 strikes by public employees in the U.S. during 1962, 42 strikes in 1965, more than 150 in 1966, and twice as many walk-outs anticipated in 1967 as in 1966.[1]

In California, where public employee strikes used to be a rarity, averaging less than two a year, the number jumped to 18 in 1966. It tapered off to five stoppages (involving 1,800 workers) during the first 10 months of 1967, but this still was much higher than in previous years.

Note another statistic: man-days lost by public employee strikes in the U.S. during 1961 were 15,300. The comparable figure for 1966 was 455,000.

Reasons for Increase in Strikes

One hears the explanation that these strikes are but part of the new pattern of social turbulence, just another symptom of the impatience with the status quo that has led thousands of Americans to march for civil rights or for peace in Vietnam and has sent conveys of middle-class youth off to the pads of hippiedom. Analyze the psychological drive which impels people in these directions, the argument goes, and you may find a clue as to why thousands of formerly decorous public employees have hit the bricks with picket signs in the past two years. This mass-neurosis view of the problem may have some validity, but digging out such subtleties is no job for a mere personnel director.

Another explanation for the upsurge in strikes is purely statistical. Most of the labor unrest has been in state and local government, especially in the local jurisdictions. State and local public employees now total more than eight million—double their number at the outbreak of the Korean War in 1950—indeed, this is the most rapidly growing field of employment in the United States. State and local government employment rose 65 percent from 1955 to 1965, as compared with only 9 percent for the federal government and only 13 percent for the total civilian work force. Labor unrest, it is said, could have

Excerpted from 28 *Public Administration Review*, 2: 126–132, March/April 1968. Copyright © 1968 American Society for Public Administration. Reprinted with permission.

been expected in view of the much greater numbers on the payroll; that is, more workers, more chance for strikes.

The uneven pattern of public employee strikes over the past 20 years casts doubt on this explanation. If the frequency of strikes had been tied to the size of the work force, there should have been a rising curve in the number of manhours lost in government for that reason since the end of World War II. Instead, Bureau of Labor Statistics figures show a relative calm in the late 1940s, with 7,290 man-days lost in 1947, 8,830 in 1948, and 10,300 in 1949. This was followed by a rising (but not dramatically) incidence of work stoppages in the early 1950s, with 32,700 man-days lost in 1950, 28,800 in 1951, 33,400 in 1952, and 53,400 in 1953. Then there ensued six relatively quiet years, with only 8,850 man-days lost in 1959. The strike activity shot upward in 1960 with 57,200 man-days lost, traceable mostly to a half-dozen strikes in large cities involving transit, sanitation, and school employees; but in 1961 it dropped back again to 15,300 man-days. This was about half of what it had been in the early 1950s when the public payroll was much smaller.[2] From the preceding figures it is difficult to see how anyone could place much blame for public strikes on the sheer increase in the number of government employees.

Yet this increase would seem to have had an *indirect* effect. The swelling ranks of public employees apparently became an irresistible target for the AFL-CIO. A leveling-off in the size of the private industry blue-collar work force had slowed labor recruiting in these ranks to a walk. It was only natural that the AFL-CIO should divert organizing energy to the more promising field of government.

As the trade unions moved into the government field they collided with the long-established professional associations of teachers, technicians, policemen, firemen, and others. The unions and associations became rivals for the loyalties and the due dollars of the public employees. This conflict undoubtedly had had much to do with heightening labor turmoil in the public sector during the past two years.

Teacher and Other Strikes

The biggest battleground has become public education. There the relatively young American Federation of Teachers, AFL-CIO (at least 155,000 reported members), is challenging the older, bigger National Education Association (more than one million members).

Both organizations displayed their muscle last September as schools opened—or tried to. In New York City, the AFT pulled out its 49,000 teacher members, crippling the city school system for 18 days. In Detroit the AFT, with nearly 11,000 teachers on its rolls, forced the schools to close for two weeks. Meanwhile, in 35 other Michigan cities NEA-affiliated teacher associations struck schools with a half-million pupils. Both AFT and NEA units staged smaller-scale teacher walkouts or near-walkouts simultaneously in many other parts of the nation.[3]

The September teacher strikes, while shocking to many because of their severity (particularly in New York City and Michigan), did not arrive without warning. For a decade before, teacher walkouts had been negligible, only a few each year. The first indication of a change came in 1964 with nine work stoppages involving more than 14,000 teachers.

However, like earlier walkouts, those in 1964 were brief, averaging about two days each. The situation seemed easier in 1965 when seven stoppages, in which only 1,800 persons participated, occurred, but the walkouts were of greater duration than they had been for many years, specifically, an average of four and one-half days.

The lid began to jiggle dangerously in 1966 when there were 33 work stoppages, involving 37,400 teachers. Michigan was the major trouble spot with 12 strikes in the spring and late summer. Most of the outbreaks, however, did not last long. An average of 1.8 days per teacher was lost. The lid finally blew off last September. The likelihood was that teacher strikes in 1967 would cause approximately *three times* as great a loss in man-days as did all such strikes during the preceding 25 years.

While striking teachers have received most recent headlines, they are by no means the only public employees playing a role in the 1966–67 upsurge of labor disputes. In Los Angeles County, for instance, the Social Workers Union Local 535 (AFL-CIO) persuaded almost half the county's 2,800 social workers to walk off their jobs May 31, 1966, following a pay controversy with the County Board of Supervisors. The strikers returned after 18 days. Four days later the County Board of Supervisors granted the desired pay increase, but at the same time voted $20 to $50 compensation for the extra work required for the 4,600 social workers, clerks, and other welfare employees who had remained at their desks during the strike. This action caused the social workers union to call another walkout a few days later, but this time only a fourth of the social workers stayed off their jobs and the second strike collapsed after four days. The only other sizable strikes of public employees in Los Angeles in recent years had been two walkouts against the Metropolitan Transit Authority (now the Rapid Transit District), one in June 1964 for eight days and another in November 1960 for five days.

Welfare departments also proved trouble spots in Chicago and New York. Cook County welfare workers struck for 14 days only a few weeks before the May 1966 strike in Los Angeles. In 1965 union members in the New York City welfare department staged a marathon work stoppage for 28 days.

Rubbish collection departments have had their share of work interruptions. One June morning in 1966, for instance, some 900 refuse collectors reported to the City of Los Angeles yards but refused to move their trucks out on the collection routes. After a day of hurried conferences, the men were all back at work and the trucks moving the following morning. The president of the city board of public works, true to his word, went before the city council and pleaded successfully for a pay raise for the rubbishmen. Also in 1966, Detroit's 1,400 sanitation workers walked off the job and stayed out for five days. York, Pennsylvania, had an even messier experience last winter. Collection crews there let rubbish pile up for 25 days until they gained a pay increase.

The Disguised Strike

So far we have been discussing work stoppages frankly and openly labeled as strikes. Nobody tried to call them anything else. But an equally serious source of labor trouble has been the quasi-strike, the disguised strike.

The disguised usually is pretty thin. When 80 per cent of the Pontiac, Michigan, police force called in sick for two days in 1966, no one had much trouble deciphering what was happening. A similar outbreak, termed "blue flu," hit the Detroit police department last summer after Mayor Jerome Cavanagh announced the 1967–68 budget contained no money for police pay increases. One of the most lingering illnesses of this type afflicted social workers in Westchester County, New York. The 155 workers telephoned in sick every day for most of last March and April.

There is a second kind of quasi-strike in which the employees report for duty but do not do much work. New York City firemen in April 1967 indulged in one of these partial stoppages. They went into action whenever there was a fire or an emergency rescue call, but otherwise they simply sat, refusing to carry out firehouse drills, maintenance work, or fire hazard inspections. Several cities have experienced "lazy finger" slowdowns by unhappy police. Traffic officers patrol the streets but refuse to issue citations to motorists. Perhaps the most discriminating use of the partial-work tactic took place in Duluth in 1965 when public golf course employees refused to mow the fairways but continued to cut the greens.

Young interns and resident physicians at Los Angeles County General Hospital staged a "heal in" to dramatize their demands in 1965 for more pay. They began to admit more patients than usual to the huge institution and to slow down discharges. As the hospital reached its 3,000 patient capacity, county officials promised to consider the doctors' demands, and the hospital population gradually returned to normal.

Last June the Los Angeles County public health nurses adopted a different tactic to emphasize their salary demands. They announced they would not work overtime on a Saturday and Sunday when a countrywide mass vaccination against measles was scheduled. Health officials proceeded anyway and thousands of children were immunized by volunteer technicians at the 24 county health centers, while the nurses marched outside with their signs and leaflets.

Yet another device, the threatened strike, is a sword-of-Damocles maneuver which often makes use of withholding of contracts. School teachers give their contracts for the coming year to a negotiating agent who is authorized to deliver them to the school board—but only after a satisfactory agreement has been reached. Or a group of employees may threaten mass resignations, as did members of the Fire Fighters Union in St. Louis in 1966. Their written resignations reportedly were given to the union leaders to use in case negotiations failed.

Anti-Strike Laws

The increase in government labor difficulties the past two years, characterized by strikes, disguised strikes, and threatened strikes, has led to fresh examination of what once was regarded as the ultimate answer: the anti-strike law.

For generations most Americans saw no need for laws prohibiting strikes by public employees. It was accepted almost as gospel chiseled in stone tablets that nobody would, or could, strike against the government.

For New Yorkers, this happy belief was shattered when Buffalo public school teachers struck in 1947. The New York legislature reacted by passing the Condon-Wadlin Act. It forbade strikes by public employees, provided automatic dismissal for violators, and prescribed long probation and pay freezes for any violators who were rehired. Eight other anti-strike laws were passed that same year: seven by state legislatures and one by Congress. The latter was the Taft-Hartley Act which, among other things, outlawed strikes by federal employees and specified that violators be dismissed and deprived of their civil service status.

Other legislatures have acted in the years since, until now about a third of the states have some form of legislation prohibiting work stoppages by state and/or local employees. Two of the best known are Michigan's Hutchinson Act and Ohio's Ferguson Act. Both of these looked more like beanbags than big sticks in strikes last September. Alabama has perhaps the most hardnosed measure: it prohibits *any* unions of government employees.[4]

In 12 states court decisions have been interpreted as making public employee strikes illegal. California is among them, although some doubt was raised in 1966 by a superior court decision that is now on appeal. The judge in that case (*Social Worker Union, Local 535, v. County of Los Angeles*) wrote at one point: "It cannot be stated, without considerable doubt, that . . . the Government Code does not authorize public employees . . . to go on strike." That ruling, to say nothing of the syntax, has caused considerable pondering.

The debate over the strike issue continues, growing hotter and spreading to arenas other than state capitols and courts. In many cities local elected officials and administrators have plunged into the debate after encountering the first employee defiance. Their reactions, while not identical, tend to follow a pattern. First come surprise: nothing like this has ever happened in Thingumabob County or Tweedledee City before. Then may come exasperation, perhaps anger, and a feeling of helplessness. As officials experience these different emotions they are bound to start thinking about anti-strike laws and court injuctions. If anti-strike laws are already on the books, they may start demanding, "let's use them." If such laws are lacking, they may say, "let's get one quick." Such demands draw the predictable response from employee organizations: strong counter-pressure.

The Pros and the Cons

The debate over anti-strike laws has proceeded on two planes, the moral-theoretical, let us call it, and the pragmatic. At the moral-theoretical level the argument is whether public employees have the *right* to strike. Should they have the same freedom to walk off the job as private industry workers? Or do they have a higher duty or at least a different duty from other workers, so that striking becomes an immoral act, a breaking of faith?

When debate leaves this abstract level and descends to the pragmatic, questions such as these arise: What do anti-strike laws accomplish? Do they prevent strikes? If strikes do occur, does the presence of an anti-strike law shorten them? And, in the long run, do anti-strike laws serve or harm the public interest?

"Sovereignty" Concept

The theoretical case favoring anti-strike legislation rests basically on the familiar "sovereignty" concept. Proponents contend that government, while perhaps no longer the creation of God through his chosen instrument the king, is still something special—a creation of all the people. As such it has a higher claim on citizen loyalties, and anyone who defies it is guilty of a form of treason.

The Boston police strike of 1919 evoked two much-quoted expressions of this attitude. President Wilson called the stoppage "a crime against civilization"; Governor Coolidge declared, "There is no right to strike against the public safety by anybody, anywhere, any time." More recently, New York State Supreme Court Justice Emilio Nunez, in fining the United Federation of Teachers $150,000 for its September 1967 walkout, stated: "From time immemorial, it has been a fundamental principle that a government employee may not strike."[5]

Adherents of the "sovereign" viewpoint believe public employee strikes are political rather than economic weapons, and thus represent anarchy; they are really "demonstrations" against the government and not part of a lawful procedure.

Those favoring anti-strike laws also point out that in private industry the workers strike against a company, an identifiable group of managers and owners. But when public employees strike, they strike against—whom? Who is the employer in local government: the top administrator (e.g., city or county manager), the elected officials who choose him, or the voters who choose the officials? In state government who is the employer: the governor, the legislature, the senior bureaucrats, or the sovereign voters of the state?

Furthermore, a private industry strike takes place within certain economic boundaries. The company struck has only so much income, depending upon the market, the competition, and similar factors. Wages paid can be only a proportion of this income, and so the workers' demands have to be limited if the business and their jobs are to survive. In government, however, there are no such constraints from the marketplace. Government need not make a profit to survive; indeed, it has no choice but to survive. It cannot go out of business. And if its workers resort to strikes to enforce unreasonable demands, its only choice is to resort to punitive measures to break the strike. For this reason, proponents say, anti-strike laws are necessary.

To this the opponents of anti-strike legislation reply that government strikes face practical limits, too. The amount of revenue available for salaries is limited by political and legal factors, including statutory tax ceilings, the political competition for government funds, and the ultimate power of the voters to force out any official who becomes overly generous with public moneys.

"Freedom" Concept

Just as the theoretical arguments in favor of anti-strike laws revolve around the concept of "sovereignty," so the rebuttal of opponents centers around "freedom." Note the following statements:

Public employees have a free people's right to refuse to work no matter who the employer is. This is a fundamental right in a free society (Thomas T. Jordan, chief counsel, California State Employees' Association).

Conflicts in human relations are not solved merely by prohibition. Nor is prohibition congenial to the American tradition of liberty (Leonard D. White).

Nearly 20 per cent of the nation's work force is now employed by government, and one cannot deprive 20 per cent of the work force of the essentials of democracy in employment relations without harming the basic freedoms of all Americans (Jerry Wurf, president, American Federation of State, County and Municipal Employees).

A free collective bargaining system contemplates that at the end of the road there can be a strike . . . If you don't like that, then take out the word "free" (George Meany, president, AFL-CIO).

Unionists and others also dispute the contention that government work is "more essential" than private employment. A nurse in a public or private hospital, a city rubbish collector or an employee of a private company performing such service, a bus driver on a government-owned or private line, a charwoman at city hall or in the Empire State Building—what's the difference, they ask, and who is more essential? Union spokesmen hem and haw a bit when it comes to the case of policemen and firemen, but in general they stand by their contention that collective bargaining in both the public and private sectors should be run by the same rules.

In summary, when the theoretical arguments for and against anti-strike laws are reduced to simplest form, they seem to boil down to this: one side says, "Strikes against the public cannot be tolerated!" and the other side says, "Why not?"

When the debate enters the pragmatic realm, opponents of anti-strike laws can reduce their argument to a single sentence: Anti-strike legislation has proved powerless to prevent the only strikes that matter, the big ones, so why have such laws at all?

Opponents point to New York's Condon-Wadlin Act as a notable failure. It did not prevent the massive New York City transit strike in January 1966 when Michael Quill's 34,000 transport workers tied up the system for 12 days. That failure led to passage of the 1967 Taylor Act which continues to outlaw public employee strikes, but directs the penalties largely against the union treasury (up to $10,000 a day) rather than against the individual employee, as in the case of Condon-Wadlin. The Taylor Act went into effect last September 1 and within weeks flunked its first test: the big New York City school strike. At the same time, Michigan's Hutchinson Law was being flouted in the widespread teacher strikes in that state, and in Florida an anti-strike law did not prevent school shutdowns in the Fort Lauderdale area. Furthermore, there had been earlier instances of defiance of such legislation: by the Woodbridge, New Jersey, teachers in February 1967; the Youngstown, Ohio, teachers in December 1966; the New York City welfare workers in 1965; and by others.

Most state anti-strike laws contain no criminal penalties, usually providing nothing more than dismissal for the public employee who walks out. Yet even where the threat of jail exists, it has not always deterred those who want to strike. Mike Quill and his lieutenants went to jail in 1966 after defying an injunction. Striking teachers in New York, New Jersey, and elsewhere have also spent a brief time behind bars. In February 1967,

41 Sacramento County, California, social workers were hauled off in paddy wagons for hit-run picketing in defiance of a court's no-picketing order.

Mere passage of an anti-strike law, in short, is no guarantee that it will be obeyed. That much the records make clear, but what is not so clear is how many potential strikes by public employees have been prevented by anti-strike laws. Neither does anyone know how many stoppages have lasted only a matter of days because the club of an anti-strike law hung over the employees' heads. The work stoppage by Youngstown police and firemen last September has been cited as an example of a strike shortened by threats of legal sanctions.

The Future Picture

We have been talking about the dimensions of the public strike problem today. What about its dimensions tomorrow? On this score one can only guess. And that guess will be determined by the answers to certain questions.

Will governmental managers, as the size of their organization increases, tend to drift further and further out of touch with their employees? Or will they give high priority to establishing fast, easy, up-and-down communications so that no one feels left out and ignored?

Will elected officials and top administrators tolerate the existence of employee organizations that demand the right to discuss pay and working conditions? Or will they attempt to suppress them as outlaws, or at the least, undesirable pests?

Is the U.S. social climate to be permeated with ever-growing turmoil and outbreaks of citizen defiance over issues like the Vietnam War and Negro rights? Or will this turbulence decrease as its causes disappear, or as fatigue and boredom set in?

Is the recent upsurge in militancy among teachers, social workers, and certain other government workers the beginning of a permanent aggressiveness, as some AFL-CIO leaders contend? Or will this militancy subside, after a period of adjustment, into a pre-1965 pattern in which government managers, officeholders, and workers get along reasonably well?

These are some of the questions. Many other relevant ones could be asked. Each observer must supply his own answers. If he believes that government managers will become increasingly remote from their subordinates, that the elective and appointive officialdom will try to stifle all employee attempts to organize and express themselves, and that social turmoil is to become the norm in this nation, then he can only conclude that walkouts by public employees are likely to become more common in the years ahead. The dimensions of the strike problem will expand.

But if he believes that government managers will learn how to communicate with all their coworkers (and not just other managers), that elected officials and administrators will learn to live with responsible employee organizations, and that today's sociopolitical schizophrenia in the U.S. is a temporary ailment rather than a progressive one, then he may fairly conclude that the strike problem will diminish.

After all, a public employee strike is a confession of failure by both sides. And we are supposed to learn by our mistakes.

Notes

1. Randy H. Hamilton, "The New Militancy of Public Employees," *Public Affairs Report,* August 1967, Institute of Governmental Studies, University of California, Berkeley.

2. *Work Stoppages, Government Employees, 1942–61.* Bureau of Labor Statistics Report No. 247, U.S. Department of Labor, April 1963.

3. *Government Employee Relations Report No. 209,* Bureau of National Affairs, Inc., Washington, D.C., September 11, 1967, pp. B4-B8.

4. William B. Gould, "The New York Taylor Law: A Preliminary Assessment," *Labor Law Journal,* June 1967.

5. See Robert B. Moberly, "The Strike and Its Alternatives in Public Employment," *Wisconsin Law Review,* Spring 1966, 549–582; Eugene J. Berroclin, "At the Bargaining Table," *National Law Review,* July 1967, 392–396; and George W. Taylor, "Public Employment: Strikes or Procedures?" *Industrial and Labor Relations Review* 20, 617–636.

CHAPTER 35

PUBLIC SECTOR COLLECTIVE BARGAINING

Is the Glass Half Full, Half Empty, or Broken?

DONALD E. KLINGNER

A Paradoxical Forecast

Public unions continue to be effective, at least as measured by membership figures. The number of state and local government employees climbed from about 13.2 million in 1982 to 15.5 million in 1991 (Executive Office of the President 1992). Although the percentage of unionized state and local employees fell sharply between 1979 and 1981, it has since climbed steadily to almost 1979 levels (30 percent of state employees, 43 percent of local employees). Membership in AFSCME (the American Federation of State, County and Municipal Employees), the largest union of state and local government workers, rose from 450,000 in 1970 to 1.3 million at the end of the 1980s (Walters 1993).

But other indicators show an underlying erosion of public unions' organizational, economic, and political power. Collective bargaining has declined from its position as a dominant public personnel system in many state and local governments in 1970, to a much more diminished and defensive position today. Within public sector unions' jurisdiction, strikes have been replaced by givebacks, furloughs, and layoffs. And even in areas such as New York and Connecticut where unions have been historically powerful, state and local politicians have won popular support by campaigning against unions, and by gaining bargaining concessions under threat of layoffs or privatization (Walters 1993). Essentially, the problem is that while there may be many legitimate targets for public concern with government waste and inefficiency—including unclear policy objectives, mismanagement, and political corruption—the high percentage of operating budgets going to pay and benefits for unionized civil service employees is a visible and vulnerable point of attack. And in an era where many unionized employees in the private sector face the threat of losing their jobs, it is difficult to generate political support for pay and benefit increases for civil service employees with job security.

From 13 *Review of Public Personnel Administration*, 3: 19–28, Summer 1993. Copyright © 1993 Sage Publications. Reprinted with permission.

This paradox of apparent strength and underlying weakness reflects not only day-to-day events, but also underlying societal trends: *economic* pressures on collective bargaining *outcomes, organizational* pressures on collective bargaining *processes,* and *political* pressures on collective bargaining *systems.*

Economic Pressures on Collective Bargaining Outcomes

The percentage of unionized employees in the United States has dropped from one in three (1950) to one in six today, due to the erosion of manufacturing industries in favor of non-unionized service and white collar employment, a gradual shift of jobs away from the Rust Belt to the Sun Belt (toward parts of the country without a strong tradition of industrial unions), intensified economic competition due to deregulation, and adoption of effective union avoidance strategies by management (Coleman 1990). Some consider unions a structural inefficiency in the new and more competitive global economy, in that they hinder unionized firms' competitiveness (Mishel and Voos 1992), employment growth (Leonard 1992), and investment activity (Hirsch 1992). Unions combine with other factors to increase personnel costs; these factors include rising health care costs and related workers compensation, sick leave, and disability retirement expenses (Allan 1988; Blostin, Burke and Lovejoy 1988). The economic restructuring and increased corporate debt that characterized the 1980s have led many employers to underfund pension plans, or to eliminate them altogether to avoid ERISA compliance (McClain 1992). And demands on the Social Security system will increase due to changing demographics and budget pressures on federal entitlement programs.

Employers have responded to pay, health care, and pension costs by increasingly hiring employees into non-benefitted positions. According to Doeringer and Piore (1975), employers differentiate between a *primary* labor market comprising applicants for skilled managerial, professional, and technical positions characterized by high pay, high status, and job security; and a *secondary* labor market comprising applicants for less skilled laborer and service positions filled on a temporary or part-time basis. Secondary labor market mechanisms are attractive because they enable personnel administrators to reduce benefit costs, and to circumvent personnel ceilings and civil service rules. Where positions are covered by collective bargaining agreements, the threat of privatization or contracting out is a powerful tool for breaking unions or gaining give-backs during contract renegotiation. While employers will increasingly utilize minorities and women because of changing workforce demographics, most new jobs will be created in the service sector and filled through the secondary labor market (Hudson Institute 1988). Divergent views of employees as assets or costs are one organizational implication of dual labor market theory. Skilled managerial, professional, and technical employees hired through primary labor market mechanisms into career positions are considered human resource assets who bring human capital to the labor market (Johnston and Packer 1987). Employees hired through the secondary labor market are more likely to be considered personnel costs. Employers utilize personnel practices predicated on cost reduction through elimination of benefits and advancement opportunities (O'Rand 1986). Finally, employers also reduce legal liability risks in using the secondary labor market because temporary employees have fewer rights.

Organizational Pressures on Collective Bargaining Processes

There is a societal trend away from adversarial dispute resolution techniques (such as civil suits or formal grievance procedures) because of a growing awareness that they build acrimony, harden bargaining positions, and delay the resolution of the original conflict. In a number of areas (such as family law, consumer complaint resolution, and workplace disputes), mediation is supplanting adversarial dispute resolution procedures. There has been a similar transition within organizations from adversarial bargaining to participative decision-making through total quality management (Deming 1988, Swiss 1992) and organizational development (French and Bell 1990).

The challenge of channeling diversity into productivity is complicated by the breadth of expectations members of diverse cultures bring to their work, both as individuals and as members of those cultures. Without an organizational commitment of respect, tolerance, and dignity, differences lead only to divisiveness that consumes organizational resources without positive results (Thomas 1990). Therefore, non-adversarial techniques for protecting organizational justice and fair play are increasingly recommended by proponents of workforce diversity as a better alternative to the adversarial complaint resolution process favored by traditional affirmative action programs (Solomon 1989).

Pressures for public agency accountability and performance have also undermined traditional union emphasis on seniority as a criterion for personnel actions. Objective measures of merit and performance are more defensible and rational than seniority as a criterion for promotion eligibility, pay increases, or retention during a reduction-in-force. This change has affected civil service systems as well as collective bargaining. In both systems, it has meant increased flexibility in job matching for individual employees (based on competency-based job matching, rank-in-person personnel systems, and individualized development plans); and on competency-based job matching systems (such as results-oriented job descriptions, delegation and management by objectives) to "manage to mission." Seen in this light, traditional criteria for determining merit and retention preference during a reduction-in-force (seniority and "blanket" qualifications standards for a range of positions), are simply not considered valid enough to be used as the sole basis of selection, promotion, or layoff decisions. What many observers see as the politicization of personnel actions is in fact the application of more flexible definitions of merit based on situational competencies required of an employee on the job, and a reasonable managerial effort to end the over-rationalization of personnel procedures.

Political Pressures on Collective Bargaining Systems

These generalized and persistent economic and organizational pressures have interacted with demands for "reinventing government" to intensify political pressure on public personnel systems to measure outputs, increase efficiency, and enhance political accountability (Osborne and Gaebler 1992). Critics have argued that the private sector can often provide services more cheaply and efficiently by eliminating unnecessary personnel costs and employee rights. And desires for both political payoffs and political accountability make provision of public services through the private sector more attractive (Holzer 1988). Consequently, much government growth has been through a secondary labor market of part-time, temporary, and seasonal employees which at least give the appearance of controlling the size of the public "bureaucracy," and through alternative instrumentalities which share responsibility: purchase of service contracting, franchise agreements, subsidy arrangements, vouchers, volunteers, self-help, regulatory and tax incentives (International City Management Association 1989; Naff 1991; Chandler and Feuille 1991). The watershed event in the political attack on the validity of collective bargaining systems was the 1981 strike of the Professional Air Traffic Controllers' Organization (PATCO). Union supporters learned painfully that a small union, without strong public support, and without a monopoly on the supply of air traffic controllers, would lose a political showdown with an incoming President with an ideological and pragmatic bias against unions. The results: PATCO was broken, its leaders faced criminal charges, and its members were barred from future federal employment.

This pattern of confrontation and retreat has been repeated in numerous state and local governments during the past decade, as officials are forced to cut payrolls to balance budgets (Kearney 1992). For example, Coleman Young, who rose to political power in Detroit as a union organizer, last year offered Detroit AFSCME officials the choice of losing 1000 of the city's 16,500 jobs, or agreeing to a 10 percent pay cut for all employees. Connecticut Governor Lowell Weicker gave state police unions a choice between layoffs and wage freezes. And Massachusetts Governor William Weld successfully sued to abrogate public-sector union contracts signed by his Democratic predecessor, forcing employees to continue working under the terms of previous contracts without pay raises (Walters 1993).

"Crossover" Issues: From Private Privilege to Public Interest

Public sector collective bargaining's current malaise is therefore based not only on recent events, but also on persistent underlying realities. The combined economic pressures on collective bargaining outcomes and organizational pressures on collective bargaining processes may simply overpower unions' ability to effectively organize workers around political action as well as internal bargaining issues. And "right to work" laws mean that unions will not be able to increase membership in many states unless "free riders" are required to pay their fair share of benefits (Voltz and Costa 1989, and Masters and Atkins 1990).

Yet unions could overcome even these daunting economic and organizational disadvantages through a concerted effort to increase their political strength. What public unions must do, if they can, is to rebuild their political constituency by championing broad public interests rather than what opponents consider the private privilege of jobs, benefits, and due process protection for their members. And current social and economic conditions present unions with some potent issues for political action: (1) supportive career opportunities for a diverse workforce; (2) organizational justice in the allocation of benefits, training, and involvement opportunities; (3) workforce productivity: and (4) retirement and health care.

• *Supportive career opportunities for a diverse workforce.* Traditionally, unions have been more concerned with protecting members' seniority rights than promoting equal job opportunities for minorities, women, and persons with disabilities. Indeed, public employee unions have been party to many lawsuits involving the relative priority accorded individual rights based on seniority, and social equity based on affirmative action (Klingner and Nalbandian 1993). This historical opposition to social equity may be simple economic self-interest by current members, or a more complex function of discrimination within union leadership (Melcher, Eichstedt, Eriksen and Clawson 1989).

But whatever the historical basis of discrimination, the brightest prospects for union organizing are in the service jobs dominated by women and minorities. Unions must focus on employment access issues critical to blacks (Mladenka 1991), Hispanics, women (Riccucci 1990), and Americans with disabilities. Unions can also increase organizing efforts in growth sectors of the economy such as prisons and health care (American Federation of State, County and Municipal Employees 1989). They will need to sensitize themselves to workforce diversity, pay equity, and those employee services that help employees meet family obligations. These include flexible benefits (Cafeteria Plans 1990), parental leave (Taylor 1991), child- and elder-care support programs (Child Care 1987), alternative work locations and schedules, and employee-centered supervision.

• *Organizational justice in the allocation of benefits, training, and involvement opportunities.* From a societal human resource perspective, the United States currently is suffering from the absence of concerted public policy which ties together educational development, national human resource development, industrial policy, and economic growth (Dunlop 1992). Public and private employers uniformly express alarm at the ineffectiveness of our educational system in producing the skilled workers needed by high-technology industries. Lack of high-tech job training or retraining capacity is a major obstacle to retention of manufacturing jobs, which have fallen to their lowest level in twenty years. But the organizational implications of economic pressures for increased productivity and lower personnel costs are clean a "shake-out" between "asset employees" and "kleenex employees."

Increasingly, employers reduce costs by hiring *"kleenex employees"* through secondary labor market mechanisms into low wage and non-benefitted jobs. Skill requirements of these jobs are reduced by job-redesign or work simplification (which ironically contributes to the perpetuation of segmented labor markets and the "glass ceiling" by reducing developmental opportunities for employees "stuck" in secondary labor market jobs). Where commitment and high skills are required on a temporary basis, employers may seek to save money or maintain flexibility by using contract or leased employees.

"Asset employees" continue to receive comparatively liberal health benefits, at least compared to other employees, to help ensure retention and loyalty. But health insurance

carriers (and self-insured employers) have responded to rising health care costs by increasing premiums, reducing benefits, lengthening the waiting period for exclusion of preexisting conditions, or adopting sub-benefit limitations on coverage for health problems that may be considered "lifestyle choices" (Faden and Kass 1988). Whenever possible, given the limits of available technology and the applicability of handicap laws protecting applicant rights, employers have sought to reduce benefit costs by excluding applicants for career positions who pose long-term health risks (Rowe, Russell-Einhorn and Weinstein 1987).

Although personnel directors are accustomed to applying contradictory human resource management models simultaneously in an organization that values both human resource asset maintenance and cost accountability, these models often lead to conflicting personnel techniques in such areas as recruitment, benefits, and employee rights. While the secondary market offers the advantage of lower short-term pay and benefit costs, many examples support the conclusion that viewing employees as assets results in long-term benefits, not just for employees but also for the employer as well (Morgan and Tucker 1991). This trend threatens middle class employees who lose a "career job" and are forced into a succession of "kleenex jobs" because there is nothing else available. This is a powerful, explosive issue that union leaders may use to promote a national agenda for education, economic reform, and job creation. It remains to be seen whether they will be able to do so by taking advantage of the relatively favorable climate characterized by Democratic party control of both the White House and Congress.

Public unions have taken advantage of public support for fair and decent wages by supporting pay equity for women, minorities, and the disadvantaged—groups that have been traditionally discriminated against in the private sector because market-based pay plans allow employers to pay them less than the wages offered their white male counterparts. For example, in 1983 AFSCME won more than $500 million for female members in the state of Washington when federal courts found the state guilty of sex-based pay discrimination (Persinos 1989). Pay equity has been a fruitful AFSCME organizing issue for ten years, particularly in agencies with disproportionately high employment of women and minorities in service jobs (Orazem, Mattila and Weikum 1992). But again, this has required unions to shift their emphasis away from traditional seniority systems and toward the issue of wider employment access by women, minorities, and persons with disabilities. And unions must be cautious in supporting "two-tier" pay and benefit systems that establish economic differentials between current employees and new hires. While it may be tempting to protect the economic status of current members at the expense of new employees' pay and benefits, this tactic undermines union support among the new hires and the general public.

• *Workforce productivity.* Unions may succeed in building a broader constituency if they can demonstrate that union strength is critical to employee involvement, and that employee involvement is critical to enhanced workforce productivity (American Productivity Center 1987; Grenier 1988; U.S. Department of Labor 1989; Herrick 1990). As one example, Los Angeles union negotiators turned themselves into budget analysts to cooperate with the County at cost-cutting efforts that helped the county develop a budget that eliminated an anticipated $750 million shortfall while protecting union jobs (Walters 1993). As another, unions can cooperate with management to reduce costs by encouraging competitive bids on employee health care programs.

At the workplace level, unions can emphasize cooperative labor-management productivity improvement efforts through quality circles or other participative management techniques. For example, one recent study (Cooke 1992) investigated the effectiveness of employee participation in achieving product quality improvement in union versus nonunion settings and in programs unilaterally administered by management versus programs with joint union-management administration. Findings suggest that among unionized firms, those with jointly administered programs achieved significantly greater improvements in product quality than did those with more traditional adversarial collective bargaining relationships (that is, with no participation programs), but those with programs administered solely by management fared no better than those with no programs. The gains associated with jointly administered programs in unionized firms were at least equal to the gains associated with participation programs in nonunion firms. And Jacoby and Verma (1992) indicate that enhanced industrial productivity may be possible by combining the advantages of company-based employee involvement programs with those of independent local unions, especially in a high-tech industry which has moved away from adversarial management employee relations.

In the public sector, there is some evidence that cooperative efforts between federal unions and agencies have resulted in a more hospitable climate toward cooperative efforts to improve organizational climate and increase productivity (Levine 1991; Government Employee Relations Report 1990). But obviously, more research is needed that investigates the impact of labor-management committees, quality management teams (Levine 1992), and independent local unions on organizational productivity in the United States.

• *Employer pensions and health care programs.* There is widespread public concern with the financial condition of public health and pension systems. Union strength will increase to the extent that the public perceives problems with private pension systems and employer-financed health benefit programs to be major public policy issues (Labor Leaders 1990). For example, the government agency that guarantees private pensions for 40 million Americans covered by ERISA recently reported an increase in underfunding of defined benefit programs. This in turn increases pressure on Social Security, just as increases in non-benefitted positions increase pressure on public health systems (U.S. Congress 1992). Second, self-funded employer health benefit plans are currently regulated only by state laws, rather than by federal legislation (such as exists under ERISA to regulate private sector pension systems). The managerial cost containment strategies discussed previously place additional pressure on public health systems, to the point where the majority of those without adequate health care coverage are employed full time. As recent national election results show, access to adequate and affordable health care is a public policy issue.

Summary

Public sector collective bargaining faces an uncertain future because of economic pressures on collective bargaining outcomes, organizational pressures on collective bargaining processes, and political pressures on collective bargaining systems. Its continued viability will depend on unions' ability to persuade the public, and political leaders, that strong unions are tied to vital public policy concerns that go beyond members' self-interest. Some potent political issues are: (1) supportive career opportunities for a diverse workforce; (2) organizational justice in the allocation of benefits, training, and involvement opportunities; (3) workforce productivity; and (4) retirement and health care.

References

Allan, I. (1988). "Financing and Managing Public Employee Benefit Plans in the 1990's." *Government Finance Review* 4:32.

American Federation of State, County and Municipal Employees. (1989). *The Public Employee* (November/December) 54: 4.

American Productivity Center (1987). *Participative Approaches to White-Collar Productivity.* Washington, D.C.: U.S. Department of Labor, Bureau of Labor-Management Relations and Cooperative Progress.

Blostin, A., T. Burke and L. Lovejoy (1988). "Disability and Insurance Plans in the Public and Private Sector." *Monthly Labor Review* (December): 9–17.

"Cafeteria Plans, Wellness Programs Gaining in Popularity" (1990). *Employee Benefit Plan Review* (July): 90–92.

Chandler, T. and P. Feuille (1991). "Municipal Unions and Privatization." *Public Administration Review* 51 (June): 15–22.

"Child Care and Recruitment Boost Flexible Plans" (1987). *Employee Benefit Plan Review* (March): 32–33.

Coleman, C. (1990). *Managing Employee Relations in the Public Sector.* San Francisco: Jossey-Bass.

Cooke, W. (1992). "Product Quality Improvement Through Employee Participation: The Effects of Unionization and Joint Union-Management Administration." *Industrial and Labor Relations Review* 46, 1: 119–127.

Deming, W. (1988). *Out of the Crisis.* Cambridge, MA: MIT Center for Advanced Engineering Study.

Doeringer, P. and M. Piore (1975). "Unemployment and the "Dual Labor Market." *The Public Interest* 38: 67–79.

Dunlop, J. (1992). "The Challenge of Human Resources Development." *Industrial Relations* 31, 1 (Winter): 50–79.

Executive Office of the President, Office of Management and Budget (1992). *Budget of the United States Government—FY 1993.* Washington, D.C.: U.S. Government Printing Office.

Faden, R. and N. Kass (1988). "Health Insurance and AIDS: The Issue of State Regulatory Activity." *The American Journal of Public Health* 78: 437–38.

French, W. and C. Bell (1990). *Organizational Development,* 4th edition. Englewood Cliffs, NJ: Prentice-Hall.

Government Employee Relations Report (1990). *Employee-Management Cooperation in the Federal Service: A Selective Look.* Washington, D.C.: Bureau of National Affairs.

Grenier, G. (1988). *Inhuman Relations.* Philadelphia: Temple University Press.

Herrick, N. (1990). *Joint Management and Employee Participation: Labor and Management at the Crossroads* San Francisco: Jossey-Bass.

Hirsch, B. (1992). "Firm Investment Behavior and Collective Bargaining Strategy." *Industrial Relations* 31, 1 (Winter): 95–121.

Holzer, M. (1988). "Productivity In, Garbage Out: Sanitation Gains in New York." *Public Productivity Review* 11 (Spring): 37–51.

Hudson Institute (1988). *Opportunity 2000: Creating Affirmative Action Strategies for a Changing Workforce.* Indianapolis: The Hudson Institute.

International City Management Association (1989). *Service Delivery in the 90s: Alternative Approaches for Local Governments.* Washington, D.C.: ICMA.

Jacoby, S. and A. Verma (1987). "Enterprise Unions in the United States." *Industrial Relations* 31, 1: 137–158.

Johnston, W. and A. Packer (1987). *Workforce 2000: Work and Workers for the Twenty-first Century.* Indianapolis: The Hudson Institute.

Kearney, R. (1992). *Labor Relations in the Public Sector, 2nd edition.* New York: Marcel Dekker, Inc.

"Labor Leaders Call for Moving Health Care Issues from the Bargaining Table to Political Front" (1990). *Government Employee Relations Report* (February 12):179–180.

Leonard, J. (1992). "Unions and Employment Growth." *Industrial Relations* 31 (Winter): 80–94.

Levine, M. (1991). "Legal Obstacles to Union-Management Cooperation in the Federal Service." *Labor Law Journal* 42 (February): 103–110.

———. (1992). "Labor and Management Response to Total Quality Management." *Labor Law Journal* 43 (February): 107–116.

McClain, J. (1992). "Report: Pension Gap is Growing." *Tampa/St. Petersburg Times* (November 20): D-1, 6.

Masters, M. and R. Atkins (1990). "Public Policy, Bargaining Structure, and Free-riding in the Federal Sector." *Journal of Collective Negotiations in the Public Sector* 19: 97–112.

Melcher, D., J. Eichstedt, S. Eriksen and D. Clawson (1992). "Women's Participation in Local Union Leadership: The Massachusetts Experience." *Industrial and Labor Relations Review* 45: 267–273.

Mishel, L. and P. Voos, eds. (1992). *Unions and Economic Competitiveness,.* Armonk, NY: M.E. Sharpe.

Mladenka, K. (1991). "Public Employee Unions, Reformism, and Black Employment in 1,200 Cities." *Urban Affairs Quarterly* 26 (June): 532–548.

Morgan, H. and K.Tucker (1991). *Companies that Care.* New York: Fireside.

Naff, K. (1991). "Labor-Management Relations and Privatization: A Federal Perspective." *Public Administration Review* 51 (January/February): 23–30.

O'Rand, A. (1986). 'The Hidden Payroll: Employee Benefits and the Structure of Workplace Inequality." *Sociological Forum* 1: 657–683.

Orazem, P., P. Mattila and S. Weikum (1992). "Comparable Worth and Factor Point Pay Analysis in State Government." *Industrial Relations* 31 (Winter): 195–215.

Osborne, D. and T. Gaebler. (1992). *Reinventing Government.* Reading, MA: Addison-Wesley.

Persinos, J. (1989). "Can AFSCME Parlay Its Social-Issues Savvy into Another Decade of Growth?" *Governing* 3 (July): 46–48.

Riccucci, N. (1990). *Women, Minorities and Unions in the Public Sector.* Westport, CT: Greenwood.

Rowe, M., M. Russell-Einhorn and J. Weinstein (1987). "New Issues in Testing the Work Force: Genetic Diseases." *Labor Law Journal* 38: 518–23.

Solomon, J. (1989). "Firms Address Workers' Cultural Variety: The Differences Are Celebrated, Not Suppressed." *The Wall Street Journal* (February 10): B-1.

Swiss, J. (1992). "Adapting Total Quality Management to Government." *Public Administration Review* 52 (July/August): 356–362.

Taylor, P. (1991). "Study of Firms Finds Parental Leave Impact Light." *The Washington Post* (May 23): A9.

Thomas, R. (1990). "From Affirmative Action to Affirming Diversity." *Harvard Business Review* 68: 107–117.

U.S. Congress, House, Select Committee on Aging, Subcommittee on Human Services (March 9, 1992). *Left at the Gate: The Impact of Bankruptcy on Employee and Retiree Benefits.*

U.S. Department of Labor (1989). *An Orientation to Joint Labor-Management Initiatives,* Washington, D.C.: U.S. Department of Labor, Bureau of Labor-Management Relations and Cooperative Programs.

Voltz, W. and D. Costa (1989). "A Public Employee's 'Fair Share' of Union Dues." *Labor Law Journal* 40 (March): 131–137.

Walters, J. (1993). "Labor's Pain." *Governing* 6 (January): 26–30.

CHAPTER 36

PUBLIC EMPLOYEE UNIONIZATION AND COLLECTIVE BARGAINING IN THE SOUTHEAST

RICHARD C. KEARNEY

The tremendous growth in public employee unionization and collective bargaining is a phenomenon whose beginnings are generally traced back to the issuance of Executive Order 1098 by President John F. Kennedy in 1962, which formally legitimized bilateral relationships between unions and management in federal government. Since that time more than one-half of all state and local government workers have joined employee organizations and forty states have enacted legislation enabling collective negotiations or meet and confer arrangements for one or more employee groups. A 1977 symposium in *Southern Review of Public Administration* examined developments in unionization and collective bargaining in the Southeast up to that time. (Nigro 1977) The purpose of this article is to assess the current status of public sector labor relations in the Southeast and consider the major factors related to the limited success of organized labor in this section of the United States. The "Southeast" as discussed here includes the quadrant of states bordered by Virginia and Kentucky to the north, the Atlantic Ocean to the east, the Gulf Coast to the south, and the Mississippi River to the west.

Present Status of Unionization in Southeast

Table 36.1 displays the percentage of state and local government employees belonging to employee organizations in 1972 and 1979, the earliest and latest dates for which census data are available. "Employee organization" is rather generously defined by the Bureau of the Census (1980:182) as one which "exists for the purpose, in whole or in part, of dealing with the employer concerning personnel policies and practices, employee grievances, labor disputes, wages, rates of pay, hours of employment and other conditions of work." This definition includes organizations running the gamut from professional associations with no bargaining or meet and confer experience to full-fledged labor unions.

From 5 *Southern Review of Public Administration*, 4: 477–499, Winter 1982. Copyright © 1982 Southern Public Administration Education Foundation, Inc. Reprinted with permission.

Table 36.1

Percentage of Full-Time Employees Belonging to an Employee Organization, By Type of Government, 1972 and 1979

State	State Government			Local Government		
	1972	1979	% change	1972	1979	% change
Alabama	44.8%	23.2%	−21.6	39.3%	32.0%	−7.3
Florida	3.2	46.8	43.6	30.7	34.7	4.0
Georgia	2.0	9.3	7.3	33.7	19.1	−14.6
Kentucky	6.9	3.1	−3.8	45.7	33.4	−12.3
Louisiana	19.3	15.6	−4.0	33.2	25.0	−8.2
Mississippi	1.9	12.9	11.0	23.7	10.2	−13.5
North Carolina	45.0	34.0	−11.0	40.3	21.4	−18.9
South Carolina	28.7	14.1	−14.6	26.6	17.8	−8.8
Tennessee	8.3	19.2	10.9	44.2	39.1	-5.1
Virginia	26.9	22.3	−4.6	44.2	28.6	−15.6
U.S. Total	40.7	38.7	− 2.0	53.2	51.4	−1.8

Source: U.S. Bureau of the Census (1975, 1980). *Labor-Management Relations in State and Local Governments.*

In 1979, Florida state employees were most heavily organized (46.8 percent), while local governments in Tennessee reported the highest level of local organizational membership (39.1 percent). Of all the southeastern states, only Florida exceeds the national average for state government; none of the states approach the national average for local government organization. Kentucky, Georgia, and Mississippi have the fewest organized state employees while South Carolina joins Georgia and Mississippi at the bottom of the local government rankings. The most interesting aspect of Table 36.1 is the decline in reported membership throughout a majority of state and local jurisdictions over the seven year period. Six states indicate decreases in state organizational membership and all except one (Florida) report decreases in local government organization. Although slight reductions in public employee organization were indicated nationwide, most of the southeastern states substantially exceeded the decline in national percentages. The aggregate data do not permit examination of the reasons for these declines, but some of them may be attributed to reductions-in-force or the vicissitudes of government data collection.

Another means for analyzing the status of labor relations is provided in Table 36.2, which presents the percentage of subnational governments engaged in meet and confer or collective bargaining relationships during 1974 and 1979. The lack of union success is again apparent as only Florida, Tennessee, and (to a limited extent) South Carolina report gains in formal bilateral relationships. The termination of collective negotiations in Virginia is attributable to a Virginia Supreme Court decision which declared existing bargaining arrangements illegal because they had not been sanctioned by legislation

Table 36.2

Percentage of State and Local Governments Engaging in Collective Bargaining and/or Meet and Confer, 1974 and 1979

State	1974	1979	% Change
Alabama	3.2%	3.0%	−0.2
Florida	12.4	21.9	9.5
Georgia	2.2	1.2	−1.0
Kentucky	4.7	3.9	−0.8
Louisiana	4.0	5.2	1.2
Mississippi	3.6	1.3	−2.3
North Carolina	1.2	—	−1.2
South Carolina	1.0	1.5	0.5
Tennessee	3.1	6.7	3.6
Virginia	9.8	—	−9.8
U.S. Total	14.9	17.4	2.8

Source: U.S. Bureau of the Census (1975, 1980). *Labor-Management Relations in State and Local Governments.*

(McCollum 1980). Excluding Florida, the level of bargaining in the southeastern states falls well below the United States as a whole.

Although the Census Bureau data do not permit a breakdown on how many of these bilateral relationships are authorized by statute or other legal means and how many constitute de facto bargaining, it is likely that a large proportion of the arrangements falls into the latter category (Nigro 1977). If the precedent established in Virginia carries over into other states, some of these relationships may be endangered. Nonetheless, every southeastern state except Mississippi has some sort of labor relations policy for public employees, and at least five permit collective bargaining or meet and confer for one or more employee functions. Table 36.3 shows how the states compare in selected labor relations policy characteristics.

Florida is the only state in the Southeast with a comprehensive collective bargaining law covering all public employees, which probably accounts in large part for that state's recent gains in union membership. Interestingly, the Public Employee Relations Act of 1974 was enacted by the legislature in compliance with a Florida Supreme Court decision which held that public employees in Florida have the right to bargain collectively and that the legislature was required to develop statutory guidelines governing collective bargaining. (*Dade County Classroom Teachers' Assn. v. Legislature of Florida,* 269 S 2d 684 [1969]) When the legislature balked at passing labor relations legislation for three consecutive years, the Florida Supreme Court ruled that it would issue its own labor relations guidelines if the legislature continued to refuse to carry out the judicial decision and appointed a Commission to recommend appropriate regulatory actions when the legislature again failed to act the next year. Finally, the labor relations bill was passed by the Florida legislature and signed into law in August of 1974 (Waldby 1977).

Table 36.3

Selected Characteristics of Public Sector Labor Relations Policies in the Southeastern States, 1980

State	Legal Basis	Bargaining Policy		Other Labor Relations Policies					
		Bargaining Relation-ship	Employee Functions Covered	Admin. Agency	Union Se-curity	Impasse Procedures	Grievance Procedures	ULP's	Strike Prohibition
Alabama	Statute	Meet and Confer	Teachers, Firefighters	x	x	x		x	x
Florida	Statute	Coll. Barg.	All Public Employees	x	x	x	x	x	x
Georgia	Statute Att. General	Coll. Barg.	Firefighters[a]			x			x
Kentucky	Statute Att. General	Coll. Barg.	Firefighters, Police,[b]	x	x	x	x	x	x
Louisiana	Statute Att. General	None			x				x
Mississippi	No Policy	None							
North Carolina	Statute	Prohibited							
South Carolina	Statute Att. General Court Decision	Prohibited					x		x
Tennessee	Statute	Coll. Barg.	Teachers, Transit	x	x	x		x	x
Virginia	Statute Court Decision	Prohibited					x		x

[a] Local jurisdictions > 20,000 population

[b] Local jurisdictions > 300,000 population

Tennessee and Alabama provide for bilateral relations for teachers; firefighters may engage in meet and confer in Alabama and collective bargaining in Georgia and Kentucky. However, the Georgia statute applies only to jurisdictions of 20,000 or greater population; the Kentucky law in reality applies only in the City of Louisville. Police officers may also bargain in Louisville and transit workers are covered in Tennessee. Although collective negotiations may occur in other state and local jurisdictions, these are *de facto* rather than *de jure*.

Public employers are prohibited from bargaining with their workers in Virginia, North Carolina, and probably South Carolina. The Supreme Court of Virginia held that public sector bargaining was illegal in the case of *Commonwealth of Virginia v. Arlington School Board* (1977, *94 LRRM* 2291). In North Carolina, a 1969 statute prohibited public employees from joining unions or engaging in collective bargaining. Although the union membership provision was later struck down by the courts as a violation of the First and Fourteenth Amendments to the U.S. Constitution (*Atkins v. City of Charlotte* [1969, *70 LRRM* 2732]), the portion of the Act prohibiting collective bargaining was upheld.

The situation in South Carolina is somewhat murky. A lower court decision in the aftermath of the 1969 Charleston Hospital Workers' strike held that union recognition was prohibited in the absence of state enabling legislation (*Medical College of South Carolina v. Drug and Hospital Union, Local 1199* [1969, 9th Cir. Ct. S.C.]). Shortly after that decision, during the strike, a concurrent resolution of the South Carolina General Assembly was issued in support of Governor Robert McNair's policy declaration that no public employer could enter into collective negotiations with his employees without constitutional or statutory authority. In addition, the Attorney General issued an opinion that state and local governments can neither recognize nor bargain with representatives of an employee organization. The *Medical College* decision was not appealed and the concurrent resolution and Attorney General opinion do not have the full force of law. In toto, however, these various decisions have created an environment strongly inimical to unionization and collective bargaining.

In Table 36.3, other labor relations policies in southeastern states may be observed. All states except Mississippi and North Carolina provide for at least one of the six-listed policies, even though bargaining relationships have not been legally established. Four states have designated administrative agencies to oversee labor relations; five states permit some form of union security arrangement; procedures for resolving impasses resulting from negotiations are available in five states; grievance procedures are found in four; and unfair labor practices are stipulated in four. Strikes by public employees are formally prohibited in all states except Mississippi and North Carolina.

Taken together, the data presented above demonstrate that public employee unions have not been as successful in efforts to organize workers and gain bargaining rights in the Southeast as they have been in other sections of the country. With the exception of Florida, Tennessee, and Alabama, union membership is low and bilateral relationships are rare or de facto. The remainder of this article will examine some of the reasons why unionization and collective bargaining have not achieved the same levels of success in the Southeast as they have elsewhere.

Why the Southeast Is Different

It is probably a safe assumption that most individuals who have had occasion to reflect on the South as a region and as a society, whether they lived within the area, outside of it or both, have concluded that the South is indeed "different" in certain respects. Myriad popular writings have been devoted to an elaboration of these differences through historical treatments, novels, and poetry (Woodward 1951, Tindall 1967, Cash 1940). Others have examined the political peculiarities and characteristics of the region (Bass and DeVries 1976, Key 1949, Bartley and Graham 1975). Few, however, have systematically treated the snail-like pace of labor's emergence in the South (but see Marshall 1967).

In approaching the labor issue in public employment, one should at the outset distinguish between two related, but different, dependent variables initially examined in Tables 36.1–36.3. The first is concerned with the propensity of public workers in the Southeast to join employee organizations; the other measure of union success is the incidence of collective bargaining legislation. It has already been determined that the Southeast lags well behind the rest of the United States on each of these dimensions. But which comes first—unionization or collective bargaining laws?

Logic and the literature (Burton 1979) tell us that the relationship is reciprocal. On the one hand, collective bargaining laws are not passed in a vacuum; labor interests must be strong enough to influence elected officials to enact enabling legislation. This implies a substantial organizational base which, at least in the minds of political office-seekers, can influence the outcome of elections. More specifically, the level of union political pressure affects the outcomes of the legislative process regarding labor legislation. On the other hand, union organizational efforts are aided greatly by legislation permitting or mandating collective bargaining policies, especially union security provisions such as the union shop, fair share, or dues checkoff. In a legislative vacuum, in other words, it is difficult for the union to attract new members and effectively represent those whose allegiance it already claims. While resolution of this chicken-and-egg case is beyond the scope of this article, collective bargaining legislation and unionization will be examined as separate phenomena in order to gain some understanding of why both have been slow to develop in the Southeast.

Collective Bargaining Policy

Three empirical studies yield some insight into the question of what determines the enactment of state public employee bargaining policy. The first by Kochan (1973) develops an index of state labor relations policy characteristics and then uses regression analysis to predict the index scores with a series of state socioeconomic, environmental, and political variables. Kochan finds that one-third of the variance in formal public sector labor relations policies is explained by three variables: per capita state expenditure, 1968–1970 change in per capita personal income, and state innovation scores developed in an earlier study by Walker (1969). All are directly related to the strength of public employee bargaining policy. Thus, states with high levels of expenditures, rising personal income, and a tradition of policy innovations are likely to have enacted strong labor relations policies. Unfortunately, the generalizability of Kochan's study is limited by the absence of meaningful theory, the somewhat arbitrary and unvalidated nature of his index, and the use of cross sectional data in a changing state policy environment.

A later study by Moore and Newman (1975) employs discriminant analysis by dividing the states into three categories on the basis of their collective bargaining policy: comprehensive bargaining law, permissive policy or no policy, and using assorted independent variables to predict the policy category. Results indicate that labor climate variables (the size of state government employment, population density, the absence of right-to-work laws, location outside of the South, and urbanization) are directly related to the different categories of bargaining laws.

More recently, Gryski (1980) utilizes discriminant analysis to predict the presence or absence of comprehensive, mandatory state bargaining laws in existence in 1978. He finds that two variables show significance in explaining state policy–interparty competition and Walker's (1969) innovation score. Gryski concludes that high levels of interparty competition and state policy innovativeness, along with certain socioeconomic factors, predispose a state to enact comprehensive public sector labor legislation.

What do these findings imply with respect to public employee labor legislation in the Southeast? Clearly, the southeastern states do not, as a whole, possess characteristics correlated with strong public employee bargaining policy. Few of them are statistical outliers with high scores in policy innovation, state expenditures, wealth, interparty competition, or the labor climate variables employed by Moore and Newman. Just as clearly, however, the South is changing with the continuing flow of people and industry to the region (Perry and Watkins 1977). At the risk of stating a truism, only time will determine the long-term impact of Sunbelt growth and change on the policy climate of public sector labor relations. In the short run, empirical research indicates that significant policy changes must be considered unlikely.

Unionization

As shown in Table 36.1, just as the Southeast has trailed the rest of the United States in public sector labor legislation, so too has it reported lower levels of employee organizational membership. There are two principal ways of looking at the propensity for unionization: in the aggregate and through data on individual workers.

Individual Data

A recent summary of research (Coffinberger 1981) concludes that workers in the American private sector join unions for three basic reasons: economic, social, and psychological. They desire increased wages and fringe benefits (economic), respond to pressure to join the union from their co-workers (social) and wish to enjoy job security, participate in on-the-job decision-making, and protect their rights (psychological). The labor movement in the United States historically has shown little concern or interest in ideological or political matters, preferring instead to utilize collective bargaining to improve employment conditions. Dissatisfaction with compensation and working conditions and the belief that a union can improve the situation motivate workers to join the union (Kochan 1980:143).

Bread-and-butter issues tend to take precedence over social and psychological motives for unionization, especially for blue-collar workers; white-collar employees' propensity to organize is somewhat more affected by psychological motives, although economic concerns remain important (Kochan 1979:26). For most private sector workers, however, dissatisfaction with the job "must be quite severe before a majority will support unionization as an option for improving these conditions" (Kochan 1979:26)

Results of various surveys indicate that, in general, 55–70 percent of the American public approve of unions and the right to join them with the strongest support among nonwhite workers (GERR 1979). Interestingly, Southern blue-collar employees are as supportive of unions as their counterparts in the heavily-unionized Northeast. When asked in the 1977 Department of Labor's Quality of Employment Survey whether they would vote union in an election held at their own place of employment, 35 percent of the Southern workers answered in the affirmative (Kochan 1979:28).

In general, the following traits are descriptive of those employees with greatest propensity to join unions: they are products of families characterized by low socio-economic conditions; they are not well-educated; they do not feel "involved" with the employing organization; and their employer is a large organization (Smith and Hopkins 1979).

For many years it was presumed that public employees joined unions for the same reasons as their industrial brethren (Christrup 1966) and to a certain extent this appears to be true. Economic, social, and psychological factors are salient in public employees' decisions to join unions, but social concerns are much less important than for private sector workers. Surveys of locals of the American Federation of Government Employees at Tinker and Wright Patterson Air Force Bases determined that economic and psychological reasons were most important in decisions by white and blue-collar federal employees to join the union; social or peer pressures were of little consequence (Imundo 1975). Similar findings are reported for state social service workers by Warner, Chisholm, and Munzenrider (1978) who found that the three primary motives for unionization were wages and benefits, job protection, and unfair management practices. Finally, a 1975 survey of state government employees in five states determined that pro-union attitudes are a product of "work situation dissatisfactions, lower occupational status, negative life experience, a large work setting, and less involvement with the organization" (Smith and Hopkins 1979).

In sum, public employees join unions for many of the same reasons as private sector workers: improved compensation and benefits, better job security and working conditions, protection against adverse actions by management, and more participation in decision-making. However, social pressures from co-workers to join the union are less influential in government. As far as the Southeast is concerned, public workers would seem to have unionization motives at least as strong as those of their counterparts in other regions.

Aggregate Data

Several empirical studies have used data aggregated at the state, municipal, or school district levels in efforts to uncover the determinants of public employee unionization (Moore and Newman 1975). Using a model developed earlier to predict private sector unionization, Moore (1977) finds that the percentage of unionized state and local government employees throughout the 50 states is significantly affected by four factors: the percentage of nonwhite government employees, age of the state work force, urbanization, and the presence of comprehensive public bargaining laws. Another study by Moore (1978), this time of teacher union growth, uses cross sectional and time series data to predict membership in the National Education Association (NEA) and American Federation of Teachers (AFT). He finds that a statistical proxy for changes in the business cycle exercises a strong positive effect on teacher union growth and that levels of union membership are significantly influenced by and directly related to a predominantly white work force, strong private sector labor organizations, mandatory bargaining laws, high teacher salaries, and urbanization. Interestingly, a south/nonsouth dummy variable is not significantly related to teacher unionization.

Summarizing the rather atheoretical work by Moore (1977, 1978) and several more rigorous studies predicting union growth in private employment (Ashenfelter and Pencavel 1969, Blum 1968, Hirsch 1980, Freeman and Medoff 1979), aggregate union membership appears to be a product of the following: the business cycle, race, urbanization, private sector labor strength, region, public employer resistance, and bargaining laws. Each will be examined in turn in relationship to unionization in the Southeast.

The influence of the *business cycle* on union membership has traditionally been viewed as follows: improving business conditions leads to membership growth. Higher profits and the strong need for high levels of output and uninterrupted production combine to encourage firms to buy labor off rather than suffer a strike; when business conditions are deteriorating into a recession or depression, a labor surplus develops from production cutbacks and layoffs—unions cannot demonstrate enough success on the all-important bread-and-butter issues to increase membership. Thus, other things being equal (and they seldom are), one would expect that periods of economic growth would enhance union membership gains. The southeastern states for the past decade or so have been gaining on their wealthier brethren in many parts of the country in terms of a number of economic indicators, but apparently unions have not benefited to any substantial degree in either government or industry. This phenomenon may reflect the strong attraction of the non-union southeastern work force to "Frostbelt" employers wishing to escape or avoid unions and the policy decisions (both overt and covert) of many southeastern states to seek out new industries which are likely to remain unorganized.

The relationship between race and unionization is not a clear one. Unions in both government and industry have been known to discriminate against minorities, but at the same time minority workers probably have the most to gain economically from unionization (Hirsch 1980:149). In public employment in the Southeast, blacks have been in the vanguard of unionization drives in sanitation and low-wage functions in hospitals, public works, and other fields where the work force is predominantly non-white (Stepp 1974). However, white-dominated functions, especially in local government services like police and fire protection, have historically discouraged minority recruitment. As noted by Cramer (1978:33 fn):

> It is evident that the race issue has affected unionization efforts in the South for a century. Unions seem always to have faced a dilemma of how to attract white members while at the same time dealing with blacks who either potentially or actually occupied similar jobs. Even when unions focused only on white recruitment and permitted exclusion or segregation of black workers, many whites seemed not to have been attracted because of suspicions about the long-range racial goals of unions . . .

Racial attitudes are changing in the Southeast (Erickson and Luttbeg 1973), however, and state and local government employees increasingly function in integrated work environments. Therefore, the impact of the race factor on future employee organization may be diminishing (Cramer 1978).

Empirical research on determinants of unionization is virtually unanimous in finding that an urban environment is highly conducive to union organizing success in both government and industry. As a general rule, industry is attracted to urban areas. One consequence is a concentration of industrial labor which presents an attractive organizing target for unions. But most of the southeastern states are not highly urbanized in comparison to the strong union states of the industrial Northeast and Midwest. Only Florida and Louisiana rank in the upper one-half of all states in urbanization in the 1970 Census. Furthermore, in those metropolitan areas in the Southeast which are benefactors of Sunbelt population shifts and rapidly growing labor markets, the work force tends to be highly mobile and lacking in attachment to the job. The result is less demand for unionization and higher union organizing exists (Hirsch 1980:151).

Private sector labor union strength and *activity* contribute to a favorable union political climate for public employees. This relationship has been demonstrated in research on the determinants of public employee bargaining legislation discussed earlier. Throughout the United States, the acceptance of organized labor in the private sector has preceded and enhanced union activity in government. However, private sector union membership, measured as a percentage of organized workers in non-agricultural employment, decreased from 33.4 percent of the workforce in 1956 to 26.9 percent during 1976 (U.S. Department of Labor 1980:109). The deterioration in union members is partly attributable to shifts in the nature of the work force from blue-collar to white-collar positions, but even in traditional industrial strongholds unions have declined in membership.

Recent data from the U.S. Department of Labor (1980:109) demonstrate that states in the Southeast exhibit low levels of organization in industry, ranging from 25.4 percent of the non-agricultural workforce in Kentucky to 8.9 percent in South Carolina. Five of the seven least unionized states are found in the region: Virginia, Mississippi, Florida, North Carolina, and South Carolina. In spite of several highly publicized union campaigns to organize the South over the past 40 years such as "Operation Dixie" following World War II, membership gains have been sporadic. Thus, a strong and potentially influential private sector union infrastructure has not been available to aid public employee organization. Recent union victories in the Southern industry notwithstanding, the future prospects for substantial union gains in industry do not appear particularly hopeful.

Region as an explanation for social, economic, and political behavior is intuitively appealing but difficult to contend with theoretically or operationally. Attempts to grapple with the concept pervade the literature of political science (Elazar and Zikmund 1975; Johnson 1976; Patterson 1968; Sullivan 1973) and generally focus on the notion of political culture. The landmark work in the field is by Elazar (1966) who characterizes states in accordance with their "dominant" political culture as individualistic, moralistic, traditionalistic, or combinations thereof. According to Elazar (1966:108), the southeastern states are almost entirely traditionalistic, with the exception of Florida which is "traditionalistic-individualistic." He characterizes the traditionalistic states as reflecting a "paternalistic and elitist conception of the commonwealth" and accepting "a hierarchical society as part of the ordered nature of things . . ." Political power resides with a small elite which claims the "right" to govern through social position or birth. These traits and tendencies lead the southeastern states to rate highest in terms of deviation from national policies. (Elazar 1966:18) Although not dealt with directly by Elazar, labor-relations policy would seem to present an excellent case-in-point. Hierarchy, paternalism, and elitism most definitely do not blend well with unionization and collective bargaining.

The paternalistic tendencies of employers in the Southeast are firmly grounded in the social and economic history of the region. Paternalism developed as part of the plantation system. After the Civil War: (McLaurin 1967:24)

> The mill president replaced the plantation owner; the mill village replaced the slave quarters . . . (and) like the planter, the entrepreneur looked after the social and moral, as well as the socioeconomic well-being of his work force.

The mill owner not only ran the mills, he also provided housing for former share-croppers who left the fields to toil in the factory, furnished them with food and clothing from the company store, sent their children to schools financed by the mills, provided a hospital, library, and recreation center, and even built their church and hired the minister with company money. (Conway 1979:15; Van Osdell 1966) The importance of the company ministers to union avoidance is illustrated in the following example: (Skelton 1964:103)

> In August, 1949, four ministers in McCall, South Carolina spoke to members of that community in a radio broadcast urging them to vote against the union. (They) pointed out that the Plymouth Manufacturing Company controlled the town and that the future wealth and happiness of wives and children . . . depended on the results of the scheduled election.

The broadcast was paid for by Plymouth Manufacturing.

While the southeastern textile industry today has replaced paternalism with methods of production more akin to those advocated by Frederick Taylor (Van Osdell 1966:129), the vestiges of paternalism continue to discourage unionization in industry.

A striking development over the past few years has been a marked increase in the sophistication of union resistance tactics by employers. With ineffective and unresponsive labor organizations also to blame, the number of union decertification elections nationwide has grown from 154 in 1954–5 to 735 in 1976–7); 74 percent of these elections resulted in union losses during the latter period (Krislov 1979). Even though less than one percent of all union members nationwide participate in a decertification election during any given year, the trend is not a healthy one from the perspective of organized labor.

New union organizing efforts today are facing their most difficult challenge since the Wagner Act protections were enacted in 1935 and nowhere is this more evident than in the Southeast. In that bastion of anti-union activity in the region—the textile indus- try—J.P. Stevens Company has been charged with over 1200 violations of the Wagner Act and convicted by the National Labor Relations Board (NLRB) in more than 100 cases. In one finding of guilt involving particularly egregious violations, Administrative Law Judge Bernard Reis was moved to declare that "the record as a whole indicates that Respondent approached these negotiations with all the tractability and open-mindedness of Sherman at the outskirts of Atlanta" (Conway 1979:11). Although Stevens suffered a serious setback by the federal courts in early 1980 in its longstanding struggle to keep the Amalgamated Clothing and Textile Workers Union (ACTWU) out of its mills, company policy continues to be unrelenting hostility toward the union.

Most corporate union-suppression activities today are more sophisticated than the dismissals, lockouts, and employee intimidation tactics of J.P. Stevens. "Union-busting" has become a "new growth industry" fueled by approximately 300 management consult- ing firms (Farmer 1979) which direct the union election strategies of corporations, hold seminars throughout the country in "union avoidance" tactics, offer educational materials on union prevention, and design personnel selection systems to screen out potential union supporters. Although most of the methods advocated by the "union-busters" seem to be legal "positive personnel management" strategies (Kilgour 1981), some are questionable or patently illegal (Chernow 1980; Dunbar and Hall 1980; Farmer 1979).

Public employers, usually alert to effective business practices which are transferable to government, have begun practicing some similar management strategies in efforts to keep government services non-union. As Johnstone (1980:10) explains, the positive per- sonnel management approach to government is "neither pro-management or pro-union" but "pro-people," concerned with:

> effective, open two-way communication between management and employees, fair wages and benefits. . . , good safe working conditions, and fair treatment for employees through appropriate rules and procedures which are fairly and consistently applied.

Few employees or unions would quibble with such a personnel system. Unfortunately, all employers cannot afford the added costs in time and money necessitated by advanced personnel systems (Kochan 1980:185). Hiring a "union-buster" might be less expensive; already there is evidence that public hospitals, universities, and other jurisdictions have retained firms to help fight unions (Farmer 1979). In some southeastern states, business interests have joined forces with public employers in efforts to keep unions out even at the cost of losing prospective new industry. For example, the President of the South Carolina Chamber of Commerce has been quoted as follows (Stucker 1980:14):

> Philosophically we are opposed to unions for South Carolina, and as far as new industry coming into the state, we oppose new companies bringing unions with them. With very few exceptions—and I can't think of who they might be—what I'm saying reflects the business attitude as a whole in South Carolina.

Stepp (1974:60) cites a Charlotte, North Carolina municipal official's attitude as an example of the "prevailing southern anti-union sentiment":

> In our environment, if we are going to deal with the community . . . we are not striving for a climate of good labor relations. We are striving to do the same thing practically every company in this area is doing, keeping the damn unions out, and any other position on that would be so politically unpopular we really couldn't survive.

If such attitudes are prevalent on the part of public officials in other states of the Southeast—and there is little reason for doubt in the most fervently anti-union states— public employee unionization will continue to face a struggle as formidable as that of Sisyphus.

Summary and Conclusions

In relation to national figures collected by the Bureau of the Census, the Southeast shows low levels of public employee organizational membership, with only marginal growth over the 1972–1979 time period. Formal meet and confer, collective bargaining, and other labor relations policies are also quite restricted. Florida, Tennessee, and Alabama are the most heavily organized, probably in large part because of their more permissive labor policy environments. Three southeastern states prohibit collective bargaining altogether: Virginia, North Carolina, and South Carolina. Empirical research indicates that the states of the Southeast do not possess those traits which are correlated with unionization and collective bargaining elsewhere in the United States.

Public employees join unions for economic and psychological reasons; unlike private sector workers, they are not influenced greatly by social concerns such as peer pressure. In the aggregate, public employee unionization appears to be related to economic conditions, race relations, urbanization, private sector union strength, regional and political culture, and the strength of resistance to unions by public employers. All of these factors, of course, tend to be closely related.

Future union growth in members and political influence in the southeastern public sector does not appear very promising, at least in the short term. Although Sunbelt growth and development continue to be accompanied by increased industrialization, urbanization, and other socioeconomic conditions associated with unionization in the past, union successes in both public and private sectors have been limited. Strong anti-union biases on the part of political and economic elites pervade most of the region, reflecting the traditionalistic and paternalistic political culture which continues to prevail. Meanwhile, "union-busting" has become an accepted means of preventing and decertifying unions. With a national shift to the right in domestic politics, unions are likely to confront hard times throughout the United States.[1]

For the unions, a vicious cycle seems to be in effect. The conservative political climate and lack of public employee organizational strength discourage the passage of new collective bargaining legislation. But without enabling legislation union membership gains do not come easily. Florida, the only comprehensive bargaining law state in the region, owes its statute not to the legislature but to an activist State Supreme Court.

It must be noted, however, that some conditions are conducive to public employee unionization in the Southeast. The socioeconomic changes noted earlier, along with increasing per capita incomes, heightened two-party competition, a large non-white work force, and other characteristics of a changing region may help the unions. Furthermore, according to one survey (Kochan 1979), there exists a substantial reservoir of potential union support in the Southeast. For the unions to tap this reservoir, they must somehow adapt themselves to the social, economic, and political peculiarities of the region and become a part of the overall Southern culture. The problems, however, are immense. As one observer has reflected (Dennis 1981:1):

> All the cords of anti-unionism in the South . . . are tied into the cords of some of the best and worst traditions of the South and made to sound as if anyone who would join a union would spit on their mother's grave and repudiate Southern traditions.

The traditional bread-and-butter issues which have fed unionization in other areas of the United States are important in the Southeast as well. But union organizers face an obstacle in the region which they have not been forced to contend with elsewhere—the individualistic, traditionalistic Southern culture.

Note

1. Recent changes in the composition of the National Labor Relations Board (NLRB), for example, portend some of the future difficulties to be confronted by private sector unions. President Reagan has appointed two pro-management lawyers to the five-member Board. One of them is a former consultant to management on avoiding unionization. The other is a former aide to conservative Senator Orrin Hatch of Utah.

References

Ashenfelter, Orley and John H. Pencavel (1969). "American Trade Union Growth: 1900–1960." *Quarterly Journal of Economics* 83 (August): 434–448.

Bartley, Numan V. and Hugh David Graham (1975). *Southern Politics and the Second Reconstruction.* Baltimore: Johns Hopkins Press.

Bass, Jack and Walter DeVries (1976). *The Transformations of Southern Politics.* New York: New American Library.

Blum, Albert (1968). "Why Unions Grow." *Labor History* 9 (Winter): 39–72.

Burton, John F., Jr. (1979). "The Extent of Collective Bargaining," in Benjamin Aaron, Joseph R. Grodin, and James L. Stern (eds.). *Public-Sector Bargaining.* Washington, D.C.: Bureau of National Affairs.

Cash, Wilbur J. (1940). *The Mind of the South.* New York: Knopf.

Chernow, Ron (1980). "The New Pinkertons." *Mother Jones* 4 (May): 50–59.

Christrup, H.J. (1966). "Why Do Government Employees Join Unions?" *Personnel Administration* 11 (September/October): 49–54.

Coffinberger, Richard L. (1981). "A Primer on Unionization Motives." *Journal of Collective Negotiations* 10(2).

Conway, Mini (1979). *Rise Genna Rise: A Portrait of Southern Textile Workers.* Garden City, N.Y.: Anchor Books.

Cramer, M. Richard (1978). "Race and Southern White Workers' Support for Unions." *Phylon* 39 (December): 311–321.

Dennis, Bob (1981). "Textile Union Rethinking Strategy in the South." *The Charlotte Observer* (May 1). Section CL: 1, 4.

Dunbar, Tony and Bob Hall (1980). "Union Busting: Who, Where, When, How, and Why." *Southern Exposure* 8 (Summer): 27–48.

Elazar, Daniel J. (1966). *American Federalism: A View from the States.* New York: Thomas Y. Crowell.

Elazar, Daniel J. and Joseph Zikmund (eds.) (1975). *The Ecology of American Political Culture.* New York: Thomas Y. Crowell.

Erickson, Robert S. and Norman R. Luttbeg (1973). *American Public Opinion: Its Origins, Content, and Impact.* New York: John Wiley.

Farmer, James (1979). "A Boom in Busting Unions." *Business and Society Review* 31 (Fall): 55–58.

Freeman, Richard B. and James L. Medoff (1979). "New Estimates of Private Sector Unionism in the United States." *Industrial and Labor Relations Review* 32 (January): 143–174.

Government Employee Relations Reporter (September 10, 1979): 24–25.

Gryski, Gerald S. (1980). "A Model of the Enactment of State Public Employee Bargaining Laws." *Social Science Quarterly* 60 (March): 702–708.

Hirsch, Barry T. (1980). "The Determinants of Unionization: An Analysis of Inter-area Differences." *Industrial and Labor Relations Review* 33 (January): 147–161.

Imundo, Louis V., Jr (1975). "Why Federal Government Employees Join Unions: A Study of AFGE Local 1138." *Journal of Collective Negotiations* 4: 319–328.

Johnson, Charles A. (1976). "Political Culture in the American States: Elazar's Formulation Examined." *American Journal of Political Science* 20 (August): 491–509.

Johnstone, Stephen R. (1980). *Measures for Avoiding Unions in the Public Sector*, PERL No. 60. Chicago: IMPA.

Key, V.O., Jr. (1949). *Southern Politics in State and Nation.* New York: Knopf.

Kilgour, John G. (1981). *Preventive Labor Relations.* New York: AMACOM.

Kochan, Thomas A. (1973). "Correlates of State Public Employee Bargaining Laws." *Industrial Relations* 12 (October): 322–337.

——— (1979). "How American Workers View Labor Unions." *Monthly Labor Review* 102 (April): 23–31.

——— (1980). *Collective Bargaining and Industrial Relations.* Homewood, Ill.: Richard D. Irwin.

Krislov, Joseph (1979). "Decertification Elections Increase but Remain No Major Burden to Unions." *Monthly Labor Review* 102 (November): 30–32.

Marshall, F. Ray (1967). *Labor in the South.* Cambridge: Harvard University Press.

McCollum, James K. (1980). "Bilateral Interaction v. Unilateral Fulfillment." *Public Personnel Management* 9 (July/August): 296–301.

McLaurin, Melton A. (1967). "The Southern Textile Operative and Organized Labor." Unpublished dissertation, University of South Carolina.

Moore, William J. (1977). "Factors Affecting Growth in Public and Private Sector Unions." *Journal of Collective Negotiations* 6(1): 37–43.

——— (1978). "An Analysis of Teacher Union Growth." *Industrial Relations* 17 (May): 204–215.

Moore, William J. and Robert Newman (1975). "A Note on the Passage of Public Bargaining Laws." *Industrial Relations* 14 (October): 364–370.

Nigro, Felix A. (ed.) (1977). "Public Sector Collective Bargaining in the Southeast: A Symposium." *Southern Review of Public Administration* 1 (September).

Patterson, Samuel C. (1968). "The Political Cultures of the American States." *Journal of Politics* 30 (February): 187–209.

Perry, David C. and Alfred J. Watkins (eds.) (1977). *The Rise of the Sunbelt Cities,* vol. 14. Urban Affairs Annual Reviews. Beverly Hills: Sage.

Skelton, Billy E. (1964). "Industrialization and Unionization in North Carolina and South Carolina: An Economic Comparison." Unpublished dissertation, Duke University.

Smith, Russell L. and Anne H. Hopkins (1979). "Public Employee Attitudes Toward Unions." *Industrial and Labor Relations Review* 32 (July): 484–495.

Stepp, John E. (1974). "The Determinants of South Public Employee Recognition." *Public Personnel Management* 3 (Jan./Feb.): 59–69.

Stucker, Jan (1980). "Industrialist Sees South Essentially Union Free." *The State* (December 21), Section B.

Sullivan, John L. (1973). "Political Correlates of Social, Economic, and Religious Diversity in the American States." *Journal of Politics* 35 (February): 70–84.

Tindall, George B. (1967). *The Emergence of the New South.* Baton Rouge: LSU Press.

U.S. Bureau of the Census (1980). *Labor Management Relations in State and Local Government:* 1979. Series Gss No. 100. Washington, D.C.: Government Printing Office.

U.S. Department of Labor (1980). Directory of National Unions and Bargaining Associations, 1979. Bulletin 2079. Washington, D.C.: Government Printing Office.

Van Osdell, John G. (1966). "Cotton Mills, Labor, and the Southern Mind." Unpublished dissertation, Tulane University.

Waldby, H.O. (1977). "The Florida Public Employee Relations Commission: Its Functions and Operations." *Southern Review of Public Administration* 1 (September): 150–163.

Walker, Jack (1969). "The Diffusion of Innovations Among the American States." *American Political Science Review* (September): 880–892.

Warner, Kenneth S., Rupert F. Chisholm, and Robert F. Munzenrider (1978). "Motives for Unionization Among State Social Service Employees." *Public Personnel Management* 7 (May/June): 181–190.

Woodward, C. Vann (1961). *Origins of the New South,* 1877–1913. Baton Rouge: LSU Press.

PART 8

EMPLOYEE PARTICIPATION AND LABOR MANAGEMENT COOPERATION

Labor-management cooperation refers to arrangements where representatives of unions and management engage in cooperative efforts to promote issues of mutual concern. Such arrangements are intended to supplement rather than substitute for collective negotiations. It is common for unions and management to form joint committees to address such long-term concerns as health and safety, quality of worklife, and diversity. Ad hoc or temporary labor-management committees are also sometimes formed to address strategies for minimizing the effects of layoffs or reductions-in-force (rifs). While management and labor find both advantages as well as disadvantages to forming such committees, cooperative efforts have become a staple of labor relations in the public sector.

In an article appearing in a 1943 issue of *Public Administration Review*, "A New Frontier for Employee-Management Cooperation in Government," Emmett Rushin points to a successful experience with a joint labor-management committee, "the Victory Council," of the National Youth Administration (NYA). As Rushin points out, labor-management cooperation became important at the federal level of government during World War II, when unions and government officials within the Federal Security Agency and the War Production Board were seeking ways to fulfill and execute President Roosevelt's directive to "bring home to labor and management alike the supreme importance of war production" (Rushin 1943: 158). Rushin, the Chief Personnel Officer of the NYA, provides a comprehensive review of the organization and functioning of his agency's Victory Council as well as of the overall importance of labor-management cooperation to effective government performance.

In the next selection, Jim Armshaw, David Carnevale, and Bruce Waltuck point to the positive experiences with joint labor-management partnerships in the U.S. Department of Labor (DOL). Writing just prior to the creation of formal labor-management partnerships, as called for by the National Performance Review (NPR),[1] the authors review the experiences of labor-management committees in more than 800 regional and field locations of the DOL. They find that the DOL's experience with joint committees has been very successful, leading to mutual gains for both management and labor, and ultimately, clients of the DOL.

Finally, Richard Kearney and Steven Hays, in "Labor-Management Relations and Participative Decision Making: Toward a New Paradigm," examine the relevance of participative decision making to labor relations in government. They point to evidence that participative decision making strategies can improve the quality of labor-management relations to ultimately enhance governments' delivery of public services. As they point out:

Increased experimentation in labor-management participation provides a rare and interesting opportunity for the public interest to be served. By fostering a new cooperative spirit between public management and public employees, organizational democracy becomes a natural extension of dominant societal values, and represents a promising new chapter in the American democratic experience (Kearney and Hays 1994: 50).

Note

1. The National Performance Review (NPR), recognizing the salience of labor unions to the operations of government, called for the creation of Labor-Management Partnerships to ensure that unions and management jointly participate in decision making in order to make government work better. In February of 2001, President George W. Bush, just a month after taking office, revoked Bill Clinton's executive order calling for labor-management partnerships in federal government and the creation of the Labor-Management Partnership Council to oversee their activities.

Additional Classics

Goldoff, Anna C. and David C. Tatage. "Joint Productivity Committees: Lessons of Recent Initiatives." 38 *Public Administration Review*, 2: 184–186, March/April 1978.

Krim, Robert M. and Michael B. Arthur. "Quality of Work Life in City Hall: Toward an Integration of Political and Organizational Realities." 13 *Public Administration Quarterly*, 1: 14–30, Spring 1989.

Patton, W. David. "A Choice Between Paleontological and Contemporary Approaches." 14 *Review of Public Personnel Administration*, 4: 52–64, Fall 1994.

Schwarz, Roger M. "Participative Decision Making and Union-Management Cooperative Efforts: Attitudes of Managers, Union Officials, and Employees." 11 *Review of Public Personnel Administration*, 1, 2: 38–54, Fall 1990/Spring 1991.

CHAPTER 37

A NEW FRONTIER FOR EMPLOYEE-MANAGEMENT COOPERATION IN GOVERNMENT

EMMETT R. RUSHIN

One of the most interesting and worthwhile developments in public administration during the past year has been the transplanting of the labor-management committee idea from industry to government. Basically, the employee-management committee, as it should be called in government, is nothing dramatically new. It is a combination of the old suggestion-box type of employee suggestion plan and several modern ideas of employee-management cooperation; the latter components have added enough vigor and novelty to an old idea to account for a significant contribution to public service employee relations.

The introduction of the employee-management committee into governmental agencies followed, and was perhaps derived from, the basic provisions of the War Production Drive plan for industry initiated by Donald M. Nelson, chairman of the War Production Board. This provided for the establishment of management and labor committees to give effect to the President's direction of February 27, 1942, "to bring home to labor and management alike the supreme importance of war production." The initial proposal for the formation of such committees in government agencies originated in an employee-management conference within the office of the administrator of the Federal Security Agency. Following that conference Mr. Paul V. McNutt on May 18, 1942, directed a memorandum to the heads of all constituent agencies within the Federal Security Agency, announcing the establishment of an employee-management committee, the "Victory Council," to consider suggestions of employees for the furtherance of the Agency's contribution to the war effort, and suggesting that the constituent units of the organization establish similar councils. As one of these constituent agencies at that time (it was transferred to the War Manpower Commission by executive order on September 17, 1942), the National Youth Administration established its Victory Council on June 1, 1942. After approximately ten months of operation of this council there are certain observations to be made concerning the organization and functioning of the employee-management committee idea in relationship to government agency administrative problems.

From 3 *Public Administration Review*, 158–163, 1943. Copyright © 1943 American Society for Public Administration. Reprinted with permission.

Organization of a Victory Council

The size and composition of the Victory Council is dependent upon the usual considerations which apply in the formation of any representative committee group within a formal organization structure. It is desirable to have management and employee representation equal, the chairman being one of the management representatives. At the departmental level each constituent agency should be represented in the departmental council. In order to avoid having the council unduly large, however, it may be necessary to have employees throughout the department represented by several union representatives chosen by the union regardless of whether they hold positions within the parent agency or in one of the constituent agencies.

At the constituent agency level the problem of organization is simpler. For effective operation membership of the council should be limited to eight members; a six-member council is ideal for purposed of expediting discussion and for ease of assembling members.

Victory Councils at successively lower administrative levels within departments and within constituent agencies should be integrated with the higher councils, both through having lower councils represented in the higher councils and through permitting the former to refer to the latter suggestions sufficiently broad in scope to be applicable to the entire department or to all government agencies.

The council gains maximum potentialities as an implement for employee-management cooperation when its membership is carefully selected. Employees should be represented by their best leadership, and management by representatives who are respected within the organization, who have authority to act, and who represent a cross-section of management responsibilities. The organizational relationships of personnel offices have accounted for the fact that the administrators have turned in many cases to their chief personnel officers for initiation of the council and for active leadership in its activities; in several instances the personnel officer has been chosen as the logical person to serve as chairman.

The employee group should be represented on the council by members of an employee union or similar formal employee organization. Such persons are accustomed to negotiating with management on questions involving special interests of employees; they have steady access to large segments of employees; and they provide an organization through which projects can be publicized and effected. While a theoretical case can be advanced for selecting general employee representatives, this is undesirable from a practical standpoint. In the first place, the formation of the council organization is unduly complicated when special elections of such representatives must be held. In the second place, general employee representatives have no permanently available channel through which to advise or consult employees, and no organization framework within which they can be held responsible and accountable for council activities—a most essential factor. These considerations make it unwise for an agency without a formal employee organization of any kind to attempt to form an employee-management council; such an agency had best employ the straight employee-suggestion plan supported by an awards committee appointed by the agency head. An agency whose formal employee organization does not include all its employees may feel that unorganized employees should be represented on the council. However, the union organization usually tries to represent all employees from the point of view of the advancement of projects involving employee interests, and for the reasons that have been cited this type of agency also will do better to restrict council membership to employee organization representatives.

Initiation and Promotion of the Council

The effectiveness of a Victory Council will parallel the degree to which it is accepted by management from its inception as a practical method with which the agency can put all its resources to work for war purposes. Its objectives should be explained to all employees during the initial stages of its formation. This is best done by a formal memorandum followed by a meeting of all employees at which the council is explained and the participation of all employees is urged by the agency head. The basic objectives of the council should be explained clearly, the identity of the council members and their alternates announced, and a description given of the way in which suggestions should be submitted and the method to be employed in evaluating them and determining suitable awards. The employees should be told that they will be given maximum credit on efficiency ratings for noteworthy suggestions accepted and used and that a good suggestion will entitle an employee to first consideration for promotion to positions in higher grades for which he is qualified. It is important also to remove any misconceptions which may block employee acceptance of the plan and hinder its effective operation. The following points should be stressed: (1) the work of the council is considered official agency business, so that employee participation, as well as official council meetings, may be conducted during regular working hours; (2) if the application of a suggestion should result in the elimination of the job of the employee making it, he will be given another job equally good, or if possible better; (3) suggestions made by supervisors or by employees under their supervision resulting in reduction of personnel or of volume of work when applied in their units will not be the cause of their losing either grade or salary status.

In order to keep the Victory Council idea dramatized to employees, the council should consider issuing a bulletin periodically. There is practical value also in special bulletin boards to permit all council announcements, the official bulletin, and colorful posters illustrating council objectives to be posted in an established, well identified place. As various refinements to internal procedures of the council are developed the employee group should be notified; they should also be told periodically about awards made by the council and be kept aware of the projects sponsored by the council which have demonstrated their usefulness.

Relationship between the Council and Supervisors

A sound plan will take cognizance of the relationship between the employee and his supervisor as the most important single consideration underlying an agency policy of encouraging suggestions from employees. For this reason, particular stress should be placed upon the principle that suggestions made by employees to the Victory Council shall in no sense replace or take precedence over the normal obligation of the employee to cooperate with his supervisor in improving work operations in their own organization unit. Employees and supervisors alike should understand the Victory Council as an organization designed primarily to encourage suggestions that are (1) broad enough in scope to demand all-over agency consideration, (2) smaller in scope but such that their application cuts across responsibilities of more than one organizational unit, or (3) pertinent to operations or work conditions in a unit other than the one in which the employee is working.

When an employee submits a suggestion of a type which should normally be discussed and settled between him and his supervisor, the council should ascertain whether he has approached his supervisor with it. If not, in many cases it is preferable simply to return the suggestion to him with the recommendation that he take the matter up with his supervisor. Another procedure is to discuss the matter in the presence of both employee and supervisor, so that the employee may be educated on the point of proper relationships with his supervisor, at the same time that the application of the suggestion is settled. If, however, the suggestion is one which the supervisor has refused to consider, or has rejected, then the council has a special task cut out for it. The employee must be protected in any event, particularly if the suggestion is a good one and should be used. All the facts in the case should be carefully presented to the head of the division or office in which the supervisor and employee are located and the responsibility left at that point for weighing the value of the suggestion against the possible overruling of the supervisor.

Some of the past efforts to establish employee suggestion plans have foundered on the difficulty of supervisors' seeing in such plans an effort to override their judgment on responsible parts of management. The task of avoiding this attitude on the part of supervisors while providing for the utilization of worthy suggestions rejected by the supervisors and for the protection of employees making such suggestions represents a real challenge to the employee-management committee. If its role is interpreted to supervisors as one of service to employees and supervisors alike, if it assumes no authority as such which transcends normal employee-supervisor relationships, and if it restricts its function to that of being an expediter and interpreter for *all* suggestions, there is every reason to believe that the obstacles can in the main be overcome.

Procedure for Handling Suggestions

One of the first questions confronting a Victory Council is the determination of the way in which suggestions are to be routed to the council and of the method for processing them after they are received. The NYA plan provides for suggestions to be sent to the council headquarters bearing the date, room number, and name of the employee making the suggestion. Each suggestion is acknowledged when it is received and a date stamp is placed on it and receipt noted in a card register.

Another method which has been employed by certain agencies is the serially numbered employee suggestion form. With a two-part form the employee may leave his name off the part carrying the suggestion, retaining the stub for identification purposes if the suggestion is used. With a three-part form the main section is devoted to space for the suggestion and a serial number; one stub carries the employee's name and the serial number, to be retained in the Victory Council files for identification purposes; and a second stub, retained by the employee, carries only the serial number. Aside from encouraging suggestions from employees who would not respond unless they could remain anonymous until their ideas were passed upon, the use of such forms has the additional advantage of dissociating the employee's name from his suggestion during the entire process of evaluating and investigating the practicability of the suggestion.

Several different methods have been used by Victory Councils for testing the practicability of suggestions. One of these involves the simple procedure of referring the suggestion direct to the division, office, or unit head having jurisdiction over the subject matter or administrative function most nearly related to the purpose of the suggestion. There are two objections to this method: (1) suggestions are not always confined in their application to one organizational function; (2) a substantial preliminary investigation should be made of most suggestions before they are recommended by the council to management, and neither the council nor the division or office head should be burdened with this function.

The NYA Victory Council handled this matter by establishing four fact-finding committees composed of employees who are not members of the council, with one member of the council designated for liaison between each of these committees and the council. Each committee is concerned with suggestions which fall into one of four categories: (1) employee activities and morale, (2) civilian participation, (3) staff utilization, and (4) utilization of materials, equipment, and facilities. All suggestions received by the council are read briefly and, if practical enough for further consideration, are routed to the appropriate liaison member of the council. The latter outlines council recommendations for implementation of the suggestion and forwards it, plus his own recommendations, to the fact-finding committee. After the committee members have made all the investigations deemed necessary they submit a report of their findings and recommendations through the liaison member to the council.

Administration of an Awards Plan

The various employee suggestion plans now in effect among government agencies have used three methods of giving awards: the cash award, meritorious within grade salary advancements, and citations of merit. Each has individual advantages and disadvantages, and it is necessary to choose the one which best fits the methods employed to evaluate suggestions.

The cash plan is flexible in that it permits considerable latitude for making the award somewhat commensurate with the value of the suggestion. Critics of this plan, however, make the point that cash awards have the cold effect of straight payments of money and do not place sufficient emphasis upon the prestige values contained in recognition of the employee contribution.

The major argument in favor of the meritorious within grade salary advancement system is that it does, if carefully administered, combine the elements of monetary award and appropriate recognition for meritorious performance. Its principal disadvantages are that it can be used only for the exceptionally good suggestions; it is not as flexible as the cash award; and its origin in law makes for certain technical difficulties in administration.

The awarding of citations or certificates of merit is undoubtedly sound from the standpoint of recognition of meritorious performance. The main difficulty with the citation system is its lack of adaptability; if citations are used for the small idea as well as for the important one, their prestige value is of doubtful significance in motivating continued suggestions from employees.

Both cash awards and citations have the disadvantage of being temporary. The meritorious within grade salary advancement, on the other hand, has continuous value with respect to both money and prestige.

The use of meritorious within grade salary advancements as awards can be strengthened by adding certain features to the awards plan to offset their disadvantages. One of these is combining it with the citation plan by giving citations for small-scale suggestions that are accepted and making an accumulation of such citations lead to the award of a meritorious within grade advancement. In addition, the plan may be supported by the adoption of a merit-point system to provide for objective consideration and equitable grading of suggestions.

The awards plan used by the National Youth Administration employs meritorious promotions supported by a merit point system. Numerical values are assigned to adopted suggestions under three separate categories: (1) From one to three points are awarded an idea on the basis of its degree of practicability. All suggestions must stand the test of this category before being measured in the two remaining categories. (2) From one to four points are awarded with respect to the suggestion's effect upon morale, efficiency of operations, and saving of money and manpower. The sum of the numerical values accorded an idea under these first two categories is then multiplied by (3) one to four points assigned under the third category, scope of application. The accumulation of eleven points is tentatively set as deserving of a meritorious within grade increase.

The Awards Committee of the NYA Victory Council, composed of the four liaison members, administers the merit point system subject to the guidance and advice of the entire council. After suggestions have been returned to the council with the recommendations of the fact-finding committees, the council (1) passes the suggestion to the Awards Committee immediately if the suggestion has already been put into practice, (2) formally presents the suggestion to the division or office head concerned if it has not already been put into practice, referring it to the Awards Committee after it has been accepted by part of the agency concerned with its use; (3) acknowledges to the employee the action of the Awards Committee on his suggestion, telling him definitely what disposition has been made of his idea and that a specified amount of merit point or a meritorious within grade increase has been earned; (4) acknowledges also suggestions which have been decided to be impractical; these are not, of course, referred to the Awards Committee at all.

Conclusions

A progression of frontiers must be passed from the old-fashioned "suggestion box" concepts on through to an enlightened type of employee participation that is soundly integrated with management planning. Consequently, there is considerable room, both inside and outside normal administrative processes, for experimentation with employee participation in certain phases of management. With several different approaches being made to the matter of encouraging and utilizing properly a broader type of employee participation in activities of government agencies, it is not possible, and for that matter not logical, to build up the employee-management committee idea as either the only way or the best way of doing the job. However, it is pertinent to note that recognition has been accorded the employee-management committee plan by the President's Committee on Deferment of Federal Employees, which included as a collateral recommendation in its report of March 10, 1943, the following statement:

> We recommend that all Federal departments and agencies institute, under the supervision of the personnel officer or other appropriate ranking executive, management-employee suggestion committees which shall hold regular conferences on methods of maximizing efficient operation.

The Victory Council grew out of war-time necessity, but its application should be useful in peace time as well. A great deal of good can be salvaged from simple techniques developed in war time which in normal times have been either ignored or inadequately exploited, and it seems likely that the employee-management committee idea will prove to be a real contribution to public service administration.

CHAPTER 38

UNION-MANAGEMENT PARTNERSHIP IN THE U.S. DEPARTMENT OF LABOR

Cooperating for Quality

JIM ARMSHAW, DAVID CARNEVALE, AND BRUCE WALTUCK

Employee involvement and participation in decisionmaking is accepted as a crucial factor in achieving quality improvement and organizational effectiveness. While an expanding body of research underscores the importance of employee participation systems, less consideration is given to the role of unions in such ventures. The issue of union partnership in quality undertakings is especially important in the public arena where the extent of labor organization is roughly twice that of the private sector. What follows is a description of a highly successful joint labor-management program in the U.S. Department of Labor (DOL) known as "Employee-Involvement/Quality Improvement" (EIQI). Lessons learned from this innovative arrangement can be introduced in other unionized jurisdictions to heighten organizational performance and enrich the work life of employees.

Employee Participation

The appeal of employee participation has intensified in recent years. Elevated interest in the concept originated in the private sector primarily as a result of competitiveness issues. With increasing economic pressures, especially following the 1982 recession, American managers escalated their search for different means of ordering work organizations and processes to compete better in world markets and take advantage of emerging technologies. The public sector is similarly challenged. It faces its own stresses exemplified by an ongoing taxpayers' revolt, resource scarcity, the allure of privatization programs, a deepening crisis of legitimacy, and a host of other problems. The challenges facing government today require involvement and empowerment of workers.

The importance of capitalizing upon staff know-how to strengthen production and service delivery is underscored by interest in Japanese management techniques (Ouchi 1981), prescriptions on how to promote excellence in organizations (Peters and Waterman 1982), a surge of concern about organizational culture (Deal and Kennedy 1982), and a passion for developing quality (Deming 1986; Juran 1988).

From 13 *Review of Public Personnel Administration*, 3: 94–107, Summer 1993. Copyright © 1993 Sage Publications. Reprinted with permission.

Despite recent enthusiasm, these are not new ideas. They build on earlier research which investigated the effects of participation on leader and group effectiveness, the motivational needs of a changing workforce, productivity, job satisfaction, decisionmaking, and adjustment to change (Lewin 1953; Likert 1961; *Work in America* 1973, Coch and French 1948; Morse and Reimer 1956; Marrow, Barrows, and Seashore 1967; Porter, Lawler, and Hackman 1975). In fact, appreciation of the possible salutary effects of participation dates from the classic Hawthorne Experiments (Roethlisberger and Dickson 1939).

There are several theoretical virtues attributed to participation (Levine and Strauss 1989: 1900–1901):

1. Participation may improve decisions.
2. People tend to be more committed to the implementation of decisions they make themselves.
3. For some people, participation satisfies needs for creativity, affiliation, achievement, social approval and elevates their sense of power.
4. Participation improves communication and can increase identification with organizations if suggestions are adopted.
5. Participative workers learn to supervise themselves and develop leadership skills.
6. When labor and management leaders learn to participate in a non-adversarial way, integrative problem-solving skills are bred that help both parties address their needs.

When people work together in teams, these theoretical assets result in a synergistic effect. The decisions and recommendations made by the team as a whole generally surpass those made by individual members and elevate the decision capacity of each person in the group.

Methods to encourage staff participation include Scanlon, Rucker, and Improshare Plans, socio-technical systems, job enrichment and redesign programs, assorted organizational development (OD) interventions, management-by-objectives (MBO), quality circles, and various Quality of Working Life (QWL) initiatives (Lawler 1986). Recently, implementation of Total Quality Management (TQM) in government continues the trend (Hyde 1992; Swiss 1992). Employee dedication is a critical element of TQM which relies on individual employee attention to customer service and continuous improvement of products and services (Carr and Littman. 1990). While there are differences among these processes, they generally share three principal aims: (1) to increase the involvement of individuals and work groups to affect operational flexibility and costs, (2) to boost the motivation, commitment, and problem-solving potential of persons and teams, and (3) to overcome perceived negative effects of confrontational, adversarial labor relations.

Union involvement. Labor and management have worked together since the early part of the century on the types of programs detailed above. They have also cooperated on health and safety, wartime production, apprenticeship and training, employee assistance, energy and resource conservation, new technology, joint community fund drives, and other concerns (Cohen-Rosenthal and Burton 1987). All of these efforts are based on the simple, enduring proposition that greater collaboration benefits both parties. This does not suggest that the factions lose their identities. It is accepted that the groups have areas of interest which are distinct and separate, but these do not preclude capitalizing on opportunities to work together for mutual gain.

Despite a history of alliance, some union leaders and managers remain both skeptical and resistant to participation plans. The primary reason is that employee involvement (EI) policies hold different assumptions about the underlying nature of the employment relationship than traditional labor relations processes. Some union officials fear that participation programs undermine the local union, its officers, and collective bargaining. Unionists also know that participation programs, in all their forms, have been used in union-avoidance strategies. Behavioral science consultants, who have strongly supported employee involvement, have been seen as unfamiliar with unions and closely associated with management interests (Parker 1985; Kochan, Katz, and McKersie 1986). This view is summarized as follows:

> . . . early proponents of QWL largely ignored the history of industrial relations and collective bargaining. . . . While industrial relations recognizes the need for both hard bargaining and mutual cooperation, the behavioral science theories upon which the QWL advocates derived their strategies ignored the conflict side of the employment relationship and stressed only the need for and value of cooperation. In their crudest form, the behavioral science theories were really theories of management developed for managers rather than theories of the employment relationship from which policies and practices could be derived for balancing the diversity and maximizing the commonality of interests at the workplace (Kochan, Katz and Mower 1984: 5).

Managers have their own worries. They fret that collaboration is "soft," undercuts their authority, and threatens their livelihoods. Supervisors, for example, are jeopardized because the agenda of work teams can cut deeply into their jobs or eliminate them altogether (Hecksher 1988). Middle managers, in particular, have been accused of subtly sabotaging more EI efforts than any other group (Huszczo 1991). Flattened hierarchies have accompanied many recent employee involvement efforts and first-level supervisors and middle managers have seen their jobs threatened as a result. At bottom, employee participation and union cooperation procedures menace the ideology that it is the principal job of managers to command and control work operations and employee behavior.

These perceptions about cooperation breed distrust between employers and unions and make buying in to any program difficult. Overcoming such obstacles occurs one day at a time as the parties have opportunities to work together to see if the espoused theories match those actually practiced. These problems have had to be confronted in the evolution of the EIQI program in the Department of Labor.

EIQI

The joint Employee Involvement and Quality Improvement Project (EIQI) is a partnership between the National Council of Field Labor Locals (NCFLL) and the U.S. Department of Labor. Employees covered by the agreement work in hundreds of DOL field offices nationwide. The goals of the program are to improve: (1) the day-to-day quality of working life of employees, (2) the effectiveness of DOL operations, (3) the quality of agency products and services, and (4) the caliber of the labor-management relationship.

EIQI is premised on the belief that cooperative and participative work relationships among employees, union officials, and managers is the way to make continuing improvement in DOL products, services, and work conditions. The spirit of the endeavor is captured in a 1991 memorandum to all DOL employees which encourages the idea that the Department should be a model workplace" which "practice[s] what it preaches" and is "able to point to successes in improving our own workplaces when making suggestions to private employers on how to improve theirs" (U.S. Department of Labor 1991).

The governing body of the EIQI is its National Executive Committee (NEC). The NEC is comprised of one union and one management representative from each of DOL's five largest agencies: Bureau of Labor Statistics (BLS), Mine Safety and Health Administration (MSHA), Occupational Safety and Health Administration (OSHA), Employment Standards Administration (ESA), and the Employment and Training Administration (ETA). There is also one representing the Office of the Assistant Secretary for Administration and Management (OSAM). These Union-Management Pairs (UMPs) have the responsibility and the authority to help initiate, guide, and monitor EIQI drives within their agendas. Each pair consists of a senior manager named by DOL's administrative head and a union official identified by the national union president. In effect, each UMP is a two-person steering committee. The NEC is co-chaired by the Deputy Secretary of Labor and the NCFLL President. The NEC is staffed by two national coordinators, one each appointed by the union and management. The Coordinators are responsible for day-to-day leadership, information dissemination, and monitoring of project activities nationwide. In short, the program is pervasive and jointly operated.

The NEC is the primary implementation vehicle for EIQI and its structure satisfies the first objective of the program's design—minimal bureaucracy. The two staff coordinators, who developed the model, studied examples of employee involvement programs in both the public and private sectors to identify ideal design arrangements. Their investigation showed that the formation of staff participation or quality improvement programs should not establish excessive layers of fresh bureaucracy that would repress rather than encourage creativity and innovation. In other words, there are limited levels of administration and staff requirements are lean. The primary appeal of the overall model is that it is responsive and relatively inexpensive to execute and administer, especially in an organization with hundreds of offices dispersed throughout the United States.

A second feature of EIQI is that there is no "one best way" approach being pushed. Instead, DOL agencies are encouraged to develop enterprises that address the exceptional circumstances found in their particular operating domains. However, they are guided by certain norms and assumptions that underlie the project. These are that (1) the union is a full partner and its legitimacy is respected, (2) UMPs are responsible for all projects within their respective agencies, (3) the union will name its representatives to the UMP teams, (4) employee participation is voluntary, (5) all decisions are made by consensus, and (6) employee time spent on EIQI is considered work time. These operating values set the foundation for the venture by establishing a common language and shared vision on how to proceed.

Empowering employees through involvement in problem-solving and decision-making is another core concept behind this cooperative enterprise. Empowerment means removing unnecessary constraints that obstruct people from doing their jobs. Despite the fact that the term has been overworked recently, the abiding truth is that liberating the hands-on, experiential "know-how" of those who do the actual work is the real key to realizing quality and organization achievement (Schon 1983, Hummel 1987, Zuboff 1988). The vehicle used to release this special knowledge is the self-managing team. Self-directed teams are egalitarian undertakings where roles (e.g., member, leader, scribe, and facilitator) vary and are determined by team members. Everyone must come to the same understandings and be able to support decisions.

Another important aspect of EIQI is that it supplements, rather than substitutes for, traditional labor relations processes like collective bargaining.

How EIQI Coexists with Collective Bargaining

Virtually all union-management cooperation programs like EIQI are kept separate from the bargaining process and grievance procedure. It is important to recognize, however, that collective bargaining is the foundation of EIQI. For without a secure union, with rights guaranteed by law and regulation, EIQI is not possible. The union's legitimacy is ensured as is its ability to file unfair labor practices and grievances as necessary for review by third parties. Nothing in EIQI replaces, limits, or modifies the rights and duties of the parties in their mutual obligation to bargain and administer contracts. This traditional *rights-based* system is maintained and EIQI operates parallel with it (Figure 38.1).

When an issue arises that is considered a contractual matter, it is processed under the terms of the contract. However, if a new element surfaces that is not covered by the agreement, the parties may by expressed mutual consent waive the formal contract procedures and permit a quality improvement team to work on it. Once a team determines a recommendation for action, its impact on the rights of either party under the contract are determined prior to implementation. If either party believes that their contract rights are affected by the recommendation, then they can have it removed from the EIQI mechanism and addressed by collective bargaining. The overwhelming majority of issues addressed by EIQI do not conflict with collective bargaining. EIQI was specifically designed to get at those things outside the normal scope of negotiations where the union had an interest and management wanted employee involvement. Of course, that is easier to realize in theory than in actual practice.

• *Making the bargaining compatibility theory work in practice.* Despite a history of fairly cordial relations between the Department of Labor and the NCFLL [American Federation of Government Employees, AFL-CIO], labor-management relations had generally been based on an adversarial model. This approach, as discussed above, relies on rights reserved to each party by law and regulation. Where disputes arise, union and

Figure 38.1 **Sorting Issues: Traditional LMR and EIQI**

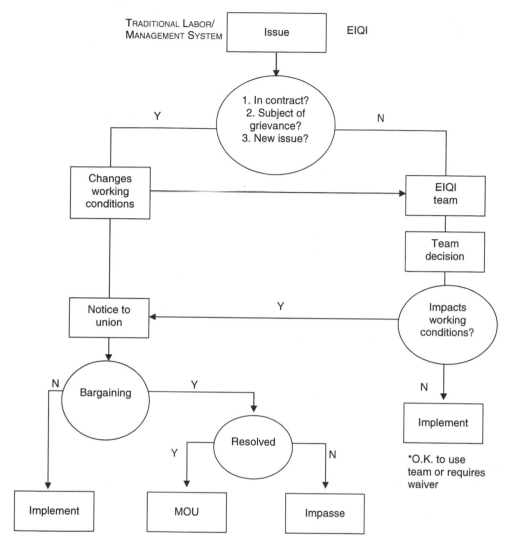

management either negotiate within the context of their collective bargaining agreement or seek third party resolution of their problems through grievance arbitration or appeals to the Federal Labor Relations Authority.

Before EIQI, the parties engaged one another at "arms length." There was little focus on areas of shared interest or chances for mutual gain. Positional bargaining was the rule. Principled or interest-based negotiations were non-existent.

In November 1989, when attendees at a conference on Total Quality Management were asked how they perceived barriers to a successful partnership to accomplish quality improvement, their answers centered on issues of trust, commitment, and co-optation. More union representatives cited concerns about co-optation—the fear that the union would somehow lose its organizational identity by participating in a joint venture with management.

The Executive Board of the NCFLL did not universally embrace the notion of cooperating for quality. Despite a significant majority vote approving the venture, union leaders had many concerns. Chief among these was the fear that a labor-management cooperative effort would circumvent the collective bargaining system.

Implementing a cooperative system for quality improvement, separate from the Agreement worried some union leaders. A quality improvement team might have a supervisor on the team, and that supervisor might influence the group to change working conditions without proper notice to the union. Or, as has happened in other settings, teamwork itself might be used by management to raise questions about why unions were needed at all (Parker and Slaughter 1988). In the Spring of 1990, as the NCFLL-DOL Employee Involvement/Quality Improvement initiative took shape, speculation about threats of circumvention was uppermost in the minds of union leaders. As EIQI's design evolved, this threshold issue had to be addressed. The procedure described in Figure 38.1 above represents the theoretical solution to the problem. It envisions an accommodation between the joint quality initiative and the traditional labor-management relations process. It looks good on paper, but how has this design actually worked in practice? So far, the results have been encouraging.

For many years, for example, the NCFLL has struggled with a policy in the DOL's Mine Safety and Health Administration (MSHA). The procedure involves taking notes in the field by Mine Safety inspectors. This note-taking procedure had been the subject of numerous debates at labor-management relations meetings.

To address the note-taking problem, the Mine Safety and Health Administration and the NCFLL formed a group consisting of their UMPs at all levels. This group was assembled to review the inspection notekeeping process. The group was successful in developing a new approach. This method was piloted at several locations within MSHA's Metal and Nonmetal Mine Safety Health division. Encouraged by the results of the pilot, the parties planned to implement the procedure nationwide. In expanding the program nationally, agency management sought mandatory participation. This required submitting the proposed national pilot to the NCFLL and the Department's Labor Management Relations Committee (LMRC) for approval. This brought implementation within the scope of the collective bargaining agreement. The NCFLL and the Department indicated that the MSHA UMP should continue to monitor implementation and maintain EIQI involvement in the expanded pilot.

Another case of how the theory works in practice involves the Bureau of Labor Statistics (BLS). The Bureau has long maintained a culture of strict management control over its operations. In response, the NCFLL typically is obliged to negotiate every proposed change in working conditions. When the San Francisco regional office of BLS had to relocate its offices in 1992, both management and the union agreed on EIQI as an effective system for change. The NCFLL's Union Pair for BLS worked in the San Francisco office and persuaded agency managers and local union officials to expand their options to include EIQI for the first time as a suitable method to address contingencies associated with the move. As with the MSHA note-taking issue, details of the BLS office transfer were jointly determined and represents another success for EIQI. The configuration of the new office space was done in less time, with less expense than before. In addition, the inclusion of employees in the decision process resulted in a measured boost in morale.

These examples (and there are others) suggest that the design theory of EIQI has been supported in practice. Both managers and union officials have agreed to move issues from bargaining processes to EIQI. The results have been very positive. Difficult work processes have been improved with less confrontation, at less cost, and with increased worker satisfaction. What then of the union's initial fear of the bargaining process being circumvented and union security being undermined? These examples suggest that union and management officials can prevent infringement of the collective bargaining procedure and still cooperate for quality. The two objectives are not naturally incompatible.

Not every case, of course, has been as positive as the ones cited above. In a few incidents, agencies have tried to implement quality improvement decisions without union consultation or participation. In each situation, the parties have been able to resolve these threats to cooperation. As time goes on, it is expected that the parties will adapt better to the requirements of a mutual adjustment, rather than a mainly adversarial, labor relations approach.

In summary, both unions and managers have legitimate fears about entering into cooperative relationships. Admittedly, there is risk involved. Both groups worry that their perceived prerogatives, power, and security will be eroded. Ultimately, security for each faction is guaranteed by the existence of the traditional collective bargaining process which can be used if need be. Perhaps even more significant is the observation of one labor leader who indicated that involvement in quality enhances the visibility of the union throughout the workplace, associates it with positive change, enables it to increase employee authority over working conditions, and dispels the myth that unions do not care about quality or customers. Contrary perceptions of unions have reduced, rather than enhanced, union security and growth.

At bottom, the underlying principles of the EIQI system and the evidence from the actual experience of using it suggest that EIQI strengthens, rather than weakens, both union and management participants. Of course, there is nothing magic in the model that automatically overcomes mistrust and confrontational tendencies. At this point, the parties have been able, if not to overcome their learned wariness of one another entirely, at least to begin to discover ways to cooperate. So far, it is fair to conclude that neither party feels harmed by the process.

Simplifying structure, recognizing the legitimacy of the union, empowering employees through the use of teams, separating quality issues from traditional labor relations processes, creating trust, and committing sufficient resources make the EIQI partnership work. In the relatively short time it has been in operation, the program has produced impressive results.

Results

The NEC is an "umbrella" organization that does not advance an exclusive scheme to enhance involvement and quality. It is expected that the shape and nature of agency approaches will vary. This is perhaps one of the most powerful features of the design. It is not a top-down strategy based on some number of commandments that must be strictly followed. As a result, a variety of quality improvement plans have ensued.

1. In the Wage and Hour Division, Employment Standards Administration, for instance, a nationwide TQM effort was launched three years ago. Some 1400 field and national office Wage and Hour employees were given 40 hours of TQM training in quality tools and techniques, group dynamics, problem solving, and work process improvement methods. At any given time, there are presently more than 200 quality improvement teams working on more than 450 projects or issues. Some of the matters include the delegation of decision authority to lower levels, improving case management, correspondence control, strategic planning, and customer service.

The Wage and Hour Division's San Francisco region was awarded the 1992 Quality Improvement Prototype (QIP) Award by the Federal Quality Institute which recognizes model organizations that achieve high standards of quality based on employee involvement and participation. Examples of high performance through employee participation include faster delivery of unpaid back wages and the reduction of backlogs in the registration of farm labor contractors. Problems in migrant labor camps were also addressed, as well as issues concerning child labor violations (Federal Quality Institute 1992; U.S. Department of Labor 1992).

In Wage and Hour's Atlanta region, cooperating for mutual gain enabled the Georgia State district office to experience dramatic outcomes. For example, when the cooperating for quality program began, there were 682 complaints over 240 days old. Within twelve months, these were reduced to 169. To achieve such impressive results, the Atlanta district initiated twelve distinct TQM projects. A team identified and charted the complaint handling and work flow process, and developed an enhanced computer application to track all complaints as they moved through the office. Other teams addressed staff utilization, work related travel, audit procedures, and technical assistance services. The 75 percent reduction in complaint backlog enabled staff to spend its time on the worst violators, and to concentrate more on providing education and bringing about voluntary compliance with the law (Bremer, 1992).

2. The Mine Safety and Health Administration (MHSA) has used EIQI team building and customer service projects at its major field locations. As referenced previously, the mine inspection process has been improved as a result of EIQI. A multitude of health and safety issues arise in mine environments. These place considerable pressure on MSHA inspection forces. Both physical conditions in the mines, as well as the need to identify violations and issue citations—that can withstand legal challenge—add to the demands

of the mine inspection process. For example, an inspector in "low coal" must often crawl around in a 30-inch coal seem for several hours. At the same time the inspector must produce notes that are legally adequate to support any MSHA action taken against the mine operator. An EIQI task force of inspectors and supervisors were able to develop a new approach to notekeeping. It includes simplified inspection information requirements, checklists to aid inspectors, breakdowns of the most cited violations, and streamlined forms. The improved system meets legal standards, is easier for inspectors to use, and is scheduled for broad implementation throughout the system in the near future.

3. The Occupational Safety and Health Administration (OSHA) has named and trained Pairs in all ten OSHA regions. The Kansas City region recently used EIQI to develop its annual Regional Performance Plan, to modify complaint handling procedures, design new computer applications for the management of case files and records, streamline case file processes, and enable the issuance of some regional level documents without review by the national office.

4. The Bureau of Labor Statistics (BLS) launched EIQI pilot projects in Kansas City, Denver, and San Francisco. Teams have examined a wide range of issues including telephone etiquette, electronic mail applications, general communications, and scheduling travel assignments. In the San Francisco region, for instance, the travel team developed plain-language travel guidelines that are consistent with government regulations and the collective bargaining agreement. Moreover, the team developed a database which allows better coordination of travel assignments which benefit the organization, the employees, and their families.

5. The Boston, Philadelphia, Chicago, Dallas, Kansas City, and San Francisco regions of the Office of the Assistant Secretary for Administration and Management (OSAM) have individually charted quality improvement teams, working on processing commercial invoices, requisitions, and purchase orders; communications between payroll and personnel units, utilization of office and storage space; and a wide variety of other operational issues (*Working Together* 1992).

6. All the regions of the Employment and Training Administration (ETA) have named and trained UMR, to implement EIQI. Some regions have adopted TQM; others have adopted more generic approaches to employee involvement and quality improvement. The Seattle region's TQM effort achieved remarkable results. There, UMP chartered teams include mission work schedules, program monitoring and technical assistance, correspondence, peer and subordinate performance appraisal (of supervisors), and computer applications. A team developed an "ALL-Together Training" model that provides that all employees in the region will have access to the same TQM training. The training team was also involved in the training needs survey, course design and acquisition, and course delivery.

In addition to the above illustrations of the diffusion of EIQI within DOI, a major EIQI enterprise is the department-wide Serving Our Customer (SOC) program. Over 750 SOC work groups at more than 500 field offices have met and generated between 8,000 to 9,000 improvement decisions that are already in various stages of implementation. SOC is based on training generated by an instructional video conceived by the EIQI National Executive Committee. This joint union-management cooperative undertaking involved the entire DOL field organization and resulted in the on-the-job training of more than 7,000 department employees.

Conclusion

Innovations in workplace practices in the public sector, based on quality improvement schemes, are on the rise (Hyde 1992). Reports of successful cases are increasingly prevalent (Bowman and French 1992; Gilbert 1992). However, the role of unions in such ventures and the effects on their interests have received little direct examination (Kochan, Katz, and Mower 1985; Cohen-Rosenthal and Burton 1987). Since quality improvement plans depend upon employee involvement and teamwork, their success in unionized environments hinges on the willingness of labor leaders to become champions of such programs and management's agreement to embrace collaboration with unions as a key aspect of implementation strategies.

The Department of Labor's EIQI venture was inspired by successful joint ventures in the private sector, Saturn and Xerox in particular, and is based entirely on labor-management cooperation and the idea of equal partnership. As such it strengthens the "voice\response" face of unionism (Freeman and Medoff, 1984) and lends credibility to management's claim that it is interested in empowering employees. It supplements, rather than substitutes for, collective bargaining. It recognizes that the quality movement presents opportunities for mutual gain for both management and labor. Cooperation strategies also reduce the "we-they" mentality that can pervade employee relations systems to the detriment of both parties.

EIQI, on balance, is clearly successful. However, it must be noted that it does have its problems. Not every initiative succeeds. Sometimes relationships can worsen rather than get better. As a practical matter, such programs are hardly worthwhile if they are not integrated into a comprehensive program of system change which empowers employees to improve, not only the instrumental concerns of organizations, but also the terms and conditions of their own employment.

Both parties experience frustrations about the extent to which the traditional personnel system is able to reward cooperative behavior and teamwork. Specific personnel practices like classification, job design, performance appraisal, and the entire reward and incentive structures in organizations need to be examined to determine the extent to which they support innovations in modem work processes. Employees need to be rewarded, not penalized for the time they devote to group accomplishment.

The federal government must also do much more to improve levels of cooperation between labor and management. As noted in a recent GAO (1991: 71) study on the state of the federal labor relations system, agency and union respondents indicated that levels of teamwork should be increased. Factors necessary for successful collaboration were identified: (1) respect and trust between the parties, (2) commitment to training, (3) support from top union and management officials, (4) incentives for cooperation, (5) mutual objectives, and (6) management's willingness to involve workers in decision processes. DOL's EIQI program responds to each of these principles and, while it is far from perfect it must be considered a "best practice" in the federal government in the area of labor-management cooperation for quality improvement.

As government confronts increasing resource scarcity, sparse public support and outright political hostility, it is imperative that public employees cooperate to improve the quality of goods and services produced by their organizations. What is needed is a combination of flexibility and "collective entrepreneurialism" where groups work creatively together in pursuit of common goals and a new management philosophy exists premised on a different view of labor-management relations (Reich 1987). Cooperation between employers and labor organizations is an essential ingredient in such strategies, and more direct examination of these experiences is required.

References

Bowman, J. and B. French (1992). "Quality Improvements in a State Agency Revisited." *Public Productivity & Management* XVI, 1: 53–65.

Bremer, D. (1992). "Success—Only Ten Steps Away." *TQM News* (July).

Carr, D. and I. Littman (1990). *Excellence in Government*. Chicago: Coopers and Lybrand.

Coch, L. and J. French (1948). "Overcoming Resistance to Change." *Human Relations* 1, 4: 512–532.

Cohen-Rosenthal, E. and C. Burton (1987). *Mutual Gains*. New York: Praeger.

Deal, T. and A. Kennedy (1982). *Corporate Cultures*. Reading, Mass.: Addison-Wesley.

Deming, W.E. (1986). *Out of Crisis*. Cambridge Center far Advanced Engineering Study, Massachusetts Institute of Technology.

Federal Quality Institute (1992). *Quality Improvement Prototype Award: U.S. Department of Labor Wage and Hour Division San Francisco Region*. Washington, D.C.

Freeman, R.B. and J.L. Medoff, (1984). *What Do Unions Do?* New York: Basic Books.

Gilbert, G.R. (1992). "Quality Improvement in a Federal Defense Organization." *Public Productivity & Management Review* XVI, 1: 65–77.

Government Accounting Office [GAO] (1991). *Federal Labor Relations: A Program in Need of Reform*. GAO/GGD-91-101. Washington, D.C.: General Government Division.

Hecksher, C. (1988). *The New Unionism: Employee Involvement m the Changing Corporation*. New York: Basic Books, Inc., Publishers.

Hummel, R. (1987). "Behind Quality Management: What Workers and a Few Philosophers Have Always Known and How It Adds Up to Quality Management." *Organizational Dynamics* 16: 71–78.

Huszczo, G.E. (1991). "The Long-Term Prospects for Joint Union-Management Worker Participation Processes," pp. 13–36 in *Workplace Topics*. AFL-CIO Department of Economic Research.

Hyde, A.C. (1992). "The Proverbs of Total Quality Management Recharting the Path to Quality Improvement in the Public Sector." *Public Productivity & Management Review* XVI. 1: 25–39.

Juran, J.M. (1988). *Juran on Planning for Quality*. New York: Free Press.

Kochan, T, H. Katz and R. McKersie (1986). *The Transformation of American Industrial Relations*. New York: Basic Books.

Kochan, T., H. Katz and N. Mower (1984). *Worker Participation and American Unions: Threat or Opportunity?* Massachusetts Institute of Technology, The W.E. Upjohn Institute for Employment Research.

—— (1985). "Worker Participation and American Unions," pp. 274–306 in T. A. Kochan (ed.) *Challenges and Choices Facing American Labor*. Cambridge, Mass: The MIT Press.

Lawler, E.E. III (1986). *High Involvement Management*. San Francisco: Jossey-Bass, Inc.

Levine, D. and G. Strauss. (1989). "Employee Participation and Involvement," in Commission on Workforce Quality and Labor Market Efficiency. Investing in People: A Strategy to Address America's Workforce Crisis (Background Papers, Vol. II). Washington, D.C.: U.S. Department of Labor, 1895–1918.

Lewin, K. (1953). "Studies in Group Decision." in D. Cartwright and A. Zander (eds.) *Group Dynamics*. Evanston. Ill.: Harper.

Likert, R. (1961). *New Patterns of Management*. New York: McGraw-Hill.

Marrow, A., D. Barrows and S. Seashore (1967). *Management by Participation*. New York: Harpers.

Morse, N. and E. Reimer (1956). "The Experimental Change of a Major Organizational Variable." *Journal of Abnormal and Social Psychology* 52 (January): 120–129.

NCFLL-USDOL Collective Bargaining Agreement, October, 1991.

Ouchi, W. (1981). *Theory Z: How American Business Can Meet the Japanese Challenge*. Reading, Mass.: Addison-Wesley.

Parker, M. (1985). *Inside the Circle*. Boston, Mass.: South End Press.

Parker, M. and J. Slaughter (1988). *Choosing Sides: Unions and the Team Concept*. Boston, Mass.: South End Press.

Peters, T. and R. Waterman (1982). *In Search of Excellence: Lessons from America's Best-Run Companies*. New York: Harper & Row.

Porter L., E. Lawler and R. Hackman (1975). *Behavior in Organizations*. New York: McGraw-Hill.

Reich, R. (1987). *Tales of a New America*. New York: Times Books.

Roethlisberger, F. and W. Dickson (1939). *Management and the Worker*. Cambridge, Mass.: Harvard University Press.

Schon, D. (1983). *The Reflective Practitioner*. New York: Basic Books.

Swiss, J. (1992). "Adapting Total Quality Management (TQM) to Government." *Public Administration Review* 52: 356–362.

U.S. Department of Labor (1991). Memorandum for All DOL Employees, from Lynn Martin, Secretary of Labor, Subject: DOL Model Workplace. Washington, D.C.

—— (1992). "Labor Department Honored for Achieving High Standards of Quality Service," *News*. Washington, D.C.

Work in America (1973). Report of Special Task Force to the Secretary of Health, Education, and Welfare. Cambridge, Mass.: MIT Press.

Working Together (1993). "15 New Beginnings." Newsletter of the Ten Regional OSAMs, January.

Zuboff, S. (1998). *In the Age of the Smart Machine: The Future of Work and Power*. New York: Basic Books, Inc., Publishers.

CHAPTER 39

LABOR-MANAGEMENT RELATIONS AND PARTICIPATIVE DECISION MAKING

Toward a New Paradigm

RICHARD C. KEARNEY AND STEVEN W. HAYS

During recent years, a chorus of voices has risen in support of a new era in labor-management relations. Drawing on the Japanese experience, which has become a virtual icon of the contemporary management culture, advocates representing all segments of the labor economy have called for greater employer-employee cooperation (Brock 1987, Hatch 1987, Kochan 1987, Thomann and Strickland 1992). Despite our long traditions of adversarial labor relations in union environments and authoritarian or paternalistic management approaches in union-free settings, many commentors assert that one solution to the crisis in government is to emphasize the mutuality of interests between management and labor. The process is already well underway, as shown by the numerous experiments with such innovations as Total Quality Management (TQM), Quality Circles (QC), Labor-Management Committees (LMCs), and quality-of-worklife (QWL), and organizational development (OD) schemes.

This article explores the question of the employee involvement or participative decision-making approach, including the key role of public employee unions in facilitating or obstructing employee involvement programs. No new theory of labor-management relations is offered here. The intent is to integrate the existing theory and assumptions of the participative decision-making model with the empirical research to determine the factors necessary for, impediments to, and prospects for, a new paradigm in labor-management relations. Our finding suggest that participative decision making provides personal benefits to the individual employee as well as desired organizational outcomes. Generally, we are cautious yet hopeful that such an approach can contribute significantly in advancing employee, institutional, and public interests.

Toward a Participative Management Model

Since the 1940s, the management literature has paid lip service to the so-called human resources model of administrative behavior. As the name implies, this approach to leadership begins with the premise that an organization's workers are its most important asset, and should be treated accordingly. Once this norm is internalized, then a predictable set of attitudes and administrative practices follows naturally. Training and employee development will be emphasized, worker security and long-term employment will be the rule, and participative decision-making strategies will prevail. Bottom-up authority structures are envisioned as the only appropriate means for managing an organization adhering to the human resources model. Top-down, conflictual, nonparticipatory leadership styles are regarded as antithetical to, and destructive of, the worker-as-asset approach to management.

Although management theorists have long been obsessed with the human resources philosophy, even the most starry eyed Pollyanna would agree that until recently, this approach to administration was rarely implemented within the American workplace. Where they existed, participative decision-making styles were most likely found in very small organizations or in large corporations that were attempting to ward off union organizing efforts. The unionized setting was perhaps least likely to follow a human resources approach to management.

In recent times, however, eternal pressures have forced a heightened level of management and labor interest in employee-involvement programs. Among the plethora of factors contributing to this near-biblical conversion are declining rates of worker productivity, worsening difficulties encountered in recruiting and retaining "knowledge workers," increased demands made on employees because of the requirements of new technology and the information age, diminishing international competitiveness of U.S. firms, citizen demand for more efficient government service performance, and a national economic malaise that impedes the ability of organizations to increase workers' material incentives (Volcker 1989). The refrain heard time and again in both public and private organizations is that managers must do more with less. There is a growing realization that this charge simply cannot be accomplished by managers alone; the cooperation of all workers is essential.

Predictably, managers searching for ways to adapt their organizations to a human resources model have looked in Japan's direction first. One of the most appealing characteristics of Japanese personnel practices is their people-centered approach to management. Japanese organizations are bound together by such guiding principle (but not guarantees) as lifetime employment, harmony and consensus in decision making, and a preoccupation with the quality and price of goods and services produced (Hasegawa 1986). These factors, in turn, interrelate and foster such byproducts as reduced worker insecurity, a heavy emphasis on training and the development of worker talents, and small salary and status differentials among employees. The organizations are rewarded by extremely high levels of worker loyalty, amazingly low rates of absenteeism, and a work force that is generally willing to sacrifice personal gains for the greater good.

Legitimate questions are routinely raised concerning the applicability of Japanese-style management practices to the American cultural setting. Whether or not one agrees that such an approach can be superimposed upon the heterogeneous United States, there can be no denying the fact that the familial managerial model has been a major contributor to Japan's "economic miracle." Because the Japanese approach to administration closely resembles many elements of the human resources model, managers in the United States have been busily identifying facets of Japanese management practice that can be expeditiously emulated. Total Quality Management (TQM) eloquently reflects the worker-centered tradition that is evident throughout Japan. Undergirding TQM's emphasis on customer-driven decision processes, concentration on production system design, and "continuous improvement" is the unambiguous message that all employees must be empowered by management to participate in decision making and that they must be allowed to do so "without fear" (Deming 1986, Swiss 1992). The common, unifying element in TQM, QCs, QWL programs, Labor-Management Committees, and related approaches is meaningful employee participation in organizational decision making wherein a formal vehicle for an employee voice is operative, and employee views and decisions are given serious consideration. That is what we mean by participative decision making (PDM) in this article.

Participative Decision-Making Theory, Assumptions, and the Empirical Record

For American managers, a question of critical common is: To what extent are current assumptions concerning the benefits of the human resources approach valid? That is, what evidence exists concerning linkages among worker participation, productivity, job satisfaction, and other relevant consideration? Although few definitive conclusions can be drawn, the theory and research—most of which has been recorded in an American setting—points to a number of potential benefits if the PDM model is widely embraced in public and private organizations. These benefits may accrue to the individual employee, as a person and as a worker, and to the organization in terms of both managing and maintaining resources and achieving its production or service-related goals. Figure 39.1 shows the principal personal and organizational benefits attributed to PDM.

A long intellectual trail of motivational theories, beginning with Maslow (1954) and including McClelland (1953), McGregor (1960), Likert (1961), Herzberg (1968), and numerous other major figures, leads to the conclusion that employee participation produces *instrinic, personal benefits*. Although a wide variety of personal employee benefits are described in the literature, three of the most important, and most widely noted, are personal growth and development, job satisfaction, and willingness to change (Lawler and Hackman 1969, Armstrong 1971, Grunenberg 1979, Goodman 1980, Mohrman and Lawler 1988, Lincoln 1989).

These factors are believed to contribute, directly or indirectly, to desired organizational outcomes. For instance, high job satisfaction results in lower turnover, fewer unexcused absences, and slightly lower accident rates (Vroom 1964). Job satisfaction has also been

Figure 39.1 **Linkages Between Participative Decision-Making Model and Personal and Organizational Benefits**

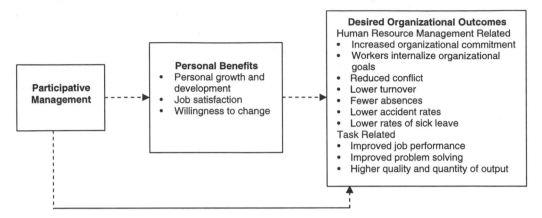

shown to lead to a better quality of output and to a healthier work force, measured in terms of the frequency of sick days and stress-related illnesses. Other research has correlated high levels of job satisfaction with reductions in "lax and disregardful behavior" (Kolarska and Aldrich 1980), and to "good citizenship" among employees (Bateman and Organ 1983). Job satisfaction has been associated with stronger organizational commitment, which is broadly defined as the "psychological bond between people and organizations" (Buchanan 1974: 533). Organizational commitment has been defined more pragmatically by Porter (1968), who holds that it consists of (a) a willingness of employees to exert high levels of effort on behalf of the organization, (b) a strong desire to remain in the organization, and (c) an acceptance of the organization's major goals and values. Using these and other definitions, researchers have linked organizational commitment to high performance levels, low turnover (commitment is thought to be even more predictive of turnover than job satisfaction), and other measures of organizational effectiveness (Angle and Perry 1983, Verma and McKersie 1987, Morris and Steers 1980, Goodman 1980, Straw and Heckscher 1984, Steers 1977).

A significant finding in this line of inquiry is that organizational variables such as structure, span of control, and the level of decentralization directly influence commitment. The linkage is predictable, in that flatter structures and more consultative work environments tend to enhance levels of worker commitment (Morris and Steers 1980). Employee willingness to change and adapt to a work environment in a constant state of flux is considered an important work force characteristic for high technology and information-age organizations. A major appeal of Quality Circles, TQM, team management, and similar arrangements is their purported ability to accomplish tasks in a rapidly changing environment. PDM has been shown to exert a positive effect on workers' willingness and ability to innovate, to accept change, and to upgrade their skills so they are better able to deal with workplace uncertainties (Wexley and Yukl 1977).

In addition to, and in conjunction with, the personal benefits derived from PDM, there are convincing arguments that this approach is "organizationally desirable because it enables the organization to perform the technical tasks required to achieve its mission" (Mohrman and Lawler 1988: 47). Making the case for this technical rationality argument are numerous organizational theorists who insist that centralized organizations are unable to respond to turbulent environments (Bennis 1966, Pfeffer 1978). Such contemporary challenges as increased societal competition for resources and greater demands for responsiveness among client groups require rapid and innovative responses. The high transaction costs and delays that accompany hierarchical and control-oriented decision-making systems (Galbraith 1973) make them unsuitable to today's management setting. What is needed is a "boundary spanning" capacity that enlists all workers—especially those on the front line who work with clients on a daily basis—as management's representatives. That is, the workers who are closest to the problems have the understanding and knowledge necessary to make all but the most nonroutine decisions.

Although not completely conclusive, a growing body of research tends to support the contention that PDM strategies reap major dividends for organizations in other ways as well. Much of the easy research is summarized in Anthony's (1978) *Participative Management.* Worker involvement has been found to improve job performance in difficult settings (Marrow 1972, Davis 1972), to improve the quality of decisions thanks to increased information flow and the effective transfer of ideas (Frost, Wakeley, and Ruh 1974), to enhance workers' willingness to become more psychologically involved in their tasks (i.e., to internalize organizational goals) (Patchen 1970), and to achieve improvements in product quality (Cooke 1992). Conflict has been shown to decline in conditions of collaborative decision making, thereby promoting effective problem solving and adding to job satisfaction (Locke and Schweiger 1979). Also, participation leads workers to greater trust in the organization and the decisions that are made, thereby reducing resistance to change and contributing to more enthusiastic program implementation (Gabris and Kenneth 1986, Carnevale and Wechsler 1992).

Although some research indicates that the personal benefits of PDM are linked to desired organizational outcomes (Marshall 1992: 43–46), a less optimistic conclusion emerges from the research focusing on concrete measures of worker and organizational productivity (Locke and Schweiger 1979). While PDM is consistently shown to improve worker attitudes and job satisfaction, clear productivity or efficiency gains can only be verified in about 50 percent of the cases studied (Miller and Monge 1986; Holzer 1988; Cooke 1989; Kelley and Harrison 1992). The difficulties that researchers have experienced in "proving" productivity gains have been variously attributed to contextual factors including form of participation (Cotton 1993: 17–22), methodological incapacities, insufficient explanatory theory, and to the assertion that happy workers simply do not necessarily produce more than unhappy ones in some settings. In other words, a worker may derive enormous satisfaction from doing virtually nothing from 9 to 5.

Although the jury is still out, the theoretical and empirical support for a participative approach to organizational decision making is reasonably compelling. PDM styles have always had some allure, but they are especially appealing in the current economic and political climate. In the next section, conditions required for establishing a successful PDM program are discussed before turning to a more problematic question; namely, what factors assist or impede collaborative decision making, particularly in the unionized setting?

Conditions Necessary (but Not Sufficient) for a Successful Participative Decision-Making Program

PDM implies a near-revolutionary shift in perspective and practice on the part of both employer and employees. Based on a thorough review of the relevant literature, we conclude that in order for this approach to develop successfully and thrive, four necessary but not sufficient conditions must be met:

1. Viable collaborative mechanisms must be available and understood by management and employees;
2. Win-win expectations (and realizations) must be present among the parties;
3. The parties must be committed to investing the time and effort needed for a successful program;
4. A basic level of trust and mutual respect must exist among the various parties.

The first condition is perhaps the most easily met. Viable collaborative, consultative mechanisms for PDM are available, and their usefulness has been demonstrated in a number of public and private sector settings. Quality Circles have been used to foster participation and have been shown to enhance employee and organizational performance (Ouchi 1981). Specifically, QCs can produce significant improvements in participants' attitudes, behavior, and job effectiveness (Griffin 1988), and can increase job satisfaction and reduce absenteeism (Marks et al. 1986, Hanlon 1985). QCs have operated successfully at all levels of government for nearly a decade. For example, positive results have been reported for the U.S. Postal Service and other federal agencies, the Missouri state government, and numerous local governments.

A related technique is the Process Improvement Team (PIT). PITs consist of large groups of employees assembled on a short-term basis to solve a designated problem, whereas QCs are small groups designed to address ongoing problems. PITs have been used productively at Department of Defense sites (GERR Special Report 1990).

Labor-Management Committees (LMCs) offer another collaborative decision-making strategy. Typically, unions and management engage in cooperative efforts in an attempt to resolve troublesome issues, commonly including incentive pay plans (Schwarz 1990–91). The Internal Revenue Service (IRS) and the National Treasury Employees Union (NTEU) have successfully used Labor-Management Committees, and even incorporated them into their national contract. The IRS-NTEU approach has also embraced a Joint Quality Improvement Process (JQIP), in which voluntary, joint problem-solving teams address quality improvement issues. A similar cooperative approach has been utilized in the Selective Service System (SSS) and the Department of Energy to create gainsharing programs. For example, savings resulting from personnel attrition at the SSS are shared with productive personnel on a quarterly basis. At the state and local level, Labor-Management Committees and related mechanisms have been used to negotiate agreements concerning such difficult topics as productivity, privatization, and potential layoffs (Dawson 1991: 18–22).

The current management rage, TQM, embraces a participative decision-making strategy in its focus on continuous product and service improvement, error prevention, and customer needs. Various cooperative mechanisms are employed to involve and empower the TQM employee (Levine 1992). Indeed, it is difficult to conceive of TQM efforts enjoying even a modicum of success without early, meaningful, and ongoing employee participation in organizational decisions (Kochan 1987).

The second prerequisite for successful PDM, win-win expectations, may be somewhat more elusive than determining a suitable collaborative mechanism, especially where unions and collective bargaining inhabit an organization's human resource environment. Even when win-win expectations are expressed initially, in order to maintain them over time there must also be at least an occasional realization of those expectations. In particular, management must take action on collaborative decisions or give a convincing reason why it cannot.

Despite predictable opposition in many quarters from union officials and midlevel managers, who fear the loss of power far more than other employees (Klein 1986), progress has been recorded in implementing a win-win philosophy both within the collective bargaining process and outside of it. The origins of win-win bargaining may be traced to Walton and McKersie's (1965) behavioral theory of collective bargaining, which set out two major negotiating strategies. The first, distributive bargaining, encompasses the conventional, adversarial, zero-sum model. The second, integrative bargaining, embraces a collaborative, win-win approach to bargaining, in which each party leaves the negotiating table savoring a "victory." Today, the win-win strategy may be referred to as interest-based, principled, or collaborative bargaining, among other rubrics. It is most popularly represented in the book *Getting to Yes* (Fisher and Ury 1981). *Getting to Yes* has been criticized for a lack of analytical content, giving short shrift to the role of power and bargaining resources, the inherently zero-sum nature of dividing up a finite pie, and other omissions (White 1984; McCarthy 1985; Lobel 1992), but the concept itself has won widespread support among labor and management representatives in the private sector and in all levels of government.

Some of the most extensive public sector experience with win-win bargaining is in the schools, where effective reform depends largely on a cooperative role for teachers (nearly 80 percent of whom belong to labor organizations). Teachers' high degree of control over the classroom and the learning process, their extensive responsibilities for decision making in work assignments and student evaluations, and, in general, the substantial degree of individual teacher responsibility for what happens in the classroom make public education especially amenable to a participative approach, including win-win bargaining (see Bacharach, Shedd, and Conley 1988; Crisci, Giancola, and Miller 1987; Schachter 1989).

Win-win experiences have been achieved through vehicles other than collective bargaining. QCs, TQM, LMCs, QWL programs, and other cooperative endeavors have reported integrative outcomes in a variety of jurisdictions. A GERR Special Report (1990) relates success stories for federal agencies, including the IRS and the Postal Service, where productivity and other gains have been shared by the agencies and their employees. For example, the number of employee grievances in the Postal Service has been reduced significantly, and delivery routes have been reconfigured for efficiency improvements.

The third condition for effective PDM is the commitment of the principal parties to invest the necessary time and effort to bring the collaborative approach to fruition, and to keep the relationship fruitful. This means management—from agency and department heads to front-line supervisors—and union officials—from state, local, and even national presidents to stewards—must be "actively committed to supporting these innovations and make the strategic decisions necessary to reinforce and sustain them" over time (Kochan 1987: 33). Active support and endorsement may entail top management's willingness to release employees from regular job assignments for training in problem-solving techniques, interpersonal relations, and other collaborative decision-making skills. Long-term commitment may also mean that parties must periodically "reinvent" or rejuvenate their approach to PDM to keep it vital and effective (Cooke 1990).

Finally, effective collaboration is constructed from a foundation of mutual respect and trust—not a simple thing to build in the face of years of fierce adversarialism and bitter battles across the bargaining table. A management-employee partnership requires both sides to sacrifice some former "rights." Mutual respect and trust are predicated on management giving up plenary decision-making authority in certain areas and, where relevant, its sincere acceptance of a legitimate role for unions in decision making. Union leaders and officials must develop a coherent strategy for "selling" participative mechanisms to the rank-and-file. Management and union leaders need to stand together in a common front to avoid divisiveness, and whenever possible, to work out their problems so that each wins something and neither sacrifices too much.

Impediments to Participative Decision Making

Of course, in the day-to-day world of employer-employee relations, myriad creatures lurk around every turn and corner, waiting to destroy incipient or ongoing cooperative enterprises.

Mechanisms may exist to structure PDM, but in many jurisdictions the NLRA model upon which collective bargaining is premised interferes with the development of viable cooperative vehicles by perpetuating a never-ending power struggle through adversarial provisions and processes. The most patent example is Title VII of the Civil Service Reform Act of 1978. Section 7106, the management rights clause, through both its content and OPM's interpretations of it, excludes from the scope of bargaining many subjects that must be addressed if PDM is to take place, including such issues as performance standards, seniority, contracting out, reduction in force, and virtually all agency rules and regulations. Under the CSRA (Section 7114c), federal agency heads may (and often do) review and reject contract clauses negotiated by union and management representatives. Negotiability disputes go to the Federal Labor Relations Authority which has earned a reputation for inconsistency and illogic in its decisions (Rosenbloom 1989). When we consider that Title VII also prohibits bargaining over wages and benefits, it is no wonder that the federal labor-management relations program is characterized by constant legalistic conflicts over relatively trivial matters. The power imbalance between management and labor often defies meaningful cooperation through participative mechanisms. Valiant efforts to develop collaborative mechanisms are being made, but where they succeed it is *in spite of* the CSRA (Levine 1991). Disequilibrium in bargaining power is conducive to unilateral directives, not PDM. Win-win expectations tend to be naive.

Also undermining win-win expectations, even in jurisdictions where a bargaining power equilibrium exists, is the historical (and natural) mutual suspicion of union leaders and managers at all levels. Indeed, the absence of win-win expectations is largely attributable to the lack of trust between parties. As noted, management fears the loss of authority and control, and typically evinces an innate distrust of unions (Levine 1992: 110–111). Obviously, however, cooperation with employees inevitably implies cooperation with the union. Union leaders, for their part, fear that QCs, TQM, and other devices "are spawned from an antilabor seed and tend to subvert collective bargaining" (cited in Levine 1992: 115). They also need to be convinced that productivity gains do not translate into job losses.

According to some critics, American-style labor-management relations may be so ingrained with adversarialism that sustained collaboration is virtually impossible, that labor-management perspectives are too profoundly divergent to permit PDM (Reisman and Compa 1985). Unions have *existed* to oppose management and fight for zero-sum outcomes. Labor leaders cut their teeth on adversarialism. More broadly, American society itself is characterized by individualism and adversarialism. Our litigious propensities support countless numbers of lawyers. Even our education system is premised on individual competition—not cooperation.

Nonunion settings are not necessarily conducive to PDM, either. Political and operational cultures in states hostile to unions and collective bargaining lean toward traditionalistic, authoritarian approaches to management. In the absence of unions, a collective employee voice is problematic. Where management itself designs a representational structure for employee participation in decision making, the employee response is likely to be a presumption of management insincerity, manipulation, or corruption. In a December 1992 ruling, the NLRB reached a similar conclusion in a case involving Electromation, a firm that unilaterally established worker-management teams to improve efficiency. The administrative law judge found that the farm had violated a provision of the NLRA prohibiting employer efforts to interface with union organizing efforts (the Teamsters began an organizing campaign shortly after the worker-management teams were formed).

Indeed, one can argue that unions are *necessary* for meaningful employee participation in organizational decision making, and that participative systems are most likely to emerge in collective bargaining situations. Should one be bold enough to suggest that perhaps it is time to revive the long-dormant proposal for congressional legislation to establish a minimum floor for state and local government union recognition and bargaining rights?

Finally, as observed above, the commitment of time and effort necessary to implement PDM is problematic in a society focused on the short term. Sustained effort and long-term time horizons do not characterize management or union leadership at any level, and perhaps it is unreasonable to expect that they will (Lobel 1992). Truncated time horizons are serious enough in the private sector, but tend to be even more common and confounding in the public sector, where elected officials and their political appointees enter and depart government with startling rapidity, and where budget shortfalls can disrupt even the most peaceful labor relations setting.

Is the Public Sector Ready for Participative Decision Making? Toward a New Paradigm

It is not entirely flight and fancy to envision a scenario in which common sense and the public good win over tradition, the status quo, and mistrust. Simply stated, an eloquent case can be made for PDM. It has already been recognized by many notable policy makers, managers, and labor leaders as one of the few available options to improve government performance in the next century and to address the needs of women and minorities and the aging work force. Likewise, considering the fact that both public workers and their managers are glumly trying to ride out a hurricane of seemingly intractable fiscal and political problems in the same leaky boat, there is a natural commonality of interests that is similar to the one that exists in corporate America (where, incidentally, cooperative labor-management relations have been most successful in organizations facing the *worst* economic crises) (Levine 1991). Management theory, bolstered by a growing body of empirical evidence, lends additional credence to the assertion that PDM strategies can make government work better. In fact, it is perhaps the best available alternative for simultaneously advancing organizational, employee, and public interests.

Employees, whether union members or not, tend to exhibit strongly positive attitudes towards PDM and other worker involvement programs (U.S. General Accounting Office 1991: 63–75, Kochan, Katz, and Mower 1984: ch. 5). Public employers should seek to build on these positive attitudes while emphasizing the sometimes forgotten, shared mission in public service, as well as mutual employer-employee vulnerability to the machinations of elected officials in executive and legislative bodies.

PDM promises to inject a greatly needed element of flexibility and adaptability in public organizations. If public agencies are truly to be customer-oriented, as TQM and good sense demand, and if they are to resemble a public sector model of the "high performance production system" that corporate America is pursuing (Marshall 1992: 36–37), then organizational decision making must be moved as close to the point of service delivery as possible. Effective delivery of services to increasingly diverse client groups requires an adaptive, learning, cooperative work environment.

Elected officials have a critical contribution to make in terms of creating the legal and procedural mechanisms necessary to foster participative approaches. Successful programs are predicated on a facilitative legal environment with statutes, rules, and regulations that provide incentives for cooperation—not obstacles to it. Legal and procedural barriers to PDM must be taken down, but it will not be easy. In federal employment, it will require reform of Title VII of the CSRA to foster union-management participation instead of hindering it. Similarly, state bargaining laws and state and local civil service rules and regulations that impede PDM must be amended. For example, rigid position classification schemes and archaic work rules should be eliminated to enhance flexibility, adaptation, and responsiveness, and performance appraisal systems should be modified to facilitate employee cooperation, group rewards, team building, and decentralized decision processes. It is important that legalized procedural reforms not threaten job security. Employees treated as disposable assets and periodically confronted with the prospect of losing their jobs will not likely commit themselves to the sustained effort necessary for participative program success. Agency managers at all levels, and particularly in lead personnel units, have a key role to play in educating political officials and lobbying for needed statutes, regulations, and attitudinal changes. A fundamental adjustment in organizational and work culture is required, and it will not come quickly or easily.

Instead of becoming fossilized in the face of change, unions need to do well what they do best: collectively express the voices of those whom they represent (Freeman and Medoff 1984). In order to attract, retain, and effectively represent members, unions must do a better job of identifying and meeting the needs and desires of a rapidly changing work force, including participation in organizational decisions. In short, the unions must remain relevant. As suggested above, where unions are not present or recognized in state and local settings, perhaps they should be fostered by federal or state enabling legislation or by voluntary recognition by employers.

Cooperative, participative labor-management relations should not automatically be perceived by the unions as a threat. Empirical research implies the existence of a basic foundation for cooperative labor-management relations. Employees can be loyal and committed to both their organization and to their union (Gallagher and Clark 1989). Where workers view the relationship between their union and their employer as positive, commitment to each tends to be elevated (Angle and Perry 1986, Levine 1991: 112, Kochan, Katz, and Mower 1984). Such "dual loyalty" may be enhanced through employee involvement schemes, which, in turn, boost job satisfaction (Verma and McKersie 1987, Conlon and Gallagher 1987, Gallagher and Clark 1989, Clark 1989).

The change in work culture demanded by PDM may seem overwhelming at first, but a wide assortment of trust-building, cooperation-inducing interventions are proven and readily available. Arising largely from the organizational development (applied behavioral science) tradition, these techniques use such strategies as fact-finding, feedback, and confrontation to stimulate frank problem solving among adversarial and warring factions. Common examples include process consultation (essentially a structured problem-definition and goal-setting exercise), "organizational mirror" strategies (which are intended to get combatants to understand and respect each others' perspectives), and team-building approaches (ranging from "role analysis/negotiation" to "responsibility charting"). Quality of work life approaches can also help overcome skepticism and cynicism (Kochan, Katz, and Mower 1984: 8–9). All of these interventions have identical objectives: to enhance interpersonal trust and communication among all organizational citizens. As such, OD has scored many successes (and quite a few failures) as the techniques have been refined and applied in different settings (French and Bell 1984, Neilsen 1984). In all possible instances and approaches, unions should be directly involved as full partners in program design and implementation.

Of course, for every new story of successful PDM, there is probably one of failure. Unfortunately, a comprehensive, empirical assessment of participative labor-management cooperation efforts has not been conducted in government. Many individual experiments have been reported and analyzed (Herrick 1983, U.S. Department of Labor 1983, U.S. OPM 1990), but the vast majority have gone unreported. The U.S. Department of Labor's (Bureau of Labor-Management Relations) initially promising effort to serve as an informational clearinghouse and resource for cooperative programs has suffered from a lack of top-level support and currently faces termination by OMB and/or Congress.

Clearly, such a clearinghouse and analytic function are called for to evaluate accumulating successes in PDM and to disseminate findings, so that one jurisdiction can learn from another's experiences. Just as important is the need for technical assistance to government employers and unions determined to develop participative programs. If leadership does not soon emerge from the federal government, then perhaps an existing interstate organization will step forward. For their part, scholars could contribute significantly by empirically examining the purported linkages between participative decision making, personal benefits, and organizational outcomes.

Increased experimentation in labor-management participation provides a rare and interesting opportunity for the public interest to be served. By fostering a new cooperative spirit between public management and public employers, organizational democracy becomes a natural extension of dominant societal values, and represents a promising new chapter in the American democratic experience.

References

Angle, Harold and James L. Perry, 1983. "Organizational Commitment." *Work and Occupation,* vol. 10 (2), pp. 123–146.

———, 1986. "Dual Commitment and Labor Management Relations Climates." *Academy of Management Journal,* vol. 29 (1), pp. 31–50.

Anthony, William, 1978. *Participative Management.* Reading, MA: Addison-Wesley.

Armstrong, T.B., 1971. "Job Content and Context Factors Related to Satisfaction for Different Occupational Levels." *Journal of Applied Psychology,* vol. 55, pp. 57–65.

Bacharach, Samuel B., Joseph B. Shedd, and Sharon C. Conley, 1988. "School Management and Teacher Unions: The Capacity for Cooperation in an Age of Reform," *41st Annual Proceedings of the IRRA,* pp. 60–69.

Bateman, Thomas and Dennis Organ, 1983. "Job Satisfaction and the Good Soldier: The Relationship Between Affect and Employer 'Citizenship.'" *Academy of Management Journal,* vol. 26 (December), pp. 587–595.

Bennis, Warren, 1966. *Changing Organizations.* New York: McGraw-Hill.

Brock, William E., 1987. "Labor and Management Must Forge New Partnership." *Journal of State Government,* vol. 60 (January/February), pp. 3–5.

Buchanan, Bruce, 1974. "Building Organizational Commitment: The Socialization of Manager at Work." *Administrative Science Quarterly,* vol. 19 (December), pp. 533–546.

Carnevale, David G. and Barton Wechsler, 1992. "Trust in the Public Sector: Individuals and Organizational Determinants." *Administration and Society,* vol. 23 (February), pp. 471–494.

Clark, Paul F., 1989. "Determinants of the Quality of Union-Management Relations: An Exploratory Study of Union Members' Perceptions." *Journal of Collective Negotiations,* vol. 18 (2), pp. 103–115.

Conlon, E.J. and D.G. Gallagher, 1987. "Commitment to Employer and Union: Effects of Membership Status." *Academy of Management Journal,* vol. 30 (1), pp. 151–162.

Cooke, William N., 1989. "Improving Productivity and Quality Through Collaboration." *Industrial Relations,* vol. 28 (Spring), pp. 299–319.

———, 1990. "Factors Influencing the Effect of Joint Union-Management Program in Employee-Supervisor Relations." *Industrial and Labor Relations Review,* vol. 43 (July), pp. 587–603.

———, 1992. "Product Quality Improvement Through Employee Participation: The Effect of Unionization and Joint Union-Management Administration." *Industrial and Labor Relations Review,* vol. 46 (October), pp. 587–603.

Cotton, John L., 1993. *Employer Involvement: Methods for Improving Performance and Work Attitudes.* Newbury Park, CA: Sage Publications.

Crisci, Pat E., Joseph M. Giancola, and Cynthia A. Miller, 1987. "Win/win, Effective Schools and Reform: An Agenda for the 1990s." *Government Union Review,* vol. 8 (Winter), pp. 1–24.

Davis, Keith, 1972. *Human Behavior at Work.* New York: McGraw-Hill.

Dawson, Irving O., 1991. "New Approaches to Collective Bargaining and Workplace Relations: Do They Work?" Paper presented at the Annual Meeting of the American Political Science Association, Washington, DC: August 29-September 1.

Deming, W. Edwards, 1986. *Out of the Crisis.* Cambridge: MIT Press.

Fisher, Roger and William Ury, 1981. *Getting to Yes.* New York: Penguin Books.

Freeman, Richard B. and James L. Medoff, 1984. *What Do Unions Do?* New York: Basic Books.

French, Wendell and Cecil H. Bell, 1984. *Organizational Development.* Englewood Cliffs, NJ: Prentice-Hall.

Frost, C., J.H. Wakeley, and R.A. Ruh, 1974. *The Scanlon Plan for Organizational Development.* East Lansing: Michigan State University Press.

Gabris, G.T. and M. Kenneth, 1986. "Personnel Reforms and Formal Participation Structures: The Case of Biloxi Merit Councils." *Review of Public Personnel Administration,* vol. 7 (Summer), pp. 99–114.

Galbraith, Jay, 1973. *Designing Complex Organizations.* Reading, MA: Addison-Wesley.

Gallagher, David G. and Paul F. Clark, 1989. "Research on Union Commitment: Implication for Labor." *Labor Studies Journal,* vol. 14 (Spring), pp. 52–71.

GERR Special Report, 1990. *Employee-Management Cooperation in the Federal Service: A Selective Look.* Washington, DC: Bureau of National Affairs.

Goodman, Paul S., 1980. "Realities of Improving the Quality of Work Life: Quality of Work Life Projects in the 1980s." *Proceedings of the 1980 Spring Meeting.* Philadelphia: April 16–18, 1980, Madison, WI: Industrial Relations Research Association, pp. 487–494.

Griffin, Ricky, 1988. "Consequences of Quality Circles in an Industrial Setting: A Longitudinal Assessment." *Academy of Management Journal,* vol. 31 (2), pp. 338–358.

Grunenberg, M.M., 1979. *Understanding Job Satisfaction.* New York: Wiley.

Hanlon, Martin, 1985. "Unions, Productivity, and the New Industrial Relations: Strategic Considerations." *Interfaces.* (May/June), pp. 48.

Hasegawa, Keitaro, 1986. *Japanese-Style Management: An Insider's Analysis.* Tokyo: Kodansha International, Ltd.

Hatch, Orrin, 1987. "U.S. Labor Law and the Future of Labor-Management Cooperation." *Labor Law Journal,* vol. 38 (January), pp. 53–62.

Herrick, Neal Q., ed., 1983. *Improving Government: Experiments With Quality of Working Life Systems.* New York: Praeger.

Herzberg, Frederick, 1968. "One More Time: How Do You Motivate Employees?" *Harvard Business Review,* vol. 46 (January/February), pp. 53–62.

Holzer, Marc, 1988. "Productivity In, Garbage Out: Sanitation Gains in New York." *Public Productivity Review,* vol. I (Spring), pp. 37–51.

Kelley, Maryellen R. and Bennett Harrison, 1992. "Unions, Technology, and Labor-Management Cooperation." In Lawrence Mishel and Paul Voos, eds., *Unions and Economic Competitiveness.* Washington, DC: Economic Policy Institute, pp. 247–285.

Klein, Gerald D., 1986 "Employee-Centered Productivity and QWL Programs: Findings From and Area Study." *National Productivity Review* (Autumn), pp. 345–364.

Kochan, Thomas A., 1987. "Strategies for Sustaining Innovations in U.S. Industrial Relations." *Journal of State Government,* vol. 60 (January/February), pp. 30–35.

Kochan, Thomas A., Harry C. Katz, and Nancy R. Mowrer, 1984. *Worker Participation and American Unions: Threat or Opportunity?* Kalamazoo, MI: Upjohn Institute.

Kolarska, L. and H. Aldrich, 1980. "Exit, Voice, and Silence: Consumers' and Managers Responses to Organizational Decline." *Organizational Studies* (March), pp. 41–58.

Lawler, Edward E. and J.R. Hackman, 1969. "Impact of Employer Participation in the Development of Pay Incentive Plans." *Journal of Applied Psychology,* vol. 53 (6), pp. 467–471.

Levine, Marvin J., 1991. "Legal Obstacles to Union-Management Cooperation in the Federal Service." *Labor Law Journal,* vol. 42 (February), pp. 103–110.

————, 1992. "Labor and Management Response to Total Quality Management." *Labor Law Journal,* vol. 43 (February), pp. 107–116.

Likert, Rensis, 1961. *New Patterns of Management.* New York: McGraw-Hill.

Lincoln, James R., 1989. "Employee Work Attitudes and Management Practices in the U.S. and Japan: Evidence from a Large Comparative Survey." *California Management Review* (Fall).

Lobel, Ira B., 1992. "Labor-Management Cooperation: A Critical View." *Labor Law Journal* (May), pp. 281–289.

Locke, E.A. and D. Schweiger, 1979. "Participation in Decisiion-Making: One More Look," In B. Staw, ed., *Research in Organizational Behavior.* Greenwich, CT: JAI Press.

Marks, M.L., P.H. Mirvis, E.J. Hackett, and J.F. Grady, 1986. "Employee Participation in a Quality Circle Program." *Journal of Applied Psychology,* vol. 71, pp. 61–69.

Marrow, Alfred J., 1972. *The Failure of Success.* New York: AMACOM.

Marshall, Ray, 1992. "The Future Role of Government in Industrial Relations." *Industrial Relations,* vol. 31 (Winter), pp. 31–49.

Maslow, Abraham, 1954. *Motivation and Personality.* New York: Harper and Row.

McCarthy, William, 1985. "The Role of Power and Principle in 'Getting to Yes.'" *Negotiations Journal* (January), pp. 59–66.

McClelland, David, 1953. *The Achievement Motive.* New York: Appleson-Century-Crofts.

McGregor, Douglas, 1960. *The Human Side of Enterprise.* New York: McGraw-Hill.

Miller, X.I. and P.R. Monge, 1986. "Participation, Satisfaction, and Productivity: A Mem-Analytic Review." *Academy of Management Journal,* vol. 29 (4), pp. 727–753.

Mohrman, Susan A. and Edward E. Lawler, 1988. "Participative Managerial Behavior and Organizational Change." *Journal of Organizational Change Management,* vol. I (1), pp. 45–59.

Morris, James and Richard Steers, 1980. "Structural Influences on Organizational Commitment." *Journal of Vocational Behavior,* vol. 17, pp. 50–57.

Neilsen, Eric H., 1984. *Becoming an OD Practitioner.* Englewood Cliffs, NJ: Prentice-Hall.

Ouchi, W., 1981. *Theory Z.* Reading, MA: Addison-Wesley.

Patchen, Martin, 1970. *Participation, Achievement, and Involvement on the Job.* Englewood Cliffs, NJ: Prentice-Hall.

Pfeffer, Jeffrey, 1978. *Organizational Design.* Arlington Heights, IL: AHM.

Porter, Lyman, 1968. *Management Attitudes and Performance.* Homewood, IL: Irwin.

Reisman, Barbara and Lance Compa, 1985. "The Case for Adversarial Unions." *Harvard Business Review* (May–June), pp. 27–30.

Rosenbloom, David H., 1989. "The Federal Labor Relations Authority." *Policy Studies Journal,* vol. 17 (Winter).

Schachter, Hindy Lauer, 1989. "Win-win Bargaining: A New Spirit in School Negotiations." *Journal of Collective Negotiations,* vol. 18 (1), pp. 1–8.

Schwarz, Roger, 1990–91. "Participative Decision Making and Union-Management Cooperative Efforts." *Review of Public Personnel Administration,* vol. 11 (Fall), pp. 38–54.

Steers, Richard, 1977. "Antecedents and Outcomes of Organizational Commitment." *Administrative Science Quarterly,* vol. 22 (March), pp. 46–56.

Straw, Ronnie J. and Charles C. Heckscher, 1984. "QUs: New Working Relationships in the Communication Industry." *Labor Studies Journal,* vol. 8 (Winter), pp. 261–274.

Swiss, James E., 1992. "Adapting Total Quality Management in Government." *Public Administration Review,* vol. 52 (July/August), pp. 356–362.

Thomann, Daniel A. and Donald E. Strickland, 1992. "Managing Collaborative Organizations in the 90s." *Industrial Management,* vol. 34 (August), pp. 26–29.

U.S. Department of Labor, 1983. *Resource Guide to Labor-Management Cooperation.* Washington, DC: U.S. Government Printing Office.

U.S. General Accounting Office, 1991. *Federal Labor Relations: A Program in Need of Reform.* GAO/GGD-91–101. Washington, DC: U.S. Government Printing Office.

U.S. Office of Personnel Management [OPM], 1990. *Federal Labor Management Relations: A Guide to Resources.* Washington, DC: U.S. Government Printing Office

Verma, Anil and Robert B. McKersie, 1987. "Employee Involvement: The Implications of Noninvolvement by Unions." *Industrial and Labor Relations Review,* vol. 40 (July), pp. 556–568.

Volcker, Paul, 1989. *Leadership for America: Rebuilding the Public Service.* Lexington, MA: Lexington Books.

Vroom, Victor, 1964. *Work and Motivation.* New York: Wiley.

Walton, Richard E. and Robert B. McKersie, 1965. *A Behavioral Theory of Labor Negotiation.* New York: McGraw-Hill.

Wexley, Kenneth and Gary Yukl, 1977. *Organizational Behavior and Personnel Psychology.* Homewood, IL: Irwin.

White, James J., 1984. "The Pros and Cons of 'Getting to Yes.'" *Journal of Legal Education,* vol. 34 (March), pp. 115–124.

PART 9

CRITICAL DEVELOPMENTS IN PUBLIC SECTOR LABOR RELATIONS

A critical issue that persists in the field of public sector labor relations is the conflict between seniority systems and equal employment and affirmative action policies. Unions have historically supported and collectively bargained for the use of seniority as a criterion for such employment decisions as promotions and layoffs. However, given the fact that systematically, women and people of color are the last to enter most workforces—due to discrimination—they systematically lack seniority. Hence, they are the first to be laid off and are last on the list for promotions. Despite this incongruity, unions continue to push for seniority systems, mainly because they are viewed by unions as an objective way to make employment decisions.[1] While the U.S. Supreme Court has upheld the use of affirmative action in promotion decisions (see *Johnson v. Transportation Agency, Santa Clara County*[2]), the Court has been unwilling to support the use of affirmative action when bona fide seniority systems are in place (see *Wygant v. Jackson Board of Education*[3]).

In "'Last Hired, First Fired' and Public Employee Layoffs: The Equal Employment Opportunity Dilemma," Robert Roberts addresses the issue of layoffs and seniority systems prior to the U.S. Supreme Court's *Wygant* decision. He begins by pointing to the employment progress that women and people of color began making in the 1960s and 1970s, after contemporary civil rights laws were passed. He then illustrates how seniority or "last hired, first fired" systems threaten to erode this progress.

Wilbur Rich, in "Bumping, Blocking, and Bargaining: The Effect of Layoffs on Employees and Unions," provides a case study of events surrounding the 1981 fiscal crisis in Detroit, Michigan. Rich points to various concessions (e.g., around wage increments) the union made in order to avoid layoffs, which would have adversely affected the least senior workers, viz., women and people of color.

In the final selection here, Joan Pynes examines another critical issue to labor relations in government: adjudication of union or management actions by courts and labor relations boards. Pynes looks at the patterns of decisions made by state courts and public employee relations boards across the country, specifically around the scope of bargaining. Her analysis shows that decisions by these bodies have expanded the scope of mandatory items of bargaining to include such topics as class size, drug testing, and smoking in the workplace. These topics have traditionally been seen as nonmandatory items of bargaining, or management prerogatives.

Notes

1. However, some evidence shows that unions have manipulated seniority systems when women or people of color stood to benefit from seniority policies. See, Norma M. Riccucci, *Women, Minorities and Unions in the Public Sector* (Westport, CT: Greenwood Press, 1990).

2. 480 U.S. 616 (1987).

3. 476 U.S. 267 (1986).

Additional Classics

Barnum, Darold T. and Edward L. Suntrup. "Multilateral Labor Relations in the Public Sector: Citizen Involvement." 5 *Review of Public Personnel Administration*, 2: 56–69, Spring 1985.

Chandler, Timothy and Peter Feuille. "Municipal Unions and Privatization." 51 *Public Administration Review*, 1: 15–22, January/February 1991.

Loney, Timothy J. "Formal Discussions in Federal Labor Relations: A Case of Goal Deflection." 45 *Public Administration Review*, 5: 609–615, September/October 1985.

Perry, James L. "The 'Old Testament': A Litany of Beliefs About Public Sector Labor Relations—Introduction." 5 *Review of Public Personnel Administration*, 2: 1–4, Spring 1985.

Perry, James L. and Carder W. Hunt. "Evaluating the Union-Management Relationship in Government." 38 *Public Administration Review*, 5: 431–436, September/October 1978.

Riccucci, Norma M. and Carolyn Ban. "The Unfair Labor Practice Process as a Dispute-Resolution Technique in the Public Sector: The Case of New York State." 9 *Review of Public Personnel Administration*, 2: 51–67, Spring 1989.

Seroka, Jim. "The Determinants of Public Employee Union Growth." 5 *Review of Public Personnel Administration*, 2: 5–20, Spring 1985.

Stanley, David T. "Trying to Avoid Layoffs." 37 *Public Administration Review*, 5: 515–517, September/October 1977.

West, Jonathan P. and Richard C. Feiock. "Support for Sunshine Bargaining in Florida: A Decade Later." 9 *Review of Public Personnel Administration*, 2: 28–50, Spring 1989.

Wurf, Jerry. "Merit: A Union View." 34 *Public Administration Review*, 5: 431–434, September/October 1974.

CHAPTER 40

"LAST HIRED, FIRST FIRED" AND PUBLIC EMPLOYEE LAYOFFS

The Equal Employment Opportunity Dilemma

ROBERT N. ROBERTS

Introduction

During the 1960s and 1970s, public employees made substantial gains in pay levels and other types of employee benefits. In fact, the level of pay for certain public sector personnel has caused debate over whether public employee compensation has exceeded the ability of the governments to pay (Pierce 1975:1199). Yet, the most important non-monetary benefit of public employment has been the job security provided to the majority of civil servants at the local, state, and federal levels. Since the depression, public service employment has grown steadily, particularly within state and local governments. The growth in government has insulated public employees from the recession-induced layoffs that periodically hit the private sector. When cuts in government expenditures have occurred, the majority of public employers have used hiring freezes, attrition, and early retirement incentives to avoid employee layoffs.

Recent trends indicate that the unwritten rule of no public employee layoffs is becoming an anachronism for a period of deepening financial problems for government at all levels. As efforts to slow the growth of government expenditures continue, public employers will find it increasingly difficult to avoid the layoff of some employees (Stanley 1977; Slack and Weisshaar 1976).

The education community has been the first to experience necessary layoffs. Large numbers of teachers in school districts across the country have been laid off because of declining enrollments at the elementary and secondary school levels (*U.S. News and World Report* 1976:65). Many of those laid off entered the teaching profession with the expectation that their positions would be secure as long as they satisfactorily performed their assigned responsibilities.

From 2 *Review of Public Personnel Administration*, 1: 29–48, Fall 1981. Copyright © 1981 Sage Publications. Reprinted with permission.

During the 1960s and the 1970s, significant progress has also been made in the area of equal employment opportunity for minorities and women. Over the last two decades, numerous statutes, executive orders, and administrative regulations have been enacted or issued to prohibit discrimination in employment because of race, color, religion, sex, or national origin.[1] Besides the more prominent provisions of Title VII,[2] other statutory grounds have proved effective in ending employment discrimination by state and local governments.[3]

In addition to the trends of fiscal austerity and the drive to end discriminatory employment practices in both the private and public sectors, the increase in the size and power of public employee unions has made collective bargaining the most important means of resolving disputes over the level of compensation for public employees. Following the practice of private sector unions, public employee unions have directed their resources towards obtaining better monetary and non-monetary benefits. Of the non-monetary benefits, the awarding of seniority, providing job security to those employees with the longest service, has been regarded as one of the most important.

Briefly, seniority is the measure of time an employee accrues with an employer. A seniority system contains "rules of when and how to apply this measure of time" (Weiner 1980:440). Both public and private employee unions have regarded negotiated seniority provisions an essential element of any comprehensive collective bargaining agreement. The rule of "last hired, first fired" determines the order in which employees receive layoff notices. As the phrase implies, those hired last are laid off or furloughed first. Accordingly, the longer an individual stays with one employer, the less likely it is that the employee will receive a pink slip.[4]

The Equal Employment Opportunity Dilemma

Through the mid-1960s legal commentators, civil rights groups, and public and private employee unions raised a few questions regarding the use of seniority as the basis of making employee layoffs. Employers and employee unions regarded seniority systems as a fair and equitable way of deciding what employees would lose their jobs. But within a few years of the enactment of Title VII of the 1964 Civil Rights Act, legal scholars began to raise questions about the impact of the "last hired, first fired" rule on equal employment opportunity programs.[5] At first, these writers directed their attention to the effects of seniority systems on the promotion opportunities for minorities and women (Cooper and Sobal 1969). They expressed concern that promotion systems based on the seniority of employees would unfairly discriminate against minorities recently hired pursuant to affirmative action plans.[6]

Subsequently, other writers shifted their attention to the impact of the "last hired, first fired" rule on the long-term success or failure of Title VII to eliminate discriminatory employment practices. They argued that the strict application of seniority for purposes of layoffs had a disproportionate impact on minorities and women, since they were the last to be hired. In other words, the operation of the seniority system perpetuated the effects of previous employment discrimination. Employees recently hired had little opportunity to build up sufficient seniority to avoid being laid off during periodic downturns in the economy. Years of effort to increase the representation of women and minorities could be wiped out in a few months.

Title VII and the Bona Fide Seniority System

Supporters of seniority-based layoffs directed the attention of critics to section 703(h) of Title VII:

> Notwithstanding any other provisions of (Title VII), it shall not be an unlawful employment practice for an employer to apply different standards of compensation, or different terms, conditions, or privileges of employment pursuant to a *bona fide seniority* or *merit system*. . . provided that such differences are not the result of an intention to discriminate because of sex. . .

The language of 703(h) and its legislative history tend to support the interpretation that Congress intended to immunize otherwise neutral seniority systems from attack even if such systems tended to perpetuate the effects of past discriminatory employment practices. However, Congress failed to provide much guidance on what it meant by a *bona fide* seniority system. Critics of this interpretation of 703(h) argued the Congress could not have intended to permit the continuation of employment practices that institutionalized the effects of past discrimination.[7]

Through the early 1970s the debate over the meaning of 703(h) remained basically an academic exercise. But the recession of 1974–1975 brought home the reality of the "last hired, first fired" rule to millions of workers.[8] The recession had a particularly severe impact on minorities and women who had entered the labor force as the result of increased employment opportunities brought about by the enforcement of equal employment opportunity laws. Not unexpectedly, many of those laid off brought suit to block the layoffs on the grounds that the seniority systems operated to perpetuate the effects of past discrimination and therefore violated Title VII.[9]

While the 1974–1975 recession did not directly affect the operations of state and local governments, the financial crisis that rocked the foundation of the City of New York demonstrated that public employees were not immune from large-scale layoffs. In response to the financial crisis, the City of New York laid off thousands of employees during the spring and summer of 1975. As part of these layoffs, some 2,500 police officers received pink slips. The New York Civil Service Law requires that employees hired last be laid off first in event of a reduction in force.[10] The same requirement was contained in the contracts negotiated with the police officers' bargaining representatives.

The layoffs had a devastating impact on women and minority police officers of the New York Police Department. The action reduced the number of women on the police force by 73.5 percent. It required the discharge of only 23.9 percent of male police officers. Of the male police officers released, a significant number were black or Hispanic. Shortly thereafter, women and minority police officers brought suit to block the layoffs (*Acha v. Beame* 1975).

The layoff of significant numbers of minorities and women in the private and public sectors shifted the debate over the scope of 702(h) to the federal courts. It is the purpose of this article to examine the developments regarding the legal status of neutral seniority systems allowed to operate in such a manner as to throw a disproportionately large percentage of women and minorities out of work. There is still much confusion about the authority of the federal courts to modify seniority systems to prevent the layoff of certain classes of employees. This confusion remains, notwithstanding a number of important decisions by the United States Supreme Court on the meaning of 703(h).

This article will also suggest how the courts might apply existing legal theory to a number of different types of layoff situations.[11] Although the law dealing with employee layoffs has changed significantly over recent years, it is important for public administrators to familiarize themselves with current application of the appropriate case law on the subject.

The Legal Setting of Equal Employment Opportunity Litigation in the Public Sector

Before the litigation surrounding the application of the "last hired, first fired" rule is reviewed, it is essential for the reader to understand that employment discrimination suits may be brought on a number of different constitutional and statutory grounds. The existence of multiple causes of action, thus, complicates employment discrimination litigation involving both the private and public sectors.

Title VII of the 1964 Civil Rights Act

Students of equal employment opportunity programs and public administration are familiar with Title VII of the 1964 Civil Rights Act and the 1972 amendments to the legislation. Title VII prohibits employment discrimination on the basis of race, color, religion, sex, or national origin. With the passage of the Equal Employment Opportunity Act of 1972, all government employees were brought within the coverage of Title VII. Hence, Title VII provides civil remedies for acts of employment discrimination by either public or private employers.

The Civil Rights Acts of 1866 and 1871

Long before the passage of the 1964 Civil Rights Act and the Equal Employment Opportunity Act of 1972, Congress sought to prevent state officials and private citizens from depriving other citizens of their civil rights (Brooks 1977). The Reconstruction Acts of 1866 and 1871 have provided individuals with a number of effective weapons against employment discrimination; namely, sections 1981 and 1983 of Title 42 of the United States Code. However, neither section 1981 nor section 1983 expressly prohibits employment discrimination.

Nonetheless, the courts have interpreted section 1981 as protecting an individual's right to contract from racial discrimination.[12] In addition, a Supreme Court decision in 1975 upheld the position of a number of federal courts that section 1981 and Title VII created separate and independent causes of action.[13] In other words, it is possible to use section 1981 or Title VII or both to redress discriminatory hiring practices involving racial discrimination.[14]

Section 1983 makes it unlawful to deprive "'under color of state law' any person of rights guaranteed by the Constitution or other statutory right" (Noble 1979:49). The most important characteristic of section 1983 is that it does not provide a specific cause of action. The cause of action arises from the violation of a constitutional or statutory right. With respect to the area of employment discrimination, the action of a state or local official "under color of state law" that deprives an individual of the opportunity to "ply one's trade may constitute a violation of the individual's right to due process under the Fifth and Fourteenth Amendments of the Constitution" (Brooks 1977:270). In addition, "either section 1981 or Title VII can satisfy the operative cause of action requirement for section 1983" (Brooks 1977:270).

Although Title VII is available as a remedy for employment discrimination based on race, sex, religion, or national origin, there are reasons for bringing a suit for employment discrimination under section 1981 or 1983. First, Title VII requires claimants to exhaust a series of administrative steps with the Equal Employment Opportunity Commission before bringing a Title VII action to the federal courts. In contrast, the Reconstruction statutes do not require the exhaustion of other administrative remedies. Second, Title VII contains two time limitations of Title VII actions.[15] Action brought pursuant to section 1981 or 1983 must meet only the time limitation imposed by the appropriate state statute of limitations.[16] Third, and more important to the issue of seniority systems, the remedies for violations of Title VII are limited to equitable relief and back pay. The Civil Rights statutes permit the awarding of compensatory and punitive damages as well as equitable relief.[17]

In sum, any discussion of the legality of the operation of the "last hired, first fired" rule must take into consideration the existence of multiple grounds for challenging different employment practices as discriminatory. Therefore, it may not be possible to modify the layoff provisions of a seniority system as part of an action based upon Title VII. Yet, a court may find that it has sufficient equitable powers in actions brought under section 1981 or 1983. The legality of seniority-based layoffs that have a disproportionate impact upon minorities and women remains uncertain as a result of the availability of this "full arsenal" of statutory weapons for employment discrimination litigation.

The Supreme Court and the Bona Fide Seniority System

As noted, the Senate added 703(h) to Title VII in response to fears that Title VII would destroy existing seniority rights. Senators Clark and Case, responsible for leading the fight for the passage of Title VII, placed an interpretive memorandum in the Congressional Record to allay fears that Title VII would alter existing seniority rights (*Congressional Record* 1964:7213). The memorandum stated that Title VII would not affect established seniority rights.

A number of years later, the Supreme Court in *Griggs v. Duke Power Company* (1971) held that "under (Title VII), practices, procedures, or tests neutral on their face, and even neutral in terms of intent, cannot be maintained if they operate to 'freeze' the status quo of prior discriminatory employment practices." In other words, the courts had the responsibility to evaluate the impact of employment practices on those groups who had been subject to employment discrimination. If those practices acted to perpetuate the effects of past discrimination, they could not be maintained.

The language of the *Griggs* decision created a serious dilemma for the lower federal courts. On the one hand, 703(h) and its legislative history appeared to insulate *bona fide* seniority systems from Title VII suits. On the other hand, the *Griggs* decision said that employment practices could not be maintained if they acted to "freeze" the *status quo* of prior discrimination.

Relying on the *Griggs* interpretation of Title VII, those laid off argued that the court should award them "retroactive seniority" to compensate them for damages caused by the discriminatory employment practices of their employers. The advocates of the "rightful place" remedy reasoned that "but for" the prior discrimination they would have been hired many years earlier. With the added years of service, they would have accumulated sufficient seniority to prevent their layoffs. An award of retroactive seniority would be an equitable way of compensating those women and minorities who had experienced the discrimination.

During 1975, a number of lower federal courts reached conflicting decisions on the authority of the courts to award retroactive seniority and on the issue of who would be eligible for such awards.[18] In July of 1976, Judge Duffy of the United States District Court for the Southern district of New York held that the layoff of women police officers did not violate their civil rights. The court pointed to the fact that Section 2000e-2(j) of Title 42 of the United States Code did not allow "any employer. . . to grant preferential treatment to any individual or to any group because of sex" (*Acha v. Beame* 1975). In addition, Judge Duffy noted that Section 80 of the New York Civil Service Law required that layoffs be made on the basis of seniority.

On appeal, the United States Court of Appeals for the Second Circuit reversed the district court's ruling on the awarding of retroactive seniority (*Acha v. Beame* 1976). In holding that the district court erred in apparently concluding that because of section 703(h) layoffs under the facially neutral formula of section 80 of the New York Civil Service Law could not violate Title VII, the United States Court of Appeals concluded that the federal courts had broad equitable powers to fashion remedies to restore "aggrieved persons to (a) position where they would have been had there not been unlawful discrimination" (*Acha v. Beame* 1976).

The Court of Appeals proceeded to detail the rule that it would apply in determining which female police officers were entitled to retroactive seniority:

> If a female police officer can show that, except for her sex, she would have been hired early enough to accumulate sufficient seniority to withstand the current layoffs, then her layoff (violates Title VII) (Acha v. Beame 1976).

The decision placed the burden on the laid-off police officer to show that she had attempted to gain employment or had expressed interest in a position with the police department before any award of retroactive seniority may be made.

A short time after the Second Circuit Court reached its decision in the case of *Acha v. Beame*, the Supreme Court ruled on the issue of the legality of awarding retroactive seniority. In *Franks v. Bowman Transportation Company* (1976), the Court upheld the authority of the federal courts to award retroactive seniority under limited circumstances.

Equally important, the court reaffirmed the authority of the courts to fashion equitable remedies to eliminate the effects of past discrimination:

> We are of the view, however, that the result which we reached today, which, standing alone establishes that a sharing of the burden of the past discrimination is presumptively necessary, is entirely consistent with any fair characterization of equity jurisdiction, particularly when considered in the light of our traditional view that 'attainment of a great national policy. . . must not be confined within narrow canons' for equitable relief deemed suitable by chancellors in ordinary private controversies (*Franks v. Bowman Transportation* 1976:777–778).

In answering the question of which employees might qualify for awards of retroactive seniority, the Court followed a pattern of reasoning similar to that relied upon by the Second Circuit in the *Acha* case. It limited relief to "identifiable parties" who could provide evidence that they would have been hired "but for" the discriminatory employment practices of the employer (*Franks v. Bowman* 1976). The Court did not accept the argument of the plaintiffs that the entire class of minority employees should receive back seniority.

The *Franks v. Bowman* decision left unanswered two important questions. First, did the authority to award retroactive seniority extend to the period of time before the effective date of Title VII of the 1964 Civil Rights Act (private employees) and the Equal Employment Opportunity Act of 1972? Second, did Title VII permit substantial modification of a neutral seniority system beyond that of the awarding of retroactive seniority to identifiable parties? The Court answered both these questions in the 1977 case of *International Brotherhood of Teamsters v. United States* (1977).

The Court held that 703(h) immunized *bona fide* seniority systems from direct challenge even if the system perpetuated the effects of pre-Act discrimination. Specifically, it held that "an otherwise normal, legitimate seniority system does not become unlawful simply because it may perpetuate pre-Act discrimination" (Weiner 1980:438). In other words, the court accepted the argument that Congress had intended to protect existing seniority systems from Title VII litigation as long as the post-Act seniority systems "applied equally to all races and locked in whites as well as blacks" and women (Weiner 1980:438). If a seniority system applied equally to all employees, then it qualified as a *bona fide* seniority system under the language of 703(h).

At the same time, the decision made it clear that retroactive seniority would be available only to job applicants who sought relief from an employer's post-Act hiring discrimination. As applied to public employees, it meant that only those individuals hired after March 24, 1972, fell within the class eligible for an award of back seniority. The decision did not alter the burden on the employee to show that "but for" the employee's sex or race the employee would have been hired at some time after March 24, 1972. Evidence that discriminatory hiring practices took place prior to March 24, 1972 would not justify a court's awarding retroactive seniority to compensate the employee for the discrimination that occurred prior to the effective date of the Equal Employment Opportunity Act of 1972. The decision effectively limited the availability of "rightful place" relief.

The Implications of Franks and Teamsters for Public Sector Reductions in Force

The decisions of the Supreme Court in *Franks v. Bowman* and *International Brotherhood of Teamsters v. United States* have important implications for public sector reductions in force and for equal employment opportunity programs. The most immediate impact of the decisions was to force a number of federal courts to reconsider their treatment of 703(h) and their awards of back seniority.[19]

What does the recent clarification of the status of *bona fide* seniority systems mean for local governments faced with the prospect of laying off significant numbers of public employees? How will the courts be likely to view such layoffs if they result in the dismissal of disproportionate number of minorities and women? The following hypothetical fact patterns will provide illustrations of the practical effect of these decisions with respect to action brought under Title VII. They do not apply to actions brought pursuant to other statutes available to redress acts of employment discrimination.

Example One

Assume that city X has been an equal employment opportunity employer since the early 1960s. However, the percentage of women and minorities employed remained fairly low through the early 1970s. But after 1972 the city showed significant progress in recruiting those groups previously underrepresented on the employment rolls of city agencies and departments. Early in 1982, City X faces a severe financial emergency resulting from a sharp drop in funds from a number of different federal categorical grant programs. After failing to find additional revenues to make up the projected shortfall, the mayor and city council agree that it is necessary to make across-the-board cuts in personnel except in the city's police department. The collective bargaining agreements previously negotiated with the public employee unions require that the layoffs be made on the basis of seniority in each of the departments.

The resulting layoffs reduced the percentage of women in city departments by 50 percent and of minorities by 70 percent. It reduced the percentage of white males by only 20 percent. If the women and minorities brought suit to stop the layoffs, the courts would have to decide which of the laid-off employees were entitled to an award of retroactive seniority.

According to the test laid down by the Court in *Franks* and *Teamsters*, it is unlikely that any of the laid-off employees would prevail in the courts.

First, any award would be limited to discriminatory employment practices taking place after March 24, 1972. Second, the facts as presented indicate that City X had not been guilty of a Title VII violation either before or after the effective date of the Equal Employment Opportunity Act of 1972. Arguably, the seniority system operated by City X had a disproportionate impact upon minorities and women. Yet, there is no indication that the seniority system operated to perpetuate the effects of past discrimination. Thus, it is improbable that any of the laid-off employees could show that "but for" prior employment discrimination they would have been hired at some earlier point in time.

Example Two

Assume that City Y administered general knowledge examinations for most city openings through 1969. Subsequent analysis showed that there was little correlation between the examinations and job performance. The city used these examinations to put together employment eligibility lists. Through February 1972, city departments used these eligibility lists to make civil service appointments. Minority applicants fared poorly in obtaining appointments under the general examinations. After strong criticism from a number of community groups, the city scrapped its existing examinations and replaced them with new tests. With the introduction of the new tests and the commitment of the city to a program to increase the percentage of minorities in city departments, the number of minorities on the city payroll increased dramatically between 1972 and 1981.

In December 1981, the state legislature voted to cut sharply state aid to local governments. The city manager realized that the loss of state aid would put the city in a precarious financial situation. Looking for ways to cut city expenditures, the city manager opened talks with the three principal public employee unions to determine whether they would agree to pay cuts to prevent the possible layoff of a number of union members. The unions refused any reduction in salary or fringe benefits. At the recommendation of the city manager, the city council approved a 15 percent reduction in expenditures. The plan included a 10 percent reduction in the city workforce immediately. The resulting layoffs reduced the number of minority employees 75 percent and of white male employees 15 percent. The laid-off minority employees filed a complaint with the Equal Employment Opportunity Commission and subsequently filed suit in federal district court to stop the layoffs. How would a court rule, if faced with this type of controversy?

Applying the *Franks* and *Teamsters* decisions to the fact pattern in this case, a court would not have the authority to block the operation of the seniority system as the basis for determining which employees received pink slips. The decisions did not prohibit the awarding of "retroactive seniority." Since the city had adopted valid selection procedures prior to March 24, 1972, those hired after that date would not qualify for an award of retroactive seniority. This rule applies regardless of the fact that the operation of the seniority system after March 24, 1972 may perpetuate the effects of the discrimination that took place before the city replaced its examination early in 1972.

Example Three

Under a third set of facts, City Z has a long history of resisting outside pressures to increase the number of women and minorities in city government. The city argued that its selection procedures adequately measured the qualifications of applicants and the city departments employed so few minorities and women because they failed to score high enough to qualify for city positions. In June 1975, a group of minority and women applicants sued the city to have its selection procedures declared illegal and to force the city to replace the selection practices with others that would not have a disproportionate impact upon minorities and women. Before the suit reached trial, the city agreed to introduce new selection procedures and to try to recruit minorities and women for new openings. At the time of this agreement only 4 percent of the personnel of the police department were women, and only 2 percent were minorities. By January 1975, the city had completed revamping its selection procedures for the police department and had begun an active minority recruitment program. The reform had immediate results. By October 1980, the percentage of women increased from 4 percent to 8 percent, and of minorities from 2 percent to 6 percent.

Shortly thereafter, a state initiative was approved by the voters, mandating a sharp drop in property taxes collected by local governments. In an effort to make up the loss of revenues, the mayor supported an increase in the city income tax. That recommendation failed in a special election to gain the support of the majority of city residents. Since the state constitution requires that all cities operate with a balanced budget, the mayor prepared a reduced budget calling for substantial pay cuts for all city employees or drastic reductions in staff. The unions representing teachers agreed to a temporary reduction in pay and fringe benefits. However, the employees association representing police officers refused to accept pay reductions and informed the mayor that he would have to lay off employees. Subsequent layoffs of police officers brought the percentage of women down to 4 percent and of minorities, to 2 percent. The layoffs eliminated the gains that had been made between 1975 and 1980.

How would the women and minority police officers fare if they went to court to stop the layoffs in an action based upon Title VII?

As noted in the previous two examples, the *Franks* and *Teamsters* decisions authorize the award of back seniority on an individual basis. The *Teamsters* decision limited such awards to post-Act discrimination. When dealing with layoffs of public employees, the federal courts are bound as of March 24, 1972, the effective date of the Equal Employment Opportunity Act of 1972. Consequently, the court would be permitted to make awards of retroactive seniority to those police officers who could show that "but for" the discriminatory hiring practices of City Z, they would have been hired at an earlier date.

The facts provide evidence that the hiring practices of City Z violated Title VII through January 1975. Hence, the class of police officers hired after January 1975 might qualify for awards of back seniority if they can show that they would have been hired at an earlier point in time.

Certain kinds of admissible evidence might be used to meet the burden of proof required for an award of back seniority. The *Franks* decision and the opinions of a number of lower courts support the position that other evidence besides that of an employment rejection may be sufficient to meet the "but for" burden of proof. Specifically, proof that an employee had filed an application for employment, had written a letter complaining about the hiring practices of the city, or was declared by public statement to have been deterred from seeking employment with the employer may be sufficient to meet the plaintiff's burden.

Finally, the award of retroactive seniority may still not be sufficient to block the layoff of the minority and women police officers. The fact that an individual receives back seniority means only that the position of the individual changes on the seniority ladder used for determining the order of layoffs. Unless the employee moves high enough on the ladder to bump another employee lower, the layoff will still be permitted under the *Franks* and *Teamsters* decision.

Summary: Title VII and Public Employee Layoffs

The preceding examples explain the application of the law regarding public employee layoffs and Title VII of the 1964 Civil Rights Act and, in particular the meaning of 703(h) and its exemption for *bona fide* seniority systems. Recent Supreme Court decisions leave little doubt about the treatment of neutral seniority systems that may appear to perpetuate the effects of past discrimination. In sum, Title VII has proven to be an effective weapon against an employment discrimination, but it is the position of the Supreme Court that Congress believed that established seniority system should be immune from challenge under the provisions of Title VII.

Challenges to Seniority-Based Layoffs on Other Statutory Grounds

The fact that the Supreme Court holds that a Congress intended to immunize neutral seniority systems from challenge under Title VII does not preclude bringing action on other statutory or constitutional grounds to block the operation of the "last hired, first fired" rule. As discussed earlier, Sections 1981 and 1983 provide independent grounds to redress discrimination in employment. Accordingly, the decisions in *Franks* and *Teamsters* immediately raised questions about whether the reasoning applied to Title VII action also applies to suits brought pursuant to 1981 and 1983. The unsettled nature of the law at this point makes it difficult to answer this question with certainty. Nevertheless it is important to be aware of the implications of the use of these alternate statutory grounds to bypass the road block established by the present interpretation of 703(h).

As to the issue of the application of 703(h) to 1981 actions, two Courts of Appeals have reached different conclusions. In *Johnson v. Ryder Truck Lines Inc.* (1977), the Fourth Circuit held that facially neutral seniority systems that perpetuated the effects of pre-Act discrimination do not violate Section 1981 (*Johnson v. Ryder Truck Lines* 1979). In making its determination, the Court relied upon an interpretation of a 1976 civil rights statute, Section 1988. Part of that statute requires that federal courts enforce the civil rights statute "in conformity with the laws of the United States . . ." (42 U.S.C. 1988). The Court reasoned that failure to apply the *Teamsters'* limitations on 703(h) to 1981 action would violate the language of Section 1988.

The Fifth Circuit has also held that a *bona fide* seniority system is not subject to attack under Section 1981. It concluded that the congressional decision to immunize *bona fide* seniority systems from attack by its inclusion of 703(h) in Title VII made it apparent that Congress could not have intended to permit a similar challenge under another decision. The words of the decision read:

> Assuming as we must, that Congress intended section 703(h) to accord absolute protection to pre-Act seniority rights which accrued under *bona fide* seniority systems, Congress could not have intended such rights to remain subject to revision under section 1981 (*Pettway v. American Cast Iron Pipe Co.* 1978:1192).

A number of commentators have strongly criticized the application of the 703(h) limitation to section 1981 employment discrimination actions.[20] They point out that the courts have recognized the independent character of 1981 and the other Reconstruction Era civil rights statutes. Without specific evidence in the legislative history of Title VII or Section 1988, it was inappropriate for the courts to limit the remedial relief available to the federal courts when dealing with the problem of eliminating the effects of past discrimination.

In contrast to the two decisions cited above, the Court of Appeals for the Third Circuit rejected the theory that 703(h) limitations applied to remedial relief available under section 1981 actions (*Bolden v. Pennsylvania State Police* 1978). The case involved a series of complaints charging the Commonwealth of Pennsylvania with racial discrimination in the hiring and promotion practices of the State Police.[21] Subsequently, a consent judgment was entered that required the State Police to take a number of steps to end discriminatory hiring and employment practices. As part of the consent judgment, the Court ordered the state to end the practice of using seniority as a criterion for promotion and directed the awarding of retroactive seniority to a significant number of minority applicants. A short time after the Supreme Court decisions in *Franks* and *Teamsters*, the Fraternal Order of Police and other groups representing non-minority police officers asked the federal district court to modify significant elements of the consent judgment previously entered by the district court. In upholding the denial of the request for intervention, the Court of Appeals addressed the issue of the applicability of the *Franks* and *Teamsters* decisions to actions brought under section 1981:

> But the statute involved in the three recent decisions, Title VII of the Civil Rights Act of 1964, was not the predicate for relief in the case. Before we could find those three cases relevant here, we would have to impute to the second session of the Eighty-eighth Congress the intention to circumscribe the remedial powers of the federal courts under sections 1981, 1983, 1985, and 1988. We find nothing in *Franks v. Bowman Transportation Co.*, *International Brotherhood of Teamsters v. United States*, or *United Airlines, Inc., v. Evans* to support such a construction of 703(h) of Title VII (*Bolden v. Pennsylvania State Police* 1978:921).

The *Bolden* Court was not prepared to imply that Congress had intended to limit remedial relief for actions brought pursuant to the Civil Rights statutes.

It remains to be seen whether the Supreme Court will extend the limitation of 703(h) to neutral seniority systems challenged under section 1981.

Besides the issue of the scope of 703(h) with respect to section 1981, a recent decision has raised the question of the impact of the *Franks* and *Teamsters* decisions on 1983 actions (*Brown v. Neeb* 1981). As stated earlier, a complaint "starting a section 1983 cause of action must allege, in addition to jurisdiction, a deprivation, under color of state law, of rights, privileges, or immunities secured to the plaintiff by the Constitution or federal law" (Brooks 1977:269).

Recent years have seen a dramatic increase in the use of section 1983 to provide citizens with a remedy against unconstitutional acts by state and local officials acting under color of state law.[22] As part of the expanded use of 1983 to deal with the violation of federal statutory and constitutional rights, the federal courts have become increasingly involved in the fashioning of remedies to eliminate the effects of unconstitutional acts by state and local officials. The fashioning of school desegregation plans, the action of the federal courts to improve conditions in prisons and mental hospitals, and other simi- lar remedial steps have involved the federal courts in the day-to-day administration of government programs.

The authority of the federal courts to fashion remedial relief for violations of 1983 was dealt with by the Court of Appeals for the Sixth Circuit. In August 1972, black and Hispanic plaintiffs filed suit against the city of Toledo, alleging that the employment policies and practices of the city's fire department violated the civil rights of the plaintiffs under 42 U.S.C. 1981 and 1983 and the United States Constitution (*Brown and Neeb* 1981). Other plaintiffs brought suit against the Toledo Police Department, alleging that the department was guilty of discriminatory employment practices (*Sarbabia v. Duck* 1977). In a third suit, black and Hispanic police officers challenged the promotion prac- tices of the Police Department as discriminatory (*Afro-American Patrolman's League v. Duck* 1973).

Early in 1973, Judge Young of the Northern District Court of Ohio found that the Toledo Police Department was guilty of discriminatory employment and promotion practices. Shortly thereafter, the city of Toledo and the plaintiffs involved in the three suits moved to find a solution to the suits without further litigation. On November 27, 1974, all the parties to the suits signed a consent decree, which Judge Young approved. The city agreed to begin the process of validating its examinations and to submit a comprehensive plan for affirmative recruitment to the court within ninety days. In addition, the decree specified that it would be the goal of the city to recruit a sufficient number of blacks and Hispanics to "reasonably reflect the ratio of each minority group to the total population of the City of Toledo" (*Brown v. Neeb* 1981:555). Under the provisions of the consent decree, the city agreed to meet this goal within a period of five years.

For a number of reasons, the city made little progress between 1973 and 1977 in its effort to recruit substantial numbers of minorities for the fire department. [Table 40.1] details the recruitment efforts of the fire department.

The present controversy arose as the result of a serious financial crisis that hit the city in March 1980. Anticipating a short-fall in revenues of some $3.7 million, "the city manager ordered a 7 percent cut in the budget of every department except the police department" (*Brown v. Neeb* 1981:556). These severe budget cuts led the city to layoff 61 firefighters. The collective bargaining agreement with the firefighters' union and Ohio law required that layoffs be made strictly on the basis of seniority. As described by the court, the layoffs had a devastating effect on minority firefighters and on the affirmative action program of the city:

> The layoffs had a devastating effect on the slow progress which the Toledo fire department had made toward integration. As a result of the layoffs, nearly one-half of the blacks and Hispanics hired since the consent decree was entered were laid off. The percentage of black firefighters in the department fell to 5.48 percent; the percentage of Hispanic firefighters fell to 0.78 percent (*Brown v. Neeb* 1981:557).

Understandably, the affected minority firefighters asked the District Court to enjoin the layoff of minority firefighters on grounds that they violated the terms of the consent

Table 40.1

Toledo Fire Department Recruitment 1973–1980

Date	Authorized number of uniformed personnel	Breakdown by race		
		White	Black	Hispanic
1/1/73	546	536	10	
		98.16%	1.83%	
1/1/74	567	543	22	2
		95.76%	3.88%	0.36%
1/1/75	583	553	26	4
		94.85%	4.46%	0.69%
1/1/76	566	529	33	4
		93.46%	5.83%	0.71%
1/1/77	576	540	32	44
		93.75%	5.56%	0.69%
1/1/78	576	537	33	66
		93.23%	5.73%	1.04%
1/1/79	576	532	37	7
		92.30%	6.43%	1.22%
1/1/80	572	523	42	7
		91.43%	7.34%	1.22%

decree. After a hearing to consider the argument of the minority firefighters, the city, and the firefighter's union, Judge Young issued a preliminary injuction to enjoin the city from reducing the number of minority firefighters below 8.21 percent black and 1.22 percent Hispanic.

On appeal, the Court of Appeals upheld the action of Judge Young in issuing the preliminary injunction against the layoffs. But two questions are raised: How did the Court of Appeals reconcile the decision of the district court with the *Teamsters* and *Franks* decisions? And why did the court accept the reasoning of Judge Young that the court had the authority to enjoin the layoffs?

In the first place, the Sixth Circuit accepted the argument that the consent decree entered into by the plaintiffs and the City of Toledo could be treated as an enforceable contract. As a result, "the district court retained broad authority to make sure that nothing interfered with the implementation of the consent decree" (*Brown v. Neeb* 1981:559). The court placed great weight on the fact that it regarded the consent decree as imposing an affirmative duty on the city of Toledo to eliminate the effects of its prior discriminatory employment practices. Specifically, it argued that the city of Toldeo had agreed to the consent decree as a way of avoiding further litigation.

Moving to the difficult question of reconciling the injunction with the *Teamsters* decision, the court emphasized the differences between Title VII and 1983 actions. In a brief, but extremely important paragraph, the court made it clear that it accepted Judge Young's position that the *Teamsters* decision did not strip the federal courts of their equitable powers under section 1983:

> Nor do we believe that *Teamsters* mandates a different result. In *Teamsters* the court held that a *bona fide* seniority system was immune to attack under Title VII of the Civil Rights Act of 1964, even if it perpetuated past discrimination . . . (We) do not think that *Teamsters* can bar relief sought to remedy constitutional violations under 1983, or under a consent decree. While a *bona fide* seniority system may not itself violate the law, such a system cannot be allowed to obstruct remedies designed to overcome past discrimination (*Brown v. Neeb* 1981:564).

This opinion leaves little doubt that at least one Court of Appeals believes that a federal court responsible for eliminating the effects of unconstitutional employment discrimination is not required to apply the *Teamsters* line of reasoning to actions brought under section 1983. It is too soon to predict whether the interpretation adopted by the Sixth circuit will be accepted by other federal courts and the United States Supreme Court.

The Law, Public Employee Layoffs, and Equal Employment Opportunity: Implications for the Future

The preceding discussion has summarized recent developments in the law relating to the conflict between the application of the "last hired, first fired" rule and its impact upon equal employment opportunity programs in the public sector. Up to this point, relatively few public employers have worked to avoid laying off employees unless other alternatives proved unworkable. Yet, present trends lead to the conclusion that units of government will increasingly face the prospect of using employee layoffs as a way to make significant cuts in expenditures.

While critics of the "last hired, first fired" rule have suggested that alternatives to seniority-based layoffs be used more frequently by employers in both the private and public sectors, there is little indication that the most frequently mentioned alternatives will gain wider acceptance.[23]

In the first place, public employee unions have strongly resisted attempts by local governments to accept pay or benefit cuts in lieu of the layoff of union members. In the second place, recommendations that layoffs be based on the performance and qualifications of the employees have been tried by only a few public employees and have met strong resistance from public employee unions (Johnson 1980).

At the same time, as local governments continue the process of cutting back services and programs, competition for public sector jobs will increase. Equally important, with fewer job openings, it will be more difficult to increase the number of minorities and women in government. Thus, the subject of public employee layoffs has important implications for the future of affirmative action programs in government.

In sum, the litigation surrounding the impact of the "last hired, first fired" rule on employment discrimination cases and on the operation of equal employment opportunity programs has thrown the federal courts into debate over the extent of the national commitment to end employment discrimination in both the private and public sectors. While the decisions of the Supreme Court in the *Franks* and *Teamsters* cases have helped to clarify the status of *bona fide* seniority systems under Title VII, a number of other important questions remain unanswered. More important, the prospect of increased layoffs by public employers is likely to aggravate the controversy over the impact of layoffs on minorities and women. Regardless of future developments in the law, the debate over the operation of the rule of "last hired, first fired" will continue during this period of government retrenchment.

Notes

1. See, for example. Back Pay Act of 1966, 5 *U.S.C.* 5596 (1970), as amended, 5 *U.S.C.* 5596 (Supp. V, 1975); Federal Anti-discrimination in Employment Act, 5 U.S.C. 1751–1752, 7154 (1970), as amended, 5 *U.S.C.* 7152, 7154 (Supp. V, 1975); Title VII of the Civil Rights Act of 1964, 42 *U.S.C.* 2000e to 2000e-15 (1970), as amended. Equal Employment Opportunity Act of 1972, 42 *U.S.C.* 2000e to 2000e-17 (Supp. V, 1975).

2. See 42 *U.S.C.* 2000e to 2000e-17 (Supp. V, 1975).

3. See sections 1981 and 1983 of Title 42 of the *United Slates Code*.

4. It is important to note that procedures for reductions in force vary among public employers.

For example, the federal government does not use the strict application of the "last hired, first fired" rule for determining employee layoffs.

5. Note, *Harvard Law Review* (1967); *North Carolina Law Review* (1968); *Texas Law Review* (1969) and *Rutgers Law Review* (1969).

6. For a more comprehensive discussion of this issue see, *Georgia Law Review* (1975).

7. See *Harvard Law Review* (1975).

8. See, for example, *Business Week* (1974:166); *Business Week* (1975:51); *Time* (1975:58) and *U.S. News and World Report* (1975:73).

9.See *Watkins v. United States Steel Workers of America, Local 2369* (1975); *Franks v. Bowman Transportation Co.* (1974) and *Jersey Central Power and Light Co. v. Local Union 327* (1975).

10. See Section 80 of the New York Civil Service Law, McKinney (1973).

11. These examples apply only to suits brought pursuant to Title VII and not sections 1981 or 1983.

12. See *Jones v. Alfred H. Mayer Co.* (1965).

13. See *Johnson v. Railroad Express Agency, Inc.* (1975).

14. While state and local government employees may bring employment discrimination suits either under 1981 or Title VII, the Supreme Court in *Brown v. General Services Administration* (1976), held that Title VII was the exclusive remedy for discrimination suits by federal employees.

15. A charge must be filed with the EEOC within 180 days of the "unlawful act" and the plaintiff must file within 90 days of the time when the EEOC receives the complaint.

16. Depending upon the state in which the action is brought, the statute of limitations for a tort contract, or state civil liberties action may be applied to the suit by the federal court.

17. The recent decision of the United States Supreme Court in *Newport News v. Facts* (1981) held that local governments are immune from "punitive damages" that go beyond compensating the victim for injuries caused by the constitutional violations by a local government.

18. Decisions upholding the award of retroactive seniority included *Watkins v United Steel Workers of America, Local 2369* (1975); *Franks v. Bowman Transportation Co.* (1974). Decisions not permit-

ting the award of retroactive seniority include *Jersey Central Power and Light Co. v. Local Union 327* (1974); *Waters v. Wisconsin Steel Works* (1974).

19. See *Guardians Association v. Civil Service Commission* (1979); *Acha v. Beame* (1977) and *Acha v. Beame* (1978).

20. See *Harvard Law Review* (1980).

21. The action claimed that the hiring and promotion practices of the State Police violated the Thirteenth and Fourteenth Amendments to the Constitution and 42 *U.S.C.* 1981, 1982, 1985(3), and 1988.

22. See *Harvard Law Review* (1977).

23. See *University of Pennsylvania Law Review* (1976).

References

Acha v. Beame (1975). 401 *F. Supp.* 816.

———— (1976). 531 *F. 2d* 656.

———— (1977). 438 *F. Supp.* 70.

———— (1978). 570 *F. 2d* 57.

Afro American Patrolman's League v. Duck (1973). 366 *F. Supp.* 1095.

Back Pay Act of 1966 (1970). 5 *U.S.C.* 5596.

Bolden v. Pennsylvania State Police (1978). 378 *F. 2d* 912.

Brooks, R. L. (1977). "Use of the Civil Rights Acts of 1866 and 1871 to Redress Employment Discrimination." *Cornell Law Review* 62 (January).

Brown v. General Services Administration (1976). 425 *U.S.* 820.

Brown v. Neeb (1981). 644 *F. 2d* 551.

Business Week (1974). "Last Hired, First Fired, Takes It On The Chin." (March 9).

———— (1975). "Women: Last In, First Out in Detroit." (February 16).

———— (1975). "Seniority Squeezes Out Minorities In Layoffs." (May 5).

Civil Rights Act of 1964: Title VII (1970). 42 *U.S.C.* 2000e-15.

Equal Employment Opportunity Act of 1972 (1975). 42 *U.S.C.* 2000e-17 (Supp. V).

Franks v. Bowman Transportation Co. (1976) 495 *F. 2d* 398.

Georgia Law Review (1975). "The Problem of Last Hired, First Fired: Retroactive Seniority As A Remedy Under Title VII." Vol. 9.

Guardians Association v. Civil Service Commission (1977). 431 *F. Supp* 526.

———— (1979). 466 *F. Supp.* 1273.

Harvard Law Review (1967). "Title VII, Seniority Discrimination, and the Incumbent Negro." Vol. 80.

———— (1969). "Seniority and Testing Under Fair Employment Laws: A General Approach to Objective Criteria of Hiring and Promotion." Vol. 82.

———— (1975). "Last Hired, First Fired, Layoffs and Title VII." Vol. 88.

———— (1977). "Development in the Law: Section 1983 and Federalism." Vol. 90.

———— (1980). "Development in the Law: Civil Rights, Civil Liberties." Vol. 15 (Spring).

Jersey Central Power and Light Co. v. Local Union 327 (1975) 508 *F. 2d* 637.

Johnson, S.M. (1980). "Performance-based Staff Layoff In The Public Schools: Implementation and Outcomes. *Harvard Education Review* 50 (May): 214–33.

Johnson v. Railroad Express Agency, Inc. (1975). 421 *U.S.* 454.

Jones v. Alfred H. Mayer Co. (1965). 392 *U.S.* 409.

Newport News v. Facts (1981). No. 80-396 (June 26).

New York Civil Service Law (1973). Section 80.

Noble, A.A. (1979). "Civil Rights—An Analysis of section 1983 and Title VII: A Comparative Strategy." *Trial Lawyer's Guide* 23.

North Carolina Law Review (1968). "Comment, Layoffs and Title VII: The Conflict between Seniority and Equal Employment Opportunities." Vol.46.

Pettway v. American Cast Iron Pipe Co. (1978). 576 *F. 2d* 1157.

———— (1979). 440 *U.S.* 1115.

Pierce, N.R. (1975). "Federal-State Report/Public Worker Pay Emerges as Growing Issue." *National Journal* 7.

Rutgers Law Review (1969). "Seniority and Equal Employment Opportunity: A Glimmer of Hope." Vol. 23.

Sarbabia v. Duck (1977). 601 *F. 2d* 914.

Slack, W.E. and M.G. Weisshaar (1976). *"Reduction in Force: A Guide for the Unitiated."* George *Washington Law Review* 44 (May): 642–676.

Stanley, D.T. (1977). "Trying to Avoid Layoffs." *Public Administration Review* 37 (September/October): 515–517.

Texas Law Review (1969). "Seniority and the Black Worker: Reflections on Quarles and Its Implications." Vol. 47.

Time (1975). "Who Gets The Pink Slip? Conflict Between Ban on Hiring Discrimination and Layoffs." (February 3).

University of Pennsylvania Law Review (1976). "Work Sharing As An Alternative to Layoffs by Seniority, Title VII Remedies in Recession."

CHAPTER 41

BUMPING, BLOCKING, AND BARGAINING

The Effect of Layoffs on Employees and Unions

WILBUR C. RICH

Introduction

Layoff statistics alone, depressing as they are, don't fully tell the story of the anguish and uncertainty now faced by hundreds of public employees. Their's is a story of first time unemployment, overqualification in an unstable job market, resentment toward the arbitrariness of the seniority system, and disillusionment with unions' inabilities to save their jobs. Recession layoffs have penetrated their civil service security and have exposed them to career uncertainties. Many young employees feel betrayed and older employees are asked to work twice as hard to cover the losses in manpower. Although layoffs in the public sector are not new, the current round of staff reductions comes at a time when American taxpayers blame big government for the sluggishness of the economy, waste, corruption and the general breakdown of society. Blaming public employees for what ails the country is also not new. What is new is the virulent tone of the accusations. The growth of government has been slowed by these attacks. It is unlikely that the number of public employees will ever reach the high point of the seventies. We are now in an era of cutback management.

Cities are particularly affected by these new attitudes and trends. Of the nation's 2.4 million city employees, "full time government workers decreased 49,000 (2.4 percent) and part-time workers decreased by nearly 43,000 (8.7 percent) from October 1980 to October 1981" (U.S. Bureau of the Census 1981:1). As the government closest to the people, cities are first to encounter the wrath of the public. However, the voice of the electorate is often contradictory. On the one hand it seems to want less government and fewer city employees; on the other hand it demands no cuts in services. Many taxcutting crusaders believe that the way to reduce personnel cost is to refuse to pay higher taxes. The myth is that cities can be forced to provide the same services with fewer resources. Fewer resources mean the reduction of bus schedules, fire and police department personnel, and

From 4 Review of *Public Personnel Administration*, 1: 27–43, Fall 1983. Copyright © 1983 Sage Publications. Reprinted with permission.

garbage collections. These reductions in services are realities in American cities. Faced with continuing revenue problems, the city is caught on the horns of a layoff dilemma. If it reduces the workforce then it must reduce more services. The revenue saved by a pared down workforce will not solve the cities' cash flow problems. Hence the taxpayer will be asked to pay more for less services. The deterioration of services triggers more middle class flight and lessens a city's chances of diversifying a limping economy.

This article will analyze the problems associated with the use of layoffs as a cutback management strategy. Examined are the impact of layoffs on employees, unions, job market behavior, affirmative action, and productivity. In addition, the paper attempts to develop a typology of the phases of layoffs in cities. Lastly, it will suggest conditions under which the response by elected officials to cut back management is more likely to be effective.

Detroit: A City in Transition

As one of the nation's largest urban centers, Detroit is also a classic example of the decline of the Midwest as an important American manufacturing region. The domestic auto industry, once the staple of the city, now finds itself challenged by foreign imports, high interest rates, and unstable gas prices. Detroit, which has been losing population to the suburbs for years, is now losing its skilled workers to other parts of the country. The reversal of these economic trends is a recurrent theme in city politics.

Below the apparent themes of Detroit lie the hidden themes of city politics. Black succession to elective office and city department directorships is the most controversial. The new black elite, like their counterpart in the earlier ethnic takeover of cities, is understandably self-conscious. Just as the white Yankee Protestants used the media to question and attack the Irish and Italian-Catholic ascendancy to power in the 19th century, today's white suburbanites subject black powerwielders to second-guessing and criticism. Although the minority white voters generally support the mayor's policy, many do not share the ethnic pride shown among black voters.

The other unspoken theme is the city's tough residency law. This ordinance forces city workers to live in Detroit. Many white public employees feel trapped below Eight Mile Road (city limits). As the city changes, the once white-only neighborhoods have become integrated. The pressure of more black neighbors has caused some white flight for those who do not work for the city (Wurdock 1981). In 1970 there were 838,877 whites; now there are 444,730. The black population actually increased from 660,428 to 758,939.[1] Although at-large election assures white representation on the city council, their political influence in the city has diminished. However, there is no evidence of a systematic effort to force the whites out of the police and fire departments, a favorite career choice among white job seekers. High ranking white bureaucrats and department heads have not been pressured to retire early to make room for blacks, nor has the city affirmative action program been shelved until after the fiscal crisis.

The political and racial transition often upstages the important population changes in the city. Although it can still boast a population with 1,203,339 residents and a city workforce of 19,600, these statistics belie the profound demographic transformation of Detroit. The city has lost 20.5 percent of its population since 1970.[2]

An inevitable correlate of these population losses has been elimination of approximately 6,000 city employees' jobs. The continual attrition of city employees has created a zero-sum environment in various city departments. Losses of personnel have become permanent as the city budget office has been forced to reduce personnel costs.

Despite federally mandated and funded programs which justify some agencies requesting more personnel, manpower has not grown substantially. Unfortunately, with each new federal administration, the government has been interested in different programs. Accordingly, department administrators have been unable to depend upon federal funds. The result has been an uneven growth of city bureaucracies. Table 41.1 shows selective major city department change from 1972 to 1982.

Table 41.1 shows "no growth" in the city planning department and a decline in growth in the housing department. Although these data are selective, they are consistent with budget data which indicate not only shifts in manpower but also reveal that there was attrition of city personnel preceding the onset of the 1981 fiscal crisis. In fiscal year 1972–73 the city had 25,519 employees; now it has approximately 6,000 less. In 1972 the city budget, minus state and federal dollars, was 6 million dollars. The fiscal 1982–83 budget was 1.5 billion dollars which includes grant funding. Salaries and wages alone account for a total of approximately $500 million of the total budget. Pension and fringe benefits come to a total of $300 million. As a result, personnel costs account for 55 percent of the city budget.[3] Although attrition reduced the number of employees, the cost of maintaining the extant city employees did not decrease. The cost of personnel remained high because of what economists called a monopsony. The labor market in Detroit is dominated by

Table 41.1

Selective Department Personnel Changes, 1972–1982

Departments	1972/3 Staffing	1982/3 Staffing	Percent Change
Budget	37	30	−18.9
Treasury	159	101	−36.4
Fire	1,557	1,733	+11.3
Police	6,276	4,802	−23.4
Park & Recreation	1,382	1,161	−15.9
Economic Development	210	305	+45.2
Planning*	49	49	0
Personnel	104	135	+29.8
Water	1,788	2,068	+15.6
Sewerage**	177	1,466	+728.2
Law Department	80	108	+35.0
Housing Department	522	398	−23.7

Source: City of Detroit Budget Office.

*There are actually two planning departments, the City Planning Department and the City Planning Commission with an additional staff of 12.

**The Department of Water and Sewerage is now a single agency the automobile industry, which traditionally has maintained high wage levels. When the industry was at its peak in the seventies, it raised the cost of labor for the entire region. The city of Detroit had to raise its wages to be competitive with the private sector and allow its workers to keep up with the cost of living. Responding to the job market, wages for city workers continued to increase until the late seventies. Wages are now frozen as a result of the 1980 negotiations. It could be argued that city wages have tracked the automobile industry so closely that an industry slowdown was a harbinger of bad news for city workers.

Layoffs and the Marketplace

Economists who monitor unemployment in the private sector find that reduction in force is a cyclical phenomenon which responds to shifts in the marketplace. When the demand for goods is down some workers become redundant. The supply of labor exceeds the demand. Firms resort to layoffs to reduce labor cost and redirect capital to other parts of the organization. To remain competitive, firms reorganize and retool to meet the new market realities. Mortenson (1978) argues that the latter strategy allows the employer to search for more appropriate workers, i.e., a better match between the firm's needs and the worker's skills.

Human capital theory and search theory hold that workers have different opportunities in the marketplace.[4] The skill of a computer programmer has a higher market value than that of an assembly line auto worker, although they may be receiving similar incomes. The computer programmer has more mobility and opportunity for advancement in the marketplace, whereas the assembly worker has few options and a limited search pattern. According to these theories, layoffs and resignations can be explained as a marketplace phenomenon. Workers in the public sector, although insulated from the market forces in past recessions, are now exposed to shifts in the economy. The market is forcing the city to make manpower choices consistent with new service needs and new technologies. The city no longer needs the types and numbers of workers it now employs. The recession may be viewed as an opportunity for housecleaning and gearing up for the new economic realities. The dissent to this argument comes from Martin Feldstein (Feldstein 1976:938). He argues:

> Most workers remain with a single firm for a very substantial period even though they may experience frequent spells of temporary unemployment. Most of those who are laid off know that they will soon return to their employer protected by seniority arrangements and by their job specific human capital. For them, the theory of job search is largely irrelevant. Moreover, in contrast to search theory, it is the employers who determine the duration of these individuals' spells of unemployment.

The Feldstein argument seems to be supported by the Detroit experience. City employees are among the most optimistic about the possibility of recall and department manpower expansion. Few laid-off workers take jobs in other fields and many quit temporary jobs to resume working for the city. Worker loyalty may be explained by the city's liberal working conditions, salaries, and benefits. These items, according to Howard Becker

(1960) constitute an individual's investment in the organization. The degree of organizational commitment is proportional to the amount of investment or what Becker calls *side bets*. These side bets serve as a disincentive for members to leave the organization. The individual often finds that "side bets have been made for him by the operation of impersonal bureaucratic arrangements." Union contracts and state pension laws further lock the employee into the personnel system. The longer one remains in the civil service system, the more one invests. In time, resignation and job switch become too costly. If the investment is heavy, the individual will view organizational decline in personal terms and may often interpret it as a test of his or her commitment. Albert Hirschman (1970:78) offers an alternative explanation for employee loyalty under conditions of organizational relapse. He argues that such actions, e.g. expressions of optimism and dedication, are more than an act of faith. Employee loyalty under conditions of pending cut-backs and organizational decline may be considered a *reasoned calculation*. According to Hirschman, relatively uninfluential city employees might draw support for the collective plight of all city residents, rich and poor. This attitude may account for the often heard refrain: "Detroit is our city, surplus or elicits." Hirschman (1970:78) argues that the "possibility of influence is in a fact cleverly intimated in the saying by the use of the possessive 'our.' The intimation of some influence and the expectation that, over a period of time, the right turns will more than balance the wrong ones, profoundly distinguishes loyalty from faith." For Hirschman, loyalty serves to keep a crippled organization from experiencing precipitous decline. Leaving (exit) is delayed, speaking out (voice) exercised in hope of reform from within. Indeed, many city workers have psychological attachments to the workplace and the community. These attachments are especially helpful to the city in retaining young, highly skilled workers. In sweeping the nation, the recession protected Detroit from personnel raids by other cities. However, the continuing recession has had a debilitating on the city's cash flow situation.

The 1981 Fiscal Crisis, Attrition, and Layoffs

The 1981 Detroit fiscal crisis was a watershed in the city's history. The recession and continued decline of the auto industry produced a devastating effect on expected tax revenue. In January, 1981, Mayor Coleman young established a blue-ribbon committee to study the city's finances and to make recommendations for changes. The Secrest Committee Report, named after its Chairman, Fred Secrest, a retired businessman, found that the city had an accumulated deficit forecasted at $132.6 million as of June 30, 1981. The report recommended that the city issue medium term notes to cover the immediate cash flow problem. The report also recommended an increase in the city income tax rate for both residents and nonresidents. Finally, the report suggested freezing wages, salaries, and benefits for all city employees. Upon receipt of the report, the mayor moved quickly to implement the recommendations. To alleviate the city deficits the mayor proposed the following plan: 1) city residents were asked to vote themselves a one percent increase (from 2 percent to 3 percent for residents and from .5 percent to 1.5 percent for nonresidents in city income tax rate); 2) the unions were asked to give up scheduled wage increments for fiscal years 1982 and 1983; and 3) the city asked state permission to issue 5-year Budget Stabilization Bonds for $113 million. These actions followed a previous city decision to turn over the Detroit Municipal Hospitals to a new hospital authority and the Detroit Recorders Court to the state court system. The city also eliminated all 100 percent federally funded (e.g. CETA) jobs. In July, 1981, the city was able to get 52 of the city's 57 bargaining units to agree to wage concessions. The unions agreed, in return for no layoff, to forego wage increases scheduled for fiscal years 1981, 1982, and 1983. Only the Building Trades Council, which represented construction workers, balked at the agreement and experienced some layoffs. Many city job vacancies were not filled, and all departments were asked to increase productivity. The mayor's plan worked: the city was spared massive layoffs. The Secrest Report had the effect of supporting the mayor's initiative, legitimating and facilitating the wage concession strategy. The cooperation of the major interest groups played a key role in averting the fiscal collapse.

Interest Group Politics and the 1981 Fiscal Plan

At first glance it appears that interest group politics should have remained unchanged as a result of the reprieve from massive layoffs. A closer look at the actions of the mayor and the unions reveals an interesting configuration of Detroit power wielders. The process of obtaining agreements among the various interest groups was less disruptive than a similar crisis in New York City. Among the differences between the two cities are size of the workforce and New York City's tradition of strong independent city department directors. The mayor of Detroit has fewer interest groups with which to negotiate in times of crisis. There are no active civil service reform groups evaluating Detroit's personnel decisions. Detroit public employee organization leaders, unlike their counterparts in New York, are not political kingmakers. These organizations have been preempted in that role by the United Auto Workers (UAW). In a previous study of city politics it was found that the UAW had co-opted the Michigan Democratic party as early as 1948 (Greenstone 1969). Having transformed the party into an ally of the UAW, the union has been able to dominate Wayne County politics. Most of the public employee organizations defer to the UAW and seek to avoid confrontations. This affords the mayor, who has strong UAW support, tremendous leverage against the less powerful public employee unions.

As described by Rich (1982) in *The Politics of Urban Personnel Policy,* the 1975 New York City fiscal crisis changed the staffing calculations of city agency commissioners and heads. The mayor and his staff had a set of goals, policy choices, and audiences that differed from the operating departments. The goal of the mayor was to reduce expenditures to impress the investment community, while department heads wanted to retain services and staff. The conflict between the mayor and agency heads was joined by civil service reformers, agency constituencies (i.e., clients and interest groups), and the unions. Each interest group seemed to have a separate public agenda. The fragmentation of New York City politics forced the mayor to negotiate with various interest groups. This proved to be a time consuming and generally disruptive procedure.

In Detroit the mayor had only to negotiate with the unions. These organizations were in poor bargaining position throughout the fiscal crisis. City workers had good salaries/benefits and were not anxious to enter the job market already saturated with laid off auto workers. Therefore, the mayor could safely organize a rescue package with no fear of rejection by the unions.

Detroit residents, in contrast to their New York counterparts, supported the political positions taken by the mayor and the unions during the fiscal crisis. The Detroit media did not second-guess the mayor, especially after the Secrest Report, nor were citizen groups defending the public interest. Since Detroit had no neutral broker (civil service reformer) to represent other fiscal and personnel options to the public, there was no widely discussed alternative plan to the city plan. Absent any alternatives, the mayor had little trouble selling the fiscal prescriptions needed for the city. The mayor was also helped by private union endorsements of the plan. In a pro-union town such endorsements are usually sufficient to facilitate public approval. Under these conditions Detroit agency heads were left with no policy options other than compliance with mayoral directives and union contracts. They could not take their case to the public or reform groups. Unlike agency heads in the New York crisis, Detroit department chiefs had no highly organized constituency which would support them against the mayor. Ignoring the mayor's directive would have cost the agency heads their positions. The crisis also demonstrated that the locus of political power had not changed with the growth and development of public employee unions.

Union Politics in a Pro-Union City

Detroit, which enjoys relatively good labor relations with its employees, is a city with a rich labor tradition. As a pro-labor city, Detroit residents have generally supported the aims of public sector collective bargaining. This receptive environment allows city officials to maintain labor peace. Although this labor peace was not enough to avoid a fiscal crisis, it played a major role in the mayor's successful fiscal rescue plan.

The largest public employee union is the American Federation of State, County and Municipal Employees (AFSCME) which represents approximately 6,935 employees of the city's 19,600 workers. This big union is the pacesetter for the remaining smaller organizations. Although AFSCME workers are not the highest paid city workers, their numbers make them the key to labor peace. The AFSCME unions were among the first to sign the wage concession agreement. Table 41.2 shows the distribution of workers among the bargaining units.

This type of membership distribution suggests that AFSCME is more powerful politically than it actually is. The leadership of the union has yet to assume a meaningful political presence (i.e., the veto of political candidates). This relatively weak political position belies the fact that AFSCME has been extremely successful as a negotiator. Michigan's liberal labor laws have been one of the reasons for the success of these public employee organizations. However, the combined strength of all of these public employee organizations does not match the UAW political expertise and campaigning skills.

Table 41.2

Major Public Employee Unions in Detroit

Name	Approximate Number of Employees Represented	Percent of Total
AFSCME	6,935	33.3%
Amalgamated Transit Union	1,049	5.0
Teamsters	1,050	5.0
Detroit Police Officers Assn.	2,922	14.0
Detroit Police Lt. & Sgt. Assn.	1,075	5.2
Detroit Firefighters Assn.*	1,396	6.7
Building Trade Council	677	3.3
Other Unions**	2,807	13.5
Non-Union	2,827	13.9
	N = 20,738	

Source: City of Detroit Budget Office. Figure based on 1981 count.
*The Firefighters Union also represents 44 non-uniformed personnel.
**Unions with less than 500 members.

In Detroit, at-large elections of the city council further limit the potential for influence of the public employees. Under a local district system the public employee unions could concentrate their resources in selected districts and thereby compete with the UAW for the loyalty of local politicians. The so called civil service vote does exist but it has not been mobilized. In Detroit, political issues are not framed as pro- or anti-civil service. Instead, the mayor has cast political issues as pro- and anti-Detroit, black versus white, and central city against suburbs. In the 1981 tax vote, the mayor used all three themes to mobilize the yes vote.

The Layoff Process in Detroit

If the mayor's strategy of wage concessions had failed and massive layoffs were needed to prevent a fiscal crisis, then the process of reducing the city's workforce would have unleashed a plethora of bumping and blocking procedures which would have left some departments with mismatched staffs and individuals in positions for which they were overqualified or ill-suited. Employees would have discovered nuances and pitfalls in a perplexing layoff system. Far from being simple, the decision rules for layoffs are among the more complicated rules in the civil service. In fact, for anyone who is not an employee in the certification division of the City Personnel Department, the whole layoff process sounds rather confusing. In Detroit, layoffs are described as "reductions in force which are due to lack of work or lack of funds." Layoffs are further defined "as the removal of employees for reason not due to individual acts or delinquencies." Citywide bumping is defined as the right of an employee with high seniority to displace a lower seniority employee within this title. The bumping rules hold that an individual can only bump someone who holds the same title at the time of layoff. If bumping is impossible then the individual is placed on a blocking list. Individuals on that list have blocking rights (i.e., a right to the job before any other individual) to any vacancies in the civil service in their titles, or any lower titles in their occupational series.

The first type of reduction in force is intradepartmental demotions (i.e., internal bumping) in title series or to former titles. The individual is removed from a position in one class to a lower class. If this occurs the employee has the right to be reconsidered for a higher title and the right to block others in line for that title. A special register or blocking list is maintained for this purpose. These rights continue even if the individual continues to work in a lower title. To retain rehire rights, a laid-off employee must remain a resident of the city of Detroit. A laid-off individual who is a city resident retains his or her blocking rights up to four years. A working city employee retains his or her blocking rights indefinitely.

Section No. 2 of Rule I specifies the order of the layoffs. The first to go are the provisional employees, probationary employees, and limited term employees. In the second round of layoffs, permanent status employees can be laid off in accordance with total city seniority, the least senior employee to be removed first. In most cases total city seniority applies regardless of department location or bargaining unit. The permanent status employee has blocking rights if he or she elects to be demoted to a lower rank in which there are individuals with less seniority. Laid off employees who elect layoff in lieu of demotion go on a preferred eligibility list. This preferred status means the laid-off employee is recertified for the rank held at the time of layoff. If the individual refuses a job offered, then he or she loses the right to remain on the eligibility list. Reemployment is also governed by total city seniority rules (i.e., across city departments). Section 9 empowers the personnel director to void changes of status made by a department to avoid layoffs.[5]

The Sequence of Layoff Development

Layoffs seem to occur in four stages or phases, each with its particular causes and effects. The strategy of the layoff actors also changes in each of the four stages. The environment for negotiation and the prospects for reemployment diminish as a city enters the next stage. In order to understand the sequence of layoffs in cities in general, a typology of the stages of layoffs is outlined as a developmental process.

Phase I. In the first phase, layoffs are threatened in order to achieve concessions from public employee organizations. The need for layoffs can be documented but wage concessions from employees can serve as an alternative to across-the-board layoffs. Unions make wage concessions which have the effect of delaying the "inevitable" for one or two fiscal years. Phase I allows actors—the mayor, personnel directors, and union leaders—to play the role of statesmen, willing to compromise in the spirit of the public interest. Phase I is a classical example of the politics of municipal labor relations with layoffs being just one of the negotiable issues. If layoffs are only threats to create condi-

424 DEVELOPMENTS IN PUBLIC SECTOR LABOUR RELATIONS

tions for negotiations, do people actually lose their jobs? Yes and no. Yes, there are a few individual workers who no longer appear on the payroll. These laid-off workers are not exactly exiled as there are civil service regulations and union contracts that provide them rights to any new openings caused by retirement, firing or death. In most cases laid off workers return to their jobs within a one-year period. This stage reflects the Detroit situation. As stated earlier, the Building Trade Council did have layoffs since they did not sign the wage concession agreement.

Frank Thompson's study of Oakland, California characterized the struggle to maintain certain staffing patterns as the politics of manpower. Thompson (1975) observed that during times of budget paring, department administrators utilize a variety of personnel saving strategies. Many imperialistic departments justify requests for new staff by arguing that their additional functions require more personnel. Some departments claim that additional personnel would generate new revenue on the grounds that these new staff members would not be a burden, as they would pay for themselves (e.g., parking meter monitors). Other departments offer to reduce manpower in order to gain a reputation of frugality. This tactic creates obligations with the city budget office and improves the agency's chances for success in future personnel negotiations. Still other agencies exchange personnel lines for other budgetary concessions. A few agencies exchange a senior position for a junior one (e.g., secretary 111 for a clerk typist). During the Fiscal Crisis the budget office was only willing to negotiate replacements for critical department personnel. Departments had to convince the budget office that nonreplacement would imperil their functions. In such cases personnel requisitions were granted. The fiscal situation has deteriorated so rapidly that the city budget has become more parsimonious in manpower negotiations.[6]

Phase II. In this phase actual layoffs are now mandated by the worsening fiscal situation, since the stopgap measures did not work. A city which has reduced services continues to suffer expenditure losses and higher service costs. The union reluctantly concedes layoffs, but demands that the reductions must be made by seniority. The less senior workers (1–2 years) are released, and moderate seniority workers (3–5 years) are bumped by 6-and-above seniority employees. This systematic layoff strategy is not without its problems. Title VII of the 1964 Civil Rights Act prohibits arbitrary dismissal of minorities and women during periods of layoff. City departments with successful affirmative action programs are usually the first to feel the effects of reduction in force (RIF). These departments harbor disproportionate numbers of workers with little seniority. In Highland Park, a city surrounded by Detroit, all the black firemen hired under the 1970 court ordered affirmative action program were laid off. There were 28 percent and 29 percent layoffs in the policy department (75) and Department of Public Service (85) respectively.[7]

Phase III. In phase III layoffs are accelerated, but this occurs systematically and in accordance with union contracts. Permanent status employees now join the ranks of the laid-off affirmative action hires, temporaries, provisionals, seasonals, and clerical workers. These layoffs take place where continuing and deteriorating revenue forecasts exist. In this phase confrontation between unions and city officials becomes more strident. Each accuses the other of misrepresentations and distortions. Unions now call for job actions to demonstrate their disagreements with the city administration. Media coverage is increased and the entire city now becomes an audience for the layoff drama.

The city's political problems are exacerbated by its fiscal problems. Uncertainty feeds on fear and rumors. The bond rating services downgrade the city bonds. The city begins to limp along hoping that the economic situation will improve, tax revenue will hold steady, and the unions will agree to forego some benefits and workrule victories in exchange for a reduced layoff schedule. We are now in a "giveback" stage of contract negotiations. In this phase the unions and city officials will have to defend the city's image against charges of a mismanaged corporation of overpaid workers. The bond rating service usually likes to see significant changes before it reverses its rating decision. New York reached this stage in the middle part of the 1975 fiscal crisis.

Phase IV. In this phase, layoffs now involve workers with considerable amounts of seniority—the "untouchables." Police and fire departments see significant reductions of staff. There are also periodic shutdowns of essential services. To keep the city functioning, many city bills and obligations are left unmet. A small city workforce scrambles to meet the needs of the city. Supervisory personnel are returned to the street. All remaining workers are forced to work more to cover the loss of manpower. This phase may also force the mayor to ask the governor for assurances that if further cuts are necessary, then the state will maintain safety and security. The city bond rating situation sinks below the negotiations stage. To manage the city cash flow problems, local officials begin borrowing from local sources (i.e., banks and pension funds). Aside from making emergency loans, the state acts as a day-to-day monitor of the city's fiscal activities. Ironically, the final phase forces all public officials, union leaders, and citizen groups to work together in order to keep the city from the edge of bankruptcy. The City of Highland Park, Michigan, is at present in this stage of fiscal complications. The city has had to lay off 200 or 500 employees since 1979. No department has been spared reduction in force. In July, 1982 the entire health department staff of 15 was laid off.

The orderly layoff procedures outlined in Detroit's personnel rules are only possible in what may be called Phase I and Phase II of the layoff or downsizing process. The next two stages, phases III and IV, restrict the ability of the personnel office or the union to protect workers. Table 41.3 summarizes conditions and responses within the sequence.

Although the sequence of the phases are developmental, a particular city's fiscal situation may skip one phase and go directly to the second and third step. In other words, the categories are neither mutually exclusive nor inevitable for all cities.

Layoffs and Productivity

It is difficult to gauge the effect of attrition on productivity in city departments since there are no before and after data. The Mayor's Office of Productivity does not keep statistics. Its role is to inform agency heads of productivity techniques. However, the general consensus is that an understaffed department has an unsettling effect on the employees of an organization. Aside from disturbing the routine of oldtimers and the learning schedule of

Table 41.3

The Sequence of Layoff Developments

Stage	Conditions	Responses
I	Cash flow problems; decline in anticipated revenue	Wage concessions by unions; delay of COLA; few actual layoffs
II	Worsening fiscal situation; severe cash flow problems	Moderate layoffs; moderate bumping; non-essential departments reorganized or merged
III	Negative fiscal forecast; deteriorating political situation; downgrading of city bonds	Accelerated layoff of non-tenured personnel; moderate-major layoffs, giveback negotiations
IV	Bonds rating reach low point; a major fiscal crisis (near default); improving political situation	Major layoffs; essential services reduced or temporarily terminated; possibility of payless paydays

newcomers, being "shorthanded" tends to reduce the staff's ability to perform any tasks not considered essential to the department's future. Charles Levine (1978:32) makes the following warning about hiring freezes:

> A *hiring freeze* is a convenient short-run strategy to buy time and preserve options. In the short run it hurts no one already employed by the organization because hiring freezes rely on "natural attrition" through resignation, retirement, and death, to diminish the size of an organization's work force. In the long run, however, hiring freezes are hardly the most equitable or efficient way to scale down organizational size. First, even though natural and self-selection relieves the stress on managers, it also takes control over the decision of whom and where to cut away from management and thereby reduces the possibility of intelligent long-range cutback planning. Second, hiring freezes are more likely to harm minorities and women, who are more likely to be the next hired rather than the next rehired. Third, attrition will likely occur at different rates among an organization's professional and technical specialties. Since resignations will most likely come from those employees with the most opportunities for employment elsewhere, during a long hiring freeze an organization may find itself short on some critically needed skills yet unable to hire people with these skills though they may be available.

With staff inadequacies so ubiquitous, long range planning becomes less relevant. Crisis management becomes the norm. City departments which are reduced to minimum services also have trouble keeping more able staff members stimulated. Some young people leave city employment rather than await the next round of layoffs. Demoted older workers often have tremendous psychological problems adjusting to less pay and status. For older employees, personal energy becomes a real factor in an environment of continuous overtime and stress.

Since layoffs are the tactics of last resort, they are often preceded by relaxation of equipment purchases, delays in management upgrading, and cancellation of training and development programs. These budget paring tactics can have a debilitating effect on employee morale. Fewer personnel means more overtime and more stress. Generally productive and cooperative employees often question working twice as hard only to have the vacant positions permanently eliminated in the next department budget. Why not hire additional staff rather than pay extra for overtime? Increased productivity in a fiscal crisis then presents a dilemma for the employee. If he or she increases productivity, then department chances for new staffing or recalls are jeopardized. On the other hand low productivity invites public resentment and unwanted attention from higher officials.

Layoffs and Equal Opportunity

Although the recession has claimed many municipal affirmative action programs, Detroit still believes it is on the track for a successful equal opportunity city. However, the last hired and first fired principle, which has traditionally dominated the working life of minorities, still attains as a byproduct of a rigid seniority system. Since minorities were the last hired, they have less seniority and are thus targets for any future layoffs. Title VII of the Civil Rights Act of 1964 prohibits discrimination by employer on the basis of race, color, religion, sex, or national origin. Section 703 (h) of the Act provides for bona fide seniority systems which do not have discriminatory intent. In *International Brotherhood of Teamsters v. United States* (1977), the Court held that a seniority system adopted before the 1964 Act but maintained without discriminatory intent was not a violation of Title VII. These seniority systems were permissible even though they had an adverse effect on minorities. Recently the Court has broadened the immunity of seniority systems to legal challenges. In *American Tobacco Company v. Patterson* (1982) the Court held that a seniority system adopted after the effective date of Title VII was subject to the same broad immunity under Section 703 (h) as one adopted before Title VII. In *Pullman-Standard v. Swint* (1982), the Supreme Court held that appellate courts could not overturn a trial court finding in suits involving seniority clauses unless the ruling involved errors of procedure rather than substance. The latter ruling had the effect of insulating most seniority clauses from civil rights suits. After *American Tobacco* (1982) and *Pullman-Standard* (1982), municipalities were left with less flexibility in saving low seniority affirmative action hires from layoffs.

The new immunity means that the next round of layoffs could fall disproportionately on minorities. In ruling that bona fide seniority systems are permissible, the Court has abetted their adverse effects on minorities, women, and young workers. Conversely, the Court has strengthened the city's hand in layoffs in eliminating challenges by mandating strict compliance with seniority rules. It appears that seniority rules will remain a source of tension between the generations, sexes, and races.

Conclusion

Today's public employees are confronted with a variety of pressures including a backlash from the taxpaying public. In the sixties public employee unions were very successful in securing favorable work rules, benefits and political recognition. As these organizations approached parity with their private sector counterparts, they were also exposed to the pressure of the market place. The decline of the automobile industry in Detroit has caused a secondary effect on the institutions of municipal government. Traditionally, the wage settlements of auto workers set the pace for other workers in the region. The monopsonist theory of economics argues that the automobile industry had inflated wages when it expanded its production. During the period of expansion, the area's economy was at or near full employment. Other employers were forced to match compensation and benefits to attract workers. Now the situation has reversed itself. There are fewer auto industry jobs and other workers have been forced to make concessions. These workers range from steel workers at McLouth Steel to grocery clerks at Kroger's. The recent layoffs of auto workers have also made it easier for the city to obtain wage concession deals because negotiators can argue that city workers are being treated like other workers.

In a sense, Detroit is luckier than some snowbelt cities. The city residents have been willing to increase taxation. Unions have not attempted to use the fiscal crisis to embarrass the mayor. Nevertheless, layoffs are still in the city's future. The auto industry has not yet recovered and new industries are not yet on the Michigan horizon. An inevitable correlate of this economic condition for the city is its continued image as a dying city. Layoffs may not assuage the public apprehensions about the future of the city. Since each passing month had brought more negative news about the city's economy, the mayor received an overwhelming vote in his tax increase campaign as an act of faith. It is unlikely that any other big city mayor would have been able to make such an appeal and receive a tax increase in a recession. The credibility points gained in the 1981 fiscal crisis gave politicians more leverage in dealing with workers and their unions. If more budget paring is in the future, then the affirmative action program, total seniority system, and union cooperation could disappear overnight.

In the Detroit case study, wage concessions proved to be sufficient to avoid Phase II of the layoff sequence. In the next round of negotiations the city might consider other alternatives to layoffs, some of which can be negotiated. The obvious alternative for negotiation in non-wage items (e.g. personal days, break time, vacation times and schedules). If the layoff sequence continues, however, the unions may be amenable to rotated layoffs, unpaid furloughs, and reduced work days. With any of these alternatives, face to face consultations with employees will relieve the anxieties and help facilitate the process. Such counseling should enable the worker to maintain psychological contact with the workplace. If recall and rehiring are impossible, then outplacement and retraining should become negotiable items. The city worker who is a victim of indefinite layoffs is entitled to assistance from his union and employer.

Unfortunately, layoff politics have always been the underbelly of the personnel system. As the soft and vulnerable part of the system it can be easily manipulated by the politicians. In an atmosphere of uncertainty, a few politicians will panic and call for a return to a leaner and more exclusionary government service consistent with new fiscal realities. By insisting on equity in layoff decisions, personnel professionals can help protect the integrity of the entire system. This can be done without adopting the moral tones of Marvin Reder's (1960) "ethics of queues" (i.e., maintaining that layoffs by seniority are the only moral procedure possible) or by adding to the heavy burden of proof imposed by the United States Supreme Court. If a discriminatory case can be made, then minorities and women are entitled to the full cooperation of the personnel department in their challenge of the seniority system. The affirmative action gains, many won after numerous court battles and human relations training programs, are essential if society is to achieve its goal of a representative bureaucracy. Rich (1982:156) observed:

> The open bureaucracy has to be considered a truly American invention. Our society's choice of a decentralized representative democracy precludes an absolutely efficient bureaucracy. Episodic mismanagement is the price of democracy. The occasional demonstration of massive inefficiency con-firms the system has not succumbed to the "closing tendency," or the propensity of bureaucrats to deny public access to the internal management of an agency.

Whereas some mismanagement is inherent in our system of government, a fiscal crisis should not be seen as an opportunity to close off public access to decision making nor should it force us to make a choice between equality and efficiency. Nevertheless, competing interest groups demand that choices be made. The personnel director, then, is forced to represent a variety of conflicting values and avoid the appearance of bias toward any one of them. This can be accomplished by developing a coherent retrenchment strategy. Accordingly, the personnel director must prepare the city for episodic layoffs by insisting on cross-training of personnel within and between departments, by maintaining good working relations with union representatives, and by planning for the full sequence of layoffs. Union leaders and politicians can help by not overpromising employees or using the layoff issue to get elected or reelected. If these simple prescriptions are followed, then the management of retrenchment can be less disruptive and more humane.

Notes

1. The population data are based on U.S. Census data. The manpower data were obtained from the City of Detroit Budget Office.

2. The population data are based on U.S. Census data.

3. The fiscal data were based on a report by the Budget Planning and Stabilization Committee (1981): 1–2. Current fiscal data were obtained from the City of Detroit Budget for 1982–83.

4. For a lively discussion of human capital theory, see Parson (1972).

5. This is a summary of the rules entitled, "Reduction in Force," Personnel Department. Rule X.

6. City departments sent their personnel requests directly to the budget office, bypassing the personnel department. The personnel department is only aware of those requisitions approved by the budget office. The budget office does not keep data on the number of requisitions received. Therefore, data are not available to determine the percentage of requests denied or of which departments were more successful.

7. These manpower data are based on the Highland Park police department and personnel data.

References

American Tobacco Company v. Patterson (1982). 102 S. Ct 1534

Becker. H. (1960). "Notes On The Concept of Commitment." *American Journal of Sociology* 66 (July):36.

Budget Planning and Stabilization Committee, City of Detroit (1981). Report submitted to Mayor Coleman Young, April.

Feldstein, M. (1976). "Temporary Layoff in the Theory of Unemployment." *Journal of Political Economy* 84, 5 (October):938–937.

Greenstone, D. (1969). *Labor in American Politics.* New York: Vintage Books.

Hirschman, A.O. (1970). *Exit, Voice and Loyalty.* Cambridge: Harvard University Press. *International Brotherhood of Teamsters v. United States* (1977). 431 U.S. 324.

Levine, C. (1978). "Organizational Decline and Cutback Management." *Public Administration Review* 38, 4 (July/August):316.325.

Mortenson, D. (1978). "Specific Capital and Labor Turnover." *The Bell Journal of Economics* (August):572–586.

Parson, D.O. (1972). "Specific Human Capital: Application to Quit Rate and Layoffs." *Journal of Political Economy* 80, 6 (November/December):1120–1143.

Pullman Standard v. Swint (1982). 102 S. Ct. 1781.

Reder, M.W. (1960). "Job Scarcity and the Nature of Union Power." *Industrial and Labor Relations Review* (August):353–357.

Rich, W.C. (1982). *The Politics of Urban Personnel Policy Reformers, Bureaucrats and Politicians.* New York: Kennikat Press.

Thompson. F. (1975). *Personnel Policy in the City.* Berkeley: University of California Press.

U.S. Bureau of Census (1981). *City Employment.* Washington, D.C.: U.S. Government Printing Office.

Wurdock, D.J. (1981). "Neighborhood Racial Transition: A Study of the Role of White Flight." *Urban Affairs Quarterly* 17, 1 (September): 75–89.

CHAPTER 42

WHAT PUBLIC EMPLOYEE RELATION BOARDS AND THE COURTS ARE DECIDING

Mandatory Subjects of Bargaining

JOAN PYNES

The scope of collective bargaining addresses what subjects are negotiable. Specific topics have generally been classified on a case by case basis into three types of bargaining: mandatory, permissive, and illegal. Mandatory topics must be bargained if either side requests it. Either side can bargain to impasse on a mandatory topic if the parties can demonstrate that they made a good faith effort to reach agreement on it. Mandatory topics typically include wages, salaries, union security, and working conditions. A permissive topic may be subject to bargaining if there is mutual agreement between labor and management, but neither side may unilaterally insist on such bargaining. There is no duty to bargain over permissive topics. In many states permissible topics of bargaining may include insurance benefits retirement benefits, and productivity bargaining.

An illegal topic cannot be bargained and any agreement to bargain with respect to an illegal topic will be void and unenforceable. Examples of illegal or prohibited subjects of bargaining include the negotiation of the organization's objectives, how the objectives should be implemented, how work is to be performed, the agency's organizational structure, and employment standards.

The authority to control the mission of the agency is generally considered to be nondelegable since it involves the power of the agency to govern itself. To the extent that an issue can be classified as controlling the mission of the agency, it will be considered an unlawful topic. Illegal topics typically must be resolved through the legislative process.

This article presents a review of the trends that have challenged or expanded the topics covered under mandatory subjects of bargaining as permitted by state and local public employers, state public employee relations boards, and the state courts. This review is not all inclusive; rather it focuses on discernible trends and relevant public administration research findings.

Management rights. The principal goals of government are politically determined. Government goals are decided by a legislative body. The management responsible for

From 13 *Review of Public Personnel Administration*, 3: 58–62, Summer 1993. Copyright © 1993 Sage Publications. Reprinted with permission.

the performance of these functions is accountable to that legislative body and ultimately to the people. The administrative process and standards devised by management for the delivery of services are subject to the scrutiny of elected officials. Major decisions made in bargaining with public employees are inescapably political decisions. They involve critical policy choices. The matters debated at the bargaining table and decided by the contract are not simply questions of wages, hours, and working conditions. Directly at issue are political questions of the size and allocation of the budget, the tax rates, the level of public services, and the long-term obligation of the government. These decisions are political in the sense that, within a democratic system of government, they must be made by elected officials who are politically responsible to the voters. These decisions are generally considered legislative and not subject to delegation (Edwards, Clark, and Craver 1989). Therefore, public sector employers tend to have more discretion in exercising their management rights than private sector employers.

Provided below is the management rights clause of the Illinois Public Labor Relations Act (Section 4, p. 5); it is rather typical of public sector practices generally.

> Employers shall not be required to bargain over matters of inherent managerial policy, which shall include such areas of discretion or policy as the functions of the employer, standards of services, its overall budget, the organization structure and selection of new employees, examination techniques and direction of employees. Employers, however, shall be required to bargain collectively with regard to policy matters directly affecting wages, hours and terms and conditions of employment as well as the impact thereon upon request by employee representatives.

Data

The data for this investigation were obtained through a content analysis of abstracts/summaries published by Bureau of National Affairs (BNA), *Government Employer Relations Report,* and the Commerce Clearing House's, *Public Employee Bargaining* services through the years 1988–1991. These services were selected because they deal exclusively with public sector labor relations and are recognized as providing an exhaustive compilation of recent developments in public sector labor relations. They provide information about new laws, regulations, and pertinent judicial and administrative decisions (Elias 1986).

Management Rights or Mandatory Topics of Bargaining

Described below are a number of employment issues that have been decided by state courts and public employee relations boards (PERBs) as to whether the topics fell within the parameters of mandatory topics of bargaining or management rights.

Smoking. Smoking has become a controversial issue in the work environment. Many states have passed legislation prohibiting smoking in government buildings. Many employers have instituted smoking policies in the workplace and the courts have gotten involved in the smoking vs. non-smoking dispute (Colosi 1988; Upton 1988; Wilson

1989). As of summer 1992, 20 states had enacted laws regulating smoking in the work-place. However, 22 other states have adopted smokers' rights legislation (Vaughn 1992). Disagreement over employees' right to smoke in and away from the workplace is found across the states and also across public employee relation boards/commissions.

Public employee relation boards/commissions in the states of New York, Washington, and Iowa ruled that cigarette smoking is a mandatory subject of bargaining and does not fall within the purview of management rights. California, however, ruled that smoking policies fall within the range of managerial prerogative.

The New York State Public Employee Relations Board held that in order to unilater-ally implement smoking regulations a public employer must demonstrate there is a need related to its mission for the restrictions it imposed on employee smoking in its facilities. To ban smoking in libraries and cafeterias—areas not customarily used by the facility's patients—was ruled to be not mission related. [Niagara County Unit, Local 832, CSEA, Local 1000, AFSCME and County of Niagara (Mount View Health Facility), 1988].

In New York City, the Office of Collective Bargaining ruled that New York Health and Hospitals Corporation improperly implemented a no-smoking policy and must negotiate workplace smoking with the union. Prior to the adoption of the policy the employees had been permitted to smoke in designated non-public areas of the facility and lounges. The union argued that the smoking ban was a mandatory bargaining subject since it was a work rule affecting employee terms and conditions of employment. The administrator of the health care facility argued that implementing its policy was within its managerial prerogatives under the bargaining law and thus not a mandatory subject of bargaining. Because employees were allowed to smoke before the ban in designated areas, the smoking ban had an effect on at least some of the employees' personal convenience and comfort on the job. Now employees who wished to smoke had to do so outside; thus, a work rule banning smoking is germane to the work environment. On this logic, the smoking policy was held to be a mandatory bargaining subject (Hill 1991).

The Washington Public Employee Relations Commission determined that the city of Seattle could not implement a policy on tobacco use on city property without bargaining with unions representing its employees. The bargaining law requires employers and unions to bargain wages, hours, and working conditions which may be peculiar to an appropriate bargaining unit. The PERC stated that an employer is required to bargain on imposing a smoking policy unless it can establish a compelling business need to restrict smoking in the work environment. No compelling business need was shown in this case (International Federation of Professional and Technical Engineers Local 17 and Seattle, 1989).

In California, the Public Employee Relations Board ruled that a school district could change its policy in regard to smoking and the use of tobacco products by employees without bargaining about the decision and the effects of the policy. The school district was under no obligation to bargain because bargaining would significantly abridge its freedom to exercise managerial prerogatives essential to the achievement of its mission (*California School Employees Assn. et al. v. Riverside Unified School District* 1989).

A different case concerns the city of Clinton, Iowa which adopted a resolution stating new employees hired after January 1, 1987 must sign an employment agreement not to smoke, chew, or use tobacco products on or off duty. The union (AFSCME) filed an unfair labor practice charge, contending that the policy was a mandatory subject of bargaining falling under the "health and safety matters" provisions of the Act.

The city, however, defended its position by claiming that this was not a health and safety matter but one of "management rights." The management rights clause in the state act gave public employers the right to hire, promote, demote, transfer, assign and retain public employees and to determine and implement methods, means, assignments and personnel by which the employers' operations are to be conducted. The city said that neither the public employee relations act (PERA) nor the parties' existing agreement precluded it from unilaterally adopting such a policy as a job qualification. The intent of the no-smoking and tobacco use policy, as expressed in terms of the employment condition agreement and the enabling resolution, was to affect city employees' health directly by prohibiting smoking on or off the job and thus reduce the city's health care costs. Tobacco products have an adverse effect on the health of an employee that directly affects the ability of the employee to perform his job while increasing health care costs that are borne by the city. The board decided that the subject matter of the policy as it related to employees concerned a "health and safety matter" under PERA. The board said the important policy issue here "clearly addresses the protection of employee health in the workplace by requiring employees to refrain from using tobacco products." To the extent the condition of employment agreement directly affects employee working conditions by trying to protect workers beyond the normal hazards inherent in their work, the agreement is also a health and safety matter.

The board acknowledged that the state's PERA health and safety matters provision requires that a subject must be bargained if it bears a direct relationship to the health and safety of employees as a means of protecting them beyond the normal job hazards, so long as it does not substantially interfere with the employer's authority to set basic policies for government to accomplish its mission. Therefore, any unilateral changes in health and safety provisions are prohibited under the PERA (American Federation of State, County, and Municipal Employees Council 61 and City of Clinton, 1988).

At this time, there is no constitutional right to smoke nor is there a right to a totally smoke-free environment. There is no court decision setting precedent nor federal statute which governs smoking in the workplace. Decisions in regard to workplace smoking are being made on a state by state basis by the legislatures and courts. However, concerns about passive smoke endangering the health of non-smokers may provide the impetus for standardized smoking policies. Studies have shown that diseases caused by passive smoke are generally the same as from direct smoking (Ballard 1992). The evidence linking passive environmental smoke to cancer, heart disease and respiratory ailments is so convincing that the National Institute for Occupational Safety & Health (NIOSH) recommends banning smoking in the workplace (Smith 1992). The Surgeon General has called for a smoke-free society by the year 2000, meaning that no one could smoke in the presence of others without their permission (Ludington 1991). I believe that in the future, the conflict over smoking in the workplace will be removed from the grasp of management and labor, and a resolution will be imposed by legislative imperatives.

Drug testing. Testing public employees for drugs has received considerable attention in the public personnel literature (Cowan 1987; Elliott 1989; Klinger, O'Neill and Sabet

1990; Riccucci 1990). Public employers and unions usually disagree over the implementation of drug testing policies. The examples below illustrate different positions in regard to testing. In the first example, the city of Miami cited managerial prerogative in its attempt to implement a compulsory drug testing policy. The union insisted that drug testing was a mandatory subject of bargaining since it would be a term and condition of employment that would impact upon the employment relationship.

The Florida District Court of Appeals agreed with the Florida Public Employee Relations Commission (PERC) that drug testing is a mandatory subject of bargaining. The Florida constitution provides that the right of employees, by and through a labor organization, to bargain collectively shall not be denied or abridged. Because the Florida Constitution grants public employees the same rights as private employees, and because private employees have the right to bargain over compulsory testing for drugs, it follows that public employees in Florida have a state constitutional right to bargain over drug testing *(Miami v. Fraternal Order of Police Lodge 20* 1989).

In this next case, the union was reluctant to negotiate drug testing. The city of Annapolis filed an unfair labor practice with the Maryland Mediation and Conciliation Service because the union representing police and firefighters refused to negotiate in good faith about a drug testing program. There was no agreement before the present contract expired and still no formalized agreement on drug testing one year later. The city proposed a drug testing program requiring its uniformed police and firefighters to submit a urine sample to determine the presence of illegal drugs during their regularly scheduled physical examinations during their 'birthday' month, with 30 days' prior notice of the week of the test and 48 hours' notice of the exact time.

The union filed suit in the circuit court to enjoin the city from implementing its proposed plan, and the circuit court held that mandatory testing was unconstitutional because "there is absolutely no evidence that a drug problem exists within a governmental department or any suspicion of an individual's drug use, as the city has conceded." The city appealed the decision to the court of appeals which found that drug testing of safety personnel was a mandatory subject of bargaining. The court held that there is a compelling government interest to ensure that employees do not use illegal drugs even while off duty. It would be difficult, if not impossible for the employer to detect drug impairment until the employee is called into action, which would be too late. Therefore, the city may constitutionally require uniformed police officers and firefighters to submit to drug testing, even if they are not suspected of taking drugs during their annual physical examinations (*Annapolis v. United Food and Commercial Workers Local 400* 1989).

In both of the above cases, drug testing was considered to be a mandatory subject of bargaining. It is interesting to note that the respective postures of the unions and cities were not consistent. In the first example, the city of Miami did not want to negotiate drug testing, but the union insisted. In the second example, the city of Annapolis wanted to negotiate drug testing but the union refused. In both instances, the courts of appeal balanced the government's special needs with the union members' individual rights. Drug testing was found to be a mandatory subject of bargaining.

Fringe benefits. Fringe benefits have steadily increased over the last 50 years to an approximate 36.7 percent of payroll costs. Hence, benefits have become important topics of collective bargaining. A survey distributed to major unions or employee associations with over 90,000 members revealed that the most important benefit was health and welfare (76 percent), with 59 percent of the respondents specifically designating health (Kemp 1989). Collective bargaining agreements in the 1980s reflected the concern over rising health care costs. Health care cost containment measures included higher deductibles and employer-employee joint funding or cost sharing. During this period, the number of total employer-funded health care plans declined (Stelluto and Klein 1990). Eighteen percent of the respondents specified pensions as the most important benefit.

When asked what benefits would be important over the next ten years, 65 percent of the survey respondents again mentioned health and welfare. Pensions were cited as most important by 29 percent of the respondents. The pension concerns include protecting pension benefits and improving income supplements to social security (Kemp 1989).

The survey disclosed other benefits which have received limited bargaining attention, including dental coverage, vision coverage, employee assistance programs, alternative work schedules, sabbatical leaves, legal coverage, eldercare, childcare, and financial counseling/planning (Kemp 1989). The benefits which have recently been challenged as mandatory subjects of bargaining are broken into the following categories: health insurance, payment to annuity funds, sick and vacation leaves.

Health insurance. Below are two court decisions and three public employee relation board decisions regarding health insurance. The New York Supreme Court upheld an employer's right to change health insurance plans without negotiating with the union as long as health insurance benefits were continued. The court found that the institution of a new plan did not deviate from an established past practice. The collective bargaining agreement made no reference to any specific health insurance benefits or program, just that coverage would be offered. Although the benefit costs to employees and the administration of the new plan were substantially different, there was no deviation from a past practice because the past practice did not include any specific benefits, but rather the provisions of a benefit program that was consistently offered (*Unatego Non-Teaching Association v. New York State Public Employment Relations Board* 1988).

The Wisconsin Public Employee Relations Commission determined that negotiation over providing certain health benefits to current employees who retire during the contractual terms was a mandatory subject of bargaining (*Matter of City of Brookfield and Brookfield Professional Firefighters Association* 1988). In another case, the Wisconsin public employee relations board also ruled that the choice of health benefits, the choice of a particular HMO, and the level of benefits received by employees would have a significant impact on existing conditions of employment. Therefore, they were mandatorily negotiable (*Matter of Milwaukee Teachers' Education Association and Milwaukee Board of School Directors* 1989).

The Iowa Public Employee Relations Board ruled that a provision allowing an employee to elect wage credits over dependent health insurance was a mandatory subject of bargaining. The Board considered the monthly credit to an employee's pay check to be a direct link to the mandatory issues of wages. The board also considered it to be linked to the mandatory issue of insurance (Public, Professional and Maintenance Employees, Local 2003 and Clay County, 1989).

A state court in Pennsylvania ruled that the Kennett Consolidated School District could not unilaterally change the Blue Cross health care program provided to the district's professional employees because fringe benefits such as health and life insurance are wages, and wages must be bargained over (*Kennett Consolidated School District v. Commonwealth of Pennsylvania* 1990).

The above cases illustrate different circumstances and different interpretations of health benefits based on state laws. In the New York case, the issue before the court was one of procedures; whether the employer deviated from past practices and was guilty of refusing to bargain over health benefits. The first Wisconsin case addressed whether the public employer must negotiate over whether to provide certain health benefits to employees who retire during the length of the contract. This case did not address the issue of health benefits as mandatory subjects of bargaining. The last three cases did. In the second Wisconsin case, the WERC held that benefits have a significant impact on existing conditions of employment and therefore are a mandatory subject of bargaining. In Iowa, the public employee relations board found benefit credits to employees' pay checks to be "wages," and also, the Iowa PERA specifically mentions insurance as a topic within the mandatory scope of bargaining. The Pennsylvania court ruled that fringe benefits such as health and life insurance are wages and wages are a mandatory subject of bargaining.

Payment to annuity funds. Public employee relation boards in Iowa, Oregon, and Wisconsin have ruled that employer contributions to annuity, pension, and trust funds are related to wages and compensation and are therefore mandatory subjects of bargaining. The Iowa Public Employee Relations Board ruled that where payments to an annuity fund were a form of deferred compensation, the payments were mandatory subjects of bargaining. Since all wages are mandatory bargaining subjects, the annuity fund payments, although deferred, were a form of compensation (Anamosa Community School District and Anamosa Education Association, 1988).

The Oregon Employee Relations Board ruled that a union's proposal that an employer pay the employee portions of a pension was a mandatory subject of bargaining. The board determined that paying such contributions was a matter concerning direct or indirect monetary benefits to employees and fell within the statutory definition of "employment relations" (Portland Fire Fighters Association, Local 43, IAFF and City of Portland, 1988).

The Wisconsin Employee Relations Commission determined that a union's proposal that required an employer to make all contributions to the employee trust fund was mandatorily negotiable. The proposal sought to improve the level of deferred compensation that the employer's jailers would receive for their services, and that the proposal related primarily to wages (Matter of La Crosse County and Wisconsin Professional Police Association/LEER Division, 1990).

Sick and vacation leave. The Ohio Court of Appeals ruled that collective bargaining was required for sick leave payments. Payment for sick leave involves wages, hours, and terms and conditions of employment (*Deeds v. City of Ironton* 1990).

The Oregon Supreme Court ruled that public employer limits on the number of firefighters who may be on vacation at the same time is an "employment relation" and therefore a matter over which the employer may not refuse to bargain. The City permitted a maximum of 24 firefighters to take vacation on a particular day. The purpose of this rule was to maintain consistent staffing levels at optimum cost. The employment relations board acknowledged that vacations were a mandatory bargaining issue but used a test of reasonableness to determine if the issue had a greater effect on management's rights than on working conditions. The court held that it was wrong to use a test to determine whether the new vacation policy concerned a permissive subject of bargaining when the legislature had already designated that the specific topic required bargaining (*Portland Firefighters Association, Local 43, IAFF v. City of Portland* 1988).

Employer-provided benefits have joined wages, hours and job security as no-surrender strike issues. A study issued by the Services International Union reports that the incidence of health benefits as a major issue in work stoppages had quadrupled from 18 percent in 1986 to 78 percent in 1989 (Fisher 1990). The New York Philharmonic, Chicago Symphony, city of Evanston police officers, General Motors' salaried and hourly workers, five New York City bus companies, school bus drivers in Atlanta, employees at AT&T, Pittston Company coal miners, and members of Los Angeles' Local 11 of the Hotel Employees' Union are examples of public and private sector unions who were prepared to strike between 1989 and 1992 over health and pension benefits (Burden 1992; Gorman 1992; Ham 1989; Fisher 1990; Fried 1992; Kozinn 1992; Papajohn and Von Rein 1991; Seal 1992).

As illustrated above, concerns about employer provided health and pension benefits transcend employees in the public and private sector, different professions and industries, and in geographically dispersed locations. Resolving the health care dilemma has become too costly an issue to be dealt with by employers and unions struggling alone. However, until there are some statewide or national reforms, employer provided benefits will continue to dominate the issues targeted by contract negotiations.

Education Issues

Class size. Public employee relation boards in Oregon and Illinois held that class size was a mandatory subject of bargaining. Those decisions, when challenged by the respective school districts, were upheld in state courts. The courts ruled that class size is related to workload, which is a bona fide condition of employment and therefore a mandatory subject of bargaining.

The Tigard School District refused to bargain over class size. The District felt that class size was a permissive subject of bargaining. The teachers' union appealed the District's decision to the Oregon Employee Relations Board (OERB). For the past 16 years, the OERB employed a "balancing effect on each party" to decide if a topic fell under the management rights umbrella. Under this policy, if a proposal was determined to have a greater effect on management's rights than on working conditions, then it was considered to be a permissive subject of bargaining. If the proposal had a greater effect on working conditions than on management's rights, then it was considered to be a mandatory subject of bargaining. The OERB said that a matter concerning a condition of employment must be bargained over, even if the particular proposal arguably might have a greater impact on some management prerogative " . . . The proposal to limit the number of students assigned addresses a matter concerning workload, therefore, and is mandatory, regardless of its obvious effects on management's right to establish staffing levels or on other management prerogatives" (*Tualatin Valley Bargaining Council v. Tigard School District 23J* 1989).

This decision was appealed by the District to the Oregon Court of Appeals. The court affirmed the 1989 decision by the Oregon Employment Relations Board, stating that workload was a condition of employment subject to mandatory bargaining. Class size dearly relates to workload and consequently should be a mandatory subject of bargaining (*Tualatin Valley Bargaining Council v. Tigard School District 23J* 1991).

In Illinois, the Fourth District Court of Appeals upheld a decision made by the Illinois Educational Labor Relations Board that class size was a mandatory subject of bargaining. According to the court, the Decatur Board of Education District No. 61 breached the state's labor relations act by refusing to bargain over the general issue of class size. The Illinois Educational Labor Relations Act requires public employers and employee unions to bargain over wages, hours and other terms and conditions of employment. The employer rights' provisions in Section 4 exempt public employers from bargaining over matters of inherent managerial policy, including employer functions, standards of service, overall budget, the organizational structure and selection of new employees and the direction of the workforce.

However, the law requires that employers bargain "with regard to policy matters directly affecting wages, hours and terms and conditions of employment as well as the impact thereon upon request by employee representatives." The court noted that the words "directly affecting and impact thereon" were important.

The Illinois Educational Labor Relations Board, after finding that a direct effect existed, adopted a balancing test to decide this issue. The interests of the employees were weighed against the district's interest in maintaining unencumbered control over managerial policy. The court held that the same balancing test could be used to determine when the impact of a particular policy decision would be subject to bargaining. The court decided that class size was an element that obviously affects financial planning, and that the bargaining requirement will create administrative problems, such as the need for additional teachers or even additional buildings. The Court recognized that school boards face substantial fiscal problems, but a teacher's work hours and disciplinary requirements definitely are affected by class size and the IELRB acted in the parameters of its discretion (*Decatur Board of Education District No. 61 v. Illinois Educational Labor Relations Board and Decatur Education Association* 1989).

Layoffs. In Illinois, the Educational Labor Relations Board ruled that a school district's decision to adopt a reduction of force which resulted in the dismissal of four teachers was permissively negotiable. The board found that the effect on the teachers' conditions of employment, while substantial, was "indirect." The district's need to freely determine educational policy outweighed the interests of employees in bargaining over such decisions (*Matter of Central City Education Association IEA/NEA and Central City School District 133,* 1989). This decision was overruled by Appellate Court of Illinois Fourth Division on May 24, 1990. The court held that a reduction in force was a mandatory subject of bargaining if the reduction directly affects employee wages, hours and terms and conditions of employment. The court found that the layoff of four teachers in a 18 teacher district would directly affect the terms and conditions of employment of the remaining teachers. Therefore, the reduction in force was a mandatory subject of bargaining. Whether or not the court would have reached the same decision in a larger school district is uncertain.

Evaluation criteria. The evaluation of teachers has received considerable attention (Crisci, March and Peters 1991; Gainey 1990; Geisert and Chandler 1991; Rieck 1989; Root and Overly 1990; Rynecki and Linquest 1988; Zerger 1988). Teachers, principals, union representatives, labor and school board attorneys, and academics all have opinions on the efficacy of teacher evaluation. Below are two cases that specifically address the role of teacher evaluations in school.

The Kansas Supreme Court held that the evaluation procedures of professional employees are mandatorily negotiable, but evaluation criteria are not. The school board refused to negotiate the portion of the plan regarding evaluation criteria, but was willing to negotiate the portions of the plan regarding the evaluation procedure. The court found that appraisal procedures were distinct from appraisal criteria. Evaluation criteria is a managerial policy solely within the dominion of the board, whereas the evaluation procedure is the mechanics of applying such criteria (*Board of Education, U.S.D. No. 352 v. NEA-Goodland* 1990).

This next case dealt with how a new evaluation procedure implemented by a school board affected the supervisor/ teacher relationship. The focus of this case was employee working conditions. The Indiana Educational Employee Relations Board held that the unilateral implementation of an evaluation procedure which ran contrary to longstanding policy concerning the effects of supervisor observation and written evaluation of teachers on the supervisor/ teacher relationship must be bargained. Supervisors were affected under the new evaluation strategy and the role of the supervisor was a mandatory subject of bargaining under the Collective Bargaining Act *Board of School Trustees of the Gary Community School Corporation v. IEERB* 1990).

On matters that affect the workload of teachers, state courts and PERBs have sided with the unions and not with school boards in deciding if an issue falls within the mandatory scope of bargaining. The courts and PERBS have interpreted class size, layoffs, and evaluation procedures to fall within the domain of working conditions as opposed to managerial policy. These rulings have promoted the role of unions in governing schools. Unions may influence/obstruct what were previously administrative decisions.

Health and safety. The Connecticut State Board of Labor Relations ruled that a union's proposal that the employer screen all inmates for AIDS and other infectious diseases before their inclusion into the prison population was mandatorily negotiable. The proposal involved health and safety conditions of employment concerning the protection of bargaining unit members from contracting such diseases (Matter of State of Connecticut Office of Labor Relations and Council 4, AFSCME (NP-4), 1989).

The Michigan Court of Appeals held that minimum staffing requirements for fire fighters are mandatory subjects of bargaining if the staffing requirement is related to the safety, or inextricably intertwined with safety issues. Safety issues fall within the context of terms and conditions of employment (*Manistee, City of v. Manistee Fire Fighters Association, Local 645, I.A.F.E.* 1989).

In regard to police officer staffing, the Massachusetts Supreme Court ruled that a police commissioner possessed the authority to implement a patrol and deployment plan that provided for the assignment of one officer per marked patrol car vehicle instead of two. The court held that the plan's content contained exercises of management prerogative in which no bargaining was required (*Boston, City of v. Boston PPA, Inc,* 1989).

Grooming. The Minnesota Supreme Court ruled that the implementation of a grooming policy applicable to personnel of a sheriff's department was a matter of inherent managerial policy and not subject to mandatory bargaining. The union contested that the implementation of the new policy without negotiation was an unfair practice because it related to terms and conditions of employment. The court held that the policy did have an impact on the employee working conditions. However, the policy was so interwoven with its implementation that to require the employer to negotiate its implementation would also force it to negotiate the underlying policy decision. The court stated that respect and confidence are integral to a sheriff's success and the grooming policy was to foster and enhance respect and confidence. Therefore, it involved an inherent managerial policy (*Law Enforcement Labor Services, Inc. v. County of Hennepin* 1990).

In another case dealing with law enforcement, a different interpretation of grooming policies was made by the Florida Public Employee Relations Commission. The Commission ruled that the city of Fort Lauderdale's no beards policy was a mandatory bargaining subject. The policy affects employees' comfort, convenience, appearance, and self-expression, both on and off the job, and has a significant impact on job security where violations of the policy might result in discharge or other disciplinary measures. Therefore, the policy must be negotiated (*Fraternal Order of Police, Fort Lauderdale Lodge 31 v. City of Fort Lauderdale* 1988).

Bowman and Hooper (1992:331) acknowledge the role that dress and grooming play in communicating credibility and responsibility. Their review of some legal/case law indicates that in most instances a balancing test is used to determine whether the interests of an employee as a citizen outweigh the public employer's interest in promoting efficient and effective service.

Conclusion and Summary

This review has scanned the published findings of the scope of negotiations in the public sector. What has been reported is not all inclusive. Instead, the focus is on topics of bargaining which are consistent with topics researched in the public administration literature. Topics such as smoking in the workplace, drug testing, fringe benefits, staffing requirements, evaluation, safety concerns, and grooming are frequently found in private sector labor relation contracts and are considered without question to be mandatory topics of bargaining because they affect working conditions and/or compensation.

However, in the public sector the distinction is less clear. Public administrators need to be concerned with efficient and effective service delivery within budget restrictions consistent with the political winds. There is a tension between management rights and mandatory subjects of bargaining. Deciding whether an issue is a mandatory topic of bargaining has generally been accomplished on a case by case basis. Public employee relation boards (PERBs) and state courts have devised varying and flexible tests rather than establishing fixed rules. The decision is often difficult because many issues affect both the terms and conditions of employment and management policy making. Examples of this dilemma surface frequently in teaching and law enforcement. Teachers want to negotiate issues such as class size, evaluation, and layoffs. Public safety officers want to bargain over staffing requirements, drug testing, grooming, and vacation schedules. Those issues address working conditions but are also important dimensions of management policy.

From the cases presented above, it appears that the state courts and public employee relation boards, through their interpretations, have expanded the scope of mandatory subjects of bargaining. With few exceptions, there is consistency in the decisions made across the states. This serves notice to public employers that unless there is specific legislation either mandating or prohibiting certain subjects from bargaining, topics that they consider to be permissive may be held to be mandatory by an adjudicatory body.

References

American Federation of State, County, and Municipal Employees Council 61 and City of Clinton (1988). Iowa PERB No. 3391. 26 Government Relations Reporter 1291.

Anamosa Community School District and Anamosa Education Association, PERB, 145,087 (1988). *Public Employee Bargaining* 268 (February 23).

Annapolis v. United Food and Commercial Workers Local 400 (1989). 27 Government Employee Relations Reporter 1341.

Ballard, J.A. (1992). "Health Effects of Passive Smoking." *Professional Safety* 37: 28–32.

Board of Education, U.S.D. No. 352 V. NEA-Goodland (1990). *Public Employee Bargaining* 322 (March 20).

Bowman, J.S. and H.L. Hooper (1992). "Dress and Grooming Regulations in the Public Service: Standards, Legality, and Environment." *Public Administration Quarterly* 15: 328–340.

Boston, City of v. Boston PPA, Inc. (1989). *Public Employee Bargaining* 309 (September 19).

Burden, B. (1992). "Officials Say Schools Today Will Be Normal." *Atlanta Constitution* (September 16): 1.

California School Employees Assn. et al. v. Riverside Unified School District (1989). *Public Employee Bargaining* 308 (September 5).

Central City Education Association, IEA-NEA v. Illinois Educational Labor Relations Board, and Central City School District 133 (1990). Appellate Court of Illinois, First District, Fourth Division. No. 1–89–0919. May 24.

Colosi, M.L. (1988). "Do Employees Have the Right to Smoke?" *Personnel Journal* 67: 72–78.

Cowan, T. (1987). "Drugs and the Workplace: To Test or Not to Test." *Public Personnel Administration* 16: 313–322.

Crisci, P.E., J.K. March and K.H. Peters (1991). "Empowerment with Accountability: Teachers Evaluating Teachers." *Government and Union Review* 12: 1–21.

Decatur Board of Education, District No. 61 v. Illinois Educational Labor Relations Board and Decatur Education Association, IEA-NEA (1989). Appellate Court of Illinois, Fourth District, No. 4–88–400. February 9.

Deeds v. City of Ironton (1990). *Public Employee Bargaining* 324 (April 17).

Eberts, R.W. (1984). "Union Effects on Teacher Productivity." *Industrial and Labor Relations Review* 37: 346–358.

Edwards, H.T., R.T. Clark Jr. and C.B. Craver (1989). *Labor Relations in the Public Sector.* 3rd ed. Charlottesville, VA: The Mitchie Co.

Elias, S. (1986). *Legal Research: How to Find and Understand the Law.* 2nd ed. Berkeley, CA: Nolo Press.

Elliott, R. (1989). "Drug Testing and Public Personnel Administration." *Review of Public Personnel Administration* 6: 15–31.

Fisher, M.J. (1990). "Health Benefits Found Surging as Strike Issue." *National Underwriter* 94: 7, 31.

Fraternal Order of Police, Fort Lauderdale Lodge 31 v.City of Fort Lauderdale (1988). *Public Employee Bargaining* (November 29).

Fried, J.P. (1992). "Five Bus Lines and Union Settle Strike." *New York Times* (June 11) 1.

Gainey, D.D. (1990). "Teacher Evaluation and Supervision for School Improvement Myth or Reality?" *NASSP Bulletin* 527: 14–19.

Geisert, G. and C. Chandler (1991). "Learning the ABCs the Hard Way: Teacher Unionism in the 1990's." *Government Union Review* 12: 1–23.

Gorman, J. (1992). "Evanston and City Police Union Meet with Federal Mediator." *Chicago Tribune* (March 23) 3.

Gruenberg, G.W. (1988). "Smoking in the Workplace: The Issues Heat Up." *The Arbitration Journal* 43: 8–14.

Ham F.L. (1989). "Who Will Pay for Health Benefits? Management and Labor Face Off." *Business and Health* 7: 29–39.

Hill, S.H., executive director, AFSCME Council 37 and Raymond Baxter, acting president, New York City Health and Hospitals Corporation (1991). 29 Government Employee Relations Reporter 1414.

International Federation of Professional and Technical Engineers Local 17 and Seattle (1989). 27 Government Employee Relations Reporter 1341.

Jones, W.J. and J.A. Johnson. (1989). "Aids in the Workplace: Legal and Policy Considerations for Personnel Managers." *Review of Public Personnel Administration* 9: 3–14.

Kanungo, R.N. and M. Mendoca (1988). "Evaluating Employee Compensation." *California Management Review* 31: 23–39.

Kemp D.R. (1989). "Major Unions and Collectively Bargained Fringe Benefits." *Public Personnel Management* 18: 505–510.

Kennett Consolidated School District v. Commonwealth of Pennsylvania (1990). *Public Employee Bargaining* 317 (January 9).

Klingner, D.E., N.G. O'Neill and M.G. Sabet (1989). "Drug Testing in Public Agendas: Public Policy Issues and Managerial Responses." *Review of Public Personnel Administration* 10: 1–10.

Klingner, D.E., N.G. O'Neill and M.G. Sabet (1990). "Drug Testing in Public Agendas: Are Personnel Directors Doing the Things Right? *Public Personnel Management* 19: 391–397.

Kozinn, A. (1992). "Orchestra Reaches Pact with Musicians." *New York Times* (January 22): 13.

Law Enforcement Labor Services, Inc. v. County of Hennepin (1990). *Public Employee Bargaining* 319 (February 6).

Ludington, D.M. (1991). "Smoking in Public: A Moral Imperative for the Most Toxic of Environmental Wastes." *Journal of Business Ethics* 10: 23–27.

Manistee, City of v. Manistee Fire Fighters Association, Local 645, I.A.F.E (1989). *Public Employee Bargaining* 309 (September 19).

Matter of City of Brookfield and Brookfield Professional Firefighters Association (1988). *Public Employee Bargaining* 289 (December 13).

Matter of La Crosse County and Wisconsin Professional Police Association/ LEER Division (1990). *Public Employee Bargaining* 327 (May 29).

Matter of Milwaukee Teachers' Education Association and Milwaukee Board of School Directors (1989). *Public Employee Bargaining* 310 (October 3).

Matter of State of Connecticut Office of Labor Relations and Council 4, AFSCME (NP-4) (1989). *Public Employee Bargaining* 307 (August 22).

Miami v. Fraternal Order of Police Lodge 20 (1989). 27 Government Employee Relations Reporter 1303.

Mitchell, D.J.B. (1986). "Concession Bargaining in the Public Sector: A Lesser Force." *Public Personnel Management* 15: 23–40.

Murphy, M.J. (1985). "The Impact of Collective Bargaining on School Management and Governance." *Public Budgeting and Finance* 5: 3–14.

Niagara County Unit, Local 832, (SEA, Local 1000, AFSCME and County of Niagara [Mount View Health Facility] (1988). *Public Employee Bargaining* 274 (May 17).

Papajohn, G. and J. Von Rein (1991). "The Sound of Silence Fills Orchestra Hall." *Chicago Tribune* (September 13): 1.

Portland Fire Fighters Association, Local 43, IAFF and City of Portland (1988). 288 *Public Employee Bargaining* (November 29).

Portland Firefighters Association, Local 43, IAFF v. City of Portland (1988). *Public Employee Bargaining* 276 (June 14).

Public, Professional and Maintenance Employees, Local 2003 and Clay County (1989). *Public Employee Bargaining* 304 (July 11).

Riccucci, N. (1990). "Drug Testing in the Public Sector. A Legal Analysis." *American Review of Public Administration* 20: 95–104.

Rieck, W.A. (1989). "This Veteran Principal Tells What You Need to Know About Teacher Evaluation." *American School Board Journal* 7: 33–34.

Root, D. and D. Overly (1990). "Successful Teacher Evaluation: Key Elements for Success." *NASSP Bulletin* 527: 34–38.

Rynecki, S.B. and J.H. Linquist (1988). "Teacher Evaluation and Collective Bargaining: A Management Perspective." *Journal of law and Education* 3: 487–506.

Seal, K (1992). "L.A. Union Contract Talks Falter." *Hotel and Motel Management* 207: 3,24.

Simpkins, E., A.V. McCutcheonm and R. Alec (1979). "Arbitration and Policy Issues in School Contracts." *Education and Urban Society 11:* 241–254.

Smith, B. (1992). "Gearing the Air." *Occupational Health and Safety* 61: 24.

Stelluto, G.L. and D.P. Klein (1990). "Compensation Trends into the 21st Century." *Monthly Labor Review* 113: 38–45.

Tualatin Valley Bargaining Council v. Tigard School District 23J (1989). 27 Government Employee Relations Reporter 1330.

Tualatin Valley Bargaining Council v. Tigard School District 23J (1991). 29 Government Employee Relations Reporter 1408.

Unatego Non-Teaching Association v. New York State Public Employment Relations Board (1988). *Public Employee Bargaining* 278 (July 12).

Upton, R. (1988). "Has Workplace Smoking Become a Burning Issue?" *The Journal of the Institute of Personnel Management* 20: 44–49.

Vaughn, D.H. (1992). "Smoking in the Workplace: A Management Perspective." *Employee Relations Law Journal* 18: 123–139.

White, J.B. (1992). "GM is Headed for Clash with Workers Over Reductions in Jobs, Health Benefits." *Wall Street Journal* (August 24): 3.

Wiatrowski, W.J. (1988). "Comparing Employee Benefits in the Public and Private Sectors." *Monthly Labor Review* 111: 3–8.

Wilson, T.M. (1989). "Smoking in the Workplace." *Review of Public Personnel Administration* 9: 32–45.

Zerger, K.L. (1988) "Teacher Evaluation and Collective Bargaining: A Union Perspective." *Journal of Law and Education* 3: 507–525.

INDEX

Boldface page references indicate graphs and illustrations. *Italic* page references indicate charts and tables.

ABOUT THE EDITOR

Norma M. Riccucci is a professor in the School of Public Affairs and Administration at Rutgers University, Newark Campus. She has published extensively in the areas of employment discrimination law, affirmative action, and diversity management. Her most recently published books are *Managing Diversity in Public Sector Workforces* (Westview Press) and *How Management Matters: Street-level Bureaucrats and Welfare Reform* (Georgetown University Press). She is the recipient of several national awards, including ASPA's 2006 Charles H. Levine Award, ASPA/NASPAA's 2002 Distinguished Research Award., and ASPA's Section on Personnel Administration and Labor Relations 2000 award for Scholarship in Public Sector Human Resources. In 2005, she was inducted into the National Academy of Public Administration.